CHANGING SELF-DESTRUCTIVE HABITS

For the first time in one volume, self-harm, substance abuse, eating-disordered behavior, gambling, and Internet and cyber sex abuse—five crippling, self-destructive behaviors—are given a common conceptual framework to help with therapeutic intervention. Matthew D. Selekman and Mark Beyebach, two internationally-recognized therapists, know first-hand that therapists see clients who have problems with several of these habits in varying contexts. They maintain an optimistic, positive, solution-focused approach while carefully addressing problems and risks. The difficulties of change, the risk of slips and relapses, and the ups-and-downs of therapeutic processes are widely acknowledged and addressed.

Readers will find useful, hands-on therapeutic strategies and techniques that they can use in both individual and conjoint sessions during couple, family, and one-on-one therapy. Detailed case examples provide windows to therapeutic processes and the complexities in these cases. Clinical interventions are put in a wider research context, while research is reviewed and used to extract key implications of empirical findings. This allows for a flexible and open therapeutic approach that therapists can use to integrate techniques and procedures from a variety of approaches and intervention programs.

Matthew D. Selekman, MSW, is a family therapist and a licensed addictions counselor in private practice, and the co-director of *Partners for Collaborative Solutions*, an international family therapy training and consulting firm in Evanston, Illinois, USA. He is an approved supervisor with the American Association for Marriage and Family Therapy, and also received the Walter S. Rosenberry Award in 2006, 2000, and 1999 from the Children's Hospital in Denver, Colorado, for having made significant contributions to the fields of psychiatry and the behavioral sciences.

Mark Beyebach, PhD, is a clinical psychologist, and a licensed family therapist and family therapy supervisor in Spain. For the past 18 years, he has served as the director of the Master's Degree Program in Systemic Therapy in the Department of Psychology at the Universidad Pontificia de Salamanca, Spain. He also serves as a clinical research consultant and trainer for *Partners for Collaborative Solutions* in Evanston, Illinois, USA. He is currently a board member for the European Brief Therapy Association, and has been on the executive board of the Spanish Federation of Family Therapy Associations.

CHANGING SELF-DESTRUCTIVE HABITS

Pathways to Solutions with Couples and Families

Matthew D. Selekman and Mark Beyebach

Routledge
Taylor & Francis Group
NEW YORK AND LONDON

First published 2013
by Routledge
711 Third Avenue, New York, NY 10017

Simultaneously published in the UK
by Routledge
27 Church Road, Hove, East Sussex BN3 2FA

Routledge is an imprint of the Taylor & Francis Group, an informa business

© 2013 Taylor & Francis

The right of Matthew D. Selekman and Mark Beyebach to be identified as authors of this work has been asserted by them in accordance with sections 77 and 78 of the Copyright, Designs and Patents Act 1988.

All rights reserved. No part of this book may be reprinted or reproduced or utilised in any form or by any electronic, mechanical, or other means, now known or hereafter invented, including photocopying and recording, or in any information storage or retrieval system, without permission in writing from the publishers.

Trademark notice: Product or corporate names may be trademarks or registered trademarks, and are used only for identification and explanation without intent to infringe.

Library of Congress Cataloging in Publication Data
    Selekman, Matthew D., 1957-Changing self-destructive habits : pathways to solutions with couples and families / Matthew D. Selekman & Mark Beyebach.pages cm
    Includes bibliographical references and index.
    1. Self-destructive behavior. 2. Brief psychotherapy.
    3. Marital psychotherapy. 4. Family psychotherapy.
    I. Beyebach, Mark. II. Title.
    RC569.5.S45S45 2013
    616.89'1425—dc23
    2012038136

ISBN: 978–0–415–82073–8 (hbk)
ISBN: 978–0–415–82076–9 (pbk)
ISBN: 978–0–203–38601–9 (ebk)

Typeset in Baskerville
by Swales & Willis Ltd, Exeter, Devon

Printed and bound in the United States of America
by Edwards Brothers, Inc.

To my loving and supportive wife Åsa and Hanna,
my angel and other love
Matthew D. Selekman

To my sweet daughter Lara and my love Maite
Mark Beyebach

CONTENTS

About the Authors viii
Acknowledgments ix

1. Self-Destructive Habits: A Collaborative Strengths-Based Brief Family Therapy Approach   1
2. Key Elements for Co-creating a Therapeutic Climate Ripe for Change   31
3. Major Therapeutic Experiments and Rituals   60
4. Self-Harming Habits   82
5. Eating-Distressed Habits   112
6. Substance-Abusing Habits   144
7. Problematic Gambling Habits   174
8. Internet and Cyber-Sex Dependency Habits   204
9. Working with Reluctant and Complicated Multi-Habit-Dependent Clients and Couple and Family Systems   235
10. Couple and Family Relapse Prevention Tools and Strategies   285
11. Self-Destructive Habits: Future Directions with Treatment, Training, and Research   309

References 316
Index 346

ABOUT THE AUTHORS

Matthew D. Selekman, MSW, is a family therapist and a licensed addictions counselor in private practice, and the co-director of *Partners for Collaborative Solutions* (www.partners4change.net), an international family therapy training and consulting firm in Evanston, Illinois, USA. Matthew specializes in the treatment of couples and families presenting with self-injury, eating disorders, substance abuse, Internet abuse, school disruptive behaviors, oppositional defiant disorder, and anger management difficulties. He is an approved supervisor with the American Association for Marriage and Family Therapy. Matthew received the Walter S. Rosenberry Award in 2006, 2000, and 1999 from the Children's Hospital in Denver, Colorado, for having made significant contributions to the fields of psychiatry and the behavioral sciences. Matthew is the author of numerous family therapy articles and five professional books: *Collaborative Brief Therapy with Children*, *The Adolescent and Young Adult Self-Harming Treatment Manual: A Collaborative Strengths-Based Brief Therapy Approach*, *Working with Self-Harming Adolescents: A Collaborative Strengths-Based Therapy Approach*, *Pathways to Change: Brief Therapy with Difficult Adolescents (Second Edition)*, and co-authored with Thomas C. Todd *Family Therapy Approaches with Adolescent Substance Abusers*. He has presented workshops on his collaborative strengths-based brief therapy approach with challenging children, adolescents, and adults and their families extensively throughout the United States, Canada, Mexico, South America, Europe, Singapore, Indonesia, Hong Kong, Australia, and New Zealand.

Mark Beyebach, PhD, is a clinical psychologist, and a licensed family therapist and family therapy supervisor in Spain. For the past 18 years, he has served as the director of the Master's Degree Program in Systemic Therapy in the Department of Psychology at the Universidad Pontificia de Salamanca, Spain. Mark is frequently invited to serve as a guest lecturer in universities throughout Spain and Europe. He also serves as a clinical research consultant and trainer for *Partners for Collaborative Solutions* in Evanston, Illinois, USA. He is currently a board member for the European Brief Therapy Association, and has been on the executive board of the Spanish Federation of Family Therapy Associations. He is the author of *24 Ideas para una Psicoterapia Breve* [24 Ideas for Brief Psychotherapy], and co-author of *Terapia Familiar: Lecturas* [Readings in Family Therapy], *Avances en Terapia Familiar Sistemica* [Advances in Systemic Family Therapy], and *200 Tareas en Terapia Breve* [200 Homework Tasks in Brief Therapy]. Mark has written over 50 articles and book chapters on brief and family therapy, family dynamics, and process-outcome research on solution-focused brief therapy. He has presented over 200 workshops and consulted in Europe, South America, North America, and Asia.

ACKNOWLEDGMENTS

There are a number of people we would like to thank who paved the way for the creation of this book. Each one of us would like to separately pay homage to these key individuals as being instrumental in our professional growth as therapists, supervisors, and trainers. First, Matthew would like to thank Michele Weiner-Davis for showing me a number of effective and respectful ways to rapidly empower clients to "Solution Land." While on this solution-focused brief therapy training journey, I had the great fortune of training with Eve Lipchik, a master systemic interviewer and trainer, and several wonderful intensive training experiences with Steve de Shazer and Insoo Kim Berg. From "down under," the late Michael White and David Epston get my undying appreciation for introducing me to narrative therapy and particularly to the creative therapeutic pathway of externalizing the problem. Many thanks to the brilliant family therapy pioneers Harry Goolishian and Harlene Anderson for reminding me to never lose sight of the client's story, to avoid being a narrative editor, and the art of respectful collaboration with involved helping professionals from larger systems. I would like to thank my good friend, mentor, and colleague Thomas Todd for helping cultivate my passion for working with couples and families plagued by alcohol and substance abuse issues, eating-distressed behaviors, and other habit difficulties. I also would like to thank my friend Scott Miller and his colleagues for reminding us through their important research that ultimately it is the clients who know what is best for them and should have the lead voice in determining what they want, what works, and regularly soliciting from them what we need to do differently to better improve our relationships with them.

There are many people who have contributed to and shaped the ideas that have found their way into this book. First and foremost, I (MB) want to thank the late Steve de Shazer, whose brilliance and elegant teaching turned my views of clients, therapy, and training upside down. Another big thank you goes to the rest of the solution-focused community, organized around the *European Brief Therapy Association*, as well as my colleagues and friends of the *International Alliance of Solution-Focused Training Institutes*, who provide ongoing inspiration and so many thought-provoking conversations. Among them, my friends Luc Isabaert, Yvonne Dolan, and Michael Hjerth have been inspirational over the years.

A very big thank you goes of course to my clients, the individuals, couples, and families who over the last 25 years have had the courage to share with me their stories of pain, hope, and survival. My post-graduate students of the Master's Degree Program in Systemic Therapy at the Universidad Pontificia de Salamanca served as my team with some of the cases I describe in this book, and over the years helped me to clarify my thinking with their never-ending questions and reflections.

My mentor and friend Pepe Navarro made our small Eating Disorders Unit possible, and shared his profound views and contagious passion for family therapy and psychotherapy with me. I am also grateful to the many distinguished therapists and researchers in family and brief therapy who over the years visited our training programs in Salamanca and offered Pepe Navarro and I their wisdom: John Rolland, Bill Pinsoff, John Carpenter, Peter Hawkins, Scott Miller, Frederike

ACKNOWLEDGMENTS

Jacob, Adriana Uken, Annete Kruez, Eero Riikonen, Ben Furman, Matthew Selekman, and many more. I would also like to thank Alberto Rodriguez Morejon and Marga Herrero, with whom I have shared for 20 years ago the exciting adventure of practicing, researching, and training in solution-focused brief therapy; Emilio Gutiérrez, always eager to share his ground breaking research on anorexia nervosa; Valentin Escudero, who helped me to advance my understanding of the therapeutic alliance; Lenore Walker and David Shapiro, for their inspiring conversations on violence and survival; and Esther Opi and Joserra Landa, who were always happy to vehemently discuss sex and couples therapy.

Finally, we both would like to thank Adam Ornstein for his technical assistance with most of the figures and client worksheets in our book and Marta Moldavi and Teri Pichot for their helpful editorial recommendations.

1

SELF-DESTRUCTIVE HABITS

A Collaborative Strengths-Based Brief Family Therapy Approach

> I count him braver who overcomes his desires than he who conquers his enemies, for the hardest victory is the victory over self.
>
> *Aristotle*

Introduction

This book presents a brief family therapy approach for five different, broad categories of self-destructive habits, each of which would surely merit a text on its own: self-harm (self-injury), substance abuse, eating-distress, gambling, and Internet and cyber-sex abuse difficulties. Why have we chosen to include the treatment of these five different self-destructive habits in the same book?

First, all five self-destructive habits share a number of important features that create similar therapeutic dilemmas. These shared elements include the role that brain functioning and neurochemistry play in all of them, the major impact they have on the couple and family relationships of our clients, and the therapeutic challenges they are likely to present even to the most seasoned clinician.

Second, in our clinical experience clients are very likely to present with not only one, but probably two or even three different self-destructive habits at the same time. Therefore, it makes sense to cover all five self-destructive habits in one text.

A third reason is that, as couple and family therapists, we may not only work with a client presenting with various self-destructive habits, but also encounter different members of the same family engaging in some of them as well. In these not so uncommon cases, co-morbidity will interact with multi-problem families increasing complexity and creating entirely new challenges.

Our fourth and final reason for writing a book for clinical problems for which a number of well-researched treatments exist, many of which have been deemed "empirically supported," is a clinical one. There are indeed a number of "empirically supported treatments" for the kinds of problems we cover in this book, but the truth is that, although the majority have been demonstrated to be effective to a certain extent, they are not entirely satisfactory; many of the clients who undergo these treatments do not improve, many of those who improve are still symptomatic at termination, and many of those who are not symptomatic at termination relapse shortly after completing treatment or less than a year down-the-road (Dennis et al., 2004; Gutiérrez, 2011; Westphal, 2007). If on top of this we take into account that the average attrition rate for all these treatments (before, during, and after treatment) is in the 30–50% range (Roth & Fonagy, 2005), the hard fact is that less than one-third of clients who were meant to receive treatment end up completely recovered. This is not to say that these treatments should be dismissed, but it is a reminder of how much ground there is still to be covered.

Orford (2008) contends that researchers may have been asking the wrong questions, by pitting competing treatments against each other instead of recognizing the basic equivalence of outcomes between bona fide treatments and refocusing on what are likely to be more relevant therapeutic processes than the theory-driven differences: the therapeutic alliance, the unaided self-change processes, the social support and broader provider systems, and therapists' and clients' views of change. This also is the reason why, in this book, we do not wish to propose yet another therapy model, to create another therapeutic approach by emphasizing all that is different or supposedly better in our way of intervening. On the contrary, we would like to bring to the fore the similarities, the common change processes that seem to be at work in the successful treatments for a variety of self-destructive habits. Furthermore, we certainly have no problem in bringing aboard the most promising elements of different therapeutic approaches, like for instance cognitive interventions with gamblers (Ladouceur & Lachance, 2007; Marceaux & Melville, 2011), biological heat interventions with eating-disordered clients (Birmingham, Gutiérrez, Jonat, & Beumont, 2004), or the strategic engagement of the families of young drug addicts (Szapocznik, Hervis, & Schwartz, 2003; Szapocznik & Kurtines, 1989). However, we do that with an acute awareness that these elements will only contribute to therapeutic change in the context of other powerful factors: the therapeutic alliance (Diamond et al., 2006; Friedlander, Escudero, & Heatherington, 2006); the ongoing feedback processes between therapist and clients (Lambert, 2010); and the skill and competence of each individual therapist (Anderson, Ogles, Patterson, Lambert, & Vermeersch, 2009); all of them in interaction with the strengths and limitations of each individual client and the broader systemic forces of family, cultural, peer, and larger systems influences. In other words, *collaborative strengths-based brief family therapy* is a way to take common therapeutic factors and accumulated psychotherapeutic practice evidence-based wisdom seriously, and to do so by both offering therapists ideas and tools to better serve their clients, and emphasizing the important role of therapists' creativity and risk-taking in therapy (Selekman, 2009; Selekman, Wilson, & Beyebach, 2005).

Understanding the Territory of Self-Destructive Habits

We provide here a comprehensive overview of how self-destructive habits can develop, are maintained, and can be transformed into virtuous habits by harnessing clients' self-change processes and unique quitting styles, and by using a collaborative strengths-based brief family therapy approach. We begin by discussing four major societal aggravating factors that can fuel self-destructive habits; present our Buddhist and wellness perspective on self-destructive habits; compare and contrast self-destructive habits with other behavioral and mental health difficulties; present the pathways model as a useful framework for understanding how self-destructive habits develop and are maintained (Blaszczynski & Nower, 2002); and discuss the key brain systems and neurochemistry involved in maintaining self-destructive habits. We cover how, for many clients, self-destructive habits have served as gifts and resources for coping with life difficulties; and we present important self-change research that can inform our clinical practices in the treatment of the five self-destructive habits featured in this book.

Self-Destructive Habits in the Age of Dysregulation

It has been our clinical experience that the five self-destructive habits featured in this book are fueled by a wider consumerist cultural and media-driven societal climate that primes us for getting and overspending, and overrides our capacities for self-control and self-regulation by bombarding us with multiple temptations that can rapidly and temporarily elevate our moods or "numb out" any emotional distress or external stressors. We can quickly anesthetize ourselves with the help of a razor blade, pick up fast food, get drunk or "stoned," play video-games, and thanks to the advancements in digital technology, we can shop, gamble, and have cyber-sex 24 hours a day! Unfortunately, the more we consume and engage in these risky habits for temporary rewards of pleasure and to obliterate stress, the more physical health, psychological, social, and financial consequences we will incur over time. It becomes a vicious cycle that we become ensnared in and takes on a life of its own.

There are four major aggravating factors that we believe are playing a central role in the development and maintenance of self-destructive habits today: *economic upheaval and nihilistic fear about the future*; *high levels of anxiety and stress*; *the increasing popularity of quick fix solutions*; and *the primacy of the virtual world over human contact*.

Economic Upheaval and Nihilistic Fear about the Future

The devastating economic aftermath of the Wall Street and home loan crisis in 2008 has wreaked havoc around the world. In both of our countries, the United States and Spain, unemployment rates, personal indebtedness, loss of savings, and home foreclosures have skyrocketed. For many, the freedom to make choices has been replaced with restraint, and happiness has been replaced with gloom and pessimism about our governments being able to resolve the economic crisis (Salecl, 2010). In response to financial stress and worry, many of the young people and adults we work with have increasingly turned to unhealthy and inexpensive fast-food consumption, excessive use of cigarettes, heavy drinking, abusing cheaper and readily available substances, and long hours surfing the Internet in search of pleasurable activities to escape into as attempted solutions to quell their anxieties and fears.

High Levels of Anxiety and Stress

In our clinical practice settings and at our workshops, therapists are reporting that they have been seeing an increase in clients presenting with severe anxiety and stress-related difficulties. College-bound adolescents and young adults already in college are highly stressed about being able to fund their education. Adults are fearful of losing their jobs and pensions (or have already lost them), and are reporting having panic attacks; couples are presenting with multiple habit and serious financial difficulties.

Some high-achievement oriented parents believe that by over-scheduling their children in multiple college level classes and in several extracurricular activities they will become highly marketable to top colleges and universities and possibly secure them scholarships. What these parents are totally oblivious to is that their children are stressed and struggling to stay afloat. Many of these young people are leading the "vampire" lifestyle to stay ahead of the game: pumping themselves up with heavily-caffeinated drinks and abusing attention-deficit disorder (ADD) medications and other stimulants to keep them going. A recent study found that 25–40% of college students across the country abuse the ADD medication Adderol for late night studying and to improve their academic performances (Razzano & Pashka, 2012). Both college students and adolescents have reported also relying on cutting, substance abuse, binge-eating and purging to soothe them and get quick relief from their emotional distress (Levine, 2006; Selekman, 2009; Selekman & Schulem, 2007; Whitlock, Muehlenkamp, & Eckenrode, 2008).

Quick Fix Solutions: Obliterate Stress and Discomfort at all Costs

Television and the Internet are full of advertisements for medications for just about every physical health and psychological ailment, presented as the ultimate quick fix solution for all human troubles. The underlying message from major pharmaceutical companies about their popular money-making products is: "Take this and it will quickly obliterate your physical and psychological discomfort." Unfortunately, the wider public are not being exposed to alternative healing methods, like mindfulness meditation and yoga, that in the long run will likely produce many more positive physical and psychological health benefits. Instead, young people are exposed to advertisements on the Internet, television, and in magazines about how a particular medication will enhance their sexual performance, help them rapidly lose weight, or cure their psychological ills. In addition, they also may be observing their stressed parents relying on prescription medications, alcohol, illicit substances, and nicotine just to cope. They soon discover that cutting oneself, binge-eating, abusing certain substances, video-games, and cyber-porn can function as fast-acting sedatives for their stress or as mood elevators to make themselves quickly feel better.

Alone Together: The Virtual World Has Become More Valued and Meaningful than Human Contact

Thanks to significant advances in digital technology, the popularity of social networking sites like *Facebook* and *Twitter*, and highly successful marketing strategies by the leaders behind these companies, having the next popular digital device and interacting in the virtual world has become more highly cherished than having human contact in the offline world. Interestingly enough, recent research on *Facebook* has found that rather than bringing us closer to others, it is isolating and distancing us from the very people we care the most about. This is increasing feelings of loneliness, and in some cases psychologically contributing to our being more depressed and anxious (Burke & Kraut, 2011; Cacioppo & Patrick, 2008; Marche, 2012; Ryan & Xenos, 2011). Chellappan and Kotikalapudi (2012) found that excessive users of the Internet exhibited high levels of anxiety and the depressive symptom of "flow duration entropy," which occurs when there is frequent switching among Internet applications like excessively checking one's e-mails, downloading files (movies and music), spending lots of time in chat-rooms, and engaged in online games. Turkle (2011) has written extensively on and researched the addictive quality of digital technology and how, once hooked, craving for "the next new thing" (digital device) and spending excessive amounts of time in the virtual world not only psychologically entraps users but promotes emotional distance in offline intimate relationships. Recently, when one of us (MB) went to the waiting room to invite a family in for their first session, all four members were connected to a different digital device and disconnected from one another: the father was having a work conversation from his mobile phone, with headphones and speaker; the mother was texting on her Blackberry; the 10-year-old daughter was writing on her iPad, and the 8-year-old was absorbed by his Nintendo—"alone together."

In many families today, parents are not providing any firm boundaries or guidelines for screen usage time nor do they know what websites their children and adolescents are regularly visiting (Selekman, 2009; Taffel, 2009). Excessive screen usage can drive emotional wedges in parent–child relationships. As far as we are concerned, nothing replaces parental presence and spending regular high-quality time together as a parental couple or family group, even in this age overloaded daily agendas and highly stressed parents. In fact, research has indicated that not only is spending time together as a family one of the six characteristics of strong families but simply having dinner together has been found to serve a preventative function for the initiation of adolescent drug experimentation and preventing substance dependency with young people already experimenting, and for helping prevent obesity with young people (Califano, 2007; DeFrain & Stinnett, 1992; Fulkerson et al., 2006; Stinnett & O'Donnell, 1996).

Why "Self-Destructive Habits" rather than "Addictions"?

Our choice of the words "self-destructive habits" over the more traditional term "addictions" grows out of our basic therapeutic assumptions regarding how we view self-destructive behavior and the treatment for these difficulties. We have adopted the Buddhist perspective in our clinical practices that self-destructive habits, like all life difficulties, are impermanent and in a constant state of evolutionary flux (Bien, 2010; Chodron, 2010; Gregson & Efran, 2002; Hanh, 1998; Rinpoche, 1993; Selekman, 2009; Trungpa, 1984). With this open-minded and hopeful view, we operate from the assumption that our self-destructive-habit clients already are changing well before we see them for the first time. As Berg and Reuss (1997) put it, "Recovery does not start the day our clients show up in our offices. It starts the day they say, 'I got to do something about this'" (p. 19). They are taking constructive steps to prevent their problem situations from getting much worse, may have already greatly reduced their time spent engaging in their choice habits, or possibly have quit engaging in their self-destructive habits altogether by the time we see them for the first time. Research and clinical evidence-based practice experiences on client pretreatment change and the self-change literature on self-harming, substance abuse, and gambling strongly support the notion that individuals with diagnosable *Diagnostic and Statistical Manual-IV* (DSM-IV) disorders can and do change on their own (Allgood, Parham, Salts, & Smith, 1995; Dawson, Goldstein, & Grant, 2007; Dawson et al., 2005; Klingemann & Klingemann, 2009; McKeel, 2011; Pietrusza, Rothenberg, & Whitlock, 2011; Selekman & Schulem, 2007; Shaffer, Martin, Kleschinsky, & Neporent, 2012; Sobell, 2010; Toneatto & Nett, 2010; Vaillant, 1983; Weiner-Davis, de Shazer, & Gingerich, 1987; Whitlock, 2008). In fact, many self-changing individuals have not only conquered self-destructive habits but had the ingenuity to know that what worked in the past can serve as a model for future success for resolving a new self-destructive habit or some other current difficulty they are faced with (Selekman, 2009; Sobell, Sobell, & Agrawal, 2002).

The self-change literature also critically challenges the disease-model belief that clients presenting with serious self-destructive habit difficulties must have progressive diseases that only can be brought into remission with total abstinence goals, participating in Twelve-Step self-help groups, and with treatment. We find this rigid one-size-fits-all disease model quite limiting in terms of avenues for intervention and it counters our belief and that of pioneering psychotherapy outcome researchers that we need to tailor-fit what we do with clients' unique stages of readiness for change and honor their preferences, expectations, theories of change, and goals (Hubble, Duncan, Miller, & Wampold, 2010; Norcross, 2010; Prochaska, Norcross, & DiClemente., 2006; Selekman, 2009). However, we will completely support the preferences and theories of change of those of our clients who are actively attending Alcoholics or Narcotics Anonymous or think they should first pursue treatment in traditional Twelve-Step programs. After their inpatient treatment experiences, we will work with them to consolidate their gains and provide relapse prevention work.

Finally, we believe self-destructive habits, like all habits, are made to be broken and we have witnessed they can indeed change quite quickly in a couple or family therapy context. It has been our clinical experience that it is not necessary to wait for the habit-dependent person to achieve abstinence or to "hit bottom" before beginning couples or family therapy. On the contrary, we have found that quickly intervening with help-seeking couple partners, family members, and concerned members from the clients' social networks at the point of their initiating counseling, has not only contributed to engaging them but has promoted changes in their problematic behaviors without there even being present in sessions.

Habits and Self-Destructive Habits

Habits are chains of behavior with their accompanying cognitions and emotions that are performed in a patterned way in certain contexts and that make our behavior more predictable. Psychiatrist Luc Isebaert (2005), building on Aristotle's wisdom, differentiates four elements of habits: ethos/ETHOS, pathos, logos, and oikos. At the behavioral level (ethos), habits are made of chains of observable and non-observable behaviors that tend to follow a certain sequence. The repetition of behaviors also reflects a moral dimension, ETHOS, as they define the type of person that we choose to be. These behaviors are accompanied by states of arousal and a range of emotions (pathos). The cognitive side (logos) of habits is represented by the thoughts that accompany the behaviors and the emotion, which take place in a given context (oikos). Aristotle, in his *Nicomachean Ethics*, was the first theorist to introduce the notion of harm-reduction or tapering down one's engagement in the choice self-destructive habit as a pragmatic pathway to conquering it. He would recommend experimenting with gradually limiting the amount of time indulging in one's choice habit(s) with increasingly longer time intervals between each episode. As a result, the individual learns how to delay gratification and strengthen his or her self-regulation capacities and abstinence self-efficacy (Bartlett & Collins, 2011).

At the brain level, the repetition of the behaviors that constitute the habit creates a neuronal model of the habitual behavior, with the participation of both cortical and sub-cortical structures. Doidge (2007) contends that neuronal pathways or deep tracks become ingrained in our brains by repeated engagement in our choice self-destructive habits, which is analogous to our strong proclivity to taking the fastest sled-riding tracks (often well carved into the snow) down a hill for the thrills and the pleasure when we are out sled-riding with friends or family. Thus, the more we use a particular neuronal pathway or track, the deeper that pathway becomes established in our brains. Finally, since our brains are involved in so many activities at any given moment and do not distinguish between healthy and unhealthy habits because of reward-distinction blindness, they will go into an automatic pilot default mode, and compel us to pursue the quickest pathway to pleasure and emotional distress relief, which may be our choice self-destructive habits.

Self-destructive habits are those habits that have a negative effect on the person, but in which the person engages repeatedly in spite of their short- or long-term negative consequences, creating emotional distress, behavioral constriction and cognitive impairment, reducing personal freedom, and causing couple, family, school, and occupational difficulties. Self-destructive habits include problems like abusing illegal drugs or alcohol, physical self-harming, reckless driving, over-exercising, binge-eating, compulsive shopping, and so forth. From a traditional diagnostic point of view, these self-destructive habits are classified as different types of disorders. For instance, in DSM-IV substance abuse is one diagnostic category, which is different from eating disorders, with pathological gambling falling under "impulse control disorders." Self-harming behavior does not receive a separate diagnosis, but is often considered a symptom of borderline personality disorder or post-traumatic stress disorder. Internet and cyber-sex dependency are being considered for representation in DSM-V. However, from a clinical point of view, it makes sense to cover these five groups in one book,[1] for a number of reasons:

- As we will see in the next section, these five types of self-destructive habits share a number of clinical features that create *similar challenges* in therapy. For instance, clients often keep their self-destructive habits secret and try to conceal them, they are usually not motivated for therapy, and their risk for relapses is quite high.
- They are highly *co-morbid*, and many clients present with various self-destructive habits simultaneously. For instance, a bulimic girl who cuts herself and abuses alcohol; the pathological gambler who is also hooked on cyber-porn and abuses cocaine; or the poly-substance-abusing teen who engages in risky self-harming behavior and indulges in binge-eating.
- Self-destructive habits also share their co-morbidity with other mental health problems. For instance, the lifetime prevalence of co-morbid depression for anorexia and bulimia is between 24 and 88% (Mitchell, Specker, & de Zwaan, 1991), with a higher likelihood of anxiety disorders (Laessle, Kittl, & Fichter, 1987) and obsessive symptoms (Holden, 1990); bulimic persons and binge-eaters are also prone to abuse alcohol and other drugs, to self-harm, and possibly gambling (Yip, White, Grilo, & Potenza, 2011). Persons suffering from a mood or anxiety disorder are at least twice as likely as the normal population to have a drug

---

[1] We will be focusing on these five groups of self-destructive habits because our clinical expertise lies in these five areas. We are not implying that other self-destructive habits like kleptomania, compulsive shopping, or risky sexual behaviors are (or are not) different.

abuse disorder also; and persons who abuse drugs are twice as likely to present with a concurrent mood or anxiety disorder than those who do not (Kessler, 2004).

- Three-quarters of problem gamblers manifest symptoms of depression (Blaszczynski & McConaghy 1988; Linden, Pope, & Jonas 1986; Petry, Stintson, & Grant, 2005), and 96% of cyber-sex dependent persons present signs of diagnosable anxiety disorders and 71% some form of mood disorder (Raymond, Coleman, & Miner, 2003). Co-occurring obsessive-compulsive disorder, addictive disorders or ADD/ADHD have also been described (Kafka & Hemen, 2003).

- When self-destructive habits coexist, they usually *reinforce each other*. For instance, the drug-abusing, self-harming client is more likely to cut herself when under the influence of substances. A pathological gambler is more likely to have inappropriate and/or unprotected sex when in a "gambling rush," and is likely to wager more money and lose more control if he consumes alcohol while gambling; conversely, his gambling losses are likely to lead him to abuse alcohol more heavily.

- Furthermore, research suggests that one self-destructive habit may *set in motion* the appearance of others. Within the same class of self-destructive habits, we often find that anorectic behaviors lead to bulimia and vice versa, or that abusing one kind of drug paves the way for others. This "switching addiction model" (Hodgins, Peden, & Cassidy, 2005) also applies from one category of self-destructive habits to another. For instance, research suggests that substance abuse may facilitate later pathological gambling (Potenza, 2008).

- All five types of self-destructive habits seem to share an *addictive quality*, presenting withdrawal symptoms, tolerance, and craving, and (as we will discuss in detail below) are likely to share some basic underlying biological mechanisms that involve the dysregulation of the endorphin system in the brain, and specially the dopamine system. As Blaszczynski and Nower (2002) contend:

  > It is hypothesized that a lack of dopamine receptors cause individuals to seek pleasure-generating activities, placing them at high risk for multiple addictive, impulsive, and compulsive behaviors, including: substance abuse, binge eating, sex addiction and pathological gambling. Thus, the genetic research suggests that the drive toward intense and, sometimes, detrimental pleasure-seeking is biologically prescribed, though the choice of behavior differs by individual. (p. 450)

- These common mechanisms are likely to be the reason why biological treatments originally developed for one type of self-destructive habit are showing promise in the treatment of others. For instance, some research suggests that opioid antagonists originally designed to treat substance-abusing clients may provide good results with pathological gamblers (Grant, Brewer, & Potenza, 2006). On the psychological treatment side, our point is that these five types of self-destructive habits respond well to similar interventions, so that, for instance, the therapeutic process with a bulimic adult may be similar to the therapy of a drug-abusing adolescent; or the therapy of a pathological gambler and his couple partner may share important features with the treatment of a self-harming individual and her/his spouse.

We wish to make clear that we are not suggesting that self-destructive habits are a homogeneous phenomenon. On the contrary, we are well aware of the enormous differences both between and within each of the five groups, and of the risk of assuming any "homogeneity myths" (Kiesler, 1966) in their description or treatment. For instance, there are many obvious differences between eating disorders on the one hand and pathological gambling on the other. Furthermore, there are also clear differences between anorexia, bulimia, and binge-eating (within eating disorders) or between problem gamblers who compulsively bet on horses at the race track and individuals hooked on slot machines (within gambling). Many relevant variables, such as the gender of the client, the chronic nature of the self-destructive habit, and level of family involvement, create further differences. However, self-destructive habits also have an important number of commonalities, some that they share with other problems that present in therapy, and some that make them different from other disorders. We will discuss both separately.

What Self-Destructive Habits Share with Other Mental Health Problems

There are a number of features that self-destructive habits share with other mental health problems like mood and anxiety disorders:

- As with other mental health problems, self-destructive habits act like powerful "black holes" (Hjerth, 2005) attracting the *attention* of the person who engages in them, who usually gets progressively more and more preoccupied with them, and discovers there is no escape from them. For instance, the heroin-abuser spends increasingly more time not only using the substance, but figuring out ways of getting it; or the anorectic's thoughts center increasingly on food and calories. Effective therapy can be seen as a way to pull the client out of this compulsive tendency and create a powerful ritual that allows him or her to focus the attention elsewhere (Frank, 1973; Gutiérrez, 2009). In our approach, this translates into the creation of powerful, engaging "therapeutic themes" during our sessions and into a deliberate effort to help clients structure their leisure time and engage in meaningful activities.
- Although in a large proportion of clients the natural course of their self-destructive habit is towards recovery, even without any therapeutic help (as we will see below in our discussion of self-change), in many other cases the course is progressive and leads to major *impairment* in important areas of clients' lives, in a way analogous to that of serious mental health problems. In some cases, clients reach us after a long history of involvement with the self-destructive habit, and with the perception that they have big "blank spaces" in their autobiographies. A therapeutic implication is that sometimes it is necessary to help the client restore as much as possible those missing chapters from their lives.
- Another feature that self-destructive habits share with other mental health problems is the perceived *lack of control*. As systemic writers cogently pointed out decades ago (Haley, 1963; Watzlawick, Beavin, & Jackson, 1967) the uncontrollability of symptoms is the hallmark of any mental health problem: the anxious person feels she cannot escape her anxiety; the obsessive client cannot help but ruminate for hours. Lack of control is a common feature of clients with self-destructive habits, but it also takes a different nuance in the form of *loss of control* once the engraved habit sequence starts. One implication for therapy is that pattern intervention strategies (Haley, 1973, 1983; O'Hanlon, 1987; O'Hanlon & Weiner-Davis, 1989; Selekman, 2005, 2009) can be seen as ways to re-introduce a sense of control.
- Loss of control is related to another feature that self-destructive habits share with other mental health problems: the serious *risk of relapses*, with the difference being that for self-destructive habit relapses, they are more likely to take the form of a sudden re-emergence of the old behavior, which on top of it all is likely to be initially very pleasurable due to the sensitization effect. A habit cannot be unlearned; one can learn new, alternative virtuous habits, but any old habits remain as a possibility (Isebaert, 2005). As will be seen in the case examples presented later, this increased risk of relapses with self-destructive habits implies the need to dedicate considerable therapy time to relapse prevention training, and to be prepared to constructively manage relapses should they happen.

Differences with Other Presenting Problems

There are also a number of issues in which self-destructive habits share as a group, elements that pose unique challenges to therapists, couples, and families alike:

- Although arguably for most non-psychotic disorders, the *borders between normal and pathological behavior* are also ill-defined, in the case of self-destructive habits the progression from behaviors perceived as normal to clinical problems is even more subtle. In fact, most self-destructive habit problems begin with the person engaging in what initially may be perceived as a harmless, recreational activity (playing blackjack in a casino; having some drinks after work; playing online wargames) that only at later stages increases and gets out of hand. Furthermore, except for illegal drugs and self-harming behavior there is an enormous *social and commercial pressure* to engage in most of these activities, from drinking alcohol to smoking, dieting, or spending money on lotteries. The therapeutic challenges that derive from this situation are that, on the one hand, many clients with self-destructive habits find it difficult to realize that they have a problem, when so many other people behave in the same way, and on the other hand, maintaining changes and preventing relapses is more difficult in a social environment that is saturated with invitations or "temptations" to relapse.
- The positive side of this situation is that for some self-destructive habits abstinence is not necessarily the only therapeutic goal, and that *controlled engagement in the behavior* might be a valid therapeutic aim. Although this is a controversial issue, our reading of the research literature is that both controlled gambling and controlled substance use are viable treatment outcomes (Klingemann & Sobell, 2010; Miller & Rollnick, 2002; Shaffer et al., 2012); and in fact happen as often as abstinence after treatments; continued dieting is also a common (and acceptable) outcome in the treatment of eating disorders.
- Another relevant issue, related to the previous one, is that most self-destructive habits are *ego-syntonic*, whereas most other non-psychotic problems are usually *ego-dystonic*. The person who starts feeling depressed or anxious, or the person who suffers from tics or psychosomatic abdominal pain, is distressed by these symptoms and wants to get rid of them from the beginning; in contrast, most self-destructive habits begin by being pleasurable and are not perceived as a problem. Only at later stages, when the negative consequences of the self-destructive habit become evident, is the person prepared to see it as a problem. The clinical implication is that more often than not persons with self-destructive habits are not voluntary clients for therapy, but are brought in by concerned others who see their behavior as problematic. In other words, clients with self-destructive habits are likely to show up in therapy in a precontemplative stage of readiness for change (Prochaska & DiClemente, 1982, 1985, 1992; Prochaska, DiClement, & Norcross, 1992; Prochaska et al., 2006) and may even feel proud of their "accomplishments": the anorectic girl feels superior to other girls who are not able to restrict their food intake as successfully as she does; or the pathological casino gambler is proud of the "system" he has figured out for winning.
- An almost natural consequence of the ego-syntonic nature of most self-destructive habits and of clients' lack of initial motivation to change is the high likelihood that clients with self-destructive habits may *lie or act deceivingly* in order to continue with their habits. This is different from most clients with non-psychotic problems, who may feel ashamed by their problem, more or less frightened by the prospects and risks of change, or demoralized by their inability to change, but who basically are in the same boat with their therapists in wanting to get relief from their problems. Self-destructive habits, in contrast, usually need a certain degree of concealment in order to be carried out, varying in its degree from the bulimic girl who binges at night while other family members are asleep, to the chronic gambler who has created a whole system of deception to conceal that he is broke and keeps securing financial resources. As an unfortunate consequence, the clinical literature is full of descriptions of substance-abusing clients as "liars," of gamblers as "self-entitled," "deceitful," and "manipulative" (Selvini-Palazzoli, Boscolo, Cecchin, & Prata, 1978). In our view, it is important not to make any moral judgments on these behaviors, but to understand that they are a logical consequence if the person feels they are being forced to change something that they do not want to. This

calls for an accepting and understanding position of the therapist, and for a motivational enhancement approach to collaborating with initially reluctant clients (Miller & Rollnick, 2002).

- Another therapeutic challenge is that, once self-destructive clients have moved into contemplation and start to see their habit as a problem, powerful bio-psychological mechanisms like *withdrawal symptoms* and *craving* will make it more difficult to cut down on their habits. This is an obstacle that other psychotherapy clients do not have to face, and for therapists it implies the need to make sure their clients get enough support and extra motivation.
- An additional source of difficulty in overcoming self-destructive habits is that in many cases they play important *functions* for the person: for instance, the cutting helps the teenager to numb her emotional pain; online gambling helps a client escape his boredom; or being thin works as a valuable source of self-esteem for an abused and neglected young woman. It has been our clinical experience that the longer our clients have been engaging in their choice self-destructive habit practices, the unique functions for their use in their lives appear to increase as well. We will return to this issue later in the chapter.
- Although we favor couple and family therapy for most presenting problems (Beyebach, 2006, 2009; Selekman, 2005, 2009, 2010), in the case of self-destructive habits the *role of the family and/or couple partner* is even more important than for other mental health problems. The client may not see a problem and that the only persons willing to seek treatment are the family members or the couple partner; as a consequence, families and couples often play a crucial role in motivating and engaging the client in therapy (Meyers, 2012; Smith & Meyers, 2004). The self-destructive habits usually have a massive negative impact on families and couples, erode family functioning, and are liable to traumatize family members (Kalischuk, Nowatzki, Cardwell, Klein, & Solowoniuk, 2006). Therefore, couple and family sessions can be a highly supportive and healing context for couple partners and family members. The therapeutic challenge, in our view, is to mobilize families and couple partners as allies in the treatment of the person with self-destructive habits and at the same time keep an eye on their personal needs. The creation of a therapeutic united front of therapist, client, and family member or couple partner against the problem (often including key resource people from our clients' social networks) is often hampered by the negative emotional arousal and by the secrecy and deceit that often accompany self-destructive habits. Therefore, an additional therapeutic task is to restore trust and stop negativity and mutual blaming, guilt-inducing processes that are often reinforced by the unfortunate social construction of certain self-destructive habits as "vices" or as expressions of bad will.

The Pathways Model: A Framework for the Development and Maintenance of Intractable Self-Destructive Habits

As we have seen in the previous sections, there are a number of clinical similarities between the five types of self-destructive habits, but also important differences not only between them but also within each of them. For instance, for pathological gamblers, impulsive men are more likely to wager bets in horse races or soccer matches, whereas depressed, problem-gambling women are more likely to play slot machines; in eating disorders, restrictive anorectics tend to behave differently from purging bulimics; self-harming individuals who choose to cut themselves can be quite different from self-injurers who prefer self-battery. There is no common personality profile for individuals who engage in self-destructive behaviors and co-morbid personality disorders also vary greatly: for instance, anti-social personality disorder is common for some gamblers and some drug users; self-harming clients often receive a borderline personality disorder label; restrictive anorectics are frequently described as obsessive-compulsive. An alternative way to make sense of both heterogeneity and commonalities of self-destructive habits is to examine how self-destructive habits fit into the life-stories of the persons who display them. Building on the theoretical framework that Blaszczynski and Nower (2002) proposed for gambling, we like to differentiate three different pathways in the development of self-destructive habits, which lead to three different types of clinical pictures:

- Pathway I: Self-destructive habits that develop in individuals with no previous vulnerability or psychological problems, in a process of pure behavioral and cognitive conditioning, which is later biologically and interpersonally reinforced.
- Pathway II: Self-destructive habits that develop as coping mechanisms for personal or interpersonal distress in individuals with emotional vulnerabilities or relational difficulties, or are impacted by past traumatic events.
- Pathway III: Self-destructive habits that develop in highly disturbed individuals, as part of a broader picture of antisocial behaviors and impulsivity.

The starting block common to the three pathways is the availability and accessibility of the substance and/or equipment of abuse. Epidemiological surveys indicate that availability and access to gambling facilities are associated with a higher incidence of pathological gambling (Shaffer, Hall, & Vanderbilt, 1999;Abbott & Volberg 1996; Welte, Barnes, Wieczorek, Tidwell, & Parker, 2001; Volberg, 1996); that availability and access to drugs and alcohol increase the incidence of substance abuse and dependence problems (Moos, 2007; Peterson, Hawkins, & Catalano, 1992); and that the more people who voluntarily diet in a given population, the higher the incidence of eating disorders in that population (Hsu, 1997). Environments in which gambling, substance abuse, and/or dieting are socially accepted and promoted increase the risk of people engaging in these behaviors. The social construction or perception of risk is a relevant mediator of this relationship, something well established by research both for substance abuse (Johnston, O'Malley, Bachman, & Schulenberg, 2012) and pathological gambling (Jacques, Ladouceur, & Ferland, 2000; Shaffer, LaBrie, & LaPlante, 2004; Shaffer, Hall, & Vanderbilt, 1999). In the case of self-harming behavior, the social encouragement of self-destructive or risky behaviors appears to happen when endorsed by popular and powerful peers, music and entertainment celebrities, toxic online support groups and websites, and in confined institutional spaces such as schools and residential treatment facilities (Selekman, 2006, 2009).

Once the problematic behavior is initiated, the next process commonly applicable to all three pathways is the influence of classical and operant conditioning, which leads to increasing engagement in the self-destructive behaviors and to the development of habitual patterns of gambling, dieting/bingeing, or excessive Internet use. Operant conditioning occurs through positive reinforcement by the direct pleasurable and physiological effects of drugs and alcohol or by the release of dopamine and other neurotransmitters that self-harming, dieting, or winning in gambling produce. This arousal is also conditioned to stimuli associated with the habit environment, so that certain stimuli act as cues and as powerful reinforcers for the habit. In addition, negative reinforcement is produced when aversive anxiety states or depression are reduced by the consumption of substances, the excitement of gambling, video-gaming, or risky self-harming behaviors. Eventually, a habitual pattern emerges: a "neuronal model" of the habitual behavior is built through a process of cortical excitation (McConaghy 1980, cited in Blaszczynski & Nower, 2002). Once triggered by habit-related cues, the behavior completion mechanism underlying this neuronal model is stimulated to produce a drive to carry out the habitual behavior to completion. Attempts to resist completing the habit provoke a state of aversive arousal experienced as a compulsive drive to carry out the habitual pattern. The more the client goes down the chain of behaviors that constitute the habit, the more difficult it is to resist this urge.

Cognitive processes intervene at the very start of the process, putting the person at risk of engaging in self-destructive behavior: for instance, a teenage girl may start to think that she would be more popular at school if she succeeded in losing weight, and starts a restrictive diet that puts her at risk for developing anorexia; or an adolescent may try MDMA tablets out of the erroneous belief that they are not "drugs," but harmless recreational devices that will make him or her more "social." Then, as the frequency of engaging in the self-destructive habit progresses, cognitive functioning gets impaired and erroneous, and distorted cognitive schemas appear, as a direct effect of the habit (for instance, impaired decision-making due to the psychotropic effect of drugs or alcohol) and/or as an attempt to reduce cognitive dissonance (over-evaluation of wins and underestimation of losses in problematic gamblers; wrong appraisal of body shape in eating disorders). These schemas shape expectations, attributions, and evaluations of one's own performance, leading to erroneous perceptions, superstitious thinking, and in general what is usually described as distorted cognitions, self-defeating, negative automatic thoughts that tend to perpetuate the negative habit. Some of these cognitions take certain predictable forms for certain types of problems, in what we like to describe as "the traps of alcohol" (for instance, minimizing such as "everybody drinks"), "the lies of anorexia" (for instance, distorted cognitions such as "If I eat this sandwich I will put on two pounds"), the "traps of slot-machines" (superstitious thinking such as "this is my lucky machine"), or "the false promises of cutting" (self-defeating thoughts such as "I have to punish myself"). The potency and pervasiveness of distorted beliefs strengthen with increasing levels of involvement in the self-destructive habit and with deeper effects on the brain.

On the biological side, the repeated enactment of the habit eventually leads to the brain's reward system malfunctioning, especially through the alteration of the dopamine system, which may lead to physiological dependence with withdrawal and tolerance symptoms. In the case of eating disorders, the starvation syndrome, with hypothalamic dysregulation and the alteration of the intake/exercise/body temperature feedback mechanisms, adds another layer of biological constraint.

Relational aspects are also important factors in the development and maintenance of self-destructive habits, although probably more so for the first and second pathway. Couple partners, immediate and extended family members, and peers may play a crucial role both in the initiation of the problematic behavior (for instance, peer pressure to smoke marijuana or to gamble in a casino; the mother criticizing her daughter for being overweight) and in the later mismanagement of the self-destructive habit, either by failing to take action or by involuntarily reinforcing it.

Pathway I: Behaviorally Conditioned Self-Destructive Habits

Individuals without previous psychopathology or serious emotional or relational problems may enter this pathway at any age, prompted by exposure to the problematic behavior through chance, relatives, the couple partner, or friends. They may maintain their behavior at a non-problematic, low-risk level, as in the case of social gamblers, social drinkers, non-anorectic dieters, and even occasional recreational drug users. However, in other cases they reach a point where the behavior escalates through the process described above and transforms into a fully fledged self-destructive habit that affects the person at various levels, creating emotional distress and functional impairment. This escalation may be triggered by chance events like a "big win" in gambling; a digestive illness in anorexia, or a move into a new neighborhood with more drugs available.

Clients who develop their self-destructive habits through this pathway are expected to present with less severe problems and to be more likely to be initially motivated for treatment than those who follow Pathways II and III. For gamblers, Blaszczynski and Nower (2002) predict that these clients are more likely to be able to engage in controlled gambling (as opposed to abstinence) after therapy.

Pathway II: Self-Destructive Habits as Coping and Escape Mechanisms

Self-destructive habits that develop through this pathway are established through the same process of behavioral conditioning, cognitive distortion, and relational feedback as in Pathway I, but in this case the person enters the cycle with an emotional or relational vulnerability, so that the problematic behavior is sought as a way to cope with emotional distress or meet specific psychological or relational needs.

Relational factors are often the initial motivators for bulimia, which may start as a response to family or couple conflict, in a similar vein as alcohol abuse in women; the extreme dieting that paves the way to anorexia may initially be a means of improving low self-esteem (Le Grange & Lock, 2010; Robin & Le Grange, 2010). Post-traumatic stress disorder symptoms, and especially intrusive memories and flashbacks, might be handled by low-skill gambling (Anderson & Brown 1984; Jacobs 1988), taking drugs such as cannabis derivatives, and engaging in certain forms of self-harm such as cutting (Selekman, 2009) that alleviate the emotional distress through the effect of dissociation and narrowed attention ("numbing out bad feelings"). When the initial vulnerability stems from depression or boredom, clients may try to increase their arousal through high-skill gambling or cyber-sex practices that counteract their dysphoria, by abusing stimulants such as cocaine or amphetamines, or by engaging in highly arousing risk behaviors. In contrast, individuals who try to reduce their arousal level to cope with their intolerable *anxiety* may resort to low-skill gambling to focus their attention, abuse depressants (alcohol) or tranquilizers (over-the-counter hypnotics), or engage in forms of self-harm (cutting, burning) that create a dissociative effect.

Blaszczynski and Nower (2002) have found that Pathway II gamblers will be more resistant to treatment than Pathway I gamblers and that their treatment needs to address the underlying vulnerabilities. In our experience, Pathway II self-destructive clients are not necessarily more reluctant to participate in therapy, but it is possible that they request help for their emotional distress only, without wanting to address their self-destructive habit, which they perceive as alleviating their distress. In these cases, it is necessary to help our clients find alternative ways to cope with their emotional problems before taking away their cherished "ally" and resource (choice habit), and then help them to address the emotional or relational issues.

Pathway III: Self-Destructive Habits as Part of a Broader Antisocial and Impulsive Pattern

According to Blaszczynski and Nower (2002), clients who follow Pathway III can be described as highly dysfunctional individuals, with both psychosocial and genetic vulnerabilities such as the presence of the dopamine D2A1 allele receptor gene, an alteration strongly associated with impulse control disorders which has been found more frequently in pathological gamblers and substance abusers (Commings et al., 1996; Linden, 2011). Clients who later develop self-destructive habits through this pathway display impulsivity, antisocial behavior, and/or ADD, and from an early age engage in a wide array of problematic and even illegal behaviors (Welte, Barnes, Tidwell, & Hoffman, 2009, 2011), with devastating negative effects on their lives and relationships. Their self-destructive habits are only one part of this broader picture, and are likely to be more severe and chronic than for Pathway I and Pathway II habits. Indices of diagnosable mental health problems and of suicidality are also increased in comparison to Pathways I and II. These individuals are likely to display several mutually reinforcing self-destructive habits simultaneously, and to be in multi-habit-dependent couple relationships or families. The "anti-social impulsivist" gamblers described by Blaszczynski et al. (1997) would fit this pathway, as well as Cloninger, Sigvardsson, Svrakic, and Przybeck's (1995) Type II highly anti-social and genetically influenced alcoholics; and in general poly-substance-abusing individuals with histories of violent and criminal behaviors. Although this pathway applies more to substance abuse and gambling, and is in our view less common among self-harming clients, the extreme self-harming and daredevil behaviors of "thrill seekers" (Selekman, 2009) can be included in this pathway. Among eating disorders, only binge-eating and some cases of extreme purgative bulimia would fit this pattern. Blaszczynski and Nower (2002) describe Pathway III gamblers as unlikely to seek treatment on their own, with poor compliance, and having a poor prognosis. We have found Pathway III clients to be initially reluctant to enter treatment and very difficult to engage; in these cases it is likely that we end up working with the concerned others only, and more often than not the therapeutic goal is merely to reduce the negative impact of the self-destructive individual's challenging behaviors on our clients. However, with some Pathway III reluctant clients their engagement into couple or family treatment was made possible only after significant changes had occurred with their couple partners and/or concerned family members (see Chapter 9 for examples of effective engagement strategies for reluctant habit-dependent clients).

Implications of the Pathways Model

Before we discuss some of the possible implications of the pathways model we have described, we would like to acknowledge that there are several caveats to be taken into account. First, we are not assuming that different pathways necessarily require different curative procedures. In other words, therapeutic solutions do not necessarily have to match exactly the structure of a given problem, but simply to fit successfully into a given presentation (de Shazer, 1988, 1991). Furthermore, the factors that contributed to the initiation and perpetuation of a self-destructive habit may not play a major role in its maintenance, and factors that initially had no bearing on the etiology of the habit may come into play only once it is established. What makes a difference in terms of treatment planning are the current problem-maintaining causes of the habit, which may or may not coincide with the ones that lead to its formation (Pinsof, 1995). Finally, although we have focused on risk factors, there are a number of protective factors that play an equally important role in the evolution of self-destructive habits, sometimes moderating their course and sometimes preventing even very vulnerable persons from developing any self-destructive habits. These protective factors operate at various levels: individual (for instance, personal resilience, self-control, capacity to establish and maintain strong and meaningful connections with supportive others), family (for instance, positive parenting practices, emotional availability of parents and/or couple partners), peers (for instance, supportive peers engaged in healthy lifestyles and offline activities), school (academic environments that foster individual competencies; cooperation versus competition), community (positive social support; opportunities to get involved in service work and social organizations), and wider societal level (tough no-drug use policies and enforcement, eating disorders prevention, etc.).

In any case, we believe that conceptualizing the formation of self-destructive habits with the three-pathway model has the advantage of giving justice to the heterogeneity of self-destructive habits while at the same time explaining their commonalities:

- It allows us to understand that, on the one hand, "everybody is at risk" of developing a self-destructive habit (Pathway I), given that no previous psychopathology, personality disorder or "character flaw" is necessary to fall into the trap of self-destructive habits. On the other hand, it acknowledges that some individuals do indeed have more opportunities than others to fall prey to self-destructive habits, due to their pre-existing vulnerabilities or lack of protective factors (Pathways II and III).
- It allows us to see the emotional or relational origin of self-destructive habits as a possibility (Pathway II habits) but not as a necessity. From this vantage point, we see the automatic description of relational functions to any self-destructive habit as a "circularity bias," espoused by systemic therapists (Boscolo, Cecchin, Hoffman, & Penn, 1987; Madanes, 1981;

Onnis, 1988; Selvini-Palazzoli et al., 1978). We consider the failure to recognize the relational functions of Pathway II as a "linearity bias," not infrequent in cognitive, behavioral, and traditional disease model approaches.

- The pathways model also makes sense of the startling discrepancies between different clinical descriptions, research data, and therapy outcomes for clients with self-destructive habits. For instance, many of the negative biological and genetic elements that characterize Pathway III clients, as well as their gloomy prognostic outlook, would not apply to Pathway I and Pathway II clients.

Self-Destructive Habit Maintenance Factors

As mentioned above, it is important to understand how different self-destructive habits can become established, but it is therapeutically even more crucial to be able to describe what factors contribute to their maintenance even in the face of their negative and often catastrophic effects. We will briefly review some of the most important ones, which also can be understood as determinants of relapse (Witkiewitz & Marlatt, 2004):

- On the biological level, all self-destructive habits can be conceptualized as physiological dependencies: the person needs to engage in the habit with increasing frequency and/or intensity to get the same pleasurable effect (tolerance) and, if they cut down on the habit, they are likely to experience unpleasant withdrawal symptoms, ranging from slight irritability and restlessness to craving and full-blown organic withdrawal syndromes. If the person has a lapse after a period of abstinence, the sensitization effect will make their first experience of re-engaging in the habit especially rewarding, and therefore will increase the risk of a relapse. We will discuss this level more fully in the next section.
- On the behavioral level, self-destructive habits are, as we have seen, both positively and negatively reinforced. In addition, there are a number of interrelated phenomena that make established self-destructive habits resistant to change. On the one hand is *inertia failure* (Ciarrocchi, 2001): as the person advances in the chain of behaviors that constitute the habit, it is more difficult to stop and the person feels an increased urge to complete the habit. In *acquiescence* (Ciarrocchi, 2001), people contribute to their self-regulation failures by intentionally or unintentionally placing themselves in the high-risk situation: the recovering addict who wants to visit "old buddies"; the self-harming teenager who plays the music she knows is associated with cutting; or the cyber-sex abuser engaged in inappropriate online sex who wants to "only check who contacted me." The *abstinence violation* effect first described for alcoholism (Marlatt & Gordon, 1985) and the *counter-regulation* of eating-disordered persons refer to the tendency of those exercising restraint to give up completely once a lapse or slip occurs, thereby falling into a full-blown relapse.
- Negative cognitions brought about by the self-destructive habit also contribute to the maintenance of self-destructive habits: low expectancy of success ("I will never be drug-free"), external expectancy of locus of control ("To overcome this problem is not in my hands") or lack of abstinence self-efficacy ("I don't have enough self-control to kick this habit") become self-fulfilling prophecies, and are therefore both the result of and contributors to the persistence of self-destructive habits. More pervasive depressive negative cognitive schemas about oneself ("I am a loser and bound to fail at everything"), the world and the future also invite paralysis and failure, and catastrophic fears nurture the tendency to escape through abusing substances, gambling, self-harming, or escaping into the virtual world. Furthermore, as mentioned before, each self-destructive habit is usually associated with certain problem-specific distorted cognitions, what we like to call the "traps of the self-destructive habit," for instance low-risk perception in substance abuse or illusions of control in gambling. A

positive expected outcome of the self-destructive behavior ("If I smoke a joint it will relax me") contributes to the motivation of engaging in it.
- At the level of emotions, the negative consequences of self-destructive habits in the long run create negative affective states that further fuel the habits themselves. For instance, the person who has lost his home or family due to the financial consequences of gambling or drug abuse is likely to feel anxious and depressed, which may trigger new substance-abusing or gambling behavior. Or the adolescent female who has disfigured her legs through cutting and may feel so bad about it that she escapes even more into self-harming, that is thereby negatively reinforced. Baker, Piper, McCarthy, Majeskie, and Fiore (2004) have identified the escape from negative affect as the primary motive for drug use.
- At the interpersonal level we have already mentioned that immediate and extended family members, couple partners, and peers may contribute to the maintenance of the self-destructive habit both by failing to take adequate action (for instance, the mother who ignores or minimizes the cuts on her daughter's arms), by taking action that worsens the problem instead of relieving it (scolding the daughter who has cut herself is likely to induce more cutting), or by inadvertently reinforcing it (lecturing at the daughter about how she is disfiguring her body and getting overweight). More generally speaking, high levels of low-quality support (i.e., interpersonal pressures to engage in the self-destructive behavior) and low levels of high-quality support (support for abstinence) can trigger relapses for substance abuse (Witkiewitz & Marlatt, 2004), gambling behavior, some forms of eating-distressed and self-harming behaviors (Ciarrocchi, 2001; Le Grange & Lock, 2010; Selekman, 2009; Witkiewitz & Marlatt, 2004).
- Finally, another source of difficulty in giving up a self-destructive habit is that the habit often plays a useful and important role for the individual, their family, or couple relationship, as described by early family systems theorists (Haley, 1976; Minuchin, Rosman, & Baker, 1978; Selvini-Palazzoli, Boscolo, Cecchin, & Prata, 1978). For instance, the bulimic daughter's symptoms may be helpful to her mother, in that by defocusing her attention on to her distracts the mother from having to face her unresolved marital conflicts with her father.

Figure 1.1 summarizes our view on the development and maintenance of self-destructive habits. The upper part illustrates the three pathways we discussed for the development of self-destructive habits; the bottom portion of the figure portrays the roads to both chronicity and recovery. In the evolution towards chronicity, the maintenance factors we have just described interact in a mutually reinforcing way; in the evolution to recovery, this negative feedback loop is interrupted in such a way that alternative, healthy virtuous habits replace the self-destructive ones. As we will explain in outlining our collaborative strengths-based brief family therapy approach, we understand that on the road to recovery, although it may be enough to change one of the factors (biological, behavioral, cognitive, emotional, or relational) to create a major change in the whole self-destructive habit problem-maintenance system, therapists stand more chances of bringing about meaningful change if they intervene on as many levels as possible.

Self-Destructive Habit Maintenance and the Brain

We have mentioned before that although we prefer not to use the label *addictions* for the self-destructive habits covered in this book, they are often placed under this heading. The biological basis of the addictive nature of self-destructive habits can be found in the pleasure circuit in the medial forebrain, what David Linden aptly calls "the compass of pleasure" (Linden, 2011, p. 3). The central axis of this pleasure circuit (see Figure 1.2) is the dopamine-containing neurons of the ventral tegmental area (VTA) and their axons, which project to the nucleus accumbens, the ventral striatum, the anterior cingulated cortex, the prefrontal cortex, parts of the hippocampus,

SELF-DESTRUCTIVE HABITS

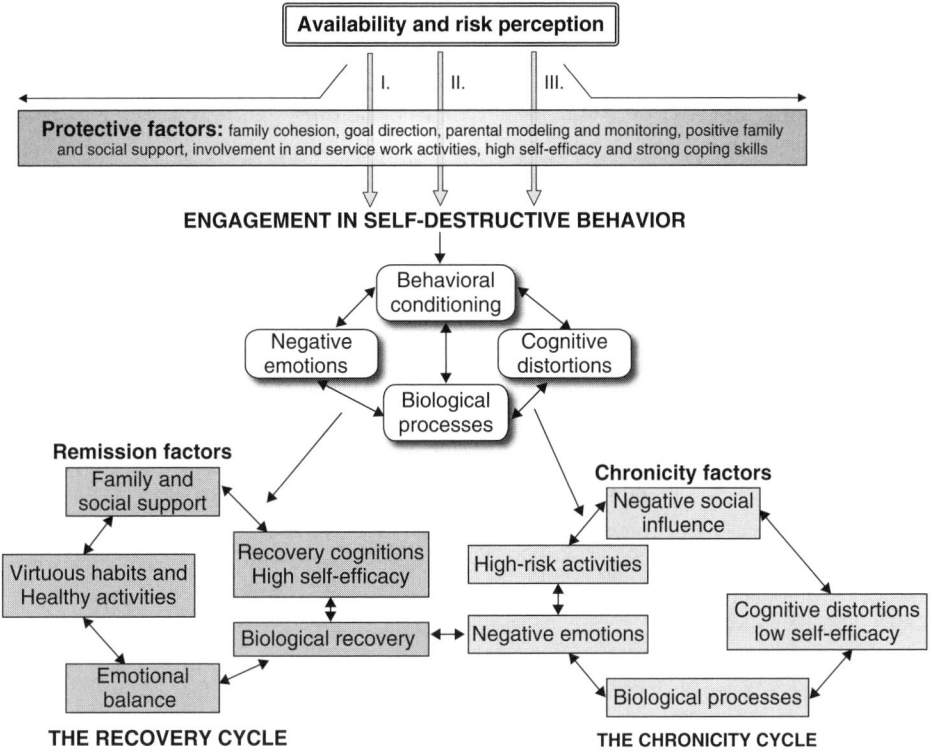

Figure 1.1 The formation and maintenance of self-destructive habits.

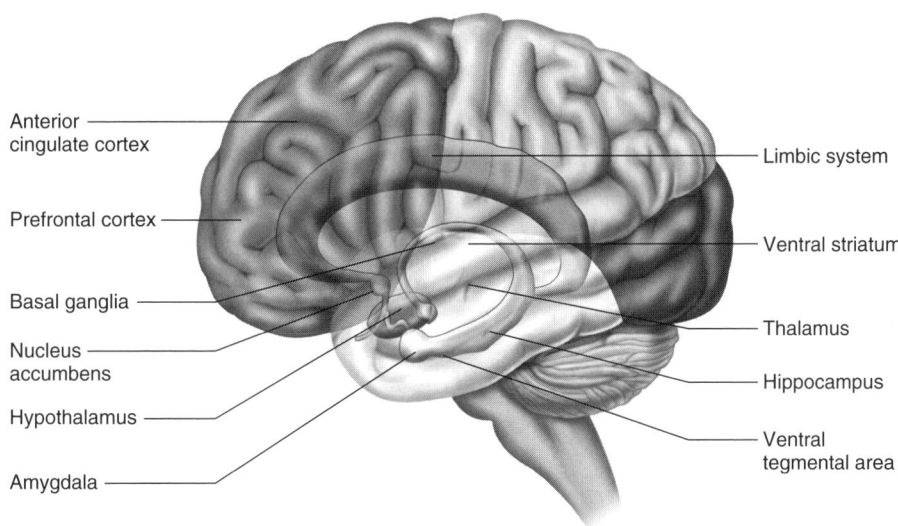

Figure 1.2 The key brain systems.

thalamus, hypothalamus, and amygdala, where they release dopamine. The reception of the released dopamine by the dendrites of receiving neurons is subjectively experienced as pleasure, which will not only depend on how much dopamine is released, but also by how much is effectively bound by the dopamine receptors versus re-uptake by dopamine transporters. The release of dopamine will of course depend on the levels of other excitatory and inhibitory neurotransmitters, like GABA or glutamate.

As Linden (2011) contends, the addictive potential of a given substance or behavior (in interplay with individual and environmental factors) depends on three main variables:

- The more a given drug or behavior activates the pleasure circuit, the more addictive it becomes. This is why heroin, cocaine, and amphetamines are more addictive than alcohol, nicotine, and cannabis.
- The faster a given substance reaches the brain, the greater its addictive potential. This is why smoked or injected cocaine is more addictive than snorted cocaine; or why injected opioids are more addictive than ingested opium.
- Finally, from a human learning perspective, the addictive potential also depends on the number of pleasure or behavior associations that a given substance or habit typically generates. For instance, a heroin addict may get two strong, rapid "hits" per day, whereas a pack-a-day cigarette smoker will get two hundred weak, rapidly delivered hits per day. This is one of the reasons why 80% of people who smoke become addicted to nicotine, whereas only about 35% of all people who have injected heroin become addicts (Linden, 2011). The addictive potential of video-games can also be accounted for by the very intensive reward schedule they offer: the stimulation of the pleasure circuit is weak, but is provided dozens of times during a given match.

These biological elements help us to better understand the *key brain systems and major neurotransmitters involved with the self-destructive habit maintenance loop* (Amen & Smith, 2010; DiSalvo, 2011; Hanson & Mendius, 2009; Linden, 2011; Schwartz & Gladding, 2011) (see Figure 1.3.):

1. Once the person has acquired the habit, the maintenance loop is set in motion by a variety of stimuli/triggers, such as external (relational conflict) and internal stressors (negative emotion and self-defeating thoughts), and other environmental cues that have become associated with the self-destructive habit (images, pleasurable memories, music, certain objects, people, places, activities, etc.).
2. In response to these stimuli/triggers, our limbic system induces craving and urges in us to engage in our choice habit(s) with the anticipation that we will get rewarded with immediate relief and pleasure.

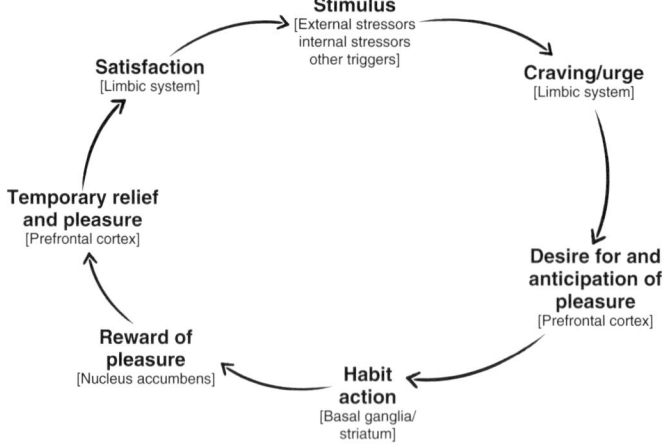

Figure 1.3 The self-destructive habit maintenance loop.

3. The craving and urges set in motion by the limbic system are then registered in our prefrontal cortex as a conscious desire to seek relief as quickly as possible, which then compels us to engage in our choice habit(s) actions.
4. The habit actions send signals back to our limbic system and to the ventral tegmental area (VTA) of our brain, which releases dopamine and other neurotransmitters in their trigger areas. This activation of the neuronal pleasure circuit triggers euphoric feelings and emotional and physical pain relief.
5. The prefrontal cortex provides the conscious experiencing of pleasure. The dopamine and other neurotransmitter levels increase and rapidly circulate throughout our blood systems, which create powerful feelings of satisfaction within us.
6. Alcohol, opioids, and stimulants artificially co-opt the dopamine reward system either by inducing an increased release of dopamine, by reducing its re-uptake, or by locking onto the dopamine receptors. In any case, the subjective experience of the person is one of pleasure and euphoria. Regular to heavy abuse of these substances leads to suppression and malfunction of the reward circuits, which makes it necessary for the users to increase the amount of their choice substances of abuse in order to get the same pleasurable effect. Gradually, the euphoria produced by the drug drains away, and pleasure is replaced by desire; liking becomes wanting. In addition, the enjoyment of other pleasurable experiences also becomes affected.
7. Cyber-sex/porn abuse habits not only trigger the dopamine release systems but also other "feel-good" chemicals like adrenalin, serotonin, vasopressin, oxytocin, and testosterone (Maltz & Maltz, 2010). Oxytocin is produced by our pituitary gland, controlled by the hypothalamus, and released by stimulation of sex and reproductive organs and during orgasm. It produces a pleasurable "rush" feeling that promotes bonding with intimate others. Both oxytocin and vasopressin help with the processing of social cues involved in the recognition of certain intimate others and the creation of positive shared memories. However, by taxing the systems involved in the manufacturing of these "feel-good" chemicals, they may start to malfunction, particularly in offline intimate relationships, leading to sexual dysfunction and intimacy difficulties, and the system circuitries becoming limited to and primed for online cyber-sex and porn-related activities (Maltz & Maltz, 2010).
8. Gambling and on- and offline video-gaming trigger not only dopamine release, but an increase in adrenalin, noradrenalin, and testosterone levels as well. All of these chemical substances produce autonomic arousal and the "rush" sensation gamblers and gamers experience while playing.
9. With self-injury, an endogenous opioid manufacturing system is directly involved. The endorphins manufactured by this system can provide immediate pleasure in the form of euphoria or a "rush" sensation. The endorphin effect also can provide for the self-injurer a "numbing" sensation to deaden any emotional distress or physical pain he/she may encounter. Finally, for some self-injurers their lack of impulse control and attempt to take back control when feeling emotionally and physically out of control, can be related to their having much lower levels of serotonin than the average person (Favazza & Selekman, 2003).

The fact that self-destructive habits are deeply ingrained in the brain chemistry does not imply, however, that their treatment has to be biological. In fact, the most effective treatments for self-destructive habits like substance abuse tend to be of psychological nature, with medication playing a subordinate role (National Institue on Drug Abuse, 1999). This makes sense from a systemic perspective (Bronfenbrenner, 1979; von Bertalanffy, 1968), as biological, cognitive, emotional, behavioral, and interpersonal interaction levels are constantly interacting, and changes in one can be brought about by changes in others. For instance, the effective parental monitoring of a substance-abusing adolescent his (behavioral/interactional level) may contain his self-destructive habit and produce a rebalancing of his pleasure circuitry (biological level); the understanding of the "gambler's fallacy" (cognitive level) may help the pathological gambler to reduce his gambling (behavioral level) and to overcome his dependency (biological level), and so on. As Linden (2011) contends:

> In the brain, causality is a two-way street. Yes, our genes and our neural circuits predispose us to certain behaviors, but our brains are malleable, and we can alter their neural circuits with experiences. When an addict goes to talk therapy or engages in mindfulness meditation to reduce stress or to create associations between drug abuse and negative life consequences, these actions don't just occur in some airy-fairy non-biological realm. They create changes in the pleasure circuitry to reverse or otherwise counteract the rewiring produced during addiction. This is the biological basis of social and experiential therapy (pp. 65–66).

Habits as Gifts and Resources: The Multiple Meanings and Functions of Self-Destructive Habits in Clients' Lives and Social Ecologies

As we have seen, one possible maintaining factor for self-destructive habits is that they provide important functions in and have served as gifts and resources in our clients' lives. This is illustrated below by the following case examples:

- Alberto, a 28-year old single man, had been a social drinker since his teenage years and smoked marijuana occasionally on weekends when he hung out with his friends. Two years before coming to therapy, he had started a very demanding job, working long hours in a state of continuous stress. He found that smoking "one or two joints" at night relaxed him enough to "disconnect from the hassles at work" and would help him "sleep well through the night." When he started therapy, he was smoking four or five joints every night, plus one or two in the morning.
- 17-year-old Pedro dropped out of school when he was 16, after a long history of academic failure. His ADHD and his difficulties in relating to his fellow students had made him a very shy, socially avoidant person. When he discovered on-line gaming he finally felt "important and competent." When his mother found out that he spent 8–10 hours per day playing on-line games, she decided to bring him to therapy.
- Erica, a married housewife in her fifties, had always resented her husband's working hours and business travels abroad, but her feelings of loneliness and worthlessness escalated when her only child left home to start college. She had been a very moderate social drinker, but began to drink alcohol more heavily alone at home, in the evenings, as a way to cope with her feelings of abandonment. One year later, she asked for therapeutic help when she realized that she was drinking more than one bottle of wine per day and that her marital relationship and the relationship with her offspring were deteriorating.

The first case, marijuana-abusing Alberto, is an example of Pathway I development of a self-destructive habit, where the negative habit is seen as a possible solution by the client, who tries to solve his perceived problems by smoking marijuana. His self-destructive habits are an ineffective *instrumental* solution. Pedro, hooked on online video-games, illustrates the Pathway II route to a self-destructive habit, with a pre-existing vulnerability that makes him fall prey to a self-destructive habit. The self-destructive habit fulfills an important *emotional* function for him, as it allows him to escape from his negative emotional states. Finally, the case of alcohol-abusing Erica (Pathway II) shows how self-destructive habits may play a *relational* function for our clients, playing an important role to stabilize their most intimate couple, family, or peer relationships.

This is what we mean when we talk about self-destructive habits as "gifts" and "resources": self-destructive habits are maintained not only because of the powerful psychological and physiological reinforcement they provide, or through their engraving in the brain circuitry, but also because in specific ways they are useful for our clients, serving some important functions in their lives and relationships. The important therapeutic implication is that, if we want to motivate our clients to reduce or quit their self-destructive behaviors, we first need to know how their self-destructive habits have benefited them and fit into their unique life stories, and then we need to help them find other ways to fulfill what the habit produces for them. Otherwise, they will continue to engage in their choice habits because they will feel that they need them. Returning back to the examples mentioned earlier, Alberto will need to find alternative ways for relaxing and coping with stress at work in order to reduce his marijuana use; Pedro will probably not drop his online gaming unless he has some alternative activities in which he can feel competent; and for Erica, directly confronting her issues with her husband will be an important area to work on in couple's therapy to help insure her successful recovery from alcohol abuse. In Chapter 2, we will present useful questions to ask clients about the multiple meanings and functions of their self-destructive habits and practical guidelines for how to collaboratively transform with our clients their self-destructive behaviors into healthy virtuous habits.

Self-Destructive Habits and Self-Change

Out of the five self-destructive habits presented in this book, the substance abuse field has been amassing the largest body of research evidence on individuals self-changing and self-healing without treatment or participation in self-help groups (Blomqvist, 2010; Burman, 1997; Carballo et al., 2010; Cohen, Feinn, Arias, & Kranzler, 2007; Dawson et al., 2005, 2007; Ellingstad, Sobell, Sobell, Eickleberry, & Golden, 2006; Klingemann, 1991; Klingemann & Sobell, 2010; Price, Risk, & Spitznagel, 2001; Raimo & Schukit, 1998; Robins, 1993; Robins, Helzer, Hesselbrock, & Wish, 1980; Rumpf, Bischof, & John, 2010; Shaffer & Jones, 1989; Smart, 2010; Sobell, Cunningham, & Sobell, 1996; Sobell, Ellingstad, & Sobell, 2000; Sobell & Sobell, 2011; Sobell, Sobell, & Agrawal, 2002; Stall & Biernacki, 1986; Tuchfeld, 1981; Tucker, Vuchinich, & Gladsjo, 1994; Vaillant, 1983; Vaillant & Milofsky, 1984; Waldorf, 1983; Winick, 1962). Similar reports of self-generated strategies for self-change and staying quit are also being found with self-harming, problem gamblers, eating-distressed, and more recently, Internet and cyber-sex dependent individuals (Hodgins & el-Guebaly, 2000; Pietrusza et al., 2011; Polivy, 2010, 2001; Selekman & Schulem, 2007; Shaffer et al., 2012; Toneatto & Nett, 2010; Turner, 2000; Whitlock, 2008). For some self-destructive habit individuals, all it took was a single psycho-educational or motivational interviewing session to serve as the catalyst for setting in motion the self-quitting process and eventual total abstinence (Shaffer, 2010; Carey, Purnine, Maisto, & Carey, 1999; Dimeff, Baer, Kivlahan, & Marlatt, 1999; Edwards et al., 1977; Miller & Rollnick, 2002; Orford & Edwards, 1977; Selekman, 2009; Selekman & Schulem, 2007; Sobell, 2010; Sobell & Sobell, 2011).

Two famous cocaine self-changers, Sigmund Freud and William Halsted, are masterfully described by Howard Markel in his fascinating book, *An Anatomy of Addiction: Sigmund Freud, William Halsted, and the Miracle Drug Cocaine*, which nicely illustrates how self-changers can have unique and personalized quitting styles. What helped Freud to kick his cocaine habit was structure-building, that is, filling his free time up with seeing many patients, doing research, writing, and attending meetings with colleagues daily. Halsted, a famous surgeon, whose innovative surgical procedures are still being used today, also employed structure building and adopted a moderation of use quitting style. Markel (2011) was struck by Halsted's amazing ability to be a "high-performing addict," conducting intricate and challenging surgeries with great precision and maintaining control of his cocaine consumption.

In spite of the existing body of evidence on self-change, many professionals in both the mental health and addiction fields are skeptical when they hear the words *self-change, spontaneous remission,* or *natural recovery* used to describe individuals who supposedly without intervention and participation in any self-help groups achieved abstinence from alcohol and/or substance abuse and from other serious self-destructive habits. Often we hear at our workshops or when consulting with treatment programs worldwide responses like: "How can that be?," "He must be in denial!," "She is a good manipulator," "Borderlines are good liars." In some cases, rather than focusing on what the client may want to work on changing presently, the therapist or addiction professional consumed with disbelief will return the focus to the so-called self-changed client's denying that he or she has a problem or is concealing his or her self-destructive habit activities. Why is there such skepticism about self-change? For one reason, because of the popularity and proliferation of the disease model in the addiction field and its being extended as the choice treatment method for other self-destructive habits, such as eating disorders, problem gambling, and Internet and cyber-sex dependency difficulties. Another reason has to do with the belief held by many in recovery and now working in the addiction field that "What worked for me must work for you." Therefore, self-change is impossible unless you admit you are an alcoholic or addict and are either working a Twelve Step program and/or have been in treatment for your choice addiction. After all, it is believed that he or she has a progressive, irreversible disease that can only be resolved through total abstinence goals, treatment and life-long abstinence (Shaffer & Jones, 1989; Sobell, 2010). A third reason that contributes to this disbelief about the possibility of self-change is the fact that indeed, a sizeable number of individuals with self-destructive habits do not recover and progress to a state of chronicity or even death. The tendency for both professionals and lay people to conceptualize phenomena in single categories, makes this apparently incompatible with the complementary fact that there is another great proportion of persons that do indeed change spontaneously.

However, research on self-change from the 1940s up to this very day is challenging this fundamentalist view and supporting the perspective that individuals with self-destructive habits *do* and *often* change on their own or set this process in motion with minimal therapeutic intervention necessary (Klingemann & Klingemann, 2009; Selekman, 2009; Selekman & Schulem, 2007; Shaffer & Jones, 1989; Vaillant, 1983). With numerous longitudinal studies demonstrating how individuals deemed alcohol and substance-dependent change on their own without treatment and/or any participation in self-help groups, Klingemann and Klingemann (2009) contend that:

> These findings indicate that various degrees of use, misuse, and addiction must be linked to a treatment continuum ranging from unassisted individual change to residential specialized addiction clinics. At the same time, a range of outcome goals including abstinence as only one among various pathways out of addiction should be taken into consideration (p. 269).

We are in agreement with the Klingemanns' position about the importance of tailor-fitting what we do and the level of care we offer with the unique ways our clients are already changing, want to change at their unique paces, and going with the clients' goals. Similar to Prochaska and his colleagues (2006) and Miller and Rollnick's (2002) approaches of matching therapeutic interventions with clients' unique stages of readiness for change and motivational levels, we go with their goals, which may range from accentuating and consolidating their self-quitting processes and relapse prevention to stay quit; helping them advance from the contemplation stage of readiness for change to the preparation and action stages of readiness for change through harm-reduction methods like "cutting down" on use and/or involvement with their other choice self-destructive habits, if this is a more palatable goal for them and they had voiced and already appeared to be on this pathway for change. Finally, with more serious alcohol and substance abuse situations and where severe withdrawal symptoms and concerns about personal safety and the safety of others are quite evident, we will actively pursue inpatient, partial hospital, and/or short-term residential care until our clients are stable and we can consolidate their gains, do relapse prevention work, and address other problem-maintaining difficulties with them in a couples or family therapy context.

Below, we will discuss self-change with each of the five self-destructive habits, beginning with the key findings from the alcohol and substance abuse research literature where there is a wealth of information and wisdom that has been reported. Since the research on self-change is somewhat limited on the other self-destructive habits presented in this book, we will report what we do know that self-changing individuals surveyed in studies indicated worked for them and what we have learned from former clients who had conquered their habits well before we saw them for the first time. Furthermore, since the five self-destructive habits in this book share similar features and consequences for the individual and his or her couple and/or family relationships, the creative and resourceful self-generated change strategies of alcohol and substance-abusing self-changers can be quite beneficial in helping our clients presenting with other self-destructive habits.

Self-Change with Alcohol and Substance-Abusing Individuals: What Works

In reviewing the self-change literature, we have found a wide range of individual and relationship factors that contributed to how these individuals initiate self-quitting and are able to remain abstinent.

Individual Factors

Cognitive appraisals and *decisional balancing processes*, such as critically looking at the pros and cons of continued use and behavior change, have been identified as "the motor for self-change" (Klingemann & Klingemann, 2009; Miller & Rollnick, 2002; Prochaska et al., 2006). Baumeister and Tierney (2011) and Baumeister (1996) have found that when an individual's perceptions of the negative consequences of his or her behavior outweigh the positives and reach a threshold of discomfort and crystallize or solidify in his or her mind, he or she will be motivated to change the problematic behavior or kick the habit. Baumeister refers to this cognitive shift as the "crystallization of discontent." Ebaugh (1988) describes another change process called *becoming an ex*, where the individual develops a perception that his or her current role, in this case getting drunk or stoned a lot and all of the negative personal and social costs that have accrued over time are not what he or she desired when they began this role. These sudden realizations or "turning points" play a major role in behavior change, letting others know that you plan to change, helping reduce cognitive dissonance and conflict, and helping mobilize one's personal inner resources to change. Other individual thinking and behavioral strategies self-changers have successfully employed are as follows:

- Reminding oneself of the health consequences of use.
- Recognizing in early stages of their abuse "early warning signs" that they were on the brink of becoming addicted or that the use of their choice drug was not good for them.
- Maturing out of use; deciding that drug use has no future place in their life story or with future pursuits.
- Hitting personal bottom, accidents, crises, and lost family and friends as a result of their use and friends' use.
- Both a tapering down or employing a cold turkey quitting strategy may work.
- Multiple resolutions, which is using one's past successful strategies for resolving one or more self-destructive habits to help them to kick their alcohol or substance abuse habit.
- Deliberately avoiding certain people, places, objects, and other triggers strongly associated with use.
- Increased hope and self-esteem.
- Keeping written diaries or journals documenting their self-change process.

- Meaningful religious experiences and/or epiphanies.
- Public pledge to family, relatives, and friends to quit their alcohol and substance use.
- Growing sense of commitment to loved ones; internalizing that he or she does not want to lose them.
- Dramatically changing one's lifestyle and structure building, which consists of filling up one's free time with many healthy and meaningful activities.
- Expanding one's horizons through meaningful service work and new educational and career pursuits.
- Developing the capacity for affect tolerance through meditation, yoga, and cardiovascular exercise.
- Regular spiritual involvement.

Relational Factors

Often, self-change is induced, sparked, or set in motion by the positive influence of family, friends, or work colleagues. However, social support is not only offered, but also actively sought out by persons that self-change. Some of the thinking and behavioral strategies are the following:

- To self-initiate social control, which takes the form of inviting close friends to actively assist them in steering clear from certain people and places, to make themselves available for impromptu telephonic or face-to-face support when necessary, and to hold them accountable for their actions.
- To become aware of severe marital or family financial difficulties due to use.
- To give up toxic using friends and acquaintances.
- To seek out and establish non-using friendships.
- To start new, non-using couple relations
- Legal difficulties often spark the self-changing process.

Self-Change and Self-Harming Individuals: What Works

One of the first studies that examined the self-changing processes of self-harming individuals was a study of 873 college students who were part of a much larger multi-site college study on non-suicidal self-injury (NSSI) (Pietrusza, Rothenberg, & Whitlock, 2011; Whitlock, 2008). Fifty-three percent of this sample who had been past self-injurers recovered from NSSI without ever having had a discussion about it with a therapist and 32.8% of the sample did so in complete secrecy and believing that no one knew or suspected that they were self-injuring. The researchers found that many self-injuring clients did recover on their own without therapeutic intervention and without therapy for any other issues. The major individual cognitive and behavioral strategies they pursued to self-change were as follows:

- They matured or grew out of using self-injury to cope or for other purposes.
- They experienced epiphanies that self-injuring was an ineffective coping strategy.
- They pursued and regularly used alternative healthy coping strategies.
- Increased hope and self-esteem.
- They sought out and used the support of friends and family.

Selekman and Schulem (2007) found that self-harming adolescents who were part of their qualitative research project and had already begun the self-changing process, indicated that exposure to mindfulness meditation and yoga and using their natural talents in art, music, dance, and drama helped them to quit their "cutting" and conquer other habits they had such as bulimia, substance abuse, and in some cases sexually acting out. Once the therapists in the project learned about what worked from their young clients, they made a concerted effort to utilize their key strengths in remaining individual and family problem areas to empower them.

Self-Change and Eating-Distressed Individuals: What Works

Unfortunately, the self-change literature on eating-distressed individuals is quite limited because most people diagnosed with an eating disorder end up in treatment. The most frequently cited reasons for self-change have been from the obesity literature: serious health consequences, a strong psychological commitment to change, maturing out of the eating-distressed behavior, and supportive relationships outside the family (Polivy, 2010). Individuals who were overweight and obese and had never been in treatment indicate that they lost significant amounts of weight and kept it off over time by making healthier food choices, eliminating all fatty foods from their diets, and by regularly exercising (Tinker & Tucker, 1997a, b). Furthermore, Hollis and her colleagues (2008) found that out of the 1600 obese individuals in their study those participants who kept a daily food journal lost twice as much weight as everyone else. This important virtuous habit (keeping a daily food journal) led to a new attitude about food, better choice making regarding what they ate, instituting healthier diets, and discontinuing in between meal snacking.

Polivy (2010) has found that the more of a disparity there is between eating-distressed individuals' goals and their perceptions of how close or far away they are from achieving them, plays a major role in restrained or unrestrained eating behaviors. Because of this important finding in their study, it is argued that clinically it is important for therapists and treatment programs to negotiate small and realistic short-term goals with eating-distressed clients.

Self-Change and Problem Gamblers: What Works

Successful problem gambling self-changers have reported what worked best for them in reducing and eventually conquering their habits were the following: setting limits on themselves; critically evaluating the negative costs of their gambling on their core values; eliminating environmental stimuli; staying away from certain people and places; legal difficulties; reminding themselves about the severe financial costs and other consequences that had resulted from their gambling habits (Shaffer et al., 2012; Toneatto & Nett, 2010; Turner, 2000). Turner (2000) has found a correlation between self-recovery from gambling and a deeper understanding of the nature of randomness and the principles of probability. Clinically speaking, he contends that for gambling prevention and treatment purposes it may be quite useful to teach people about randomness.

Self-Change and Internet and Cyber-Sex Dependent Individuals: What Works

Since excessive Internet usage is so prevalent and cyber-sex dependent individuals are often secretive about their activities online, particularly if they are using this time to secure sexual pleasure or are doing something illegal, it is difficult to recruit them for research surveys. The research literature on self-change is non-existent. Unfortunately, only clinical anecdotes (Young, 2011) and our experiences working with these individuals are available to draw conclusions from. Those individuals that other clinical specialists and we have worked with cited the following steps they took to self-change from problem Internet usage and visiting cyber-porn sites:

- Coming to the realization that serious weight, cardiovascular, and sexual dysfunction problems required immediate attention and the need for change.
- Legal difficulties also sparked the self-changing process.

- Inviting their partners and/or parents to tightly monitor and limit their time on the Internet.
- Relinquish all hand held digital devices to partners and/or parents and move the personal computer into the living room or into some other visible and heavily trafficked room in the home.
- Partners and parents need to be made aware of all the dangerous and problem-maintaining websites they abuse.
- Surrender their passwords and have their partners and/or parents regularly check up on them.
- Have their partners and/or parents purchase special software to block visiting dangerous and problem-maintaining websites.
- Increase offline activities with partners, with their families, and friends engaging in positive and healthy activities.

The Self-Change Research and Implications for Clinical Practice

Although it is an unanswered question whether they are similar to or different from people who change in therapy, self-changers are remarkable and resilient people who offer us valuable wisdom about not only how change occurs from alcohol and substance abuse and other self-destructive habits but how to maintain a successful recovery process. As Orford and Edwards (1977) put it best, "alcoholism treatment research should embrace the study of 'natural forces' that can then be captured and exploited by planned interventions" (p. 3). This entails finding out what clients' self-generated pretreatment changes are with their self-destructive habits, that is, what are their effective coping and problem-solving strategies and those of concerned significant others that we need to harness, amplify, and consolidate to further empower them. In addition, we want to utilize their expertise and self-generated past and present successful strategies to co-construct solutions for other difficulties they may be still be experiencing in other areas of their lives. Some other important treatment considerations the self-change research literature points to are:

- Invite clients to share their goals and honour their preferences and visions for the change process.
- Assist clients with the cognitive appraisal and decisional balancing process around the advantages and disadvantages of continuing to use or engage in other self-destructive habits.
- When clients are still using substances and/or engaging in other self-destructive habits, let them determine which habit they wish to work on changing first, if they prefer to go for controlled use or abstinence, and what quitting style best suits him or her: *tapering down* or *cold turkey*.
- Negotiate small and realistic behavioral goals.
- Teach affect distress tolerance coping tools and strategies, such as mindfulness meditation and related practices and visualization techniques.
- Publicly pledge to couple partners, family members, and close friends their strong desire and plans to quit their self-destructive habits.
- Actively involve couple partners, family members, and key resource people from the clients' social networks in and out of sessions for co-generating solutions and relapse prevention purposes.
- With self-destructive adolescents, create stronger and more meaningful connections with their parents.
- Clients benefit from highly structured relapse prevention plans.
- Clients benefit from active involvement in healthy and meaningful activities like service work.

- As part of changing one's lifestyle, maintaining a healthy diet, engaging in some form of daily exercise, and getting enough sleep is critical to the recovery process.
- Spiritual involvement can serve as a resiliency protective factor.

Transforming Self-Destructive Behaviors into Virtuous Habits: A Collaborative Strengths-Based Brief Family Therapy Approach

As discussed in the previous section, we believe strongly that the primary role of the therapist who works with clients with self-destructive habits is to capitalize on their strengths, resources, and natural self-change processes to empower them to interrupt problem-maintaining patterns and beliefs and co-generate solutions that enable them to move towards recovery and the development of alternative and meaningful virtuous habits. In the next two chapters, we provide a detailed description of the major therapeutic tools and strategies of our collaborative strengths-based brief family therapy approach (Beyebach, 2006, 2009; Selekman, 2005, 2009, 2010). In this section we will only outline the basic theoretical tenets that inform our approach, and describe how it fits in with the territory of self-destructive habits.

One implication of the development and maintenance model that we have spelled out in this chapter is the need to adopt an eco-systemic, bio-psychosocial view if we want to do justice to the multiple factors that operate at the biological, cognitive, emotional, and couple and family interaction levels that maintain self-destructive habits. In addition, the complexity of this scenario calls for the use of a variety of techniques and methods that may address those factors that in each particular case may need to be modified. This is why we believe that a flexible and integrative therapeutic approach is needed, able to combine different therapeutic tools and strategies from different individual and family therapy models within a coherent conceptualization of self-destructive habits that provides an overall map of the therapeutic journey.

What techniques should be included in such an integrative, flexible approach? A common response to this question is that only "empirically supported treatments" should be used, sometimes described as the only ethical and responsible option (Chambless & Crits-Cristoph, 2006; Labrador, Echeburúa, & Becoña, 2000; Lebow, 2005). We recognize the value of the research that backs empirically supported treatments (EST), but we are also aware that the EST logic has serious shortcomings and is not the only way to advance the practice of an empirically based therapy (Duncan & Miller, 2000; Duncan, Miller, & Sparks, 2000; Duncan, Miller, Wampold, & Hubble, 2010; Garfield, 1996, 1998; Wampold, 2001; Wampold et al., 1997). Does this mean that we dismiss the impressive body of EST research for self-destructive habits? No, but it means that we are aware of the advantages of expanding the evidence base for psychotherapy practice to include valuable insights produced by process research, process outcome-research, broad community sample longitudinal studies, lab studies in different areas of psychology and neurobiology, and clinical evidence-based practice wisdom (Norcross, Beutler, & Levant, 2006). It is our contention that no closed, "empirically supported" treatment manual substitutes for the need of careful clinical decision-making for each unique case.

If in our work with self-destructive habit clients we are to use different techniques and strategies, what is their anchor point? How can we, as therapists, not get lost in what could appear to be a chaotic array of interventions? In our view, there are three central therapeutic bases from where we can integrate different procedures: the reliance on the resources and self-change strategies of our clients; the establishment and nourishment of a strong therapeutic alliance with them (Friedlander, et al., 2006; Pinsof, 1995); and a careful monitoring of how our clients improve or fail to do so from session to session (Lambert, 2010). This is why we describe our collaborative strengths-based brief family therapy model as *client-focused, alliance-centered* (Escudero, 2011) and *outcome-informed* (Duncan et al., 2010; Miller, Meyers, & Tonigan, 1999). This allows for a careful matching of each therapeutic encounter to the unique features and needs of individual clients, couples and families, a strategy that is likely to be more effective in the long run than the futile attempts to find static treatment/problem matches. We have already discussed clients' self-change strategies and resources. Here we will only briefly present the other two elements, the centrality of the therapeutic alliance and the feedback on the therapeutic process.

- One of our ways to conceptualize the *therapeutic alliance* is the conceptual framework of the System of the Observation of Therapeutic Alliances (SOFTA, Friedlander et al., 2006). In SOFTA, two dimensions, "Engagement in the therapeutic process" and "Emotional connection with the therapist," correspond with the individual "agreement on tasks and goals" and "emotional bond" aspects of the therapeutic relationship (Bordin, 1979). But, in addition, SOFTA includes two dimensions that refer specifically to the complexities of therapeutic alliances in conjoint sessions: "Safety" of each client who participates in the conversation, and "Conjoint purpose," the extent to which the couple or family feel that they are on the same boat in their struggle with their problems. Clinically, safety is seen as a prerequisite for the meaningful participation of clients in conjoint sessions; a view that a recent meta-analysis of SOFTA research confirms (Friedlander, Escudero, Heatherington & Diamond, 2011), and that is especially relevant in the therapy of self-destructive habits cases, where shame, guilt and mutual blaming are likely to be present. In collaborative strengths-based brief family therapy, safety is managed in part through careful subsystem work that allows us to strategically join with some members in the absence of others. We promote a conjoint sense of purpose by the way we ask questions and create conversational themes, as well as through the in-session and between-session conjoint experiments we will present in this book.
- The other conceptual tool we use to look at the therapeutic alliance and base our moment-to-moment clinical decision-making is the *Stages of Readiness for Change* model (Prochaska & DiClemente, 1982, 1985, 1992; Prochaska et al., 1992, 2006). Close monitoring of the readiness for change of each individual member of the therapeutic system, and painstaking attention to how it varies over the course of therapy and even during each session, helps us to adjust to the unique wishes and preferences of each client and to tailor our treatment intervention in accordance. The Stages of Readiness for Change model, which started in the field of addictions but nowadays is being applied to a variety of clinical problems (Prochaska et al., 2006), is especially relevant for the treatment of self-destructive habits, given that, as we have discussed, self-destructive habits are largely ego-syntonic, making motivation for change crucial. We are in agreement with Ciarrocchi (2001) who believes that the real challenge in therapy is not so much knowing what our clients need to do, but how to get them to do it.
- As to the *monitoring of therapeutic progress*, we are well aware that the ongoing feedback from our clients forms a more solid base for clinical decision making than any preconceived therapy/problem/client matches (Anker, Duncan, & Sparks, 2009; Lambert, 2010). On the basis of client feedback, we keep therapeutic track if things are improving, or alternatively switch gears if no change happens (Beyebach, 2009; Quick, 1996). As we will describe in the next chapter, our general strategy is to begin with a more solution-focused approach (de Shazer, 1988, 1991, 1994; de Shazer et al., 2007) capitalizing on our clients' self-generated changes and past successes, but if this strategy is not working, or is not working well enough, we prefer to do something else, moving more into the Palo Alto Mental Research Institute (MRI) brief strategic (Fisch, Weakland, & Segal, 1982; Nardone & Watzlawick, 1990), narrative (White 2007; White & Epston, 1990), structural (Minuchin, 1974; Minuchin & Fishman, 1981), and collaborative language systems (Anderson, 1997) and other postmodern therapy (Hoffman, 2002; Friedman, 1995) approaches. The fact that negative emotion, loss of control, and poor self-regulation abilities play such important roles in the development and maintenance of self-destructive habits makes the inclusion of Positive Psychology (Duckworth, Steen, & Seligman, 2005; Frederickson, 2009; Peterson, 2006; Seligman, 2002, 2002), Buddhist psychology and

mindfulness meditation (Kabat-Zinn, 1994; Kissel Wegela, 2009), and Acceptance and Commitment Therapy (Hayes, Strosahl, & Wilson, 1999) natural choices to tap therapeutically. We see this therapeutic process as a continuous evaluation-as-intervention and intervention-as-evaluation loop, so that each attempted intervention provides new information to confirm or correct the therapeutic course. In this process, it is important to keep an open, flexible state of mind, allowing ourselves as therapists to be creative and take risks with our clients, using our facilitative interpersonal skills (Anderson et al., 2009) from a position of partnership and conjoint adventure (Selekman et al., 2005). The therapeutic stance that we try to adopt in our clinical work is that of motivation-enhancers, trying to bring to the fore the resources and expert knowledge of our clients, but at the same time allowing ourselves to take risks by being creative and improvisational, making maximum use of therapeutic moments to seize.

The other defining feature of collaborative strengths-based brief family therapy is that it adopts a contextual, *relational view*. This perspective comes from the systemic and brief therapy traditions (de Shazer, 1988, 1991; de Shazer et al., 2007; Fisch et al., 1982; Fisch and Schlanger, 1999; Haley, 1976; Watzlawick, Beavin, & Jackson, 1967) and is particularly well-suited for self-destructive habits: as we have shown during this chapter, contextual influences from couple partners, family, peers, and clients' social networks play an important role in the shaping and maintenance of self-destructive behaviors. Furthermore, given that many persons trapped by their self-destructive habits stay for a long time in a pre-contemplative stage of readiness for change, perceiving no problem and no need to seek therapy, concerned others usually play a central role in their engagement and treatment. Also, they are likely to be suffering a great part of the negative impact of the self-destructive habit, and are therefore often in need of therapeutic help. We believe that the acute awareness of relational factors and the inclusion by default of relatives, couple partners, family members, peers and any other significant others as active therapeutic agents, mark an important difference to most treatment approaches to self-destructive habits, and opens many interesting possibilities for therapeutic change. In this way, we capitalize on the four common factors that Sprenkle, Davis, and Lebow (2009) consider to be unique to the relational therapies (as opposed to individual treatments): the relational conceptualization of problems, the active disruption of relational patterns, the expansion of the direct therapeutic system by inviting the key resource people from clients' social networks to the sessions, and the expansion of the therapeutic alliance to accommodate the interaction of the therapist with more than one client. We will demonstrate this therapeutic process in many of the case examples presented in this book. Figure 1.4 illustrates the multiple target areas for change that are addressed using the collaborative strengths-based brief family therapy approach.

Overview of the Book

Chapters 2 and 3 present a comprehensive overview of the major therapeutic tools and strategies of our collaborative strengths-based brief family therapy approach. In Chapter 2, we cover the session format, the key elements for co-creating with clients' therapeutic climates ripe for change, interviewing for possibilities, and practical guidelines for transforming clients' self-destructive habits into virtuous habits. Chapter 3 is chock-full of therapeutic experiments and rituals that not only tap couple partners' and family members' creativity and resourcefulness but are designed to strengthen their relationships as well.

Chapters 4–8 cover the five self-destructive habits, which are: self-harming, eating-distressed, substance abuse, problem gambling, and Internet and cyber-sex abuse habits. We begin the treatment section of each of these five chapters with a comprehensive overview of each habit, a brief review of the existing research on treatment, with special attention to family and couple approaches; these reviews help the reader appreciate some of the limitations and pitfalls of

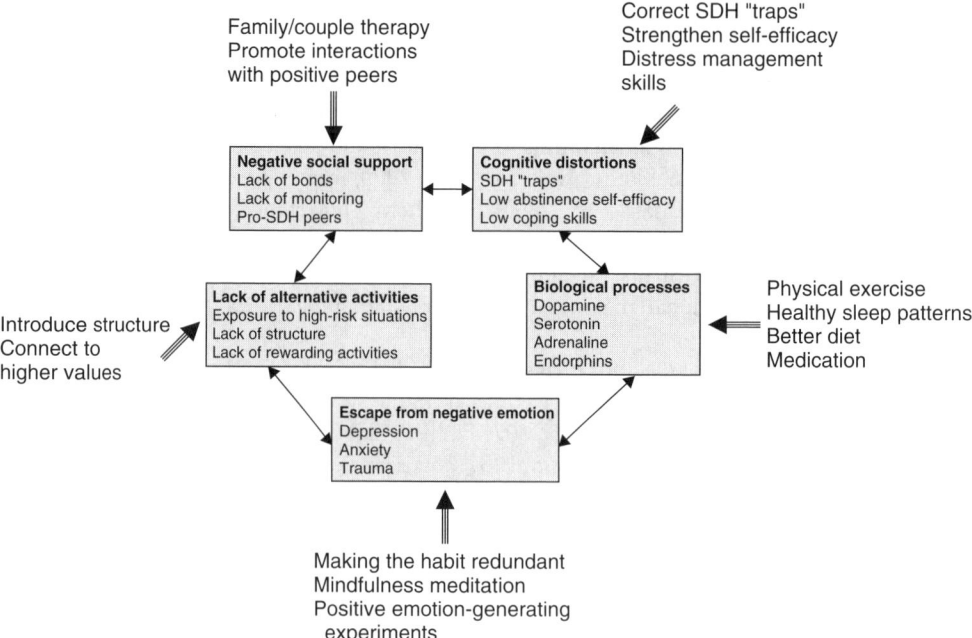

Figure 1.4 Interrupting self-destructive habits (SDH) and promoting healing with collaborative strengths-based brief family therapy.

the most researched treatments, but also the therapeutic factors that hold the greatest promise. We then move on to discuss the most important assessment questions and treatment planning. We close each of these chapters with full-length couple and family case examples that illustrate the major therapeutic tools and strategies of our treatment approach. Post-treatment analysis and reflections are provided after each case presentation.

Chapter 9 discusses effective engagement strategies with reluctant self-destructive multi-habit-dependent clients, their couple partners, and absent and powerful family members. Special treatment dilemmas are covered, such as when the referring person is the customer for change and how to treat multi-habit-dependent couples and families. Two highly complex and challenging cases are presented.

Chapter 10 presents a plethora of highly effective relapse prevention and goal-maintenance tools and strategies for couples and families. Several mindfulness meditations and related practices are presented. We discuss how to constructively manage the treatment dilemma of chronically relapsing habit dependent clients and effective therapeutic strategies for intervening with their couple partners and family members that continue to persist in unproductive attempted solutions in their efforts to change them.

Finally, Chapter 11 summarizes the major themes of the book and offers some recommendations for future directions in treatment, training, and research on the five self-destructive habits.

2

KEY ELEMENTS FOR CO-CREATING A THERAPEUTIC CLIMATE RIPE FOR CHANGE

> Habit is habit and not to be flung out of the window by any man, but coaxed downstairs a step at a time.
>
> *Mark Twain*

Collaborative Strengths-Based Brief Family Therapy

Our collaborative strengths-based brief family therapy approach has been evolving since 1986 (Beyebach, 2006, 2009; Beyebach & Rodríguez Morejón, 1999; Beyebach, Piqueras, & Rodriguez, 1991; Selekman, 2005, 2006, 2009, 2010). It is a flexible and respectful brief family therapy approach that logically integrates the best elements of solution-focused brief therapy (Berg & Miller, 1992; de Shazer, 1988, 1991, 1994; de Shazer et al., 2007); positive psychology (Haidt, 2006; Lopez & Snyder, 2009; Lyubomirsky, 2007; Peterson, 2006; Peterson & Seligman, 2004; Seligman, 2011, 2002; Snyder & Lopez, 2007), client-directed, outcome-informed therapy (Duncan, 2010; Duncan & Miller, 2000; Hubble, Duncan, & Miller, 1999; Hubble, Duncan, Miller, & Wampold, 2011), Palo Alto Mental Research Institute (MRI) brief strategic therapy (Fisch & Schlanger, 1999; Fisch, Weakland, & Segal, 1982; Nardone & Watzlawick, 1990), narrative therapy ideas (Epston, 2000; Freeman, Epston, & Lobovits, 1997; White, 1995, 2007, 2011; White & Epston, 1990), collaborative language systems therapy (Anderson, 1997; Anderson & Gehart, 2007; Anderson & Goolishian, 1988), experiential therapy ideas (Satir, 1988, 1983; Papp, 1983), and community reinforcement and family training (Meyers, 2012; Smith & Meyers, 2004).

From the worlds of individual therapy and alternative healing methods, we have incorporated ideas from cognitive-behavioral therapy (Beck, 1995; Beck, Rush, & Emery, 1979; Ryle & Kerr, 2002), motivational-enhancement therapy (Miller & Rollnick, 2002; Rollnick, Mason, & Butler, 1999; Rosengren, 2009), harm-reduction therapy (Marlatt, 1998; Tatarsky, 2007), art therapy (Malchiodi, 2008, 2003), expressive writing therapy (Pennebaker, 2004), and mindfulness meditation and related practices (Bien, 2010; Bowen, Chawla, & Marlatt, 2011; Gregson & Efran, 2002; Hanh, 2011, 2001, 1998; Kabat-Zinn, 1994; Wegela, 2009; Kozak, 2009; Lowenstein, 2005; R. D. Siegel, 2010; Taylor, 2010; Trungpa, 1984; Wilson & DuFrene, 2012). Finally, we have found the new groundbreaking neuroscience research useful to help us and our clients better understand their brain functioning, specific neurotransmitters involved in maintaining their self-destructive habits, and the power of memories, reward systems, cues, and triggers that can promote relapses (Amen & Smith, 2010; DiSalvo, 2011; Hanson & Mendius, 2009; Linden, 2011; Schwartz & Begley, 2003; Schwartz & Gladding, 2011; Shermer, 2011; D. J. Siegel, 2007, 2010a,b).

We like to begin therapy with new clients by keeping things simple and capitalizing on our clients' strengths and resources, their self-generated pretreatment changes, past successful problem-solving and coping strategies, and future visions of success. When clients have grave difficulty accessing this information or later in therapy are not making any progress, their situations are highly complex in that there are multiple habit-dependent family members, they are deeply entrenched in negative ways of interacting, or they are clinging to rigid problem views, we will use more complex interventions to better meet their needs. As part of this move towards more complexity, we will go back to our roots and employ strategic, structural, Milan systemic, and symbolic-experiential family therapy interventions in and out of sessions when necessary (Boscolo & Bertrando, 1993; Boscolo, Cecchin, Hoffman, & Penn, 1987; Connell, Mitten, & Bumberry, 1999; Fishman, 1993; Haley, 1976; Hoffman, 2002; Madanes, 1981, 1984; Minuchin, 1974; Minuchin, Colapinto, & Minuchin, 1998; Minuchin & Fishman, 1981; Selvini-Palazzoli, Cecchin, Prata, & Boscolo, 1978; Stanton, 1984; Whitaker, 1989).

There are a number of reasons why we believe that the collaborative strengths-based brief family therapy approach is a good fit for couple and family self-destructive habit difficulties. Some of the major reasons are: its strong emphasis on clients' strengths and resources, which triggers positive emotion for the clients and neutralizes their negative emotions, for disrupting negative and irrational thinking patterns, and increasing their hope and optimism levels; it is an eco-systemic and comprehensive therapy approach that targets interventions at the individual, couple, family, social network, and larger systems levels; and it is truly collaborative in that the clients are put in charge of creating their own unique blueprints for change plans, determining the goals for therapy, the frequency of visits and who attends meetings, and it is their feedback that informs therapists on how best to build and sustain strong alliances with them.

The Session Format

When we begin with new couples and families, we make an effort to include the most relevant members of the system, such as: both couple partners and both parents and children if one of the children is the main focus of concern. In cases that are referred from the school, social services, hospitals, or the legal system we may also include the referring person and other involved helping professionals in the first session if the couple or family feel comfortable with that. We share with them how we like to divide the sessions up and meet with individuals and subsystems; how our approach is collaborative and requires teamwork with co-constructing solutions and the implementation of their selected change strategies; that after some 45–50 minutes of conversation there will be an intersession break of 5–10 minutes and then a wrap-up editorial reflection, including their feedback on their session-by-session experiences. Taking an intersession break helps both the therapist and clients alike to prevent fixation on one central idea or explanation and instead, promotes diverse ideas or views flowing. We have found that simply explaining the session format to clients helps lower their anxiety levels and makes them feel more comfortable with the therapeutic process.

The session format consists of six therapeutic operations:

- co-creating a therapeutic climate ripe for change;
- interviewing for possibilities;
- walking the tightrope: subsystem work for deepening therapeutic alliances and implementing secret mission projects;
- identification of solution-determined system membership and whom to include in future sessions;
- the intersession break and editorial reflection; and
- client feedback as a guide for tailor-fitting therapeutic relationships.

Below, we discuss each of these therapeutic operations.

Co-Creating a Therapeutic Climate Ripe for Change

For us, rapport-building and the creation of a therapeutic climate ripe for change begins with our initial telephone conversation with the caller seeking help. We treat this couple partner or parent like an invited guest in our homes, conveying warmth, empathy, sincere interest in hearing about his or her problem story, how they were referred to us, and who they think is most important to bring to the first session. We also present our view that therapy is going to be easier and more helpful if all relevant persons can come to the first session, because the "more heads we have to put together, the better." If the person on the telephone has objections to bringing in a particular member of the family, we try to understand the reasons for their concern and react accordingly (for a more detailed discussion of effective engagement strategies with reluctant couple partners and family members see Chapter 9). After building rapport and securing this important client information on the telephone, we will ask him or her or both couple partners or parents to perform the following pretreatment experiment (McKeel, 2011; Selekman, 2009; Weiner-Davis, de Shazer, & Gingerich, 1987):

> My colleagues and I have been so amazed over the years about how resilient, creative, and resourceful our clients have been, that well before our first sessions with them they had not only prevented their situations from getting much worse but they had already taken constructive steps to try to resolve their difficulties. In order for me to learn more about your strengths, creativity, and resourcefulness, I would like you to pull out your imaginary magnifying glass on a daily basis over the next few days/week and carefully observe for any encouraging or responsible steps you see your (partner/son/daughter) take that you would like to continue to happen. While you are playing detective, I would like you to pay close attention to what you may be doing during those times that is contributing to his or her positive behaviors. Please write those things down and bring your list to the first session. It will be a great pleasure to meet you and your (partner/son/daughter) and I can't wait to hear what further progress you have made!

When giving this pretreatment experiment to parents where the young adults or the adolescents are the habit-dependent persons and if they appear to be equally invested in attending the initial family therapy interview, we will encourage the parents also to play detectives and carefully observe and prepare lists of all the positive behaviors they noticed that they want to see continue to happen. They are to bring this important top secret information to the family session as well.

Once the first interview begins, and before reviewing the telephone pretreatment experiment results, we spend the initial part of the session establishing rapport with the habit-dependent person, his or her partner, and/or other family members that joined us for the session. After coming to know both partners or all family members by their top strengths, talents, and life passions and injecting into the session our own humor and playfulness to lighten up the session atmosphere, we will revisit with the help-seeking couple partner or the parents what they observed that is already better with their situation. All self-generated pretreatment changes are amplified and consolidated by us through a detailed discussion of the interactive behaviors, and feelings and thoughts that were different on those occasions. Once we have a detailed picture of these improvements, we move on to "positive blaming" (Kral & Kowalski, 1989) to find out how they have made their important changes happen. One helpful question to ask to gather this information is, "Are you aware of how you did that?"

As part of the client self-generated pretreatment change discussion, we also like to inquire with couple partners and family members if they had experienced any recent meaningful coincidences or epiphanies that had brought them great joy, valuable wisdom, or some new insights about their situations or their lives. If so, we explore with them how they have already put to use certain ideas or flashes of insight from these experiences in the presenting problem or in other areas of their lives. Along these same lines, we want to learn from our clients what their key serendipitous practices and contexts are that have fairly consistently offered them good luck, the opportunity to meet resourceful others, and valuable insights and building blocks for resolving their difficulties in the past.

Once the couple partners or family members cannot think of any other significant pretreatment changes, we take the time to elicit from them any concerns they still may have, their problem theories, or how they may account for their problems (Duncan, Hubble, & Miller, 1997), details about their past attempted solutions and those of former treatment providers, their treatment expectations, preferences, and visions of change for our work together. In this way, we negotiate what we like to describe as a "conjoint therapeutic project," a "shared sense of purpose" (Friedlander, Escudero, & Heatherington, 2006). In this conversation, we pay close attention to and validate the different and sometimes contradictory positions that the persons in our therapy room may have, trying to convey a genuine interest both in their personal views and in their conjoint struggle as a couple or family. This often requires that we take the lead in structuring the conversation and block possible negativity and mutual blaming in order to make sure that each couple partner and every family member can voice his or her views in a safe and secure context (Friedlander et al., 2006).

Therapeutic Presence and Tailor-Fitting the Therapeutic Relationship of Choice

Two other ways we co-create a therapeutic climate for change with our clients are: *therapeutic presence* and *tailor-fitting the relationship of choice*. By *therapeutic presence* we mean completely being in the moment with our clients on multiple levels: emotionally, cognitively, physically, and spiritually. Present therapists are empathically attuned to their clients' feelings and keenly aware of what they are thinking and feeling in relationship to their clients in the moment (Duncan, 2010; Geller & Greenberg, 2012; Selekman, 2009; D. J. Siegel, 2010a). When we are on the same emotional wavelength with our clients, they will often convey during the conversation or when giving feedback at the end of sessions "feeling felt" and held by us, because they sense we are generously and deeply listening to and validating their stories. Present therapists also give themselves permission to take risks, improvise, and share their emotional reactions, hunches, metaphors, and humorous thoughts in response to what clients just shared in the moment that resonated with them and that they think may be worthwhile sharing with the clients. In addition to establishing strong collaborative partnerships with our clients, using words like "we," "let us," and "teamwork," help to convey to them that "we are in this together"; this type of language used by therapists has been rated by clients as an indicator of having strong alliances with their therapists in treatment outcome studies (Bohart & Tallman, 2010; Creed & Kendall, 2005).

Finally, we strive to have conversations with our clients that are so meaningful and emotionally resonate with them that they have an "afterglow effect" long after each session ends. For the German philosopher Karl Jaspers, an afterglow effect occurs after a great conversation, when both parties continue to ponder and reflect on the conversation and separately add to it and uncover new ideas or views that can open up space for transformative possibilities (Erlich, Erlich, & Pepper, 1994).

Tailor-fitting the therapeutic relationship of choice has four important dimensions to it: honoring clients' preferences, expectations, and visions of change; carefully matching what we do therapeutically with clients' unique stages of readiness for change; matching our therapeutic positioning with clients' psychological reactance levels; and soliciting client feedback on the quality of the therapeutic alliance-building process (Lambert, 2010; Norcross, 2010). Client feedback will be discussed later in the chapter.

Honoring clients' preferences, expectations, and visions of change includes the following: what type of treatment modality our clients would like to pursue among offered options (individual, couple, family therapy, or a combination of the options); soliciting from them their preferences about how they would like their therapists to interact with them in sessions; the cultural background and gender of the therapist they would like to work with; and what their theories of change are, that is, what specifically needs to be addressed or resolved so that they will be most satisfied with the treatment experience. We can gain access to this important information by asking them the following questions:

- "Which type of therapist would you feel most comfortable working with, a more action-oriented goal-focused therapist who offers you things to do between sessions to help you to quickly achieve your goals, or a more laidback therapist who is conversational and helps you to make connections and gain insight into your problems?"
- "How do you feel about working with a white therapist or would you prefer that I refer you to a Latino therapist?"
- "How do you feel about discussing your binge-eating difficulties with a male therapist or would you prefer that I refer you to a female therapist?"
- "I know I'm the sixth therapist you have been to, so what specifically has to be addressed and resolved in our work together so that you will leave here completely satisfied and glad that you chose to work with me?"

Next, it is critical that we match our questions and therapeutic experiments with each partner's or family member's unique stage of readiness for change. We need to be patient and gear our therapeutic actions to the stage each partner and family member is presently in. The key is to gradually advance them at their unique paces to the next stage of readiness for change, which can optimize the likelihood for their future success in treatment (Prochaska, Norcross, & DiClemente, 2006).

Some of our self-destructive habit clients will enter treatment with us presenting with multiple DSM-IV labels, chronic difficulties, and multiple treatment failures, and not too thrilled about being forced to go for counseling again by their partners or parents. These individuals often have high psychological reactance levels and will try to hang on to control at all costs. Tactically, it would be a big mistake on the therapist's behalf to be pushy with goal-setting and expect that these clients are eager to implement change strategies. If the therapist fails to take a one-down position and is not sensitive to the client's high psychological reactance level, the client not only will not comply with therapist's directives but may prematurely drop out of therapy. Therefore, with clients presenting with high psychological reactance levels the therapist must optimize for them to have as much control of the treatment process as possible. This includes giving these clients lots of input in therapeutic planning and decision-making and encouraging them to go slow with the change process and to have a conversation regarding their concerns about the disadvantages of change (Beutler, Moleiro, & Talebi, 2002; Fisch & Schlanger, 1999; Rohrbaugh, Tennen, Press, & White, 1981; Selekman, 2009; Stanton, 1984). Conversely, clients with low psychological reactance levels are often in the *action* stage of readiness for change and are armed with goals and eager to implement change strategies.

Interviewing for Possibilities

Questions are a formidable therapeutic tool for therapeutic intervention (McGee, Del Vento, & Bavelas, 2005; Tomm, 1987b). We use a variety of therapeutic questions to tap our clients' expertise, to ensure we are working on the "right" problem that they wish to have changed first, to establish well-formulated treatment goals, to better cooperate with more pessimistic and demoralized clients, to explore their untold stories and liberate them from the various constraints that are keeping them stuck, and to co-create with them compelling future realities of success.

Depending on our clients' responses to our questions and how they best like to cooperate in the interviewing process, we will choose different kinds of questions to promote interactive fit. It is critical when asking clients questions that we give them the time and space to think and reflect on them and avoid at all costs adopting an interrogative interviewing style, which can promote premature client drop-out (Beyebach, 2009; Beyebach & Carranza, 1997; Nylund & Corsiglia, 1994). Our bias is always to begin with honoring and celebrating our clients' strengths, past successes, stories of courage, resiliencies, talents, life passions, no matter what DSM-IV labels they are carrying or how many past treatment experiences they have had. At the same time, we must express empathy and compassion to self-destructive clients, their partners and families who have long stories to share regarding their chronic and intractable difficulties and unsuccessful multiple treatment experiences. We have to be respectful of their problem stories and be careful not to be narrative editors (Anderson, 1997; Miller & Rollnick, 2002; Rollnick et al., 1999; Selekman, 2009; Tatarsky, 2007). Below, we present eight different categories of therapeutic questions. First, we discuss where in the therapeutic process we use them and why. Second, several examples of each of the questions are provided.

Client Expertise Questions

Client expertise questions elicit from clients their self-generated pretreatment changes, key strengths and resources, past successes, stories of courage and resiliency, major talent areas, life passions, any recent 'good luck' events, epiphanies, and important serendipitous practices and environments (de Shazer, 1988, 1991; de Shazer et al., 2007; McKeel, 2011; O'Hanlon & Weiner-Davis, 1989; Selekman, 2005, 2009, 2010). As a way for therapists to gain access to important client expertise information and empower them prior to their first sessions, we invite clients on the telephone at intake to play detectives for us and carefully observe what they (parents, couple partners, the self-destructive clients) are already doing to prevent their situations from getting much worse and even improving their situations a little bit. Their information is to be written down in the form of lists by all family members and couple partners who wish to try this pretreatment experiment out and brought to their initial sessions. Family members' and couple partners' self-generated pretreatment changes serve as building blocks for solution construction. Each client self-generated change reported is to be amplified and consolidated by the therapist. Cheerleading can be used to punctuate these important sparkling moments for clients. For example, the therapist can respond with, "Wow! Are you aware of how you pulled that off?!"

Together, the therapist and clients can determine what new patterns of thinking, feeling, and doing need to be increased and utilized more, in particular relationships both within and without the couple or family and channeled into specific unresolved client concerns or problem areas that they identified. Important action steps from their stories of courage, how they overcame adverse life situations, other past successful problem-solving or coping strategies, utilizing their unique talents, recent epiphanies, and helpful serendipitous practices also can be tapped for empowering the clients to resolve their remaining concern or problem areas. These other areas of clients' expertise can be explored with them at any stage of the treatment process particularly if the couple or family is feeling stuck with resolving a piece of the presenting problem or is faced with a new life stressor or dilemma. Some examples of the nine client expertise categories of questions are as follows.

Client Pretreatment Change Questions

- "So what's better, even a little bit, since we spoke together on the telephone last week?"
- "Are you aware of how you got that to happen?!"

- "What did you tell yourself to drum up the courage to pull that off?"
- "Is that different for you to do that?"
- "How specifically has Cecilia's cutting back on the nagging helped you to cut back on your use of weed and coke?"
- "Cecilia, is there anything else you have been doing differently around Steve lately that you think might be contributing to his cutting back on the weed and coke?"
- "So side-stepping getting into arguments with Steve seems to be helping. What are you telling yourself that seems to be helping you pull that off so well?"
- "Steve, in response to Cecilia's efforts to help the two of you get along better, other than cutting back, what else are you doing differently lately that is bringing out the best in your partner?"
- "If I asked a good friend of both of you what they are seeing you do differently as a couple as a result of these changes, what do you think he or she would tell me?"

Client and Couple/Family Key Strengths and Resources Questions

- "Which of your top strengths will you call upon to help you face and resolve that conflict with your friend Mary?"
- "Can you give me an example where your family showed great teamwork successfully managing a crisis situation?"
- "If a stranger were to stop you (the mother) in the parking lot of our building, and ask you, 'What are two of your daughter's top strengths?' what would you tell that person?"
- "Can you describe for me a recent example of your daughter's 'assertiveness' in action?"
- "If you were at your best friend's house and she asked you, 'What are two things that you really appreciate about your mother?', what would you tell her?"
- "In what ways can Mr. Smith [teacher and adult inspirational other] help support you best at school with those mean-spirited girls that have been harassing you lately?"
- "What is one achievement you are proudest of?"

Client and Couple/Family's Past Successes Questions

- "You mentioned earlier that bulimia used to get the best of you in the past. What specifically did you do and tell yourself to conquer that tough habit?"
- "Which of those important steps that you took and self-talk valuable words of wisdom do you think you should use to help you to conquer your cutting habit now?"
- "Are you aware of what you told yourself or what you did that helped you six months ago when you went three weeks without partying once?"
- "You mentioned earlier that your older son used to be 'hooked on online gambling and *World of Warcraft*.' What steps did you take back then to help him to successfully conquer those habits?"
- "Do you think we could get the same results using those strategies with Kirk [younger son with Internet abuse and online video-gaming difficulties]?"
- "Are there any key people in your life that have served as your cheerleading squad and biggest supporters in the past that we may want to call upon to help you with your quest to conquer your cutting habit?"

Client Storylines of Courage Questions

- "Can you think of a time in the past or recently where you drummed up the courage to master a difficult task or situation?"

- "What did you learn about yourself that surprised you the most when you took that courageous step?"
- "What did you tell yourself that got you so fired up to pull that off so well?"
- "If we were to gaze into my imaginary crystal ball and watch you taking courageous steps over the next week to put a stop to your cutting habit, what will we see you doing to make that happen?"

Client Resiliency Questions

- "Can you think of a time in the past where you lost someone really close to you and the helpful steps you took to better cope with that painful loss?"
- "In looking back, what steps did you take to better cope with the loss of your grandmother?"
- "Which of those steps could you use now in helping you come to grips with the loss of your boyfriend?"

Client Life Passions Questions

- "You shared with me earlier in the session that one of your major passions in life is making sculptures. If you were to sculpt a new shape to your relationship with John, how would it look and what difference would it make?"
- "So, you love gourmet cooking. How do you think we can spice up your marriage so that the passion and romance comes back, add hot chili flakes or more garlic?"
- "What in your life gives you the greatest sense of satisfaction?"
- "What do you find most meaningful and fulfilling about that?"

Client Epiphany Questions

- "Sometimes we read, hear, or see something in a book, out in nature, on a TV show, or in a movie that sparks some new insights about our situations or compels us to try something new or daring. Have you had any experiences like that lately or in the past that were really meaningful to you?"
- "After experiencing that epiphany, how have you put that wisdom to use in your life and in your most important relationships?"
- "What did you start doing differently as a result?"
- "How specifically has your life been transformed by that new realization about your personal capabilities?"
- "Are there any other hunches or connections sparked by another epiphany you plan to follow up on?"

Key Client Serendipitous Practices Questions

- "Sometimes we discover that certain cherished beliefs or expectations we have or practices we engage in seem to lead to positive and surprising things happening. Do you have any cherished beliefs or certain practices like this that seem to bring good fortune or luck to you?"
- What specifically are those beliefs and practices?"
- "Do you think that accessing that belief and all the good that it can bring you might come in handy in giving you the strength to confront your parents?"
- "Do you have any hunches for today—just feelings about actions you should take or things you might do?"
- "With your keen sense of openness for possibilities, what pleasant surprises are you anticipating happening over the next week that you will be on the lookout for?"

Key Client Serendipitous Environment Questions

- "Can you think of any places you like to visit or hang out in where it seems like positive surprises or good things seem to happen that benefit you either while you are there or after leaving those places?"
- "Do you think it would be easier for you to stay quit from partying on the weekends if you were out hiking in the woods more during those times?"
- "What is it about being out in nature that seems to benefit you so much?"

Problem Clarification and Visions of Change Questions

Since self-destructive clients and their partners or families can be challenging to engage and often have had multiple past unsuccessful treatment experiences, we want to be clear in the very first session that we are addressing with our clients what they consider to be the "right" problem to work on changing first. As Charles Kettering, the famous inventor, once said, "A problem well-stated is a problem half-solved." Often, in listening respectfully to our clients' past unsuccessful treatment stories it becomes quite clear that the therapists or treatment teams acted like privileged experts who decided which of the clients' problems were the "right" problems that needed fixing, and what the treatment goals, modalities, and best course of treatment should be for them. This is why we take the time in our initial meetings with couples and families to find out in great detail about the following: what is the most pressing problem that the clients wish to change first; explore with them what specifically all of their and key members from their social networks, and past treatment providers' attempted solutions have been, including what may have been helpful in the short-run or they had stopped employing for some reason; what their treatment expectations and preferences are; what their *visions of change* are; and determining with them what their unique stages of readiness for change are, as well as their confidence and importance levels for change. All of this important information is critical for tailor-fitting the relationship we co-construct with our clients to best meet their unique needs and characteristics. *Problem-tracking questions* (Fisch et al., 1982; Selvini-Palazzoli, Boscolo, Cecchin, & Prata, 1980; Selekman, 2005, 2009, 2010) provide a step-by-step description of how the problem pattern develops. These questions are especially useful with couples and families where there are no self-generated pretreatment changes or past successes reported and it is also difficult to foster a cooperative relationship with the clients even after asking coping and pessimistic questions.

Some examples of problem clarification and vision for change questions are as follows.

Problem-Clarification Questions

- "What would you like to change today?"
- "You [the parents] mentioned three things you would like to see changed with Dylan's behavior. Out of the three, which one of those difficulties is most pressing that you would like to see changed first?"
- "If we were to break 'Dylan's explosive behavior' down into bite-size pieces, which piece of that behavior do you want to see changed first?"
- "How will you know that it is really solved?"
- "You have shared with me many things that you are really concerned about, but what do you think is the most pressing and *right* problem that we need to tackle first?"
- "What is the "real pain" point in your relationship?"

Client-Attempted Solutions Questions

- "What specifically have you [the parents] tried to do to get Sandy to stop bingeing and purging and cutting herself?"

- "What else have you tried to do?"
- "How well did it work?"
- "Has there been anything the two of you [the parents] thought about trying, even something off-the wall, but held back from trying it out because you did not think it would work?"
- "You have seen many therapists before me. What specifically did they overlook or not address with your couple situation that is important for me to know?"
- "Did any of your former therapists say or do anything that you think made your situation much worse?"
- "In what ways did that further exacerbate Jane's cutting habit?"
- "What did Dr. Rubin fail to address or resolve with your family that would have really made a difference?"
- "Can you think of anything any of your past therapists had offered you to try out at home that really seemed to work at the time?"

Treatment Expectations and Preferences Questions

- "Knowing that you have seen a lot of therapists and have been involved with a lot of different treatment programs before coming to see me, what do I need to avoid saying or doing at all costs with you that would chase you out the door?"
- "Let's pretend that you have come to this meeting today to serve as my expert consultants. In about an hour from now another family just like your family is coming to see me for the first time. What advice would you have for me about how best to connect with them? What questions should I ask? What do you think I should do that would help the most?"
- "Some teens prefer individual over family counseling sessions or a combination of both, which would you prefer we do together?"
- "Which would you (the parents) prefer family therapy or participating in our new *Solution-Oriented Parenting Group* we are going to start up this week?"
- "Is there anything happening at school with any of your daughter's teachers that you would like me to directly address with them?"

Client Vision of Change Questions

- "What was the picture that you had in your mind before you came in here today about what specific issues or difficulties we would need to cover in our work together so that you will leave here hopeful and completely satisfied?"
- "What else do you think we need to address and resolve in our work together that would make a big difference for you?"
- "If our work together proved to be highly successful beyond your wildest dreams, what specifically will have changed with your situation?"

Client Readiness for Change Questions

- "What will have to happen that will tell you that the time is now to quit cutting for good?"
- "How else will you know that you are ready to quit now?"

Client Confidence Questions

- "On a scale from 1 to 10, with 10 being you are totally confident that you could quit gambling today, where would you rate yourself?"
- "How confident are you over the next week that you are going to take one step higher up on that scale to a 5?"
- "How specifically will you get that to happen?"

Client Importance Questions

- "What would be worthwhile about not doing coke anymore?"
- "What difference would it make in your life if you stopped doing coke?"
- "How will you know that you really want to stop doing coke?"

Problem-Tracking Questions

- "So after you catch Roger visiting porn sites, what do you say to him?
- "How does he respond?"
- "Then what do you do?"
- "How does he respond?"
- "What happens after that?"

Goal-Setting Questions

Once we are clear with our clients what specifically they wish to change first, we begin the goal-setting process. No matter what brought the clients to see us, ultimately the best way to foster a cooperative relationship with them is giving them the lead voice in determining the goals for treatment. If clients choose cutting back as their initial treatment goals, we will honor their wishes and support their unique quitting styles. We also have found with clients presenting with multiple habit difficulties that when they take the lead in choosing which of their habits they wish to change first, any small changes in their selected habit areas can ripple and have a transformative impact on their other habits and trigger changes in other areas of their lives. Our job is to negotiate small, realistic, and solvable goals. Furthermore, it is important to let clients know the following: that goals are the beginning of something new, not the end of something; that achieving them requires hard work, focus, discipline; to expect bumps in the road while attempting to achieve them; and to try and enjoy the journey (de Shazer, 1994; de Shazer et al., 2007; Selekman 2009). Research indicates that when people think about their goals as steps toward learning, as opposed to performance indicators, they remain engaged in trying to achieve their goals even after experiencing failure (Martin, Haskard-Zoinierek, & DiMatteo, 2010).

As a way to elicit from couples and families signs of progress in their goal areas and their ideal treatment outcome pictures, we like to employ the use of the *best hopes* (George, Iveson, & Ratner, 1999), *miracle* (de Shazer, 1988), and *presuppositional questions* (O'Hanlon & Weiner-Davis, 1989). To help secure a clear focus for treatment and as a measurement of progress in the clients' target goal areas, we use *scaling questions* (de Shazer, 1991, 1988; de Shazer et al., 2007; George et al., 1999; O'Hanlon & Weiner-Davis, 1989; Selekman, 2005, 2009). With parents and couple partners who will not budge with or negotiate one initial treatment goal at a time but instead want to see multiple behaviors changed all at the same time, it is possible to establish separate scales for each problem behavior and weave them together by inquiring with the clients over time how a change on one of the scales is affecting changes on the others. This way they see the interconnected nature of the problem behaviors and the solution steps, and that it will not require a Herculean effort to resolve these difficulties simultaneously in a short amount of time (George et al., 1999). Some examples of goal-setting questions are as follows.

Best Hopes Questions

- "What are your best hopes that you will get out of our meeting today?"
- "Which one of your best hopes would need to be realized today to make this a really useful session?"

- "What will your everyday lives be like once these best hopes are realized?"
- "What are you already doing or have done in the past that may in some way contribute to these best hopes being realized?"
- "How will you know when another small step toward achieving your best hopes has been made?"

Miracle Questions

- "Now I want to ask all of you a fun question. Supposed that while you are sleeping tonight and the entire house is quiet, a miracle happens. The miracle is that the problem that brought you here is now solved. However, because you are sound asleep, you don't know that the miracle has happened. So, when you wake up tomorrow morning, what will be different that will tell you that a miracle has happened and the problem which brought you here is solved?"
- "How specifically will Maria be showing you tomorrow that her 'self-esteem' is higher?"
- "What effect will that have on you and your relationship with her, when she is 'smiling' and 'more open' with you about 'her life'?"
- "Maria, what will you be most surprised with after the miracle happened?"
- "Let's say your husband were sitting in this empty chair (the father was absent from the meeting) over here, what will he be the most pleased with that changed in your relationship with Maria?"
- "What else will be happening in this family after the miracle happened?"
- "I'm curious, are any pieces of the miracle already happening a little bit now?"

Presuppositional Questions

- "Let's say you left our meeting today feeling like it had accomplished everything you were hoping for. In reflecting back on how your situation was before you came in here today and how things are really different now, what changed that you are most pleased about?"
- "How specifically are those changes helping the two of you get along better?"
- "What is the next smallest and simplest step each of you will take that will have the greatest impact on your relationship situation?"
- "Let's say we are gazing into my imaginary crystal ball two weeks down the road and the two of you are no longer arguing, what will we see the two of you doing instead that is helping you get along?"
- "In what ways is that making a difference?"
- "Let's say we are watching you in my imaginary crystal ball staying quit from cutting over the next week, what are the steps we are watching you take that are making that happen?"
- "What else are we watching you do, that is keeping you quit from cutting?"

Scaling Questions

- "So, on a scale from 1 to 10, where 1 stands for when things were at their worst, and 10 means the day after the miracle, where would you say you are at today?"
- "At a 5?! I'm curious, what tells you that you are not at 3 or a 4?"
- "Are you aware of how you did that?!"
- "What else did you do that got you 50% of the way up toward that 10?"
- "Suppose things continue to improve. What will a 6 look like?"
- "What are you going to do over the next week to help you get up to that 6?"
- "Who will be with you when you achieve that goal?"

- "You mentioned that there are three things you want changed with Gina. If scale A represented her swearing, scale B represented respecting her curfew times on the weekends, and scale C represented her cutting, where would you have rated all of these behaviors a month ago on a scale from 1 to 10, with 10 being doing much better?"
- "All at a 1. So how about two weeks ago?"
- "At a 5, 6, and a 7 respectively. What steps did you see Gina take that got her up to 50–70% higher on those scales?"
- "Wow! She has been talking to you more respectfully, respecting her curfew times better, and greatly reduced her cutting behavior. Tell me, are you aware of how you contributed to Gina's great turn around?"
- "Is that different for you to cut back on your 'nagging' with her?"
- "What else are you doing that seems to be contributing to Gina's progress?"
- "Where would you rate Gina on the three scales today?"
- "Wow! At a 7, 8, and a 9 respectively."

Coping Sequence Questions

Some pessimistic couple partners or family members may have grave difficulty responding to the miracle, best hopes, or presuppositional questions, even after gently saying, "Can you try to pretend or play around with the idea?" With pessimistic and the "I don't know" adolescents who do not contribute to the miracle inquiry, we find it useful to respond with, "If you did know ..." or turn to a sibling and ask, "If your brother did know [what his miracles were], what do you think he would say?" Most adolescents do not like family members speaking for them and will often open up at this point in the session. However, in some cases these adolescents may continue to be pessimistic about the possibility of their parents' ever changing. Also, we have found that with "Yes, but ..." couple partners and parents that tend to nullify any constructive or responsible steps taken by the identified client and only want to talk about what is not right or not working, the coping sequence questions are very useful in helping foster cooperative relationships with these youth and adults (Berg & Miller, 1992; de Shazer et al., 2007; Selekman, 2005, 2009). Some examples of coping sequence questions are as follows:

- "It sounds like at times things get really out of hand in your relationship with the blaming. So, tell me what steps each of you are taking to prevent the situation from getting much worse?"
- "Are you aware of how you did that?!"
- "Since you have been 'calling time-outs' and for 'truces,' how has had that made a difference?"
- "What else are you doing to prevent your situation from getting much worse?"
- "How specifically has that been helpful?"

Pessimistic Sequence Questions

With more demoralized and highly pessimistic couple partners and parents, the coping sequence questions may lead to even more negative responses like, "Sooner or later things are really going to get out of hand" or "She will probably end up killing herself eventually." These clients can really test the integrity of therapists and it is quite easy to become inducted into their bottom-less vortex of pessimism. Depending on the clients' unique pessimistic style, will determine what type of pessimistic sequence questions we will employ with them to help foster a better cooperative and collaborative partnership (Berg & Miller, 1992; de Shazer et al., 2007; Selekman, 2009). A dramatic form of pessimistic question is the nightmare question (Berg & Reuss, 1997), where we invite our clients to imagine that their problems get as bad as they can possibly get, as if they were experiencing their worst nightmare. This may lead to constructive conversations on what steps the clients could take to prevent that nightmare from coming true. Some other examples of pessimistic sequence questions are as follows:

- "If you don't solve this problem soon, what will the dire consequences be?"
- "And after that?"
- [With laissez-faire pessimistic parents] "Let's say that this Friday night at midnight a police officer rings your doorbell and proceeds to tell you that your daughter is no longer with us. What effect would her loss have on you as parents?"
- "What would you miss the most not having your daughter present in your lives?"
- "Who will attend her funeral?"
- "What will the eulogies be?"
- [With demoralized highly pessimistic parents] "Some parents in your situation would have thrown in the towel a long time ago with counseling, would have shipped their kid off to residential treatment, made their kid a Ward of the State, or better yet, put their kid up for adoption! What has stopped you from doing that?!"
- "On a scale from –10 to –1, with –10 your situation is totally hopeless and irresolvable and –1 you have an inkling of hope that things can improve just a little bit. Where would you have rated your situation one month ago?"
- "At a –9. How about two weeks ago?"
- "At a –5. Are you aware of how you got up four notches higher on that scale?"
- "What else seems to be preventing you from dropping back down to a –9?"
- "What is the tiniest step that Sebastian could take over the next week that could give you a glimmer of hope?"

Conversational Questions

When we are referred therapy veteran and traumatized clients and their couple partners and families, it behooves us to honor their long problem-saturated stories and validate their feelings of hopelessness, despair, and demoralization. We must avoid at all costs being narrative editors and instead be like cultural anthropologists entering a native's village, wanting to learn more details about his or her culture and the untold chapters of his or her life story. Here we need to adopt a position of "not knowing" and create with clients a safe climate for the sharing of the "not-yet-said," which may take the form of couple partners or family members taking risks sharing secrets and critical life events (Andersen, 1991; Anderson, 1997; Anderson & Gehart, 2007). Conversely, we invite couples and families to speculate about the therapist's "not-yet-said," that is, what hunches, concerns, and important questions they think he or she has held off asking them due to being too cautious or some other reason. This useful client feedback can help strengthen the therapeutic alliance and move the treatment process in a much more productive direction.

Conversational questions are open-ended and designed to facilitate ongoing dialogue and transcend simple "yes" or "no" responses. These questions promote a mutual search and exploration between therapists and their clients to identify constraints that are keeping them stuck and together co-generate new meanings about their problem stories. The telling and re-telling of the problem story or certain life events can loosen up fixed beliefs and lead to *news of a difference*, which can dramatically change couple and family interactions. Conversational questions can be employed to tap the expertise of children and adolescents to help generate solutions for their parents and families. We call this subcategory of conversational questions *reversal questions* (Selekman, 2005, 2009, 2010): for example, asking an adolescent, "Do you have any advice for your parents so they can argue less?" Parents are often quite amazed how creative their kids' recommendations are and, once implemented, more often than not get good results.

Conversational questions are very useful in the context of family–multiple helper collaborative meetings. In viewing involved helping professionals as potential allies to us, we like to honor and respect their stories of involvement, concerns, best hopes, and treatment expectations for the clients and us. The practice context the helpers represent will shape their unique problem explanations and treatment expectations. In the context of these collaborative meetings, asking conversational questions honors and encourages everyone's voice around the table and conveys a strong sense of "we are in this together," which can pave the way for many high quality solutions being co-generated. Some examples of conversational questions are as follows:

- "If 'cutting' were to pack its bags and leave your life for good tomorrow, what would you miss the most?"
- "What have we not talked about that if resolved, could make a big difference in your relationship with Bill?"
- "What's missing in your relationship with your father that if it were present would make a big difference?"
- "Prior to coming in here for the first time, was there anything you told your selves that you were not going to talk about in our sessions?"
- "What questions do you think I have avoided asking you about your situation that you think are important for me to ask?"
- "If there was one question you were hoping I would ask you while we are working together, what would it be?"
- "If there was one thing that has not yet been said in order to reach a deeper understanding about your (cutting/situation), what would that be?"
- "What is the courageous conversation you have not had with your parents that once you have it, could really move your relationship with them forward in a more positive direction?"
- "It seems like all of a sudden we have run into a brick wall with our conversation. What are we not talking about that needs to be talked about?"
- [Asking involved helpers in a collaborative meeting] "Help me understand how you arrived at that conclusion?"
- [Asking involved helpers in a collaborative meeting] "Who else has faced or been involved in solving a problem like this before?"
- [Asking involved helpers, families, couples] "What is the essential question we have not asked about this situation?"
- "What do you think this problem is trying to tell us?"
- "What is it about this problem that you have been most curious about?"
- "Imagine that you fully understood the causes of these problems that have been plaguing all of you. What difference would that make for you?"
- "What do you think is keeping your situation at a stand-still right now?"
- [Asking a bulimic client] "Has there been anything that happened to you in the past or recently that has been difficult for you to stomach and digest?"
- "If you were your parents and you had a son like you, what types of consequences do you think would really work best with him and why?"
- "I'm currently working with another couple just like you and I am totally stuck. Do you have any advice for me about how I could best help that couple out?"
- "If all of you pretended to be my family therapy supervisor and you were observing me work with a family like yours, how would you change the way I was working with them? What questions should I be asking? What should I risk trying with them that might really help?"

Imagination and Future-Oriented Questions

We like to use imagination and future-oriented questions to make the session atmosphere more playful and to help the treatment system to get unstuck when the situation is at a standstill. Imagination questions can help take the sting out of clients' problems, tap their inventiveness, and make the change process more enjoyable. Often when we use imagination questions with our clients we find that it stimulates high-level creative problem-solving with clients and can pave the way for the co-construction of playful therapeutic experiments they are eager to try out. With imagination questions the sky is the limit in terms of the metaphors, subjects, themes, and contexts embedded in the questions. Some examples of imagination questions are as follows:

- [Inspired by the movie *Inception*] "If you were to 'extract' (remove certain ideas or memories) certain ideas that your parents have about you while they are asleep in deep dream states, what would they be?"
- [Inspired by the movie *Inception*] "If you had the power and the skill to perform an 'inception' [plant an important idea or hypothetical memory] in your parents' minds while they are asleep deep in dream states, what would you really want them to know about you as a person and what difference would that make in your relationship with them?"
- "Tanya, let's say you could add something special to your relationship with your parents that would make it much better. To help get your creative juices flowing, please respond to this question, 'Wouldn't it be cool if …?'"
- "Mom and dad, how would you respond to, 'Wouldn't it be cool if …?'"
- "If you could all hop into my imaginary helicopter and gain an aerial view looking down at your family, what are you seeing that we are missing and need to address?"
- "If the two of you were to come up with a [song title/newspaper headline] that would best describe your relationship, how would it read?"
- "If you [the husband] were to pretend to be George Clooney [the wife's favorite actor] and Vera you were to pretend to be Penelope Cruz [the husband's favorite actor] this Friday night when you go out on a date, what special things will happen that will really make you enjoy each other's company more?"
- "If 'cutting' were to shape-shift into an animal, what would it become?"
- "If this problem suddenly became King Kong in its size, what would that mean for you and your family?"
- "What steps would you take as a family team to defend and support one another when King Kong starts pounding his chest and gets mad?"
- "If you had special X-ray goggles and could see inside the mind of your cutting habit, what would it look like in there and what important discoveries would you make?"
- "If you were to unleash your wildest dream, what would you do first?"
- "After taking that step, how would that make a difference in your life?"
- "Let's say that Steve Jobs had been presented with your problem situation, how would he have solved it?"

The most exciting aspect of the future is that it has not happened yet and together with our clients we have the opportunity to co-create the kind of compelling future realities they desire. Future-oriented questions can be used for goal-setting, to consolidate client gains, for relapse prevention, and when the treatment system is stuck in an impasse situation (Andersen, 1991; Boscolo & Bertrando, 1993; Selekman, 2006, 2009; Tomm, 1987a,b, 1988). For highly pessimistic and demoralized clients who did not respond well to the miracle question, gaining access to a more expansive and compelling future reality of success may be the spark that provides hope and possibilities for them. Some examples of future-oriented questions are as follows:

- "Let's say we all ran into one another at the shopping mall one year from today. What will each of you be the most excited to share with me about the changes you made?"
- "How are those changes making a difference in your relationship with your parents?"
- "Let's say that Mr. Cochrane [former probation officer] and Mr. Taylor [former high school dean] just happened to run into us at the mall. Which of your biggest changes will blow their minds the most, that you are completely drug-free or that you are going to college?"
- "Let's say you were to play the role of historians and walk us back in time tracing the steps that you took as a family to get to this great place, what will you tell us were the most important initial steps that you took that paved the way for your success?"
- "What was one early obstacle you had to deal with as a family and how did you overcome it?"
- "How about you Pedro [the adolescent], were there any individual obstacles you had to overcome to pull off your big changes?"
- "Let's say we are gazing into my imaginary crystal ball four weeks down the road and you are continuing to stay quit from cutting and smoking weed, what are we seeing you do and your parents that is making that possible?"
- "What else are we seeing you do to stay on track?"
- "What do you truly want your life in the future to look like and how will you follow that vision through the unchartered waters of uncertainty?"
- "Is getting stoned/gambling moving you closer to or further from the life you dream of having?"

Externalization of the Problem and Percentage Questions

Externalization of the problem questions (Epston, 2000; White, 2007; White & Epston, 1990) offer an elegant way to enhance responsibility of clients over their self-destructive habits while at the same time putting the blame on the externalized problem instead of the person of the client, couple partner, the parents and involved helping professionals. Externalization also allows us to work on the problem cognitions that accompany most self-destructive habits, challenging these beliefs without criticizing the person (Beyebach, 2000; Durrant & Coles, 1991; Epston, 1998; Maisel, Epston, & Borden, 2004; Selekman, 2009; White 1995, 2007; White & Epston, 1990).

When externalizing clients' problems, therapists need to co-construct the problems into the language the clients use to describe them or from their beliefs about why they think they exist. In listening carefully to the clients' descriptions and problem views, behaviors, habits, DSM-IV labels, patterns, and lifestyles can be externalized. We like to find out details about the various negative effects the problem has had on the identified clients, couple partners/parents, other family members, concerned members from their social networks, including involved helping professionals from larger systems. This helps to create an adversarial position against the problem and promotes advancement in the stages of readiness for change; if the negative effects of the externalized problem become more evident, our clients will be more motivated to defeat it. We also want to learn about unique outcomes and sparkling moments when the identified clients and concerned others have been successful at standing up to the oppressive problem and have not allowed it to get the best of them individually or with their relationships.

Externalization of the problem is particularly useful with couples and families that have been plagued by oppressive and longstanding self-destructive habit difficulties. Many self-destructive habit clients develop intimate relationships with their choice habits and they often become personified like: "Coke is my lady" or "Cutting is like a good friend, I can always count on it." We have also observed that in some cases couple partners or multiple family members are being pushed around by habit difficulties and there may be a multigenerational family history of habit difficulties that seemingly have a life of their own. In these cases, externalization of the family pattern has the added bonus of uniting family members against their enemies. Some examples of externalizing questions are as follows:

- "Sonia, who is in charge of your skin, 'cutting' or you?"
- "In what ways have your scars left a bad taste in your mouth about 'cutting' being more of a foe than a friend?"
- "Sonia, have there been any times lately where you stood up to 'cutting' and you did not allow it to claim your arms as battlefields?"
- "How are you viewing yourself differently now as opposed to the former you that was held captive by 'cutting'?"
- "Mom and dad, how can you be absolutely certain that your son is being pushed around by 'Bipolar' or could it be the teen years are just like one big emotional roller-coaster ride?"
- "In what ways does bulimia coach the two of you [the parents] to disagree?"
- "Can you think of any times lately where the two of you [the parents] dug in as a united team and put bulimia in its place when it was trying to push your daughter around?"
- "Which would you prefer Timmy, for online war games to make you a passenger in life or for you to be in the driver's seat of your own life and future success?"
- "Which would you prefer, 'coke' or your wife?"
- "Which would you prefer, a self-erasing or a self-embracing lifestyle?"
- "Do you see how 'running away' puts your parents and the professionals in charge of your future or would you prefer to be charge of your own future?"
- "Tell me, who is in charge of your relationship, "blaming" or you two?"
- "I'm curious, when you were growing up, in what ways did "blaming" get the best of your relationships with your parents?"

Once we externalize our clients' problems, we like to use *percentage questions* to secure from them a quantitative measurement of the percentage of the time they thwart or neutralize the problem's efforts to get the best of them versus the percentage of time the problem gets the best of them and concerned others. To begin with, we will ask the couple or family members to give us a percentage measurement of where things were a month before pursuing therapy with standing up to the problem and not allowing it to get the best of them, and the times where the problem was victorious over them. Similar to scaling questions, we want to solicit from them percentage measurements of where things were with their situation at two weeks and presently. When progress is reported between the different time periods we want to elicit what worked and amplify and consolidate their gains. Some examples of percentage questions are as follows:

- "Sonia, one month ago, what percentage of the time were you and your parents in charge of 'cutting' versus casualty victims to it?"
- "What specifically do you think you and your parents could do to out-trick 'cutting' over the next week to help increase the percentages of you being more in charge of it to a 60/40% split?"
- "What will be the next step to put you up to 70% in charge of 'cutting'?"
- "What percentage of the time do you think 'coke' coaches Sid to lock horns with you (his partner)?"
- "Sid, what percentage of the time in a week's time do you stand up to 'coke's' attempts to seduce you to use and not fall prey to it?"

Walking the Tightrope: Subsystem Work for Deepening Therapeutic Alliances and Implementing Secret Mission Projects

In our initial telephone intake conversations with the help-seeking partner or parent, we will explore the possibility of including any key members from their social networks, including any actively involved professionals from larger systems in our first couple or family sessions. This way we can learn what their problem explanations, expectations, and recommendations are, and the couple partners or family members have the opportunity to share how the key members can best help them. However, more often than not, many couples and families feel more comfortable meeting alone with us first before bringing in the other members of the solution-determined system.

Our work with couples and families is not conjoint during the entire session, as we usually like to split up the partners or family members. We find it most advantageous to do subsystem work as a way to deepen our alliances with the couple partners and family members, to disrupt problem-maintaining interactions and power imbalances in both couple and family relationships, and to propose secret mission projects and therapeutic experiments for each of the partners, parents, young adults, adolescents, or siblings to carry out separately. Keeping one's balance as a therapist is like walking on a tightrope, carefully attending to each couple partner's and family member's unique goals and needs and demonstrating that you can deliver for each party without alienating, violating trust, or putting anyone on the defensive. During this time, the habit-dependent partner can educate his or her partner about his or her triggers, both positive and negative. By positive triggers we mean what specifically the partner does that helps and can greatly benefit him or her by increasing their frequency.

When to See Couple Partners Separately

When we are working with a couple situation where both parties share the same goals and are in the *action* stage of readiness for change we will see them together most of the time. Individual session time with the habit-dependent client will be devoted to creating his or her structured daily plan for success (see Chapter 10) and for learning a wide range of distress management tools and strategies. After this individual session time, we bring the partners back together and the habit-dependent partner is put in charge of sharing with his or her partner the specific distress management tools and strategies he or she is learning and we begin the couple relapse prevention process.

In challenging clinical situations where the habit-dependent partner is reluctant to attend couples therapy, we will offer to see the concerned partner alone. We use our session time with this partner to accomplish the following: assess any pretreatment changes with either the habit-dependent partner or the concerned partner that seem to be helping; assess past successful problem-solving strategies for gaining the other partner's cooperation that the concerned partner might want to experiment with; track the concerned partner's attempted solution patterns of interaction that may be inadvertently maintaining the habit-dependent partner's problematic behaviors; and to recommend some specific therapeutic experiments to try to disrupt all of his or her unproductive problem-maintaining patterns of interaction. In addition, we also like to devote some session time to discussing how concerned partners can care for themselves, how they can protect themselves from possible violence; what else they can do to cope with the stress that the self-destructive habit of the partner creates and how they can expand their social networks in order to get some additional support. This strategy sometimes leads naturally to the "detaching with love" Al-Anon strategy that we discuss further in Chapter 10. Future individual sessions with the concerned partner will be used to monitor progress, consolidate gains, or to experiment with other change strategies. In many cases, we have succeeded at changing the habit-dependent partner and greatly improved the couple relationship by working solely with the concerned partner. In our experience, the most difficult part is that the concerned partner understands that these individual sessions with him or her can indeed be useful for the other person as well.

Sometimes, the habit-dependent partner will accompany the concerned partner to the session but is clearly in the *precontemplative* stage of readiness for change. They may not only view the problem situation completely differently, but there may appear to be a lot of emotional distance in their relationship as well. In these situations, we will divide the partners up and conduct very different conversations with them. With the concerned partner, we will pursue the same strategies described above that we would use when working alone with him or her. However, with the precontemplative habit-dependent partner, we would use the *two-step tango* strategy. This consists of first restraining him or her from changing too quickly and then gently planting seeds in their mind about the benefits of changing, in an effort to raise their consciousness level regarding the importance of changing (Selekman, 2005, 2009). In addition, we will use this individual session time to build an alliance with him or her by coming to know them better by their strengths, talents, and life passions and find out what they would like us to work on changing with the concerned partner's most annoying or troubling behaviors. According to Prochaska, Norcross, & DiClemente (2006), if we can advance the client to the next stage of readiness for change we are increasing the likelihood for his or her future success.

In some cases, in spite of the Herculean efforts of the concerned partner to try to change the habit-dependent partner's behavior and the therapist's strong coaching support and letters to him or her, the partner may not only continue to engage in the self-destructive behaviors but also remains reluctant to attend couples sessions. In this situation we will intervene directly with him or her. Readers are encouraged to see Chapter 9 for a variety of engagement strategies to employ with more challenging and reluctant habit-dependent clients.

Parental Subsystem Work

After spending the beginning portion of the family session with the whole family group, we typically meet with the parents alone first before meeting with the young adult or the adolescent. The only times we will meet with the young adult or the adolescent first is if they are in charge of the family mood and wield most of the power in the family. It is then essential for us to build an alliance with them as early as possible in the treatment process.

During our individual session time with the parents, we try to accomplish the following in relation to their child's problems: have them identify any self-generated parenting pretreatment changes or adjustments that they may want to increase; past successful problem-solving strategies they may want to try to use to resolve the presenting problem; explore with them all of their attempted solutions, negotiate small and realistic goals; and offer them a therapeutic experiment to try out over the next week.

The parents or couple partner of a person with self-destructive habits plays a critical role in the therapy of their daughter or partner. When the self-destructive client is in the *preparation* or *action* stage of readiness for change, the couple or family provides a caring context that makes the therapeutic journey less burdensome for the client by providing assistance, comfort and emotional support. In these cases, we like to invite the client to ask explicitly for the kind of help and support she wishes to get from her family members or couple partner when needed.

The role of the parents and couple, however, is even more central in those cases where the client is in a *precontemplative* stage of readiness for change. In these situations, the family members or couple partner are likely to be the only ones who ask for therapeutic help. It will be our role to help them become a containing context for the self-destructive family member or partner, trying to minimize the harm the self-destructive behavior brings about and helping to create in their daughter or partner an awareness of the problem and a motivation for change. This usually involves two different types of action. On the one hand, it is important that the parents or couple partner cease any self-destructive habit-maintaining behaviors and take a firm stand against the self-destructive habits and take measures to, for instance, limit Internet use, supervise meals, or keep drugs out of the house. This should be done in a firm but gentle way, without criticism or hostility towards the habit-dependent family member or partner. We also make clear that the parents stand a chance only if the two of them are a united front in working together as a team, resisting any attempts from their habit-dependent son or daughter to divide them. In addition, we strive to strengthen the parent–adolescent bond, which can help infuse more positive emotion into their relationship (Selekman, 2006, 2009).

There are some other issues that we are likely to address in our conversation with the parents. With life-threatening self-destructive habits, it is very common for the mother to take on the role of the *primary caretaker* (Rolland, 1994), a role associated with high levels of stress, anxiety, and depression. Therefore, we will help the primary caretaker to "put the self-destructive habit in its place," promote that he or she takes moments of respite, and try to counteract the pervasive guilt-inducing messages that they are to blame for their child's predicament. Another likely relational effect of self-destructive habits is that the parents put all their attention and efforts into the wellbeing of their self-destructive sibling, forgetting about their own wellbeing as individuals and as a *couple*. If this is the case, it is important to work to strengthen the marital relationship and to promote "problem-free couple time."

In addition to interrupting ineffective attempted solutions around the presenting self-destructive behaviors, and to protecting the space and wellbeing of all family members, family or couple therapy might also be necessary to transform broader family dynamics: entrenched negative family and/or couple dynamics that might feed into perpetuating the self-destructive habits.

Seeing Young Adults, Adolescents, and Siblings as a Group Separately

When we meet alone with young adults or adolescents, we can use this time to deepen our alliances with them and revisit pieces of the family story or the problem situation that were not shared earlier when the parents were present. This would include certain tabooed family subjects, past traumatic events, painful losses, and other self-destructive behaviors the identified client and other family members are engaging in but had not talked about earlier in the session due to safety issues, fear of negative repercussions, or a conspiracy of silence. For example, a lot of adolescents feel much more comfortable talking about their drug use when their parents are not present. Once trust develops with their therapists, adolescents make excellent system's consultants and they may feel more comfortable revealing to us that one of their stressors is a parent's drinking or gambling problem.

With young adults living at home or with adolescents, we want to find out from them in the very first session what is in it for them in terms of agreeing to participate in family therapy. How we find out this important information is by asking them the following questions:

- "How can I be most helpful to you?"
- "What is the number one thing that your parents do that gets you the most ticked off with them that you would like me to work on changing?"
- "Is there one privilege or thing that you really want me to fight for with your parents?"
- "What would I have to accomplish here with your family that in looking back you would say, 'That was really worth my time'?"

Once we find out this important information, we can serve as an intergenerational labor relations arbitrator, working both sides of the generational fence to disrupt the identified parental problem-maintaining behaviors and negotiate what the young adult or adolescent wants from the parents. We can use this individual session time with young adults and adolescents to identify and negotiate solvable goals with them. We need to go with whatever they want help with, even if it has nothing to do with their presenting self-destructive behaviors. This is how we can best foster a cooperative relationship with them. Finally, if the young adult or adolescent is in the *preparation*, *action*, or *maintenance* stages of readiness for change, we can offer them specific distress management tools or strategies, a therapeutic experiment designed to change their relationship with one of their parents, or relapse prevention tools and strategies if they have already attained abstinence from their former self-destructive habits.

When we discover that the identified clients' *siblings* are concerned and voice a strong desire to be part of the solution construction process, we will meet alone with them to explore with them how they would like to help. In some cases, an older sibling likes to serve as a co-therapist to help his or her younger habit-dependent sibling make better choices and stay on track both at school and in the community. In cases where one of the parents is the habit-dependent client, we have given the siblings fun therapeutic experiments to implement, such as putting them in charge of their parent's happiness for a day (see Chapter 9). However, we have to be careful that the siblings' personal needs are not becoming unmet because the parents are too absorbed by the self-destructive habit child's extreme behaviors. Also, siblings may feel overwhelmed because their parents have put them in the position of being supervisors or spies of their self-destructive brother or sister. Our strategy in dealing with these situations is to acknowledge and validate the siblings' concern for their sibling, but then to free them from the responsibility of taking care of him or her. We work with the parents so that they stop hiring them as "surrogate parents"; with the kids, a letter "Giving the Sack to Surveillance" or a "Farewell Letter to the Spy" are narrative, ritualized means to this end (White & Epston, 1990).

Identification of Solution-Determined System Membership and Whom to Include in Future Sessions

As an important dimension to the treatment process, we like to have our clients identify who comprises the *solution-determined system membership*, that is, all the key people concerned about their situations and trying to solve their difficulties from their social networks, including the referring person and other involved larger systems professionals. Whether working alone or with a treatment team, we become members of the solution-determined system once we enter conversations with and accept clients from the referring professional. The beauty in actively collaborating with all of the key members from clients' solution-determined systems is that they bring to the table many creative ideas, which can spark multiple high-quality solutions and shorten clients' lengths of stay in treatment. Additionally, these individuals can serve as a supportive network of concerned others to help consolidate clients' gains between couple and family sessions and prevent relapses. When it comes to inviting concerned peers of the identified client or adult inspirational others (caring and supportive teachers, clergy, community leaders, etc.) to participate in future family sessions, it is most important to have parents and adolescents first sign off on our significant other consent form (see Figure 2.1), as well as their friends' parents, friends, and adult inspirational others to insure that client confidentiality will be respected.

In our initial telephone intake conversations with the help-seeking partner or parent, we will explore with them the possibility of including any key members from their social networks, including any actively involved helping professionals from larger systems in our first couple or family sessions. By doing so, we can learn from them what their problem explanations, expectations, and recommendations are. In addition the couple partners or family members have the opportunity

I/We _____ give my/our therapist _____
_____ permission to include in my/our counseling sessions the
following two friends/adult significant others:_____
_____ for the purpose of providing additional support
in my/our treatment. I will explain to my friends, their parents, and adult significant
others that confidential information will be shared in our counseling sessions and that
it is *not* to be disclosed outside of our meetings. I will obtain signatures from my friends,
their parents, and any adult significant others I wish to include in my/our counseling
sessions.

_____   _____
Signature of client   **Date**

_____   _____
Signature of parent/guardian   **Date**

_____   _____
Signature of friend's parent   **Date**

_____   _____
Signature of friend   **Date**

_____   _____
Signature of friend's parent   **Date**

_____   _____
Signature of friend   **Date**

_____   _____
Signature of adult significant other   **Date**

_____   _____
Signature of adult significant other   **Date**

_____   _____
Witness   **Date**

Notice to client/significant others: I/We understand that this consent shall expire in 1 year from the date of our signature(s) or until the calendar date _____. I/We understand that I/we may revoke this consent at any time during my/our treatment. I/We also agree not to hold my/our therapist responsible for any violation of my/our confidentiality by participating friends or adult significant others. I/We (friend's parents) agree not to hold the therapist responsible for any possible negative effects of having my/our teen participating in his/her friend's counseling sessions.

Figure 2.1 Significant other consent form.

to share with them how they can help them in the best way possible. However, more often then not, many couples and families feel more comfortable meeting alone with us first before bringing in the other members of the solution-determined system in future sessions.

The Intersession Break and the Editorial Reflection

We usually take 5–10 minutes' intersession break around 40–45 minutes or so in to the hour. It is during this time we put our heads together with our observing team of colleagues or (if we are working alone) we quietly reflect on what transpired in the session earlier and construct the *editorial reflection*, which consists of the following: compliments for each couple partner or family member regarding their self-generated pretreatment changes, resourcefulness, courage, resilience, great insights or wisdom; positively reframing negative behaviors and/or reflecting back the problem constructions that we conjointly developed during the session; and any questions that grew out of the session that we would like the clients to ponder over the week. Finally, during this time we select or construct therapeutic experiments to offer them that are in line with their strengths, unique stages of readiness for change, visions of change, and treatment goals. When all family members are in the preparation or action stages of readiness for change, have common goals and have been very active during the session in generating ideas and strategies, we like to use the "handing over the break" strategy (Sharry, Madden, & Darmody, 2004): we invite them to have their own "team meeting" while we are taking our intersession break, and come up with one or two experiments that they would like to implement over the next week.

Client Feedback to Assess the Quality of the Therapeutic Relationship

Lambert (2010), Hubble, Duncan, Miller, and Wampold (2010), and Duncan (2010) have found that one of the most robust predictors for successful treatment outcomes are clients reporting that they had strong therapeutic alliances with their therapists. Furthermore, one of the best ways we can optimize for our clients' treatment success is to secure session-by-session feedback from them on the quality of the therapeutic relationship. This valuable feedback can aid therapists in making necessary adjustments in their interactions with their clients to help strengthen their alliances with them and help prevent premature client drop-outs from occurring. We like to ask our clients the following questions immediately after the editorial reflection:

- "What was this meeting like for all of you today?"
- "Were there any specific ideas or things we discussed that you found most helpful?"
- "What ideas or strategies that we discussed will you put to immediate use?"
- "Was there anything that we did not talk about or that you were surprised I did not ask you about that we need to discuss the next time we get together?"
- "Was there anything that I said or did that upset any of you that you would like me to stop doing?"

Since we believe that therapy should be a collaborative process and our clients are truly the experts, regularly securing this valuable feedback from them can strengthen our alliances with them and optimize for their treatment success. Another way to secure this useful feedback is by inviting our clients to fill out the Outcome Rating Scale (ORS) after each session and to briefly review the scores with them (Duncan, Miller, & Sparks, 2000). The ORS is a four-item visual analog scale, very easy to administer, that taps into how clients perceive their relationship with their therapist, if they agree on the goals and topics of therapy, if they feel the therapeutic approach is a good fit for them, and how the session felt for them.

Two final areas we address with our clients in our very first couple or family therapy session and throughout the therapeutic process are: determining the unique functions and meanings of clients' choice habits to inform clinical decision-making and risk management for suicide attempts or violent behavior. These are two critical areas that therapists must address when working with self-destructive habit clients and their couple partners and/or families.

Determining the Unique Functions and Meanings of Clients' Choice Habits to Inform Clinical Decision-Making

As we have discussed in Chapter 1, initially our clients' habits have served as gifts and resources for them. They may serve as attempted solutions for taking back control of their lives, for finding comfort and sanctuary, for coping with challenging life dilemmas and past traumatic events. They may serve specific functions, such as to soothe our clients, to quickly elevate their moods, to make them feel more confident and powerful, or to "numb out" painful feelings and unpleasant memories. Many clients develop intimate and protective relationships with their habits and devote a great deal of time and energy in both engaging in and concealing their habits from their intimate partners, close friends, family members, school faculty, and their employers.

Another interesting dimension to our clients' habits are their metaphorical aspects such as how they may describe past or present conflicted relationship difficulties, family secrets, emotional cut-offs, or the inequity of power and control in their intimate couple or family relationships. No matter what clients' habits are symbolic of or what their unique functions serve for them, eventually they become prisoners of their habits and the costs become severe psychologically, physically, socially, and in their school or work lives.

Ultimately, our clients' unique meanings of why they gravitated toward certain habits and the multiple functions they serve for them need to be elevated high above our initial impressions, explanations, or theories about their habit stories. In determining with our clients the unique meanings of their choice habits and the different functions they serve in their life stories, we like to ask them the following questions:

- "It would be really helpful for me to come to know how _____ fits into your life story?"
- "What does _____ mean to you?"
- "In what ways has it/have they [habit(s)] benefited you?"
- "In what situations or relationships do you find _____ helps you the most?"
- "What results do you get that you were hoping for?"
- "Can you think of any times lately or in the past where _____ really backfired for you or cost you in some way?"
- "Have there been any times lately or in the past where you said to yourself, 'I am really not sure who is in charge here anymore _____ or me?'"

The above questions can greatly aid therapists in determining the unique meanings and functions of the clients' habits and help provide multiple avenues for intervention. This important client information can point us in the direction of specific couple relationship areas or family relationships to target for intervention and specific replacement coping tools and strategies that can offer him or her similar positive effects that the habits have provided for the client. It is important to remember that whatever virtuous habit ideas we co-generate with our clients, they need to match or top the powerful pleasurable or numbing effects that they had been receiving from their choice self-destructive habits. Below, we provide nine guidelines for co-transforming client self-destructive habits into constructive and virtuous habits. This will be followed by some examples of constructive and virtuous habits our clients have come up with to replace their former self-destructive behaviors for each of the self-destructive habits presented in this book.

Guidelines for Transforming Self-Destructive Habits into Constructive and Virtuous Habits

The nine guidelines presented below are designed to offer clinicians a positive and wellness-oriented framework for viewing their clients' self-destructive habits and managing the transformational process to best optimize for their success on their challenging journeys.

1. Identify the positive intent to the client's engagement in his/her choice self-destructive habit and how it is meaningfully connected to his/her current difficulties or life story. Brainstorm together some possible virtuous habits to begin to experiment with. The virtuous habits can take the form of healthy and positive activities and/or coping strategies the client would like to try out that he/she used to engage in or new ones that sparked their interest.
2. Utilize clients' key strengths, life passions, unexplored interest areas of curiosity, serendipitous practices, and learning styles to identify and tailor-fit new constructive and virtuous habits.
3. Prepare clients for the challenging journey and the territory of habit change, which includes: initial ambivalence, taking small steps at his/her unique pace, hard work, patience, bumps in the road, and possible slips.
4. Clients also need to be made aware of the fact that initially their new virtuous habits may feel unnatural and not as effective in producing the same level of pleasurable, mood-elevating, or numbing sensations as their former choice self-destructive habits did. It is important to let them know that with daily practice they will begin to see positive results in all areas of their lives.
5. The use of worst-case scenario planning (see Chapter 10) can empower clients to not cave into their deceiving brain messages attached to their choice self-destructive habits and other triggers that may try to derail them.
6. While on their journeys, therapists need to positively reinforce their clients' progress, no matter how small their gains are, and celebrate with them their successes and their storylines of courage and resilience rebounding from slips.
7. Clients may keep a detailed *habit diary* of their transformative journeys, which includes: keeping a daily record of their practice times using their selected virtuous habit behaviors both positive and negative experiences, what specifically they and concerned others are doing to help them to successfully combat urges and craving, and when slips do occur, what specifically they and others did to help them to get back on track.
8. Clients are to increase their awareness of what their triggers are and what toxic people and places they need to avoid at all costs.
9. All slips are indications that headway had been made and offer valuable wisdom about where they need to tighten up with the structure and what they learned from their slips that they can put to good use in similar stressful situations in the future.

Self-Destructive Habits Transformed into Constructive and Virtuous Habits

In this section, we present some creative and effective virtuous habits our clients have come up with over the years as replacements for their former oppressive self-destructive habits. Under each habit listed below, we include examples of the clients' virtuous habits that became part of their daily routines, brought meaning and purpose into their lives, and contributed to their remaining free from their self-destructive habit. We wish to make clear that the virtuous habits described below are interchangeable, as they are not self-destructive habit-specific.

Self-Harm Habits

- Cultivate culinary skills by taking cooking classes.
- Ceramic, sculpture, jewelry-making, and collage artwork.
- Gardening.
- Woodworking.
- Taking yoga or martial arts classes.
- Suicide prevention and outreach work at school and in the community.
- Co-facilitator for future *Stress-Busters' Leadership Groups* (see Selekman, 2009).

Eating-Distressed Habits

- Purifying the soul through yoga and/or spa treatment.
- Start a young women's empowerment school club to help combat the sexual objectification of women and the societal and media forces that push "thinness" and other unhelpful patriarchal assumptions about how women should look and act.
- Launch a school peer support group for young women struggling with body image and weight issues.
- Launch a school and/or local community initiative to help prevent and combat obesity.
- Co-facilitator for future *Stress-Busters' Leadership Groups*.

Substance Abuse Habits

- Serve as gatekeepers in their school identifying and facilitating at-risk substance-abusing fellow students, connecting them with counseling staff for support and referral information.
- Serve as sponsors and peer counselors for substance abusers trying to kick their habits and/or struggling to stay quit from future drug use.
- Provide education to parent groups at school and in the local community on the most frequent drugs being abused by young people today, signs and symptoms of use, share how they kicked their habits and are staying quit, and their recommendations about how best parents should intervene and support their kids.
- Provide creative outreach and anti-drug prevention initiatives using art, music, drama, and dance.
- Co-facilitator for future *Stress-Busters' Leadership Groups*.

Internet Dependency and Cyber-Sex Habits

- Create and coordinate in conjunction with the school career planning office an online website that provides up-to-date information for fellow students seeking community service work opportunities and involvement in social action and environmental projects in their communities and abroad.
- Provide on- and offline peer support services for fellow students who experienced cyber-bullying and harassment, including spearheading an anti-bullying/bystander school campaign in close collaboration with the school counseling department.
- Create an interesting and challenging nonviolent video or computer game that underscores cooperation and resolving conflicts among individuals, groups, and nations through negotiation and using peaceful and other nonviolent resistance methods.

- Seek adrenalin rush experiences through exciting and challenging outdoor activities like: bungee jumping, hang gliding, mountain climbing and bike-riding, and taking a challenging long-distance hiking trail.
- Launching a new business and going to great lengths to make it succeed.
- Raising as much money as possible for an important community and/or social cause in this country and/or abroad.
- Commit to one random act of kindness (good deeds) per day for a family member, a friend, a neighbor, or someone in the community.

Risk Management: Suicide and Violence Prevention

With all of the five self-destructive habits discussed in this book, it is critical as therapists that we keep our eyes and ears open for the potential for suicidal or violent behavior with our clients. As the consequences continue to build psychologically with intense emotional distress, physically with serious health problems, socially with potentially losing family and friends, and vocationally with job loss or school failure due to their chronic involvement with their choice habits, self-destructive-habit clients may turn to suicide as a way to quickly put an end to their misery. This is why we routinely inquire with our self-destructive habit-dependent clients if they or anyone in their families of origin experienced suicidal ideation or made an attempt(s) in the past. In addition, we want to assess with our self-destructive clients who have had fleeting suicidal thoughts if they have conquered their fears of death and perceive themselves as a burden to others who they feel would be better off without them around (Joiner, 2005). For us, these are potential red flags for suicide risk. We also make maximum use of self-destructive habit clients' immediate and extended family members, concerned friends, and other key members from their social networks to serve as a *circle of caring others* to provide a supportive safety net if there is some concern of potential for due to impulsivity and impaired judgment but low-grade (no plan, no major risk factors present) suicide risk (Selekman, 2009). Sometimes this family-social network intervention alone can rapidly stabilize suicidal thoughts and risk. With high-level suicide risk situations, such as the client has a clear plan, conquered their fear of death, perceives self as a burden to others, or cognitive constriction is present, we instruct the couple partner or family members to immediately take him or her to the nearest hospital emergency room.

Often, self-destructive habit dependency can lead to increased irrational thinking, poor judgment, poor self-regulation, and impulse control problems. The combination of these difficulties with a history of problems with anger management for a client can set the stage for violent behavior toward their couple partners and family members when they try to control or interfere with their compulsive desire to engage in their choice habits. When we know that the self-destructive client has a history of anger management difficulties and/or violent behavior, or couple partners and family members voice their concerns that he or she has become threatening and increasingly more out of control and they are worried about their safety, we will put in place a written violence prevention safety plan. Each couple partner and/or family member will commit to pursuing the three or four steps they identify they will take when they feel unsafe. We work with our self-destructive-habit clients in increasing their awareness levels regarding their personal warning signs when they feel like they could potentially lose physical control, such as identifying certain physiological sensations (feeling a rise in their blood pressure), certain irrational thoughts, and feelings (anger, fear). They, too, have to come up with concrete steps they can take as early as possible in the anger response cycle, such as when they begin to feel a rise in their blood pressure, to prevent themselves from hurting their partners or family members. We will do worst-case scenario planning with these at-risk self-destructive-habit clients and their partners or families so that everyone is very clear and well practiced with the steps they need to take to prevent a escalation if the threat of violence should occur in the future, which includes contacting the police immediately.

Conclusion

In this chapter we have presented the main interviewing strategies we use to co-construct with our clients a strong therapeutic alliance and a climate ripe for change. Sometimes, the session itself has such a powerful therapeutic impact that no therapeutic experiments or rituals are needed; in these cases, our end-of session editorial reflection may include only some compliments, encouragement, and are conveying with confidence our belief that the clients will continue doing what is helpful to them and are committed to pursuing a more preferred direction with their lives. However, in most cases, at the end of the initial couple or family interview, we offer them a few therapeutic experiments or rituals in order to further build on the momentum they had gained during the session and as a way to make sure that the changes that were brought about during the session generalize beyond our offices and catch on in our clients' lives. We will present the major therapeutic experiments and rituals that we regularly use with couples and families in the next chapter.

3
MAJOR THERAPEUTIC EXPERIMENTS AND RITUALS

The best way to predict the future is to invent it.
Alan Kay

Introduction

In this chapter, we will discuss the major therapeutic experiments and rituals we use with our collaborative strengths-based brief family therapy approach with couples and families presenting with self-destructive habit difficulties, including both in-session experiments and rituals and those to be implemented at home. When we select, design, and recommend specific therapeutic experiments or rituals, it is important to match them with our clients' stages of readiness for change, psychological reactance levels, goals, theories of change, and to respect their treatment preferences and expectations for the change process. It does not make sense to offer a therapeutic experiment to someone who is in the precontemplative stage of readiness for change, or a complicated ritual to a person who is in contemplation stage.

As to the position of the client, someone who sees a problem but feels that it behooves others to act upon it (a complainant relationship; de Shazer, 1988) is more likely to benefit from an observation experiment, whereas a client who feels responsible for and capable of acting on the self-destructive habit (a customer relationship; de Shazer, 1988) will benefit more from an action-oriented therapeutic experiment. Our rule of thumb is to error on the side of cautiousness and only invite clients to carry out those therapeutic experiments or rituals they are capable of and willing to do (Beyebach & Herrero, 2010). Furthermore, when we assign elaborate therapeutic experiments and rituals, we make sure that we provide clear and logical rationales (embedded with clients' key words, metaphors, and belief system material) for the value and importance of implementing the experiments or rituals. This promotes a cooperative relationship with them and increases the likelihood that the clients will accept our suggestions. In addition, we find it useful to write down the concrete implementation steps of all proposed therapeutic experiments or rituals to give to clients at the end of our sessions. This helps increase treatment compliance and follow-through. Finally, we like to give our clients plenty of room to make choices and therefore tend to offer them two or three therapeutic experiments or rituals from which to choose from each session.

Major Therapeutic Experiments and Rituals

In this section, we present six classes of therapeutic experiments and rituals: *family/couple connection-building, adventures in time-traveling, family/couple art therapeutic experiments, positive psychology therapeutic experiments, bringing Broadway, dance, and film media to the therapeutic stage*, and the *power of the written word*. Below, we discuss each of these classes of therapeutic experiments and rituals.

Family/Couple Connection-Building Therapeutic Experiments and Rituals

We employ family connection-building therapeutic experiments and rituals in family situations in which adolescents and young adults either voice a strong desire to be emotionally closer to their disengaged parents or where strengthening the parents' emotional bonds with their children could reduce the likelihood of their engaging in self-destructive habits and being strongly affiliated with negative peer groups. These experiments and rituals also can strengthen couple and family problem-solving, communications and conflict-resolution skills, and create a more positive climate in their relationships. Below, we discuss the mechanics of implementing the eleven therapeutic experiments and rituals.

Adolescents/Young Adults Mentoring their Parents

We use the *adolescents/young adults mentoring their parents* ritual in the following clinical situations: the adolescent or young adult is feeling emotionally disconnected from one or both parents and longing for a closer relationship; the parents view their son or daughter as "incompetent," "irresponsible," "sick," or as some DSM-IV label they had been given by former therapists and treatment programs; and when the parents may be so burned out with his or her self-destructive habit difficulties and all of the past treatment failures, that they have decided to throw in the towel and disengage from him or her (Selekman, 2005, 2009). The power of this ritual is that it can trigger dramatic changes on the parental belief/problem view level, strengthen the parent–young adult/adolescent relationship, and build self-confidence and self-esteem in the young adult or adolescent when he or she shines as a competent mentor for one or both of their parents.

The format for this ritual consists of having the family coming up with a daily schedule of 45–60 minutes of protected time where the young adults or adolescents will teach one or both parents some skills for the whole week, such as: technical skill on the computer, sewing and knitting, playing an instrument, wood-working, sports, baking special desserts, working in an art medium, and so forth. The house rules are as follows: the parents have to be respectful students and not challenge their son's or daughter's authority; they can only ask questions for clarification about something they do not understand or some step they need help with; and no cell phones, other digital devices, or interruptions are permitted during the scheduled training sessions.

As a result of this ritual, not only do the young adults and adolescents shine and are met with much praise from their parents about their teaching abilities, tremendous patience, and support while they were attempting to master new skills, but the family also grows much closer from this meaningful and valuable learning experience. In fact, we have had many families decide to keep the ritual going long after the first week of experimenting with it because it had injected a high level of positive emotion into their relationships.

Invisible Couple/Family Inventions

The *invisible couple/family inventions* in-session experiment taps the creativity and imagination powers of the couple partners and family members to come up with a machine or gadget that could benefit other couples and families just like them (Selekman, 2005, 2009, 2010). When introducing this experiment, they are asked the following questions:

- "If you were to invent a machine or a gadget that would benefit other teens/couple partners and families/couples just like your family/couple relationship, how would it work?"
- "What would it look like?"
- "What special features would it have?"

- "How, specifically, would it benefit you?"
- "How about parents/couple partners?"
- "How will having and using this machine or gadget regularly with your parents/couple partners improve your relationships with them?"
- "How else will this machine or gadget benefit your family/couple relationship?"

Once the couple partners or family members have discussed some of their ideas, they choose the machine or gadget that they think will benefit them the most and draw a prototype of it. They are to come up with a name for their new gadget or machine. The added bonus and fun aspect of this experiment with adolescents and their families in particular is that they get so excited and inspired by their new invention that they go home and try to build it.

One family in which the sibling rivalry and the fighting was quite intense between the 14-year-old self-battering boy and his 12-year-old brother were able to design a sound control device peacefully together. This was a reverse megaphone that was portable and had an expandable stand and a light on it so it could be taken into noisy rooms in the early morning and in the nighttime. The brothers had to contend with their 6-year-old autistic brother who was constantly making noises in the early mornings and late at night. This experiment paved the way for them to have a more positive relationship.

Couples can pretend that their chosen machine or gadget exists in reality and use it to reduce the frequency of arguments and to bring more intimacy and playfulness to their relationship. Often, this experiment can spark solutions to relationship difficulties, promote couple or family teamwork, and can be used as both a coping and a pattern intervention strategy.

Famous Guest Consultants Couple/Family Experiment

The *famous guest consultants experiment* can strengthen couples and families problem-solving, conflict-resolution, and communications skills (Selekman, 2005, 2009). This playful in-session experiment begins by inviting the couple partners or family members to write down on paper two famous people that they have been inspired by and highly respect for their accomplishments and talents. The famous people can be historical figures, artists, philosophers, scientists, musicians, authors, politicians, well-known TV, movie, and sports stars, or popular book and cartoon characters. After sharing with one another who their selected famous people were, they are to pretend to put themselves in the minds of their famous people and think about how they would view and attempt to resolve their presenting problems. As a couple or family team, they are to write down on paper what the famous people's solution strategies would be and decide which ones they would like to try to implement over the next week. By following the lead of the famous people's ideas, couples and families gain a meta-position to their relationships and difficulties, they can see and think more clearly, and find it easier to play and work together as a team. While implementing and using the famous people's solution strategies over the week, couple partners and family members often report sensing their famous others' spirits in their homes, almost like their guardian angels. The beauty with this couple or family experiment is that it is the clients who generate their own unique solutions.

The Compliment Box

With couples and families where the atmosphere at home is filled with negativity, criticism, sarcasm, and blaming, the *compliment box* can dramatically change these destructive interactions, which often fuel the self-destructive-habit clients' behaviors (Selekman, 2006, 2009). The couple partners or parents find an old shoebox and cut a slit in the box top. On a daily basis, each partner or family member writes on slips of paper compliments for one another, which consists of sharing things that they appreciate about one another as people and specific things they did for each other that they really liked. After dinner each night, they are to pass the box around and take turns reading each other's compliments. This experiment triggers positive emotion for each couple partner and family member and can dramatically alter negative beliefs and improve couple and family communications.

Positive Sticky Notes

Another way to handle negativity in couples and families is to invite family members to leave sticky notes with compliments or love messages written on them for other family members (Beyebach & Herrero, 2010). We especially like to make this suggestion to parents that spend most of the time criticizing their adolescent son or daughter; in these situations, leaving and reading the positive messages often creates a completely different emotional atmosphere. With parents we stress that they have to put the notes in places where the adolescent does not expect to find them; this surprise element makes the experiment more playful for everybody.

The Secret Surprise

The *secret surprise* (O'Hanlon & Weiner-Davis, 1989; Selekman, 2005) is a playful therapeutic experiment that not only injects positive emotion into the parent–adolescent relationship but facilitates connection-building as well. During the therapist's individual session time with the adolescent, he or she is to come up with two surprises over the next week that the parents will notice and really appreciate. The adolescent can either come up with special surprises for each parent or both of them. We like the adolescent not only to come up with some possible surprises in the session but also to write down what they plan to try. Most importantly, they are not to tell the parents what the surprises are or when they may happen. When we reconvene the family for the editorial reflection, the parents are alerted about some surprises happening over the next week and that they must pretend they are detectives and try to figure out what they were. We let them know that we will compare notes with their son or daughter in the next session to judge whether or not they should open up a private detective agency. Sometimes, we switch the roles and have the parents pulling the secret surprises and the adolescent has to play detective.

The Glass of Wishes

With couples we like to promote a more positive and intimate relationship by encouraging the exchange of pleasurable behaviors (Gottman, Schwartz Gottman, & DeClaire, 2006). A playful way to do this is by inviting the couple to create a "glass of wishes" and put it in a special place in their home (Pérez Opi & Landarroitajáuregui, 1995). Each partner writes ten wishes on ten pieces of paper; each wish has to be a specific and positive request of his or her partner ("a foot massage," "a walk in the woods together"). Each time one of our clients feels like fulfilling a wish of his or her partner, he or she takes a piece of paper out of the glass. If it feels okay to fulfill this wish, he or she will do it and take the piece of paper out of the glass. As the glasses start to get empty, both partners will write new wishes and put them into the glass so that there are always enough wishes to be filled.

Crazy and Absurd Ideas

As Albert Einstein long believed, solutions lie outside original problem explanations and *more of the same* attempted solutions. He once said, "If at first the idea does not sound absurd, then there is no hope for it." The *crazy and absurd ideas* experiment is particularly useful for couples and families who have not responded well to more straightforward therapeutic strategies and have forgotten how to play together (Selekman, 2010). Couple partners or family members are to first generate a list of the craziest and most absurd ideas that they can come up with for resolving the presenting habit difficulty or some other problem they would like to solve together. They are free to be as outrageous with their recommended solutions and their corresponding implementation steps as possible. Next, the couple partners or family members are to select at least two ideas from their list, and modify them in such a way that they become prototypes for trying out over the next week. We have found that this experiment consistently sparks laughter and playfulness for even the most demoralized and pessimistic therapy veteran couples and families. However, the greatest accomplishment for these couples and families is generating their own unique and high-quality solutions for their difficulties that we would have never thought of.

Create a Delicious Dish out of the Oppressive Habit

Another fun couple and family connection-building experiment that can generate some very creative solutions is *create a delicious dish out of the oppressive habit*. This experiment is particularly helpful to use when the couple partners or all family members identify a specific self-destructive habit that is wreaking havoc in their relationships and has fueled conflict and high levels of stress in their lives. The couple partners or family members are to decide the following: the name for the dish; if the dish will be meat, poultry, fish, seafood, or vegetarian; if the ingredients would be baked, sautéed, grilled, or steamed; what vegetables or fruits will be in it; what type of sauce would be used; and what type of herbs and spices they would use. They also have to decide to just make an entrée or whether or not to include an appetizer and a dessert. While brainstorming their dishes or different courses, they are to be mindful of how all of the main dish's or course's ingredients are related in some way to the various dimensions or effects of the presenting habit difficulty on them individually and in their relationships. For example, a family member may choose to have habanera peppers in the dish because he or she is burning up with anger about how the parents are overly involved with the bulimic sister and paying very little attention to him. Couple partners and family members can be quite creative using certain food items, spices, herbs, and food preparations as metaphors for how they see their couple relationship and family dramas. Once they have completed their entrée or three-course meal, we can process with them any new views they gained about their situation. Next, they are to pull their heads together and brainstorm how they could put their new ideas about their situations into action so as a team they can successfully counter the self-destructive habit's reign over them and eventually conquer it.

Question-Storming

With clinical situations where straightforward therapeutic experiments and rituals have not had a positive effect on the couples' or families' presenting problems and the treatment process is at a stand-still, we will have them do *question-storming* (Dyer, Gregerson, & Christensen, 2011; Roland, 1985). Unlike brainstorming sessions, where a group generates as many solutions for a problem as possible, question-storming entails having a couple or family generate five or six questions regarding why they think a particular problem exists, is keeping us stuck in the treatment process, and continues to persist in their relationships. They are to begin their questions with: "What?," "Why?," "Why not?," and "What if?" They are free to formulate different style questions as well. To help kick off the question-storming process, the couple or family can be asked to respond to the following question: "What are the best and most essential questions we need to ask right now about our situation?" Their questions can be listed on a whiteboard or a flip chart with one person writing the question down and the couple partners or family members taking the time to reflect on and dialog about each question before the next question is put up. The couple partners and family members are to defer placing judgment on or criticizing contributors' questions. Once the couple or family have compiled their list of questions, they are to prioritize and discuss the most important and intriguing questions in their search for uncovering and removing constraints and finding their own unique solutions. For some couples or families who wish to further dialogue about or reflect on their self-generated questions, they are free to request more time, take their questions home, and come back to the next session prepared to share with us what new ideas or solutions were sparked by them.

The beauty of this activity is that couples and families discover together that taking the time to craft meaningful, well thought-out, and provocative questions can help them to generate their own unique high-quality solutions for their difficulties. They also discover that they can use this problem-solving method to constructively resolve future conflict and other difficulties they are faced with.

Family/Couple Service Work

In today's digital era, excessive screen usage by youth and adults has become much more important of an activity and priority then spending time together as a couple or family (Selekman, 2006, 2009; Taffel, 2009; Turkle, 2011). Research indicates that spending time together is one of the characteristics of strong families (Stinnett & O'Donnell, 1996). We also believe that one of the aggravating factors that have contributed to the rise in young people engaging in more risky and/or self-destructive behaviors has to do with a lack of purpose and meaning in life.

One high-quality family activity that can help facilitate connection-building and underscores the important values of generosity and being compassionate to and giving to others is *family service work*. Through service work, adolescents can find meaning and purpose in the offline world and discover how one of the greatest gifts in life is the gift of giving to others. It is important that parents convey to their kids that this family activity is "a positive and meaningful way that we can be and work together." Many adolescents find that doing service work builds self-esteem, that they become more compassionate as people, and for some, this meaningful life experience may be the spark for pursuing later a career in a helping profession, getting involved in important social causes, or philanthropic work. Often, families report that their doing service work has contributed to bringing them closer together. We have found with couples who have drifted apart and do not spend enough quality time together that doing service work together can inject a strong dose of positive emotion into their relationship and help strengthen their relationship bond.

Adventures in Time-Traveling: Four Major Uses of the Imaginary Time Machine

The *imaginary time machine* is one of the most versatile therapeutic experiments we regularly use (Selekman, 2005, 2009, 2010). Most clients are intrigued by the use of time as a vehicle to help get them unstuck in the here and now, and generate exciting possibilities with their problem situations. There are four major ways we use the imaginary time machine with couples and families, they are: *bringing back the best from the past to facilitate connection-building, experiencing future selves to establish new parent–young adult/adolescent relationships in the here and now, saying "hello" in order to say "good-bye" to lost parents, siblings, or close relatives*, and *taking the time machine anywhere in time*. Below, we discuss with what types of clinical situations we employ each of the imaginary time machine experiments.

Bringing Back the Best from the Past to Facilitate Connection-Building

In family situations where there is a great deal of emotional distance between adolescents and one or both parents, or one or both parents have disengaged out of frustration or anger, we will have both the disengaged parent and the adolescent separately take the imaginary time machine back in time where they each felt much more emotionally close to one another and enjoyed their relationships. Prior to having adolescents and parents embark on their time-traveling journeys, we ask them to apply all their senses along the way, including adding color (the scenery of the place they traveled back to) and motion (what they and others are doing with and around them). The main objective of using the imaginary time machine in this way is to not only go back into the past to find out from both the parents and adolescents about the specifics of what worked back then that facilitated more closeness so pieces of their special experiences together could be reinstated in the here and now, but also as a way to inject a strong dose of positive emotion and more warmth into their current relationships as well. What we find with both parents and adolescents is that even the process of doing this experiment they are often smiling and re-experiencing joy and the mood in the office shifts toward the positive. We ask parents and adolescents the following questions to get them started on their individual journeys:

- "Where in the past are you planning to take the time machine back to?"
- "How old is your son/daughter?"
- "What are you doing together and talking about?"
- "What are you enjoying the most about this special time with your son/daughter?"
- "What are you thinking and feeling at the time?"
- "What else is special about this experience?"
- "If you were to bring back any aspects of this special experience with your son/daughter and want them happening today in your relationship with him/her, what specifically would you want to put in to place?"
- "How would those changes make a difference in your relationship now with him/her?"

We ask adolescents similar questions while on their time-traveling journeys. The next step is to have the parents and adolescents begin to experiment with their former behaviors and ways of being with one another and keep track of what seems to help the most. Initially, especially if there is a lot of conflict in the relationship, it may be most advantageous to have parents and adolescents experiment with these behaviors in small doses the first week, such as one or two days. When progress is reported, we can increase the experimenting days to three or four times over the week until the clients feel these positive behaviors and ways of being with one another have become second nature.

When working with couples who feel there is a lack of intimacy, that they have drifted apart, or are deadlocked in conflict in the here and now, we will have each partner go back into the past to capture a time in the history of their relationship where they were madly in love with one another, the passion was strong, and they shared many activities together. Similar to working with adolescents and their families, the couple partners select specific behaviors and ways of being that they appreciated about how the other partner was in the past and reinstate them in the here and now, beginning with small doses. Once we identify what works, we will have them gradually increase their positive interactions until they feel satisfied with the results and their difficulties have been resolved. With the help of using the imaginary time machine in this way, our clients' pasts can serve as a gold-mine for co-creating future possibilities.

Experiencing Future Selves to Establish New Parent–Young Adult/Adolescent Relationships in the Here and Now

In family situations where the parents are totally burned out with their son or daughter's long-standing self-destructive habits and demoralized by multiple past treatment failures, this use of the imaginary time machine can be quite effective in instilling hope and possibilities. The young adult or adolescent who is the number one source of their stress and anger, or hopelessness and despair, is to hop in the time machine: they are now 32 (the young adult) or 25 (the adolescent) years old and have come over for Sunday night dinner to update them on how well their lives are going. At these ages, they have good jobs, their own apartments, are engaged in meaningful and healthy activities and hobbies, and possibly serious intimate relationships. They are completely transformed beyond their parents' wildest dreams. We ask the young adult or adolescent the following questions:

- "What will be the first bit of exciting news that is happening in your life that you will share with your parents once you get there?"
- "How do you think they will respond to that?"
- "What effect will their positive responses have on your view of yourself?"
- "How will that help improve your relationship with them?"
- "Is there one thing that you could think of that your dad might like to do with the new you, that he would not have pursued with you in the past when you used to have difficulties?"
- "In looking back to the steps you took to become this new and special you in the future, what would you share with your parents about those specific steps?"

Co-creating with young adults or adolescents and their parents this future reality of success, triggers positive emotion, hope, and optimism for all family members. It also can lead to the identification of specific goals that can help pave the way for the young person's future success.

Saying "Hello" in order to Say "Good-bye" to Lost Parents, Siblings, or Close Relatives

When working with couple partners, young adults, or adolescents who lost parents, siblings, or close relatives and are grappling with unresolved grief issues, the imaginary time machine can be used for facilitating the mourning process. Some clients who have experienced sudden and traumatic losses of loved ones become stuck in time and prisoners of the past following their painful losses. To further complicate matters they may have turned to self-harm, substance abuse, or eating-distressed habits to try to cope with their pervasive and intense emotional pain. In many cases, they never had a chance to say "good-bye" to their lost loved one, which inhibited the mourning process.

On a cautionary note, we will not use this experiment with newly habit-free abstinent, highly depressed, or emotionally brittle clients, or those who have made past suicide attempts. With adolescents, it is critical to secure written consent from the parents to try this experiment in case there are negative repercussions from it, which is more the rare exception than the rule. We also let clients know that they should feel free to stop the experiment at any point if it feels emotionally uncomfortable or they feel like they are losing control.

When we begin the experiment, we instruct clients to apply all of their senses to the experience, including color and motion. They are to take the time machine back to a recent or past special experience they had had with their lost loved one. We ask the following questions:

- "What time in the past would you take the time machine to?"
- "Where are you and _____ at?"
- "What are you doing together and talking about?"
- "How are you thinking and feeling at the time?"
- "What is making this experience so special?"
- "Now, if you were to hug _____ , kiss him/her, say the words you never got to say to him/her and say 'good-bye,' then hop back in the time machine carrying with you certain

special qualities and aspects that you really appreciated the most about him/her, what are those qualities and aspects that you wish to make a part of you?"
- "How will making those special qualities and aspects a part of you have a positive effect on you as a person?"
- "And with others?"
- "How else will you keep his/her legacy alive in the here and now?"

Not only does this experiment open the door for talking about the painful loss for the first time but the couple partner, young adult, or adolescent is given a second chance to say their parting words and "good-bye" to their loved ones. If the couple or family thinks it may be useful, we have them bring in photo albums so they can reminisce and talk about their special past experiences that they had with the lost family member.

Taking the Imaginary Time Machine Anywhere in Time

With this last use of the imaginary time machine, couple partners, parents, young adults, and adolescents can take the time machine anywhere in time that they wish. We have had clients go back in time and meet famous historic figures, artists, musicians, philosophers, and authors. They learn about their important ideas and work, which in itself can spark for clients some creative solutions for their problem situations. Next, they are to accompany the famous other into the time machine and rejoin us in the session. Time-traveling clients can pretend that the famous others are sitting in empty chairs and ask them the following questions:

- "What advice would Ben Franklin/Gloria Steinem/Miles Davis have for you and your parents to help the three of you get along better?"
- "How about if Ben Franklin were to accompany you to Miss Smith's class (getting an 'F' grade in this class) and sit behind you, what would he whisper in your ear that you should do that will help you do better grade-wise in that class?"
- "What advice would Gloria Steinem have for you in your relationship with Tom that could help the two of you get along better?"
- "In what ways would Miles Davis suggest you improvise with your wife to help the two of you get along better, Tom?"

With the help of the famous others, often couple partners, parents, young adults, and adolescents can come up with some high-quality solutions. Some of our clients have taken the time machine into the distant future and have met up with alien beings that have offered them some very creative and useful ideas they can put to use in the present.

Family/Couple Art Therapeutic Experiments

When we discover that the adolescents, young adults, or one or both couple partners enjoy art and are strong in the visual-spatial intelligence domain (Gardner, 1993), we will use art therapy experiments with them. Some of our habit-dependent clients are used to keeping a lid on their painful thoughts and feelings and/or have grave difficulty articulating or expressing what they are experiencing inside. Art therapy activities can serve as a non-threatening way to express their inner emotional turmoil and individual and relationship struggles. Conversely, art therapy activities also can serve as a vehicle for solution-building and to underscore clients' strengths, talents, and resources. Below, we discuss eight art therapy activities that we use with both couples and families.

Imaginary Feelings X-Ray Machine

We use the *imaginary feelings X-ray machine* with children, adolescents, and young adults who have grave difficulties expressing their thoughts and feelings and/or may have somatic complaints (Selekman, 2005, 2009, 2010). They may have grown up in invalidating and high-stress family environments where one or both parents may have had serious alcohol or substance abuse difficulties and/or were emotionally distant from them and the unspoken rules in the family were: "Don't talk," "Don't feel," and "Don't trust" (Black, 1982).

The instructions for beginning this art activity are for the clients to imagine a special X-ray machine that could show pictures of what their feelings look like inside. Next, they are to lie down on a long sheet of rolled out high-grade construction paper (similar to meat-wrapping paper) that does not wrinkle and tear easily. They are to pick a crayon color and a family member to draw an outline of their body. When we turn on the machine, they are to draw pictures of what they think their feelings look like inside of them and where they tend to live the most in their bodies. Additionally, we like them to draw scenes from their lives that capture best each of those feelings.

This powerful art activity often reveals unresolved conflicts with certain family members and peers, family secrets, and other major stressors that are fueling their self-destructive habits. For the observing family members, they can feel free to ask questions and share their reactions to the feelings X-ray drawing. This process of reflection and dialogue can open up space for resolving longstanding conflicts and can improve family communications.

My/Our Couple/Family Story Mural

We like to use this art activity at the beginning and throughout couple or family therapy as another visual measurement of change (Selekman, 2005, 2009, 2010). It is particularly useful with couples and families who are very problem-focused and have grave difficulty identifying pretreatment changes, past successes, and entertaining hypothetical future success. Similar to family sculpting or choreography (Papp, 1983; Satir, 1983, 1988), couple partners and family members position themselves in their murals together in terms of closeness and distance. The first couple or family mural drawing can serve as a vehicle for goal-setting in initial sessions. The first artist can be asked questions like:

- "What steps would your dad need to take over the next week that would move him closer to you?"
- "How specifically would that make a difference in your relationship with him?"
- "What specifically could Roger [the husband] do over the next week so that you would feel more comfortable having him closer to you?"
- "When he takes that big step how will you feel differently about him and your relationship?"

Depending on the young person's or the couple partner's comfort levels they can decide whether or not to create the mural alone first or in the company of the rest of the family or their partner. As a way to facilitate connection-building, improve couple and family communications, and inject more playfulness into the couple or family relationships, we may encourage them to make the mural together. If there is an individual artist, he or she is free to portray himself/herself, the couple partner, or family members in any shape or form they wish. Most importantly, when drawing the mural they are to show closeness and distance in relationships, major couple and family themes, stressors, styles of coping, and attempted solutions to their difficulties. When the couple or family create the mural together, they need to incorporate the above-mentioned aspects, as well as discuss with one another how they want portray themselves together and come up with a title for what they would want call their couple or family problem story.

After the murals have been completed, couple partners or family members are free to reflect on the most striking features in the murals, what they learned new about one another and their situations, and what goals grew out of the activity for them that they wish to pursue. In a future couple or family therapy session, a new mural can be created depicting the changes that have been made in the couple or family story.

Our Couple/Family Miracle Story Mural

We use the *couple/family miracle story mural* as a way to bring couple partners' and family members' miracles to life visually. On a long sheet of paper after the miracle question (de Shazer, 1988) has been asked, the couple partners and family members are to create drawings on the paper to depict what their top two miracles are and their positive effects on their relationships and them individually. Alternatively, they may create a collage with journal pictures, drawings, and other objects (Dolan, 2000). It is important that each couple partner and the family members have ample space to display their desired miracle scenarios. Following the art activity, they can be asked the following questions:

- "What are you most surprised with that changed in your relationship with _____?"
- "What differences will that make for you in your relationship with him/them?"
- "What else is better?"
- "Are you aware of how you got that to happen?"
- "I'm curious, are any of these miracles happening a little bit now?"

This line of questioning can continue until the couple partners or family members identify small behavioral goals they wish to pursue over the next week. Sometimes after this discussion, couple partners or family members may return to the mural, adding the further changes they see themselves making over the next week. We like to have them take the mural home and post it somewhere so that they can always look at it and remind themselves of where they want to be and how they plan to get there.

Drawing Out Your Oppressive Thoughts, Feelings, and Habits

This art activity can empower our clients by having them externalize their oppressive thoughts, mood states, and habits. On a large sheet of white construction paper, they are to tap their powers of imagination and draw on the paper what they think the oppressive thought, feeling, or habit looks like. They can use crayons or pastels to create their art product. Some clients prefer to make a small sculpture with modeling clay. Musically talented clients may come up song titles and lyrics for their drawings. Some ambitious clients have even written the musical notes for their songs. Not only do clients really enjoy this art activity but they often feel empowered by breaking free from the tight grip of their self-destructive habits on them through this fun externalization process.

Surrealist Art Solutions

When working with clients who are strong in the visual-spatial domain and are passionate about art, we will introduce them to the *surrealist art solutions* activity. Most of these clients had had some exposure to the surrealist art movement in high school or college. However, it helps to refresh their memories and get their creative juices going to show pictures of the work of Salvador Dali, Rene Magritte, or Giorgio de Chirico. We discuss some of the major sources of inspiration for the surrealist artists, such as: symbols and themes from fairy tales, symbols and images from their dreams and forbidden fantasies, the random, the illogical and absurd, humor, and time distortion, as well as themes of wandering without a destination, and the suspension of the laws of nature (Neret, 1994; Whitfield, 1992). Furthermore, we share with clients that our dreams are like a theater of the unexpressed and the absurd where our wishes come true, we can resolve conflicts and difficulties any way we wish, our imagination can run wild, we can live with uncertainty and thrive in chaos.

To kick off this art activity, we have the couple partner, young adult, or adolescent identify a current difficulty they are really struggling with and have dreamt or had fantasies about trying to resolve it or had nightmares about what if it is not resolved and the dire resulting consequences for them and concerned others. If in their dreams or fantasies they had had absurd or off-the-wall thoughts or images about how best to resolve these difficulties that had not been expressed, they are to incorporate their unique solutions into their crayon or pastel surrealist drawings. Some clients may want the week to write down or tape record the contents of their dreams or nightmares in order to do better justice with this activity.

Once the clients complete the surrealist art solutions activity, we will ask the following questions:

- "What was your inspiration for your drawing?"
- "What are the main themes of your drawing?"
- "What do the symbols, objects, and scenes captured in your drawing mean to you?"
- "In looking and reflecting on your completed art product, did it spark in your mind any new views about or potential solutions for the current difficulty you selected to draw about?"
- "If Dali or Magritte joined us in our session and were looking at your drawing, what do you think they would be the most intrigued by and why?"
- "After learning about the contents of your dreams or nightmares portrayed in your art product, what ideas do you think Dali or Magritte might have for you about adding to your art product to produce a different outcome with your dreams or nightmares?"
- "What ideas did this spark for you about how best to approach your current difficulty?"

With the help of the surrealist art solutions activity, clients often come up with some creative ideas to begin to put into place to resolve their presenting problem. This activity also can serve as a vehicle for goal-setting as well.

Soul Collages

The *soul collage* art activity offers couple partners, young adults, and adolescents to depict what they think their souls would look like if they could look inside their minds. We invite our clients to come up with their own unique descriptions of what they think a *soul* is and its varied contents. On a large sheet of white construction paper, they are to draw a giant head shape, which represents them. Next, they are to imagine if we could take the top of their heads off, look into their minds, and reveal their souls, what images, symbols, phrases, and words would emanate out of their souls. They are to cut out of magazines and newspapers photographs and other images, symbols, phrases, and words that capture best their unique souls and then paste them on to the paper. As part of their collage work, they can draw and write on the collage as well.

Before we ask our clients questions about their completed soul collages, the other couple partner or family members are free to ask their questions and share their reflections. Three questions we like to ask our clients after they completed their soul collages are:

- "How does your soul shape the person of who you are?"
- "As a result of making your soul collage, did you learn anything new about yourself?"

- "If you had an opportunity to change your soul, what changes would you make?"
- "How specifically do you think those changes will make a difference in your life?"

Through the use of the soul collage not only do our self-destructive habit clients often gain some important insight into themselves but their couple partners and family members also find the post-art activity discussion very insightful and useful. Finally, we have found that the soul collage art activity can be quite helpful for clients in identifying their treatment goals, individual and relationship work projects to pursue, and potential building blocks for solution construction.

My/Our Gratitude Collage

Thanks to technology and the craze about owning the next new popular digital device, more adults and youths today are spending excessive amounts of time in front of some sort of screen rather than having human contact in the offline world engaged in meaningful activities with their couple partners, families, and friends. The *gratitude collage* is a reminder to savor what you do have that is more important than a digital device or other hot material item: good health, family, friends, special life experiences and memories, meaningful hobbies and skills, and so forth. The client is instructed to assemble on a large sheet of tag or poster board personal pictures of self, family, close friends, memorabilia and souvenirs from special trips, and other life experiences that they savor, and key words and phrases cut out from magazines and newspapers that capture best all that they are grateful for. We encourage clients to spend some time weekly taking a look at their completed collages as a constant reminder of everything they do have and as a way to get a dose of positive emotion when experiencing negative emotions.

My Superhero Cartoon Strip

We use this art experiment with adolescents who enjoy animation, science fiction, and on- and offline video-games. The adolescents are to tap their imagination powers and pretend that they have become superheroes with magical and special powers and have been called into action to defeat their oppressive self-destructive habit, which has now taken the form of a clever super-villain or a monster. The super-villain or monster also has magical and special powers. On a long sheet of paper, they are to create comic strip boxes depicting how they will systematically outsmart and defeat the super-villain or monster. The parents and other family members often find the adolescent's superhero cartoon strip quite interesting and can generate for them valuable insights. Not only do adolescents have a lot fun doing this experiment but it can spark creative solutions and give them the courage for conquering their oppressive self-destructive habits in the real world.

Positive Psychology Therapeutic Experiments

Many self-destructive habit clients have grave difficulty tolerating negative emotion and loss of control, respond to frustration and life disappointments with pessimistic thinking, and fall prey to rumination. In our clinical practices we have found that positive psychology therapeutic experiments can be an effective method of triggering positive emotions and successfully raising the optimism and happiness levels both in them and their significant relationships. Furthermore, the positive psychology experiments increase clients' awareness levels of their unique strengths, how to use them more in all areas of their lives, and to accurately identify specific patterns of behavior, people, and places in their social ecologies that trigger positive emotion in them and enhance their resilience and creative problem-solving abilities (Fredrickson, 2009; Peterson, 2006; Seligman, 2011).

Prior to offering positive psychology experiments to our clients we may encourage clients to visit positive psychologist Christopher Peterson's website at www.viacharacter.org to take either the *Values-in-Action Inventory of Strengths for Adults* (VIA adult version) or the *Values-in-Action Inventory of Strengths for Youth* (VIA older children and adolescents version; see Peterson, 2006; Peterson & Seligman, 2004). After completing the online questionnaire, the clients can bring in the printed out results which indicates their top five strengths, as well as the remaining nineteen in the order of their potency. Simply by taking the questionnaire, clients often are pleasantly surprised to discover their wealth of strengths and abilities, some of which they were unaware of or have yet to utilize in all areas of their lives. They also discover that by beginning to cultivate the remaining nineteen character strengths that it can contribute to further enhancing their resilience and creating for themselves more meaningful and fulfilling lives (Peterson, 2006; Peterson & Seligman, 2004; Seligman, 2011).

Although many of the positive psychology experiments were originally designed for individuals, we have found they can be modified for couple and family work. Below, we discuss the major positive psychology experiments we regularly use with our clients.

Planning Out My Perfect Day

We have found that the *planning out my perfect day* experiment is one of the most effective interventions for quickly identifying with clients *what works* and what they need to increase doing to resolve their difficulties. Additionally, research indicates that this experiment can rapidly decrease depressive and anxiety symptoms and increase positive emotion and happiness levels (Peterson, 2006; Selekman, 2009).

The clients are instructed to write down on paper each night a list of all of things they would need to accomplish, whom they would need to associate with, and what contexts they would need to be in that would make the next day a perfect day. At the end of the next day, they are to rate the day on a scale from 1 to 10. Peterson's (2006, pp. 43–44) rating scale for the experiment is as follows:

    10 = Best day of my life
    9 = Outstanding day
    8 = Excellent day
    7 = Very good day
    6 = It was a good day
    5 = It was an average day
    4 = It was a sub-par day
    3 = It was a bad day
    2 = It was a terrible day
    1 = It was the worst day of my life

What is so powerful and effective with this experiment is that we are co-creating positive self-fulfilling prophecies with them. The clearer the steps are that clients need to take, the more likely they are to make positive things happen for themselves. After having our clients do this experiment for two weeks, what emerges and becomes clear for them is what specifically they need to do, who they need to associate with, and what positive contexts they need to live in that produces days rated 6 and above. Conversely, they learn the activities, and places they need to steer clear of that can produce 3 and below days. Once we know what works with our clients, we encourage them to do more of what works.

Using Our Top Signature Strengths in Novel Ways

One way we can help expand our clients' horizons to help make their lives more meaningful and utilize their top strengths in new contexts, is the *using our top signature strengths in novel ways* experiment (Peterson, 2006; Selekman, 2009). In addition to using this experiment with individual self-destructive habit clients, we have gotten good clinical results using this experiment with couple relationship difficulties. After each partner has taken the *VIA Inventory of Strengths for Adults* questionnaire online at www.viacharacter.org and we have reviewed the results of their questionnaires in the next session, as part of the goal-setting process and in determining their relationship work projects, they are to think of novel and creative ways they can use their top signature strengths to achieve their goals and strengthen their relationship. For example, if one partner is rated high on *bravery* he or she could take the other partner out on an adventurous trip hiking through mountains or white-water rafting, especially if the other partner has not been exposed to these challenging activities before. If his or her partner is rated high on *appreciation of beauty and excellence* and is an art aficionado, he or she can take the partner to a special art exhibit to help expand his or her horizons in this area.

On the above website, clinicians will also find a more streamlined and shorter version of the questionnaire for adolescents called the *VIA Inventory of Strengths for Youth*. In a similar fashion to using the questionnaire results with couples, we have adolescents choose important relationships and presenting other difficulties in their lives they wish to experiment with using their top signature strengths in novel ways to make improvements in those areas.

Appreciation Days

Gottman and Gottman (2008) and Gable, Reis, Impett, and Asher (2004) have found that one of the most important ingredients in highly satisfied couples' relationships is each partner's daily expression of appreciation and gratitude toward one another. Based on this research, we developed the *appreciation days* couple experiment. Each partner daily is to make a concerted effort to deliver in some shape or form three or four expressions of appreciation and gratitude for the other partner. The ways that each partner expresses their appreciation and gratitude can take the form of flowers, cards, letters, texts, e-mails, or e-cards, complimenting one another on their daily accomplishments, and surprising one another with gifts and completing some household task or an errand shortly after one of the partners had requested it.

For highly conflicted couples, we would begin the process of showing appreciation and gratitude toward one another in small doses. We may have them separately over the next week pick two days to show appreciation and gratitude toward one another and each partner can write down on paper their thoughts and feelings about their experiences, which will be discussed in the next session. As the conflict level resides, we can increase the use of the number of days the partners use the *appreciation days* experiment.

My Gratitude Log

Self-destructive habit clients can greatly benefit from keeping a *gratitude log*. They are to record a few times or more often per week what they feel blessed about in their lives, such as: their good health, loving and caring partners or families, relatives, good and reliable friends, positive school or work experiences, abilities to learn and master important life skills, overcoming adverse life events or illnesses, and having greatly reduced their reliance on their choice habits to cope or achieved abstinence from their self-destructive habits. Research has repeatedly demonstrated that having and showing gratitude increases our optimism and happiness levels, decreases negative emotions and increases positive emotions, helps us to be more empathic with and socially connected to others, can calm our nervous systems, and improves sleep quality, particularly when writing in the log right before going to bed (Emmons, 2007; Emmons & McCullough, 2004). The ability to notice, appreciate, and savor life is strongly associated with life satisfaction (Peterson, 2006; Peterson & Seligman, 2004). Finally, Watkins, Scheer, Ovnicek, and Kolts (2006) found that gratitude can serve as an important resiliency protective function, aid in mood management, and reduce post-traumatic stress disorder symptoms with trauma survivors.

The gratitude log is easy to set up. Clients who are into technology may want to maintain their logs on their PCs, laptops, or iPads. In addition to writing My Gratitude Log in bold letters at the top of the page, there are two columns, a date column on the far left, and a *What I'm grateful for* column right next to it.

Clients can use their gratitude logs in three major ways. When experiencing emotional distress or craving to engage in their self-destructive habits, they can review their gratitude log to trigger positive emotion and to help stay on track. Second, to help combat sleeping difficulties, they can make it a nightly habit to review their gratitude logs or add new entries right before they go to bed. Finally, they can keep their gratitude logs in their designated *chilling out rooms* (see Chapter 10) as part of their book libraries and to use as another way to trigger positive emotion for them.

My Epiphany Log

As we discussed in Chapter 1, epiphanies can serve as a valuable resource for our clients in that they offer new perspectives, valuable wisdom, and new directions to pursue to create workable realities. Therefore, we encourage our clients to intentionally raise their awareness levels and open themselves up for epiphanies to happen in all areas of their lives and with everything they see, hear, and experience. By doing so, epiphany experiences seem to happen more often for them.

In setting up the My Epiphany Log, the clients are to create five columns: Date, My epiphany, Sparked by, Wisdom gained, and Applied to. We want them to pay really close attention to what specifically sparked their epiphanies, what wisdom or new insights they gained from the epiphany experiences, and in what ways they have started to apply these new insights and ideas in various areas of their lives (see Figure 3.1).

When clients feel stuck or are experiencing difficulties in an area of their lives, we will encourage them to review their epiphany logs for some possible ideas they can tap. We also recommend that they keep the epiphany logs in their book libraries of their designated *chilling out rooms* (see Chapter 10) if this therapeutic strategy is being employed.

Celebrating Habit-Free Days

In Alcoholics Anonymous and closely related self-help groups, members receive pins for maintaining their sobriety over periods of time to honor their hard work of protecting their sobriety and staying on the recovery track. In a similar fashion, we encourage our clients' couple partners or parents to celebrate each week their partner's, young adult's, or adolescent's efforts to maintain their abstinence from their choice habits. Couple partners and parents can reward the newly habit-free partner or young adult/adolescent with a special dinner, engaging in some fun and pleasurable activity that he or she would really like to do with them, or having a party in honor of his or her great work with family, relatives, and closest friends. At the party, the guests can give short speeches reflecting on how the client used to be during pre-abstinence days and how they have changed since achieving abstinence. This is a great way to underscore *news of a difference* for the client, the partner, the parents, and other family members. Motivational and behavioral couples therapy research indicates that when we praise and reward people's efforts and hard work it increases their drive and determination to master a task or achieve a goal, such as achieving abstinence from alcohol or drug use and maintaining it (Dweck, 2006; Halvorson, 2010; O'Farrell & Fals-Stewart, 2006).

MY EPIPHANY LOG				
Date	My Epiphany	Sparked By	Wisdom Gained	Applied To

Figure 3.1 My epiphany log.

The Gratitude Letter and Visit

The *gratitude letter and visit* has been shown to have some of the longest lasting positive effects at reducing depressive symptoms and triggering high doses of positive emotion in clients (Emmons,

2007; Peterson, 2006; Seligman, 2002). This experiment is very effective with clients who have been traumatized, depressed, and feel like prisoners of their past realities. The client is instructed to write a letter of gratitude to some past mentor or inspirational other that had offered them some valuable words of wisdom or taught them some important life skills that continue to benefit them. After completing a draft, we review it with our clients in the next session. The next step is for them to contact this individual and arrange a meeting in which they will read the gratitude letter to them. Often, clients report that tears and hugs followed this reading of their letter. In most cases, this valuable encounter turns out to be an emotionally uplifting experience for both parties. The added bonus for therapists is that we learn about a valuable resource person we may want to recruit and actively involve in our counseling sessions.

Bringing Broadway, Dance, and Film Media to the Therapeutic Stage

Some of our clients are strong in both the bodily-kinesthetic and visual-spatial intelligence areas (Gardner, 1993). These clients express themselves best through movement, art, photography, and film-making. By infusing more drama and action into our couple and family sessions, it can liven up the atmosphere in the room and make the change process playful and entertaining.

Couple/Family Choreography

When couples and families first come to see us they are entrenched or deadlocked in destructive and negative patterns of interaction, and have narrow and rigid problem-saturated views about the identified clients and his or her presenting problems, which are contributing to the maintenance of their self-destructive habit and other difficulties. *Couple/family choreography* can help the couple partners and family members gain a meta-position or bird's-eye view of their relationships and systems that can help liberate them from their unproductive ways of interacting and begin to establish more adaptive and positive ways of being with one another (Papp, 1983). With both couples and families we like to put the identified clients in charge as the lead choreographers, place themselves in the center of the room, and describe how their partners or family members move around and interact with them when the presenting problem happens. At different points in the session, we can freeze the couple partners or family members and ask them to reflect on where they were positioned and share their thoughts and feelings regarding the identified clients' choreographies. For goal-setting purposes, we will have the identified clients show us ideally how they would like their couple or family relationships and interactions to look like when their desired outcomes are achieved. Couple/family choreography can be used throughout the treatment process as a measurement of change. It also can be used in group therapy settings as well.

Our Happiest Moments Documentary

With couples who have been drifting apart, whose relationships have become humdrum, or who are deadlocked in destructive blame–counter-blame interactions, we will recommend that they try making an *our happiest moments documentary*, as a way to bring back the sparks and passion in their relationships. To begin this meaningful couple film-making experiment, the partners are asked to first generate a list of all of the most positive memories and high points in the history of their relationship together. Next, they are to decide together as the co-producers of their documentary of the happiest moments of their relationship which of the most positive memories and high points would they want to incorporate into the movie, including photographs, souvenirs, special locations, fun and meaningful activities, special vacations and life experiences they shared, the birth of children, and close friends, family, and important others they would like to feature in their documentary. Additionally, they are to create a musical score comprising the favorite tunes that they listened to during the year each happy moment occurred. After the film is completed, the couple brings it in for an advanced showing and can feel free to stop the movie at times to further elaborate on some of the most meaningful parts of the documentary.

Choreographing Habit and Habit-Free Dance Performances

Some of our young adult and adolescent self-destructive habit clients express themselves best by, and are passionate about, dancing. With these young clients, we stretch their powers of imagination to choreograph a dance number that best captures their choice habit difficulty in motion (Selekman, 2009). They are free to choose the style of dance, the title for their dance numbers, the background music for their dance numbers, and the costume or clothing they wish to wear while performing. Some of our more ambitious clients have even made their own props. In some cases, they have invited a friend or two to join them in the dance number.

With the first dance number, the client choreographs to capture all of their emotions and thoughts fueling the habit, and, through dance movements, shows what that looks like. Once the first performance is over, family members are free to ask questions and share their reactions, and the client can share the unique meanings of his or her choreographed piece. For the second dance number, the client is to perform a dance number of what he or she and their situation would look like once liberated from the habit. Again, family members can ask questions and discuss with him or her the unique meanings of being free of the habit. Both dance performances can help generate new meanings and potential building blocks for co-constructing solutions with families.

The Power of the Written Word

Some clients plagued by self-destructive habit difficulties and/or who have been traumatized have grave difficulty verbally articulating their thoughts and feelings and express themselves best through writing. Pennebaker (2004) has demonstrated repeatedly that writing about one's thoughts and feelings can produce better results on physical and psychological health, and interpersonal functioning measures, than talk therapy, particularly with traumatized clients. Some clients keep a journal about their daily lives or like to write poetry or creative stories. When we discover that our clients enjoy this pastime and are strong in the linguistic intelligence area (Gardner, 1993), we will build into our therapeutic work expressive writing experiments. Below, we describe seven of our most popular and useful expressive writing experiments.

My Habit Diary

We have received a great deal of positive feedback from our self-destructive clients regarding the use of a *habit diary* documenting their transformative journeys from being trapped in the clutches of their choice self-destructive habits to breaking free and taking back control of their lives and intimate relationships from them, as being a powerful way to underscore their courage, and highlighting their changes. Another important component of the habit diary is documenting the bumps in the road and temporary derailments in the form of slips or more prolonged relapses while on their transformative journeys, including their personal reflections and the wisdom they gained from these challenging experiences. Clients can gain valuable insight about *what* (useful self-talk, drawing, yoga) and *who* (certain family members, friends, adult inspirational others) helps them to stay on track and the *what* (negative emotions or thoughts), *whom* (toxic people), and *where* (toxic places) are their most potent triggers for slips. As mentioned in Chapter 1, habit diaries have been shown to be quite effective with empowering obese individuals to lose weight and keep it off (Hollis et al., 2008).

The Farewell Letter

This experiment comes from the narrative therapy tradition (White & Epston, 1990). Once we have successfully externalized the self-destructive habit during a session, we invite the client to write a letter to his or her externalized self-destructive habit. The letter can take the form of a "farewell letter" or of a letter by which the self-destructive habit is given the sack. In both cases, the client is first to acknowledge and give thanks for all the positive things that the negative habit brought him or her initially. Once these positive functions have been acknowledged, the client will describe in great detail all the negative effects the habit is now having, how it is spoiling his or her life and relationships, and holding him or her captive chained to it. After that, he or she will move on to summarize the reason why he or she is saying "goodbye" for good to the self-destructive habit. This exercise usually provides positive emotional momentum and creates extra motivation to begin to fight the self-destructive habit. We invite our clients to keep this letter as a reminder of their determination to conquer their self-destructive habit, and we often ask them to bring it to the session and read it aloud.

My Favorite Author Rewrites My/Our Story

When our clients mention to us that one of their favorite hobbies or interests is reading books, we will ask who their most favorite authors are, and why, and which characters in the books resonate with them the most. By doing so, we can familiarize ourselves more with our clients' favorite authors' work, learn more about them as people, and use the major themes and metaphors from the books in our conversations with them and with therapeutic experiment design. We have used this expressive writing experiment with couple partners, young adult and adolescent clients. In session, to help get their creative writing juices going, we ask the clients to respond to the following questions:

- "Let's say your most favorite author decided to rewrite your individual/couple/family story, what kind of character would you be in this new story?"
- "What special qualities, powers, talents, or interests would your new character have?"
- "Would you be the lead character?"
- "How would your favorite author rewrite how your couple partner/parents/friends are as characters in your new story about your life?"
- [After the client completes the short story or at least begins it in session, he or she can be asked] "Are there any aspects of your new character or elements/themes from your new story about you that you might want to experiment with in your current life?"
- "How do you think that can make a difference in your relationship with your partner/parents?"

Some of our most ambitious and enthusiastic clients have continued to expand their short stories into the first couple of chapters of the new book written about them by their favorite authors. Finally, this fun expressive writing experiment can help generate new views of self and others and help generate creative solutions for the clients' difficulties.

My Extraordinary Newspaper Headline

With this expressive writing experiment, the couple partners, young adults, or adolescents are to imagine picking up the *New York Times* and reading on the front page in bold black letters something extraordinary he or she had accomplished. After they come up with their headline, they are to write the interview below it, sharing with the reporter how they had achieved their extraordinary feat or accomplishment. They are to share their courageous thoughts, feelings, and specific actions that contributed to their success. Through the help of this experiment, clients often generate some creative building blocks for constructing solutions for their habit difficulties. Sometimes we will have the clients create a movie out of their extraordinary feat or accomplishment and use it as both a visualization and pattern intervention strategy when craving their habits or at risk for a slip.

The Humor Journal

One positive way clients can trigger positive emotions and seek pleasure in a healthy way when feeling emotionally distressed or craving is to review their *humor journals*. After purchasing a notebook or a larger size diary book, they are to fill it with pasted or taped in humorous newspaper or magazine cartoons, jokes, stories, and to write in their journals hilarious jokes or stories they heard on TV shows, in movies, or told to them by family, relatives, and friends. If they choose to keep their humor journals on their PCs, laptops, or iPads, they can add video clips of popular comedians' performances, and funny scenes from TV shows and clips from Youtube.com. If they choose to go the paper route with keeping their humor journals, we recommend that they keep it in their designated *chilling out rooms* (see Chapter 10) if that therapeutic strategy is being employed.

You At Your Best Story

With *you at your best story* expressive writing and positive psychology experiment, clients are to write three or four paragraphs of something they had accomplished or were at the top of their games with during their performances in a sporting, musical, or theatrical event (Peterson, 2006; Selekman, 2005, 2009). After completing their stories, we like them to underline with different color ink their *agency thinking* and their *pathway thinking*. Agency thinking consists of how we and/or family or close friends help get us fired up and motivated to achieve a goal or master a task. Pathway thinking consists of the specific steps they took to achieve a goal or master a task (McDermott & Snyder, 1999).

The power in this expressive writing experiment is that it can serve as a roadmap for clients' future success through utilizing their agency and pathway thinking in their presenting problem area. Peterson (2006) has found that when clients are instructed to read their stories of success prior to going to bed that it triggers positive emotion for them and they sleep better.

The Letter of Advice

In the final stages of therapy, once our clients have made substantial progress and therapy is no longer necessary, we like to suggest this experiment as a way to empower our clients and to put them into the position of co-therapists for other people in need of help. We invite the client to write a letter, addressed to an unknown person who may be facing the same self-destructive habit that he or she has successfully conquered, explaining his or her own success story and how he or she overcame the self-destructive habit. The letter might include encouragement and emotional support, but should also provide specific and practical advice on how to beat the self-destructive habit and how to prevent and manage possible relapses. We invite our client to write this letter as a "personal follow-up session" one or two months after our last therapy meeting and to mail it to us, with written consent to pass it on to other clients who may benefit from it.

Conclusion

In this chapter, we have presented six classes of therapeutic experiments and rituals for couples and families struggling with self-destructive habit difficulties. The beauty with most of these therapeutic experiments and rituals is that they are designed to tap the inventiveness, strengths, and resources of clients to empower them to generate their own high-quality solutions. Finally, many of these therapeutic experiments and rituals are versatile and effective and can be used with a wide range of couple or family difficulties.

4
SELF-HARMING HABITS

> From the thorn, emerges a flower.
> from the movie *La Mission*

Introduction

Non-suicidal self-harming behavior is not a new phenomenon of the twenty-first century. In fact, there are descriptions of this behavior in the Bible. It is described as "a sign of madness," "a deed of the devil," or "a way to salvation" (Mark 9: 47–49; Kings 18: 28; Mark 5: 5; Matthew 6: 22–23 (Adler & Adler, 2011; Ougrin, Zundel, & Ng, 2010; The Holy Bible, 1994). However, researchers, clinical specialists, and healthcare and school professionals have observed an increase in this behavior among adolescents over the past decade, which has been empirically supported by a number of community studies across the United States, Canada, England, the Netherlands, Germany, Bulgaria, Sweden, Australia, and New Zealand (Adler & Adler, 2011; Hawton & Rodham, 2006; Heath, Schaub, Holly, & Nixon, 2009; Lloyd-Richardson, Perrine, Dierker, & Kelley, 2007; Ougrin et al., 2010; Selekman, 2009; Whitlock & Selekman, 2012). Approximately, 6–8% of the adolescent and young adult populations report regularly and deliberately cutting, scratching, burning, bruising, and pinching themselves until blood is drawn (Klonsky, 2011). The average onset of self-harming behavior is between 12 and 15 years (Jacobson & Gould, 2007; Klonsky, 2011; Klonsky & Muehlenkamp, 2007; Muehlenkamp & Gutiérrez, 2004). Among college students who self-harm, 79.8% report stopping this behavior within five years of starting and 40% stopping within one year of starting (Whitlock, Eckenrode, & Silverman, 2006). Lifetime prevalence of self-harming behavior among adolescents and the young adult populations is 12–38% (Heath, Toste, Nedecheva, & Charlebois, 2008; Polk & Liss, 2007; Whitlock et al., 2006). Non-suicidal self-harming behavior occurs with individuals across all cultural and socioeconomic groups (Adler & Adler, 2011; Hilt & Nolen-Hoeksema, 2008; Lloyd-Richardson et al., 2007; Nasser, 2004; Newham Asian Women's Project, 2004; Whitlock, Muehlenkamp, & Eckenrode, 2008). Gender-wise, most community and university studies indicate that the breakdown for self-harming adolescents and adults is 65% females and 35% males (Favazza & Selekman, 2003; Selekman, 2009; Whitlock et al., 2008). However, male self-harming clients are on the rise due to their difficulties equally coping with high stress and the stigma of seeking out and participating in counseling being less of a barrier today for males (Gratz & Chapman, 2007, 2009).

Background: Different Methods of Self-Harming

There are six major areas we review below that are critical to explore and think about in our work with self-harming clients. Each of these areas plays an important role in the assessment and treatment planning process. The most common forms of self-harm are cutting, scratching, pinching, self-battery (to draw blood or bruise oneself), ripping or tearing the skin, picking at scabs to prevent the healing process, hair-pulling, and burning oneself (Adler & Adler, 2011; Heath et al., 2008; Klonsky, 2007a, b; Selekman, 2009; Whitlock et al., 2006). Some male adolescents and young adults engage in periodic and intense self-battery (self-hitting, having others batter them). Less common forms of self-harming behavior are bone-breaking, ingesting caustic or toxic substances, swallowing glass or other harmful objects, and embedding objects (often not sterilized) under the skin (Klonsky, 2007a, b; Lloyd-Richardson et al., 2007; Selekman, 2009; Sharples, 2008; Whitlock et al., 2006). Self-harming individuals typically cut or burn themselves on their arms, abdomens, inside their thighs, and on the bottoms or sides of their feet; locations on their bodies that can be covered up. Over 70% of the repeat self-harmers report using multiple methods with 50% reporting using two to four methods (Adler & Adler, 2011; Whitlock et al., 2006). Selekman (2009) and Whitlock and her colleagues (2008) have found that *heavy* and *severe* self-harming practice category clients tend to use multiple methods for inflicting self-injury to their bodies, with the latter category clients doing the most severe damage to their bodies, such as severing tendons and in some cases, irreparable physical damage. Finally, adolescents or adults who are cutting or burning themselves around their eyes or genitalia, which is quite rare, should receive immediate psychiatric intervention.

Functions of Self-Harm Behavior

For more than two decades, we have learned the importance of honoring our self-harming clients' stories and exploring with them how their habits have benefited them physiologically, psychologically, and interpersonally. Each self-harming story is unique and their self-harming practices have served specific and often multiple functions. In fact, research indicates that for many self-harming individuals, the longer they have been engaging in this behavior, the functions it serves for them in their lives increase (Andover, Pepper, & Gibb, 2007; Gratz & Chapman, 2009; Haines & Williams, 2003; Klonsky, 2007a; Lewis & Santor, 2010; Lloyd-Richardson et al., 2007; Selekman, 2009; Nock & Prinstein, 2005; Whitlock & Selekman, 2012). So, in a sense, self-harming can be quite a versatile and effective habit that our clients want to maintain and protect at all costs. This is one of the main reasons why it can be so challenging to engage and retain self-harming clients in treatment.

Some of the most common reasons why clients report that they self-harm for are as follows:

- "To numb out bad feelings"
- "To stop bad thoughts"
- "To vent anger"
- "As an escape from my problems"
- "To feel something"
- "To prevent suicide"
- "To punish myself"
- "To hurt others"

The most common reason why most adolescents and adults report that they self-harm are to get quick relief from emotional distress and pain (Adler & Adler, 2011; Gratz & Chapman, 2009; Hawton & Rodham, 2006; Levine, 2006; Whitlock et al., 2008; Whitlock & Selekman, 2012). Most self-harming clients fit into one of two categories: *pleasure-seekers* and *thrill-seekers*. The majority of self-injurers fit into the *pleasure-seeking* category and engage in this behavior to soothe or calm themselves and/or to "numb out" bad feelings. The *thrill-seekers*, on the other hand, may engage in extreme forms of self-battery to escape from feeling dead or numb inside. Selekman (2009), Whitlock et al. (2008), and Muehlenkamp, Yates, and Alberts (2004) have identified a subcategory of thrill-seeking self-harming male adolescents and young adults whose main method of self-injury takes the form of extreme self-battery (punching and slapping oneself, inviting others to physically hurt them with various objects, head-banging, the choking game, and engaging in other highly risky daredevil behaviors which result in serious bodily injury, etc.). Often, these behaviors are quite intense, episodic, and tend to occur over a few days, a week, or longer, sparked by a stressful life event. This subcategory of mostly males also may be concurrently engaging in heavy binge-drinking and substance abuse. More recently, professionals have been seeing a range of new self-harming behaviors in both male and female adolescents, such as: embedding a variety of objects under their skin, the choking game, and using other ways of inhibiting breathing (Selekman, 2009; Sharples, 2008). For some adolescents and adults, self-embedding occurs as a symbol of connection to close friends who also are in engaging in this behavior. Some self-harming clients can fit into both of the pleasure-seeking and thrill-seeking categories.

According to Adler and Adler (2011), the majority of their self-harming practitioners stretched out their self-injuring rituals in order to savor them. First, they would decide what equipment to use to carry out the act and how they would nurse their wounds. Next, they would amplify their negative thoughts and feelings and ruminate on the negative events of the day. Once their negative emotions peaked in intensity, they would self-inflict wounds, and focus on the blood and everything it stood for. The reward was enjoying and riding out as long as possible the "high" or "numbing out" effects that they received from the self-injuring acts. They would stop the ritual when they recognized the following: they were feeling pain, ashamed, guilty, and they did more damage to their bodies then originally intended.

Differentiating Self-Harming Behavior from Suicidal Risk

Many mental health, healthcare, and school professionals tend to view cutting behavior as a suicidal gesture and assume that the individual wants to die. However, cutting is rarely associated with completed suicide in young people and also tends to be less lethal than other forms of self-harm (Walsh, 2006). How an adult or adolescent may accidentally die is by cutting him- or herself while intoxicated on alcohol or other substances and severing a major blood vessel. This is why it is critical that therapists explore with their cutting self-harming clients if they are concurrently abusing alcohol and other substances. Self-harming clients in general are like amateur surgeons carefully cutting themselves around major blood vessels mostly on their arms, inside their thighs, on their abdomens, or on the bottoms of their feet. Favazza, a world renowned expert on self-injury, contends that the difference between truly suicidal and self-harming individuals is that the former wants to end all feeling while the latter is seeking quick relief from emotional distress and pain (Favazza & Selekman, 2003). Unfortunately, many self-harming clients are misdiagnosed and mismanaged, ending up being wrongly psychiatrically medicated or hospitalized for what is believed to be high suicide risk.

Research indicates that the majority of infrequent to regular self-harming adults and adolescents will either have never had suicidal ideation or may have thought about it during their lifetimes but never made an attempt (Adler & Adler, 2011; Muehlenkamp & Gutiérrez, 2004; Nock, Joiner, Gordon, Lloyd-Richardson, & Prinstein, 2006). A very small percentage of self-harming individuals will have made one or more attempts to take their lives in the past and are actively suicidal prior to or while in treatment. These are individuals grappling with multiple stressors, intense emotional pain, and feel that they lack a solid support system (Miller, Rathus, & Linehan, 2007). However, with long-term heavy to severe self-harming practice category clients (multiple daily self-injuring acts and inflicting deep and serious tissue damage), it may be a different story. Joiner (2005) contends that the "habituation and practice effects of repeated self-injury may be implicated in the escalating trajectory toward making a serious future suicide attempt" (p. 84). He further added, "As individuals continue to self-injure it loses its painful and fear-inducing properties and as this occurs the main barrier to suicide erodes" (p. 85). Thus, according to Joiner's theory, once clients have self-harmed for a long period of time, they have acquired the ability and fearlessness about confronting pain, serious self-harm, and indeed death. For some severe self-harming practice category clients, death may be viewed as "a beautiful thing" (Joiner, 2005).

Another important distinction between non-lethal self-harming and serious at-risk suicidal clients is the *perceived burdensomeness to others* risk factor. Truly suicidal clients reported perceiving them being a burden to others and this was one of the major reasons why they wanted to die (Brown, Comtois, & Linehan, 2002; Joiner et al., 2002). According to Brown, Comtois, and Linehan (2002), non-suicidal self-harming clients in their study reported engaging in self-harming behavior to either express their anger or to inflict self-punishment.

Nock and his colleagues (2006) and Whitlock and Knox (2007) found that individuals who attempted suicide were more likely to have longer histories of, and use of a greater number of methods, of self-harm than those without a suicide attempt. These researchers also identified a subset of self-injuring individuals who had unusually high pain tolerance levels and are at higher risk for a future suicide attempt.

Adolescents struggling with sexual orientation issues are at higher risk for both self-harming behavior and possibly suicide attempts, particularly females who are four times more likely to self-harm than boys and girls that are not grappling with these issues (D'Angelli, Grossman, & Salter, 2005; Hawton & Rodham, 2006). We have both worked with lesbian, gay, and transgendered youth who both prior to or after initiating the courageous step of trying to *come out* to their parents and friends have increased their self-harming behavior or made suicide attempts. Unfortunately, there are no longitudinal studies that could tell us whether self-harming adolescents become suicidal later in life.

The Parallels between Self-Harming Behavior and Substance Abuse and Dependency

Many believe that self-harming behavior, when done regularly and over a long period of time, is similar to a drug addiction (D'Amore & Lloyd-Richardson, 2008; Faye, 1995; Gratz & Chapman, 2009; Joiner, 2005; Miller, 2005; Newham Asian Women's Project, 2004; Nock & Prinstein, 2005; Selekman, 2006, 2009; Selekman & Schulem, 2007; Walsh, 2006; Whitlock, 2008; Whitlock et al., 2008; Whitlock & Selekman, 2012). Self-harming behavior is used as a powerful and efficient way to self-medicate because it rapidly triggers multiple neurochemical responses that produce numbing and soothing effects (Schroeder, Oster-Granite, & Thompson, 2002; Selekman, 2006, 2009; Selekman & Schulem, 2007; Walsh, 2006). According to Miller (2005), self-harming behavior follows the same predictable route in behavior, thinking, and conducting relationships as addictions do. Similar to substance dependency, we see the compulsion to self-harm, loss of control, and continued self-harming behavior despite serious consequences, such as severe physical damage and infections, family and other significant relationship difficulties, loss of friends, school and/or occupational difficulties, and poor choice-making in all areas of these individuals' lives. The self-harming individual is willing to endure serious bodily disfigurement and more severe deep tissue damage to his or her body to obtain the reward, which is all endogenous opiate (Osuch & Payne, 2008). Self-harming individuals learn that by manipulating their brain chemistry self-harm can serve as a 24-hour pharmacy for them when they need an endogenous opiate fix (Plante, 2007).

Once habituation and dependency occur with the self-harming behavior, it is very common for adolescents and adults to become cross-dependent, or more vulnerable, on other risky behaviors such as substance abuse and/or binge-drinking, bulimia, and unprotected sex with multiple partners as attempts to elevate their moods, obliterate unpleasant thoughts and feelings, or soothe themselves when experiencing emotional distress. In some cases, they are engaging in these behaviors concurrently, particularly combining bulimia with self-harming behavior often seen with adolescent and adult females. Once the analgesic properties of the endorphins wear off a few hours later, moderate to severe self-harming individuals often experience withdrawal symptoms like irritability, an increase in anxiety and/or depressive feelings, experience craving, and sleep disturbance. They are highly reactive to stressors in the home and school and/or occupational environments. Over-stimulation of the endogenous opioid system can lead to actual withdrawal symptoms (Osuch & Payne, 2008).

Similar to the chemical tolerance or dependence seen with alcohol and drug-dependent individuals, many self-harming clients report that, over time, they needed to cut themselves more frequently and deeper and/or they begin to experiment with a variety of new methods to produce the same pleasurable and/or numbing sensations they were getting from this behavior in earlier periods of their self-harming practices (Adler & Adler, 2011; Whitlock & Selekman, 2012). In a multi-college/university study, 21% of the participants indicated they had injured themselves more severely than expected at least once (Whitlock, 2008; Whitlock et al., 2008). Michel and Nock (2008) found in their research sample a subset of self-harming adolescents who had a significantly higher tolerance for physical pain and were using multiple methods for inflicting self-injury. In fact, this subset of 23% of the self-harming subjects in the study not only were much more open to submitting themselves to the physical pain tolerance task procedure of receiving a low-grade electric shock but were willing to continue engaging in this procedure for the maximum amount of time—183 seconds! The non-self-harming control group of adolescents in the study requested to stop at 61 seconds.

Joiner (2005) contended that self-harming behavior has both negative and positive reinforcement dimensions to it, which is similar to substance abuse behavior. The behavior is reinforcing because it quickly gets rid of negative thoughts and feelings, and positive reinforcing because after self-harming it induces positive feelings. Kemperman, Russ, and Shearin (1997) found in their study with adults diagnosed with borderline personality disorder that the clients reported significant mood elevation after self-harming. It is believed when individuals self-harm the body rapidly secretes endorphins, which act like a fast-acting analgesic to protect us from experiencing bodily pain and triggers a pleasurable sense of well-being and euphoria.

For some self-harming clients, pain can become something desired, and the act of pursuing this bodily sensation takes on an addictive quality. The physical pain feels like relief compared to the overwhelming psychic pain some of these clients are experiencing (Blakeslee & Blakeslee, 2007). However, for clients with moderate to heavy self-harming practices, just thinking about engaging in this behavior and having the expectation of quickly getting immediate relief from emotional pain and distress, based on many past positive experiences and memories, will release endorphins that block agony and produce pleasure and intoxicating highs. Thus, familiarity breeds positive expectations (Ariely, 2008; Linden, 2011).

Another important dimension of the addictive quality of self-harming behavior is emotional arousal. Research indicates that when we are in an emotionally aroused state, we are twice as likely to engage in risky behaviors. Furthermore, once we experience pleasure from engaging in a particular habit or behavior, no matter how risky or self-destructive, it will imprint in our memory as a pleasurable experience that will help determine whether we pursue this experience when distressed or in need of pleasure (Ariely, 2008; DiSalvo, 2011; Linden, 2011; McCauley, 2009; Schwartz & Gladding, 2011).

Finally, similar to substance-addicted individuals attempting to abstain from their former drugs of choice who are exposed to powerful negative triggers that may result in relapse, self-harming clients may get derailed from the recovery track once they are exposed to certain places, objects, musical tunes, graphic art, stories and poetry with self-harming themes, websites, and friends who continue to self-harm. The more residual craving self-harming clients experience during treatment, the more likely they will experience post-treatment slips and prolonged relapsing situations

(Iacoboni, 2008; McCauley, 2009). D'Amore and Lloyd-Richardson (2008) found in their qualitative study with self-harming college students that they both were feeling addicted to this behavior and were finding it extremely difficult for them to kick their self-harming habits. Whitlock (2008) and Whitlock and her colleagues (2008) found in their multi-college/university study that one-third of their research sample reporting self-harming indicated that it was difficult to control the urge to self-injure, and nothing else had worked as well as self-harming to calm them.

Trauma and Self-Harm

One of the most widely held assumptions made by mental health, school, and healthcare professionals is that self-harming individuals have post-traumatic stress disorder (PTSD) and more than likely had been physically or sexually abused. Similar to the borderline personality disorder often used to describe self-harming individuals, the self-mutilation behavior described as a symptom of PTSD is taken out of context by many professionals without a comprehensive assessment of how certain key interpersonal dynamics may have played a role in the development and maintenance of the self-harming behavior. In fact, the research findings are quite mixed regarding most self-harming clients having experienced past physical or sexual abuse or some other severe traumatic event. One study found that adolescents that had been physically and/or sexually abused were five times more likely to self-harm (Hawton & Rodham, 2006). Whitlock and her colleagues (2008) found in their multi-college/university study that those students more at risk and more frequently cutting were 3.5 times likely to report family backgrounds of emotional and/or physical or sexual abuse. Some individuals who had been sexually or physically abused have relied on their self-harming practices to get out of dissociative states, to stop flashback activity, unpleasant thoughts and feelings, and past painful memories from entering their conscious minds (Gratz & Chapman, 2007, 2009; Miller, 2005).

If anything, many clinical specialists who have worked for years with self-harming individuals have reported emotional neglect and invalidation and disconnection in their couple and family relationships as being powerful dynamics fueling this behavior (Linehan, 1993; Miller, 2005; Miller et al., 2007; Plante, 2007; Selekman, 2006, 2009; Whitlock et al., 2008; Whitlock & Selekman, 2012). These experiences lead to serious attachment and trust issues in both parental and significant relationships outside the home, but the client may not really know what they are feeling, or feel emotionally dead inside and experience de-realization (Selekman & Schulem, 2007; van der Kolk, McFarlane, & Weisaeth, 2007; van der Kolk, Roth, Pelcovitz, Sunday, & Spinazzola, 2005; Yates, 2004). Yates (2004) contended that the damage done to self-harming individuals who had been severely traumatized in childhood undermines their normal developmental process regarding establishing a cohesive sense of self, self-regulation of affect, impulse control, and healthy relationships with others. Some of these individuals struggle with *alexithymia*, which is impairment in the ability to recognize, label, and verbalize their feelings. These individuals often have difficulties with affect tolerance, anhedonia, self-care, and they experience psychosomatic complaints (Krystal, 1982). Thus, self-harming can become an ideal coping strategy for regulating one's feelings or for just feeling something.

For some trauma survivors, their past traumatic experiences, be they from sexual or physical abuse, surviving near-death accidents or life-threatening illnesses, can have a *steeling* effect on them which strengthens their natural self-healing and coping capacities. One important factor that contributes to trauma survivors' resiliency is incorporated in their self-narratives regarding the traumatic events. Stephen Joseph (2011), a pioneer in the new field of post-traumatic growth psychology research, contends that:

> Stories that construct meaning, in which we view ourselves as survivors and even thrivers and that establish hopefulness in us, will lead towards growth. The stories that we tell

ourselves will "work their way down," transforming first our autobiographical narratives (our life stories), then our personal goals, values, and priorities. Knowing this, we can choose to tell stories that are to our benefit (p. 134).

Research like this challenges trauma theorists' long-held belief that in order for trauma survivors to be restored to a higher level of psychological functioning and no longer have any symptoms, therapists must have their clients go back in time and "work through" their traumatic events. This may end up disempowering them or, worse yet, lead to their having suicidal thoughts. Instead, we need to elicit from our trauma survivor clients their stories of courage, persistence, and resilience to empower them.

Finally, if they wish to work on the *effects* of their past traumatic experiences (flashbacks, anxiety or depressed mood, etc.), clients should be invited to take the lead in determining which one of these effects they wish to work on changing first.

Co-Morbidity and Self-Harm

Two of the most common DSM-IV diagnoses self-harming individuals are given are borderline personality disorder and PTSD. Other popular diagnoses are: impulse control disorder, obsessive-compulsive disorder, and one of the depressive or anxiety disorder diagnoses. Many professionals view self-harming behavior as a depressive equivalent or as a suicidal gesture. However, as Walsh (2006) aptly pointed out only 1.4% of the adolescents who died from suicide used cutting as their method for taking their lives. Furthermore, although many adolescents and adult self-harming individuals have poor coping and self-regulation skills and may look clinically depressed or overly anxious, "borderline-like," "real impulsive," they often do not meet all of the criterion of the above DSM-IV disorders to use these diagnoses (Adler & Adler, 2011; Kessler, Costello, Merikangas, & Ustun, 2001; Lofthouse, Muehlenkamp, & Adler, 2008; Michel & Nock, 2008; Whitlock, 2008; Whitlock et al., 2008; Whitlock & Selekman, 2012).

Favazza has found that self-harming individuals have much lower levels of serotonin than the average person (Favazza & Selekman, 2003). Normal serotonin levels help us to maintain good impulse control and emotional balance. For Favazza, the use of Prozac or other anti-depressants can rebalance these individuals' serotonin levels and give them better impulse control and, thus, can help stabilize the self-harming behavior and other self-destructive behaviors. It is widely believed by many mental health professionals that for both self-harming and eating-distressed clients that the inner driving force behind these habits is the need to take back and maintain control when feeling like they have lost control of their habits, key relationships, and important responsibilities in their lives. However, the long-term studies that have been conducted with self-harming clients placed on anti-depressants have not shown good clinical results (Hawton et al., 2006; Sansone, Levitt, & Sansone, 2004). Some of our past self-harming clients had been placed on anti-depressants and anti-anxiety medications and had felt that they had not helped in reducing and/or eliminating these urges and other closely related habits they were engaging in. Finally, the majority of our self-harming clients have reported that they were "hooked" on the "numbing out" and "rush" sensations they received from the endorphins and this is why they were deliberately self-injuring and ambivalent about or unwilling to give up their practices.

Key Research Findings that Inform our Clinical Practice

Because self-harming behavior among adults and adolescents is rarely the sole presenting problem and it often accompanies other habits such as eating-distress, substance abuse, and sexually risky behaviors, there are no couple or family therapy outcome studies that have been conducted with subjects who only have self-harming difficulties. In reviewing the treatment and research literature, there is not even one well-controlled, well-formulated experimental study that has been conducted with couples and families where self-harming behavior was one of the more pronounced presenting problems. Most of the family treatment outcome studies that have been conducted are with self-harming adolescents presenting with other behavioral difficulties. The four family treatment approaches that have been researched integrated major therapeutic tools and strategies from empirically-supported individual and family therapy models, such as: dialectical behavior therapy (DBT) (Linehan, 1993; Miller et al., 2007), cognitive-behavioral therapy (CBT; Beck, 1995; Beck, Rush, & Emery, 1979; Weisz, Weiss, Han, Granger, & Morton, 1995), motivational-enhancement therapy (Miller & Rollnick, 2002); brief strategic family therapy (Santisteban et al., 2003; Szapocznik, Hervis, & Schwartz, 2003), and multidimensional family therapy (Liddle, 2010). Since DBT has been deemed the treatment of choice for borderline personality disorder and many health and mental health care professionals believe that self-harming individuals are "borderlines," it is no surprise that adolescents and adults who self-harm end up receiving this treatment approach even if they do not meet the other symptom criteria for this diagnosis and it is a mismatch for their unique needs and personal goals. Another popular empirically supported treatment approach used with self-harming individuals is CBT because it is believed that the clients self-harm because they have underlying depressive, anxiety, and obsessive-compulsive disorders, with which CBT has been shown to be effective. Whether or not they have underlying disorders, often self-harming clients are seen individually and couple partners and their families are either excluded from or are occasionally invited in to participate in the treatment process, even though their attempted solutions may be further perpetuating the clients' self-harming and other behavioral difficulties.

We believe strongly that self-harming difficulties are couple and family affairs, and even including concerned others from clients' social ecologies can further optimize for their treatment success. The four family treatment models reviewed here are: collaborative strengths-based brief family therapy (Beyebach, 2009; Selekman, 2005, 2009, 2010; Selekman & Schulem, 2007), therapeutic assessment (Ougrin, Ng, & Low, 2008; Ougrin et al., 2010), integrated borderline adolescent family therapy (Santisteban, Muir, Mena, & Mitrani, 2003), and multi-family psychoeducational group as developed by Miller et al. (2007), which is currently being evaluated in a randomized, well-controlled research format. Below, we list some of the key research findings that inform our clinical practice:

- Self-harming adolescents and their parents have reported that having strong alliances with their therapists and having faith in their ability to help them individually and their families contributed to their positive treatment outcomes (Ougrin et al., 2008, 2010; Santisteban et al., 2003; Selekman, 2009; Selekman & Schulem, 2007).
- Self-harming adolescents reported in qualitative family therapy research studies a strong desire "to grow into" their relationships with their parents, no matter how much conflict and emotional distance existed in their relationships. Therefore, therapists should serve as catalysts for strengthening parent–self-harming-adolescent relationship bonds (Ougrin et al., 2008, 2010; Selekman, 2009; Selekman & Schulem, 2007).
- In qualitative family therapy research studies (Ougrin et al., 2008, 2010; Selekman, 2009; Selekman & Schulem, 2007) and in follow-up client interviews with a multi-family group psychoeducational approach (Miller et al., 2007), the self-harming adolescents reported that by learning mindfulness meditation and other distress management tools and strategies played a major role in helping them individually to better manage negative emotion and be less reactive to invalidating family interactions.
- With all four of the family therapy approaches, parents found it quite useful to learn effective parent management skills, find out what their children's triggers were for engaging in their self-harming and other self-destructive behaviors, how best to respond, and learn the same

distress management tools and strategies that their kids were learning in individual or group sessions with other kids (Miller et al., 2007; Ougrin et al., 2010; Santisteban et al., 2003; Selekman, 2009).

- Self-harming adolescents in two of the family research studies indicated that they liked the solution-focused therapeutic emphasis on their strengths and resourcefulness, rather than dwelling on problems and trying to identify their deficits (Ougrin et al., 2008, 2010; Selekman 2009; Selekman & Schulem, 2007). As one adolescent participant put it best about what therapists should do with self-harming young people, "Look at the strengths built into us" (Selekman & Schulem, 2007). In these studies, self-harming adolescents also reported finding journaling, other expressive writing experiments, and art therapy methods useful.

Strategies for Assessment and Treatment Planning

The Self-Harming Practice Classification System

Over the past decade, clinical specialists and researchers have attempted to classify different types or categories of self-harming practices (Adler & Adler, 2011; Favazza, 1998; Selekman, 2009; Selekman & Schulem, 2007; Walsh, 2006; Whitlock et al., 2008). Selekman (2009) has identified five categories of self-harming practices and describes their identifying profiles, including the frequency of self-harming episodes or acts. The categories are: *experimenter/follower, episodic, regular/moderate, heavy,* and *severe*. Although some self-harming individuals may overlap category profiles with their unique self-harming practices, the different categories in this classification system are supported by empirical research and clinical evidence-based practice wisdom of self-harming treatment specialists worldwide. The self-harming practice classification system can aid therapists with treatment planning, particularly determining collaboratively with clients the best levels of care and treatment modality selection, and with selecting and designing the most appropriate therapeutic tools and strategies that best meets their unique needs. Below, we describe the five different self-harming practice categories.

Experimenter/Followers

- Infrequent solo and/or recreational self-harming with friends.
- Superficial scratching, pinching, cutting, or burning.
- Follows lead of peers for engaging in this behavior.
- No habituation.
- Precontemplators (stage of readiness to change).
- Females and males.

Episodic

- May self-harm for a few days, a week, or longer and abstain for weeks or months.
- May cut, burn, and engage in intense self-battery.
- May engage in concurrent binge-drinking and/or substance abuse.
- Self-harming and other related self-destructive behaviors may occur during high stress periods or following a critical life event.
- No habituation.
- Precontemplators.
- Mostly males.

SELF-HARMING HABITS

Regular/Moderate

- Random pattern of occurrence (daily or every other day), one to three acts of self-harming.
- Cuts, burns, or uses other methods of self-harm on a regular to moderate basis.
- May see concurrent bulimia and/or other eating-distressed, substance abuse, or sexually risky behaviors.
- May have past treatment history and be carrying a DSM-IV diagnosis.
- Habituation is developing.
- Precontemplators.
- Females and males.

Heavy

- Four or five self-harming acts per day.
- Uses multiple methods of self-harm.
- May see concurrent bulimia and/or other eating-distressed, substance abuse, or sexually risky behaviors.
- Often have extensive past treatment history and DSM-IV diagnoses.
- May be on prescribed psychiatric medications.
- May have emotional, physical, or sexual abuse background.
- May have made a past suicide attempt and has conquered fear of death.
- Habituation, strong compulsion to self-harm, loss of control, and high physical tolerance for pain have developed.
- Experiencing psychological, physical, social, and school/occupational consequences.
- Precontemplators or contemplators.
- Mostly females.

Severe

- Five or more self-harming acts per day.
- Uses multiple forms of self-harm and has done extensive and deep tissue damage.
- May see concurrent bulimia and/or other eating-distressed issues and substance abuse.
- Have extensive past treatment history and DSM-IV diagnoses.
- May be on prescribed psychiatric medications.
- May have emotional, physical, or sexual abuse background.
- May have made a past suicide attempt and has conquered fear of death.
- Habituation, strong compulsion to self-harm, loss of control, and high physical tolerance for pain.
- Experiencing serious psychological, physical, social, school/occupational consequences.
- Precontemplators or contemplators.
- Mostly females.

Important Assessment Considerations

Since it is quite common for self-harming clients to symptom switch, such as concurrently engaging in eating-distressed behavior (bingeing and purging, overeating, self-starving), abuse substances, and possibly engage in sexually risky behaviors, it is important that therapists conduct a comprehensive assessment with them regarding their involvement with these behaviors. Each of these self-destructive habits can have a synergistic effect on another, making it difficult to stabilize the self-harming behavior. Eating-distressed behaviors like bingeing–purging and self-starving can lead to bodily cramping and discomfort, which in turn can fuel self-harming behavior to get quick relief from physical pain. Substance abuse with concurrent cutting or burning of oneself is a highly dangerous combination: therapists must caution their clients about this and conduct a thorough drinking and drug history with them. The client may be willing and ready to accept a harm-reduction contract; for example, experimenting with not using drugs or alcohol prior to or during cutting or burning themselves. Furthermore, we need to inquire with clients the length of time they have been engaging in their self-harming practices, the frequency and duration of self-injury acts in a day and week, if they have ever had suicidal ideation or made suicide attempts, and if there is any past trauma history. We know that *heavy* and *severe* self-harming practice clients are at high risk for a suicide attempt and may have already attempted suicide in the past (Selekman, 2009; Whitlock et al., 2008; Whitlock & Selekman, 2012).

Another important area therapists need to gently explore with their self-harming clients is recent or past trauma. As we have seen in the previous section, clients who have experienced physical or sexual abuse or some other form of trauma use self-harming, substance abuse, and eating-distressed behaviors as a defense to ward off re-experiencing painful memories, thoughts, and feelings connected to past traumatic events (van der Kolk, 2009). By attempting to have the clients decrease or abstain from these coping behaviors prematurely before a safe and trusting therapeutic alliance has been established, and they are sufficiently emotionally stable and open to accepting and experimenting with more adaptive replacement behaviors, can precipitate crisis situations, such as suicide attempts. We must respect our clients' defenses and take them where they are at with their past trauma situations. They need to take the lead in determining whether or not we address their past traumas or what specific *effects* (symptoms and behaviors) of the traumas occurring presently they wish to work on changing.

Key Assessment Questions

The following questions can help therapists get a good grasp of the nature of the clients' self-harming practices, the various functions it serves for them and how it fits into their unique life stories. The clients' answers to these questions can guide therapists with the treatment planning process and with selecting and designing replacement coping tools and strategies and therapeutic experiments that are in line with their goals and best meet their needs. When interviewing self-harming clients, it is best to begin with less threatening, more open-ended questions so as to gain access to the central themes of their self-harming stories and the unique functions their practices have served for them. Gradually, the therapist can move on to more specific questioning about triggers and the uses of closely related habits, such as the misuse of food and substances, engaging in sexually risky behaviors, and possible past sexual and/or physical abuse histories and suicide attempts.

- "In what ways has cutting been helpful to you?"
- "What does cutting mean to you and how does it fit into your life story?"
- "Where did you first learn to cut yourself?"
- "Where on your body do you typically cut yourself?"
- "If that fresh cut mark or your most meaningful scar could talk to us what would it say about you and your situation?"
- "Do you experience any specific thoughts, feelings, or bodily sensations, before you cut yourself?"
- "What are other triggers for you?"
- "How long have you been cutting yourself for?"
- "On a given day, how often do you cut or burn yourself?"
- "How often would you say in one week's time do you cut or burn yourself?"

- "What effect does your cutting have on your relationships with your parents and siblings?"
- "Have any of your close friends expressed any concerns about your cutting or have you ever lost any friendships because of it?"
- "What would be the disadvantages of your stopping your cutting?"
- "If there were certain aspects of the cutting experience you would wish to keep, what would those aspects be?"
- "What is different during the times you don't cave into cutting yourself, what do you say to yourself or do instead that seems to really work?"
- "What do family members and close friends say or do that helps you to not cave into cutting yourself?"
- "Do you ever try to make yourself throw up, starve yourself, take laxatives, or over-exercise for weight control?"
- "Do you ever abuse drugs or get drunk to cope with stress or to escape from your problems?"
- "This is a routine question I typically ask, 'Has anybody ever hurt you emotionally or physically in the past?'"
- "Another routine question I typically ask, 'Have you ever thought about or attempted to take your life in the past?'"

Couple and Family Dynamics

Since there have not been any studies conducted with couples where the sole presenting problem was a partner's self-harming behavior, there is no research literature describing key relationship dynamics that maintain this behavior. However, from our extensive clinical practice experiences working with adult self-harming clients and their partners, we have observed the following key couple dynamics and were reported by the clients themselves to contribute to the development and maintenance of the self-harming:

- Emotional invalidation and disconnection between the partners.
- The non-symptomatic partner may play the care-taker role and there may be boundary issue complaints; the self-harming partner feels "suffocated" by the care-taking and over-involvement of his or her partner.
- Inequity of power and control in the relationship, with the self-harming partner feeling unable to voice his or her concerns and demands, sometimes even suffering physical violence.
- Poor communications, problem-solving, and conflict-resolution skills.
- The non-self-harming partner's emotional distance may be related to substance abuse, Internet and/or cyber-sex, gambling, or other habit dependencies.
- For some self-harming partners, the couple relationship is a repetition or replay of the same emotional invalidating patterns of interaction they experienced in their families of origin.

In many ways, these couples present with similar relationship dynamics described in the treatment literature on couples presenting with eating and substance abuse disorders (Birchler, Fals-Stewart, & O'Farrell, 2008; Miller, 2005; Nardone, Milanese, & Verbitz, 2005; Selekman, 2009).

There are a number of studies conducted with self-harming adolescents and their families that have identified similar family dynamics described above with couples. In addition to emotionally invalidating interactions and emotional disconnection, some of these families operate in the extremes of disengagement/emotional distance to enmeshment. They often have low family cohesion and poor conflict-resolution and problem-solving skills. The parents can oscillate from being too emotionally reactive with anxiety and anger to responding with criticism and blaming (Hollander, 2008; King et al., 2001; Miller et al., 2007; Selekman, 2006, 2009; Selekman

& Schulem, 2007; Wedig & Nock, 2007). Research indicates that there is a strong association between parental criticism triggering thoughts and feelings for adolescent self-harming behavior (Wedig & Nock, 2007). Some self-harming adolescents are overburdened as parental children or intimately entangled in their parents' marital relationship difficulties and their self-harming episodes serve a distance regulating function when the parents' unresolved conflicts come to the surface and begin to fuel arguments (Selekman, 2006, 2009; Selekman & Schulem, 2007). Self-harming adolescents from upper middle class and affluent families may never have learned how to delay gratification and tolerate frustration because of being overindulged, and thus resort to self-injury, substance abuse, eating-distressed behaviors, and other self-destructive habits to cope (Hollander, 2008; Levine, 2006; Plante, 2007; Selekman, 2009; Selekman & Schulem, 2007). In collaborative strengths-based brief family therapy, we work with the couples and families to transform these negative family interactions, as the following case example will show.

Case Example

What are We Not Talking About that Needs to be Talked About?

Courtney, 15, had been referred to me (MS) by her high school social worker Ms. Bates for "cutting, depression, poor grades, running around with a negative group of peers who were cutting and doing drugs, and for family problems." Recently, one of Courtney's teachers had noticed some fresh cut marks on one of her arms and had told her dean Mr. Stevens about it. This in turn led to his having Ms. Bates evaluate her to see if she was at suicide risk and either needed to go to a hospital emergency room or for outpatient family counseling. Ms. Bates contacted Courtney's mother Ruth. In the past, she had been unsuccessful at getting Ruth to take Courtney for counseling because of the lack of follow-through. Ms. Bates had shared with me that Courtney had disclosed to her that her mother had a "drinking problem" and had been participating in her "children of alcoholics support group" at school. On more than one occasion, Courtney had shared with her that she was "really worried about her mother" and that her stepfather also had a drinking problem and was "constantly arguing with and putting her down." Courtney had confided in Ms. Bates how she "cut herself and smoked marijuana" to "numb out" her "worries and down feelings."

In addition to her major academic decline in school, two other stressors for Courtney were her father who was described as "very strict and critical" and making her do her homework at his house twice a week after school and a popular boy named Jonas she was intimately involved with, whom she described as "playing her like a yo-yo." Apparently, this boy was known as "a player," in that he would spend time with Courtney and then move on to two of her close friends. Although Courtney did not approve of the way Jonas treated her and her friends, she was having grave difficulty breaking free from him.

After securing all of this important background information from Ms. Bates, we agreed to actively collaborate and schedule a meeting with all of Courtney's teachers to brainstorm how we can help her bring up her grades and be successful in their classes. Ms. Bates felt that Mr. Stevens should also be invited to any future collaborative meetings we scheduled. I contacted Courtney's mother immediately to schedule a family session.

SELF-HARMING HABITS

The First Family Interview

Ruth and Courtney came to the session early. However, when I greeted the two of them in the waiting room, I could smell alcohol on Ruth's breath. The good news was that she was not slurring her words or exhibiting any signs of loss of coordination, and appeared to be very present. I began the session by coming to know Ruth and Courtney by their strengths and interests. Ruth loved watching TV soap operas and cats. The family had three cats. She worked part-time in a 24-hour food mart store. Courtney loved the *Scissor Sisters* and *Muse* bands, as well as some *emo* and *rap* music. Although she had a many friends, there was a lot of peer "drama" going on with her closest friends, which was really stressing her out lately. When asked what she liked to do with her friends, she said, "Just chill together" or hang out at the local shopping mall. Courtney was not involved in any school activities or extracurricular activities.

When I asked Ruth and Courtney what their understanding was about being school-referred to me, Ruth shared that "her cutting was a big worry of hers and that she was concerned about her "D–F grades in school." Ruth went on to say that the cutting was "not a new behavior" and that she had "confronted Courtney several times before" about how "dangerous" this behavior was, especially if she is experimenting with drugs. Ruth further added that Courtney had come home a few times on the weekend after being with her friends with "red eyes" and smelling from what she suspected was "marijuana smoke." Courtney interjected that she only "smoked weed a few times" and did not have a problem with it. Ruth turned to Courtney and loudly said, "I don't want you using drugs period!" I returned the conversation back to the cutting situation. I asked Courtney what this behavior meant to her and how she thinks it benefits her. Courtney shared that her closest friends did it and it really helped her to "numb out bad feelings." Out of curiosity, I explored with Courtney what specifically those "bad feelings" were connected to and how the cutting fit into her life story. Courtney admitted to having been cutting on and off since 8th grade, doing it a few times per week lately, and sometimes daily when the stress level goes up. Although she did not make any mention of her mother's drinking problem as a major worry or stressor for her, Courtney shared that she was "stressed out by school," all of the "peer drama," particularly a love interest "Jonas," how she can't stand her stepfather Bill, her mom and Bill always arguing, and her "mean and strict" biological father Ramesh and really dislikes his "new wife Sandy." Courtney complained about how the visitation time she has with Ramesh only involves lectures about the importance of doing well in school and pressures put on her regarding getting better grades.

At this point in the session, Ruth took the floor and responded to everything that Courtney had mentioned. Ruth first expressed her concern about not really knowing that Courtney had been cutting herself so much. As far as the school grades go, she did feel that Courtney was "not staying on top of her homework" and doing poorly in school because she "spent way too much time on *Facebook* and texting her friends," particularly "Jonas." She felt that Jonas was "not good for Courtney and hurt her a lot." Apparently, Jonas would give Courtney a lot of attention and then would suddenly drop her and move on to one of her close friends. I looked over to Courtney and asked her if this was true about Jonas and she nodded her head. Next, we discussed Ruth's arguing with Bill. She openly admitted that her and Bill "argue a lot," which usually occurs when he comes home from his factory job or after having had "too many beers with his work friends." Finally, she reported how her ex-husband can be "very difficult and used to be verbally abusive toward her in front of Courtney" (which eventually resulted in her divorcing him). At this point in the session, I asked to meet alone with Ruth.

I wanted to explore all of her, Bill's, and Ramesh's attempted solutions at trying to resolve Courtney's difficulties. Ruth openly admitted that she and Bill "yell at Courtney too much." Ramesh's main attempted solutions were to "micro-manage Courtney doing her homework" at his house, "lecturing her," and encouraging Ruth and Bill to ground her for extended periods of time because her "poor attitude" about school. Ruth has tried to encourage Courtney to stay away from Jonas but she had continued to pursue him because they were "having sex." When asked about Courtney's knowledge of practicing safe sex, Ruth had talked to her about that and was under the impression that they were using condoms.

We returned our discussion back to the cutting issue, which Ruth voiced as her number one concern right now. Ruth asked what she could do that could help with this problem. I stressed the importance of her trying to keep the lines of communication open with Courtney, be emotionally supportive, be a good listener, soothe her when she appears to be experiencing emotional distress, validate her thoughts and feelings, and avoid yelling at and criticizing her. To help raise the intensity level and the need for Ruth to implement these changes immediately, I pointed out that unless these changes occur in the home environment and in their relationship, Courtney will continue to rely on cutting, drugs, and sex as attempts to emotionally comfort herself and to "numb away" bad thoughts and feelings and for stress management. I further reiterated that the combination of cutting and drug use is a prescription for death. Ruth agreed to get to work immediately. Since she was intoxicated on alcohol, I decided to write down my parental recommendations so that she would remember what to do.

Finally, I asked Ruth if she thought it would be helpful to include Bill and Ramesh in future sessions. She said that Courtney hates Bill and that he "does not believe in counseling any ways." Apparently, in past family counseling experiences, Ramesh was inconsistent with his attendance and also did not believe in counseling either. However, she did feel that Courtney's relationship with him could use some help. I said that if it were okay with Courtney, I would like to invite him in for our next family meeting. Ruth agreed.

Next, I met alone with Courtney to begin to build an alliance with her. Courtney knew I was aware of her mother's drinking problem because Ms. Bates had shared that information with me. Using curiosity, I explored with Courtney how come she did not identify this as one of the major stressors for her. Courtney pointed out that she has learned to live with it because she has grown up with it for so long. However, her catastrophic fear was that eventually her mother could die from alcoholism because her maternal grandfather and uncle used to drink a lot until they died. Courtney disclosed that her mother had confided in her in the past about "how depressed she was about her marriage to Bill because all he ever does is blame her for everything, yell at her, and gets drunk both at home and after being with his work friends." She continued to be quite vocal about her mother's choice of men. She described her biological father as being a "real jerk." She told me that he was from Pakistan and in that culture women are treated like "fifth class citizens." Courtney went on to say that she used to witness him screaming at her mother and "treating her like dirt!" Her theory was that her father drove her mother into a depression, which made it hard for her to keep jobs and led to her turning to hard liquor to cope. Courtney pointed out how she had no respect for either of her father figures. She dreaded having to go to her father's house twice a week. When asked if she would be okay with having her biological father coming to a family meeting, Courtney requested that we hold off for a while. She shared with me in past family counseling sessions her father would argue with both her mother and the therapists.

Since we were on the topic of past counseling, I wanted to know from Courtney what I needed to avoid doing with her and her family that was not helpful with former therapists. She claimed that past therapists failed to address her mother's and Bill's drinking problems. They also failed to get her biological father to stop lecturing at her all of the time. One therapist had been repulsed by the cut marks on her arm that she had shown me. Courtney jokingly said, "He looked so traumatized by it that I had to provide counseling for him!" Another therapist had his partner psychiatrist put her on Zoloft, which she refused to take on a regular basis and then stopped taking all together. I thanked her for all of her expert guidance.

I asked her what she would like me to work on changing with her family first. She wanted me to help her mother stop drinking. I shared with her that I was an addiction counselor and I would give it my best shot. However, I pointed out how it is like walking a tightrope with parents that have drinking and drug problems. The therapist has to be careful not to put them on the defensive and in any way make them feel like they are at fault for their kids' difficulties. I further added that it is important that I first help her to stop hurting herself and that it had to be a team effort with Courtney. I pointed out that this was her mother's goal and strong desire for what she wanted to see changed first. Once this would happen and depending on the seriousness of her mother's drinking problem, I shared with Courtney that her stopping cutting could have a positive effect on her mother's drinking behavior. Courtney acknowledged that this made sense and she would try to reduce her cutting.

At this point in the session, I asked her a scaling question regarding how committed she was to kicking her cutting habit on a scale from 1 to 10, with ten being totally committed. Courtney said a "6." I asked her what she was going to do over the next week to get one step higher on that scale to a lucky 7. Courtney reported that she would try to complete two past due homework assignments and try to assert herself with Jonas and express her anger with him when he mistreats her. I cautioned her that the Jonas part of the goal could potentially backfire and lead to him withdrawing from her and making her feel guilty. Courtney agreed that she would concentrate on the homework and school situation first. I also shared with Courtney that part of my job would be to collaborate with her teachers so that we can figure out together ways for her to do better in school. Courtney thanked me for being willing to do that for her. Finally, I shared with Courtney that I was concerned about her smoking weed and cutting and how dangerous this combination can be. I pointed out that I have never lost anyone to cutting before and I didn't want her to be the first. Courtney shared with me that she had only done that once and that she typically cut herself not under the influence of weed. I also acknowledged that because her mother worries about her cutting it can contribute to her desire to drink, which worked against her wish for her mother to stop drinking. Courtney could see the connection and agreed to experiment with reducing the frequency of her cutting and talking about what was bothering her with her mother, Ms. Bates, or me over the next week. I asked her if there was anything else she could do that works and prevents cutting from occurring and Courtney shared contacting her friend Tim who is trying to teach her how to play guitar and reduce her involvement time with Jonas, Cindy, and Mora who smoke a lot and cut. She pointed out that hanging out with these three together would often lead to cutting or smoking weed. She identified certain locations and musical tunes that also would trigger cutting episodes. Courtney voiced a strong desire to eventually quit her self-harming practice and to stop smoking weed. I shared with her that I could teach her some new coping tools that she may enjoy experimenting with in our next meeting. I also encouraged her to keep a *habit diary* to document her daily efforts at taking a stand against cutting and smoking weed, which would include both keeping track of what works and when cutting and smoking weed got the best of her. Courtney thought this would be helpful.

Before we parted, I offered Courtney the *secret surprise* experiment to try out over the next week. Courtney thought it would be fun to do two nice things for her mom that she would really appreciate and bring some positive emotion and "sunshine" into her life. She came up with coming home after school and doing her homework right away at least twice over the next week. Courtney also would surprise her mom by talking to her when she felt stressed out about something or if there was something positive she wanted to share with her.

Following my individual session time with Courtney, I took an intersession break to construct my editorial reflection. When we reconvened, I shared with Ruth how impressed I was with her being so committed to doing whatever it takes to help her daughter to stop cutting and do better in school. I complimented Courtney for being so open and courageous with me and how insightful she was at making connections between the major stressors in her life and how the choices she has made to try to cope have only made her situation worse. I shared with the family that cutting and substance abuse habits can be very hard to kick and it is going to require a lot of teamwork, hard work, and patience to conquer these difficulties. I also let them know that even after periods of abstinence occur, a day or two or more, these habits are like sneaky characters and strike when you're least expecting them. Thus, slips go with the territory of change and are indications that you had been making progress and are only temporarily derailed. The family was offered three therapeutic experiments:

- Ruth was to implement the new parenting strategies that were recommended and to keep track of any encouraging and responsible steps that she sees Courtney take over the next week.
- Courtney was to pay close attention to what she will do daily to stand up to cutting and smoking weed and not allow them to get the best of her, as well

as these sneaky habits' undermining her efforts to change. This is to be documented daily in her habit diary.
- Over the next week, Courtney will pull two surprises that her mother will really notice and appreciate and will shock her in a positive way. Courtney will not tell her mother what the surprises were, she will have to play detective and figure them out. In the next session, Detective Ruth will let us know what her discoveries were.

Before ending the session, I discussed the idea of having a collaborative meeting with Courtney's teachers, her dean Mr. Stevens, and Ms. Bates. Both Ruth and Courtney thought this was a great idea. I secured signatures from them on consent forms so a meeting could be scheduled.

When asked about how the session went for the family, both Ruth and Courtney reported that they were pleased with how it went. Courtney shared with me that I was unlike her former counselors in that she felt I was really interested in what she wanted and her expertise, not just spending most of the session time talking with her mother. I asked if there was anything that needed to be addressed in the next session that we had not covered and Ruth thought I should make contact with Ramesh. Courtney chimed in and said, "Please don't invite him to our next meeting." I shared with her and her mother that I will not do anything they were uncomfortable with.

Telephone Conversation with Ms. Bates

The next day, I called Ms. Bates to acknowledge that the family did show up and to tell her we got off to a good start. She had shared with me that Courtney had told her that she "liked me." We talked about the mother's drinking and marital difficulties. I explained my dilemma regarding the importance of addressing the drinking issue delicately and to be careful not to put Ruth on the defensive and prematurely exiting out of therapy. Ms. Bates completely agreed with me. She also shared with me to beware of Ramesh, who is like a "loose cannon!" I asked, "Why?" Ms. Bates pointed out how he puts a lot of pressure on Courtney with getting good grades and has sabotaged their past counseling experiences. I told her that I had planned to meet with him alone and see if I could gain his support with Courtney. Apparently, in the past he had lost a court battle to gain custody of Courtney. We agreed to stay in touch.

The Second Family Session

Ruth and Courtney came to the next session with a positive report. The other positive sign of change was that I could not smell any alcohol on Ruth's breath this time. Ruth had observed that Courtney came home three days right after school and did her homework without one reminder. I asked if this was a house record and Ruth proclaimed loudly, "Yes!" I gave Courtney a "high-five" and congratulated her. The other change that Ruth observed was that Courtney had come home earlier Fridays and Saturday nights with no signs of any drug use. She also had been steering clear from Jonas, Cindy, and Mora and went out with "nicer kids" that Ruth approved of. When I inquired with Detective Ruth about her solving the mystery of Courtney's surprises, she thought they were the homework doing, going out with her nice friends Bruce, Tanya, and Margie, and coming home earlier on the weekend nights. Courtney pointed out that she was correct but had forgotten another important surprise, which was approaching her mother to share with her both stressors in her life and some positive experiences at school. Ruth had completely forgotten about this important change. Next, I inquired with Courtney if she had observed any changes with her mother. She reported that her mother seemed warmer, more loving, and it was easier to talk to her. I asked Courtney if she could think of one time that stood out for her where she had approached her mother about something and she had felt supported by her. Courtney had shared with her mother that Jonas had been harassing her about avoiding him to such a degree that she was tempted to stab herself with a pen in the girls' bathroom but resisted the temptation to do so. I responded with, "Wow! Are you aware of how you pulled that off!? That is amazing self-control!" Courtney had told herself, "Jonas is being a real asshole and I'm not going to let him get the best of me." I asked Courtney if I could feel her bicep and after doing so shared, "I bet you he did not think you had the muscle and inner strength to not let him bring you down." Courtney laughed and acknowledged that she can be really tough when she needed to be. I shared with her that I will be really careful not to cross her or push her buttons. Both Courtney and her mother laughed. I also underscored how this epiphany and sparkling moment of not letting Jonas get the best of her by being strong and not letting a male dominate and control her, was a sign that her tough feminist side was a valuable inner resource that she could always call upon in the future when needed in situations like this. Ruth chimed in that she agreed with me and was really proud of Courtney for not letting Jonas get to her and not hurting herself. I invited Courtney to share with us other examples of how she masterfully handled stressful situations without caving into cutting or smoking weed. Courtney shared with us that she had been taking guitar lessons with Tim and was borrowing a guitar of his to practice with. She also went to a yoga class with Tanya and really liked it. I praised Courtney for being so resourceful. Ruth acknowledged that she was very pleased to observe and hear how well Courtney was doing.

Courtney did begrudgingly share with us that there had been two brief cutting episodes that had occurred during the week but that this was really good for her in that she had been cutting daily, sometimes a few times a day for the past two months. I explored with her both what the triggers were for cutting and what wisdom she gained from each of these experiences. With the first cutting incident, she had gotten a "D grade on a Math test" and started to worry about what her biological father will say. The second incident was coming home from school one day and seeing her mom strewn across the couch like she was dead. This had "freaked" her out. I validated her concerns about how her father will react to the "D grade" situation and stressed that it might be useful for me to meet with him alone to see if I can gain his support in not placing so much pressure on her about grades. In response to Courtney's dead mother on the couch scenario, I took a risk and asked the two of them the following question, "What are we not talking about that needs to be talked about?" Courtney said, "I don't know." Ruth surprisingly responded

SELF-HARMING HABITS

with, "Are you talking about my drinking?" I responded with, "How did you come with that?" Ruth went on to say that Courtney had been worried about her drinking for a long time and it has been a problem. Suddenly, Courtney chimed in with, "I am so glad that you finally admit that!" Ruth continued by sharing with me that she had really lost control of her drinking after her father died 5 years ago. She had had a very close relationship with him. Ruth had gotten deeply depressed after the loss and started drinking vodka, gin, and whiskey, at times quite heavily. Last Wednesday was the anniversary date, which was the same day that she had drank too much whiskey and passed out on the couch. Ruth went on to say that both her father and brother died from alcohol-related liver problems. Courtney moved over to her mother and hugged her, crying, telling her that she did not want to lose her to alcohol. Ruth made a commitment to Courtney that she will work on trying to quit. She did mention that she had asked Bill to move out and plans to divorce him. Ruth shared that living with him was "like living in the middle of a perpetual fire and his drinking reinforced mine." Courtney disclosed that she was very proud of her mother for standing up to Bill and kicking him out of the house.

I briefly met alone with Ruth and shared with her since I was an addictions counselor we could work on helping her gradually taper down off the alcohol and do relapse prevention work. She also agreed to see a psychiatrist I worked with who was an addictionologist and could medically detox her and effectively manage any withdrawal symptoms she may encounter. I called from the session to schedule an appointment with this psychiatrist who could best determine if Ruth can be detoxed on an outpatient basis or whether she needed to go into the hospital. She agreed to go see him for the scheduled appointment. In taking a drinking and drug history with Ruth, I discovered that at the age of 12 she was drinking hard liquor and her frequency of drinking and the amount she could consume throughout adolescence into adulthood indicated that she may have been born with a chemical tolerance system and could have primary alcoholism. She also had a history of blackouts and missing days of work. No shakes, hand tremors, sleep disturbance, or alcohol heath-related problems were reported. Apparently, with her Irish background and family history of alcoholism four generations back on the father's side of the family she was genetically predisposed to developing this condition. However, I really felt that Ruth was wedged right between the preparation and action stages of readiness for change and was getting close to trying to rewrite family history by breaking the family transmission pattern of alcoholism. I praised Ruth for taking this courageous step with resolving her alcohol problem and rewriting family history.

Ruth shared another important secret with me. Her brother's son used to self-injure for a long time and eventually sliced his wrists and died. Courtney did not know the truth about how her cousin had really died and Ruth did not want her to know about this. She pointed out to me how Courtney's cutting emotionally stirred things up inside of her, which made her worry about her daughter being on the same path to suicide as her nephew was on. I validated her concerns and provided support. I pointed out that her kicking her drinking habit will help us to conquer Courtney's cutting and marijuana use habits because they are both intertwined and were mutually reinforcing. I shared with Ruth that by taking responsibility for her drinking problem and by taking this big step it was analogous to the Chinese proverb that "One step is like traveling 1000 miles."

I briefly met alone with Courtney. I decided to capitalize on her useful self-talk tape with the Jonas incident and build it into a visualization strategy I wanted her to practice using both during non-stressful and stressful times. She was given the *visualizing movies of success* experiment. I asked her to close her eyes and capture a blank movie screen in her mind. She was then to project onto the movie screen, using all of her senses, seeing herself looking into the mirror in the girls' bathroom with the pen in her hand she was going to stab herself with after Jonas pushed her buttons, and saying, "Jonas is being a real asshole and I'm not going to let him get the best of me." I asked her to try to access her positive thoughts and emotions she had after resisting not hurting herself and not giving Jonas what he had wanted. I then wanted her to add a new scene to the movie of seeing herself in the same mirror flexing her biceps to represent her strength and mental toughness. Courtney thought this was a great idea and will help her to be more confident and mentally tougher. I also gave Courtney a *My Positive Trigger Log* to fill out over the next week to keep track of everything she does, her mother, close friends, and Ms. Bates to help her to not cave into cutting. When asked what she had rated her performance over the past week, Courtney gave herself a "+7." I congratulated her on doing an awesome job in the face of some big challenging situations over the past week. When asked what she was going to do to get up to an +8, Courtney shared that she is going to really focus on getting caught up with her back school assignments, hang out with Tim and non-cutting and non-using friends, and support her mother. She also planned to meet with her math teacher to find out how she could pick up her grade in his class after bombing the last test.

Just before taking a brief break, I wanted to strategize with Courtney how best to cope with the stressor of having to go to her dad's house and do her schoolwork. I encouraged her to blow her dad's mind and go for an Academy Award by pretending to surprise him about being real glad to be there, checking in with how his life was going, having a real positive attitude about school, and eager to get to your homework. Courtney agreed that this would "really blow his mind!" She also felt that this could help reduce some of his micro-managing with her schoolwork. I encouraged her to show him the completed work with a lot of enthusiasm. My thinking was that if this strategy really worked, I could avoid having to intervene directly with Ramesh.

After the intersession break, I reconvened the family. I began my editorial reflection on complimenting both Ruth and Courtney for their great teamwork and displaying a high level of commitment to improving their relationship. I jokingly asked Ruth if I could feel her bicep because she had shown a lot of muscle and mental toughness over the week with kicking Bill out of the house, choosing to divorce him, being more present and emotionally available to Courtney, and deciding that enough was enough with the drinking and that the time was now to kick this habit for the good of her relationship with her daughter and her own physical well-being! Ruth became teary-eyed but was smiling. Courtney shared with her mother how proud she was of her for taking such big steps. Again, I shared with the family that they have to keep working hard, be a strong team, and supporting each other because kicking habits and making major lifestyle changes often is a bumpy and challenging road to navigate. As a vote of confidence to the family for their great progress and hard work, I offered them a vacation from counseling for either two or three weeks. They elected to come back in two weeks. During this window of time, Ruth will have met with the psychiatrist and a school collaborative meeting will be held. The therapeutic experiments that were offered to Ruth and Courtney were:

- Ruth was to keep track on a daily basis of the various things she will do that works to help her to taper down from her alcohol use.
- Courtney was to practice using the visualizing movies of success coping strategy and the my positive trigger log.
- Courtney was to blow her dad's mind with novel and positive ways of acting while doing her schoolwork at his house.
- While on vacation from family counseling, Ruth and Courtney were to come up with some fun activities that they would enjoy doing together during their free time.

School Collaborative Meeting

Present at the school collaborative meeting were Ruth, Courtney, Ms. Bates, dean Stevens, Mr. Paisley (Math teacher), Ms. Spicer (English teacher), and Mr. Templeton (History teacher). Apparently, in Courtney's other classes she was at a "B" grade level and those teachers did not feel the need to attend our meeting. To begin with, Ms. Bates shared with the group that she could tell that Courtney seemed "happier," had "a much better attitude about school," and was "coping better" with family, peer, and school stressors. She also felt that Courtney had gotten under control her "cutting problem." Ms. Spicer chimed in "Thank goodness!" She was the teacher who had seen cut marks on Courtney's arm and sent her to dean Steven's office. Mr. Stevens shared that he was happy to hear that Courtney was doing better and going for counseling. He pointed out that he has had other students who had similar difficulties not follow-through with counseling.

I was curious to hear from the teachers their progress reports and concerns. Mr. Paisley had shared that Courtney was no longer at risk for failing his class and he was quite surprised when she had approached him to find out if she could do an extra-credit assignment to bring up her grade. After Courtney had done this assignment, it had brought her grade up to a "C." He was confident that if Courtney could keep working hard and consistently do her homework, she could probably pick the grade up to a "low B." Courtney chimed in, "That would be great for me!" Ms. Spicer reported that not only had Courtney caught up with her past assignments but she was getting close to a "C+/B grade." Mr. Templeton also pointed out that Courtney was now caught up and grade-wise was getting close to a "C grade" in his class. At one point, Courtney was carrying an "F grade" in his class. Everyone around the table was complimenting Courtney on her great turnaround academically. Ruth shared with the school faculty how much she appreciated their support and help and pointed out how proud she was of Courtney. We agreed to meet in a month to see what further progress Courtney had made in their classes.

The Third Family Session

Ruth and Courtney came in sporting smiles on their faces. Ruth was thrilled to report that she had not had one drink for two weeks. Dr. Jameson (the psychiatrist) had done an outpatient detox with her and put her on a low dosage of Librium, which helped reduce her withdrawal symptoms. She also was attending a local Alcoholics Anonymous group and had a sponsor. I congratulated her on her tremendous progress and shared with her that we would spend some session time on relapse prevention work. Courtney acknowledged that she was really proud of her mother. In fact, they had gone to an amusement park and had a ball together. Apparently, Ruth always loved thrilling rides like big and scary roller-coasters. They also went for some bicycle rides together in the local forest preserve.

Courtney was pleased to tell me how she had really "blown her dad's mind." Apparently, by changing the way she acted around him and having a more positive attitude about school, he treated her "nicer." They did not get into one argument. He also was delighted to hear that her grades had gone up in school. In fact, they went to her favorite restaurant and she did not get one lecture from him. Other changes Courtney reported were not cutting or smoking weed at all and regularly doing her homework. Ruth had received phone calls from Mr. Paisley and Mr. Templeton reporting that she was at a solid "B" grade level in their classes after doing exceptionally well on tests in their classes. I gave Courtney a big "high-five." In going over her my positive trigger log, Courtney showed me seven things she and others were doing to help her stay quit from cutting and smoking weed. I encouraged her to fold the log up and carry it around with her in a purse or her backpack to pull out if she ever gets stuck or if she needs to add any new helpful coping or problem-solving strategies to it. She also found the visualizing movies of success as a powerful way to boost her self-confidence and a reminder of how mentally tough she can be when she needs to be in challenging situations.

I met alone with Ruth to amplify and consolidate her gains. We discussed the importance of structure-building to fill up her free time with meaningful and healthy activities. Ruth shared with me that she was biking more both with Courtney and on her own. She also was working on eating more healthy food rather than junk food and fatty foods. I commended her on her coming up with a whole person recovery program and pointed out how a lot of alcohol and substance abusers neglect the diet and exercise aspects of recovery. I encouraged her to go to a lot of AA meetings and use her sponsor when feeling at risk to drink. To test the waters with Ruth, I explored with her what could she do that could make things go backward at this point. She pointed out excessive worrying about Courtney, allowing Bill or Ramesh to get to her in telephone conversations, not meeting with Dr. Jameson (she was seeing him once a week), and laying around the house for hours watching mindless TV shows on her days off from work.

Lately, Ruth had been dreaming about her father and feeling sad about missing him. Ruth also had felt guilty about being out drinking with her girlfriends the same evening that her father had died in the hospital. She also felt that she had not adequately mourned his loss and had not even visited the cemetery. With the loss of her father, I had encouraged her to invite her mother to the next meeting and to bring in some family albums so that they could honor and reminisce about her father. Ruth thought this was a good idea, and had been spending a lot of time lately sharing her thoughts and feelings about his loss with her mother. We decided to schedule a meeting with her mother at the end of the week since all of Ruth's thoughts and feelings were surfacing regarding the loss and she did not want this to trigger a relapse. I normalized for her that alcohol and substance abusers often dream about and experience guilt memories and feelings regarding hurting or letting down important people in their lives. I further added that all of the feelings that were anesthetized and frozen up by the alcohol in response to the painful loss she had experienced were now defrosting and present in her conscious mind.

I spent a short amount of time with Courtney amplifying and consolidating her tremendous progress. I asked if she would be willing to serve as a guest consultant to help me out with other kids experiencing similar difficulties. She confidently acknowledged her strong desire to do so. Courtney reported feeling very happy and much more self-confident. She no longer associates with Jonas, Cindy, or Mora and no longer had any urges to cut or smoke weed. Courtney rated her highly successful week at a +9. I shared with her that I thought she had established a new house record of breaking the scale and reaching a +12! Courtney laughed. As with Ruth, I asked Courtney what would make things go backward at this point. Courtney said she would start hanging out with Jonas, Cindy, and Mora, cutting and smoking weed again, excessively worrying about her mother, not doing her homework and re-adopting a bad attitude about school.

After our intersession break, I complimented Ruth and Courtney on their great teamwork and supporting one another to remain on the recovery track and not allowing their past self-destructive habits to re-assert their power and control over them and wreak havoc on their relationship. Courtney grabbed her mother's hand and they held their hands up clasped together to acknowledge their success and stronger mother–daughter connection. They both acknowledged that they felt closer than ever before. I complimented Ruth on her creativity and resourcefulness at developing her own unique whole person recovery program. I also was impressed with her mental toughness at not allowing herself to cave into drinking again in spite of grappling with a lot of painful thoughts and feelings about the loss of her father. Finally, I underscored Courtney's multitude of changes. I did caution her that although she had met with success this time around with her father did not mean that there will not be any future negative experiences with him. I also let Ruth and Courtney know that it is important to keep the structure and keep busy and engaged in meaningful and healthy activities during their leisure time to prevent slips from happening, especially when stressors or toxic people might try and shake things up. The family was offered a longer window of vacation time from counseling and could choose between three and four weeks for next appointment time. Courtney was confident that they could handle a month. Ruth agreed. However, she still wanted a meeting with her mother later in the week. I asked them to continue using the same experiments and coping strategies that working for them.

Family Meeting with Ruth and her Mother

Ruth's mother Mrs. O'Reilly was very warm and friendly. She came with Ruth armed with two big family albums filled with loads of pictures of their family, even photos when Ruth was a toddler and throughout her childhood. I could tell that Ruth was really enjoying looking at the photos and reminiscing about her father and hearing some new positive family stories about him. There were a few points in the session where they both cried and hugged one another when sharing memories and high points in their relationship with him. Ruth started to blame herself for not being at the hospital the night that her father had died. Her mother pointed out that no one saw this coming, even the doctors, and that Ruth had to stop feeling guilty about this. She went on to add that Ruth always had a special place in her father's heart and that she had seen him numerous times at the hospital. To close out the session, I encouraged them to keep their conversations going, looking at pictures and sharing meaningful stories about Mr. O'Reilly. Ruth asked her mother if she would visit his grave with her and she agreed to do so. I thanked Ruth's mother for coming and being such a big support for her daughter. Mrs. Reilly thanked me for helping out Ruth and Courtney. She was delighted that Ruth was clean, sober, strong, and confident. Ruth thanked her mother for all of her support and had shared with me that she was interviewing for a full-time job in a department store that had great benefits. I wished her good luck with the interview.

Telephone Check-In with Ms. Bates

I called Ms. Bates to update her on the wealth of progress Courtney and her mother were making. According to Ms. Bates, she had already gotten such a detailed progress report from Courtney it was as if she was "a play-by-play sports commentator." Needless to say, dean Stevens, all of Courtney's teachers, and her were very impressed with Courtney's "complete turnaround behaviorally and academically." In fact, when Ms. Bates explored with the teachers if another meeting was necessary, they all unanimously felt there was no need to meet because Courtney was doing so well in all of their classes. She now had "a solid B+ average." I shared with Ms. Bates that I had felt that Courtney and her mom were at a place where we could entertain terminating. However, I was going to offer Ruth a few more spaced out sessions for relapse prevention purposes if she wanted to continue. Ms. Bates thanked me for my help and was looking forward to collaborating on future cases together.

The Fourth and Final Family Session

Similar to my last session with Ruth and Courtney, many more important growth steps and changes were happening for both of them. Ruth was dressed up in a business-looking suit. When asked about the fancy garb, Ruth happily shared with me that she had landed the job she had interviewed for as an assistant manager in one of the store departments. Apparently, she had had a similar job in the past before the department store had closed. I complimented her on this important accomplishment. Ruth now had close to two months of sobriety, was regularly attending AA meetings, continued to see Dr. Jameson, and using her sponsor for support when she needed to. I pointed out to Ruth how she was well on her way to trailblazing new family history by breaking free from the powerful clutches of family alcoholism. Ruth confidently responded, "I feel good about that." Ruth and her mother also visited her father's grave. On her own, Ruth had written a beautiful letter sharing with him everything she could think of that she was grateful for and that she appreciated about him as a person and left it with flowers by his gravestone. She had brought in a copy of the letter for me to look at. It was very thoughtfully written and quite touching. I complimented Ruth on her fine job with the letter.

Courtney reported not having one cutting or smoking weed slip. She told me about her "B+ grade point average." Ruth shared how proud she is of Courtney. In fact, Courtney was talking about for the first time wanting to go to college and major in psychology. I jokingly asked Courtney, "You think you have problems, you want to hear about some of mine?" She said, "No thanks!" We all laughed. Courtney was getting much better on the guitar thanks to her friend Tim. She also had been going to yoga classes regularly with her friend Tanya. Courtney's relationship had continued to improve. They had not had one clash in a long time.

I asked the family what fun things they thought they might be doing together once we stop our counseling meetings. Courtney said that her and her mother would probably go biking, go out to eat, or cook a nice meal together. They both discovered that cooking different types of cuisines was a fun new pastime they enjoyed doing together. Both Ruth and Courtney felt it was time to move on with their lives. I shared with them that I had been thinking the same thing and how nice it is when my clients and I are on the same wavelength. I shared with Ruth and Courtney that the door was always open to them if they felt like they needed a tune up or if Ruth wanted to do further work and not to hesitate to call. Ruth was very confident that there was so much structure and present support in her life from her mother, with her local AA community, and seeing Dr. Jameson periodically that she was quite confident that she will stay on track. In fact, Ruth pointed out that she was no longer experiencing craving and other withdrawal symptoms.

Courtney was eager to share with me that she will get a lot of practice experience playing psychologist because Ms. Bates asked her to get involved as a peer counselor at the high school. I shared with Courtney that I am confident she will do a fine job. They both thanked me for all of my help. We mutually agreed to terminate.

Telephone Follow-Up

At six months, I had contacted Ruth to see how they were doing. Ruth shared with me that she was still clean and sober, loved her job, and Courtney was starting up her junior year of high school and had a wonderful summer doing service work in New Orleans through their church. There were no reports of cutting or marijuana use. Ruth was still attending AA and had made a lot of "straight friends" who helped her to stay on track.

When I spoke to Ruth and Courtney at the one-year mark, again there were no reports of drinking, cutting, or drug use. Ruth was still at the same job. She had finalized her divorce with Bill. Courtney's relationship with her father was getting better. Ruth and Courtney were still cooking up a storm trying dishes from around the world. Courtney was starting to look at colleges and still interested in psychology.

Reflections on the What Are We Not Talking About That Needs To Be Talked About? *Case*

Mark: This is great example of leading clients from behind by paying close attention to their treatment goals and preferences, and by celebrating and validating their small steps forward, but also gently prompting them to move forward at some critical points in therapy. You utilized the big exception in the second session (Courtney in the girl's bathroom at school resisting the urge to cut herself) as the material for the "visualizing movies of success" experiment. As for this latter experiment, I wonder: when no real movies can be accessed by clients, do you use this experiment anyway, inviting clients to create and visualize a hypothetical movie of success that they would want to see happen?

Matthew: Yes, I have had clients create their own hypothetical movies of success when they cannot access a past movie of something they had accomplished. However, I have added another option that clients can pursue first. They can try to access a past movie of some joyous event or time in their life that triggered happiness and other positive emotions for them. This can be visiting a special place or other highly positive experiences that brought them great joy with family or friends. While doing the exercise, clients often smile in my office while accessing their cherished movie with their eyes closed and it visibly elevates their moods as well. The other bonus with this experiment is that clients totally cooperate with using it on a regular basis as a coping tool they can employ when experiencing emotional distress.

Mark: To me a central element for the positive outcome of this case was how you handled Ruth's alcohol problem. It would have been quite easy to slip into a confrontational position, but you moved very slowly, asking first Courtney when you met with her alone why she had not brought up the alcohol issue, and only putting the topic openly on the agenda in the second session, as a reaction to the "dead mother on the couch" scenario. At that critical moment in therapy, your "What are we not talking about that needs to be talked about?" left the family with room enough to answer one way or the other. I wonder what you have done if the mother had also replied that she did not know, or had simply detoured to some other issue. What other questions would be useful to ask if that would have occurred?

Matthew: If my risky question had not produced any results, there were two other strategies I would have pursued. First, I would have employed the TV detective *Columbo* tactics, such as: take a one-down position, look confused, and wonder aloud with curiosity about why my gut was trying to tell me that there was still a missing piece of the family puzzle that seemed to be stressing Courtney out, and invite family members to join me in this search to find the missing piece. Second, I could have pursued the indirect strategy of sharing with Courtney and Ruth a former client family's story with a daughter who was cutting and doing drugs and it turned out that the father had a drug problem and how,

	once that was addressed, it completely transformed their situation for the better.
Mark:	The case also brings across how effective subsystem work can be, not only to deepen the therapeutic alliance with each member and to get more commitment and changes, but also to increase each member's perceived "safety in the therapeutic system" (Friedlander, Escudero, & Heatherington, 2006). In this case, your effective subsystem work started with the decision to invite just Ruth and Courtney to the first family session, a decision which in turn was based on your telephone conversation with the school social worker Ms. Bates. In discussing our book's cases with you, I am becoming increasingly aware of how much time you spend talking with the referring professionals and securing information that often turns out to be relevant and useful.
Matthew:	I view referring professionals as potential allies and integral members of the solution-determined system. Similar to the importance I place on rapidly building strong alliances with my new clients and having a high level of respect for their problem stories and explanations, I want to do the same with the referring professionals. It is important to learn from them the following information: what they and others from the school or their context are observing that prompted the referral, what their attempted solutions have been, and what they and others in the school or their context need to see changed so that they would be less concerned and satisfied. The referring person can be an important person at school for us, in that they can organize collaborative meetings on-site with all of the concerned school personnel and serve as an advocate for the adolescent client in helping them with teachers he or she is having difficulty or conflicts with. They can serve as our co-therapists in the school. I also invite referring professionals to join our family sessions to optimize other opportunities to observe changes with the clients and their families, build partnerships with the parents, and to help build a bridge from the schools or other contexts to the home. Finally, the referring professionals' presence in family sessions affords the opportunity for them to report changes they and others have observed in their settings with the identified clients, which can help alter other family members' problem views and lead to positive changes in their interactions.
Mark:	In this case it was optimal to stage the meeting with the school personnel once Courtney had made some progress already, which contributed to the positive atmosphere during the school meeting and was extra motivation for Courtney. In other cases, however, it seems that school meetings are most useful when the family sessions are stuck and we need to get some new ideas and open up different possibilities. What are your ideas on the timing of beginning school meetings in the family therapy process?
Matthew:	With school referrals, I like to begin having these collaborative meetings right after my first family therapy session. With the consent of the family

and support of the school, I will invite other involved helping professionals to these meetings as well, such as psychiatrists, probation officers, child protective workers, and so forth. By doing so, it conveys to the concerned school personnel and other helpers that the therapist and family are interested and invested in partnering up to collaboratively resolve the presenting problems. The other bonus of having these family–school–multiple helper collaborative meetings is that they tend to elicit compassion and empathy from the school personnel and other helpers about the family's difficulties and unique needs and sometimes, and often family members courageously share material in these meetings that they had never brought up before in individual family therapy sessions.

Mark: I find it very interesting how you promoted change in the Courtney/Ramesh relationship by intervening only through Courtney. This an excellent example of producing changes in a family by working solely with the adolescent. If working with Courtney had not been enough to create changes in the relationship with her father, I guess you would have taken the next step, inviting Ramesh in for a session. My hunch is that you would have tried to join with his preoccupation with Courtney's grades.

Matthew: Yes, Ramesh dwelled relentlessly on the importance of Courtney's academic success in school. What is critical here in the way of cultural sensitivity is the fact that Ramesh had immigrated to the United States with his family when he was a teenager and a lot of pressure was placed on him to excel in school and to go to college. As part of the immigration story, the belief is that the United States is supposed to be the land of opportunity and if one works hard and advances professionally, financial wealth can come. In addition, in his culture problems are kept in the family and outsiders are not involved in the family's business. These factors would help explain Ramesh's strong push for Courtney's academic achievement and discomfort with having his family affairs discussed with an outsider.

If I had to do direct work with Ramesh and Courtney, I would invite the father to be a storyteller and share with his daughter his immigrant story, some of the struggles he had had with his parents, and how he overcame adversity. I also would try to help them find the balance between talking incessantly about school and talking about other things, like planning and doing fun high quality activities together, particularly things that Courtney would wish to do with him.

Mark: You helped both Courtney and Ruth to move into the *preparation* and *action* stages of readiness for change by providing some information on the risks of cutting and more specifically, on the risks of combining cutting and drug use. You chose to do that making very clear and dramatic remarks to Ruth on how the combination of cutting and drug use is "a prescription for death," and by sharing with Courtney that you have never lost a client to cutting and didn't want her to be the first. In what other ways do you usually increase intensity?

Matthew: A good option is given by the pessimistic sequence questions, which I use as follows: "Let's say it is 1:00 AM Saturday morning and a police officer rings your doorbell and tells you your daughter is no longer with us. What effect would her loss have on the two of you? What would you miss the most not having her around? Who will attend her funeral? What will the eulogies be?" I have yet to have parents not respond to these questions with, "What do you want us to do? What can we do to prevent this? We love her, we can't let this happen." The bottom line is that we should never be working harder than our adolescent clients' parents. Our job is to serve as consultants to parents, coaching them to parent in new and more productive ways and help facilitate stronger connections in their relationships with their kids. Help them be more empathically attuned with their kids so that they sooth and emotionally comfort them when they are experiencing emotional pain and distress. Otherwise, adolescents will turn to their self-destructive habits to sooth and comfort themselves when they cannot count on their parents to provide this function.

Mark: Another theme I could see running through your therapy with this family was two women taking a stand against male patriarchy and oppression, as exemplified by Courtney's setting limits on Jonas and not allowing him emotionally to bring her down again, and Ruth taking a stand against Bill and finally divorcing him. In this process, your use of the "strong bicep" metaphor strikes me as an elegant way to encapsulate the empowerment of these two brave women. Do you think it would have been helpful to spell out more the feminist element of their quest?

Matthew: I consider myself to be a gender-sensitive therapist and it was clear to me that both of these women were being oppressed by traditional men who were interacting with them in emotionally abusive ways. I strived to empower both Ruth and Courtney to take a stand and break free from the clutches of male domination and exploitation and reclaim their identities as two strong women ready to pioneer a new direction with their lives.

5

EATING-DISTRESSED HABITS

> Habit with iron sinews, clasps us and leads us day by day.
> *Alphonse de Lamartine*

Introduction

DSM-IV-TR estimates the prevalence of anorexia nervosa in young women to be around 1%, with a greater number of clients having bulimia nervosa. Overall, including individuals with subthreshold diagnoses, the lifetime prevalence of eating disorders is estimated to be in the 5–15% range (Herzog et al., 2000; Steinhausen, 2009). This figure includes a great variety of profiles, symptoms, and problems, from restrictive anorexia to purgative bulimia, vigorexia, orthorexia or binge-eating, plus a number of intermediate conditions, all of which display a number of physical problems and run high medical risks like sudden death or starvation. The worst part is the great deal of suffering that eating disorders bring about: persons with eating-distressed habits are likely to be extremely obsessive, anxious, and/or depressed, their lives become restricted and limited, and in many cases deteriorate in a downward spiral of hospitalizations, relapses, and even death. In spite of all the alleged improvements in the treatment of eating disorders over the last 20 years, it is estimated that still up to 20% of persons with anorexia and 15% of bulimic clients remain chronically ill for the long term, and a substantial proportion of them die, either by suicide or from the medical complications of their eating-distressed habits (Arcelus, Mitchell, Wales, & Nielsen, 2011). Another 30–40% remain symptomatic all their life (Birmingham, Su, Hlynsky, Goldner, & Gao, 2005; Herzog, Keller, Lavori, & Sacks, 1991; Keel, Mitchell, Miller, Davis, & Crow, 1999; Steinhausen, 2009). For this reason, many psychotherapists feel frightened by these clients and prefer not to treat them. The good news is that the family therapy field has a long tradition of offering therapeutic alternatives for these problems, and that there are a number of strategic and cognitive-behavioral intervention techniques for bulimia and binge-eating that can be easily integrated into a more comprehensive, systems-oriented, collaborative approach.

Background: The Multiple Faces of Eating Disorders

Eating disorders can take a multiplicity of forms which may change over time and get into dangerous combinations with other self-destructive habits such as drug abuse, cutting, and unsafe sex. The traditional way to understand eating-distressed behavior is by differentiating a number of discrete disorders.

Anorexia nervosa

Anorexia is the "queen" of eating disorders, and has been scientifically documented as far back as the seventeenth century (Lasegue, 1873; Morton, 1689). Some 80% of clients with anorexia nervosa are women, with onset typically being during the mid-teen years. The basic feature of this disorder is the refusal to maintain body weight at or above normal weight, defined as 15% below that expected for the individual's height and weight; or a body mass index (B.M.I.) under 17.5. There must also be an intense fear of gaining weight or becoming fat, even though underweight; a severe restriction of food intake, often with excessive exercising; a disturbance in the way in which body weight and shape are experienced; and an undue influence of body weight or shape on self-evaluation. Anorectic patients are obsessed about food, show phobic behaviors towards food and food-related stimuli, and experience affective instability and mood swings. In postmenarcheal women, amenorrhea is also a required symptom; the equivalent for men is loss of sexual desire. Although since the influential work by Hilde Bruch (1978) psychologists have emphasized body image distortion as a patognomic feature of anorexia, more modern theories tend to see it as a subproduct of biological processes (the dieting-exercise cycle), not as a central aspect of the problem (Gutiérrez, 2011; Gutiérrez et al., 2008). DSM-IV differentiates two types of anorexia nervosa: *restrictive anorectics* get slim only by dieting and exercising; *purgative* a*norectics* also display purging behaviors such as vomiting and abuse of laxatives, diuretics, or enemas.

Persons with anorectic habits usually present in therapy in a precontemplative stage of readiness for change: they do not see a problem in their behavior or the need for any therapy. In their "honeymoon" period with anorexia, they feel proud of their achievement of having lost so much weight, have a heightened self-esteem and may even feel driven by an ascetic mission. Only in later stages may they start to complain about depression, obsessiveness, or restlessness.

Bulimia nervosa

Bulimia nervosa was first conceptualized as a distinct syndrome in the 1970s (Russell, 1979). The main feature of bulimia is recurrent episodes of binge-eating associated with a lack of control over eating behavior during the binges. Most full-blown bulimic clients are women, but partial bulimic syndromes are also common for men (Woodside et al., 2001). Bulimia has a slightly later age of onset than anorexia, typically in late adolescence or early adulthood. *Purgative bulimics* vomit or purge after their binges; *restrictive bulimics* fast or over-exercise after bingeing. As with anorexia, a persistent preoccupation with body size and shape is present, and self-evaluation is excessively linked to ideas about them. However, the weight of these persons is usually normal or slightly above normal. This makes detection of the problem by outsiders more difficult and is the reason why bulimia might be kept secret for years or even decades.

Persons with bulimia are likely to be in the contemplation or in the preparation stage of readiness for change, as they usually feel ashamed both of their binges and their inability to "control" their food intake. This is why they are more likely than persons with anorexia to ask for therapy on their own initiative. As is the case in anorexia, the spontaneous remission rate for bulimia seems to be low (Hartman, Herzog, & Driunkman., 1992); therefore bulimia is often described as a chronic disorder (Herzog, Keller, Lavori, & Sacks, 1991).

Binge-eating

According to DSM-IV, binge-eating refers to people who binge at least twice per week over six months, in the absence of other compensatory behaviors. As a result of their distressed eating habit, most binge-eaters become overweight and even obese. Binge-eating departs from the clinical picture of anorexia and bulimia in that most clients are in middle-aged and, although the majority of binge-eaters are women, the proportion of men is higher than in other eating disorders (1.5 woman to 1.0 males; Grilo, 2002). Another difference is that binge-eating tends to be intermittent rather than persistent, with most clients reporting sustained periods when they are in control of their eating (Fairburn, 2008). Binge-eating individuals are greatly troubled by what they view as a clear problem, because of both the loss of control and the implications of their binges for their weight and health. For this reason, they are likely to present in therapy in the preparation or action stages of readiness for change; however, they are also likely to get demoralized when they do not achieve fast changes.

Other Forms of Eating-Distressed Habits

Although anorexia and bulimia are the most described and researched presentations of eating disorders, between 40% and 60% of individuals seen in ambulatory practice for eating disorders do not meet full criteria for anorexia or bulimia (Fairburn & Bohn, 2005; Millar, 1998). In DSM-IV, these cases are included under the category of "eating disorders—not otherwise specified" (EDNOS); for instance, a woman who meets all diagnostic criteria for anorexia but has regular menses, or a man that binges and purges, but less than twice a week. Although EDNOS might be considered "subthreshold" from a diagnostic perspective,or as a way-station for those moving to one eating disorder to full remission or to another eating disorder (Agras, Crow, Mitchell, Halmik, & Bryson, 2009), they are not necessarily less serious than "pure" anorexia or bulimia. On the contrary, they may be even more clinically challenging. In a recent meta-analysis, Arcelus et al. (2011) found the standardized mortality rate in EDNOS clients to be higher than for bulimia clients.

The Biology of Eating Disorders

A central feature of eating disorders is the pervasive negative biological effects that dieting, bingeing, and purging bring about. As to extreme dieting, it affects every organ of the human body, including the cardiovascular system and the central nervous system. The most significant acute problems are bradycardia, hypothermia, and dehydration; all can become life-threatening. Although most of this damage is reversible, some might not be; in fact, growth retardation, peak bone mass reduction, and sterility might be life-long sequelae of anorexia. Purging by vomiting or by taking diuretics or laxatives is no less dangerous; among other risks, it imbalances the biochemistry of the blood, causing hypokalemic alkalosis, which may lead to cardiac arrest or "sudden death." Renal problems, cardiac arrhythmias, dehydration, and dental problems are also common. Given these massive medical complications, any person that starts therapy for eating-distressed habits should be routinely referred to a medical doctor to have her health checked so that if necessary palliative measures are warranted they can be can be pursued.

There is, however, an even more interesting side to the biology of eating-distressed habits. The classical, "psychological" view of eating disorders, and especially of anorexia, has been that certain personality features lead to the disorder (Bruch, 1978; Crisp, 1997). However, although certain personality traits may increase the chances of engaging in risk behaviors and eventually developing an eating disorder, most of the personality features observed in eating-distressed clients are indeed a consequence, not cause, of the biological imbalances that chronic dieting produces. This was well documented in the classic study "Minnesota experiment" conducted during the 1940s by Ancel Keys and his colleagues (Keys, Brozek, Heshel, Mickelsen, & Taylor, 1950). Their sample was 36 young, healthy and psychologically healthy men who had volunteered for the study as an alternative to military service. After three months of monitoring their normal food intake, they were placed on a semi-starvation diet for another six months. The changes were dramatic: the men not only lost about 25% of their body weight, but experienced important "attitude changes"; they became obsessed with food, and talked constantly about eating, hunger, and weight; they became irritable, depressed, and anxious, lost their sexual desire, and restricted social contacts by becoming progressively more withdrawn and isolated. They also started to play around with food, to harbor it secretly, and to binge-eat. During the three months of rehabilitation, many of the men lost control of their appetites and ate more or less continuously. In sum, perfectly healthy persons developed, by simple food restriction, mostly symptoms of anorexia nervosa first and then of bulimia.

The Keys study is a good illustration of how powerful the biological mechanisms related to food intake can be. The role that over-exercising plays in this mechanism is also known: in animal research it is a well-documented fact that experimental rats whose food intake is suddenly restricted tend to adjust to the new situation, but if they have an exercising wheel in their cage, they respond to the food restriction by exercising more and more (Epling & Pierce, 1991; Epling, Pierce, & Stefan, 1983). In the end, they spend most of their time in the wheel, stop eating and reach the point where they would die. Recent research (Gutiérrez, Vázquez, & Boakes, 2002; Gutiérrez et al., 2008) has highlighted the important role that temperature plays in this process: the death of the experimental rats only happens if the lab temperature is below a certain threshold. For humans, this finding has led to hypotheses that persons with a low basal body temperature may be more prone to develop starvation syndrome if they over-exercise and/or diet (Gutiérrez, 2011). What is already established is that eating in a warm environment decreases the stress of anorectic persons as measured by a reduction of their cortisol levels; the treatment implication is that some programs have started to re-feed clients in high temperature environments (Bergh, Eklund, Eriksson, Lindberg, & Sodersten, 1996; Berg & DeJong, 1998), or wearing health jackets (Birmingham, Gutiérrez, Jonat, & Beumont, 2004).

Another aspect of the biological trap that eating-distressed habits can create is the addictive power of endogenous endorphins. Although there is some debate over the "endorphin hypothesis" (Huebner, 1993), it seems clear that the human body responds to starvation or semi-starvation by activating all kind of mechanisms to ensure survival. Among them is an increase in the secretion of endorphins, endogenous opiates ontogenetically designed to help the starving person to keep alert, active, and looking for food. With anorectic persons, this endorphin increase has the side effect of reducing the "suffering pressure," and of making the person feel good, not only proud of the accomplishments of her diet but really hooked on the pleasurable effects it brings about. At a later stage endorphin reserves will be depleted, but by then the condition will be firmly entrenched.

The Multiple Paths to Eating Disorders

Eating disorders are described as multi-determined (Garfinkel & Garner, 1982; Garner, 1993), which means that it is not possible to identify a single cause and that the onset of an eating disorder is best understood as the result of multiple interplaying factors that involve an altered person/food intake/exercise relationship. Applying the pathways model we have proposed in Chapter 1, this relationship can get out of balance in two different ways.

Pathway I represents the "biological road" to an eating disorder, and is more likely for what will initially present as anorexia: either prolonged fasting or excessive exercising unbalance the system and trap the person (who might be a perfectly healthy, normal individual) in the starvation syndrome. This is basically what happened in the Minnesota experiment we presented above. In fact, research shows that persons who diet are more likely to develop an eating disorder than those who do not (Hsu, 1997). It is well-known fact that marathon runners, artistic gymnasts, and ballet dancers have a heightened risk of developing eating disorders. However, it is also evident that most people who exercise a lot and most people who diet do not develop an eating disorder. So what makes a dieter or an over-exerciser fall into the anorexia trap? One factor might be basal hypothermia: persons whose body temperature is naturally lower than average would be more prone to fall into the over-exercising/dieting cycle (Gutiérrez, 2011). On the other hand, most dieting people are protected from anorexia simply because they are not persistent and successful enough in their dieting efforts. Future anorectics may, in contrast, persevere and be patient enough to fast for such a long time that they start to develop anorexia.

Over-evaluation of shape and weight, so called "body image distortion" may also play an important part in leading a person to persist in their dieting efforts up to a point where she gets caught in the starvation trap. Although the dysfunctional schema for self-evaluation may only well be a result of dieting and over-exercising (Gutiérrez, 2011; Zanker, 2009), once established it becomes a powerful maintaining factor and also a risk factor for future relapses (Halmi et al., 2002).

Pathway II constitutes the "emotional road" to an eating disorder, and is more likely in cases that initially present as bulimia and binge-eating. There are a number of ways in which eating disorders can develop as emotional and interpersonal regulators:

- Eating distress can be a consequence and also a way to cope with past or ongoing trauma. In fact, data show that around 20% and 50% of eating-disordered women have suffered childhood sexual abuse; abuse being more frequent among bulimic women than among restrictive anorectics (Vanderlinden & Vandereycken, 1997; Vanderlinden, Vandereycken, & Claes, 2007). It is assumed that sexual abuse functions as a nonspecific stressor (Fallon & Wonderlich, 1997) that may lead to the onset of eating-distressed habits, as well as to other mental health problems.
- Binge-eating can develop as a way to cope with current emotional stress. The anxiolitic effect of food intake can make a person get hooked on bingeing as a means for self-soothing and relaxation. Low self-esteem is also a risk factor for developing an eating disorder: successful dieting may act as a powerful reinforcer, as it makes the dieting person feel capable and in control (Fairburn, Cooper, Shafran, Bohn, & Hawker, 2008).
- Family disturbance might play a role in reinforcing and amplifying distressed eating. For instance, the initial dietary restriction of a girl may attract her parents' attention to a degree that she does not achieve by less problematic means; reinforced by this effect, she may continue her dieting beyond normal limits and slip into full-blown anorexia. Or a boy may cope with the stress he experiences being witness to his parents' fights by secretly bingeing; later, preoccupied by his weight gain, he may "discover" vomiting as a compensatory measure and finally develop clinical bulimia.

These two pathways to eating-distressed habits developing may of course interact in multiple ways. The important thing to remember is that, as we have seen, once the starvation syndrome is activated, it tends to perpetuate itself, regardless of the initial cause or precipitant factor. The same circular patterns are evident between dieting, bingeing, and compensatory measures: dieting makes it likelier to "slip" into a binge, which will probably lead to more dieting or to purging, which in turn will make the person more aware of weight and shape issues, which will again lead to more dieting, and so on. On a more contextual level, inadequate family response to initial eating-distressed behavior, professional mishandling, or toxic peers might also act as maintaining factors (Garner, 1993; Le Grange & Lock, 2007).

Key Research Findings that Inform our Clinical Practice

Despite decades of research efforts on the treatment of anorexia, recovery rates at termination stay in a very modest 20–50% range, with a high risk of relapse or migration to bulimic symptoms at follow-up (Bergh et al., 2006; Roth & Fonagy, 2005) and only 10% of anorexia clients are symptom-free at 10 years follow-up (Von Holle et al., 2008).

Psychotropic medication may help to alleviate anxiety and depression symptoms, but has no direct effect on anorexia (Crow, Mitchell, Roerig, & Steffen, 2009; Dunican & Del Dotto, 2007). Cognitive-behavioral therapy (CBT: Pike, Walsh, Vitousek, Wilson & Bauer, 2003; Fairburn, 2008) that addresses the overvaluing of body weight and shape has shown to be of some use to reduce relapses after renutrition. A number of studies undertaken at the Maudsley hospital in London over the last two decades (Eisler, 2005; Eisler et al., 1997, 2000; Russell, Szmukler, Dare, & Eisler, 1987) have shown that for adolescent clients or young women living with their parents, family therapy achieves good results. An intensive multiple family therapy format (Dare & Eisler, 2000) has also shown some promise (Colahan & Robinson, 2002; Eisler, 2005), but the strength of the Maudsley studies has been challenged in recent years (Bergh et al., 2006). Probably the most promising results so far are those documented at the Karolinska Institute in Stockholm, Sweden (Bergh, Brodin, Lindberg, & Sodersten, 2002). This team makes use of the recent research findings on the interaction of heat, food intake, and exercise (Gutiérrez, Vazquez, & Boakes, 2002; Gutiérrez et al., 2008), and offers a treatment package that includes: reduction of physical activity; re-learning to eat via a computerized system that provides feedback on ongoing intake and satiety; resting in a heated room (up to 40°C) one hour after lunches; and the promotion of a schedule of social activities. This procedure has been recently replicated in the Netherlands, with less impressive results: after around one year of intensive, high-quality treatment and one more year of follow-up, slightly above 50% of patients reached normal weight and a similar percentage still scored above the clinical cut-off for eating pathology (Van Elburg et al., 2012).

For bulimia, CBT (Fairburn, 1985, 2008; Wilson, Fairburn, & Agras, 1997) consistently demonstrates good post-therapy effects on bingeing and purging, but with a number of unsettling findings. On the one hand, many clients still tend to exhibit significant symptoms at termination, and the percentage of clients who are fully recovered by the end of treatment is only around 40% in the treatment-completed samples (Thompson-Brenner, Glass, & Westen, 2003). On the other hand, a substantial proportion of clients who recover at termination relapse at follow-up (for instance, Fairburn et al., 1991). Finally, there is no empirical base to assume that the effect of CBT is due to its putative therapeutic ingredients. For instance, interpersonal therapy (IPT) has been found, in direct comparison, to be as effective in the long run as CBT (Agras, Walsh, Fairburn, Wilson, & Kraemer, 2000; Fairburn, Kirk, O'Connor, & Cooper, 1986; Fairburn et al., 1991). The interesting fact is that IPT examines broader interpersonal issues and focuses more on the depressive background of patients, without including any of the educational and cognitive restructuring elements considered to be central by CBT. This is also the case with dialectical behavior therapy (DBT), which assumes distressed eating patterns are an attempt to control emotional dysregulations, and which is producing evidence of its effectiveness (Safer, Telch, & Agras, 2001). In fact, CBT is evolving in the direction of accepting a broader framework that also includes working on self-esteem, perfectionism, and interpersonal issues (Fairburn et al., 2008). The benefits of family therapy with young bulimic persons are beginning to be documented (Dodge, Hodes, Eisler, & Dare, 1995; Le Grange & Lock, 2007; Le Grange & Schmidt, 2005), but the advantages of including the couple partner have not been researched so far with eating-distressed adult clients.

Below, we list the key implications of these research findings on our practice with eating-distressed habit clients:

- Given the important role that the biological processes of renutrition, exercise control, and health play in eating disorders, we do not provide therapy without having clients medically checked and followed. Healthy eating (see below) is a central element in their recovery, and, although therapy sessions should not revolve around discussing food and eating only, they should help to reestablish control over eating: education on healthy nutrition, self-monitoring of food intake, self-regulatory strategies to handle urges to binge and to purge, and the introduction of daily structure.
- Challenging anorexic/bulimic attitudes is a key element of most tested treatments; in our approach we like to do this using some narrative and brief therapy techniques like externalization of the problem (White, 2007, 2011; White & Epston, 1990).

- Studies on ITP and DBT provide good evidence for the value of working with bulimic clients to sort out the role of her distressed eating pattern in the regulation of emotions and relationships. This falls in line with our view of eating-distressed habits as "gifts and resources."
- Family therapy is useful to provide external motivation for treatment and to reduce the relational side-effects of the condition on family members. For families with low conflict, conjoint family therapy is a good therapeutic option, whereas for highly conflicted families, working with subgroups and individuals of the family, maintaining a systemic focus, is better (Eisler et al., 2000); this links in with our subsystem work strategy described in Chapter 2. Successful structural family therapy programs share their emphasis on empowering the parents in their handling of their children, while carefully avoid blaming the parents for the identified client's condition (Dodge et al., 1995; Le Grange & Lock, 2007; Le Grange & Schmidt, 2005).
- Given that relapse and symptom migration are rather common it makes sense to offer "booster" sessions with clients once they have accomplished their goals, so as to monitor their development over a longer period of time. The finding that higher self-esteem at termination might protect clients from relapse into bulimia (Fairburn et al., 1991) and that poor social adjustment worsens prognosis of bulimic clients (Agras et al. 2000), supports the importance of promoting alternative virtuous habits as protective shields against anorectic or bulimic "counterattacks."

Strategies for Assessment and Treatment Planning

Assessment Considerations

For eating disorders, DSM-IV diagnoses present a number of major problems. On the one hand, research shows that the diagnostic categories display a great deal of overlap and of variability within each diagnostic subgroup (Welch, Hall, & Renner, 1990). On the other, a high proportion of eating disorders fall into the catch-all category of EDNOS (Fairburn & Bohn, 2005; Millar, 1998). Furthermore, the symptoms of eating disorders are likely to change over time: an adolescent might start with bulimic behavior and later become anorectic; or he or she may start with a period of food restriction and over-exercising, recover, start to binge-eat, and then display full-blown bulimia. This "migration" across diagnosis is frequent (Agras et al., 2009; Fairburn & Harrison, 2003), with up to one-third of clients with an intake diagnosis of anorexia nervosa crossing over to bulimia during 7 years of follow-up, and 14% moving in the opposite direction (Eddy et al., 2008).

For these reasons, we prefer to view eating disorders as a continuum (van der Ham, Stien, & van Engeland, 1994): restrictive anorexia on one end and binge-eating at the other, with purgative anorexia and non-purgative bulimia in between. In other words, as clinicians we like to keep the wider picture in mind and look for the anorexic process that underlies any eating-disordered symptoms: the "anorexia within the bulimia" or the "anorexia within the binge-eating." This view also helps to stay alert to the risk of possible symptom reversals and emphasizes the need to discuss and prevent possible relapses.

Co-morbidity has also to be taken into account. With lifetime prevalence of co-morbid depression between 24% and 88% for anorexia and bulimia (Mitchell, Specker, & de Zwaan, 1991), working with an eating-disordered person it is important to watch out for depression, which might genetically run in the family and which would deserve some extra therapeutic input and a careful assessment of suicide risk. Bulimic persons and binge-eaters are also prone to abuse alcohol and other drugs, to engage in adolescent experimentation and risk behaviors, and to gamble (Yip, White, Grilo, & Potenza, 2011).

Eating-disordered persons (especially at the bulimic end of the continuum) are also likely to be anxious (Laessle, Kittl, & Fichter, 1987) and obsessive (Holden, 1990), and to display some other self-destructive habits too: they may self-harm, compulsively shop or gamble, or have unprotected sex with multiple partners. In many cases, this cluster of self-destructive habits is a consequence of trauma. As mentioned before, many persons struggling with eating disorders have been traumatized and their bulimic and other self-destructive behaviors can be understood as legacy of trauma, either as a way to express self-hate and chastise themselves by punishing their bodies (Ferentz, 2011), or as a way to cope, self-soothe, and gain control. Sometimes they even show a full-blown post-traumatic stress disorder. The therapeutic implication is that the trauma has to be connected to the eating-distressed behavior and carefully addressed in therapy (Fallon & Wonderlich, 1997).

Key Assessment Questions

When interviewing eating-distressed persons and their partners and/or family members, there are a number of questions we like to ask in order to get a comprehensive understanding of their situation. Most of these questions can be posed to the whole family (or both members of the couple); others are better asked separately. For instance, if we are working with a adolescent who just began starving herself, we will not ask her if she is abusing laxatives or diuretics, and instead will ask the parents about that when she is not present. Although it is likely that she is aware of that option, we do not want to make it easier to learn new "anorexic tricks."

Some of the examples of the assessment questions we ask are as follows:

- "What is your weight and height? Is there any specific weight you have in mind as an "ideal weight"? How has your weight evolved over the last years?"
- "What foods do you eat and in what quantity? How often? How fast?"
- "Are there any 'forbidden foods' for you?"
- "Do you like to eat alone or do you usually eat with your family/partner? Do you eat standing or sitting?"
- "Are you aware if she is using laxatives, diuretics, or enemas? Does she drink a lot of water? Does she vomit after eating?"
- "Is she constantly moving or restless? Does this behavior increase after meals?"
- "How much do you exercise? How often?"
- "What physical consequences of anorexia/bulimia are you experiencing *already*? Do you have frequent headaches, sore throat, dental problems ... [bulimia]? Do you have lanugo [fine, downy body hair], dry skin, bad breath, are you often constipated ... [anorexia]? Have you lost your menses?"
- "What consequences are you experiencing in the different areas of your life as a result of your problems with eating [family, friends, dating, studies, work]?"
- "How is the eating problem interfering with your social life? Do your friends support you against anorexia/bulimia, or are they supporting it against you?"
- "How are you using the Internet? Does your daughter visit proAna sites?"

To inquire about possible traumatic triggers of the eating-distressed habit:

- "What is it that you cannot stomach in your family/couple relationship? In your relations with peers?"
- "Has there been any past physical, emotional, or sexual abuse?"
- "Is there any abuse going on right now in your family, at school, with peers?"

It is also important to understand the possible positive function that the eating-distressed habit (especially bulimia and binge-eating) may serve for the person, asking the following questions:

- "In what way does bingeing/purging help you?"
- "What other alternatives do you have for soothing yourself/fighting boredom/handling anger …?"
- "What would be the disadvantage of pushing anorexia/bulimia out of your life altogether?"
- "What will you miss most once anorexia/bulimia is out of your life?"
- "What other problems would you have to face once you overcome anorexia/bulimia? Please tell me your second answer; the first one ("None") I already know … and I don't believe it" (Watzlawick, 1993).

We also like to explore the strengths of the eating-distressed person. Some exceptions-seeking questions include:

- "What is different on those occasions when you take a stand against anorexia/bulimia and eat what *you* want, not what she tries to impose?"
- "What is different during those times when you simply eat what you feel like eating, not what anorexia/bulimia says you are supposed to eat?"
- "How did you make the decision to let your partner know about the 'bulimia secret'? Where did you get the courage to do so?"

Family and Couple Dynamics

In the family therapy field, there is a long tradition of understanding eating disorders as a consequence of dysfunctional family dynamics. Anorexia has been depicted as a result of a pathological "family game" (Selvini-Palazzoli, Cecchin, Prata, & Boscolo, 1978); as one more move in the "dirty game" that the family members were playing, with the parents fighting each other and trying to gain their daughter's loyalty (Selvini-Palazzoli, Cirillo, Selvini, & Sorrentino, 1998), as a symptom of a restrictive and rigid family (Onnis, 1988); or as a strategic move to re-balance an unbalanced family structure (Madanes, 1981). Structural therapists (Minuchin, Rosman, & Baker, 1978) emphasized that families of anorectic girls were usually conflict-avoidant, rigid, and enmeshed, with over-involved parents constraining their daughters' personal space.

Nowadays, the view of the role of family and couples dynamics in the causation, maintenance, and treatment of eating disorders is more balanced, and does not blame the parents. Modern family therapy approaches to eating disorders accept that the family and couple do have an important role in the *treatment* of eating disorders, but do not see them as their *cause* (Dare & Eisler, 2000; Eisler, 2005; Le Grange & Lock, 2007; Lock, Le Grange, Agras, & Dare, 2001). In other words, it is accepted that the onset of eating-distressed behaviors can be due to a wide array of causative factors, with the future eating-distressed person basically "being at the wrong place at the wrong time." The distorted family patterns observed by so many family therapists are not the *cause*, but the *consequence* of the eating disorder, a problem that deeply affects all family members. For instance, the parents, anguished by their inability to help their daughter and scared by a life-threatening condition, are likely to disagree, to mishandle their disagreements, and to distance as a result. If there was some previous marital discord, their daughter's predicament may act like a magnifying glass and pave the way for open marital conflict and even divorce. In other words, once an eating problem is established, it becomes a potent "organizer" of the family interaction (Rolland, 1994), a theme around which the whole family is organized (Eisler, 2005). Unfortunately, this family organization eventually contributes to the problem, with the parents or the partner inadvertently reinforcing the distressed eating habits they intended to correct. Professional intervention may also contribute to the problem, if ill-informed helpers inadvertently blame the parents and therefore disempower them, or if they fail to pay attention to the biological aspects of the problem.

Another side to the relational embeddedness of an eating disorder is that, as we discussed above, it may serve important interpersonal functions for the eating-distressed person. For instance, the sense of personal control that the client feels when she succeeds with her strict diet may protect her from her feelings of personal powerlessness and of not having a voice in her family. Or a divorced mother's bulimia may effectively protect her from socializing and risking the start of a new romantic relationship.

Treatment Strategies and Major Therapeutic Experiments for Eating-Distressed Clients

With eating-distressed habit cases, it is usually not difficult to establish a collaborative partnership with the parents or the couple partner, but it is often more difficult with the client herself, especially with women at the restrictive anorectic end of the diagnostic continuum. In fact, restrictive anorectics are likely not to see a problem at all, except the incessant nagging of their parents or couple partners around food.

A basic element of building cooperation with eating-distressed clients is to show them that we are on their side, that we truly want to listen to their personal goals and find out what (besides food and exercise issues) they want from us. We carefully avoid getting into power struggles with the client around food or exercise and make every effort to show her that we respect her strengths and resources, and invite her to be our expert consultant (Selekman, 2005, 2009). The provision of choices, an ingredient of most tested treatment packages for eating disorders, can easily be part of family or couple therapy as well, and will promote the therapeutic alliance and the empowerment of the client. Possible choices are around the frequency of sessions; if the client wants some personal session time or not; if she wishes to receive some psychoeducational information or not; if she would like to learn some relaxation or mindfulness techniques or not; and so forth.

The result of our deliberate efforts to build a collaborative partnership is that we usually do not have the experience that so many therapists report of having to fight "manipulative" or even "aggressive" clients. On the contrary, we are usually able to create a true therapeutic partnership: a qualitative research conducted on a small sample of eight eating-disordered clients successfully treated by my colleagues and I (MB) showed that all clients perceived a very positive therapeutic alliance (García, 2006). During in-depth personal interviews conducted at their homes, they explained that, in contrast to their previous therapeutic experiences, they had not felt judged but accepted and understood. As one client shared, "You could really talk to the therapist without worrying that he would criticize or blame you."

Healthy Eating is the Best Medicine

With anorectic clients, we take the implicit stance that eating more and better is inevitable. Therefore the question is not whether the client will eat more or not, but of how and when she will. Nutrition and exercise are medical issues: our task as therapists is not to force clients to eat, but to help them to deal with the anxiety and discomfort that will initially go with their inevitable increased food intake or exercise decrease. With bulimic clients or binge-eaters our position is that clients gradually restore more regular eating habits; this may or may not involve increased intake. Here, our task is not to prevent clients from bingeing, but to make bingeing unnecessary by assisting clients to change their eating patterns and serve the functions of the binging/purging through less harmful means. From this position we may also provide some psychoeducation regarding food and eating, if necessary:

- The goal is not to reach a predetermined weight, but to eat in a healthy way. The only "good weight" is the weight a person keeps when eating and exercising healthily.

- "Healthy eating" means eating when hungry, and stopping to eat when full. It is also described as "intuitive" or "attuned" eating (Maltz, 2011). Eating-distressed habits disturb the normal bodily perceptions of hunger and satiety. Eating-distressed persons need some time and some training to be able to feel these perceptions again.
- Slow and mindful eating is helpful, especially for persons with bulimia or binge-eaters. This involves having enough time for meals, sitting down to eat, if possible in the company of others, and without distractions like computer games or television.
- A rule of thumb is to have three meals a day, with two or three snacks in between.
- "If you forbid something, you make it irresistible." Therefore, healthy eating includes "forbidden foods." As clients give themselves permission to eat formerly forbidden foods they start to crave less on them.
- Adequate aerobic exercise is encouraged.
- As heat appears to be helpful to re-set the exercise/food intake feedback loop in anorexic clients, we have recently began to recommend increasing the temperature at home, at least during meal times, if possible up to 78–80°C. Warm showers after eating, taking low-temperature saunas or UVA rays may also be helpful, given that there are apparently no differences between different warming strategies (Cerrato, Carrera, Vazquez, Echevarria, & Gutiérrez, 2012).

Taking a Stand Against the Eating Disorder

As we have seen, most therapeutic programs for eating-disordered clients include some cognitive work in order to re-structure "distorted cognitions." We have found that externalization of the eating disorder (Jacob, 2001; Maisel, Epston, & Borden, 2004; White, 2007, 2011; White & Epston, 1990) is an excellent strategy to challenge eating-disordered cognitions without attacking the eating-disordered person. Once the externalized eating disorder has been located as the externalized enemy, there are a number of strategies to start fighting it. On the cognitive level, we like to invite our clients to watch out for the "anorectic/bulimic traps," i.e., the eating-disordered thoughts that mislead them, for example, "If I eat just a bite of this cookie I will gain two pounds at least"; "If I start eating more, I will not be able to stop anymore." These, in turn, might be linked to thoughts like "If I put on weight, no one will love me." Typical bulimic traps are "You have eaten this one cookie, so you spoiled it; you may as well now eat all of them" (counter-regulation); "Just don't think about it, have it all and then you can purge." A first step in counteracting these traps might be to invite clients to candidly look at them and realize that they are just that, traps, not truths, and maybe even congratulate anorexia or bulimia on how credible they make them sound. Another step along the same line might be to start identifying more realistic thoughts. One good option is to invite the client to write the anorectic/bulimic thoughts on the left side of a notepad, and then to jot down the reasonable responses on the right. Ranking them by credibility (0 = feels false; 10 = feels completely true) allows the client to keep track of how the healthy thoughts slowly become more credible. Another step that can be taken is to start "rebellious action" against the tyranny of anorexia/bulimia. We invite clients to take small, symbolic steps that defy the eating disorder dictatorship, and then to watch how the tyrant tries to fight back, and how the clients manages to keep determined and not to fall into the anorectic/bulimic traps. Examples of small symbolic steps might be to eat a piece of candy while pronouncing some defying words, or to provocatively and sensually enjoy a tiny piece of chocolate.

We frame these small exercises not as a way to eat more, but as a way to fight for freedom. Pattern disruption interventions from the brief therapy (O'Hanlon & Weiner-Davis, 1989; Nardone, Verbitz, & Milanese, 1999) and cognitive-behavioral literature (Fairburn, 1985, 2008; Wilson, Fairburn, & Agras, 1997) can also be framed as ways for clients to follow their own decisions and disrupt the rigidity of her anorectic/bulimic enemy's brainwashing thoughts. From this perspective, it makes sense to ask the client for instance to put on make-up before bingeing or to put on a red hat while vomiting (Nardone et al., 1999); or to ask her to take 10 minutes before bingeing to compose a note describing how she would feel and what she would be thinking after the complete episode or, alternatively, if she avoided the episode (Orimoto & Vitousek, 1992). We like to disrupt the rigid binge/purge cycle by inviting the client to delay purging after bingeing. This is a classical behavioral intervention (Garner, Vitousek, & Pike, 1997; Vanderlinden, Norre, & Vandereycken, 1992), but we find it most useful to do it in a strategic way (Nardone et al., 1999): if the client has binged, she may vomit, but must do so after exactly 30 minutes, "not one minute less, not one minute more." In the first stages of treatment, when even delaying vomiting is too difficult, we instruct the client to repeat three times the phrase "vomiting helps me to binge more and put on weight" before purging.

Making the Externalized Eating-distressed Habit Redundant

As clients feel that they are regaining some leverage in relation to the eating disorder, we like to emphasize client choice in a broader, "existential" sense (Isebaert, 2005). If the eating-distressed habit is serving some important function for the client, like soothing herself, numbing unpleasant feelings, relaxing or getting a feeling of control over her own life, it is crucial that the client finds other choices, other ways to accomplish her goals.

There are a number of therapeutic experiments that we like to use, according to the function the habit is serving. The HALT exercise as used by Frederike Jacob (2001) invites the bingeing or overeating client to consider, when she feels like eating, how she is feeling. Is she really Hungry? Or is she Anxious, Lonely or maybe just Tired? We like to add "G" for "feeling Guilty." For each of the answers, various alternatives can be discussed and prepared. A common answer to the HALT experiment is that the client is feeling anxious and that the bingeing or purging is her way of handling anxiety. In that case, it makes the most sense to explore other anxiety-reducing options. Maybe the client has her own relaxation techniques which she uses in other contexts (taking a warm bath; painting her nails; listening to certain music), but forgets to use them when the eating-distressed habit is trying to get the best of her. Another possibility might be that she would like to learn some new techniques. In that case, we offer mindfulness meditation and related practices like those described in Chapter 10, or other traditional relaxation procedures.

Quite often, bulimic behaviors express an adolescent's or woman's dissatisfaction with important interpersonal relationships and her inability to assert herself. In these cases, learning to say "No" to other things frees the client to start saying "Yes" to food and self-care. For these clients, we like to suggest the experiment of saying "No" at least once per day to someone important and to watch what effect that has on her. If too much guilt is stirred up, some additional externalization might be useful, for instance by talking about guilt as if it were a spider that clings onto the client with its many legs, and then discussing ways to keep it at bay

One experiment that we find very useful is the "Becoming less than perfect" assignment. This experiment, inspired by early Mental Research Institute (MRI) writings (Fisch et al., 1975) is especially useful for clients at the anorectic side of the spectrum who feel compelled to be "perfect" all the time. As cognitive-behavioral therapists have also come to acknowledge (Fairburn et al., 2008), the need to be perfect (great grades, great looks, best performance) is an excellent playground for obsessiveness, rigidity, and self-imposed starvation. However, instead of analyzing perfectionism with the client and making analytical decisions on how to deal with it, we prefer to follow the "know by doing" strategy by inviting the client to try something different, to do one small thing wrong on purpose each day. As the client is very concerned about her looks, the "becoming less than perfect task" involves, of course, some imperfection in her outfit, in her make-up, or in the way her hair is arranged. This homework task can seem very scary at the beginning, but most clients end up enjoying it. An important part of it is to spend some session time using narrative questions to discuss how the "mistakes" felt, which ones were even amusing, what that means in terms of personal freedom, and what areas of their personality might start to develop in surprising ways after this discovery.

Getting Your Life Back

Many of our clients have been suffering eating disorders for a long time before they come to see us, and this means that at that point in time their lives are usually pretty disrupted. If the onset of the eating disorder was when they were teenagers, it is possible that the client did not live most of the normative experiences of adolescence like hanging out with friends or dating. Having a restricted social, professional, and/or sexual life leaves a lot of room for the disorder, for instance by leaving more time for obsessive ruminations, food rituals, and so on. For this reason, we see any step towards a more social and active life as a noteworthy exception to the rigidity that the eating problem usually imposes and celebrate and expand on any news of new acquaintances or friends, of excursion or holiday plans, new social activities or romantic relationships. If these exceptions do not happen spontaneously, we use a variety of procedures to prompt them:

- There are a number of experiments that help to rebuild self-esteem and a feeling of confidence. In addition to those discussed in Chapter 3, we may simply invite the client to pay close attention to those occasions when she feels more self-confident (or with higher self-esteem, or more …), or elaborate more and ask her to keep a "self-esteem diary" where she writes down the moments when she felt more confident, what she was doing, with whom, etc.
- We might start a "research project" on her strengths, inviting her to get positive feedback from family, friends, teachers, or even neighbors (on her values, not on her looks!). She might post some of these positive messages to herself or add some music to them to create a "self-esteem tune." Again, the main strategy is to follow the client's lead: instead of telling her what we see as her values and strengths (something we can do later), we try to create a context where she "discovers" it on her own, and with the help of others.
- Building on Giorgio Nardone's ideas on what he calls "ascetic anorectics" (Nardone et al., 1999), we like to help restrictive girls to reclaim their bodies and their sexuality. One experiment we like to use is to invite the client to take one day a week and behave as "a really attractive and sexy woman" all day long, and notice what difference that makes. If that is too much, we may start by simply asking her to pay very close attention to those occasions when she has "sensual feelings" in any part of her body, and then move on to "erotic feelings." If the person has suffered sexual abuse, it is better to go even slower, and start with some body art work, non-threatening massages, soothing hot baths, and so on (Dolan, 1991).
- An experiment of a different kind that we have also taken from Giorgio Nardone is the "anthropological task": he invites the clients to pay very close attention to the problems the people around her have. This was originally designed as a way to de-center the client from her obsessive self-preoccupation, which we have found to be a useful alternative to prompt a meaningful reconnection with the outside social world.

Working with the Family or Couple Partner

If the situation has become chronic, it is very likely that the parents or the couple partner have submitted to the demands of the eating-distressed habit, in their well-meant but ineffective effort to appease it and at least prevent the daughter/wife from getting worse: maybe a husband has accepted that he and his eating-distressed wife eat in different rooms; or the mother is doing all the cooking according to her daughter's wishes; or no one in the family is "allowed" to eat meat. We will help the family or couple partner identify what behaviors are imposed on them by the eating-distressed habit, and assist them in resisting these impositions.

It is also important that the family takes a clear stand against anorexia/bulimia. If we are working with a client and her parents this means that, as long as the daughter is not responsibly in charge of her own health, their parents will be. Therefore, they will make the decisions around food and exercising, and, if necessary, will take turns in monitoring the behavior of their daughter. This has to be done in a firm but gentle way, without criticism or hostility towards their daughter, and always giving the message that they love her. It is very important that the parents together as a team resist any attempts from their daughter to create splits in this common front. This structural family therapy strategy (Lock & Le Grange, 2005; Minuchin et al., 1978) has to be adapted working with a couple, as the partner does not have the power or the means to take over control effectively. However, instructing the partner to refuse any collaboration with the eating-distressed habit, and to give a clear and coherent message that he loves her and wants her to conquer the habit, will make a difference.

In addition to interrupting ineffective attempted solutions around eating or purging, and to protecting the space and wellbeing of all family members, family or couple therapy might also be necessary to transform entrenched negative family and/or couple dynamics that might feed into the eating problem. Take the case of Ainhoa, a 11-year-old girl who for several years had been refusing to eat. In the first session, a longstanding marital conflict was evident. The parents explained that their relationship had deteriorated some 10 years ago, long before the problems with Ainhoa had started, after the birth of Alberto, a disabled boy. In this case, we helped the parents to handle Ainhoa's behavior in a much more effective way, but this required some couple therapy. At first, the parents were reluctant to undergo any couple work, but once they saw the benefits not just for them, but for Ainhoa and Alberto, they agreed to give it a try. Once they had processed their feelings of guilt around Alberto's disability, they were able to improve their communication and to renew their intimacy as a couple. This, in turn, made it much easier for them to handle Ainhoa in an effective way.

In other cases, the eating-distressed habit does serve some important interpersonal function for the client in her family or couple relationship. If the appropriate assessment questions confirm this, it will be necessary to re-organize part of the family structure so that this function can be served in a healthier way. For instance, Elena, a 32-year-old athlete, confided to us that she was ambivalent about giving up her bulimia habit. She knew that bulimia was a big handicap for her athletic performance, but it was also the only area in her life where she felt she had a "private, secret life" apart from her partner and trainer. Based on this information, we did not involve the partner as a co-therapist for bulimia, but instead helped the couple to re-negotiate their conjoint and personal spaces. In this case, the couple partner was a great help by *not* helping. Quite the opposite happened in the family of Andrés, a 17-year-old teenager. The third of five children, less brilliant in school than his siblings and rather shy, he had always felt "invisible" in his family. When he started to over-exercise and to lose weight, he was pleased to find out how much attention he was suddenly getting. Here, therapy helped his parents to control his exercising, but at the same time to pay more attention when he was *not* showing any of his anorectic symptoms. Some work with the group of siblings helped to re-balance the relationship in the fraternal subsystem. Below, we provide a case example that illustrates the challenges of helping an eating-distressed client and her partner conquer a longstanding eating-distressed habit.

Case Example

Building Trust with Coins and Swords

Ana, 34, was referred to me (MB) by a former psychology student of mine. She lived with her husband Antonio, 35, and their son Pablo, 10, in a small village in southern Galicia. According to the referring person, Ana had been suffering from anorexia for almost 20 years, had had a couple of hospitalizations and had been in psychiatric treatment for her eating disorder the last 10 years. Now she was "very skinny," with a weight just around 43kg at 1.60m tall (BMI under 17). Some six months ago, her husband had discovered that Ana had spent all the family's savings on gambling with machines and playing bingo. No one in her family had been aware of her problem with gambling, so the discovery came as a big shock. Ana and Antonio were on the verge of divorce, but finally decided to stay together. They also decided to look for some extra help and, although they lived a five-hour drive from Salamanca, accepted the offer from my former student to be seen by our team.

The First Family Session

It was not just Ana and Antonio who showed up for our first session, but also their son Pablo and Ana's parents. After some small talk about their journey to Salamanca, I explained that I wanted to get to know them better by their strengths before going into what had brought them to therapy. I started with Pablo, a handsome kid with lively eyes, asking him what he was good at, and he proudly told me about his basketball playing. When I asked him what he loved most about his parents and grandparents, he confided that his mom was a very courageous person, that he liked Dad's quiet ways, and that he loved grandma's cooking and the stories his grandfather told him when it was bedtime. He explained that he really liked to stay at his grandparents' house, and that he usually had dinner and breakfast and slept there. I asked Ana if she would agree with her son about being courageous and she said, with a sad look in her eyes, "I used to be, but I don't know if I am courageous anymore." In fact, she looked exhausted, worn out, much older than her age. Her father chimed in and stated that his daughter was courageous indeed, and that he felt very proud of her fighting so many problems for so long. I invited him to expand on what other qualities might be helping Ana in her "fight" and he added that she was a very good-natured person, although lately she was getting a bit aggressive sometimes. As I did not want to move into problem talk that soon, I moved the conversation over to the grandpa's hobbies and interests. He explained that he loved to go fishing with his grandson. The grandma was also a nature person: she enjoyed taking long walks in the mountains near the village where they lived, but she resented that Ana would not join her anymore. Which of Ana's virtues would she underscore? I asked. She replied that her daughter had a "very, very big heart." I then joined with Ana, who lit up a little bit when she described that she liked painting in watercolors and going with Antonio to watch their son's basketball games. When I inquired what she liked most about her husband, she said that he was a very patient and kind man. Antonio got tears in his eyes. I invited him to share what he liked best about Ana, but he was obviously overwhelmed and unable to say anything. I commented that he must love his wife very deeply. He silently agreed, and took his son's hand. The grandparents and Ana seemed moved, too.

I asked them what they were expecting to get out of the meeting in order to feel that it had really been worth it to take such a long trip to see me. The grandparents were about to answer, but I said that I would prefer to hear Pablo first, and then to continue the conversation with the grown-ups only. The boy was very clear: "I want my mom to become healthy again, and that mommy and daddy won't divorce and we are a happy family again." This time, both Antonio's and Ana's eyes filled with tears, and they took each other's hand. "You must love them both also very, very deeply," I offered. Then I explained that we, the grown-ups, would do our best to improve things and also invited him to keep track of any improvements that he might witness over the next weeks. Pablo left the therapy room with a smile.

I decided to continue the conversation with Ana first, and invited her to share her expectations of therapy. She explained that she basically wanted to be trusted again, both by her husband and her parents. She furthermore described how bad she had felt being trapped in the "gambling thing," and how much she resented the way that her husband's family had treated her when everything came out. "They treated me like a thief, like a murderer. I don't deserve that." She added she was sorry for the "mistakes" she had committed in the past, and felt that gambling was now under control, because she had not gambled over the last five months. But she complained that no one trusted her to be really "clean" and that her family's mistrust made her feel depressed and anxious. When I asked what her explanation was for how she got into gambling, she said that it had been a mixture of "loneliness and boredom," as she had lost her job almost two years ago. "I just thought I could make some money, and then I got hooked on it." When I asked how she explained that she had been able to overcome this gambling problem, she said that what had helped her was to see the damage she had done to her family. Being on the verge of bankruptcy and divorce had been a "definitive cure." The problem was that after it all she now felt exhausted, depressed, and "under parole, like a criminal." "I simply sometimes feel so down in the dumps that I don't have the energy to keep on fighting. I asked her how come she had not given up. She paused for a moment, and then answered quietly that she loved her son and her husband too much. Hearing Pablo say things like what he had just shared in the session was reason enough for her to continue the fight. I asked her how she would like me to help. "I think it would be great if you helped me to trust myself, to build up some self-esteem, and Antonio and my parents to trust me." I inquired what trust would look like, and she said that her husband would not be nagging her about food and her parents would not be spying on her because of the gambling. I took the chance to ask if she wanted some help with the "food stuff," but she said no, "It is just that I don't feel like eating, I am too sad and tired."

When I turned to Antonio to find out what his expectations of therapy were, he told me that he had been the one to take the initiative to come over to see me. "Ana would have never come on her own." He explained that he had felt very hurt and badly betrayed by what Ana had done with the family savings, but for him that was of secondary importance; his top priority was Ana's wellbeing. He was very worried about his wife: He conceded that "maybe" the gambling problem was "over," but he didn't like to see Ana so depressed, so aloof, and isolated. "It is as if she were 8 years old again, she is not taking any responsibility, she is letting her parents do everything for her. I mean, that is very nice and caring of them, but I think she is letting herself go." I asked Antonio what would be a small sign of progress for him. He said that he would need to feel that he could trust Ana again. When I asked what he needed to see in order to trust his wife, he did not mention the gambling, but replied that he would love to see Ana taking the initiative, cooking again for the family, and also eating. "Would that help you trust her again?" "Yes," he said.

When I asked the grandparents what their best hopes for therapy were, they both said that the gambling issue had been a great shock for them, but that now they wanted, more than anything else, to see their daughter "happy again." I inquired what would be a small sign that she was happy again. "To see her smiling, to see her doing things again, taking care of Pablo, going out with Antonio and Pablo" said the grandmother. "Yes, to feel that we can trust her again, that we all can trust her," the grandpa added. "So what would be the smallest sign that you can trust her?" "Well, to see that she can take care of herself, that she gets up in the morning, that she eats well, that she starts looking for a job."

In order to instill some positive emotion in the session and also get clear on goals, I asked the family to imagine that, that very night, a miracle would happen while they were sleeping and all the problems that brought them in would be solved. How would they notice, the next morning, that a miracle had happened? I turned to Ana and Antonio and asked them first: "What would be the first sign, for your son, that this miracle has indeed happened?" Antonio did not hesitate. "He would see more of his mother, instead of spending so many hours at his grandparents'." I tried to get some specifics by asking, "And what would you be doing together that you don't do now?" "We would have breakfast together, the three of us, and then I would go to work and Ana would take Pablo to school, instead of leaving that to grandpa. That would be a big change." He added that Ana would also take charge of Pablo in other ways, and that therefore she would not spend so many hours in her room ruminating. "How will you react when you see that, Antonio?" "I would be the happiest man in the world!" "What do you imagine doing with Ana, the two of you alone?" Antonio paused for a moment and, looking at Ana, he said that they would go out together for walks along the river, again. They would also plan for an excursion with Pablo, over the weekend. "That would be great," Ana added.

I felt that was a good moment to hear about Ana's miracle: "What would be the first sign for you?," I wondered. "I would not feel so ashamed," she said, "I would go out for walks on my own, without wondering what neighbors and family might think of me. I would feel that people trust me again." I tried to get specific and wondered who would be the first person that she would like to see trusting her and how would it show. "Antonio. We would communicate more. He would talk to me when he arrives home, not just sit in front of the set and drink a beer. He has been doing that for months, now. It is so depressing." I asked Ana how she saw herself reacting when Antonio changed his ways. "I would be nicer to him, also." "And you would take those walks?," I offered. "Yes," she replied.

I tried to get the eating into the picture, by asking how the miracle would show when it came to food. But Ana did not seem very interested in the topic: "Nothing special, I don't think that would change a lot." I asked if she imagined eating less or more. "Well, maybe I would feel like eating a bit more," she conceded, "But, more than that, I would feel proud of myself and my family. I would feel like a competent mother again."

I sensed that Ana did not feel comfortable talking about food at the moment, so I shifted gears and asked the grandparents about their view of the miracle. They both said they wanted to see their daughter "happier," and explained that would show in her not gambling anymore, finding a job, and eating more. I asked them what they imagined they would see going on between Antonio and Ana; they said they would see them growing closer again. Would they also like to see Pablo and his mother getting closer? Yes, they said. "But I don't think he should stop staying at our place," the grandpa added. I wondered if they would feel like they were losing him. He conceded that he would miss Pablo a lot if he started to come over less often. I invited Ana and Antonio to share their views on that. Both of them assured grandpa that he would never lose Pablo, even if Ana felt better and could be more in charge of him.

As we were running out of time, I asked everyone where they saw their problems, on a scale from 1 (problem at its worst) to 10 (completely solved). Ana said "2, but only because I have quit gambling, otherwise I would be at a 1." Antonio said 4, and the grandparents 5. I wondered what Antonio and Ana's parents were seeing, that she did not, that came into their "4" and "5" ratings. They explained that the fact that Ana had accepted to go to therapy was a plus. Antonio also said that he could see Ana making some more efforts at home lately, and that she was also talking about taking Pablo to school. "So maybe you are about to get one point up soon?" I asked Ana. She nodded. "So how will you know you are at a 3?" She shrugged her shoulders and said, "I don't know. But I will know when I am there. I will not stay at home all day, down in the dumps, brooding." I then asked, "Is there anything Antonio could do, your parents could do, that would help you get one point higher?" She paused. Then she spoke in a very clear and calm voice. "It would help if my parents offered help, but without insisting. It makes me feel like I am handicapped, like I can't do it by myself. And I would also like them to stop spying on me." "How would that show?" "They would not ring me up every hour. They would not show up without notice. They would ask me to help them out, for a change!" I asked what Antonio could do to help. "Just talk to me when he comes home." All three of them listened attentively while Ana was making her point. I felt they had gotten the message.

After the break, I started by complimenting Ana for having been able to overcome gambling and to be fighting so hard, in spite of her feeling so exhausted, for herself and for her family. I also complimented the family for being so caring and supportive. I emphasized Antonio's patience and his wish to trust Ana again. I underscored the effort he had made during the session to communicate his views, hopes, and fears clearly. Ana nodded. The team and I could see how much Ana and Antonio loved and cared for one other. They held their hands in response to my compliment. As for the grandparents, I said it struck me how important their help had been in the most difficult times, and how willing they were now to slowly step back in order to allow their daughter to recover more fully. They all nodded their heads.

I further explained that I could see they had a long way to go in order to slowly rebuild trust and happiness, and that it would be hard work for all of them, especially for Ana. Again, Ana agreed. I added that it would be important to go really slow, in order to keep a good energy level and not to overburden anyone. Looking more at the grandparents, I expressed my confidence that now they had all heard each other's wishes and fears and they would be able to slowly head in that direction. I finally suggested a number of "experiments" that they could perform and that would help them make things a little bit easier.

I encouraged the four of them to keep track of any small signs that parts of the miracle started to happen, and also to keep track of anything they did in the following weeks that helped the situation to improve just one point on the scale. I stressed that the grandparents should not share their observations with Ana or Antonio, but should write them down instead and tell me when they came back.

I gave Ana a big Mexican coin. I told her that, whenever she felt "down in the dumps" at home, she should toss the coin. If she got heads, she was to go out for a short walk; if it was in the evening, she might even want to pick up Antonio at his workplace. If she got tails, she need not do anything special.

I encouraged Antonio to take a risk and take his wife for a walk at least twice per week, and notice what positive effect that had on them. I also encouraged him to plan for a trip, he and his wife with Pablo. Finally, I asked Antonio and Ana to keep track of any occasion when they felt they were communicating more, or about to do so. I would ask them about that in the next session, for which I invited only Ana and Antonio.

The Second Session

Ana and Antonio came back pleased with their progress. Ana reported that she had tossed the coin almost every day, but in the beginning she had only gotten tails. Then, when she started to get heads, she had begun to go out. The first times had been hard for her, but she found it helped to stop her "brooding" and one day she even ventured to pick up Antonio. She had enjoyed walking with him hand in hand "and feeling that he was not ashamed of me, but proud." She was also starting to feel a bit more confident "as a mother." This had not translated into her doing much different at home, but she was getting up earlier. No problems with gambling or thoughts about it.

Antonio, on his part, had taken Ana for a walk twice. He had enjoyed the walks and had even taken the step to make a trip to the mountains on a Saturday, with Pablo. Although Ana was "not 100% herself," they had enjoyed the day. When they came home, Antonio had suggested that Pablo stayed with them for the night, but Ana had preferred to leave him with her parents. I took a risk and, a bit tongue-in-cheek, asked if that meant they had taken the chance to have some "wild sex" that Saturday night. The mood in the session turned negative. "No, I was far too tired for that" said Ana in a flat voice. Antonio looked sad. "*Wild* sex? I have almost forgotten what sex is, altogether." "I can't believe you," I replied. "When was the last time you two guys made love?" There was an embarrassing silence. "One year, at least," whispered Antonio.

I decided to continue to take risks and asked, "When, do you think, will you be able to have intimacy and good sex again?" Antonio turned to Ana. She paused and then explained that first she needed to feel a stronger connection with Antonio and better communication with him. He had opened up a bit the last month, but still they were not having much of a conversation. In fact, she resented his coming home and sitting down in front of the television, having a beer, and not asking her about her day. Antonio conceded that some days he was too tired when he came home, but he also shared that he was afraid of asking Ana too many questions. "She might feel I am questioning her, that I want to find out if she has gambled again." Ana was surprised to hear that; for her, there was a clear difference between just talking about the day and going into long interrogations about her gambling. Antonio had been doing that after the whole gambling affair had come up, but he was not doing it anymore. "You mean you would not suspect me suspecting you," Antonio asked. Ana said, "Of course not." Antonio seemed relieved.

I asked them how they saw the situation on the scale. She said "4" and added "Double last month." I complimented her on that and asked her how she had done it. She explained that her parents had been very helpful but also very respectful since the first session, and that Antonio had been more trusting. "Anything *you* are doing that has helped you go up to that 4?" Ana said the coin had been very useful, and that she had been trying to be more active. Getting up earlier and accepting the trip to the mountains was part of that. "Is the effort paying off?" I wondered. "Yes, it is."

When I turned to Antonio, he said he still saw things at a 4. He certainly felt that Ana was improving, but he could not give her a 5[1] "as long as she is not eating." Ana did not seem very happy with her husband's remark. Even so, I tried to get more into that subject. "Antonio, what would be for you the smallest sign, a very small sign, that as far as eating is concerned, Ana is also slowly moving up a little bit?" "I am not sure if a small sign would be enough. She is just so skinny". I turned to Ana and asked her what a very small sign of progress would look like for her. She talked to Antonio, suddenly angry, "For me the only sign of progress would be that you and my parents stop nagging me about that." Antonio also became angry and was about to reply, so I decided to stop the conjoint session at that point.

I began my conversation with Ana validating her position. "It must be tough for you to have Antonio nagging you on this eating thing. I can see he is giving you a hard time." She agreed, and vented how tired she was of his and her parents' surveillance of her food intake. She felt "on parole in that, too," treated like a child, over-controlled. "What would it take for them to relax a bit?" I inquired. She replied that if she put on three or four pounds they would leave her alone. "But I just don't feel like eating. And I have always been skinny. Well, at least since I started with this anorexia thing." I took the opportunity to explore what the "anorexia thing" was for her. She explained that it involved eating very little, and very few things: some salads, some fruit, and some white fish. The good news was that there was no vomiting or exercising, but even so Ana felt that anorexia had messed up her life completely. I invited her to elaborate on that, and she explained that anorexia had been distancing her from her family and making her feel bad about herself. Did that mean that she wanted to take a stand against anorexia? "Maybe," she said.

I felt I was being too direct, and decided to take a step back: "You said your family would relax if you put on three or four pounds. Do you think it might be good for you, in some way, to gain those three pounds?" I ventured. "Yes, of course," she said "If I could eat more, yes." "Why would it be good?" She replied that it would help her family to worry less. "What other advantages would it have?" She would also have more energy, Ana conceded. Maybe she would also look better. "Okay, so what you are saying is that it would be good for you not to have your family on

---

[1] In Spain, the school grades go from 0 to 10, with 5 being a "pass" and 4 a "fail".

your back all the time with this, and that it would also be good for you to maybe put on some weight." She confirmed. "So what would be, just for you, not for your family, a very, very small step in that direction?" She thought for a while. "Well, I guess finding myself feeling like eating something, something tasty like a bit of chocolate or a piece of donut." "So if you felt like eating something tasty, would that also mean eating a bit more and maybe start to put on a little weight?" "Yes, it would." I asked if that would mean that she was starting to take a stand against anorexia. "Definitely," Ana answered.

After a short break I complimented Ana on the steps she had already taken over the last week, and on her willingness to take some small steps in relation to anorexia also. I encouraged her to keep track of any occasion where she might feel like eating a little bit of "something tasty." I added that it might make sense for her to write a "farewell letter to anorexia." Ana looked puzzled, and I explained that, after so many years of living with anorexia, it might be good for her to say "thank you" for the ways in which it had helped her, maybe by being good company to her, or by making her feel she had a mission, or whatever. And then of course it might also make sense to explain, in her letter, why she was making the decision to get rid of anorexia, what things she was not willing to take in any more.

After my conversation with Ana I had only some minutes left for Antonio. I shared that I was quite impressed with her willingness to talk about that issue, and that her openness was a good sign. Antonio confided how desperate he was with the situation, how deeply worried not only that Ana could relapse into gambling but that she would never overcome her anorexia. He was always telling her to eat more, trying to make her realize how skinny she was, but to no avail. He also shared that in part it was okay with him that Pablo spent so much time with the grandparents, because he felt Ana was setting a very bad example as far as eating habits were concerned. I replied that keeping Pablo away from anorexia was maybe a good idea, but not at the cost of keeping him away from his mother. Antonio accepted the idea and asked me what he could do to help Ana. I said there was something very important that he could do, but that it also was very difficult to do. I explained that I wanted Ana to really feel that she was fighting anorexia, and not Antonio. Each time he insisted that she eat something, she got detoured and started fighting him, not the real enemy. Therefore, for the next weeks I wanted him not to put any pressure on Ana as far as eating was concerned. In fact, I wanted him to encourage Ana, at least one or two times a week to eat *less*. "That is the best way for Ana to feel that you are really trusting her on this, that you are trusting her so much that you can leave her alone." Of course he should not tell Ana that this was my suggestion. Antonio was surprised, but he agreed to give it a try.

After another short break, I reconvened with Ana and Antonio, complimented them on the steps they had taken last month to get "100%" up the scale, and told them again how important it was to keep it safe and slow. I asked Ana to keep the coin tossing ritual and, whenever she got tails, give it a second try. I also asked them to spend some "catch up talking time" when Antonio came home after work: they were to sit down in the living room, the television off, and spend 15 minutes just talking about their day. I invited them to be creative and do something a little bit different each day, while talking. I also offered the experiment to have Pablo sleeping in their place at least once a week. And building on the Saturday excursion they had taken, I suggested that this time Ana and Antonio organize a "surprise trip" with Pablo. We scheduled the next appointment one month later.

The Third Session

Ana and Antonio came in smiling, with Ana looking healthier and better. She reported that she had been taking short walks every day; when she got tails with the coin, she simply had kept on tossing it until she got heads. She had also kept on being more active; a couple of days she had prepared a special dinner for her and Antonio. One day the special dinner had even led to their making love. "Wow, and you still remembered how to do it? Great!" We all laughed

Antonio and Ana also reported that they had enjoyed the "catch up talking experiment." They had used one of these moments to organize an excursion to the beach, which they had made last Saturday. They had a lot of fun and on that night Pablo stayed home with them. That allowed the three of them to have breakfast together, something they had not done for many years. In fact, the following night Pablo also stayed with his parents.

I used a scaling question to measure their progress, and both said they felt things were at a "good 5." I wondered aloud what else got things up to a 5. Ana said that Antonio was now communicating, "A little bit more," and that she also saw him trusting her more. "How does that show?" I inquired. "Well, he is not asking me so often how I am doing. And he is not on my back all the time about food." Antonio added that he saw Ana calmer and at the same time with more energy. He felt they were slowly getting closer again. "So what would you say is your recipe for your getting up to this 5?" "I think we are basically trusting each other more, communicating more, focusing on the small steps we are taking," Ana declared. Antonio agreed. I asked what they imagined the next very small step might be. Antonio said for him it would be enough to simply stay on track the following month. Ana shared that she would like to see Antonio trust her more with money management. When asked, what would that look like, she said, "Well, he will not control what I spend when I go shopping, and would simply leave the money at home." I asked Antonio if he would be willing to take that risk. He agreed.

Then I met with Ana alone for some minutes. She reported proudly that she had been able to take some "tasty little things," and that she had felt "nasty, but in a good way. "Do you mean that you are being mean to anorexia." "Yes," she said, and explained that she felt she was also eating "a little bit more." In fact, she had put on almost one pound, and felt she was looking better. "Wow! How are you doing that?" "Well, I simply felt more like eating" Then she explained that the "farewell letter" had been very important for her, although she had forgotten to bring it with her to show me. I adjusted to her "I just feel like eating" style and, instead of asking what new steps she might take, I wondered what new changes might happen. She shrugged her shoulders and smiled, "Who knows? We'll see." I closed our conversation by encouraging her to keep on defying anorexia a little bit, "in that nasty way" and to keep track of any new changes that might happen.

After the break, I complimented Ana and Antonio for the changes in their relationship and encouraged them to keep on doing what helped, especially on those days where things might feel like being a bit worse or even slipping back. I also asked them to give my congratulations to Pablo for the great job he was doing in helping them "become a family again," and to give my regards to grandma and grandpa. As there were enough improvements we decided to leave some more time until the next session, and scheduled it six weeks later.

The Fourth Session

For this session, Ana and Antonio came in with bright moods, together with Ana's parents. I began the session by asking the grandparents what improvements had struck them most. They reported that they had seen great changes in Ana: they were no longer worried about possible gambling, they saw her "mature," and becoming a competent mother again. The grandfather told me that Pablo was having dinner, sleeping, and having breakfast with his parents now. He shared that he missed spending time with Pablo, but that he could see how good it was for his grandson to live with his parents again. He was especially happy about seeing Ana and Antonio more as a couple, "I was so worried that Antonio might leave her."

The grandmother added that she saw Ana improving her eating: she was eating more and having food that before was "forbidden": chocolate, biscuits, and even some cured sausages. This time, Ana did not seem uncomfortable discussing food in front of the family. "Yes, I feel better about that, but also because Antonio and you are not on my back so much." She proudly reported that she was having regular breakfast and dinner with her husband and son. Antonio confirmed that, but pointed out that the portions were still not very large. "Well, as Mark says, let's go slow," Ana retorted smiling.

When I asked what new improvements they envisioned for the next months, Ana reported that she was about to start a three-week computing course for unemployed people, offered by the municipality of a larger neighboring town, close to their home town. She felt this would be "a start into an entirely new professional life." Antonio, however, was not so happy with the turn of events. Ana had applied for the course without telling him, and he resented the secrecy and was worried that taking the course might provoke some kind of setback. The grandparents seemed to share his concerns. The mood in the room had become suddenly negative, so I decided to tackle the issue with a series of circular questions: "What part of these concerns would you say are understandable under the circumstances, and what part do you see more as mistrust's brainchild? What do you think you could do to help keep mistrust controlled?" Ana accepted that for her family, her travelling each day to the nearby town and spending many hours there with money in her pockets could feel threatening. She also could see how her secrecy in applying for the course had sparked mistrust in Antonio, although she was disappointed by his reaction: "I kept it secret because I wanted it to be a surprise for him." She reflected that maybe ringing Antonio up around noon each day would help to calm his fears, and that it would be important to keep on spending time together now that she would start to be busier. Antonio confirmed that this would help him corner his mistrust, and added that having breakfast together would be a good way to prevent Ana from slipping back into eating too little. She accepted that.

I took some time to talk with Ana and Antonio alone and started with the progress scale. Ana felt at a 7 and Antonio at a "scared 6." I took this as an invitation to pose a confidence scale: "How confident are you that you will be able to keep things going, at least at this 7 and this 6, for the following month? 10 stands for you have all the confidence in the world, 0 no confidence at all". Ana said "an 8," but Antonio only "a 5." "So what do you think, Antonio, is Ana seeing that you don't see, and that gives her so much confidence?" Antonio had to think for a while. He then conceded that Ana might have a better knowledge of her own feelings and problems, and that maybe the fact that there was an open position to join a "Gamblers Anonymous" self-help group next week was also giving her some extra confidence. I was curious about her joining that group, now that the worst part of the gambling problem seemed to be over. "I know it might not be necessary," Ana said, "but I think it might give me some extra assurance against relapses." She explained that some six or seven years ago she had been attending an eating disorders group, and that talking to other patients had helped her. "By the way, I forgot to tell you: I have put on almost two more pounds since my last visit" I congratulated her on that, and asked if there might be anything to learn from her eating progress that might apply to the new computer course situation. "Well, as you say: Go slow!"

After taking a break, I shared with Ana, Antonio, and Ana's parents how struck I was with all the new developments. Again, I encouraged them to keep on doing what they now knew was helpful, and to do so especially whenever things might look as if they were slipping back a bit. I shared that I could see both their enthusiasm and their fears regarding the computer course, and that it is natural to feel some fear when one is about to take a major step. I encouraged Ana to calm her family down by calling them as she had offered and also to take advantage of the self-help group she was going to join. I asked her, as a private experiment, to keep track of how she successfully managed any "gambling or anorexia temptations" that might come up during the following weeks. And I encouraged Antonio and the grandparents to stay supportive and solicit regular feedback from Ana as to how they might be more helpful. We scheduled the next meeting five weeks later.

The Fifth Session

When Ana and Antonio showed up for their fifth session, something had changed. They came in bad moods, almost not looking at each other, and Ana announced right away that in fact Antonio had not wanted to come to the meeting. I thought about trying first to discuss any positive developments during the last month, but I realized they were both too angry and frustrated to follow me on that. So I decided to directly address whatever might be happening: "I see that you both look bad today. I guess that anorexia or mistrust is fighting back?" No one answered. Ana had her eyes fixed on the floor, Antonio sighed. "It is not mistrust. It is Ana," he said. I waited politely until he started to tell his version of the story. Apparently, things had gone really well for more than three weeks: Ana attended the course and was happy with that; she had started calling Antonio mid-mornings to chat with him and calm his anxieties, and after some days it had not seemed necessary. Although they were pretty busy, they had managed to keep on having breakfast together. Pablo was staying again some nights with the grandparents, but only during the week, and on weekends they had been doing things together. They were planning to do major weekend excursion to Toledo, a famous medieval city in the center of Spain. Everything seemed fine, but then Antonio found out that Ana was coming home pretty late in the evenings, three or four hours after the course finished, without telling him. So one morning he left his job earlier than usual and went home to wait for her and confront her if she came back late. As he waited, he searched her computer. He was devastated when he discovered that his wife was chatting with a fellow computer course student. The conversations were not overly sexual, but clearly flirtatious. He did not feel relieved that she was not gambling, but felt badly hurt and betrayed and, when he confronted her later that day, they got into a heated argument. Since then, they had been on an "icy standby," not having fights but also not getting any closer.

I empathized with Antonio's feelings of frustration and disappointment, hinting at how hard this last week must have been for both of them. Then I turned to Ana, to hear her version of the story. She started by saying how hurt *she* felt by Antonio's mistrust. She also reported that the first weeks were great, but in her view things had started to take a negative turn, one day Antonio failed to defend her against his family. They had met on the street during one of their walks, and she had felt insulted by how they had ignored her. She also felt that Antonio had not done anything to protect her. A similar situation occurred some days later, with former friends with whom they had cut the relationship months ago, when the gambling problem had come into the open. On top of it all, Antonio had sided with her father one day that he had blamed her for a bad grade Pablo had gotten in school. She tried to talk it over with her husband, but he was "more interested in watching soccer than in talking with me." Frustrated by Antonio's indifference and "lack of empathy" she had turned to one of her new acquaintances in the computer course. "It was never something sexual, but it is nice to have a man you can talk to and that understands your view." And then she had felt badly insulted by Antonio's suspicion about her having an affair.

I empathized with how difficult it must have been for Ana to feel left alone by her husband, and how frustrating it must have been for both of them to see that things were going well and had then taken such an unexpected turn. "I know it feels very bad to have a real crisis like this one, but for me the important thing is what you learn from it. So, what would you say, what useful pieces of wisdom have you gotten from these rocky weeks?" A long silence, again. I was starting to think that I had taken a wrong course, when Ana started to cry softly. I waited and asked her what those tears meant. "I just need to know that Antonio is 100% beside me, that he is willing to protect and take a stand for me, in spite of all the shit I brought on the family." I turned to Antonio and asked if he would like to do that. There was a hint of reproach when he said "Ana, you know that I am here for you, I have told you many times." Ana was about to retort, but I stopped her and invited Antonio to try again, "Antonio," I said, putting my hand on his shoulder, "I think you are not reaching Ana. I know you can make it better." This time Antonio physically approached Ana. His voice got very soft and gentle as he declared how much he loved her, and that he was willing to stand up against anyone or anything that hurt her. They both started to cry, and then hugged.

I waited some time and then asked Antonio what he had learned from their crisis.

"I guess that Ana is right with the communication thing. I thought I was getting it right, but now I see that I am still very bad at that. If we had talked as things started to go wrong, it would never have gotten that bad." This time, Ana offered some help. "Antonio, you are improving a lot, we are both doing it much better. It is just that sometimes you still do that coming-home-and-sitting-in-front-of-the-television thing. And sometimes that happens precisely when I need most to talk to you."

I asked if anorexia or gambling had tried to take advantage of their temporary fall-out. "Not really," Ana reported, "I lost my appetite the days after our fight, when I moved back to my parents', but I was able to eat anyway, I did not want to give anorexia a chance." I asked how she was able to do such a smart thing. "Well, it was clear to me that one problem was enough; I was having this problem with Antonio and it would have been stupid to create a second problem. So I had breakfast and lunch and dinner, even if I did not feel like it and did not have much of an appetite. And when I felt down in the dumps, I tossed the coin until I got heads." She also reported that up to that point she had been eating more, and had even put on another half pound. Antonio confirmed her report, and also said he did not have any reservations about her gambling. Ana was still going to the self-help group sessions, only once every two or three weeks, "just a reminder." "So what is different in you, Ana? I mean, it would have been relatively easy to slip back with anorexia or even with gambling, under the circumstances …" Ana thought for a while "I feel like I am a different person. I have much more confidence now. It is like anorexia and gambling belong to the past." I invited Antonio to share his thoughts: "I think Ana is a more reflective person now, she thinks twice and makes good decisions."

That was a good moment to gain some perspective and ask about the progress scale again. "If you had asked us at the beginning of the session, I would have said 1 or 2," Ana answered, and Antonio agreed. "But I feel that we are really more at a 6 or a 7 again," Ana continued. Antonio agreed again.

After the break, I shared how impressed the team and I were about the hard times they had been through, and on their ability to grow and learn from them. I agreed with their view that a "regular dose" of "communication vaccine" was an excellent way to prevent bad feelings to accumulate and explode, and I also emphasized how smart it had been not to let anorexia come back through the "back door" of their fight. I encouraged them to do more of that, as well as more of all the other things they had learned that helped them: the walks, the daily, catch-up conversations, etc. Then I turned to Antonio and explained that we had finally realized how important it is for Ana to feel he is on her side. "You know, Ana needs to feel she has a knight on her side, a strong knight who will defend her against all kind of enemies, even dragons. And that knight is you, Antonio." Without further elaboration I suggested that they did the excursion to the medieval town of Toledo as soon as possible. In Toledo, Antonio was to buy one of those miniature knight armors that are sold as souvenirs, as a present for Ana. He was to put it in some visible place in their bedroom. Antonio was intrigued with the task, and Ana displayed a bright smile. I asked her to keep track, the following weeks, of how she responded to Antonio's behaving like her knight. We scheduled the next session six weeks later.

The Sixth Session

Ana and Antonio came in with a glowing progress report. Ana had finished her computer course with excellent grades and had started a part-time job that she liked. She felt happy, competent, and very close to Antonio. He had not bought a miniature knight armor in Toledo but a replica sword, which now hung in their living room. Ana felt that he was protecting her and "defending me from nasty relatives and envious acquaintances." "So you are really using your knight sword and your imaginary armor?" I asked Antonio. "Yes," he said proudly, and added with a playful smile, "except when we make love; then I take the armor off."

Antonio added that he saw Ana stronger now, with more confidence, feeling more competent as a mother. "She is tougher with Pablo, when needed, and is also putting some more limits on her parents." Ana reported that Pablo had definitively "moved back in" with them, that her father was having a bit of a hard time with that, but that he had started to adjust. "It is good that he spends some more time with my mother," she added. Ana also shared that she was "eating well," enjoying the meals with her family and allowing herself to indulge in sweets and other treats. I asked, "With 10 standing for anorexia is defeated and kept in a small corner, a 1 meaning when it was really beating you up, where are things now?" "A safe 8 …," Ana replied, "but that is like a 10 for me." I wondered what she meant. "Well, I think it would be too much to ask for a 10, after all these years. And my 8 is good enough, more than good enough: I do not eat very much, but I eat three meals a day, I can eat with my family, I don't think all day of eating or not eating, I don't feel guilty when I eat something new or different … It is just as if it is not a problem anymore for me. And my weight is okay." Antonio confirmed that Ana was eating "normal again." He liked that his wife had put on some weight and thought she was "looking great." In fact, her BMI was at a reasonable 18. On the general progress scale, both gave an 8. When I asked what Pablo's answer would be, they both said "9."

After the break, I offered many compliments for their accomplishments. I suggested that, at this point in therapy, it might be a good idea to start thinking of having a big family celebration, a "Farewell Gambling," "Farewell Anorexia," or simply "Welcome Family" party. I offered they might start by planning this celebration, deciding who they would like to invite, what words of thanks they would like to say, what the right timing would be. As a second option, I offered the suggestion that they repaint their home, to "wash away" the bad memories and to make the point that now, with Ana functioning as a great mother and Pablo home again, they were going to be the "Lago Tejeira" family again. Finally, I offered to schedule, not a "therapy session proper," but more of a "follow-up conversation," three months later.

The Seventh Session

Ana and Antonio reported that the celebration had been very moving, with more than forty relatives and friends participating and rejoicing. Ana had organized everything, with the backing of Antonio and the enthusiastic volunteering of Pablo. After a barbecue, Antonio had made a moving speech sharing how proud he was of his wife and his family. Ana felt she and Antonio were much closer "than ever before" and were finding time for daily conversations, for walks and good sex. They had bought tickets for a four-day vacation, just for the two of them, in Barcelona. Ana's father had definitively settled in his "grandpa role" and Pablo was getting better grades at school. As far as food was concerned, Ana had not slipped back and was still at an "8 and moving up." Gambling was "absolutely out of my life." Antonio proudly reported that he had his knight sword "clean and shining," and tongue-in-cheek asked me, "Do you get the metaphor?"

After a short break, I complimented Ana and Antonio on their progress and on how well they had organized the Celebration Party, working together as a real team. I encouraged them to go ahead, reminding them that there would still be bumps on the road. Then, speaking to Antonio, I offered "another metaphor": I suggested that they took something as a souvenir from the Celebration Party, and put it in some important and visible place in their home. Antonio smiled even more broadly: "You know, that is not a bad one. In fact, we did that already: Ana asked me to write down my Celebration Party speech and framed it. Now it hangs over our bed." We all laughed, and I shared that their taking the initiative in such a brilliant way was making me redundant as a therapist. I then asked, "How about leaving six months to a final "follow-up conversation"? They agreed.

The Eighth Session

For the next "follow-up session," Ana and Antonio took a day off at work and used the travelling to Salamanca to have a short holiday with Pablo. Pablo had grown a lot since I had last seen him, and it was fun to include him in the first part of the session. He told me how happy he was with his mom and dad, and that his grades and his basketball playing had improved a lot. When I talked to Ana and Antonio, they were proud to report that there had been no relapses over the six months. Everything was going well: Ana had temporarily lost her job but had been lucky to find another, her gambling was "finally and totally over" and she had "stabilized food intake and weight." She and Antonio were "really close" again, spending quality time together and keeping good communication. As everything was so on track, we decided that no further follow-up sessions were needed, and agreed to have a simple telephone follow-up, more or less one year later. I congratulated them on their progress and their hard work, gave them some advice on Salamanca "must see" sights, and wished them good luck.

Follow-Up

Unfortunately, one year later the team was too busy and neglected all follow-ups that should have been made around that time. But some years later, we started a qualitative research project, with a researcher undertaking in-depth personal interviews with families that had been treated in our service. Ana and Antonio were included in the sample, and they happily accepted to be interviewed, three years after our last follow-up session. They reported that things were "great." Ana saw things "at a 9," and Antonio "close to the 10." Ana had had a very bad time when her father had gotten lung cancer and died the year before. By that time she had a "small relapse with anorexia," but with the support of Antonio she had been able to get back to normal slowly with no further professional help. She was over 46kg again (BMI 18), eating well, and with no gambling problems. They were very happy about their relationship, and also with their son Pablo, who had dropped basketball but was doing very well in school.

Ana felt that a big part of therapy had been improving her relationship with Antonio, and "becoming more independent" in relation to her parents. When she was asked what tasks or suggestions she remembered as making a difference, she laughed. "The coin helped me a lot. In fact, I know that I should have given it back to Mark, but I have kept it. I like it and I still use it!"

Antonio said that, in his view, what had been most useful in therapy had been improving his communication with Ana. When he was asked about experiments or suggestions he remembered, he smiled. "I loved that thing with the sword. Mark told me I had to be Ana's knight, you know, so I bought that sword. That was really useful."

Reflections on the Building Trust with Coins and Swords Case

Matthew: In this case, you did a beautiful job with the goal-setting process, subsystem work, and with boundary making with the generations. When you begin the goal-setting process with families, why do you first ask the kids what they want?

Mark: I know this practice of mine is at odds with what most family therapists would do, as it is commonly assumed that starting with the parents is the best way to join with and respect the family hierarchy (Minuchin & Fishman, 1981). I prefer to start with the kids, because that is a good way to make sure their voices get heard. Starting with the kids gives a strong message that they are important, makes it easier to engage them in therapy, and at the same time promotes the therapeutic alliance with the parents. On the negative side, an eating-disordered girl or boy might feel accused if the therapist starts directly by asking her/him. That is why, if there are siblings present, I prefer to talk with them first, and then move on to the identified client and finally the parents.

Matthew: Clearly, you elicited many signs of progress from Ana and the family members. However, in the miracle question inquiry why did you bring up the eating-disorder problem when neither Ana nor other family members mentioned it as part of the ideal outcome picture? This subject obviously triggered negative emotion and memories for Ana, which defeated the positive thrust of the miracle inquiry.

Mark: You are right, another option would have been to simply follow them in their miracle, without introducing the topic of food. However, my experience with solution-focused therapy is that it has to be adapted when we work with eating-distressed clients. When we started to work solution-focused in Salamanca, almost twenty years ago, we spent some two years being pretty "orthodox" in our way of applying the model. It seemed to work well, also with eating-disordered clients: we negotiated goals, helped clients to reach them, planned the next steps and gave compliments for achieving them. Food and eating were often out of the picture, avoided by our clients and not included by us. Then, with our follow-ups, we came to the realization that solution-focused therapy had been successful in helping our clients reach their goals, but that it had only translated into them becoming "happier anorectics," reducing the pressure to change the anorectic behavior. In other words, the changes in their social or family relationships, in their studies or other personal issues had not translated to the disturbed eating patterns. This runs counter to the solution-focused theory of the "ripple effect" from little changes, but seen from the vantage point of how powerful the biological restriction/exercising and bingeing/purging cycles are, it makes sense. That is why I now routinely ask, during the miracle question, about those issues that are part of the presenting problem and that may not come up without some prompting.

Matthew: I liked your use of the extended family as co-therapists, but then also seeing the couple alone minus the grandparents and Pablo. It was important to strengthen the marital relationship and place the grandparents in more of a caretaker role for Pablo and to serve as consultants to the parents when they would need their input or support.

Mark: I think subsystems work is one of the most useful legacies of structural family therapy. To me, it makes a lot of sense in terms of better taking into account the different needs and views of the family members. It also multiplies the chances for change and, from a narrative perspective, allows more differentiated accounts to be brought forward. On the negative side, subsystem work usually translates into somewhat longer sessions, but I feel that the extra time is worth it.

Matthew: The Mexican coin idea obviously meant a lot to Ana in that she referred to it well after discharge. How else have you used the Mexican coin strategy with other clinical situations?

Mark: The Mexican coin is an adaptation of the "toss a coin" homework task that Steve de Shazer and his team developed in Milwaukee (de Shazer, 1985) as a way to fit in with situations where exceptions were nondeliberate. In Salamanca, we have expanded the uses of this task a little bit more, and use it in more situations. It is an elegant way to ask someone to do something without asking him/her directly, like in the Ana case. For instance, we might ask someone to toss the coin every morning; if he gets heads, he is supposed to do (or pretend to do) a little piece of the miracle he has described (or of the plan he has spelled out, etc.); if it's tails, he can do what he wants. The outcome usually is that the person does a little bit every day, regardless of what the coin says. My hunch is that in these situations the coin simply works like an external cue that reminds the person of his/her plans; the ritualistic aspect adds some emotional value to it. Another situation where we use the coin is when the client is behaving in a very rigid, restrictive manner. In this case, leaving something to chance has a liberating and even "subversive" effect. Interestingly enough, in CBT (Fairburn, 2008) a similar idea is used; at some stages in treatment they ask their clients to make

Matthew: the decision on what to eat by rolling a dice. A third indication for me is to use the coin task as a pattern interruption technique that blocks the usual course of events.

Matthew: I liked your risk-taking with the couple about whether or not they were having "wild sex." After I had read this in your case description, I was wondering if you were thinking the same thing that I was thinking that the gambling had been giving her the adrenalin "rush" she was not getting from her dull and boring marital relationship.

Mark: Looking back on the case, my guess would be that I was reacting both to the distance and boredom in the marital relationship that transpired in the first session, and the "little sparks" that appeared at the beginning of the second. Also, with couples and sex I do something similar than with miracles and food when I am working with an eating-distressed client, for me, it simply does not make sense to work on a couple relationship without discussing erotic interaction, in the same way as it does not make sense to work with an eating-distressed person and not to discuss eating at all. I once heard Bill Pinsof saying that "sex is the *lubricant* of the couple dynamics," and I think it is a daring but great metaphor. Sexual intimacy is an important ingredient of couple satisfaction, and in therapeutic terms it is a wonderful resource to draw on in therapy. With eating-distressed persons, who usually have a very negative, critical, and negative relationship with their bodies, sensuality and sexuality are areas of special interest.

Matthew: You externalized "anorexia" and "mistrust." The mistrust dynamic is often present with couples and families with serious and chronic habit difficulties. Couple partners and family members watch the habit-dependent person like hawks and are highly reactive to certain cues, words, attitudes, beliefs, and patterns of behavior, which serve as the problem life support system. They become overly focused on whatever they observe or hear that confirms the dominant anorexia, gambling, or substance abuse stories.

Mark: You are right. In my view, there are three different ways in which couple partners and relatives inadvertently contribute to maintaining chronic habit problems. One is what I like to redefine as "becoming an accomplice" of the self-destructive habit, a well-intentioned but unsuccessful behavioral pattern in which the relatives or couple partner protect the client from the consequences of his/her own actions, therefore making it easier for them to go on with them. The other one is nagging/criticizing, a pattern that research in other fields like schizophrenia has linked to relapses and deterioration (Leff & Vaughn, 1985; Vaughn & Leff, 1976). Emotional over-involvement, also widely researched as part of "expressed emotion" in schizophrenia (Leff & Vaughn, 1985; Vaughn & Leff, 1976), is also ineffective and potentially linked to a negative outcome. In my view, distrust only becomes negative once the person has started to fight the problem and to improve. In that scenario, the distrust of his loved ones undermine his/her efforts, conveying the

	destructive message "we don't believe that you can do it." For me, the most important therapeutic move in counteracting distrust dynamics is to reframe distrust as a healthy "staying on guard" but at the same time discuss with the family what behaviors they need to see in order to increase their "trust account."
Matthew:	One critical work you did with this couple was validating and embracing each partner after the crisis of Antonio's discovery that Ana had flirted with a male classmate. You attended to the emotional process and provided support, turning a crisis into an opportunity for couple growth and wisdom. Finally, the "knight in shining armor" metaphor is an image that everybody can capture in their mind and an intimate partner would warm up to. However, rather than buying a miniature knight in armor, Antonio chose to buy a sword, which was an even more powerful metaphor for his commitment to protecting his marriage with Ana.
Mark:	Yes, this is another example of how meaningful and emotionally touching metaphors can be. And in this case, it is also an excellent illustration of our belief that the best metaphors are those that the clients themselves bring forth.
Matthew:	Another great example of clients coming up with their own unique solutions as an alternative of what we had proposed was Antonio's celebration party speech and framing it and placing it over their bed.
Mark:	I think we both agree that our clients are basically more creative, resourceful and brilliant than us. As Duncan and Miller (2000) say, clients are the real heroes of therapy! On the other hand, I strongly feel that there are certain therapeutic procedures that leave more room for clients' creativity and therefore promote their resourcefulness better than other approaches. In my view, psychoeducational approaches, so common nowadays and certainly useful for many clients, tend to put clients into a more passive position, whereas narrative therapeutic work in general, and rituals and metaphors in particular, promote client creativity more.

6

SUBSTANCE-ABUSING HABITS

> Any musician who says he is playing better either on tea, the needle, or when he is juiced, is a plain straight liar.
>
> *Charlie Parker*

Introduction

Substance dependency and abuse are widespread phenomena in western societies. In 2011, the National Institute on Drug Abuse (NIDA)-funded *Monitoring the Future* study showed that the proportions of 8th, 10th, and 12th graders who admitted drinking an alcoholic beverage in the 30-day period prior to the survey were 13%, 27%, and 40%, respectively (Johnston, O'Malley, Bachman, & Schulenberg, 2012). In 2009, 16 million Americans had taken a prescription pain reliever, tranquilizer, stimulant, or sedative for non-medical purposes at least once in the previous year; in the same year, more than 2 million Americans had abused inhalants. As for the abuse of illicit drugs, it has declined in the United States since the mid- to late-1990s, but is still of concern and use has recently leveled off again. In fact, in the United States, up to a 6.1% of teenagers report daily marijuana use (Substance Abuse and Mental Health Services Administration, 2012), and in the United Kingdom, it is estimated that 40% of young adults have used cannabis (EMCDDA, 2005).

Considering these figures, it is no wonder that substance abuse treatments are in great demand. According to the *Substance Abuse and Mental Health Services Administration's National Survey*, 23.5 million Americans needed treatment for illicit drug or alcohol abuse in 2009 (Substance Abuse and Mental Health Services Administration, 2012). Most treatment admissions in publicly funded substance abuse programs involved alcohol abuse (41.4%), alone or in combination with another drug. Heroin and other opiates accounted for the largest percentage of drug-related admissions (20%), followed by marijuana (17%), cocaine (8.1% crack and 3.2% non-smoked cocaine), and methamphetamines (6.1%). Every year, abuse of illicit drugs and alcohol contributes to the death of more than 100,000 Americans (Mokdad, Marks, Stroup, & Gerberding, 2004). European figures are comparable (EMCDDA, 2005).

Background

In this chapter, we use the term "substances" as equivalent to "drugs," referring to any exogenous psychoactive substance that, once taken, rapidly affects the brain of the user and impacts its functioning in varying degrees. The presence of an exogenous substance marks one important difference to behaviors that can be addictive and generate endogenous psychoactive substances, like the other self-destructive habits covered in this book. Although most drugs produce intense feelings of pleasure, the effect of drugs on the human brain varies: it can be depressant (alcohol, opioids, tranquilizers, and hypnotics), stimulant (amphetamines, cocaine, nicotine, caffeine, among others), or distort the central nervous system (LSD, cannabis derivatives, club drugs). The important fact is that drugs change the functioning and eventually the structure of the brain. These biological changes help explain the compulsive and destructive behaviors in addictions, as well as the ever-present risk for relapse.

The difference between *substance use* and abuse is not an easy one, as small quantities of a drug can have negative consequences and qualify as abuse (e.g., if it is taken by an airline pilot before take-off) and bigger ones may not. DSM-IV defines *substance abuse* as a maladaptive pattern of substance use that leads to clinically relevant impairment of distress in at least one or more of the following areas: failure to fulfill major role expectations; recurrent use in physically hazardous situations; recurrent legal problems; social problems caused or exacerbated by the effects of the drug (APA, 1994).

Substance dependence, also called "addiction," is a pattern of behavior where the consumption of substances is prioritized over other more important behaviors. The drug use, which started as a sporadic, pleasurable experience, takes over the person's life, and drug abuse becomes necessary for abusers to simply feel "normal." Liking becomes wanting as the addicted person develops dependence on the substance. Physical dependence means that the body adapts to the drug, requiring more of it to achieve a certain effect (tolerance) and eliciting drug-specific physical or mental symptoms if drug use is abruptly ceased (withdrawal). Psychological dependence is the psychological compulsion to consume the drug, in order to experience its pleasurable effects or to get rid of negative affective states. While physical dependence is relatively easy to overcome after a period of detoxification of (depending on the drug) no more than 15 days, psychological dependence is far more difficult to handle, as in the later stages of addiction users feel strong cravings for the drug, which are often triggered by drug-associated cues and are likely to lead to relapses. To make matters worse, these latter stages are also associated with strong and persistent memories of drug-taking experiences, given that the effect of drugs on the pleasure circuit in the medial brain creates deeply ingrained memories (Linden, 2011).

The Biology of Substance Abuse

Drugs work by tapping into the neuronal communication system of the brain. Although other neurotransmitter systems are also involved (endogenous opioids and cannabinoids), drugs of abuse directly or indirectly target the brain's reward system by flooding the medial forebrain system with dopamine. The over-stimulation of the dopamine system produces the euphoric effects sought by people who abuse drugs, acting like a powerful reinforcer to repeat the behavior. In a series of experiments with monkeys, Schultz (2003) demonstrated that increased dopaminergic activity is even generated by exposure to the cue, which suggests dopamine has a critical role in *anticipation* as well. On the other hand, reduced dopaminergic function has been documented in *withdrawal* and *early abstinence* (Lingford-Hughes & Nutt, 2003). The genetic contribution to the risk for addiction (estimated between 40% and 60%) is probably mediated by the dopamine system, too. In fact, carriers of the A1 variant of the gene that regulates the D2 dopamine receptors have a reduced expression of these receptors in the brain, and are as a result more likely to become addicted to drugs.

Unfortunately, the effects of drugs on the brain are not only functional, disappearing when the drug is metabolized, but also structural: a number of studies from drug-addicted individuals show a number of long-lasting alterations (Linden, 2011; Lubman, Yücel, & Hall, 2007). For instance, experiments on rats that become addicted to cocaine show that there is actually an overgrowth of dendritic spines in the neurons of the nucleus accumbens, leaving the synapse stronger than it was before drug use started (Norrholm et al., 2003); this could be the biologic basis of *drug sensitization* (Kauer & Malenka, 2007; Saal, Dong, Bonci, & Malenka, 2003). In addition, physical changes in areas of the brain that are critical to judgment, decision-making, learning, memory, and behavior control have also been documented (Fowler, Volkow, Kassed, & Chang, 2007). This creates a vicious cycle in which the poor performance of cognitive functions makes it more difficult to make sound decisions like reducing or cutting on the substance. The situation is especially dangerous when it comes to teenage drug abuse, as there is growing evidence that the adolescent brain may be more vulnerable to the effects of addictive substances than the adult brain (Monti et al., 2005; Paus, 2005; Smith, 2003). This puts drug-using teenagers at increased risk for poor choices, such as trying new drugs, continued abuse, and engaging in other risky behaviors. Also, introducing drugs while the brain is still developing may have more profound and long-lasting consequences than for adults (Lubman, Yücel, & Hall, 2007). For instance, young people who begin using cannabis before the age of 17 seem to be more vulnerable to cognitive impairments and show reduced brain grey matter (Pope et al., 2003; Wilson et al., 2000). No wonder, then, that early onset of the substance use is associated with a higher rate of dependence symptoms up to 20 years later, to using multiple substances and the onset of other mental health problems (Anthony & Petronis, 1995). One final important aspect of the effects of drugs on the brain is that the use of some substances paves the way biologically for the use of others by altering the sensitivity to later drug use (Monti et al., 2005). For instance, we know that cannabis abuse makes it easier to get later addicted to opioids: in their twin study, Lynskey et al. (2003) found that individuals who used cannabis before age 17 had increased odds of using other drugs relative to their co-twins who had not used cannabis by that age.

The structural effect of drug abuse on the brain has at least three important therapeutic implications:

- The fact that substance abuse interferes with cognitive functioning implies that therapists have to make an extra effort to engage the attention of substance-abusing clients and to get their messages across effectively. To this end, we use metaphors, externalization, and dramatization during our sessions.
- Structural brain change creates a biological basis of the high relapse rates of addictive behaviors: after chronic consumption of substances the brain is altered in such a way that it is prepared for new consumptions. This makes relapse prevention a top therapeutic priority.
- The biological effects of drug abuse are associated with mental problems like depression, anxiety and conduct disorder, especially for early abusers (Teesson, Degenhardt, Lynskey, & Hall, 2005). A review by Moore and her team (Moore et al., 2007) reveals that cannabis use increases the risk of psychotic outcomes; for heavy users, the risk to develop psychosis increased up to 200%.

The Multiple Paths to Substance Abuse

Drug use typically starts in adolescence, especially during times of transitions. It usually begins with alcohol and tobacco, and may move later to marijuana and other drugs (Kandel, 1996). However, there is no single profile for drug abusers, and also no single factor that determines whether a person will become addicted. That a person starts using drugs and escalates into abuse and/or dependency is best understood as the complex outcome of a set of risk and protective factors, which interact and can influence drug abuse in several ways. The more risks a person is exposed to, and the fewer protective factors he has, the more likely it is that he will abuse drugs. Some risk factors may be more powerful than others at certain stages in development. Building on the classifications by Peterson, Hawkins, and Catalano (1992) and Becoña (1999), and taking into account the theory-based processes that Moos (2007) proposes, we can distinguish risk and protections factors at the individual, family, school, peer, and community levels:

- At the individual level, genetic factors may create vulnerability to addiction; early aggressive behavior, poor social skills, and mental health problems are also associated to substance abuse. On the protective side, there are a number of individual factors related to resilience, like self-control and the ability to establish and maintain meaningful relationships with others. High specific self-esteem and effective coping skills are also powerful protectors (Moos, 2007).
- The family has a great impact on drug abuse, not only during infancy but also during the teenage years and in young adulthood. Family risks factors include modeling through parental substance abuse and positive attitudes towards drugs; ineffective parenting; and a lack of attachment and emotional nurturing by parents or caregivers. Protective factors are a strong emotional parent–child bond; parental involvement in the child's life and effective monitoring; and appropriate parenting that sets clear limits and enforces discipline. For adults, the couple partner is likely to play a similar role, as offering a close emotional bond, goal-directedness, and structure protects from involvement in substance abuse and is likely to aid in the recovery process (Moos, 2007).
- A major risk factor for teenage drug use is the association with drug-abusing peers. Conversely, peers with negative views on drug use and that engage in healthy lifestyles have a protective influence. However, we would like to emphasize that for adolescents peer influence is mediated by parental influence (Fletcher, Steinberg, & Williams-Wheeler, 2004; Kandel, 1996; Steinberg, Fletcher, & Darling, 1994); this is especially important to keep in mind working with disempowered parents that may feel that they have lost their kids to the influence of their "buddies."
- At the school level, academic failures and poor classroom behavior or social skills increase the chances for drug use. A protective school environment that promotes academic competence and individual resources seems to have a protective effect.
- At the community level, poverty, unemployment, economic and racial deprivation, and lack of social connections and support highly increase the risk for drug abuse. Drug availability also plays a major role. Conversely, communities with high levels of social support and opportunities to engage in alternative rewarding activities and less availability of alcohol and drugs, act as protective factors
- At the social/cultural level, a key risk/protective factor is the perceived risk of different types of drugs. Perceived risk is a social construction that shows a strong negative correlation with actual drug use (Johnston et al., 2012).

As described in Chapter 1, it is possible to distinguish clients who have developed their substance dependency without previous vulnerabilities (pathway I) and are entrapped by the reinforcing nature of the substances and their biological effects; vulnerable clients who turn to substances to alleviate their emotional or interpersonal distress (pathway II); and substance abusers for whom the alcohol and/or drug abuse is part of a broader picture of impulsivity, lack of control and antisocial behavior (pathway III).

Key Research Findings that Inform our Clinical Practice

Treatments for substance abuse have been extensively researched, producing hundreds of randomized controlled trials. Unfortunately, the effectiveness of most treatments is rather modest, with high attrition rates before and during treatment, low abstinence at termination and relapse rates at follow-up typically between 35% and 90% (Dennis, Scott, Funk, & Foss, 2005; Dutra et al., 2008; McLellan, Lewis, O'Brien & Kleber, 2000; Miller, Walters, & Bennett, 2001; Moos, Schaefer, Andrassy, & Moos, 2001; Raub, 2012). To give a recent example, the average percentage of adolescents in recovery at 12-month follow-up in the two trials of the well-designed multi-site Cannabis Youth Treatment project (Dennis et al., 2004) was only 24%. As Budney, Roffman, Stephens, & Walker (2007) declare, "Unfortunately, as with treatment for other dependencies, the rates of 'success' are modest ... clearly, there remains much room for improvement." (p. 9). The awareness of the limited effect of substance abuse treatments has led to a number of interesting developments in the drug abuse treatment field. The emphasis has changed from necessarily seeking a radical "cure" from alcohol and drug abuse to a more nuanced approach, where decrease of abuse is also considered a valuable therapeutic goal, and harm reduction programs have proliferated.

As far as *pharmacological treatments* are concerned, methadone maintenance plays an important role in the treatment of opiate addiction (Amato, Davoli, Ferri, & Ali, 2006, Gossop, Marsden, Stewart, & Kid, 2003; Gossop, Marsden, Stewart, & Treacy, 2002), and a variety of medications to foster abstinence from alcohol have been tested, like disulfiram (Krampe et al., 2006), naltrexone (Kranzler & Van Kirk, 2001; Srisurapanont & Jarusuraisin, 2002), and acamprosate (Lingford-Hughes & Nutt, 2003). For cannabis abuse, there are some pilot studies on medications that target the endocannabinoid system and may help to alleviate withdrawal symptoms (Budney, Vandrey, Hughes, Moore, & Bahrenburg, 2007; Clapper, Mangieri, & Piomeli, 2009) or block marijuana's rewarding effect (Huestis et al., 2001).

Alcoholics Anonymous (AA) popularized the Twelve-Step approach, self-help groups that adopt an illness model. They are unacceptable for many patients due to their rigid ideology, and show high relapse rates (McGowan, 2010; Raub, 2012), but a few well-controlled studies suggest they are indeed a potentially effective option for clients with more severe dependence (Brown, Seraganian, Tremblay, & Annis, 2002; Project MATCH Research Group, 1997). In our view, the message of the existing research on AA and Twelve-Step programs is that there is no evidence base to state that they are in any way a necessary ingredient for recovery from alcohol dependence (Ferri, Amato, & Davoli., 2006); but at the same time, there is evidence that they can be effective for some clients, both on their own or as an adjunct to other treatments (for instance, McCrady, 2004).

There is also good evidence that *brief interventions* can help a substantial proportion of patients, especially those who abuse alcohol (McQueen, Howe, Allan, Mains, & Hardy, 2011; Moyer, Finney, Swearingen, & Vergun, 2002). Among brief interventions, *motivational interviewing* (MI, Miller & Rollnick, 2002) has attracted a great deal of attention. Its main feature is that therapists adopt a non-judgmental and non-confrontational position, avoiding confrontational interventions, which have been shown to elicit argumentative responses. MI's moderate but positive effect has been empirically supported (Martino, Carroll, Nich, & Rounsaville, 2006; Smedslund et al., 2011; Lundahl, Kunz, Brownwell, Tollefson, & Burke, 2010). Solution-focused brief therapy, which shares some basic features with MI, has shown some very encouraging results in Europe as part of a broader framework of service provision for alcoholics that emphasizes client choice at different stages of the process (de Shazer & Isebaert, 2003; Hendrick, Isebaert, & Dolan, 2012), and has also been tested with drug abusers (Smock et al., 2008).

Social skills and *coping skills training* to maintain abstinence have been widely tested and shown to decrease substance abuse, especially with alcohol (Bottlender, Kohler, & Soyka, 2006), and marihuana (Copeland, Swift, Roffman, & Stephens, 2001; Marijuana Project Research Group, 2004; Olmstead, Sindelar, Easton, & Carroll, 2007; Sinha, Easton, Renee-Aubin, & Carroll, 2003; Stephens, Roffman, & Curtin, 2000; Walker, Roffman, Stephens, Berguis, & Kim, 2006). Their impact is probably greater when they are part of broader community reinforcement approaches (CRA; Azrin, Sisson, Meyers, & Godley, 1982; Hunt & Azrin, 1973; UK Alcohol Treatment Trial, 2005). CRA are the best supported treatments for alcohol dependence, and include a wide range of interventions, from problem solving to behavior contracting, stress management, and marital and/or family therapy. The value of including concerned others has also been supported in a number of studies on CRA for stimulant abuse (Kirby, Marlow,

Festinger, Garvey, & La Monaca, 1999; Meyers, Miller, Smith, & Tonigan, 2002). Cognitive behavioral interventions also usually include specific *relapse prevention* strategies (Marlatt, 1978; Marlatt & Gordon, 1985; Witkiewitz & Marlatt, 2007), which have shown good results for a variety of substances (Baker, Boggs, & Lewin, 2001; Baker, Lee, & Clare, 2005; Carroll, 1996; Maude-Griffin et al., 1998).

Another therapeutic element that is being added to cognitive-behavioral treatments in an effort to improve their outcome is *contingency management* (CM; Higgins & Silverman, 1999), where clients earn vouchers contingent on drug-free urine or breath analyses. It is probably the best supported treatment for cocaine abuse, usually in the context of community reinforcement programs, increasing retention in treatment and abstinence (Budney & Higgins, 1998; Higgins et al., 1993, 1994; Milby et al., 1996; Rawson, Marinelli-Casey, & Anglin, 2004; Rawson, McCann, & Flammino, 2006; Silverman et al., 2002). CM has also been added to cannabis treatments treatment, with modest results (Budney, Moore, Rocha, & Higgins, 2006; Carroll et al., 2006; Henggeler, Schoenwald, Borduin, Rowland, & Cunningham, 2006; Olmstead et al., 2007), and is also the most researched treatment for methamphetamines (Petry, Peirce, & Stitzer, 2005; Rawson et al., 2006). However, the problem with CM research is that it has still not been demonstrated that the therapeutic gains are kept after treatment discontinuation.

There are a number of family therapy approaches that have been successfully applied to drug and alcohol-abusing youth and their families. Three of them have especially solid records of outcome and process research on treating drug-abusing youth: *multisystemic therapy* (Henggeler, Schoenwald, Borduin, Rowland, & Cunningham, 1998), *multidimensional family therapy* (Liddle, 2002; Liddle, Rodriquez, Dakof, Kanzki, & Marvel., 2005); and *brief strategic family therapy* (Szapocznik, Hervis, & Schwartz, 2003; Szapocznik, Kurtinez, Foote, Pérez-Vidal, & Hervis, 1983; Szapocznik & Williams, 2000). All three were specifically developed to deal with problem and deviant behavior of youth; all three share a broad systemic view that goes beyond the family to include school, peers, and the legal system; and in all of them therapists take a proactive role to reach out into the community and provoke changes in different involved systems and their interaction. In all these approaches, family change is conceptualized in structural (Minuchin, 1974; Minuchin & Fishman, 1981) terms. Systemic reframing, especially the reframing of negativity and defensive family interactions in more positive terms plays an important role during the process.

Research on these family therapy programs has also proven that in order to work with families it is not always necessary to have the whole system in the interview; as long as the intervention is conceptualized in family terms, one-person family therapy can also be effective (Szapocznik, Kurtines, Foote, Pérez-Vidal, & Hervis, 1983, 1986). Finally, it has shown that it is possible to engage the problematic families of drug-abusing youth if it is done in an active and purposeful way (for instance, Santisteban et al., 1996).

The most researched couple intervention with substance-abusing persons is *behavioral couples therapy* (BTC; O'Farrell & Fals-Stewart, 2002, 2003, 2006), initially applied to alcohol problems but also used for other substances of abuse (Fals-Stewart, Birchler, & O'Farrell, 1996; Winters, Fals-Stewart, O'Farrell, Birchler, & Kelly, 2002). The emphasis is on improving communication and exchanging positive reinforcement in the couple; relapse prevention sessions can also be added. *Alcohol behavior couples therapy* (Epstein & McCrady, 2002; McCrady & Epstein, 1995; McCrady, Epstein, Cook, Jensen, & Hildebrandt, 2009) is a more individualized, stand-alone approach that includes some MI techniques and is more tailored to the specific needs of each couple. The therapeutic focus is typically on the control of substance abuse first, and only at a second stage moves on to relationship issues. As we will see later, collaborative strengths-based brief therapy follows the same logic.

Research on couple therapy provides evidence of some of the factors that mediate the outcome of treatment, and especially of the important role that spouses or couple partners have in the recovery process (McCrady et al., 1986; McCrady, Stout, Noel, Abrams, & Nelson, 1991). Miller and his team found that supportive partners who positively reinforced not drinking, increased positive communication, engaged in interests outside the relationship, and encouraged professional help had a greater impact on engagement than confrontational interventions (Meyers et al., 2002; Miller, Meyers, & Tonigan, 1999). Alcohol-abusing clients who perceive their partners as more critical and hostile towards them at intake have a higher relapse rate and are more likely to abuse substances in the year after treatment (Fals-Stewart, O'Farrell, & Hooley, 1999; O'Farrell, Hooley, Fals-Stewart, & Cutter, 1998; Tracy, Kelly, & Moos, 2005), and clients who at the end of therapy report less couple happiness are more likely to consume more alcohol six months after treatment (McCrady, Hayaki, Epstein, & Hirsch, 2002). Finally, there are also some good studies documenting the effect of working with the partner of clients unwilling to attend (Meyers et al., 2002; Miller et al., 1999; Smith & Meyers, 2004).

In our view, the key clinical implications of the numerous research findings in the substance abuse field are the following:

- Although substance abuse has a strong biological component, treatment of substance dependencies are basically of a psychological nature (Becoña & Cortés, 2008). Medication is necessary in some cases to manage withdrawal symptoms safely, when maintenance therapy is indicated and as an adjunct for relapse prevention, but is usually only one ingredient in the service of a broader behavioral change treatment plan.
- There is no single treatment that works for all individuals (National Institute on Drug Advice, 1999). As the effort to match certain treatments with certain clients' characteristics seems to not make a difference with outcomes (Kadden, Litt, Cooney, Kabela, & Getter, 2001; Project MATCH, 1997; UK Alcohol Treatment Trial, 2005), a better strategy might be to have therapists constantly getting feedback from their clients, providing choices to their clients, and flexibly responding to their needs. A special emphasis needs to be placed on matching what we do therapeutically with clients' expectations and unique quitting styles and the acceptance of controlled substance use or substance use reduction as a valid therapeutic goal, instead of insisting on total abstinence.
- Retention in treatment is a critical ingredient for effective therapy. It can be improved by using therapeutic strategies based on cooperation instead of confrontation; by helping clients to see the gains for their abstinence or drug use reduction; and also by including concerned significant others.
- The research on family treatments for substance abuse demonstrates the effectiveness of working with the families of adolescent and young adult drug abusers. The family structure is changed by empowering parents, helping establish clear subsystem boundaries, promoting direct, positive communications between family members, and the open resolution of conflicts. This entails strengthening the parenting functions, but also parental relations with the adolescent, as well as strengthening the parenting support exosystems (Liddle, 2010; Szapocznik et al., 2003).
- The attention to the wider social context of the drug-abusing clients and their families should translate into helping family and friends actively support the changes, promoting participation in self-help groups, and helping clients find new social networks that do not support the substance abuse (Moos, 2007). Another therapeutic ingredient of empirically supported family treatments is that therapists take a proactive role to reach out into the community and provoke changes in the different involved systems (school, juvenile justice system).
- In terms of working with couple partners, research demonstrates the therapeutic effect of reducing partner criticism and increasing the quality of marital interaction (McCrady et al., 2002, 2009; Meyers et al., 2002; Miller et al., 1999; Smith & Meyers, 2004).

- Although conjoint sessions are a central part of the tested family and couples therapies, there is direct evidence to support the value of subsystem work: both "one person family therapy" (Szapocznik et al., 1983, 1986) and therapy with the partner of a client unwilling to attend (Meyers, 2012; Miller et al., 1999; Smith & Meyers, 2004) have shown their effectiveness.
- Slips, setbacks, and relapses are normal parts of the recovery process, and therefore relapse prevention (Marlatt, 1978; Marlatt & Gordon, 1985; Witkiewitz & Marlatt, 2007) makes sense. The likelihood of relapse and the long time-course of addiction changes in general (Dennis et al., 2005; Moos, 2007) have led us to routinely offer substance abuse clients short follow-up sessions over extended periods of time.

Strategies for Assessment and Treatment Planning

Important Assessment Considerations

A comprehensive diagnosis of substance abuse habits does not only require the evaluation of what drugs are used, in what quantities, and under what circumstances. It also requires gaining an understanding of how the abuse fits into the personal history, family dynamics, and ecosystemic context of our client. One important consideration is that many clients abuse *various substances* simultaneously, the most common combination being alcohol with some other drug. This implies that, even though our clients might ask for help in relation to one substance, we should inquire about the use of other drugs, not only because the simultaneous use of various substances is more dangerous, but also because we will want to monitor the evolution of their use during therapy. If crossover phenomena are not addressed, therapy might help with one of the substances of abuse at the expense of increasing another.

Another source of concern is *co-morbidity*. Research shows that dual diagnosis is very common: 37% of persons presenting with an alcohol abuse disorder also present a mental health disorder; and 53.1% of persons abusing drugs other than alcohol also suffer a mental health disorder (Kessler et al., 1997; Klerman, 1986). Generally speaking, persons suffering from a mood or anxiety disorder are at least twice as likely also to have a drug abuse disorder than the normal population. The opposite is also true: persons who abuse drugs are twice as likely to present with a mood or anxiety disorder than those who do not (Kessler, 2004). Co-morbidity is an invitation for therapists working with substance-abusing clients to pay attention to possible problems of anxiety and depression as well as to other possible self-destructive habits (especially gambling), and to how they interact with the substance abuse. Although in this respect we try to follow our clients' preferences, we favor addressing both types of problems (mental health and drug abuse) in a conjoint, integrated fashion.

Legal issues and the ensuing complexity of professional systems must also be considered. Clients who receive criminal possession or dealing charges are likely to be involved with a number of agencies and professionals, creating the need to collaborate and coordinate efforts with other colleagues. The legal system has a logic and a rhythm of its own, which may be different from the change rhythm of therapy. The therapeutic dilemma is to find an adequate degree of involvement with this powerful system, maximizing opportunities for change while at the same time not getting sucked in by the system and losing therapeutic leverage.

Key Assessment Questions

Our assessment should establish if there is substance use, abuse, or dependence, if there are signs of physiological dependence and tolerance, and what the negative effects of the substance abuse are in the different areas of our client's life. Interviewing the client about his or her substance use habit will not only help us to gain a better understanding of the situation, but will also convey information to him or her. As discussed in Chapter 2, discussing the negative effects of a behavior promotes a greater awareness and helps to move our clients from precontemplation to contemplation. In addition to collecting data on our client's substance abuse habit, we recommend that therapists inquire with other family members about their substance use, evaluate if there is risk of violence, and inquiry about legal problems and possible delinquent behaviors. Urine and/or breath-analysis may be necessary, specially working with young unmotivated abusers and their families.

There are a number of questions that may be useful to assess the type and degree of the substance abuse:

- "What substances do you use? In what way (smoked, inhaled, injected …)? How often? How much? What are your favorite combinations of substances?"
- "How long have you been using substances? What is your pattern of use? Is your use increasing/stabilized/decreasing?"
- "What was the worst episode? Have you ever overdosed?"

As just described, the negative effects of the substance use should be carefully discussed, for instance:

- "What physical consequences of the substance abuse are you experiencing *already*? Do you have frequent headaches, restlessness, insomnia, sexual problems? Have you lost memory or concentration capacity?"
- "What emotional/psychological consequences of the substance abuse are you experiencing *already*? Are you often depressed or apathetic? Irritable, unstable or anxious? Have you had panic attacks?"
- "What consequences are you experiencing in the different areas of your life and in your relationships as a result of the substance abuse?"
- "Have you had any legal problems? Are you dealing any substances?"
- "Have you found yourself becoming violent? With what effects?"
- "Have you ever considered suicide or harming yourself?"

It is also important to understand the positive functions that the substance abuse serves for the person:

- "In what way does taking the substance help you?"
- "What would be the disadvantage of not using the substance anymore?"
- "What will you miss most once you are clean?"

Family and Couple Dynamics

One important part of assessment is to establish in what ways the family and/or couple partner are contributing to the substance-abusing habit. They might contribute by not taking action in the face of the abuse, by over-reacting in an ineffective manner (shouting, yelling, and threatening, but with no consistent consequences), by inadvertently making the abuse easier (for instance, by leaving a child unsupervised with alcohol at home, or by allowing him or her to take money), or by reducing the negative effect the abuse has on the abusing person (for instance, taking the drunk husband to bed). In order to get a clear picture of what is going on in the family or couple, questions need to be followed up until the full behavioral sequence is clearly spelled out. The information retrieved this way will be complemented by the interaction displayed during the conversation. These are some examples of questions to find out about parental monitoring and discipline:

- "How do you typically react when your child comes home under the influence of alcohol or some other drug?"
- "How do you try to monitor if your child is taking substances?"
- "What kind of disciplining measures do you take?"
- "How do you parents support each other in this?"

It is also important to keep larger systems in mind, for example by asking:

- "How do your relatives/friends/neighbors react? Do they support you or the child?"
- "What is the school telling you?"
- "Do you know your son/daughter's friends personally? Are they also using substances?"

Again, exceptions can be identified by asking about those instances when the parents were more successful in keeping their parental authority, for instance:

- "When was the last time that you were able to enforce this 'no marijuana smoking at home' policy? How did you do that?"
- "What is most useful in the way your wife supports you when you have to confront your son?"
- "How did you make the brave decision to let your own parents know that your son was abusing drugs and that you needed their help too?"

We would like to make clear that we do not see the families or couple partners as the *cause* of substance abuse habits. In fact, there is no direct scientific evidence that would support this blaming stance: drug abuse certainly can appear in dysfunctional families, but it also does in healthy families that only start to malfunction when the drug abuse problem begins to affect their functioning as a group and triggers fears and negativity in their interactions. Instead, there is good evidence that the family and/or the couple partner do have an important role in *helping* the drug-abusing person to overcome his problem, and that they can do so by changing their own behavior (Henggeler et al., 1998, 2006; Liddle et al., 2005; Meyers, 2012; Miller et al., 1999; Smith & Meyers, 2004; O'Farrell & Fals-Stewart, 2003; Szapocznik et al., 1983, 2003). Even if parents or couple partners are doing things that are obviously unhelpful, we try to understand the good intentions behind their unproductive attempted solutions, and tell them that what they have done so far could have helped, but did not; therefore, it is wise to change gears and try something different (Fisch, Weakland, & Segal, 1982). The following citation of Berg and Reuss (1997) summarizes our position perfectly:

> Our experience is that these spouses, both men and women, have enormous capacity to tolerate frustration with unlimited patience and undying hope for the problem drinker. We view these family members as tremendous resources. They have stood by their partner or son or daughter through more detoxes and attempts to quit than any professional can ever give them credit for. (p. 27)

Specialized Treatment Strategies and Major Therapeutic Experiments for Substance-Abusing Clients

In the alcohol and drug abuse field moralistic attitudes are not uncommon, with substance abuse being seen as a vice or as the consequence of a moral flaw. We prefer to adopt a non-judgmental stance, where we see the abuse as a possible problem, not as an expression of pathology or character weakness. We also take a "no drama, matter-of-fact" attitude (De Vega, 1996): because we know that substance abuse can be dangerous, we try to keep a "cool head" stance and to help all family members to do so as well. We prefer to see substance abuse habits as a series of (bad) choices that might have been adequate at some time but have outlived their usefulness and have become a self-destructive habit.

It also can be easy for therapists working with substance-abusing clients to slip into a distrustful attitude and to enter the prosecuting/distancing game with clients. As Berg and Reuss (1997) put it, "the field of substance abuse is the only professional health care discipline that does not trust an optimistic and positive client self-report" (p. 20). We prefer to believe our clients and take their reports at face value, something which comes naturally from our non-judgmental, collaborative attitude and, in turn, promotes it. However, with involuntary clients who are forced into therapy, we understand that their possibly hiding or distorting information is a logical response of not wanting to be there and not yet having a trusting relationship and meaningful therapeutic project with us. In these situations, we wait until they have found a good reason to share information with us openly.

Creating a Conjoint Therapeutic Project

Given that both alcohol and some drugs have become a normalized part of western culture, it is not surprising that many drug-abusing or even drug-dependent clients start therapy in a precontemplative position of basically not understanding why anyone should be concerned about their substance use. The dilemma for therapists is to be able to put the drug use on the therapeutic agenda, without failing to adjust to the precontemplative state of his/her client. Our way to address this dilemma is to work from a "go slow" and "leading from behind" (Cantwell & Holmes, 1994) stance. From an eco-systemic point of view, we need to keep the broader relational and biographical picture in mind. This will help us to put the drug use in its context, and will also help to de-center the substance abuse issue and therefore will make the alliance with the client easier. As with any problem, creating a strong therapeutic alliance around a conjoint therapeutic project is a critical factor for the successful therapy of drug-abusing clients (Barber et al., 1999; Diamond et al., 2006; Friedlander, Escudero, & Heatherington, 2006; Shelef, Diamond, Diamond, & Liddle, 2005). This conjoint therapeutic project should include not only the reduction or quitting of the substance abuse, but also other personal goals of the client, as well as the development of alternative ways to perform the function that the substance may serve.

To help a precontemplative substance-abusing person to progress to a contemplative stage of readiness of change is not easy, as the positive effects of drug use are quick, sometimes even immediate, whilst the negative effects often only become apparent in the long run. There are a number of strategies that we may use, alone or in combination, to shift the balance and make negative effects more visible:

- We will gently explore the possible negative effects of the abuse. We may complement this with the homework experiment of keeping track of the negative effects the substance has, or suggest a "pros/cons of quitting/abusing" log.
- We can follow the "Two-step tango" strategy described in Chapter 2 and intersperse some information on the negative effects of the abuse during "teachable moments."
- One way to deal with the short-term positive effects/long-term negative effects equation is to invite the client to imagine his or her life five years later. In one scenario, the client has kept on abusing substances; in the other, he or she has quit. Then we do the same 10 years later. What are the differences? What are the pros and cons of both lifestyles?
- If none of the above strategies seems to be making a difference, we consider asking the nightmare question: "Suppose that when you get to bed tonight, some time in the middle of the night a nightmare occurs. In this nightmare all the problems that brought you here suddenly got as bad as they can possibly get. This would be a nightmare. But this nightmare comes true. What would you notice tomorrow morning that would let you know you were living

a nightmare?" (Berg & Reuss, 1997, p. 36). Once the details of the nightmare are explored, we can discuss with the client what pieces of that nightmare are already happening and then move on to what it would take to prevent the nightmare from becoming true.
- Externalization, as discussed in previous chapters, is another option to promote the progression towards contemplation and preparation (White, 2007; White & Epston, 1990). Talking about "the voice of heroin" or "the traps of alcohol" helps to create distance between the person and the substance and to promote an adversarial position between both.

Making the Substance Redundant

As we have discussed above, besides their psychological and physiological pleasurable effects, drugs and alcohol may serve a number of other functions for our clients. The burned-out computer specialist may use marijuana to relax; cocaine helps the stressed businessman to keep his crazy work schedule, or the partying teenager to keep it up uninterruptedly. More generally speaking, most drugs help to escape reality, be it personal circumstances or social ones. When drugs are taken with peers or in the context of certain subcultures, they are a means to "fit in." If the substance abuse serves a function that is important for the client, it is unlikely that he will take a stand against it unless he finds alternative ways to serve that function. Therefore, an important therapeutic task is to help the client identify and build on these alternatives and, if necessary, offer new tools in the way of suggestions or experiments. To this end, we use the suggestions and therapeutic experiments discussed in Chapter 3.

Capitalizing on Exceptions

An important feature of substance abuse is that it is impossible to be using a substance all of the time, so there will be valuable exceptions. Especially interesting are those exceptions that represent "miniatures" of alternative, substance-free lifestyles or where the function the substance abuse serves was met in a different, healthier way. Our all-time favorite task to promote the location of exceptions and of action plans is the classical solution-focused task: "Notice carefully what is different on those occasions when you resist the temptation/the urge to use alcohol/drug" (de Shazer, 1988). This task presupposes that there will be exceptions, and opens future conversations about the unique coping strategies of our clients.

Cutting Back on the Substance Use

Except for severe alcohol dependence cases, most of our clients are able to progressively reduce and eventually quit their substance abuse without detoxification. In any case, we ask them to undergo a medical check-up in the beginning of therapy, and support them if they decide to ask for medications to reduce possible withdrawal symptoms. There are three main strategies that we use to help clients gain some control over their substance use:

- On the cognitive level, we like to invite our clients to watch out for the "*drug/alcohol traps*": What ideas promote the abuse or hinder progress? What does alcohol "whisper in the client's ear"? What thoughts are self-defeating and foster a sense of helplessness? We invite the client to ponder these questions, to identify how they work in the service of the drug abuse, and to develop more positive alternative thoughts.
- *Pattern disruption interventions* from the brief therapy tradition (Nardone & Watzlawick, 1990; O'Hanlon, 1987; O'Hanlon & Weiner-Davis, 1989) are especially useful once the client is in the preparation or action stage of readiness for change, not only because they counteract the patterned, automatic nature of drug-abusing habits, but because they are compatible with a

permissive, non-judgmental therapeutic position: given that the more dependent clients will tell us that they want but cannot abstain from taking the substance, we encourage them to do something we know they can do, to perform their substance-abusing habit in a slightly different way. For instance:

- Change the order in which the habit is performed (for instance, smoke first and then drink, instead of the other way around).
- Change the way some part of the habit is performed (smoke with your left hand, instead of with the right one).
- Change the physical context (smoke hash in the park, not at home; or in the kitchen, not in the dorm).
- Change the timing (start smoking one hour later).
- Add some elements (drink a glass of water between drinks) or some strange elements (put on a pink hat before smoking).
- Mark an arbitrary starting or ending point (you may drink, but the first beer has to be ten minutes past the hour).
- Link the occurrence of the problematic substance abuse with a burdensome but useful behavior (for instance, for each joint the client smokes, he has to iron five shirts); the client has to accept this deal before knowing what the ordeal is (Haley, 1983).

- *Delay strategies* are a type of pattern interruption interventions that merit some additional comment, as they allow drug-dependent clients to experience that craving is not the unbeatable, ever-increasing urge that necessarily keeps on growing until it finally takes over, but a feeling that comes, increases, but then decreases again. Marlatt's urge surfing (Bowen, Chawla, & Marlatt, 2011; Marlatt & Gordon, 1985) is a full-blown procedure that allows the client to experience how he can "surf" his urge with his breathing, finally mastering it (see Chapter 10).

Resisting the Invitation to Use

A central part of regaining control of their own lives is that clients learn how to deal with the invitations to consume that they will be receiving. In fact, assertiveness training and coping skills are an integral part of many successful CBT programs. We like to do this in our usual "leading from behind" mode, asking clients on what occasions they were successful in declining an invitation to do drugs/alcohol (or to do more) and trying to find out how they did that. Sometimes it is enough to discuss with the clients and/or their concerned others what their plans are to say "no" and handle the pressure to consume; on other occasions it is necessary to add some role-play to get started.

When peers are supportive of drug use, the difficult decision is either to work therapeutically in favor of a change of friends, in the direction of having the client cope better with his peers' pressures to consume, or to include peers into therapy sessions as helpful resources. All options are difficult and entail some risks. Not changing a drug-using group of reference might increase the risk of relapse, but promoting alternative social networks might create a great deal of resistance from the client, especially in those cases where the drug abuse started as a way to fit in with a specific group of friends. The necessity of a change of peers will be more evident when they are also involved in other illegal activities like drug dealing or delinquent behaviors, but in that case the pressures to stay in the group might be even greater. Our way to proceed in these cases is to follow the stages of readiness of change model: we help our clients to see the pros and cons of their current group of friends, we promote the contemplation of alternatives and gently nudge them to reach the determination to change, and help them to maintain their efforts and not relapse into the old, destructive relationships. Working with the parents of an unmotivated young drug-abusing person, we might engage the parents in an active effort to promote healthy relationships and watch out for any peers that might be supportive of our client.

Developing New Substance-Free Virtuous Habits

The greatest challenge in working with substance-abusing clients is probably to develop alternative lifestyles where the abuse is no longer present. Research demonstrates that engagement in rewarding activities other than substance abuse is one of the key predictors of remission and protectors from relapse (McCrady, 2004; Moos, 2007; Vaillant, 2003). This means developing new habits, which have to be different enough from the old ones in order not to trigger relapses (Isebaert, 2005). Developing new habits is not an easy process, but, besides detailed discussions of plans and possibilities with the clients, there are a number of procedures that we have found useful to promote it. For instance, the miracle question (de Shazer, 1988) and the time machine experiment (Selekman, 2005, 2009) are two excellent tools to generate a rich description of a desired future, provided that the therapist actively helps to spell out details and specifics. The "collage of the heart" (Dolan, 1991), also described in Chapter 2, is a more artistic variant. If future thinking is impaired, for instance with chronic and neurologically deteriorated alcoholic clients, the "three questions for a happy life" experiment (Isebaert, 2005) is a good alternative to discover what things move our clients. Here, we explain to our clients that, every night, after going to bed and just before falling asleep, they are to ask themselves questions:

- "What small thing have I done today that I am satisfied with?"
- "What small thing has someone done with me/for me that I am satisfied with? And how will my reaction lead to him/her doing more of it?"
- "What other small thing have I done today that I am satisfied with?"

Working With the Family

If the person who abuses substances is an adolescent, we will try hard to include all parental figures in the treatment. As shown by the family therapy research reviewed earlier, the engagement process is critical for the retention and success of therapy, and it is necessary for the therapist to play a strategic and pro-active role (Robbins, Turner, Alexander, & Perez, 2003; Shelef et al., 2005).

When the client is a substance-abusing adult who presents alone in therapy, it is also useful to involve family members or couple partners. Families have a great deal of expert knowledge on what works and what does not to help the client; on what the client was like before starting on alcohol or drugs; and on what his or her most valuable qualities are. When no one is available or the family member refuses to attend, we can still "have them in the session" by asking our clients relational questions from that person's perspective, sometimes leaving an empty chair in the therapy room to represent her or him. In some cases, we get permission from the client to send session summaries to the important person who is not attending the sessions.

The role of family is incredibly important when the drug-using client is a teenager in a precontemplative stage of readiness for change and refuses any help from his parents or therapists. In these situations, relatives may be the only ones who ask for therapeutic help, and they are in the best position to create in the drug-abusing person an awareness of the substance use problem and a motivation for change. This involves a careful balancing of the two different ingredients that we discussed in Chapter 2: the increase of parental surveillance on the one hand and the strengthening of the positive emotional parents–adolescent bond on the other.

Another shared feature of most empirically supported family therapy treatments for drug-abusing teenagers is the emphasis on strengthening the parent's support exo-systems. Parents of drug-abusing children are in the middle of a difficult battle that tends to divide them and isolate them from their environment; the contact with and assistance of other parents and parenting groups can help them to persist and maintain their own changes. In addition, we like to devote some therapy time to finding out how the parents take care of themselves as individuals and as a couple, and to discuss how they could take respite and be in a better condition themselves.

Another aspect of caring for the parents involves a careful assessment of violence risk by their offspring, taking preventive measures if necessary. Avoiding escalations, introducing time out, and having a third party present (neighbor, family friend) will reduce the risk of physical aggression, but the parents need to be prepared to take legal action or call the police if the situation gets out of hand. For some parents this is especially difficult to accept, and they may need some extended conversations until they can see that these extreme measures are in the best interest of the child. Protecting siblings from violence or extortion by the substance-abusing person is of course another top priority.

When one of the parents has a drug or alcohol problem, he or she is likely to be discredited in front of their children and spouse (Steinglass, Bennett, & Wolin, 1993). In that case, a careful, step-by-step approach to restoring parental authority is called for. This usually involves a careful re-balancing of power and tasks between the under-functioning partner who used to abuse substances and his or her usually over-functioning spouse, and sometimes requires a much broader reorganization of the family in order to adapt to sobriety and develop new, alcohol-free interaction patterns (Brown & Lewis, 1999; Lewis, Allen-Byrd, & Rouhbakhsh, 2004; Steinglass et al., 1993). In order to reinforce parental resourcefulness, we like to reframe the situation by pointing out that the parent who succeeded in overcoming their own substance dependency has a lot of expertise to share with their child as to how they achieved it.

Working with the Couple Partner

As we have seen earlier, a good number of studies attest to the effectiveness of including the couple partner in the treatment of substance-abusing people, even if the person who abuses is not willing to participate. When both partners come to therapy, it is important not to do "individual therapy with the substance abuser" in the presence of the partner, but to find ways to actively involve both persons in all parts of the therapeutic process. We also like to share the credit for any improvements, not only complimenting the person with the substance abuse habit, but also the partner (Isebaert, 2005), and to give the partner an active role in the homework task if he or she is a customer for change. We acknowledge in the session that both couple members are entitled to have differing views and opinions on some issues, but take the chance to access the very special expert knowledge that the partner has on the deepest strengths of his/her loved one.

It is common for couples where one or both members have been abusing substances to present with marital problems caused by the substance abuse. Maybe the husband spent the family savings on drugs; maybe the wife was repeatedly unfaithful during her periods of excessive drinking; or maybe the husband failed to support her when her mother was dying, because at that time he was intoxicated. In these cases we will help the couple to re-negotiate their relationship and develop new, healthy, and substance-free interaction patterns. Restoring trust and promoting positive interactions in the present might not be enough, as these past grievances may have created an insurmountable emotional burden. Here, rituals and metaphorical interventions can help to turn the page and move on. There are two experiments we find useful in these situations:

- We invite the couple to decide on some "penitence" that the wrongdoer could do as a way to express his or her sorrow and repentance. It has to be something difficult and painful, but harmless, and that both see as matching the seriousness of the offence.
- If both parties have grievances they cannot move beyond, we ask them to separately take some sheets of paper and write on one side the grievance they have, and, on the other side,

what an adequate repay would be (Pérez Opi & Landarroitajáuregui, 1995). This has to be something specific and doable, so that the other person has the choice of doing it.

Some couples display profound marital conflict that has preceded the substance abuse and is therefore not just a consequence of it. It may or not be a trigger for the substance abuse, but in any case therapy should specifically target the dysfunctional couple interactions, stop criticism, and promote positive alternatives (Gottman & Gottman, 2008; Gottman, Schwartz-Gottman, & DeClaire, 2006). Instead of trying to figure out what problem is central or whether to start with the drug abuse or the couple conflict, we negotiate with the couple what their theory of change is. Our preference is to work at the same time with both problems, using the substance abuse as a privileged tool to change the couple dynamics. In that way, any improvement in one area can have a positive effect on the work in the other. Below, we provide a case example that illustrates the challenges of working with a client and his partner who was not only grappling with a serious substance-abuse habit but was oppressed by concurrent self-destructive habits as well.

Case Example

"Coke is my Lady!" Having an Extra-Marital Affair with "The White Devil"

Troy and LaTisha, an African-American married couple in their mid-thirties had been referred to me (MS) by her health maintenance organization. Troy was a tall, handsome, and well-built man who used to play running back for his college football team. A severe knee injury had ended his football career when he was a junior in college. He had earned a business degree and worked as both a consultant and sales representative for his international company that had offices all over the world. LaTisha also worked for a company as a human resources director. She had regular work hours while Troy's job required him to travel almost on a bi-weekly basis.

LaTisha was seeking marital counseling for suspicions that Troy was having an extramarital affair because of the following reasons: a dramatic decline in their sexual intimacy and large amounts of money were disappearing from their two joint bank accounts, the credit card bills were getting out of hand, and Troy would not let her know what hotels he was staying at when he was out of town on business. LaTisha also had found a small gold-plated straw, a small mirror, and a razor blade in a drawer, making her suspicious that he may be currently abusing cocaine again.

Although Troy and LaTisha were college sweethearts, they had "never partied together" and back then he would drink with his friends and was described as a recreational drug user. According to LaTisha, after Troy's football career-ending knee injury, he increased his alcohol and marijuana consumption, at times abused his prescribed Vicadin (pain killer) for his leg pain, and experimented on and off with cocaine.

The First Couple Therapy Session

Troy and LaTisha came together to the session. When I greeted the couple in the waiting room, I could tell by the look on Troy's and his lack of a firm handshake that he was not too thrilled to be coming to see a marital therapist. I checked out with both partners how they felt about working with a white therapist. Without hesitation, each partner shared with me that they had appreciated my asking them about their comfort levels working with a white therapist and they had no problem with it. They also pointed out that neither of them had been in counseling before. I let them know that being first-timers makes them much "more ripe" for change than individuals and couples who have multiple therapy experiences.

I began with Troy, wanting to come to know him by his strengths, talents, interests, and life passions. Troy shared with me that he really loved having the opportunity to see the world through his job and how this was his "childhood dream to rise above" his "impoverished upbringing in the inner city to become successful in life." I learned that he chose to "sidestep gangs" and to do academically well in school and earn himself a college football scholarship. Out of curiosity, I inquired with Troy if he were aware of what he had told himself "to rise above" and get himself so fired up to transcend poverty, gang life, and be successful in life. I could tell by Troy's smile, cocking his head back, and sitting more upright that my line of questioning was making him feel more relaxed and comfortable with me. He shared the following: "My father was a janitor and slaved on his job and my mother cleaned houses. Sometimes we could barely afford groceries. One of my brothers was shot by a rival gang member from out of the hood [neighborhood] and is in a wheelchair. After my brother had been shot, I told myself, 'You got to get out of this reality, rise above, and make something out of your life.' There was no stopping me in high school. I was booking it, and not only was I the fastest runner in the whole school but I nailed down the starting running back position as a freshman. My junior year I was being heavily recruited by many universities and colleges to play football. …" "Are you done!" LaTisha interjected and further added, "We need to talk about why we are here!" Troy started to get defensive with her after her abrupt interruption. I acknowledged LaTisha's strong desire to get down to business but asked her first to help me better get to know her. LaTisha shared that she greatly disliked her management position because she had to "constantly put out fires" and "never gets any support from my superiors." I empathized with her dilemma and asked her about her hobbies and life passions. LaTisha liked listening to jazz music, particularly Miles Davis, dancing, and cooking New Orleans Cajun-Creole cuisine because she had grown up in the south and loved this kind of food. I asked Troy if he thought LaTisha was a good cook and he responded with, "She is really an awesome cook!" Next, I asked him which were his favorite house specialties, and he said, "Her seafood gumbo and shrimp jambalaya." They laughed when I shared with them that after our session I am coming over for dinner. I also shared with the couple my passion for jazz and cooking as well.

At this point in the session, I shifted gears and asked what concerns had brought them in today. LaTisha began by looking at Troy and angrily asking him point blank, "Are you having an affair?!" Troy responded with, "What makes you think that?" She went on to cite the many reasons for her suspicions, such as large amounts of money disappearing, strange credit card charges and withdrawals, and his being secretive about what hotels he was staying in, and so forth. LaTisha suddenly turned to Troy and confronted him again, "I've got to know, is it another woman, is it coke?!!!!" He responded defensively with, "Stop talking that nonsense, woman!" At this point, I jumped in out of fear that Troy would soon leave. LaTisha started to cry and was about to confront Troy again and I had suggested because things

SUBSTANCE-ABUSING HABITS

had gotten so volatile that maybe it would be best to split them up and see them individually for the remaining time of the session. They both agreed. When asked which partner would like to see me first, LaTisha voiced a strong desire for me to see Troy first, so that she could have some space "to chill." I checked out with Troy if he was okay with seeing me alone and he had no problem with that.

I began by checking in with Troy how he was holding up after the barrage of confrontation he had gotten from LaTisha. He shared that he was okay and that sometimes LaTisha can become "quite emotional and angry" with him. At this point, I decided to take a one-down position and interview Troy like the curious but confused TV detective *Columbo* would.

Scratching my head and putting a perplexed look on my face I asked Troy, "How the heck did LaTisha come up those ideas that you were having an affair or even dabbling with coke? Troy responded with, "I'm going to come clean with you Doc … Coke is my lady! However, she is the white devil, man." I first asked him what he meant by 'the white devil.' Troy responded with, "Well she seduces you with a great 'high,' like great sex, man … but then she bites you hard in the ass." I asked, "What do you mean by 'biting you hard in the ass'?" He went on to say that 'coke' was making him empty out their bank accounts and run up big credit card bills by paying off dealers through buying them material things they wanted and wining and dining them as well to eliminate drug debts. I asked Troy, "Which lady would you prefer to be number one in your life, LaTisha or the White Lady?" Troy quickly responded with, "LaTisha of course." Next, I explored with Troy if the White Lady had any close friends that she liked to bring a long for the ride, like alcohol, weed, or gambling. Troy quickly said, "Yes, there are times when we are all together." He pointed out how when the friends come along for the ride he goes for "long runs of dancing with all of them." When asked what he meant by 'dancing with all of them.' Troy responded with "coking up for long periods of time, curbing the crash with alcohol and weed, and when staying in hotels with casinos blowing wads of cash on blackjack." He went on to add, "I lose myself completely."

Since the drawbridge had been lowered and we were on a roll with Troy's "coming clean" with me about his drug use and gambling problems that dated back to high school "playing poker all of the time and hustling people at pool a lot." I used this wonderful opportunity to take a mini drinking and drug history with Troy. I found out that alcoholism problems ran in his father's side of the family and that he suspected that his father's death from liver disease was due to his heavy drinking. No other family drug problems were reported. Troy began experimenting with alcohol and marijuana in junior high school years and throughout the high school. Once he was a high school senior, he abandoned all alcohol and drug use and focused on his academics and excelling in football and in track and field as a sprinter. In college, Troy occasionally used alcohol and marijuana with friends but greatly limited his consumption to remain in top shape for football. Where Troy began to really lose control with alcohol, marijuana, Vicadin, and cocaine was after his football career-ending knee injury, as he put it best, "My whole life crashed and burned at that point." In response to his deeply depressed emotional state, he said, "I got ripped to oblivion almost every weekend." After meeting LaTisha in college and falling in love with her, Troy had dramatically reduced his use and began focusing on academic work and doing well in his business school program. He landed an excellent job with a Fortune 500 international company. For a time, on his new job he would go for long stretches of not drinking, doing any drugs, or gambling. When asked how he pulled off the long periods without partying or gambling, Troy responded with, "I told myself that I need to be on top of my game on the job and make my mark." I asked if he had any other strategies that seemed to work at thwarting the White Lady and her friends' dirty work, Troy added, "I stopped going to certain bars with partying work friends after I left the office and instead, would go right home. Sometimes on work trips, I will go directly to my hotel room right after dinner and not hang around with the guys in the restaurant bar." Where Troy tended to be most vulnerable was when he traveled. Apparently, having a great meal with expensive wine with customers and partying work friends who were single would often result in wild hotel room parties with women or going out gambling (playing blackjack) at the hotel casino. Presently, he was snorting "a few lines of coke" every other day and drinking a couple of glasses of wine and/or a few beers daily. He limited his marijuana consumption to the times that his friends had some to share with him.

Since we were running out of session time, I wanted to get some sense from Troy how committed he was to saving and improving his marriage. I asked, "On a scale from 1 to 10, with 10 being totally committed to doing absolutely anything to save and improve your marriage to LaTisha, and 1 ready to run off for good with the White Lady and her close friends, where would you rate yourself today?" Troy said, "An 8." Out of curiosity, I asked him what would have to happen for him to get one step higher up to a 9. Troy responded with, "For LaTisha to stop interrogating me all of the time." When asked, what specifically it was about LaTisha and his marriage that put him way up at an 8, Troy had shared with me that he loved her and did not want to lose her. His eyes were watery when he shared from the heart this with me with a lot of conviction, which made me hopeful that we could work together as a couple to improve the relationship. Troy appeared to be in the *preparation* stage of readiness for change (Prochaska, Norcross, & DiClemente, 2006) with the biggest obstacle for conquering his self-destructive habits being on the road work-wise with his partying work friends.

I then asked Troy how confident he was today on a scale from 1 to 10, with 10 being to close the door for good on the White Lady and her friends, and he said, "At a 7." I shared with Troy not only is 7 a lucky number for good fortune just ready to happen but that many of my clients have completed counseling successfully at a 7. He responded with a surprised, "Really, man?!" When asked why he selected the lucky 7, Troy shared, "I'm a realist, man. There is no way I can quit everything all at once this time around. When asked about what quitting strategy he wished to pursue with me, Troy felt that it should be a systematic process of reducing use with one drug at a time and then we could address the gambling. He wanted to start with tapering down with the coke and then move to the alcohol. Troy felt that it would be easy to just quit weed without any problem and he was ready to begin staying quit today. He also had pointed out that a few years back he had completely stopped taking the Vicadin because he felt "like a zombie" on them and it had made him "real tired." I decided to set an individual goal with Troy using the confidence scale. I asked him what specifically he was going to do over the next week to get one step up higher on the confidence scale to an 8. Troy shared that he would "come home right after work instead of going out for drinks with my coke-using work friends." He also thought it would be helpful to "get rid of his coke-using drug paraphernalia" and music he typically listened to while "coking up."

Before meeting alone with LaTisha, I explored with Troy if he was ready to take the courageous step of letting her know the truth about what he had been doing and where the money was going. I also shared with him that this could also be another milestone in his life where he proves to himself and others that he can "rise above" adversity and make special things happen again. Troy smiled and acknowledged that he was ready to tell LaTisha.

I quickly met alone with LaTisha to see if she had re-grouped and was feeling more "chilled out." LaTisha was curious to know if Troy opened up to me, since I had spent so much session time alone with him. I shared with her that our time alone was very productive and that Troy was ready to tell her the truth about everything. At that point, she asked me to invite Troy in to join us. Troy joined us and told LaTisha everything. LaTisha started to cry and get worked up about what Troy had been doing and the dent he had put in their finances but was able to contain her emotions enough and asked me, "Where do we go from here?" I first validated her feelings and then shared with her that this was a courageous step for Troy to finally "come clean" with her. I also pointed out that on a commitment scale from 1 to 10, with 10 being doing absolutely anything to save his marriage with her and improve the relationship, he rated himself at an "8." LaTisha smiled and shared that she was encouraged by this. I then asked LaTisha, "On a scale from 1 to 10, with 10 being you totally trust Troy again and 1 not at all, where would you place Troy on that scale right now after taking this courageous step with you?" LaTisha said, "A 5." Prior to this session, I asked her to rate Troy on that same scale and she responded with, "minus 10 … I had absolutely no trust, it was well below your scale." To set a goal, I asked each partner what they needed to see each other do over the next week to take one step up higher to a 6. LaTisha shared, "For Troy to come right home after work when he was in town, keep the lines of communication open when on the road, such as sharing details about his whereabouts, what he is doing, and using her for support when he is feeling vulnerable for partying and gambling." I inquired with Troy if he felt those steps were possible. Troy agreed to work on making "LaTisha's requests happen." For Troy, he felt if LaTisha would work on "not interrogating me" and being "more supportive" that it would greatly help him. I wrote the partners' goals down on their blueprint for change plan and we discussed which of their key individual and relationship strengths they would call upon to help them to achieve their goals.

We only had five minutes left in the session and I took a very short break to put my editorial reflection together and offer the couple therapeutic experiments to try out over the next week. After I reconvened the couple, I shared with them how impressed I was that in spite of the way the White Lady and her friends had created so much devastation and mistrust in their marital relationship, they clearly were committed as a team and could still see daylight for scoring touchdowns and winning back control of their lives from these tough opponents. I praised LaTisha for not giving up on Troy, being understanding, and so supportive with hearing the real truth about the situation and being committed to helping him conquer these challenging habits. I complimented Troy on his big courageous step of letting LaTisha know the truth about the White Lady and her friends. Again, I underscored how this was another beautiful example of him "rising above" adversity and getting his relationship and life priorities straight. I turned to LaTisha and asked her if she felt like Troy had scored a touchdown with her today and she completely agreed. I pointed out to the couple that it would be a long bumpy road ahead and required solid teamwork because the White Lady and her friends are quite clever and could strike when they were least expecting it. In fact, I shared with the couple that slips go with the territory of change, even after some days of abstinence and solid teamwork and not to worry or give up if they should occur. The following therapeutic experiments were offered to the couple:

- I encouraged Troy over the next days to educate LaTisha on what his triggers were that would lead him to fall prey to the White Lady and her friends' evil ways, so that she could quickly intervene to help him stay on track.
- Troy was to carefully notice daily what he and LaTisha did that helped him to not cave into the White Lady and her friends' attempts to undermine his efforts to remain abstinent.
- To help inject some positive emotion back into the relationship, I wanted each partner daily to let one another know what they appreciated about one another in the forms of e-mails, e-cards, and offline gestures of affection. In the same spirit, I encouraged them to reinstate a fun and mutually enjoyable activity that they used to do together in the past and make a date to do it.

As far as future sessions went, both partners thought it would be best to divide the sessions up and for me to meet with Troy alone part of the time to teach relapse prevention tools and strategies. When asked if there were any other key people from their social network that they would like to involve in future sessions, they felt that their pastor Thomas Martin would be a good bet because for Troy he was someone he looked up to like "a father." However, the couple decided to work on themselves first before bringing in the pastor. We scheduled our next session.

Prior to ending our couple session, I solicited feedback from them what this meeting was like for them. Troy shared that it turned out to be a lot more positive than he had originally thought it would be. He also found it useful to finally see the White Lady and her friends were ganging up to try to ruin his marriage and his life and that he was not going to allow that to happen! LaTisha thanked me for "reaching Troy" and "helping him to see the light that he has to change to save his marriage." The couple did not have anything negative to say about the session experience nor did they want me to do anything differently with them. They both shared that they felt very comfortable working with me.

The Second Couple Therapy Session

The couple came back one week later all smiles. Troy was able to go a whole week without any coke and greatly reduced his alcohol consumption to one drink a day. When asked about his recipe for success, he quickly corrected me and proclaimed, "Our recipe for success!" Apparently, the couple really enjoyed the appreciation days experiment and found that it had brought them closer together. Troy was coming straight home from work and was grateful that he did not have to go out of town at all over the week so he could get off to a great start at turning his life around. He rated his week's performance at an 8. The couple started going to their health club and working out together every other day. According to LaTisha, Troy did a beautiful job of educating her about his triggers for drug using and gambling, and would even come to her for a hug and support when he would experience craving to use coke. They had gotten rid of Troy's drug paraphernalia, music, photos saved on his iPhone and laptop of him partying with friends, and he even "came clean" with LaTisha, showing her his hidden drug stash locations in the house. In fact, Troy even flushed down the toilet with LaTisha some cocaine he had hidden in one of the drug stash locations. LaTisha thought this was "a huge step for Troy!" I turned to Troy and said, "Wow! Are you aware of how you pulled off that huge step?!" Troy responded with, "Yeah, it was really hard man and I had my doubts, believe me, but I really love LaTisha and I don't want to lose her." LaTisha smiled and hugged and kissed Troy. I shared with Troy that with this huge step, he spun off the White Lady's attempts to undermine his decision to get rid of the coke and to show her that his number one lady is LaTisha and that he had scored another touchdown with her! I gave Troy a 'high-five' and LaTisha did the same.

I amplified and consolidated their gains. On the commitment scale to his marriage, Troy rated himself at "a 9." I checked in with LaTisha where Troy was on her trust scale and she had felt that he had shot up to "a 7!" According to LaTisha, his coming home right after work, regularly communicating both during and after work hours, and turning over the management of financial matters had shot him up to a lucky 7. When asked if Troy wanted to meet with me alone to discuss relapse prevention tools and strategies, they both agreed that they would like to do this activity together. I pointed out to them that the best way to optimize for their further success at conquering the White Lady and her friends for good was their continued solid teamwork.

First, I underscored with the couple that they should continue to increase doing what is already working, such as keeping the lines of communication regularly open and Troy's asking for a hug and support from LaTisha when experiencing craving to use coke. Since Troy's first big test was about to happen in a few days where he would have to fly out to Hong Kong on business, I felt it would be best to do *constructive worst-case scenario planning* (see Chapter 10) with the couple. I pulled a constructive worst-case scenario planning worksheet for the couple to fill out while we talked. Troy identified the following three worse-case scenarios that he could imagine happening:

- He would go out for drinks after the dinner meeting with his coke-using colleagues.
- He would walk into a casino either alone or with his coke-using friends.
- He would fail to regularly communicate with LaTisha via e-mail or cell phone during the day or in the evenings each day he was away.

Next, we discussed each one of these scenarios and steps Troy would take and anything LaTisha could do long distance to help. Troy felt that with the first worst-case scenario, he needed to stick with his new routine of coming home right away after work, but in this case, after dinner go right to his hotel room alone to call LaTisha or e-mail her and stay there for the rest of the evening. If there was a casino in his hotel or close by, he had to force himself to stay away and go right to his hotel room. I suggested if the White Lady's gambling friend started to mess with his mind and was heading toward the casino, he was to try to picture a stop light turning red in his mind and after the light changes, make a U-turn and head quickly back to his hotel room. Finally, with the last worst-case scenario situation, on his daily schedule planning feature of his iPhone, he would type in each day in capital letters: CALL OR E-MAIL LATISHA! He also would handwrite notes all over his hotel room reminding him to stay in regular communication with her. LaTisha shared that she would leave him both e-mail and cell phone supportive messages as well. I recommended as part of one of her supportive messages that she would include the following: "Remember, you can 'rise above' this and keep scoring touchdowns with me!" Troy thought that would be a big help. I made copies of the constructive worst-case scenario planning worksheets for the couple to take with and review.

During the remainder of the session time, I introduced the couple to the following relapse prevention tools and strategies: *my structured plan for success*, *my positive trigger log*, the "*Taking a Trip to Popcorn Land*" meditation, and *visualizing movies of joy and/or success* (see Chapter 9). I pointed out that the recipe for success for many people being pushed around by powerful habits like substance abuse and gambling is to have a highly structured and tight relapse prevention plan. I handed the blank structured plan for success form to Troy to begin to fill in and complete at home. He began to fill in their every other day visit to the health club, having breakfast and dinner together, and other hobbies he could spend time alone doing and do with LaTisha, such as taking a cooking class after work together.

Next, I introduced the couple to the positive trigger log. With this relapse prevention strategy, Troy was to keep track on a daily basis and write in things that he did (useful self-generated coping and problem-solving strategies), LaTisha, close non-using or gambling friends, his family members, and what key resource people from his social network have said (words of wisdom and support) or done, such as his pastor would say or do that helped trigger positive emotion for him and prevent him from caving into substance use or gambling. I gave Troy a positive trigger log to take with and fill out over the week and bring it into the next session.

I walked the couple through the steps of doing the "Taking a Trip to Popcorn Land" meditation. I gave each partner a piece of popcorn so they could practice doing the meditation in my office. I stressed the importance of doing each step slowly and to simply label any intruding thoughts or feelings that should enter their minds while doing the meditation by saying silently to themselves, "There goes an anxious feeling or a worrying thought." The meditation is to last for 10–12 minutes. LaTisha shared that she would find this meditation very helpful to do for her work stress.

Finally, I taught the couple how to implement the visualizing movies of joy and/or success strategy. Using all of his senses, including color and motion, Troy transported himself back to his best college football game as a sophomore, where he had scored three touchdowns and had gained 150 yards on the ground. I had him pick his best touchdown run in the game to focus on. In addition to describing to himself the complete sensory experience, I had him access his thoughts and feelings when he was running for the touchdown. With his eyes closed, Troy was smiling while accessing this movie, and had shared how happy he felt by reliving this memorable run and game in general. Troy liked this visualization experiment so much that he wrote it in daily to practice on his structured plan for success weekly schedule. He also wrote in on his schedule practicing daily the "Taking a Trip to Popcorn Land" meditation.

After my intersession break, I complimented the couple on their excellent teamwork and great efforts to improve their relationship through open lines of communication, showing and giving more affection, and generating their own creative solutions. I let them know that they were already doing what works to prevent relapses from occurring, such as: keeping the relationship climate positive and loving, structure-building, keeping regular routines like going to the health club together, and Troy's coming straight home after work. I commended Troy on his many big steps over the week, such as: educating LaTisha on his triggers, showing her where the drug stashes were, and even flushing down the toilet a large quantity of cocaine! I shared, "You really burned your britches with the White Lady on that move!" Both Troy and LaTisha laughed. I also complimented Troy on his two creative methods for reminding himself daily to communicate with LaTisha. Finally, I complimented LaTisha on being so loving, supportive, and understanding and how other partners in a similar relationship situation would have absolutely no trust, blame their partners, emotionally distance, or, worse yet, would have exited from their relationships. I predicted that the White Lady and her friends more than likely will try to stage a coup with Troy while on his work trip but if he stands strong by practicing using his relapse prevention tools, keeps the lines of communications open with LaTisha, and goes right to his hotel room after business dinners, he will "rise above" this challenging situation. Since the therapeutic experiments given in the first session were so useful and effective, I encouraged them to do more of what works. Before we adjourned, I gave the couple a sheet of paper that concretely explained how to implement each of the relapse prevention tools and strategies we had discussed. The next appointment was scheduled for two weeks later.

The Third Couple Therapy Session

When asked what further progress they had made, LaTisha began with pointing out that Troy had two bad days (a disastrous Thursday and Friday) on his weeklong work trip. On Thursday he had used coke, got drunk, and gambled away a few thousand dollars. On the second day, he had forgotten to get a wake-up call and missed a very important meeting that almost cost him his job. Troy looked very dejected and voiced that he was acting like "a real loser." Rather than allowing us to keep going down this dark pathway of failure and upset, I changed direction and explored with Troy what was different on Monday, Tuesday, and Wednesday. On those days, he used all of his relapse prevention tools and strategies, regularly contacted LaTisha, and went straight to his hotel room after business dinners. I stressed to the couple that considering how historically most business trips for Troy would have consisted of daily alcohol, drug use, and possible gambling and that these were longstanding habits, the fact that he had gone three whole days of not using or gambling was amazing! I also shared with the couple that we could not have made any headway without this slip. I asked Troy what he had learned from this slip on Thursday and he responded with, "The one line theory is true and you should not mess with the system that works." Troy was under a lot of stress on Thursday because he had to give a big presentation Friday morning for his company. According to Troy, "It was like the White Lady was in my mind, sensing that I was in a vulnerable state and brainwashed me to think that if I try just one line that it would be okay." All of a sudden, Troy was doing several lines of coke, drinking, and so intoxicated that he had blown $3000 at the blackjack table of the casino next to their hotel. The major epiphany for Troy was that "one line was too much." He also saw clearly the synergistic effects of how alcohol use can rapidly trigger cocaine use and gambling. The next day, after discovering that he had already missed the early part of the morning meeting, he quickly got on the telephone and contacted one of his most reliable colleagues who could step in for him and save the day for his company. Apparently, his colleague had done so well with the sales presentation that the customer company representatives decided to contract with their company. I shared with Troy that he owes his colleague big time! Troy acknowledged, "Yeah, I plan to take Stuart out for dinner for covering my back." LaTisha chimed in, "I'm going to hold you to that. You really could have lost your job, you know …" At this point, I jumped in to disrupt this negative blaming pattern that was in motion.

Next, I shifted gears with the couple and adopted a coaching position. I shared with them that it is pointless for us to continue to dwell on what happened on the work trip and continue to be negative and that we need to pick ourselves up and "rise above" adversity. I pointed out to the couple, that "Change is a funny thing, three steps forward and two steps back, but we are not back to square one." Both partners agreed, and I explored what steps we needed to take at this point to get us back on track to those high numbers on our confidence and commitment scales. Although Troy was nervous about his upcoming out-of-town trip, he was feeling a little more confident the next time around that he would use his relapse prevention tools and stay in close communication with LaTisha. I had explored with Troy if he had any work colleagues who either did not drink or use drugs or just drank and did not use coke. There were two close colleagues: Mike and John. I suggested that he use them as his sponsors on the trip. To begin with, I recommended that he "come clean" with them, go public with them about his coke and gambling habits and strong desire to change, and ask them to help him to avoid the temptation to indulge in the habits when they travel together. Next, I had two empty chairs in my office that I wanted Troy to pretend to be both Mike and John in each of their designated chairs and I would pretend to be him. I asked him to speak for both of his colleagues in terms of what they could say or do that would prevent him from using coke. Mike would say to Troy, "You have been drinking a lot at dinner and I will accompany you to your hotel room." John would say, "I really care about you man and I don't want you to almost lose your job again. So, I think it would be best that you go up to your hotel room and chill tonight." Troy truly believed that his work colleagues would respond this way, would protect his confidentiality, and were totally committed to helping him not lose his job. He planned to schedule a meeting the next day with Mike and John to seek their support as sponsors to help aid him in his crusade to conquer his vicious habits. I asked Troy to call me to let me know how his meeting went with Mike and John.

After my intersession break, I complimented the couple on their resilience and how quickly they could bounce back from their setback. I stressed the importance of good teamwork, using the relapse prevention tools and strategies, and to work on bringing back the good feeling in the relationship through using the appreciation days experiment. I also shared with them trying out Thich Nhat Hanh's *"Two Garden"* couple mindfulness practice (Hanh, 2011) (see Chapter 10) of daily attending to each other's gardens with loving-kindness and compassion, which will help strengthen their loving bond together. Since Troy would be gone for three weeks, we scheduled our next session for after he got back.

Telephone Call from Troy

The next day, Troy called me to let me know that his meeting with Mike and John was a success! Both of them were very compassionate and understanding of what Troy was going through. It turned out that John used to have problems with cocaine abuse and he shared with Troy what worked for him to get clean and sober. Troy shared with his colleagues how they could help him best on work trips. They also had some other helpful strategies in mind to help Troy out as well. Finally, they both agreed to serve as his loyal sponsors.

The Fourth Couple Therapy Session

The couple came to our fourth session in great spirits. The great news was that Troy reported not having used any substances and not gambling once for over the past three weeks! LaTisha chimed in how proud she was of Troy's great accomplishment. I explored with Troy if he was aware of how he pulled this great feat off. According to Troy, not only were Mike and John tightly monitoring him but Mike had remained abstinent from alcohol for the duration of their business trip to help Troy out. John did not drink and stopped using all drugs after he kicked his coke habit. He provided Troy with a lot of support and encouragement that he could get on the recovery track like him. Other helpful steps that Troy took were the following: Troy was using all of his relapse prevention tools and strategies, not drinking at business dinners, going to his hotel room right after the dinners, working out daily, and contacting LaTisha throughout the day and in the evening via e-mail, Skype, and telephone calls. LaTisha also would leave "sweet and loving messages" on both his cell and hotel room phones. Troy also reported no longer craving coke, feeling the urge to drink, or gamble. He was feeling really proud of himself. To test the waters, I asked Troy, "What would have to happen for you to go backwards at this point?" He confidently stated, "There's no stopping me now, I can't even fathom going back to how things were before." Reaching over to hug and kiss LaTisha, Troy further proclaimed, "My number one special lady LaTisha and I have chased the White Lady out of town for good!"

The couple had shared with me that their relationship was now stronger than it ever was before. They were being much more "romantically intimate" with one another. Troy's theory was that by eliminating the White Lady and her friends out of his life he got his libido back and was more emotionally available to LaTisha. The couple were cooking together more. After amplifying and consolidating all of the couple's gains, I asked them how they planned to use our session time when they stopped coming to see me. Interestingly enough, over lunch the couple had asked themselves the same question. Apparently, they had felt things were going so well and in control now that they were even thinking about calling me to cancel our session. There was an Italian cooking class that LaTisha and Troy were thinking of taking together that would overlap with our session time.

Next, I shifted gears and asked the couple, "Let's say we were to run into one another six months down the road at the shopping mall and you ran over to me eager to share with me what further changes you made. What will you tell me that had further improved with your situation?" LaTisha responded with, "I'm pregnant! We had decided to start a family." Troy confidently shared, "I have remained drug and gambling-free and going strong." Troy also shared with me that they "bought a new house to make way for the new family members."

After my intersession break, I complimented the couple on their wealth of changes and asked them, "What is your consultation fee so I can invite you in to help me with other couples that are grappling with drug and gambling habits?" Troy said, "For you, Matthew, it will be on the house!" We all laughed. The couple saw no need for a future session. I told them that I have an open door policy and that if they should ever need a future tune-up, they should not hesitate to contact me. I wished them the best of luck and we mutually terminated.

Telephone Follow-Up

I spoke to both Troy and LaTisha at six months. Not only was LaTisha pregnant but Troy had been clean and sober and "going strong" like he had said to me in our last couple therapy session. The other great news was that Troy had gotten a big promotion and they were relocating to the west coast. In fact, his company had furnished them with a beautiful new house and covered their moving expenses. I wished them well.

Reflections on the "Coke Is My Lady!" Case

Mark: This case really shows how potent couple therapy is as the healing context for the successful treatment of substance abuse. For me the most important therapeutic ingredient is how you handled the initially explosive couple situation and utilized Troy's wishes to stay in the relationship with LaTisha as a powerful motivating factor. This case is also a great example of using some time at the beginning of therapy to find out about our clients' hobbies and strengths, which can provide powerful themes and metaphors for therapy. With Troy, the *"rising above"* metaphor obviously created a powerful narrative thread that informed all the rest of therapy, together with the "White Lady" theme – in much

	the same way as in great movie soundtracks there are usually two or three themes that go back and forth playing with each other. Could you explain how you prepare yourself to keep attuned to these "musical themes" in your conversation with clients?
Matthew:	You are absolutely right about the importance of taking the time at the very beginning of therapy to come to know what our clients' key strengths, talents, life passions, and metaphors are as a vehicle for identifying those powerful "musical themes" that you can utilize throughout the whole therapeutic process to empower them. You can embed them in your questions, as a rationale and a hook for trying out a therapeutic experiment, and even when celebrating with clients sparkling moments of achievement, such as bouncing back from a substance or other self-destructive habit slip.
Mark:	I think the first session is also a great example of using a variety of scaling questions to help this couple appreciate their improvements and figure out the next steps they want to take. Over the years I have found that scaling questions are among the most useful therapeutic tools for me and for my trainees (and, by the way, most of my clients do also feel satisfied with therapy when they reach a "7"). But on top of that, I feel that in the Troy and LaTisha's case, it made a big difference that in the first session, instead of using a Progress Scale only, you decided to build a Commitment Scale for Troy and a Trust Scale for LaTisha. What gave you the clue to create these two different scales?
Matthew:	With Troy, I wanted to gauge both how committed he was to saving his marriage with LaTisha and not allowing the "White Lady and her close friends" to continue to destroy and ultimately dissolve his marriage. By framing it this way, Troy could see how the marital difficulties and cocaine abuse and other self-destructive habits were interconnected. It was beneficial to use the trust scale with LaTisha because this trust issue, which mostly centered on her suspicions that he was having an affair was at the core of what was driving her conflicts with Troy. By having LaTisha concretely spell out the steps that Troy would have to take to win back her trust again, was quite beneficial for both them to accurately assess signs of progress over time. It was also helpful to have Troy share with LaTisha what she could do differently in relationship to him that could improve their relationship and aid him in his quest to drive the "White Lady and her friends" out of their lives. My experience when we fail to address the trust issue head on in a positive way is that the non-trusting partner will continue to play detective, ask questions, and anticipate more affair and other sneaky activity behind the scenes with his or her partner. This creates a negative self-fulfilling prophecy—"What you expect is what you will get."
Mark:	In the second session, you taught relapse prevention strategies and coping skills to both Troy and LaTisha conjointly, instead of focusing only on Troy. Are there any situations where you think that it may be more useful to teach the relapse prevention tools and coping skills only

to the client presenting with the substance abuse, and not to his or her couple partner?

Matthew: The only time I will do solo relapse prevention training with the substance abuser is when the partner's or parents' severe substance abuse and/or mental health issues or other difficulties overshadow the client's needs and ability to focus with me. When working with multi-habit-dependent couples or families, it makes a lot of sense to do relapse prevention training with individuals at least initially. Once things stabilize enough with the individual partner or family members, I will bring them back together for worst-case scenario planning and to consolidate their gains.

Mark: One thing that I can see us doing differently is that you often offer at least two or three relapse prevention, stress management, or coping skills tools to your clients, whereas I prefer to teach them one-by-one, one session each, so that my clients have time to train with one tool before starting with the next. It seems to me that here you are putting more of an emphasis on clients' choice, while I am underlining training time. What are your thoughts on this?

Matthew: Yes, there is a lot of research in the substance abuse field and psychotherapy process and treatment outcome research that indicates with substance-abusing clients or clients who have high psychological reactance levels, that giving them coping tool and strategy options to choose from increases their motivation levels to change and helps to insure treatment compliance. Therefore, I like my clients to give the different options a test run and see which ones suit them best. Once they decide which of the tools and strategies they like the best they can practice using those specific ones as their trusty tools.

Mark: In the third session it would have been very easy, as a therapist, to either get demoralized by the serious relapse of Troy or, conversely, to overlook it by focusing only on the three "good days" (the "solution-focused bias"). However, you discussed the couple's accomplishments first and then moved on to discuss the lapse in detail. In what situations do you prefer to do it the other way around, start by discussing the lapse and then move on to talking about the good days that had preceded it?

Matthew: First I will test the waters and see if the clients will allow me to be curious with them about the "good days" and all that was working and particularly noteworthy on those days. If I am met with a lot of strong affect and defensiveness, I will shift gears and revisit all that lead up to the slip. This would include identifying the specific triggers and tracking the sequence of events and key players involved with the slip.

Mark: Another part of this case that I love especially is how you involved Troy's colleagues as real "sponsors" who would help cover the back door to relapse. Using the two empty chairs technique added a great deal of drama and liveliness to the dialogue. If that had not been enough to engage them, would you have considered inviting Troy's colleagues to a session?

Matthew: My first thought was to see if we could sneak in a meeting with Troy and his colleagues just before they left on their business trip. However, a lot of different things had come to my mind about how difficult this might be to pull off: it might be very difficult to get everyone to come to my office together at the same time because of differing work schedules and commitments and because of confidentiality and discomfort; it would not make sense to meet at Troy's office; and I also thought this would be a great opportunity to encourage the client on his own to "rise above" and take responsibility for meeting with his work colleagues and enlisting their support. My gut told me that the latter option was the best option and to provide a coaching role and prepare Troy for what to say to his colleagues in their important meeting. Since we had such a solid working alliance, I was totally convinced that he would make this meeting happen.

Mark: I think that the pregnancy of LaTisha at follow-up marks a real turning point not only in the biography of this couple, but also in the substance abuse career of Troy. It is the kind of change that contributes to "turning the page" on drugs for good. However, I do have some concerns with timing. I think if I had been the therapist in this case, I would have insisted on scheduling another session after the fourth, maybe one or two months down the line, just to make sure there were no further lapses and to help the couple stay on guard. In order not to undermine the couples' confidence, I may have labeled this last session as "just a follow-up."

Matthew: I hear your concerns. However, I must say that I and the couple were extremely confident that they were pioneering a solution-determined direction with their lives. I think if Troy had had another slip, things were still shaky with the marital relationship, or there was some unexpected crisis like Troy having lost his job, I would have pushed hard for them to stay in therapy until things were more solid. I think the fact that I bore witness to consistent solution-maintaining patterns of interaction, regular use of the relapse prevention tools, the increase in positive emotion and bonding in the marital relationship, and the talk of starting a family made me a believer they were done with this chapter in the their story. I found the talk of having a baby in six months in response to my future oriented question to be noteworthy, and with my six month follow-up call discovered that LaTisha was pregnant. Talk about clients creating their own positive self-fulfilling prophecies!

7

PROBLEMATIC GAMBLING HABITS

The future ain't what it used to be.
Yogi Berra

Introduction

It is estimated that in the United States, around 78% (Kessler, 2004) of the population gambles over their lifetime. In 2007, Americans spent about $60 billion in legal casinos, $52.7 billion in legal lotteries, and an estimated $7 billion in illegal Internet gaming (Quinn, 2009; Lottery Vendor Data, 2008). There are many different opportunities for legal gambling: lotteries, including lotto games, instant games or scratch tickets, bingos, and video Keno; stand-alone slot machines; blackjack, roulette, and other casino games; horse race betting; and sports wagering, which in Europe has become legal in recent years.

Although a majority of adults in western societies gamble occasionally without encountering significant problems, prevalence of gambling problems is high. In their benchmark meta-analysis of 120 North American studies up to 1997, Shaffer, Hall, and Vanderbilt (1999), estimated a lifetime prevalence for DSM pathological gambling between 1% and 2%, a figure that with a more liberal cutoff point including both problem and pathological gambling went up to 2–5%. A recent worldwide update found a 3% of current prevalence of problem and pathological gambling, with a notorious convergence for different classification criteria (Stucki & Rihs-Middel., 2007). This figure increases several-fold for young adults, people with mental health disorders and prison inmates. Given that the prevalence of pathological gambling is related to the availability of gambling opportunities, legal or illegal (Grun & McKeigue 2000; Jacques, Ladouceur, & Ferland, 2000; Ladouceur & Walker, 1996; Rush, Veldhuizen, & Adlaf, 2007; Volberg, 1994, 2004; Welte, Barnes, Tidwell, & Hoffman, 2011) the boom of online gambling and the recent legalization of sports wagering is likely to increase the figures of pathological gambling in the future. In fact, online gambling is ideally suited to foster gambling dependency, as it can be engaged in 24 hours a day with little social constraint (Linden, 2011).

Background: The Multiple Faces of Gambling

Gambling can be defined as an attempt to win money by staking money on an uncertain event (Toneatto & Ladouceur, 2003). *Gambling problems* are difficulties or frictions that arise because of gambling behavior, for instance differences of opinion with a couple partner regarding the amount wagered or the time spent gambling, or a big loss during a occasional casino visit. *Pathological gambling* involves something more, a persistent and recurrent pattern of maladaptive behavior, characterized by the inability to control gambling, that leads to important deleterious personal, familial, professional, financial and/or legal consequences (APA, 1994). DSM-IV considers pathological gambling an impulse control disorder, but includes as characteristic features a number of symptoms that mirror the pattern of substance abuse, like preoccupation with the habit, the appearance of tolerance and withdrawal, and loss of control.

Besides showing symptoms of dependency (craving, withdrawal, tolerance), and a destructive way of handling adverse financial consequences (bail outs, illegal acts, risking significant relationships and opportunities), gamblers usually display specific behavioral and cognitive patterns. On the behavioral side, loss of control appears in the form of inertia failure abstinence violation and in rigidly patterned, often ritualistic, gambling customs. The betting behavior of problem gamblers is typically more impulsive than that of non-problem gamblers: they gamble faster, with higher and more frequent bets and take more risks (LaBrie & Shaffer, 2011).

On the cognitive side, one of the distinctive features of pathological gambling is *chasing*: most pathological gamblers keep an informal tally of their losses, and when they lose, they return another day to "get even," instead of accepting their losses. They also typically show more superstitious thinking than non-gamblers (Källmén, Andersson, & Andren, 2008):

- *Illusions of control* (Langer, 1975) and *illusory correlation* (Ciarrocchi, 2001; Källmén et al., 2008; Toneatto, 1999) lead gamblers to think that they can increase their odds of winning a chance event by personal choice (for instance, by choosing their lottery tickets themselves), by practice, by having early wins ("the slot-machine is hot now"), by familiarity (for instance a preferred table at bingo), or by playing against an inferior competitor. Illusions of control increase risk taking (Martinez, LeFloch, Gaffie, & Villejoubert, 2011), especially with slot machines, bingo automats, and the Internet (Lund, 2011).
- The "*gambler's fallacy*" (Corney & Cummings, 1985) consists of believing that a chance event is dependent upon previous events (for instance, believing that, because in the last decade no first lottery prize ended in a 9, the 9 is likelier to come out in the next lottery).
- A number of studies have also experimentally documented that gamblers show greater "*delayed reward discounting*," the tendency to de-valuate long-term outcomes and favor immediate ones (MacKillop et al., 2011) and are more likely to become entrapped by "near misses" than non-gamblers (Karlsen, 2011).
- Pathological gamblers are more likely to recall past wins as opposed to past losses (*availability bias*) and to display a peculiar *attributional style*, in which they attribute their wins to their skill (Towfigh & Glöckner, 2011) and explain away their failures attributing them to external circumstances.
- Problem gamblers are also likely to have *negative metacognitions*, with negative views of self, the world and the future (Ciarrocchi, 2001) as well as in relation to the possibility of self-control (Lindberg, Fernie, & Spada, 2011).

Genetic studies carried out by Wendy Slutske and her team (Slutske et al., 2000) suggest that "problem gambling" is not an etiologically distinct disorder but a milder form of "pathological gambling." The notion that pathological and/or problem gamblers do not differ qualitatively from non-problem gamblers, and should simply be seen as different points on a continuum, is supported by numerous clinical and community studies (for instance, Stucki & Rihs-Middel, 2007) has also recently been supported by a taxometric analysis of actual Internet sports gambling behavior (Braverman, LaBrie, & Shaffer, 2011). The clinical implication is that the classification of a person with gambling problems as being a pathological gambler is less important than a personalized assessment of the features of the gambling habit and the harm it is producing (Blaszczynski, 2009).[1]

---

1 A person who meets five or more DSM-IV criteria is traditionally considered a "pathological gambler" and, if s/he meets three of four criteria, a "*problem gambler.*" Given that these criteria are arbitrary and have been questioned by relevant authors (Carragher & McWilliams, 2011; Petry, 2009) we will use the terms "problem gambling," "pathological gambling," and "disordered gambling" interchangeably. In citing reviews and research that focus differentially on problem or on pathological gambling, we will stick to the term that the authors use.

Taken as a group, problem and pathologic gamblers are more likely than the normal population to lose their jobs, to declare bankruptcy, to have legal problems, to divorce and to suffer physical health problems. Heavy gambling is liable to create havoc in families, to disrupt personal biographies, and to become a major problem for the person who gambles and his or her loved ones (Kalischuk, Nowatzki, Cardwell, Klein, & Solowoniuk, 2006). However, in spite of this clinical observation, the truth is that most problem and even pathological gamblers do not seek therapeutic help (Cunningham, 2005; Slutske, 2006; Suurvali, Hogins, Toneatto, & Cunningham, 2008).

Although there is, as in the case of substance abuse, a certain degree of cross-over from one type of game to others, gamblers usually prefer one way of wagering their money. The choice of game is gender-influenced, with women preferring bingo and lotteries, and men being more likely to abuse slot-machines (Echeburúa, González-Ortega, De Corral, & Polo-López, 2011) and horse-race wagering and sports betting in general. Men tend to prefer skill games where the player has a (limited) degree of influence on the outcome, and women, luck games (Odlaug, Marsh, Kim, & Grant, 2011). Women are less likely to seek therapy (Ciarrocchi, & Richardson 1989; Lesieur & Blume, 1991;); if they do, they are more likely to report gambling as a way to escape problems and to be affected by depressive symptoms (Echeburúa et al., 2011) and psychosocial stress (Tschibelu & Elman, 2011). Finally, problem gambling becomes more common as socioeconomic status gets lower, with lower social status individuals pursuing gambling as an unfortunate way to make money (Quinn, 2009; Welte et al., 2011).

Gambling has increasingly become a normalized part of western leisure culture and is firmly established throughout the fabric of social life: gambling is not only tolerated, but even promoted by governments, which profit from taxation or even directly participate in or own gambling enterprises, playing a dual role of regulators and beneficiaries (Blaszczynski, 2011; Orford, 2011). This social embeddedness of gambling behavior makes it necessary for therapists to convey the complex message that something which is apparently normal and fun for most citizens, is in fact harmful and potentially dangerous. Superstitious thinking also is culturally and socially fostered in an environment where TV fortune-tellers, horoscopes, and all kinds of divination are shamelessly promoted and marketed. This cultural context makes cognitive distortions like the illusions of control or the "gambler's fallacy" more resistant to critical examination.

The Multiple Paths to Problem Gambling

Gamblers are usually described as a very heterogeneous group. Jacobs (1988), Blaszczynski, Winter, & McConaghy (1986), and Blaszczynski (1988) argued that there exist at least two subsets of gamblers who differentially seek to reduce or augment arousal states. "Reducers" suffer anxiety and select low-skill activities to narrow their focus of attention and produce states of dissociation, while "augmenters" or "action seekers" may choose high-skill games to overcome states of dysphoria and boredom. Ciarrocchi (2001) also distinguishes two different profiles: low-self-esteem gamblers who gamble to escape, and high-self-esteem gamblers, self-entitled individuals that think they can beat the odds and gamble to make money. Blanco, Petkova, & Ibanez (2002) also differentiate two models, one of addiction without substance, which comes close to substance abuse disorders, and another resembling obsessive-compulsive disorder. Furthermore, a number of studies and clinical reports converge in identifying an 'antisocial impulsivist' subtype of gamblers (Blaszczynski, Steel, & McConaghy, 1997; Steel & Blaszczynski, 1996). These gamblers exhibit a family history of problem gambling, early onset, more severe levels of gambling, a history of suicidal ideation and/or attempts, co-morbid substance dependency, antisocial traits, affective instability, widespread dysfunction in non-gambling-related areas and unresponsiveness to treatment.

To summarize, there is consistent evidence to support the argument that there are different subgroups of disordered gamblers, with distinct clinical features and etiological processes. In an effort to provide a coherent model for the development of gambling, Blaszczynski and Nower (2002) proposed the three pathways model that we described in Chapter 1 and applied to all self-destructive behaviors: pathway I gamblers, who lack previous pathology but fall prey to gambling because of the highly addictive schedule of behavioral reinforcement that gambling provides; pathway II gamblers, vulnerable persons who gamble to escape from negative affective states; and pathways III gamblers, antisocial and impulsive gamblers.

The Biology of Gambling

A mounting research base is suggesting that gambling disorders are closely related to substance use disorders, not only because they display similar symptoms and because of their co-morbidity, but also because they share a number of biological mechanisms and genetic features, raising the issue if problem gambling might best be characterized as a "behavioral addiction" (Brewer & Potenza, 2008; Goudriaan, Oosterlaan, deBeurs, & Van Den Brink., 2004; Linden, 2011; Potenza, 2006; Tamminga & Nestler, 2006).

Recent experiments in animal and human psychology suggest that our brains are hardwired to find certain kinds of risk and uncertainty pleasurable in their own right. Wolfram Shultz and his team (Fiorillo, Tobler, & Schultz, 2003; Hollerman & Schultz, 1998) implanted electrodes into the brains of monkeys to record the activity of individual dopamine neurons and found that, when the monkeys received visual stimuli with an *uncertain* outcome, the dopamine neurons were activated both at the presentation of the stimuli and during the period of time leading to the delivery (or not) of the reward. As Linden (2011) points out, this is analogous to the activation of a gambler during the time period when he is watching the slot machine or the roulette wheel spin, and implies that the uncertain nature of the payoff is pleasurable in its own right. Furthermore, Clark, Lawrence, Astley-Jones, and Gray (2009) have demonstrated that "near misses" activate the same neurons as wins, as long as the person believes that he or she has some personal control over the event. This explains why the illusion of control adds to the habit-forming and maintaining power of gambling, and also why many gambling devices are designed and built to foster the illusion of control and provide near misses.

Research is also beginning to uncover the genetic mechanisms involved in problem gambling. Lobo and Kennedy (2009) estimated the heritability of pathological gambling to be 50–60% and showed that disordered gambling shares genetic vulnerability factors with anti-social behaviors, alcohol dependence, and major depressive disorder. Commings et al. (1996) report that, similar to substance users, pathological gamblers are significantly more likely than controls to possess the dopamine D2A1 allele receptor gene, which is associated with reduced D2 receptor density. It is hypothesized that this reduction of dopamine receptors causes individuals to seek pleasure-generating activities, placing them at high risk for multiple addictive, impulsive and compulsive behaviors, including substance abuse, binge-eating, sexual compulsive behaviors, and pathological gambling (Blum et al., 2000).

However, this impressive biological research does not mean that problem and pathological gambling are rigidly determined by biological factors, or that they should be treated pharmacologically.[2] Although genetic factors clearly play a predisposing role for at least a significant subset of gamblers, it is the very act of engaging in gambling and of repeating the behavior which affects the human brain and strengthens the neuronal mechanisms involved in gambling, establishing

---

2 The evidence that many gamblers have altered levels of various neurotransmitters has led to the testing of various psychopharmacological treatments for this population (Carrasco, Saiz-Ruiz, Moreno, Hollander, & Lopez-Ibor, 1994; DeCaria et al., 1996; Grant, Brewer, & Potenza, 2006; Mutschler et al., 2010; Müller & Banas, 2011), but so far the American Food and Drug Administration (FDA) has approved no medication for treating pathological gamblers (for a review, see Achab & Khazaal, 2011).

a circular feedback loop that leads to a "biological trap" not very different from that into which substance-abusing persons fall (Potenza, 2008). In other words, some problem gamblers may be biologically predisposed to be at risk for gambling and for relapse, but this does not mean that psychosocial interventions cannot interrupt this negative cycle effectively. On the contrary, we will show that, while psychopharmacological treatments are still in their infancy, there are a number of purely psychosocial interventions that have documented their effectiveness both in the short and the long term.

Key Research Findings that Inform our Clinical Practice

According to existing research (for a review, see Gooding & Tarrier, 2009; Pallesen et al., 2005; Toneatto and Ladouceur, 2003), the overall outcomes of gambling treatments are probably better than those of most therapies for substance abuse and eating-distressed habits. However, there are still big challenges in the treatment of problem gambling. On the one hand, with dropout rates in the 14–50% range (Melville, Casey, & Kavanagh, 2007) retention needs to be improved. On the other, relapse is a very common phenomenon in gambling treatments, reaching up to 90% of treated samples, and high attrition rates in gambling treatment research probably hide additional cases of relapse (Westphal, 2007; Wohl & Sztainert, 2011). Finally, the most successful research studies so far have focused on homogeneous samples of gamblers with little or no comorbidity; given that a diagnosis of alcohol abuse or depression worsens prognosis, this subpopulation merits further attention.

On the behavioral therapy side, exposure plus response prevention is well supported, both for "*in vivo*" and for imaginal exposure (Echeburúa, Baez, & Fernández-Montalvo, 1996; Toneatto & Ladouceur, 2003). Cognitive approaches are based on the premise that gambling is maintained primarily by distorted gambling cognitions; therefore, they emphasize the assessment of these erroneous cognitions, education on the laws of chance, and the substitution of erroneous beliefs by healthier ones (Ladouceur & Lachance, 2007). Cognitive behavioral approaches are the most researched treatments for problem gambling (Ladouceur, Sylvain, & Boutin., 2001; Marceaux & Melville, 2011; Melville et al., 2004; Sylvain, Ladouceur, & Boisvert, 1997) and have documented good results (Gooding & Tarrier, 2009). However, although these studies show decreases in gambling behavior in response to cognitive therapy; they do not directly address whether the cognitive changes are responsible for the changes in gambling behavior. The fact that in two recent direct and controlled comparisons two cognitive behavioral therapies were found to be effective, but not superior to Twelve-Step therapy procedures meant as controls (Marceaux & Melville, 2011; Toneatto & Dragonetti, 2008), raises additional doubts as to their therapeutic ingredients. Toneatto (2008) remarks that the traditional Twelve-Step procedures embody a number of interesting therapeutic principles: accepting that gambling outcome cannot be controlled and that gambling has caused severe problems in the gambler's life and relationships; the monitoring of one's own behavior and thoughts in order to maintain abstinence; the decision to change one's own behavior and re-orient it in the direction of higher values; the chance to act as a role model for other gamblers once recovered. Although attrition tends to be high in Gamblers Anonymous (GA) research by Petry (2003) suggests that adding GA may enhance the effect of psychotherapy intervention, at least for some gamblers.

So far, a number of authors have developed different proposals for couple therapy with pathological gambling. Ciarrocchi (2001) chose to adapt Jacobson and Christensen's (1996) *integrative behavioral couple therapy* to problem gamblers and their partners. In his approach, the first goal of couples therapy is to support the client's desire to stop gambling by using various strategies: enforcing environmental controls, restoring the financial situation, handling financial issues, and "disarmament" of the problem gambling person. Beyond these task-oriented goals, Ciarrocchi (2001) contends that couples need to heal their relationship wounds, and to that end he proposes to emphasize mutual tolerance and acceptance. He also helps couples to "view the gambling as an 'it'" (Ciarrocchi, 2001, p. 234), and to join against this common enemy. This corresponds to our use of the narrative strategy of uniting the couple/family in their fight against their common externalized problem, a procedure that was described by narrative therapists (White, 1988, 2007; White & Epston, 1990) some years before the concept found its way into the cognitive-behavior therapy (CBT) literature.

The *systemic couples therapy* (SCT) proposed by Steinberg (1993) also starts by focusing on the containment of the gambling problem and the survival of the couple and then moves on to cover deeper relational issues. In Quebec, Canada, Bertrand, Dufour, Wright, & Lasnier (2008) have recently proposed *adapted couples therapy* (ACT) for pathological gamblers. A central feature of ACT is that it handles the engagement process for couples to work strategically, using principles of motivational interviewing and inviting the spouses to explore the pros and cons of becoming involved in this modality of treatment. To our knowledge, no controlled study has so far examined the effectiveness of any couple approach with problem gambling. Family therapy interventions have also not been properly researched.

This body of research has a number of interesting implications for our clinical work:

- Most tested treatments include initial behavioral procedures to enforce environmental controls, first avoiding and then controlling exposure to high-risk situations and analyzing the chain of events that lead to gambling (Echeburúa & Fernández-Montalvo, 2005). We like to do this in our collaborative, strengths-based way of working.
- Identification of gambling cognitions, education on the laws of chance, and the substitution of erroneous beliefs with healthier ways of thinking are central elements of empirically supported CBT (Ladouceur et al., 2001; Ladouceur & Lachance, 2007; Marceaux & Melville, 2011; Melville et al., 2004; Sylvain et al., 1997) and should be included in any treatment approach.
- Research also supports the necessity of paying attention to the motivational processes of gamblers, to monitor their stage of readiness for change (Gomes & Pascual-Leone, 2009; Petry, 2005; Wohl & Sztainert, 2011) and manage relapse episodes (Echeburúa & Fernández-Montalvo, 2005). Connection to higher values may promote a sustained gambling-free lifestyle (Toneatto, 2008).
- As retention in treatment seems a critical variable, working with the concerned partners and family members is a promising approach both to engage clients and to prevent dropout from therapy. Including the couple partner or the parents in therapy not only helps to increase engagement, but may also allow therapists to intervene more effectively and to identify possible negative effects of the problem gambling on family members and offer them help (Bertrand et al., 2008; Ciarrocchi, 2001; Kalischuk et al., 2006). Once the gambling behavior is controlled, trust-building measures should be used and only then deeper relational issues tackled.
- Research by Petry, Weinstock, Ledgerwoo, & Morasco (2008) provides some clues as to how gambling can be handled in the course of therapy and can be applied as a method for managing other self-destructive habits, which is as follows: it may be enough to give feedback on the extent to the gambling problem, to clarify that gambling is not an effective way to make money, and to advise restricting the time and money spent on gambling and performing other activities instead.

Strategies for Assessment and Treatment Planning

Important Assessment Considerations

One important aspect that a comprehensive assessment should take into account is possible *co-morbidity with depression*. Research shows that three-quarters of problem gamblers manifest symptoms of depression (Blaszczynski & McConaghy 1988; Linden, Pope, & Jonas, 1986; Petry, Stintson, & Grant, 2005). For some gamblers, gambling may be used as a means to induce dissociation in order to reduce or escape states of chronic depression, while for others, depression appears to represent the emotional reaction to financial crises and other problems created by excessive gambling behaviors. In any case, we recommend keeping a watchful eye on depressive symptoms and specifically on suicide risk, especially in those cases where clients seem unable to cope with the adverse consequences of gambling.

Gambling is also strongly associated with substance abuse (Cunningham-Williams, Cottler, Compton, Spitznagel, & Ben-Abdallah, 2000; Lorains, Gulishaw, & Thomas, 2011; Toneatto & Brennan, 2002; Welte, Barnes, Wieczorek, Tidwell, & Parker, 2001). Petry, Stintson, & Grant (2005) found that almost three-quarters of pathological gamblers in treatment had an alcohol use disorder, and four out of every ten, a drug disorder; the relevance of this association is given by the fact that individuals with both substance abuse and disordered gambling tend to have more severe problems than individuals with either disorder alone (Petry, 2009). The clinical implication for therapy is that our gambling clients are also very likely to be abusing substances, and that therefore therapists should explicitly inquire about possible substance use, and include it in the treatment plan or refer for appropriate treatment.

An interesting question is how to deal with co-morbidity: a client may be willing to work on the gambling problem, but not to cut down on alcohol; conversely, might ask for help for his or her alcohol dependency but see the gambling behavior as irrelevant. Sometimes, gambling clients apply their impulsive logic to the therapeutic setting, demanding a "quick fix" for their problem, with not much willingness to examine the broader picture of which their gambling difficulties are part. In this case, we try as always to adjust to the views and preferences of our clients, attempting at the same time to expand the framework in order to get meaningful change to happen. One way to do this is to explore in what ways the different problems interact. On the problem side, we may ask the client in which way one of these behaviors makes others more likely, as for instance alcohol is likely to be a gambling trigger, or vice versa; on the side of exceptions, we will show our curiosity about how keeping away from some of them makes it easier to keep others under control. In this way, both problems can be dealt with simultaneously, as cognitive-behavioral theorists have also pointed out (Petry, 2009). Finally, for the more impulsive gamblers, a possible co-morbidity with attention-deficit hyperactivity disorder (ADHD) should also be checked for (Grall-Bonnec et al., 2011).

Financial difficulties brought about by problem gambling are one of the hallmarks of this self-destructive habit, and are the main cause of the devastating effect gambling behavior can have on the families of the gambler. For therapists, often not used to dealing with money issues in a professional way, the financial situation is often too complicated to accurately assess, and referral to a financial advisor might be necessary. Possible legal charges of our clients for writing bad checks, not paying taxes, fraud or stealing company money, and so on, are another source of complication, especially given that the legal system has its own, slow timing: the sentence might come when the person is already in recovery.

Key Assessment Questions

Our assessment of gambling should first establish what games the gambler likes to play and under what circumstances: how often, where, at what time of the time, sparked by what triggers, for how long, how much money is typically lost, at what pace the gambling is increasing (tolerance), if there are signs of withdrawal, and what negative consequences the gambling has had on the different areas of our clients' lives. As shown in previous chapters, a detailed inquiry on the negative effects of the gambling habit promotes greater problem awareness and helps clients to move from precontemplation to contemplation in their stages of readiness for change

(Prochaska, Norcross, & DiClemente, 2006). Here, the presence of concerned others is important, as the gambler is likely to minimize the impact or extent of his or her gambling behavior, and the information of relatives or couple partners might help to correct the information. As just discussed, in addition to collecting data on our client's gambling habit, we recommend asking also about possible drug or alcohol abuse by our client and family members; to evaluate if there is risk of violence or suicide; and to inquire about legal problems and possible delinquent behaviors.

Superstitious thinking should also be mapped out, because it will give us some clues for cognitive work. Possible questions include:

- Do you have a favorite slot machine/a lucky number?
- What things do you do in your attempt to attract "good luck"?
- How come those beliefs took over? Do they lead you to gamble more, or to gamble less?
- How do you account for the fact that, in spite of the bullet-proof system that you have developed, you are still losing much more money than you are winning?

It is impossible to gamble constantly, so there will be valuable exceptions, occasions when the person is not gambling, avoids gambling although he has the chance to do so, gambles less money or stops gambling earlier:

- How many days in a week are you able not to gamble? What do you do different on those days?
- What is different on those occasions when you resist the temptation to gamble?
- On what occasions are you able to stop even though you are losing?

Family and Couple Dynamics

It is estimated that each problem gambler affects between eight and seventeen individuals, including family members and co-workers (Lobsinger & Beckett, 1996). The most typical effects that problem gambling of a parent has on his/her family are related to the financial losses that the self-destructive habit brings about; to the neglect of the parental and marital role because gambling and gambling-related behaviors are prioritized; to the loss of mutual trust; and to possible complications like violence, substance abuse, or legal problems (Kalischuk et al., 2006). Children of gambling parents often describe what Darbyshire, Oster, and Carrig (2001) define as *existential loss*, the sense that the parent has changed into someone their child no longer recognizes, together with a feeling of rejection, abandonment, and neglect. The neglect of the family duties and the construction of the gambler as an irresponsible person (Garrido, Jaén, & Domínguez, 2011) often displace the gambling parent into a peripheral position in the family.

The impact of problem gambling is usually more evident on the couple relationship. Gambling is likely to create a considerable degree of *emotional disengagement* in the couple relationship, often compounded by a decline in sexual interest on the part of the gambler (Lorenz & Shuttlesworth, 1983) and possible extramarital affairs (Lorenz & Yaffee, 1986). As a result, *marital satisfaction* in gamblers and their partners decreases and they are more likely to separate and divorce (Ciarrocchi, 2001; Kalischuk et al., 2006). The concealment, lies, and deceit on the part of the gambling person usually generate deep *distrust* in the partner, and lead to a persecutory cycle in which guilt, distrust, and resentment increase progressively (Garrido, Jaén, & Domínguez, 2011).

Interestingly enough, the preoccupation of gamblers about the impact that their uncontrolled gambling has on their loved ones is often a major incentive to stop gambling (Hodgins & el-Guebaly, 2004). Some examples of questions that we like to use in order to capitalize on this motivational force are:

- In what way is gambling standing in the way of you being the father that you want to be?
- What do you think is the most difficult part for your wife and children of losing you to gambling?
- What parts of your relationship with your spouse/child do you miss most when gambling gets the best of you?

Related questions to ask to the non-gambling family members are:

- What have you done so far to protect yourself and your family from the negative effects of gambling? How have you done that?
- What parts of your couple partner/parent do you miss most, as they are now hidden under the dark cloak of gambling? Which ones will you be most happy to recover?
- In what occasions do you see your husband/wife as a responsible partner/parent? In what way does your reaction to his/her responsibility help to foster it?

In relation to gambling problems we like to take the same position as with other self-destructive habits: we think that the most parsimonious explanation of research data is not that families are to blame for the gambling of their relative or partner, but to understand that they suffer the impact of gambling, cope with the stress it creates, and have an important role in supporting the gambler's recovery (Krishnan & Orford, 2002). This position is different from the systemic notion that problem gambling necessarily reflects and compensates for some family dysfunction, but is compatible with the idea that families and couple partners may sometimes play a role in the initiation and maintenance of the gambling problem. For initiation, a number of studies document that children of problem gamblers are more likely to become problem gamblers themselves, which may be due both to genetic influences as discussed above (Lobo & Kennedy, 2009; Potenza, 2006), and by social modeling processes (Ariyabuddhiphongs, 2012; Ladouceur et al., 2001). As far as maintenance is concerned, relatives of problem gambling may inadvertently contribute to gambling behavior by denying, minimizing, or enabling it. Once the gambling has been discovered, overprotective surveillance, negativity (for instance, criticizing past gambling behavior), and excessive distrust on the part of family members may act as self-fulfilling prophecies that contribute to relapse, with gamblers feeling an increased need to gamble in reaction to the controlling behaviors of their significant others (Lorenz & Yaffee, 1989). However, we would like to emphasize that, in our view, the role of couple partners is much more important for the initiation and maintenance of recovery than for in the formation and maintenance of the problem.

Specialized Treatment Strategies and Major Therapeutic Experiments for Problem Gambling

In most cases the gambling person comes in reluctantly, without admitting to having a gambling problem, referred by a concerned other who may have threatened divorce or kicking him or her out. Here, we proceed as discussed in previous chapters: after intensive joining with the clients, we set out to discover what habit problem the gambling person has and what he or she would like to get out of therapy. We then try to connect this goal to the habit problem. With gambling habits, our default position is to promote gambling abstinence. If the client is clear in that he or she prefers to go for controlled gambling, we accept it, but explain that the first part of controlled gambling should be to be able to spend at least three months without gambling; after that period of time, they will be in an optimal position to decide whether they want to gamble in a controlled way, or if instead, it seems safer to pursue abstinence. If the client insists on cutting down slowly on gambling, we also accept it; but if it does not work, we will take it as evidence that for that client an abstinence approach is preferable.

In our settings the most frequent scenario is that of a gambler who is brought in by a concerned other, in crisis after the devastating financial consequences of the gambling habit have been discovered. In this situation, the gambler is likely to present ashamed and overwhelmed by the havoc he or she has created. However, it may well be that he or she acknowledges and even feels guilty for the harm they have caused, but is not really putting the blame on the gambling habit, but on his or her (transient) bad luck. In that case, the risk of chasing behavior is very high, and therefore also the risk of relapse. That is why even in these cases, with an apparently compliant and rueful gambler, it is important to fully discuss all the negative consequences the gambling habit has on the life and relationship of the person, not just the financial side of it, and to help the gambler see that gambling is not a way to make money, but to lose it. We also like to create some kind of overarching, positive framework that redefines the therapeutic enterprise as a reconnection with the higher values of the person; for instance, themes like "being a father again," "getting back to the real me," "becoming a couple again." As Toneatto (2008) has cogently pointed out in his cognitive behavioral reading of GA, this connection of healthy cognitions and habits to personal higher values seems to be a common factor of successful therapy.

Our consciousness-raising strategies with problem gamblers are the same as with other self-destructive habits: examining the negative effects of gambling; doing the "two-step tango"; projecting the client into various future scenarios; using the "nightmare question" (Berg & Reuss, 1997); and/or externalizing the gambling problems and exposing its "dirty tricks." The basic stance behind our questions and remarks should not be that gambling is bad or stupid, but more that "gambling is a logical response *if* you feel… (the negative affect from which the client may be trying to escape) and *if* you believe that … (irrational cognitions), the problem is that gambling is having these negative effects on you and your loved ones."

Taking a Stand against Gambling: Building a Fence around Temptation

Once the client is ready to take action against gambling, the first step usually involves building what Ciarrocchi (2001) calls "building a fence around temptation," i.e., to discuss very specific measures to enforce abstinence and ensure that in these beginning phases the client does not gamble again. It is important that both the gambler and the parents or the couple partner participate in this conversation, but that the gambler is given the conversational initiative, with the concerned others only adding ideas or support. Otherwise, we might create the unwanted outcome of having the concerned others and the therapist telling the gambler what to do, which is likely to create reactance and withdrawal.

Abstinence control includes various different processes:

- To analyze the problem sequence from the triggers that start the chain of events that typically led to gambling and decide on several locus points in the chain where the sequence can be stopped. The general idea is to begin stopping at first and then move slowly further down: for instance, during the first week the gambler does not go out; during the second week he or she goes out but not to bars; then he or she goes to a bar, but not to a bar with slot machines; and so on.
- To decide on additional protection measures, which can also be gradual: for some time the gambler may need a support person to accompany him or her; or to go out without money; or to go out with some money but get the tickets for all purchases. If the type of gambling permits it and self-exclusion is legally possible, the gambler is encouraged to go to the gambling premise with the support of a concerned other, and sign in so that he or she is no longer allowed to play at that place (casino, bingo).
- To decide on financial protection measures for the relatives or couple partner, so that they run no additional financial risk: to close access of the gambler to the bank accounts

or limiting it by requesting that a co-signer is required for all cash withdrawal; to cancel his or her credit cards; to instruct friends and co-workers not to lend the gambler money, etc.
- *Disarmament* (Christensen & Jacobson, 2000; Ciarrocchi, 2001) involves that the problem gambler tells the couple partner, relative or support person all the tell-tale signs that he is gambling or about to gamble, all of his or her tricks to deceive others and conceal his or her gambling, and all his tricks to get money to gamble. This allows the concerned other to stop being in the dark about the gambling and to recover some degree of confidence and trust. It also allows for beginning the relapse prevention process by figuring out ways to act if the gambler starts to show signs that he is gambling or about to gamble again.

Making the Gambling Habit Redundant

When clients or their concerned other identify an important emotional or relational role that gambling is playing, it is important to help them fulfill that role in alternative, healthier ways, as discussed in other chapters. In many cases one important motivation for gambling is to make money in order to "get even" and/or to get out of a difficult financial situation due to debts. For gamblers who believe that they need to gamble as a way to improve their financial situations, we will help them realize that along that road failure is guaranteed and will try to encourage the development of a more realistic and constructive plan to improve their financial situations. This plan should not include getting more credit from other persons or financial institutions, because that could increase the risk of renewed gambling.

Challenging Gambling Beliefs

Illusions of control, the gambler's fallacy, and skewed attributions are core elements of problem gambling. Although we do not routinely provide psychoeducation, we take advantage of "teachable moments" (Smock et al., 2008) to educate our clients and their couple partners about the laws of causality and correct some of these erroneous cognitions:

- To counteract the "gambler's fallacy" we explain that in chance games, events are independent and that therefore a future outcome cannot be predicted based on previous outcomes. For instance, if we have tossed a coin seven times, and have gotten six tails and one heads, this does not alter the probability of the next toss: it will still be 50% for heads and 50% for tails.
- As to the "illusions of control," we gently remind gamblers that there is no way to influence a chance game or increase the chances of winning. The chances of winning at a slot machine are always the same, no matter what machine it is, where it is, how the buttons are pressed or for how long the gambler has played that machine or seen others playing it.
- We point out to gamblers that their evaluations of their gambling outcomes are skewed: they tend to remember the wins, and to downplay and forget losses, and this feeds into the other two cognitive "gambling traps."

In order to avoid the demoralization of the gamblers when it dawns on them how foolish their decision making has been so far, we make clear that the "gambling traps" are not really their fault, but a natural outcome of the clever strategies of the gambling industry, combined with the bad luck they had of "being in the wrong place at the wrong time," for instance, by having a "big win" with their first gambling experience.

Managing Urges

The first step in managing urges is to find out what the client's "best tricks" are to fight them, and how the spouse or parents are helpful in those occasions. These client self-generated techniques can be complemented by some of the interventions and experiments we describe in Chapters 3 and 10, such as cloud and wave watching, body scanning, mindfulness meditation, or other related practices.

Once the client feels confident in their managing of urges and once the most deleterious gambling cognitions have been questioned, exposure with response prevention can be safely undertaken. After all, sooner or later the client will find him- or herself close to a gambling venue, stumble upon a betting page on the Internet, or have a drink in a bar with slot machines. Although research is clear in that imaginal exposure can be effective, we usually prefer to go directly to "*in vivo*" exposure, if necessary with the support person present at the first attempts, and invite the client to approach the gambling device and then focus on how he or she accepts and resists the urge to gamble. Following the strategic tradition (Fisch, Weakland, & Segal, 1982; Nardone & Watzlawick, 1990) we like to use the pattern interruption interventions described in Chapter 6. An option is to add a number of apparently absurd elements, that paradoxically make more sense for the more superstitious persons: for instance, we like to give slot machine gamblers a foreign coin (one that does not work) with the instruction to go to a slot machine, and only use that coin; or to perform some strange movement in front of the machine and then kiss her goodbye; or say some ritualistic phrase that counteracts the distorted cognition ("I am not putting in this coin because I hate to lose").

Getting One's Life Back

Implementing alternative, virtuous habits is critical in working with problem gamblers, especially with more severe cases, where life might have centered almost exclusively on engaging in the gambling habit. A complaint that both gambling and substance-abusing clients sometimes voice is that nothing gives them a thrill like their self-destructive habit, and that life without gambling/doing drugs is shallow and boring. For us, this is an indication to promote as much as possible authentic relational experiences, and to help clients appreciate how these interpersonal emotions are much more exciting than gambling or taking drugs.

Another side to regaining one's life has to do with reparation to all the persons that have been affected by the gambling. On the most obvious level, it implies paying back debts and solving financial irregularities; but this attitude of humility and reparation applies also to all persons who were lied to, let down, or ignored due to the gambling. In this process, letting the couple partner take on the role of the mediator should be avoided, something which for male gamblers and their wives is often a big temptation. Instead, the gambler must take the initiative, with his couple partner playing only the role of a valued witness. Reparation is an important step, that on the one hand may ease the remorse and anxiety the person who used to gamble might feel, and on the other is also important in reconnecting with his social network and therefore to be in the position to again receive important social reinforcement and emotional nurturance.

If the problem gambler is a mother or a father, some help to reintegrate him or her in the family and become again a respected father/mother might be necessary (Kalischuk et al., 2006). This often means that the over-functioning partner moves slowly back again into his or her former role (Rolland, 1994; Steinglass, Bennett, & Wolin, 1993).

Working with the Family and Couple Partner

Besides having the couple partner in therapy from the beginning as a support to the gambler in recovery, in the control of the gambling episodes, and in the relapse prevention process, there are a number of additional couple issues that we like to address. The suspicion that the gambler might be gambling again or is still gambling creates a great deal of distrust and stress in concerned others, and sparks criticism and ineffective attempts to over-control the gambler. This is also the case for substance abuse, but for gambling problems the situation is worse because there are no clear physical signs of the problematic behavior and there is no way to monitor it objectively (as with urine analysis for drug abuse). In our view, the first step to restoring trust is the participation of the couple partner in the therapeutic sessions. Having the chance of being heard, of sharing his or her observations, and of witnessing the gambler struggle in therapy has a reassuring effect on the couple partner. In addition, we like to use some other techniques to booster trust:

- Disarmament is a useful strategy to identify early negative signs of an impending slip, but is not enough to build trust, because it centers on negative indicators only. It needs to be complimented with a discussion of positive signs of progress/abstinence, signs that can "feed trust" or "fill the trust tank" of the couple. In a solution-focused manner, these positive signs have to be concrete, specific, and reachable behaviors.
- We also like to use trust scaling questions in a circular manner, first asking the gambler to rate from 0 to 10 how much trust he or she perceives from his or her partner, and what the positive signs of that level of trust are, and then inviting the partner to share what number on the scale she or he had thought of. Once we identify what allows both to have that level of trust, we discuss with them what they would need to see and do to get one point higher.
- In an analogous way, we use risk-taking scales to help the partner (and the gambler) to take "reasonable" risks and slowly let go of the controlling behavior. As we have seen in other chapters, it is important to reframe the controlling behavior as "protection" and "care" instead of control, and to get both members of the couple to side against the traps and tricks of gambling.

Forgiveness and reparation are also common issues in the treatment of gambling problems. The non-gambling couple partner has the right to be angry at the gambler, and more so if shared property, savings, or third persons have been affected, but at a certain point this anger is not useful. The situation sometimes escalates into a pattern where the more the non-gambling partner reminds the gambler of what he or she did, the more likely the gambler gets to dismiss the issue under the theme "it is over, why don't you forget it?" which in turn makes the other person feel that the gambler in recovery is not really willing to accept responsibility and to change. To counteract this process, we first invite the gambler to give his or her partner ample space to voice their anger and disappointment, sometimes suggesting a variation of the "structured discussion task" (de Shazer, 1988) so that the conversation can take place in a safe way, and sometimes move on to paradoxically prescribe a "minimum dose" of complaining/listening every day. Once that is done, it may be adequate to use some forgiveness ritual developed with the couple or suggest the grievances/repay task (Pérez Opi & Landarroitajáuregui, 1995) described in Chapter 6.

As we have mentioned, the couple partner of a problem gambler is likely to be traumatized on receiving the news on the extent and catastrophic consequences of the gambling (Ciarrocchi, 2001). Therefore, it is important to promote the wellbeing of the partner by opening it up as a topic of conversation and by encouraging that the partner takes care of herself. In addition, it might be appropriate to invite the couple partner to experiment and use some self-soothing techniques (Chapter 3 and 10) him- or herself, and to promote the reconnection with the wider social network.

A persistent gambling problem is likely to expose the couple relationship to intense stress, but it may also aggravate other, often independent, problems that predate the onset of the pathological gambling behavior (Garrido et al., 2011). In therapy, once the gambling behavior is under control, trust has been restored and inappropriate guilt has been dealt with, these pre-existing couple problems should also addressed. In our view, this often requires that a new therapeutic contract is established and clearly spelled out. This new contract will help to position both partners at the same level of responsibility, overcoming the polarity that had been established around the gambling issue. In the course of this couple work, attention should be given to the risk that the intense emotional up-and-downs that sometimes accompany couple therapy do not precipitate a relapse. Therefore, we like to check the status of the gambling temptations regularly, even if therapy is focusing completely on the relational couple issues. Below is a case example of a couple grappling with severe gambling difficulties.

Case Example

Outsmarting "Vampy"

Helena, a 36-year-old married woman, called me (MB) to ask for help for her husband Jorge, 38. With a shaking voice, Helena told me that she had discovered that her husband was a "pathological gambler" when she found out that he had spent all of the family savings on slot machines. It had been a terrible blow for her, because she had been totally in the dark about Jorge's gambling, and she had considered taking the kids and moving back to her parent's place, but then she had decided to ask for some help first. When I asked about Jorge's willingness to come to therapy, she replied that right now he was eager to do anything. When Helena asked me if she had to come too, I explained that for us it is most useful to have both couple partners in therapy, as this makes therapy more effective and faster. Therefore, I offered my first opening for both of them four days later. I gave Helena the pre-treatment change experiment, asking her to keep track of any improvements, however small, that she might see over the next days, and invited her to explain this experiment to Jorge too.

The First Meeting

On the day of the appointment, only Helena showed up. She explained that Jorge felt "too ashamed" and had refused to come to the session. She believed that he had not gambled again since her phone call the other day, but that morning she had gone to the bank and discovered that over the last months he had also been taking money out of her personal bank account. After this shocking discovery she took him off as a co-holder of the account, and then had gone to his workplace to confront him; there she found out that his boss had given him an advance payment for three months' salary, that Jorge had also spent already. "It is even worse than I thought when I phoned you; that is why I had to tell my parents too, and that is why Jorge is so ashamed." I empathized with her state of shock and rage, and wondered whether she thought that Jorge would be willing to come to therapy when the waters had calmed a bit. Helena said he would, and so I shared that in that case I preferred not to have a session now, and to start therapy proper with both of them two or three days later. I asked her for permission to phone Jorge, so as to decide together what day would suit him best, but I could not reach him. We decided to settle the appointment for two days later at the same time. Helena asked me what she should do over the two next days to help her husband. I explained that I preferred to discuss that with both of them together, but that it had been an excellent idea to protect herself from any possible new financial losses, as she had done with her bank account. Any further steps she could take in that direction would be helpful. I finally explained that if Jorge by any chance happened to change his mind about coming to the session, I would be very happy to start therapy with her, to discuss further ways she could help him even if he kept on refusing to come.

The First Couple Session

Two days later, both Helena and Jorge, a skinny, sad-looking man who looked older than his age, came in. I congratulated them for having been able to make it, and opened by explaining that I wanted to get to know them by their strengths. When I asked Jorge about his hobbies, he said that there was not much that interested him. He worked long hours at a car repair shop and when he came home he liked to watch television. Helena chimed in, with an undertone of bitterness, that in fact Jorge would sit by the television set, drinking a beer and not talking at all, while she was preparing dinner and tending to the kids. I wondered what happened on weekends, and again I did not get much of an answer. I was finding it difficult to connect with him so I asked Jorge what he thought his kids would say if I asked them what they love best about him as a father. I saw the first smile in Jorge's face when he answered that the young one, Jorgito, 7 years old, was able to recognize all the different car brands. "He is even better than me at that," he said proudly. I asked, "And Sandra?" "She is ten now, and she and her father do not get along at all," Helena added. "I think she resents that Jorge has been kind of away". I asked what she thought Sandra missed most of her father. A moment of silence followed, and from the tears in Helena's eyes I could tell that she was speaking not only for her daughter. "I think she misses everything. It is like during these last years, Jorge has been away. Now I know why." I resisted the invitation to go into the gambling issue: "So, when Jorge is fully back again, what do you think Sandra would feel most happy about?" I persisted. "Just everything. He used to be a good father. On weekends he used to take Sandra and Jorgito to the mall, and they had a lot of fun. He invented great stories for them." "How about you? What are you looking forward to get back? "He used to be a very kind, a very loving man," Helena said, and to me it sounded as if she were speaking of a dead person. "Do you think that he is gone for good?" "No," she whispered. I let that answer sink in.

Then I decided to shift gears and I gave Jorge a summary of my conversation with Helena four days earlier, and asked him what his best hopes for our meeting were. He replied that he wanted to "get back to normal again." When I wondered what that meant for him, he explained that he had quit gambling for good, and that he wanted Helena and her parents to trust him again. "And what is your idea of what needs to happen so that they trust you again?" I wondered. "That is difficult, I guess," he replied, and went on to tell me that he had been cheating on his wife for more than three years. He had started to play some money when they installed a slot machine in the bar where he used to play cards with his friends in the evenings. Then he had begun to play more and to go alone to that bar also during the midday breaks, and eventually started to go to a slot-machine casino that was some 15 minutes' walk from his workplace. I wondered how much money he was losing in a typical week by then. He hesitated, and I could see how uncomfortable it was for him to talk about that with Helena present. "I don't know. Maybe one thousand euros a week, maybe more, some weeks." Helena sighed. "Let me go back to the issue of trust. You said you want Helena and her family to trust you again. What do you think you can do so that they trust you again, and how could I be helpful with that?" Jorge said again that he had quit gambling for good and he just needed to stay on track, in order to show them that he was not gambling anymore. He thought I could help him to resist the temptations to gamble.

When I moved on to Helena, she said that she also wanted therapy to help Jorge not to gamble ever again, but that she was not sure if she could trust him again. It had been a terrible blow to discover that Jorge had been cheating on her, telling her he was doing extra hours at work when in reality he was working less and spending all the evening hours gambling. She had found out by coincidence when one day she went to pick Jorge up with the kids and did not find him at the car repair garage. "I was really lucky to find out," she said. "Yes," Jorge added in a whisper. I took the chance to further build Jorge's motivation for change and asked him what he thought would have happened if Helena had not found out. Jorge conceded that it would have gotten worse, that he would have kept on losing money, and that eventually he would have lost his job. "What would have happened to your family?" Jorge looked down, and in a whisper said that he would have lost them "And to you?" "I guess I would have gone more and more into that, it is like a quicksand, the more you try to escape, the more you sink into it."

"Okay," I summarized, "so you both want to build trust, and an important part of that is that you resist the temptations to gamble that might come up. What will trust look like, once you have it back?" Helena explained that she would not feel the need to phone the car repair shop repeatedly to make sure Jorge was there and not gambling. When I asked what she would be doing instead, she described a "normal" day, where she would focus on her own work and in the evening would pick up the kids from school; she would prepare a nice dinner, and then Jorge would come home early without her having to tell him. She would also like to see Jorge giving her a hand with the kids. Jorge added that he would have paid his debts off and be able to walk around with money in his pockets, without being controlled by Helena. Helena chimed in that Jorge would be more talkative, and they would have more of a sex life again. Jorge said they would be talking about other things, not only the gambling or the money he had lost. He also wished for a good sex life again.

When I asked what improvements they had both seen since Helena's first telephone conversation with me, Helena said that the number one thing was that Jorge had not been gambling since then. When I wondered how she knew, she explained that he was not taking any money or any credit cards with him since the discovery of his gambling problems, that he was coming home early, straight after work, that he was spending some more time with the children now, and that he had not gone to play cards with his friends. I asked Jorge how Helena was reacting to these improvements. He responded that she was not "pissed off all of the time" and that she was a little bit more relaxed sometimes. "How does seeing her relaxed help you to keep on track?" I wondered. Jorge found it difficult to answer, but finally said that seeing Helena more relaxed made him feel that she trusted him, and that in turn helped him to trust himself. When I asked what he thought his biggest improvements were, Jorge said that not carrying any money was being helpful, although he did not like it. Helena added that they had taken Jorge's name off the bank account, that they had talked to his boss and asked him not to lend Jorge any more money, and that she had talked to Jorge's friends to let them know what was happening and ask for their help. I asked Jorge what else he thought they could do for the time being to protect him and his family from gambling, but he had no further ideas. Helena chimed in that Jorge should tell her if he ever felt the temptation to gamble. Jorge got a bit defensive, but when I asked him if he thought that could be helpful for the time being, he agreed, although he insisted that right now he had "no temptations at all."

I asked them how confident they were, on a scale from 10 to 0, that they could keep these "provisional protection measures" in place, Jorge said 10 ("but I hope they are provisional indeed") and Helena gave a 7. When I asked Helena what she thought Jorge was seeing that she did not, she replied that precisely that was the problem, that she could not see what was going on in Jorge's head, and therefore she did not know if he was thinking of gambling or not. "So what needs to happen for you to see that things are at a 8?" I wondered. "Just seeing that for another week he keeps on track, coming home early and all that stuff."

The session time was almost over, but I had the feeling that maybe I was missing something important, so before taking the break I asked them if there was something important that I had failed to ask them, or just something they wanted to share at this point, before finishing the session. Helena hesitated and then said Jorge was drinking too much alcohol and maybe that had contributed to the problem; in the past, when he came home at night he would usually smell of alcohol. I asked her in what way the drinking might have contributed to the gambling problem, and she replied that her best guess was that drinking made Jorge more irresponsible and more likely to gamble. "So you think alcohol is in a way a bit of an accomplice of gambling, like it makes Jorge more vulnerable?" She confirmed. I asked Jorge if it was possible that alcohol and gambling worked hand in hand sometimes to get the best of him. Jorge shrugged his shoulders. "Maybe. But I don't drink that much. Maybe four of five glasses of wine, not more." "Is it possible that these four or five glasses do favor gambling?" Jorge nodded.

After the break, I complimented the couple for their courage and determination to fight gambling and not let it ruin their lives and their family. I empathized with what a shock it must have been for Helena to find out the extent of the gambling and the damage done, and said that under these circumstances it was perfectly normal to go from hope to despair, anger, and distrust, and that it was great that she had not allowed these feelings to get the better of her in her relationship to Jorge. I also empathized with Jorge on how painful it must have been for him to realize how trapped he was by gambling, and to what extent it had put his job and his family at risk. It was clear to me how embarrassed he was about what had happened, but also how hard he was working to protect himself and his family from further gambling, by making the clever decision of letting Helena take the lead right now. I went on and explained that I agreed with them that for the time being the most important thing they could both do was to stick with the "protective measures" they had taken so far. "These are provisional measures, that you will soon be able to drop gradually, but that are very important to keep right now, because gambling will want to counterattack," I emphasized. In fact, I added, slips and bumps in the road were to be expected. Therefore, I gave Jorge the suggestion that he keep track of whatever he did that helped him in case he had some sort of gambling temptation again. I invited Helena to keep track of all those moments, even small ones, when she could see the "loving and kind" husband again, and of all those moments when he acted like the loving father their kids, especially Sandra, were longing for. I offered to see them one week later.

Helena's Phone Call

One day before our scheduled session, Helena phoned to cancel the session. She explained that two days earlier Jorge had not come home until midnight, obviously drunk. He had confessed that he had some "gambling money" hidden in his locker at the workplace and that he had gambled it all away. They had had a big argument and she had sent him to sleep on the sofa that night. Now, she was considering moving in with her parents. I asked her what had happened after the argument, and she told me that Jorge had been fine again, coming home on time and apparently not gambling again. "But I don't trust him anymore, I lost trust completely," she said. I seized the opportunity and explained to Helena that with gambling problems lapses are very common, and I asked her how she accounted for the fact that this one-evening lapse had not led to a full-blown relapse. She was apparently taken aback by this question and did not know how to answer. I took the chance and further explained that a lapse like this was painful, but also a very useful opportunity to really get some "deeper" changes going. Therefore, I thought that it would be a very good idea to keep the appointment that we had, even in spite of her hurt feelings and disappointment. She thought it over for a while, and then accepted.

The Second Couple Session

The day of our scheduled meeting, only Jorge showed up. He explained that Helena had refused to go with him. "What does that mean to you?" I asked. Jorge thought for a while and then replied, "That I have to solve my own stuff, she is not going to do it for me." I asked Jorge if he thought that was a good idea. "Yes," he said. "Would you do with some help?" "Yes!" "Okay, so let's get down to business."

I told Jorge what I had heard from Helena, shared with Jorge that lapses can be excellent teachers and invited him to describe for me the whole movie of the lapse, step by step, from the very beginning to the end. After careful reconstruction, it came out that the morning of the lapse, Jorge had felt the impulse to change his way to his job and walk by the slot machine casino. He had no money and no cards in his pockets, so he felt that it was safe, but on seeing the lights at the entrance he started to feel a strong craving (on a scale of 0 to 10, with 10 being absolutely irresistible craving, an 8). He was able to walk by and go to his job, but the idea of gambling "kind of lingered on all day," with a "tingling feeling on my back." After work he phoned Helena to tell her he had to work some extra hours, and then went over to the casino. We discussed what other options he would have had instead, and then moved on to what happened at the casino. "When I was there, I guess I repented or something, so I decided I would not really gamble the money, but then I thought I would just throw in 10 euros to get rid of the cravings." The craving had gone up to a 9 by then. "Did it work out that way, did you get rid of the cravings?" I asked. "No. I played all the money I had" "In looking back now, what were your real chances of throwing in 10 euros and stopping thereafter?" I asked. He responded with "0%" "So what would you say," I continued, "How did the machines override your better knowledge?" "I guess I wanted to win back some of the money I had lost there all these last months, to win it back and pay some of my debts back," Jorge said. "Seen with some perspective, was that a reasonable idea?" "Not really." I asked why not. This time Jorge took some more time to answer: "Because in the end, I guess you always lose more than you win." I responded with, "Exactly, those machines give back 70% of what you play. No way to get more. You know that, but even so, the machine whispered in your ear: 'Come on, Jorge, let's win that money back'?" "Yes."

I put one empty chair on top of another, close to Jorge's seat. "So this is the machine, your 'lucky machine'. What do you call her?" Jorge had given her no name, but gave a vivid description of the lights and the drawings on it, a sexy Vampirella in a cave. "Okay, so this is your favorite machine, let's call her Vampy, what are her tricks? How does she lead you to spend your money on her, in spite of your knowing, in the back of your mind, that you will lose in the end?" Jorge got more and more into the conversation. He talked about the sounds of the machine, about the colors, about the sound of coins falling down when he won. I took advantage of this teachable moment and explained about how near misses activate the same pleasure circuit in the brain as a real win, without giving out any money. I added that machine builders know this, and therefore more near misses are displayed on the lines above or below the winning lines. I further added "So Vampy, all 'vampires' in fact, are playing all kind of dirty tricks on us…What else does she tell you?" Jorge replied with, "Well, it is not that she tells me, but I know when she is hot." We discussed that for a while. "So you get this feeling that the machine is 'hot,' but what do you think, is it really more likely to give out prizes?" As he hesitated, I explained that slot machines work randomly, and that therefore the likelihood of winning is exactly the same each time, irrespective of what has happened with the previous events. As I felt Jorge was not really getting the idea, I took a coin, "Imagine I told you I have tossed this coin before our session, five times, and all five times I got heads. If I toss it again, do you think it is more likely to be heads or tails?" "I guess tails" I asked why that would be. "Well, because you got all those heads, so a tail is bound to come out soon." "Exactly. That is the kind of things we all believe. But it is not true. If I tossed the coin again, the chances of heads and tails are exactly 50% each. And if I tossed it again, again it would be 50/50." I explained randomness again. "And the problem is, if I now tossed the coin and got tails, you would say, 'See, I knew it had to be tails.' But if I tossed the coin and got heads again, you would say 'Well, right, but the next has to be tails.' So this theory of yours, which by the way all of us are tempted to believe, is wrong, but is very difficult to prove wrong." Jorge seemed to accept the explanations. He looked down again, "Now that I see all this, I realize how stupid I have been…" I took the chance to explain that this was not about him or anyone else being stupid, but about the gambling machine builders playing dirty tricks and taking advantage of how we usually see things.

After that, we spent some time discussing the little exceptions that were hidden in the lapse story. How come Jorge had walked past the casino in the morning? How come he was able to spend the day at work, in spite of this tingling feeling in his back? What had helped him to stay in the cafeteria during the lunch break, instead of walking to the casino? Jorge identified that what had helped him was: to think of his kids; to think of Helena and her suffering if he kept on gambling; to remember his decision to prove his work colleague wrong; to think of the bad feelings after losing money; to focus on his work and to engage in "mental conversation" with the car he was repairing; and to smoke some cigarettes.

Finally, we spent some more minutes discussing the alternative actions that he could have taken and the alternative thoughts that would have been helpful at each stage of the relapse process: taking a different route to work; telling Helena about his cravings; asking her to pick him up after work; seeing a movie at home with his kids after work. I asked Jorge if it made sense if I taught him some relaxation technique, and as he agreed I taught him the "Trip to Popcorn Land" meditation. I also wondered aloud if it made sense to write a list of the alternative behaviors and thoughts that we had discussed. He thought it was a great idea, so we agreed that he would write alternative, constructive actions on one side and "strengthening thoughts" on the other. He would carry that "emergency plan" in his pocket.

I asked Jorge how confident he was that he could follow his emergency plan for the next week. He paused for a while, and then said "9." I asked him what came into that 9, and he explained that his decision was now for real, that he knew he would have no further opportunities with Helena, and that he felt stronger now to resist the temptations. "Okay," I said, "So it looks like Vampy is going to leave your life for good…" and, pointing at the "slot machine" we had built with the chairs, I added: "What do you think you will be missing most, as she gets definitely out of the picture?" Jorge was surprised by the question, and took some time to answer. Finally, he conceded that in a way, gambling was good company for him, and also offered the excitement he did not get from work, marriage, or family. I wondered aloud if it made sense for Jorge to try to put back some excitement into his marriage and family life again, and invited him to start thinking what he liked to see happening more with his family and his kids. I left him thinking about it and took a break.

In my editorial summary, I congratulated Jorge for having learned so much from his lapse and for having summoned up the courage to come and share his learning with me. Now that he had found out more about "Vampy" and how she had been fooling him, it was a good moment to write her a "farewell letter." I suggested that he start thanking Vampy for the positive services she had rendered, and then making a list of the negative consequences she had brought about and the reasons to say goodbye for good. After that, he might want to create a collage of his dreams to represent the way he wanted his life without Vampy to be. I also encouraged him to pay attention to whenever Vampy would "whisper in his ear," tempting him to gamble and he countered these temptations. Then Jorge asked me how he could get Helena to trust him again; he feared that, although he was sure to "keep on track" this time, it would not be enough to reach her. I thought for a minute and then offered him two more experiments to choose from. One was "disarmament": to sit down with Helena and explain to her all of the little and subtle signs by which she could recognize that he was having a craving, as well as sharing with her the "little tricks" he had had, as for instance the "gambling money" he had hidden. "This will make her feel less in the dark about the gambling, and at the same time reassures you; it is like burning the bridges behind you." The second experiment I offered was the "secret surprise": to do something that would be a positive surprise for his family, and then another thing that was a positive surprise for Helena. We scheduled the appointment for two weeks later.

The Third Couple Session

Both Helena and Jorge came in for the session, and they were both very pleased with the improvements that had taken place. Helena was confident that Jorge had not gambled at all since the last session, and Jorge confirmed that he had been successful in "overcoming all temptations." Helena was also pleased that Jorge had surprised her some days ago by reading to her the "farewell letter to gambling," which she felt was very moving, and some days later by bringing in hamburgers, French fries, and a family comedy DVD, which they watched with the kids. I congratulated Jorge for his good ideas and asked what effects they had had. He explained how pleased his kids, and especially Sandra, had been with the "movie evening," and how Helena was being "nicer" to him again. When I asked for details about that, Jorge said that they were talking less about the gambling and the money lost, and more about "our own lives" and that he felt "under surveillance, but also more trusted by Helena." Helena chimed in that for her it had been very important that in Jorge's "farewell letter" she, Helena, had been reason number one to say "goodbye" to gambling. It had also helped that Jorge had "put all his gambling tricks in the open," giving her clues as to how she could recognize that he was starting to cheat again. "Not that I discovered anything new, but the fact that he had the courage to sit down and tell me was important to me." I took a chance and inquired where she thought that courage came from, what the story of that courage was. Helena paused for a while, with Jorge silent and expectant. "Jorge has always been very courageous. He proved that when we started dating. I was 16 then, he was 18 already, and my father firmly opposed our dating. My old man is a very strong character, and a policeman too. But Jorge just summoned up the courage to come to our place and talk with him. They talked for one hour, and then my father gave us his blessing, so to say." I was amazed by the story, which stood in a sharp contrast to the rather shy, subdued, and embarrassed Jorge that I had witnessed up to now. I wondered in what ways Helena thought Jorge's courage would help him defeat gambling for good, and she shared that "once Jorge makes a decision, he sticks to it." She added that he would also need a lot of courage to sit down with her parents again, 20 years later, to have a conversation about the gambling story. I checked with Jorge, and he confirmed that he planned to have that conversation. However, they both felt that it would be sensible to let at least one more month without gambling pass before talking to his in-laws.

We spent some time reviewing how Jorge had fought his "temptations" to gamble over the last three weeks. I decided to do that with Helena present, as a way to further promote "disarmament" and to give her further reasons to trust Jorge. Jorge shared that he had had cravings on the way home after work. He had some coins that he had not spent on lunch or coffee, and thought of gambling "just those coins." The first time, he had fought the temptation by changing his route in order to walk a completely different way home; on that occasion, it had also helped to just think that he was eating a popcorn in a mindful way. The second time, he had used the ideas he had written down in his "emergency plan," and then had the sudden inspiration of giving the coins he had to a beggar. I wondered what the next step could be. Jorge explained that right now he was still handing over the receipts for his expenses at the end of each day; that was reassuring for Helena, but humiliating for him, so he wanted to stop doing that and simply go out with "some money, not much," without having to be held accountable for his expenses. At this point, Helena hesitated; she did not feel "prepared yet" to take that step. I wondered what she would need to see happening to take it, and she said she needed more time. When I asked Jorge how he could help Helena to be more courageous with this issue, he seemed at a loss and basically insisted that she *had* to trust him. The atmosphere in the room had frozen suddenly, and the enthusiasm had gotten lost, so I decided to externalize: "I can see that gambling is being successful here in creating a split between the two of you, getting you (Helena) to become suspicious and you (Jorge) to feel hurt. How would you know that you are being successful in keeping a united front and not allowing gambling to get the best of your relationship?" They did not answer, so the question had obviously been too complicated. I stood up and built the "two chair machine" again, and placed it in between Helena and Jorge. "What do you think? How could you move it away?" Helena offered that maybe doing some more things together as a couple would help. I checked with Jorge, and as he nodded, I asked them to expand on what kind of things they could do as a couple. They listed several: talking after the kids had gone to bed; going out on a Saturday leaving the kids at their grandparents'; saying hello with a kiss on arriving home. I invited the couple to push the chair a little bit away with each of these descriptions and checked how that felt. "Better," said both. When I asked what else could help to slowly move gambling out of their couple space, Jorge ventured that maybe going with Helena to a bar with slot machines, so that she could see how he did not care about it. Helena found that to be a great idea, so I invited them to push the chairs away a little bit more.

At that point the emotional atmosphere was positive again, and I asked the couple how confident they were, on a scale from 0 to 10, that they could "keep on track" doing the things they had just discussed. Both Helena and Jorge were at a "9," so I asked each of them what they saw in the other person that gave them so much confidence. Jorge said that for him it was important to see that Helena was standing by him. Helena appreciated that Jorge was making a big effort to be more open and communicative, "and not only about the gambling thing." When I checked if there were any other things that I should ask them, Helena surprised me by telling me that, in her view, Jorge was also refraining from drinking too much, and that this was helpful too. Jorge confirmed that, and explained that he had come to realize that alcohol was in fact not really helping him with gambling, "nor with anything else." I congratulated Jorge on that and took a break.

I complimented Jorge and Helena for the improvements in their situation and the courageous and inventive steps they had both taken to outsmart the machines. They were obviously taking their "protection measures" seriously, practicing good teamwork, and were already starting to bring some fun and closeness back into their marriage. I shared that I could sense and understand Jorge's impatience with changes he found too slow, but also the fear and caution on Helena's side in considering steps that she found too big; the important thing for me was that they were both able to accept this discomfort for the time being, knowing that the more they kept on walking together, the more they would fall in step. I encouraged them both to keep doing what had been helpful and to keep track of any new positive developments that they might see happening in their relationship and their family. In any case, I cautioned them to go slow and watch for any signs that "Vampy and her gang" would try to fight back.

Telephone Call from Helena

Two and a half weeks later, I got another phone call from Helena. Things had "gone backwards" again and she wanted to reschedule and have the session earlier. She explained that everything had gone fine for two weeks, but that two days ago Jorge had not come home until three in the morning, without leaving a message nor taking the phone when she called him. She had understood that he was gambling again, and had taken the kids and slept at her parents' house. The next day, she had refused to take the phone when Jorge called her, but that evening he picked her up and they talked. He confessed that he had been out with his buddies and drinking a lot, but he insisted that he had not gambled a single euro.

The Fourth Couple Session

Two days later, both Jorge and Helena came in. They did not seem as cheerful as in our last session, but certainly not as depressed as in the first. I decided to start with a very focused question: "I know from Helena that something happened some nights ago and I understand that you must have both been through some hard times since I saw you last. We will have time to go into that today. But let me ask you first, what would you say is better now as compared to our last session?" No one answered. I waited and then decided to give it another try: "Jorge, when I ask Helena now, what do you think she will say is better in her eyes, in spite of whatever happened?" Jorge took some time to answer, but then replied that his wife would probably say that his not gambling since last session was an improvement, and that she would also say that up to "that night" he had spent more time with the children and with her. I asked Helena if those would be the improvements that she would emphasize, and she confirmed that the first two weeks after our last session had been "very good." "But not good enough for you," Jorge whispered.

I understood that there was no way but to discuss the problematic night, but decided to first reinforce what I had heard so far: "Okay, so you are both saying that no gambling has happened over these three weeks?" They confirmed. "That you have accomplished that?" They nodded. "That even on that night that you went out and everything, you did not gamble?" Jorge nodded. I shared how impressed I was with that, and put it on the agenda by remarking that I would like to discuss that in more detail later in the session. Then I invited them to share what had happened on "THAT night" and how they accounted for it.

Helena started by complaining about Jorge's lack of consideration in simply going out without telling her and without taking her phone calls. Because they had had an argument the night before about her controllingness, she understood that this was some kind of revenge game that Jorge was playing on her, and had reciprocated by leaving home with the kids. Jorge's story was in fact not very different: he was "fed up" by her "mothering me all the time" and when his buddies invited him to go out with them for a beer, he took the chance to "let the steam off" and just "let go." He soon was quite drunk, and although he was aware that his mobile phone was ringing, simply did not take it. When I asked him if, in hindsight, it had been a caring thing to do, he said no, and that he really repented for having been so rude. I decided to take a risk and asked Helena if, in hindsight, leaving home with the kids was the right thing to do. She took some time to answer, but then she acknowledged that it had been quite a "stupid" thing to do, especially because it meant involving her parents again, which was certainly not helpful.

Given that the atmosphere was not very conflicted or aggressive, I took the risk of pushing my position further. "So if there is something to be learned from this story, what could it be?" After some hesitation, Jorge shared that one thing that was clear for him now was that the "buddy night" was not a good way to handle his bad feelings with Helena. I wondered what Jorge thought he could have done instead. "Just talking, I guess," he said. But instead of hiding in silence again, he then surprised me by starting to talk. He explained that he was feeling pushed around and patronized by Helena since the gambling problem had become public, with all the money control and the constant surveillance, but that in fact he had felt like that for many years. "It is not that I am behaving like a child, it is that she is treating me like a mother all the time." Helena tried to object, but I stopped her gently and invited Jorge to continue. He explained that since the birth of their children he had felt more and more in the back seat of the family car, with Helena being a more and more competent mother who left no room for him, and who on top of that also made more money than he did, which made him feel even more worthless in his job. Helena started to object again, so I decided to try a more active approach that had worked in our last session. I invited Jorge to build a living sculpture representing how he saw himself in relationship with Helena. As I had no team in this case, I offered myself to be the "Jorge sculpture." Jorge got the idea immediately. He put me (the Jorge alias) kneeling on the floor, looking down, and then he put Helena standing upright and pulling his/my arm. I stepped out of my Jorge role and invited Jorge to take my/his position. I then asked him how he felt there, and then I asked Helena. They both felt uncomfortable, Jorge because he felt "little, useless, stupid," Helena because she felt "tired of pulling and lonely up here." I then invited them to put themselves in the position they preferred to have. Jorge stood up and put his arm around Helena. She got closer to him and also put his arm around him. I allowed some time to let the emotion sink in and then invited them to take a seat again.

I felt that not much more needed to be said and shifted gears slightly, asking Jorge and Helena what their next steps were going to be. Helena explained that now she felt that they could take some more risks; she would like to see Jorge come and go with money in his pocket and with no need to control tickets or expenses. Jorge offered to be more present at home, especially with the kids, and he also shared that he would like to go out again one night, but with Helena. Helena chimed in that this would be a funny thing to do, and added that she would also like to go out with her girlfriends one night. Jorge encouraged her to do so, and offered to take care of the kids. I stood up and built the chair-machine again. "Your doing all this, where would it put Vampy?" "In that corner!" said Jorge. "Or even on the balcony!" Helena added. I refused to put the chairs on the balcony (it was raining), but put them in the farthest corner.

To wrap it all up, I asked the couple how confident they were that they would be walking "arm in arm" the following weeks. They both said 10 and I asked if it would be okay to talk with both of them separately some minutes.

With Jorge, I focused on how he had been able to go out with his buddies plus drink too much and avoid gambling. He explained that he had exercised some restraint and not drunk too much, but what had helped most is that he did not look at the machines in the same way now, even under the influence of alcohol. I congratulated him on his insightfulness and discussed with him what other thoughts or actions were helping him to keep the temptation at bay. Then we did some worst-case scenario planning: what if he had another falling out with Helena? Or if his work colleague found a way to put him down? What if he got fired? One interesting issue that came up is that, if he had some disagreements with Helena, he not only would try harder to talk it through with her, but that he could also turn to one of his closer buddies, his only "real friend" for some company and advice. Jorge said that he also felt like having a talk with his father in law to apologize and get a new start. We discussed this option and Jorge decided that he would like to do that two months later, on the wedding anniversary of his in-laws.

Alone with Helena I wondered if there were any other concerns she had, and she confided that she was worried that her husband and her parents were not on speaking terms anymore and she did not know how to bring them closer together again. I shared that Jorge had the same worry and told Helena that in my view it would be helpful if she did not try to help, but simply stepped back and kept track of how Jorge would work on the issue. Helena was intrigued but agreed to stop mediating.

In my final message to the couple, I complimented them for the courage they had shown in the session and for all the steps they were taking. I reframed the "crazy night" as a useful crisis that had helped them to see how they could re-balance some important aspects of their relationship. I encouraged them to go on, to watch out for any new positive steps they will take and added a little suggestion: the first 15 minutes they spent together each day after coming home from work, they were to keep track, in secret, of what the other person did that satisfied each of them (Isebaert, 2005). I asked when they wanted to have another session and they decided to schedule it for one month later.

PROBLEMATIC GAMBLING HABITS

The Fifth Couple Session

Helena and Jorge showed up in excellent mood. Before I could even ask, they started to give a detailed account of all their improvements: Jorge had kept abstinent from gambling and had not had any further "temptations" to do so; he was more active at home, "helping" with the chores and spending more time with the kids; Helena had reciprocated being "nicer" and was much more relaxed about the risk of gambling; they had left the kids with her parents on two occasions and had even gone out dancing, something they had not done for more than five years! They were both feeling closer and had had sex again, and were planning to spend a romantic weekend at home (as they had no money to travel anywhere and Helena did not want to borrow any money), leaving the kids with Helena's parents. Jorge chimed in that he had had a good talk with his father in law, who had taken the initiative before he could do so and had sat down with him to find out about his recovery. Helena was very proud that the "two men are on good terms again."

When I asked them to rate the situation on a scale from 1 to 10, they both said "7." We spent some time discussing what their "recipe for success" had been to go up from 1 to 7, and then I wondered what the first small sign of an "8" would look like. Helena answered that one thing that bothered her, and that she wanted to see changing, is that now Jorge did not want to talk about his gambling problem anymore. "I don't want to keep on discussing it all day, but sometimes I still do feel angry and hurt, like when I see something I cannot buy for the kids, or when our old television set is not working, and then Jorge simply refuses to talk and goes like 'Forget it, that is past, now is the present'." When I wondered what she would like to see Jorge doing instead she explained that she wanted him to listen to her, even if she got angry at him, and to take responsibility what he had done. I wondered what that would bring her, and Helena said that it would help her to share the emotional burden and to trust Jorge more by seeing that he really repented. For Jorge, the first sign of an 8 would be that he could relax and not fear that at any time Helena would bring up the gambling/money problem. "I feel bad enough about how I spoiled it; I don't need your reminding me," he added bitterly. When I wondered what he imagined them doing instead, he said that he simply wanted to turn the page; he felt that his in-laws and his friends had forgiven him, and he wanted Helena to forgive him and forget about it too. I sensed the opposite views that Jorge and Helena had here, and decided to take the risk of playing more from Helena's perspective: "Jorge, I can see how badly you wish for Helena to forgive you, and how much you wish that she let go of all that you did. It is reasonable that you wish for that. Do you think it is also reasonable to expect Helena to do it just like that, overnight so to say?" Jorge conceded that Helena had every right to be angry at him and that she deserved to be listened to, but added that he did not want to see the "gambling issue" spoil the good things they were bringing back into their relationship. I asked if they would be willing to try out an experiment that would help them to incorporate both things, conversation on the past problem if needed and moving forward, and they said "of course." I promised to offer the suggestion after the break.

After the break, I complimented the couple for their accomplishments and for their determination to keep on track, and encouraged them to do more of what they knew worked well. I also warned them that there would probably be more bumps along the road, but shared my confidence that they would find ways to open the "stress release" on the one hand and to support each other on the other. Coming back to our conversation of what an "8" would look like I suggested that they decide on a special room or spot in their home that would be the "gambling talk area." It should not be the bedroom, and it would be a place to go and sit down to discuss the past gambling problem whenever Helena felt she needed it. The rest of the house would be a "gambling-free area". They both liked the idea, and decided that the small room with the washing machine would be their "gambling talk area"; there they could "wash the dirty gambling laundry," Helena added smiling.

The Sixth and Seventh Couple Sessions

We had two more sessions, one month after the fifth and then two months later. Things kept improving and no further gambling episodes or cravings were reported. Helena found that having the "problem laundry place" to talk about what had happened, together with Jorge's willingness to listen to her complaints, led to a decrease in her need to discuss the topic. Jorge found that spending more time with the kids was an excellent antidote to his negative ruminations, and he also found that now he was "the kind of loving father I want to be." They were consistently taking care of their marital relationship, but also making some time for their individual needs. On the progress scale, Helena went up to an 8 and a 9; and Jorge to an 8.5 and a 9.5, so we decided to simply have a short "follow-up session" six months later. When I called some days before the appointment to confirm the meeting, Helena told me that it was not really necessary because "everything" was "all right," and we agreed to have a telephone follow-up one year later.

Follow-Up

One and a half years after our last session, I talked with Jorge on the phone. He explained that he had not gambled again and had also not even thought of gambling. Unfortunately, his son had been diagnosed with a rare disease half a year ago, but this stressful news had only strengthened his determination to "keep on track." He had also lost his job and had not yet found another one, but thought this was in a way a blessing in that he had more time to care for his son and go with him through all the medical procedures. He said that he and Helena were really supporting each other in these difficult times, and so were his in-laws.

Reflections on the Outsmarting "Vampy" Case

Matthew: In the first telephone conversation with Helena, you made it quite clear that having both partners attend and working as a couple is the best way of resolving the other partner's difficulties. By doing so, you did not accept Helena's possible desire of having you "fixing" her husband alone. In what couples therapy situations would you accept this contract and work alone with one partner and why?

Mark: If a client calls me wanting to make an appointment for his or her couple partner, I will certainly insist that both partners come for the first

Matthew: session. However, if one of the partners refuses to come in, I will of course work with the one who is willing to initiate therapy, as we discussed in Chapter 2, but in that case one of the topics of our therapeutic conversation will be how to include the missing partner. However, as we both know, in some cases it is simply not possible to have both members of the couple in therapy.

Matthew: Interestingly enough, Helena ended up showing for the session alone. We soon discover that Jorge's boss had given him a three-month's salary advance, which had already been spent. When working with problem gamblers, at what point in the treatment process do you secure signed consent forms from clients to begin intervening with bosses, friends, and family members who further perpetuate their habits by giving them loans and/or cover up for them?

Mark: Working with problem gamblers I include relevant family members routinely, but I usually don't work directly with bosses or friends. With them, my first option is to work with the client and the partner to get them to change their interaction with these relevant others, for instance by asking them not to loan them any more money, to stop covering up for them, or simply to support them, as you did with Troy and his colleagues (Chapter 6).

Matthew: Some therapists' initial impressions of Jorge might have been that he has an undiagnosed form of depression or attention deficit disorder. What useful self-talk or other personal thinking strategies do you employ to help you not fall prey to going beneath the surface searching for underlying psychological causes for his problem gambling?

Mark: Yes, Jorge certainly looked depressed, and I think that on any standardized depression questionnaire he would have scored in the clinical range. However, the fact that a problem gambler is depressed should not be taken to mean that the depression is the "root cause" of the gambling problem: depression is as likely to be a consequence of gambling as to be one of its causes, or simply a coexisting problem that functions as an aggravating factor. I like to remember Ben Furman and Tapani Ahola's (1992) assertion that systemic thinking does not mean that whenever various problems coexist in a person, couple or family, they are necessarily causally related: it may well be that a given person or family has simply the bad luck to be facing various problems that happen to be present at the same time.

Matthew: I appreciate your efforts to try to engage Jorge and not give up. You also did a nice job of playing cultural anthropologist with him by asking Jorge the meaning of his words: "get back to normal again." Too many therapists make the assumption that they completely understand the meaning of clients' words even when they are quite vague and also miss a goldmine opportunity to discover what could potentially pave way for co-constructing solutions.

Mark: I think this is really the influence of Steve de Shazer and Insoo Kim Berg, who always reminded us that solution-focused thinking invites

	us to keep a non-normative stance, an open mind, and to get specific details from our clients.
Matthew:	With this couple, you made ample use of externalization of problems, such as with "Trust," "Alcohol," "Gambling," and "Vampy." What was telling you to use narrative therapy strategies here versus working in a more solution-focused brief therapy way with this couple?
Mark:	I tend to intersperse narrative techniques into most of my solution-focused work because I find it useful for clients and also more fun for them and for me. In the case of Jorge, I started to externalize when I realized that he was not really following me as I explained some of the cognitive bases of problem gambling. With the couple work it was the same: I found it was much easier for Jorge and Helena to get my message when I built the two-chair gambling machine. As the proverb says, "a picture is worth a thousand words." For me, the intuitive part of this process is about choosing the right moment to start to externalize. However, the truth is, you never know beforehand if it will catch on or not, so I see it more as a trial and error process where as a therapist you have to be very sensible to clients' feedback and adjust accordingly.
Matthew:	Creating in your office a Vampy slot machine really brought to life for Jorge the gambling experience and helped to provide a little psychoeducation around the hooks of gambling: probability and randomness. Interestingly enough, Turner (2000) has found that teaching gamblers about probability and randomness is an effective intervention in itself. Do you routinely use this therapeutic strategy with problem gambling clients?
Mark:	I started to do that routinely when I read some of the Cognitive Therapy literature on gambling (Ladouceur & Lachance, 2007; Ciarrocchi, 2001). However, I do not necessarily offer pyschoeducation as a necessary therapeutic component at the initial stages of therapy, but wait for "teachable moments" to share the information. Paraphrasing Prochaska, Norcross, and DiClemente (2006), I would say that there are also "Stages of Readiness for Learning," so that the matter of timing makes a difference for psychoeducation too. The other solution-focused twist is that, as McCollum and his colleagues describe, I like to "teach last" (McCollum, Stith, & Thomsen, 2012, p. 188), i.e., I prefer to first elicit what knowledge the person has about his or her problem and only then offer the information I want to share.
Matthew:	As in your case in Chapter 5, there were again many metaphorical twists in your sessions, such as the Vampy slot-machine, the farewell letter to the externalized problem, and the collage of dreams. Can you say something about what is driving your therapeutic decision-making?
Mark:	My use of metaphors and rituals is part of a deliberate attempt to make therapy more emotional and personally meaningful for my clients. I agree with those therapists who, like Eve Lipchik (2002), consider that solution-focused therapy runs the risk of ignoring the emotional part of our clients' lives. Focusing on specific observable behaviors is of

course a central and useful aspect of therapy but may make therapy too "behavioral" and too "cognitive." Here I find that metaphors and rituals from the Ericksonian and the narrative therapy traditions (Rosen, 1982; White & Epston, 1990), but also from great solution-focused therapists like Yvonne Dolan (1991, 2000), are an excellent complement to the more rational elements of standard solution-focused practice.

Matthew: You worked hard with this couple in covering the back door with relapse prevention work. As we both know, in spite of our best efforts to prepare clients for slips or prolonged relapsing situations, they still seem to happen. What if Helena had decided to permanently leave therapy after the third session, how would your therapeutic strategy had changed if you only had Jorge present in sessions?

Mark: I guess I would have worked with Jorge as I did, but I would have added some extra time to discuss with him how to include Helena again in the sessions, or at least let her know about what was going on in therapy. Possible options would be to invite Jorge to share his sessions with Helena, to write her some e-mails or make some phone calls to let her know how things were progressing. However, without Helena fully involved it would have been more difficult to contain lapses like the night Jorge went out and got drunk.

Matthew: One really critical thing you did in the fourth session was giving both partners balanced floor time to express their frustration and concerns. However, solution-focused purists would call this "problem talk," and push hard for the couple to report non-problem times, reinstating past successful strategies, or using the future to create new possibilities. How come you did not pursue that therapeutic pathway with the couple?

Mark: Even orthodox solution-focused therapists accept that we have to listen closely to our clients and cooperate with their views and preferences, otherwise solution-focused therapy becomes *solution-forced* therapy (Lipchik, 2002; Nylund & Corsiglia, 1994). Also, it is important to recognize that the "problem talk/solution talk" distinction may be misleading, in that one can listen to problems in a solution-focused way, for instance by gently underscoring the more positive (or less negative) elements of the story, or by using the problem story to highlight the resourcefulness or resilience of our clients –for instance using the "coping questions" described by the Milwaukee team (de Shazer et al., 2007).

Matthew: In looking back, if you had another shot at working with this same couple, would you have done anything different?

Mark: If I had the chance to travel back in time, I would try harder to avoid the two lapses, which both carried a considerable risk of spiraling into a destructive marital crisis and possibly therapy drop-out. Seen in perspective, it might have been useful to do some cognitive work with Jorge earlier in therapy, and it would have been safer to tackle the control/escape pattern already in the first session. This would have reduced the pressure on Jorge and maybe would have prevented the lapse.

8

INTERNET AND CYBER-SEX DEPENDENCY HABITS

> People never touched one another. The custom had become obsolete, owing to the Machine.
>
> *E. M. Forster*

Introduction

E. M. Forster, author of *The Machine Stops* (1909/1997), had tremendous foresight on how technologically advanced machines can contribute to social isolation and other negative consequences. In his novella, people spend their lives alone in underground rooms endlessly teleconferencing with one another. However, having a strong and instinctual desire to have human contact, the rebellious characters in his book attempt to go to the surface, seeking to re-connect with the rest of humanity. For us, Forster's story is a wonderful metaphor for the psychological and social costs of excessive Internet usage.

Internet dependency and cyber-sex are not only growing problems among adolescents and adults in the United States but Internet dependency has been declared a national health problem in South Korea, Taiwan, and China. In fact in China, 10% of the 30 million Internet online gamers were deemed addicted (Young & Nabuco de Abreu, 2011). A team of researchers at Stanford University's Medical Center found that one in eight Americans suffered from one or more signs of Internet dependency (Aboujaoude, 2011; Aboujaoude, Koran, Gamel, Large, & Serpe, 2006). Aboujaoude (2011) found that compulsive use of the Internet occupied up to 11 hours of the Internet dependents' days. They also learned from their participants that excessive use of the Internet was creating major difficulties for them in all areas of their lives, such as: having intrusive thoughts and preoccupation with the Internet when offline; fueling relationship conflicts and difficulties for them, including their children complaining about their not spending enough time with them and not being emotionally and physically present; having a need to escape to the virtual world to ward off negative mood states; affecting their work lives due to late night runs on the Internet producing physical fatigue and difficulties concentrating the next day on the job; going to great lengths to hide their Internet use; regularly staying online much longer than they originally intended; and finding it quite difficult to stay off the Internet for longer than a day or so. Finally, Internet dependency has been shown to be a major legal liability as well as a productivity problem in the corporate world. Xerox, Dow Chemical, IBM, and Merck Pharmaceutical have all terminated employee contracts for incidents of Internet abuse (Young, 2011).

Background: The Dark Side of the Internet

With the advancement of digital device products and computer technologies, accessibility to the Internet is made possible 24 hours a day, 7 days a week. Turkle (2011) refers to the next new digital device product that today's techno-savvy consumers are eager to get their hands on as "the robotic moment." She contends that we have become much more emotionally excited about and eager to connect with the next new digital device or computer model and launch ourselves into the highly rewarding and stimulating virtual world rather than having focused, face-to-face interactions with humans in the offline world. Thus, because we are falling prey to the next new digital product craze, the strong psychological and social pull to buy, and are spending more time in the virtual world, in reality we have become increasingly more alone and inattentive to and emotionally unavailable to significant others in our offline relationships. Rosen, Cheever, and Carrier (2012) contend that our enmeshed relationship with technology and its psychological and social costs has created a new disorder of the twenty-first century, the *iDisorder*.

Some of the most enticing features of the Internet are the following: it is inexpensive, and you can be anonymous, quickly and deeply engage in fantasy, experience your personal power extended and amplified, be more self-confident, receive endless reinforcements and social rewards, temporarily escape from life stressors, and quickly connect and communicate with anyone, anywhere, at any time in the world (Greenfield, 2011; Leung, 2007; Suler, 2004). In the virtual world users have the opportunity to try on different personalities and identities like one would try on new fashion clothing.

Unless hacked into, or an Internet history check is conducted by a concerned intimate partner or parents, the Internet abuser can lead a safe and private separate life in the virtual world and engage in whatever pleasure-seeking activities that he or she believes will quickly and best meet his or her unique needs. Miller (2007) put it best by comparing the Internet experience to the immediate euphoric effect a heroin intravenous user experiences after shooting up, by saying:

> The Internet is the equivalent of an electronic needle ... a potent and efficient delivery system that provides ready access to a wide range of rewards and pleasures. Shopping, gambling, and pornography can be infused directly and in high doses from the Internet, anywhere and anytime (p. 8).

Hence, once hooked on the rewards from online spending, gambling, cyber-sex, video-gaming, and social networking sites, to name a few of the plethora of stimulating and intoxicating activities offered in the virtual world, it can be quite difficult for users to resist and overcome the Internet's seductive grip and euphoric rush effect on them in spite of the resultant severe relationship, work, or school performance consequences they may eventually experience. One important factor that keeps some users hooked on the Internet well beyond normal use of it, such as for mostly checking e-mails and to conduct searches for certain resources or subjects, is the *online disinhibition effect* (Delmonico & Griffin, 2011; Ko et al., 2006; Suler, 2004).

According to Suler (2004), there are six major thought processes that occur with us when we experience the online disinhibition effect:

- *You Don't Know Me*
- *You Can't See Me*
- *See You Later*
- *It's All in My Head*
- *It's Just a Game*
- *We're Equals*

The first two interconnected thought processes are related to anonymity and its role in people's behavior. In the virtual world, we can conceal our true identity. Individuals can decide not to use their real names or make up new or a few different personas to use on the Net. When we can separate are actions from our identities, we can become bigger risk-takers and do not have to be accountable for our actions. The *disinhibition effect* makes it possible for us to explore and experiment privately with confidence our sexuality beyond how we typically operate in our real world face-to-face relationships. Some individuals convince themselves that what they say or do online, no matter how extreme, is really not them, which is called *dissociation* (Suler, 2004).

With the third mode of thinking, we discover that it can be easy to escape from the consequences of our actions in the virtual world, simply by turning off the computer or our hand-held digital device. Mean-spirited adolescents can pull an emotional hit-and-run with peers they wish to psychologically and socially hurt in status by posting nasty words, vicious rumors, or embarrassing photos of them during awkward moments (nude in the gym locker room, in the school bathroom, etc.) on their *Facebook* walls or create web pages posting this material for the whole worldwide web to see. This is cyber-bullying at its worst. Since we cannot be seen online with whoever we are communicating with, it gives us the courage to say, do, and go to places we would never visit in the offline world. Thus, it sets the stage for more risky online behaviors and sexual activities.

The fourth and fifth thought processes together blur the boundaries between reality and fantasy, particularly when sexual activities are involved. Users come to believe that all online sexual behavior is fantasy-oriented, which allows them to have more cognitive dissonance when they reflect on their online sexual activities (Delmonico & Griffin, 2011). For heavy cyber-sex abusers, the virtual world experience is like an ongoing fantasy game without any rules or norms. In the extreme, this can lead to child pornography involvement and possibly becoming a sexual predator online.

Finally, in the virtual world there are no hierarchies or rules, all is fair game, and everyone is an equal. For many Internet and cyber-sex abusing individuals, they feel liberated by and like to escape into the virtual world since there is an absence of power and control dynamics, fears of being hurt or rejected, conflicts, and unreasonable expectations that they either may feel or may really exist in their offline world face-to-face relationships.

Excessive use of the Internet can fuel severe relationship difficulties and/or eventually lead to marital and other important relationship break-ups. In a study conducted by the American Academy of Matrimonial Lawyers, 63% of the divorce cases were due to unfaithful partners' online affairs, romantic sexual relationships, and regular cyber-porn activities (Dedmon, 2003). In another interesting study with 546 adult men and women 18–59 years of age seeking love and intimacy in the virtual world, Scott, Mottarella, and Lavooy (2006) found that offline face-to-face relationships clearly have the edge in establishing truly intimate and more loving relationships than virtual relationships. *Virtual relaters*, who had intimate relationships both on- and offline, had significantly lower intimacy ratings and relationship difficulties in their offline face-to-face relationships. The *traditional relaters* in the study who only had offline face-to-face relationships on the other hand, had higher intimacy rating scores and fewer relationship difficulties. Clearly, this study indicates the importance of individual partners and couples trying to identify and resolve their conflicts and intimacy difficulties in the offline world rather than trying to escape from them in the fantasy world of the Internet as the solution for emotional relief and gratification. However, what keeps virtual relaters returning to the Internet for emotional salvation and to escape from real world relationship difficulties is their access to and ability to quickly establish intense online intimate relationships, known as *hyper-personal relationships* (Tidwell & Walther, 2002; Walther, 2007).

Popular new online services that can be quickly accessed by cyber-sex abusers and unfaithful partners are infidelity websites like: *AshleyMadison*, *Meet2Cheat*, *AdultFriendFinder*, *Marital Affair*, and *Second Life*. All of these websites glamorize infidelity and have catchy slogans about the benefits of marital and significant relationship infidelity. On the popular dating site AshleyMadison.com the motto is "Life is short, have an affair." On this website, visitors can choose from a wide range of different types of relationships and encounters they desire, such as: "Long-Term," "Cyber-Affair," "Erotic Chat," or "Whatever Excites Me" (Kolhatkar, 2011; Lee, 2011; Whitty, 2011).

With the growing popularity of social networking sites like *Facebook* and *Twitter*, a lot of adolescents today not only are spending most of their leisure time on these sites and blogging but are increasingly becoming more transparent with disclosing their risky behaviors online to others. Williams and Merten (2008) found in their study that 84% of the social network profiles of adolescents disclosed such risk-taking behaviors as alcohol and drug use, stealing, vandalism, and committing other crimes. Twenty-seven percent of these youth's profiles included statements and images of harming oneself or others, disclosing suicidal thoughts, and plans to stage a fight or gang activity.

Jaron Lanier, digital pioneer and critic, and author of the provocative book *You are not a gadget: A manifesto* (2011), contends that another troublesome aspect of *Facebook* and *Twitter* for teens is that they spend excessive amounts of time vigilantly maintaining their online reputations, but they do so "driven more by fear than by love" (Kahn, 2011, p. 46). We frequently hear this concern from our adolescent clients that *Facebook* in particular is all about staying on top of the inner and wider peer groups' politics, rumor mill, and protecting one's social status at all costs. Since young people spend a good part of their social lives online communicating with friends, they feel quite comfortable with trusting of this medium with what they say or do. However, a new form of self-harm by young people via the use of *YouTube* has been identified where they post a video of themselves asking questions like: "Am I pretty or ugly?" Rather than meeting with positive feedback, the majority of these youth are bombarded with over 100,000 worldwide responses that are vicious and humiliating and could clearly drive one to engage in severe and intense self-destructive behavior, or worse yet, suicide (Italie, 2012).

Gibson (2010), in an interview with pioneering social psychologist John Cacioppo, contends that when someone substitutes online relationships for face-to-face ones, they become lonelier and more depressed. He further adds that lonely people are likely to use the Internet as a crutch, while the non-lonely for social leverage. "So," Cacioppo says, "the rich get richer and the poor get poorer" (p. 41).

Online Gaming

Adolescents who engage in excessive and unmonitored Internet usage can fuel depression, social withdrawal from key offline relationships, aggressive and violent behavior, and drive a big wedge in and fuel parent–teen relationship conflicts (Beard, 2011; Gentile et al., 2011; Kraut et al., 1997; Lam & Peng, 2010; Messerly, 2009; Park, Kim, & Cho, 2008; Williams & Merten, 2008; see the case example of Chad later in this chapter). Online gaming is one Internet activity that can become highly addictive and can emotionally and physically pull people away from their families. Kwon (2005) found in her research that adolescents' high self-escape tendencies and low tolerance for negative affects were predictive of online gaming addiction. Three other factors that have been implicated in adolescent on- and offline video-gaming dependency: *novelty seekers*, *low reward dependence*, and *harm avoidance* (Ko et al., 2006; Rosen et al., 2012). Novelty seekers get bored very easily and constantly crave and pursue new stimuli or activities to increase their arousal levels. Some adolescents have lower reward dependence levels than the average youth in their responsiveness to verbal praise and social reinforcement, and lack the drive to want to persevere with challenging tasks and activities. They have little tolerance for life's disappointments and frustrating situations. Online gaming provides for them a world rich in resources for novel experiences and personal success without unpredictable frustration. Finally, for many adolescents the virtual world is a safe place to take lots of risks and there is no real need to be accountable for their actions.

In comparing the brain circuitry and chemistry of substance-dependent individuals with those of heavy online-gamers, both Frascella, Potenza, Brown and Childress (2010) and Ko et al. (2009) discovered that they are practically identical. These researchers also found that heavy online-gamers have higher levels of dopamine in their brains, and are really addicted to the pleasurable effects of this substance, not the activity itself. Another study examining the dopamine production systems of online-gamers indicated that adolescents who are allowed to spend six or more hours a day playing violent on- and offline role-play video-games, such as *The Elder Scrolls Skyrim*, *Modern Warfare III*, *World of Warcraft*, *Call of Duty*, and *Grand Theft Auto*, not only tend to psychologically dissociate while playing but also trigger the release of the same dopamine pleasurable-effects which can be found in the dopamine action release systems of alcohol and nicotine-dependent individuals (Han et al., 2007).

Kwon (2011) contends that on- and offline violent games can be very reinforcing for adolescents because of their interactivity and the sense of belonging, competence, social status, and power they provide. Not only do adolescents find these types of violent games highly engaging and quite stimulating to play for endless hours of time solo and/or with friends but they learn that aggression is necessary, desirable, and rewarding, there are no consequences for one's actions, and victims do not deserve pity (Aboujaoude, 2011). The added bonus, and another positive reinforcement for aggressive behavior, is that the more skilled players become at killing others in these games, the more points they are rewarded with and the more their status will increase with both their online and offline friends. Violent games *desensitize* us to violence because they bypass the moral centers of our brains, which robs us of the opportunity to empathize with others. These exciting and action-packed games do not provide the user with enough time to reflect on the moralistic aspects of his or her actions and no time to relate to opponents on any deep emotional level (Funk, 2005). In fact longitudinal research with children and adolescent long-term violent on- and offline video-gamers indicates that it does increase users' aggressive behavior over time (Anderson et al., 2008).

Online Compulsive Spending

Another enticing way that the Internet seduces users' mind is online shopping. Today, we can buy virtually anything our heart desires on websites like *eBay* or on *Amazon.com* with one click. Chaey (2011) found that "purchase happy video-gamers" spent online in 2011 $653 million on virtual goods. For compulsive shoppers, the Internet can be a dangerous place because of the endless choices of material items, which helps insure that they won't get offline empty-handed. The tendency for compulsive shoppers to spend well beyond their financial means is quite great. Teenagers tend to be the most reckless of shoppers (Roberts, 2004). Ditmar (2005) found in her study of 195 16–18 year-olds that 40% of her subjects met the criterion for compulsive shopping disorder. In a later study, Ditmar, Long, and Bond (2007) found in her study with 126 men and women averaging about 22 in age that their reasons for heavy online shopping were rooted in psychological motives and identity gains. Online shopping made them feel better about themselves, it triggered pleasurable mood elevation, and it brought them closer to the ideal self-images they were seeking. However, the Internet encourages us to adopt a materialistic attitude and fall prey to becoming a *maximizer* (Schwartz, 2004). Maximizers are not content with the bargain buy but instead, must own the *best* and *most popular* and often the most expensive material item. However, once this rigid maximizing pattern gets set in motion, a vicious cycle develops where the individual's "high" and satisfaction with the purchase is short-lived and he or she begins to feel empty, anxious, and depressed and must seek out the next best or expensive material item to purchase to feel good and *special* and special about oneself. Unfortunately, maximizers continue to over-spend despite pummeling further into emotional instability and financial debt (Schwartz, 2004).

Online Cyber-Sex Activities

Cyber-sex difficulties cut across all socio-economic and cultural groups. It is estimated that 40 million people a day log on to some 4.2 million pornographic websites, according to the *Internet*

Filter Software Review. Research also indicates that chronic masturbators engage with online porn for up to 20 hours a day and suffer a bad "hangover" effect as a result of a major dopamine level drop-off (Lee, 2011). One out of every three visitors of adult pornography websites is a woman. Twenty percent of these women struggle with online sexual compulsivity issues. In 2006, Internet pornography accounted for $3 billion (23%) of the total market share of the pornography industry earnings in the United States (Family Safe Media, 2010). Worldwide, pornography is a $100 billion revenue-generating industry (Ropelato, 2009). On pornographic websites, one can not only have erotic fantasies met through gaining access to stimulating sexually arousing images and downloads but on some websites have live chats with porn stars. Some experts believe that regular involvement with cyber-porn is like a "gateway drug" for offline marital or intimate relationship infidelity. Other ways one can gain access to cyber-sex and engage in marital or relationship infidelity is through *news groups*, *chat areas of major Internet search engines*, *peer-to-peer file sharing*, and on *social networking sites*. News groups can exchange sexualized texts (sexting), photos, videos, and erotic sounds on the Internet with others anywhere in the world who share similar sexual interests. Chat areas on major Internet search engines provide the opportunity for live conversations and flirting, which can lead to marital and relationship infidelity. With peer-to-peer file sharing it is possible to share pornographic images, videos, and software with others. Finally, social networking sites like *Facebook* can be used to engage in sexualized activities and to arrange offline sexual encounters. *Twitter* allows visitors to follow online diaries, which can be filled with sexual content (Delmonico & Griffin, 2011). Sexual addiction specialists Patrick Carnes and David Delmonico found in their research that 10% of adults who regular use porn believed they were cyber-sex addicted (Carnes & Delmonico, 2007).

Many adolescents turn to pornography to fulfill their sexual curiosities and fantasies, and to cope with life stressors; they look to porn stars to serve as the ideal for physical and sexual prowess (Earle & Bell, 2010; Maltz & Maltz, 2010). With the increase in accessibility and exposure to pornography and other sexually explicit forms of the media, adolescents are getting bombarded with confusing and harmful messages about what healthy sexual intimacy truly is. The majority of porn films youth are exposed to graphically display women as submissive, reduced to objects of desire to please their men, and the recipients of aggressive and humiliating sexual maltreatment. Rather than objecting to their mistreatment, the female porn stars in these movies convey that they are either enjoying or not troubled by being humiliated and treated roughly. As Wosnitzer and Bridges (2007) aptly point out, this conveys to adolescents that violence is normal in sexual relationships.

In a 2008 survey conducted by the National Campaign to Prevent Teen and Unplanned Pregnancy with 1,280 male and female adolescents and young adults, the researchers found that 20% of the teen girls had *sexted* (sent nude or semi-nude sexually charged and provocative images of themselves via text messaging and e-mails). Eighteen percent of the teen boys reported sexting. For the young adult male and women participants in the survey, their percentages were much higher with the use of sexting. Thirty-six percent of the women reported having done sexting while 31% of the adult males reported engaging in this activity (National Campaign to Prevent Teen and Unplanned Pregnancy, 2008).

British director Steve McQueen's provocative and realistic movie *Shame* graphically displays the powerful "psychological imprisonment" grip that severe sexually compulsive behavioral difficulties have on an individual. In the movie, Brandon, masterfully played by Michael Fassbender, is a highly successful businessman who has an insatiable sexual appetite. When not engaging in love-less cyber-porn, he is compulsively hiring prostitutes and picking up women at trendy bars for one-night stands. Any attempt that Brandon makes to have a normal non-sexual encounter with women, get in touch with his latent healthy feelings and venture out of his psychological jail cell, results in the cell door eventually slamming when the repeated outcome is intense but loveless stormy sex. Over time, we bear witness to Brandon's self-destruction psychologically, socially, and occupationally from his imprisonment to his sexually compulsive behavioral difficulty.

The Brain, the Internet, and Cyber-Sex Dependency Habits

Excessive Internet use can lead to significant changes in our brains and make us more vulnerable to developing a wide range of habit difficulties and psychological disorders. Recent research has indicated that there are significant differences in the grey and white matter of the brains of Internet-dependent and non-Internet-dependent youth (Yuan et al., 2011). Other neuroscience studies have found that individuals who have obsessive compulsive tendencies are not only at risk for developing a wide range of self-destructive habits but that excessive use of digital technology can accelerate that process. In a sense, our brains are seduced by the Internet as a path of least resistance to get our needs met quickly (DiSalvo, 2011; Doidge, 2007; Rosen et al., 2012). Thus, the Internet can function as a drug for the user (Grant, Brewer, & Potenza, 2006).

Klingborg (2009) found in his research that excessive Internet use overloads our working memory because we are bombarded with too much information to process and we are unable to retain the information or to draw connections with the information already stored in our long-term memory. Our ability to learn anything in depth suffers and our understanding remains shallow. We become mindless consumers of information. Thanks to the hyper-linking system (one item embedded into the next items) on the Internet, we not only run astray from what we originally sought out to accomplish but end up for lengthy periods of time surfing all over the Net, clicking on one intriguing item after the next. When our brains become overtaxed by information overload, it is difficult to concentrate and we are easily distracted. Individuals who meet the DSM-IV criterion for ADD/ADHD struggle with working memory overload, which explains why they often have grave difficulties with concentration, staying on task, and are easily distracted.

The largest study in the world that looked at the relationship between ADHD and excessive Internet use was conducted in South Korea with 752 adolescents who had been diagnosed with ADHD. Thirty-three percent of the research sample were using the Internet excessively daily and were deemed "addicted" (Ko, Yen, Chen, Chen, & Yen, 2008). In a study with 216 college students in Taiwan, Yoo (2004) found that 32% of the sample met the criterion for both ADHD and Internet dependency. Although the direction of causality is not yet clear, studies like these provide some empirical support for the link between excessive Internet usage and attention difficulties (Aboujaoude, 2011; Carr, 2010; Rosen et al., 2012).

Viewing pornographic images can have a major effect on our bodies, which can be as powerful as cocaine, methamphetamine, alcohol, and other drugs. Our brains recognize sexual activities faster than any other forms of stimulation presented to it (Anokhin et al., 2006; Maltz, 2009). Pornography and other sexually related activities stimulate the median forebrain, which is filled with many receptors for the neurotransmitter *dopamine*. The dopamine is released when you get sexually aroused, kiss, masturbate, have intercourse, or take drugs. The dramatic increase in dopamine production triggers a drug-like high that is as potent as crack cocaine. Other 'feel-good' chemicals that are triggered by viewing pornographic images are adrenalin, endorphins, testosterone, serotonin, and the powerful hormones oxytocin and vasopressin, which are released when we are falling in love and bonding (Maltz & Maltz, 2010). However, once our body has become accustomed to being overloaded by the manufacturing of these chemicals, it fails to produce them when needed for normal life circumstances, such as with our offline world intimate relationship encounters. According to Carnes and Carnes (2010),

> No spouse or partner can compete with the Internet. The brain has the extraordinary ability to rewire the synapses for intense pleasure and keep repeating the self-administration. The digital production of multiple stimulations intensifies that adaptation implicit in synaptic rewiring (p. 12).

Thus, the neurochemical production system becomes limited to and geared for porn-related activities (Maltz, 2009; Maltz & Maltz, 2010). This can contribute to sexual dysfunctions and conflict difficulties in the cyber-sex abuser's intimate relationships.

Key Research Findings that Inform our Clinical Practice

Since Internet abuse and dependency treatment is a relatively new field of specialization, there have been no well-controlled couple or family treatment outcome studies with Internet and cyber-sex-abusing adults or adolescents respectively. The most popular treatment method with Internet-abusing clients used today is cognitive-behavioral therapy (CBT) (Davis, 2001; Young, 1998, 2007, 2011). It is believed that, since CBT has been widely established as the empirically supported treatment for such impulse control disorders as compulsive-shopping, pathological gambling, obsessive-compulsive disorder, and bulimia nervosa, it should produce equally positive treatment results. Young's (2007, 2011) expanded CBT approach has some couple partner involvement and integrates motivational-enhancement (Miller & Rollnick, 2002) and harm-reduction (Marlatt, 1998), and employs strategic therapy pattern intervention strategies (O'Hanlon, 1987). Maltz and Maltz (2010) and Bercaw and Bercaw (2010) have developed couple therapy approaches that have shown clinical promise with cyber-sex abusers and individuals with other sexually compulsive difficulties and their partners. Beard (2008, 2011) has had positive treatment outcome results using the empirically supported multidimensional family therapy approach (Liddle, 2010) with Internet-abusing and dependent adolescents. However, with all of the aforementioned treatment approaches we only have anecdotal and immediate client feedback on their treatment experiences to go with. Below, we still feel it is worthwhile mentioning some of the important findings that these therapists have identified as key target areas for intervention, appear to contribute to positive treatment outcomes, and can inform our clinical practices:

- Maltz and Maltz (2010) and Bercaw and Bercaw (2010) both have found that the unfaithful cyber-sex-abusing and/or sexually compulsive partner must take responsibility for their actions, be completely open and honest about all present and past extra-relational acts of betrayal, and in an apology session, seek forgiveness in order to begin to rebuild trust in their main offline relationship. Maltz and Maltz (2010) have the betrayed partner establish a self-healing plan to empower him or her and aid with the recovery process.
- Young (2007, 2011), Beard (2008), Maltz and Maltz (2010), and Bercaw and Bercaw (2010) all believe that the Internet and cyber-sex abuser must have increased involvement in meaningful activities with their partners, families, and friends in the offline world. This includes involvement in healthy individual hobbies, other creative pursuits, and service work.
- The use of pattern intervention strategies employed by partners and parents can be quite effective at reducing problem Internet use, particularly during times of the day when the cyber-sex or Internet abusers were more likely behind the scenes visiting porn sites or chat rooms or engaging in other risky activities online, such as overspending or gambling (Beard, 2008, 2011; Maltz & Maltz, 2010; Young, 2007, 2011).
- Beard (2008, 2011) has found that by empowering parents to be a united front and consistently enforce firm guidelines around Internet, other digital device, and video-game usage can be quite effective with Internet-abusing and dependent adolescents.

Strategies for Assessment and Treatment Planning

To date, there has never been an official diagnostic category for Internet or cyber-sex dependency in any of the existing volumes of the DSM. However, Internet dependency will be included in the Appendix section of the DSM-V volume due out in 2013 (Block, 2008; Dell'Osso et al., 2008; Rosen et al., 2012; Young, 2011). Internet abuse experts are in agreement that Internet dependency shares many of the same clinical features as substance and gambling dependence, and impulse control disorder diagnoses. Young (2011) and Dell'Osso and his colleagues (2008) have identified the following criterion to be present with an individual in order to diagnose Internet dependency:

- excessive use
- withdrawal
- tolerance
- negative consequences.

Excessive use of the Internet involves losing track of time and loss of control. Some Internet-dependent individuals have been known to spend up to 20 hours in a day and 40–80 hours in a week online (Greenfield, 1999; Young, 1998). Such lengthy periods of time on the Internet have caused emotional and physical distance in intimate partner and/or family relationships and other important responsibilities or obligations were not being attended to on a regular basis.

The Internet dependency withdrawal picture often includes the following: mood swings, depression, sleep disturbance, excessive fatigue, anger, irritability, craving, and intrusive thoughts regarding past pleasurable experiences while on the Net. An individual may experience anxiety and can become aggressive and potentially violent when personal computers and hand-held digital devices are not available or they are prevented from using them.

Tolerance takes the form of increasing one's time on the Internet, pursuing greater and varying degrees of stimulating content, seeking out and purchasing "must have" new computer games and digital hand-held devices. Similar to the rapid absorption process of certain drugs that can greatly enhance the addiction potential, the rapid access and short time between clicking and receiving desired digital images and other content can increase the addiction potential of getting hooked on the Internet (Greenfield, 2011). At this stage of the dependency process, we might see the individual turning toward even more risky behaviors for immediate and potent pleasures and rewards like cyber-sex and infidelity, child porn, or illegal gambling activities. The tolerance pictures for adults and adolescents hooked on online and/or offline video-gaming will take the form of engaging in even more challenging and violent interactive games to achieve the same level of pleasure and excitement they have been accustomed to receiving previously.

Internet-dependent individuals experience severe consequences in all areas of their lives, such as: serious intimate and family relationship conflicts and negative interactions, relationship separations and break-ups, problems with mistrust and lying, excessive fatigue, weight gain or loss, difficulties with concentration, depression, social isolation, financial difficulties related to spending beyond one's means on new computers, hand-held digital devices, and software, possible legal difficulties, and a serious decline in academic and work performance possibly resulting in job loss.

In addition to determining whether or not a client meets the criterion for Internet dependency and for treatment planning purposes, it is important to determine if his or her problematic Internet use is *specific* or *generalized* (Davis, 2001). With specific problematic Internet use, the individual is over-involved in or heavily abusing content-specific functions in the virtual world, such as: gambling, stock trading, gaming, and visiting pornographic websites. The generalized pattern of Internet abuse, on the other hand, is not linked to any specific content; individuals are engaged in a wide range of online activities, and much prefer to spend most of their lives in the virtual world then engaged in face-to-face offline relationships. Finally, as part of the assessment process we need to identify an individual's key strengths and life passions in the offline world, present and past successes at reducing their use of the Internet and what specifically contributed to that. In addition, we need to know about key supportive others that we can call upon to aid in the change effort and for relapse prevention.

Co-Morbidity and Common Characteristics of Internet-Abusing and Cyber-Sex-Dependent Individuals

In reviewing the Internet dependency and cyber-sex abuse literature, specialists have identified some common characteristics that Internet and cyber-sex dependent individuals share: poor social skills, being socially avoidant or phobic, having a history of being unsuccessful with forming and maintaining intimate relationships, being conflict-avoidant, feeling lonely, having low self-esteem, depression, anxiety, mood swings, poor self-regulation and coping skills, having poor impulse control, sleeping difficulties, excessive fatigue, weight gain or loss due to leading a sedentary lifestyle and not eating in a healthy way, and school and work performance problems (Aboujaoude, 2011; Black, Belsare, & Schosser, 1999; Block, 2008; Cacioppo & Patrick, 2008; Caplan, 2007; Dell'Osso et al., 2008; Gibson, 2010; Greenfield, 1999; Rosen et al., 2012; Young, 2011; Young & Rodgers, 1997). However, it is important to determine with the client if these symptoms or difficulties existed prior to their getting more heavily involved with their Internet activities or developed as a result of excessive abuse of this medium. Furthermore, some of these symptoms and difficulties can be caused by other habit abuse withdrawal from illicit substances, gambling, or abstaining from self-injury.

In our clinical practices, we have found that parents of adolescents diagnosed with autistic spectrum disorders such as Asperger's, nonverbal learning disorders, sensory integration issues, who are socially phobic, shy, and even ADD or ADHD, are increasingly allowing their children to spend excessive amounts of time to escape into the virtual world on their personal computers or with their hand-held digital devices to help keep them "happy," "to entertain themselves," or "just to bring fun and joy" into their lives, since they were experiencing such grave difficulties establishing and maintaining friendships in the offline world. The Internet becomes a safe place of refuge and a cocoon for them, which can, over time, set in motion a serious dependency habit. Unfortunately, this attempted parental solution fails horribly because their teens end up further into social isolation and are robbed of the opportunity to confront their social skill deficiencies and master new skills in order to function better interpersonally in the real world.

According to Skinner (2005), one out of four females and one out of six males who are cyber-sex-dependent reported past sexual abuse and/or childhood experiences of being primed for sex. Many of these individuals grew up in home environments with diffused generational boundaries where they were exposed to pornographic movies and magazines and had been involved in sex play with siblings and friends. Because of these early and confusing experiences with sexuality, some of these individuals developed distorted and unhealthy views about what normal human sexuality and intimacy is. Some of these long-term cyber-sex-dependent adults, who spend excessive amounts of time on pornographic websites, may venture into more risky and illegal offline behaviors, such as seeking out prostitutes, visiting adult bookstores, and possibly getting involved in child pornography and sex offending (Maltz & Maltz, 2010).

As far as co-morbidity goes with cyber-sex dependent clients, research indicates that 96% of these individuals show signs of diagnosable anxiety disorders and 71% some form of a mood disorder (Raymond, Coleman, & Miner, 2003). Ko et al. (2008) and Kafka and Hemen (2003) found that these individuals had co-occurring problems with obsessive-compulsive disorder, addictive disorders, or ADD/ADHD. We have observed in our clinical practices that for individuals who are struggling with poor social skills, have difficulties with reading social cues, have been diagnosed with Asperger's and nonverbal learning disorders, or are inherently shy or socially phobic, the Internet has served as the perfect solution for them, or at least they have convinced themselves and their parents of that. It allows them to socially connect comfortably and seamlessly with others without any anxiety or having to read social cues.

Many cyber-sex abusers turn to alcohol and other drugs to quickly obliterate feelings of shame, which over time can lead to multiple habit dependency with each habit reinforcing the other. Individuals with cyber-sex and other compulsive sexual behavioral difficulties experience psychological and physiological withdrawal symptoms like intense craving when not engaged in sexual activity or trying to abstain, which is very similar to what alcohol and substance-dependent people go through (Denizet-Lewis, 2009).

Key Assessment Questions

When interviewing the Internet-abusing and cyber-sex-dependent clients and their partners and/or parents, there are a number of questions we like to ask them to help gain a better understanding of the various functions these habits serve for them, how specifically they have benefited them, and the costs they have experienced in key relationships and individually as a result of continuing to engage in these self-destructive habits. Some examples of the questions we may ask are as follows:

- "How many hours in a week do you spend online?"
- "What activities do you engage in and websites do you like to visit while online?"
- "How often do you find yourself staying online longer than you had originally intended to?"
- "How often do you feel preoccupied with the Internet when offline, or fantasize about being online?"
- "Have you experienced any consequences in any areas of your life as a result of your Internet use?"
- "[Asking the partner/parents] What effect has your partner's/son's/daughter's Internet misuse had on your relationship with him/her or in any other important areas of his/her life?"
- "[Asking the partner/parents] Have you ever complained about or tried to outlaw your partner/son/daughter from engaging in any specific activities or from visiting any specific websites while online?"
- "When your partner/parents try and block you from or limit your time online, how do you typically respond?"
- "What is the longest amount of time you have been able to abstain from engaging in your favorite online activities?"
- "Are you aware of how you were able to pull that off?"
- "What specifically do you tell yourself or do instead that helps you not cave into using the Internet to visit porn sites?"
- "What specifically does your partner/parents say or do that helps you not cave into using the Internet to visit porn sites?"
- "What would be the disadvantages of reducing your Internet use time and not visiting your favorite websites?"
- "Can you think of any advantages for reducing your Internet time that could have a positive effect on your relationship with your partner/parents?"
- "What specifically would those advantages be?"

The above questions can greatly assist therapists in assessing the severity of the client's Internet or cyber-sex dependency level and with treatment planning. Some of the questions may be uncomfortable for the client to respond to in the company of his or her partner or parents and we need to honor their desire to privately respond if they would feel more comfortable with this arrangement.

Family and Couple Dynamics

Since the Internet or cyber-sex-dependent partner or parent tends to prioritize spending most of their leisure and waking hours on the Internet, this will eventually dissolve whatever important attachments they have in their most important offline relationships, particularly with their intimate partners and children. Couple interactions are characterized by mistrust, lying, manipulation, arguments, blaming, secrecy, and emotional distance in the relationship.

According to Bercaw and Bercaw (2010), once a partner discovers that their cyber-sex-dependent partner is regularly visiting porn sites and chat rooms, and/or having online affairs for sexual gratification, it is analogous to a bomb going off in their relationship, as it is an emotionally traumatizing experience. They believe that it is much more difficult for these couples to move beyond the devastation of this painful explosion in the relationship than couples trying to recover from alcohol and drug dependencies. After the disclosure of these painful Internet activities, some couples separate or divorce. In other cases, the couple may play a cat and mouse game where the Internet or cyber-sex-dependent partner tries to outsmart the other partner by sneaking on the Net for their fixes both at and outside the home.

We have worked with some mistrusting partners who like to play detective with their partners by either installing special software to check-up on their Internet activity or even hire someone to hack into their system to secure this private information. Once their partners found out about their counter-sneaky behaviors, intense arguing and blaming often erupted and, with the worst cases, aggressive and violent behavior occurred.

In families of Internet-abusing and dependent adolescents, parents have often failed to provide any firm guidelines around computer or hand-held digital device use. Many of these youths have PCs, laptops, and hand-held digital devices in their bedrooms, making it highly tempting to be online throughout the night. These families tend to be characterized by poor conflict resolution skills, emotional disconnection, destructive interactions between the parents and their adolescents, and poor family cohesion (Beard, 2011; Selekman, 2009). Kwon, Chung, and Lee (2009) and Yen, Yen, Chen, Chen, and Ko (2007) have observed with Internet-dependent youth that their difficulties expressing themselves, being validated, and inability to get beyond conflicts in their families, makes it easy for them to escape to the Internet where they feel safe, less restrained, and can express themselves freely. The parents may also have difficulties with Internet abuse and may model for their kids the mismanagement of stress through excessive use of nicotine, alcohol, prescription medications, or illegal drug use (Beard, 2008, 2011; Park et al., 2008; Selekman, 2009).

A major challenge for parents today is that their kids are much more tech-savvy then they are, making it easier for them to get away with their online potentially risky activities without their parents having any idea of what they are doing. One of the biggest challenges we have had in our clinical practices is the family dynamic of the Internet-dependent adolescent who has a parent who also has Internet use difficulties. The Internet problem use parent models for the children that when there is a conflict or family problem, or you are stressed out, you retreat to the Internet to escape from your difficulties and the challenges of life. This has made a big challenge for therapists to unify and empower the parents as a team to resolve their son or daughter's Internet dependency problem.

Specialized Internet-Based Couple and Family Therapy Change Strategies

We have developed a variety of therapeutic change strategies that can successfully harness the strengths and resources of the Internet and cyber-sex abusers and his or her partner and/or parents to transform negative habits and problem-maintaining relationship patterns into virtuous habits and constructive actions. These therapeutic experiments can dismantle outmoded beliefs that have also contributed to maintaining the Internet or cyber-sex-problem life support system. Since in our digital age we rely so heavily on the Internet for much of our communications and information for school or work, for sending and reading e-mails, and for other normal everyday reasons, it is highly unrealistic to push for total abstinence goals. Therefore some of our therapeutic experiments are designed to increase the Internet or cyber-sex abuser's leisure time on the Internet with positive and productive on- and offline activities.

Digital Technology-Free Days During Couple and Family Leisure Times

One powerful way we can help couples and families reduce the centrality of digital technology in their relationships is to have them experiment with implementing policy regarding at least one or two days of weekly *digital technology-free days* during their leisure times together. It is during this time that they can rediscover the pleasures of truly being present with one another face-to-face without any digital device obstacles between them. This includes their beloved smart phones. During this digital technology-free time couples and families can be creative together in reinstating former pleasurable activities they used to engage in and generate some new enjoyable activities that can bring them closer together to help strengthen their relationships. Once couples and families begin experimenting with the digital technology-free days policy, they often report that they greatly enjoyed their offline activities and it was helping build more closeness in their relationships.

Sending e-Mails, e-Cards, and Texts to Share Loving Words to and Appreciation for One's Partner

One powerful way more positive emotion can be infused into couples' relationships and bring the partners closer together is through the use of random e-mails, e-cards, or text messages expressing one's love and appreciation toward one another. We encourage couple partners to strive to give each other two or three compliments a day. Gable, Reis, Impett, and Asher (2004) found in their research with happy and highly satisfied couples that when partners regularly shared what they appreciated about one another and the positive events in their lives and the partners responded with mutually positive feelings, strong interest, with a lot of enthusiasm, and complimented them, it enhanced their positive affect and wellbeing, and the interpersonal benefits resulted in increased satisfaction and emotional intimacy.

Making Online Sexual Fantasies a Reality in the Offline World Intimate Relationship

Once we discover in the early stages of couples therapy what the cyber-sex-abusing partner's unique sexual desires and fantasies are and highly stimulating and sexual experiences have been on the Internet, we can attempt to replicate these experiences in their offline world intimate relationship: fetishes, specific sexual acts and positions, dramatized scenes, sexually arousing lingerie and other types of dress, sexually arousing settings and role-play activities, seductive talk, music, and other sensory experiences. However, this therapeutic experiment can only be pursued once the cyber-sex-abusing partner has committed to the change process by making a full disclosure of all of their sexual activities in the virtual world and offline and has apologized to their partner, and he or she in turn has forgiven them and is willing to work toward rebuilding trust in the relationship. Some of our house rules that we reinforce with couples when proposing that they try this experiment is that no potentially harmful sexual activities are included; if the other partner is being asked to try something sexually that feels very uncomfortable to him or her, they have the right to refuse. We also recognize that some couples have a long history of problems with sexual intimacy due to very little experience, psychological or physical reasons, or past negative experiences with sexual relations. In these situations, the couple may need some psychoeducation and may want to learn some sex therapy techniques and exercises to help them to overcome these barriers to confidence and sexual freedom of expression before they try out this experiment.

After the cyber-sex-abusing partner has fully disclosed what turns him or her on the most, and the details about what specifically led to his or her using the virtual world, the other partner has the opportunity to learn, possibly for the first time, what the other's unique sexual desires and fantasies are, what specifically was missing in their relationship, and what he or she can do differently which can be experimented with in their offline relationship. So what was initially an emotionally devastating and traumatizing experience for the non-cyber-sex abuse partner and the relationship in general can become an opportunity for growth, improving emotional and sexual intimacy, and taking the relationship to new heights.

In the early implementation phase of this experiment, couples should be encouraged to begin with more low-scale sex play and gradually move into more challenging sexual activities that are totally new to their relationship. Along the way, they need to openly communicate with one another about their sensory experiences, what works, or what feels uncomfortable. The therapist needs to predict that they may experience some bumps in the road while experimenting with new sexual behaviors and to be supportive and patient with one another. This may help alleviate some of the performance anxieties partners may experience. They can dress up and role-play and be the producers and directors of the kind of romantic and sexually charged scenes they wish to create together. It also is critical to ensure that the other partner's voice is heard regarding their sexual desires, fantasies, and unique needs with sexual intimacy. What can grow out of this experiment for the first time in the history of the couple's relationship is that each partner is better meeting the unique emotional and sexual needs of the other, communications will improve, and they will have a much more exciting and spiced up sex life.

Adolescents as Expert Digital Technology and Internet Consultants to the Parents

The majority of adolescents today are much more tech-savvy than their parents. This has contributed to a generational hierarchical reversal where young people in this technical skill area wield more power and control than their parents. They know the virtual world and how to operate with great precision all of the popular hand-held digital devices on the market.

One way to empower the parents and help rebuild trust between the Internet-abusing adolescent and his or her parents is to place the adolescent in the expert position so he or she can educate the parents about the most popular activities adolescents engage in on the Net and their favorite websites. The adolescent can educate the parents about any online tricks of the trade that he or she may know as well as their tech-savvy Net interventionist friends, such as the art of hacking, visiting porn-sites, cyber-harassment and bullying, and so forth. He or she can be encouraged by the therapist in session to inform the parents of some of the major psychological, family, and social reasons why kids today escape into or spend so much of their leisure time in the virtual world, which includes their personal experience for doing so. The adolescent also can educate the parents about the signs and symptoms that were telling them that he or she was getting hooked on the Internet experience and inform them about how they can best help him or her with this problem. Finally, this therapeutic experiment also serves a helpful prevention function for the parents with younger siblings in that they can intervene early to prevent them from developing Internet abuse difficulties.

We have found by employing this therapeutic experiment that adolescents often begin to open up about how they became Internet abusers and some of the consequences of their behind-the-scenes actions that the parents may not have known about. Rather than over-reacting in a negative way, the parents often view this as a courageous step taken with them by their kids. At this point, honest and open communications can be fostered between the parents and the adolescents about how to best improve their relationships and help their children kick their Internet abuse habits and other difficulties they are struggling with in their lives.

Adolescent Service Work Website on the Net

Another effective way to help Internet-abusing adolescents kick their habits and stay quit from engaging in risky and self-destructive activities online is to channel their negative energy into constructive action by having them develop and launch service work websites. They can be as creative as they want to be with website design, artistic images and photographs, catchy and powerful kid-friendly text, posting testimonials of positive service work experiences of youth visitors to the site, and posting a variety of community or societal causes that they are involved with, including places in the community that welcome high school-aged youth volunteers for service work. In their offline worlds, they can regularly communicate with community volunteer service work sites, facilitate youth placements, troubleshoot when necessary, and closely collaborate with a community advisory committee of parents and professionals. A website blog can be added as well.

This therapeutic experiment is quite effective with adolescents who may already possess or have not been empowered to unleash their latent and unexpressed leadership abilities, possibly have already had some previous experience with service work, and/or are concerned about local community and societal causes. Increasing their involvement in meaningful and positive on- and offline activities will help fill their free time with structure, prevent relapses, and increase their sense of purpose and meaning in life by giving to others and remedying environmental problems.

The Teen Cyber-Bullying-Busting Activists' Website

An effective therapeutic experiment for empowering Internet-abusing adolescents who may have been involved in cyber-bullying is to channel their negative use of time and energy on the Net into constructive action by having them create a website for other youth struggling with Internet abuse and cyber-bullying difficulties to visit as a helpful and free resource for support and teen expert consultation. However, our experience has been that this experiment cannot be successfully implemented unless the adolescent is in the *preparation, action, maintenance,* or *termination* stages of readiness for change (Prochaska, Norcross, & DiClemente, 2006), committed to the change process and receptive to taking steps to improve the situations. In addition, this experiment cannot be launched unless the adolescent has partnered up with a professional therapist, team of therapists, or school counseling staff who will regularly supervise and provide consultation to him or her and fellow peer counselors, so as to tightly monitor the operations for risk management. Written parental consent, confidentiality, and liability issues must be addressed as well. Some schools have offered office space to students and supervising counselors interested in providing this service on site in order to provide offline support.

Similar to the adolescent service work experiment, adolescents get excited about being empowered as leaders and making their mark with their peers and schools, as well as making a difference in their communities. They can construct their website any way they wish to make it most inviting to young people, such as having bright and colorful graphics and photography, popular music, and kid-friendly text. Regular professional supervision and consultation is provided for the teen counselors running the program. For serious and complex identified at-risk students, an emergency referral service is provided, managed by the professional therapist team monitoring the program. In addition to having the opportunity to receive support and advice from the adolescent host or with his or her peer counseling colleagues of the site, youth visitors will have the opportunity to participate in both on- and offline support groups with the host, peer counseling colleagues, and a professional therapist. Offline support groups can be offered onsite at the school or in community-based and affiliated with the program.

Some of the adolescents that we have worked with who launched websites like this not only got involved in other peer counseling and youth outreach and prevention work, but ended up pursuing professional careers in psychology and social work.

Pattern Intervention Strategies to Change the Couple or Family Dance

Once we have successfully tracked central problem-maintaining patterns of interactions in which the Internet or cyber-sex abusing behavior is reinforced by, we can use pattern intervention strategies to disrupt them (Beard, 2011; O'Hanlon, 1987; Young, 2007, 2011). This entails adding something new to the context in which the problematic behavior occurs, such as: using alarm clocks or kitchen timers, or having a partner or family member present in the room where the Internet is being used to monitor and limit their time online. Special software can be installed that prohibits negative Internet activities or visits to forbidden websites. We can change the order of involvement of when certain family members typically intervene. Another way to disrupt problem patterns is to change the locations in which the Internet is accessed and the times of the day when it can be used. Couple partners and parents can experiment with novel and surprising ways of intervening to throw the Internet or cyber-sex abuser off balance, which can lead to a positive shift in his or her behavior.

Case Example

"King of the Castle," or just the "King of COD and World of Warcraft"

Chad, 16, was referred to me (MS) by his school social worker Barbara for falling asleep in class, mouthing off to some of his teachers, missing days of school, rapidly declining grades, verbally clashing with peers, and problems with ADD. Barbara had given my name to Kimberly, Chad's mother, to seek family therapy for him. According to Barbara, who had spoken to Kimberly on numerous occasions about Chad's academic and behavioral difficulties, she had learned that Chad had been adopted at 12 months, had problems with ADD since age 13, occasionally steals cash from the parents, that Kimberly believed that she and her husband may have spoiled him by buying digital devices and video-games all of the time that he desired, and that he spends all of his week day and weekend leisure time playing the on- and offline games *World of Warcraft* and *Call of Duty* (COD). Barbara also shared with me that not only does Chad "blow off" their scheduled meetings at school but the parents had been referred for family counseling in the past but either never followed through or they would go for a few sessions and prematurely drop-out, particularly when Chad would refuse to go.

Before we hung up from one another, Barbara shared with me, "This is going to be a tough one Matthew, good luck!" After hearing from Barbara the list of Chad's difficulties and about his great dislike of counseling, I thanked her for the referral and joked with her about how she really knows how to test the integrity of the therapist by sending me such a challenging case situation. We both laughed and promised to collaborate with one another regularly.

INTERNET AND CYBER-SEX DEPENDENCY HABITS

The First Scheduled Family Therapy Session

After establishing rapport with Kimberly on the telephone, I offered her a pre-counseling experiment of keeping track of and writing down on a daily basis any responsible and respectful steps Chad takes and anything she or her husband did that contributed to Chad's responsible, respectful, or any other positive behaviors they have observed individually or in their relationships with him prior to our first family session. Kimberly was quite enthusiastic about trying the experiment.

However, one day prior to our scheduled appointment, Kimberly called to say that "Chad refuses to come" to the session. When asked to describe the steps she and her husband Paul had taken to try to convince him to go to the session with them, it was reported that Kimberly first pleaded with Chad and then resorted to bribery by offering to buy him the new *Call of Duty* video-game he really wanted. However, they were met with a big "Fuck you! I'm not going!" Paul then retorted with, "You're going!" This was followed by Chad's slamming his bedroom door, locking it, and then breaking the door by throwing his desk chair at it. At that point, the parents completely backed off. Kimberly shared with me that as parents they had been totally dethroned by Chad and that he is like, "the king of the castle." She also pointed out to me that Paul and Chad have a very strained relationship and they rarely communicate or do things together because of Paul's long work hours for his company and regular business travel.

I first provided empathy and support to Kimberly. I also inquired about any pre-counseling examples of cooperative behavior on Chad's behalf. Apparently, there were two occasions where he helped her out around the house without a fight. When asked about if she was aware of how she pulled this off, all Kimberly could remember was asking him in "a relaxed and matter-of-fact way." I asked Kimberly if she could remember anything she or Paul had done in the past that seemed to gain Chad's cooperation. The only thing she could think of was bribing him by offering to buy him new video-games or digital devices he really wanted. I asked Kimberly to revisit her approach with Chad and experiment with "a relaxed and matter-of-fact way," requesting he go to the session with you alone to help you to better cope with family and your individual stress stuff. After the session, you can tell Chad that you will take him to his favorite pizza restaurant for dinner and then you will pop over to the Apple Store so that you can check out Mac Books and get his advice about which model would be best to buy in the future. Kimberly thought this was a good plan and may have a shot at working. I strongly encouraged her and Paul to still come to the session even if Chad is reluctant to attend.

The next day, only Kimberly showed up for our family session. Once she had failed with our planned strategy and was "met with a barrage of verbal obscenities from Chad," Paul forced his way into Chad's bedroom and began to reprimand him for his disrespectful behavior and "a shoving and wrestling match took place after Chad became explosive and had pushed over and busted up one of his bookshelves." Kimberly called the police to break it up out of fear that someone would get hurt. Chad even "mouthed off to the police officer," who had learned from Paul about why Chad was so upset and encouraged him to get some help for his anger, as well as lecturing him about how his parents were entitled to press charges for damaging their property if they wanted to. Chad got himself together at this point and apologized to the police officer. After the police officer left their house, Paul told Kimberly alone that he was done with Chad and threatened to send him off to a "boarding school for troubled kids." Kimberly started to cry and shared that she wished she could bring back the "old Chad" again as a pre-adolescent who was less explosive and irritable, and pleasant to be around, participating in activities with her and Paul. I explored with Kimberly was there anything she and Paul were doing differently back then that seemed to bring out the best in Chad. She could not think of anything specific but felt it was more Chad's being "more cooperative and not combative." Apparently, when Chad played Little League baseball Paul practiced with him all of the time to help perfect his skills. I discovered that Paul was a much celebrated high school and college baseball star but decided to go on for his MBA degree rather than being on a farm club of a professional baseball team and possibly not ever making it to the big leagues. I asked Kimberly to try to get Paul to come with her to the next session and to stress to him that they have to be a team and that we cannot turn things around without him.

After complimenting Kimberly on her perseverance and high level of commitment to improve the family situation, I reiterated the importance of getting Paul to the next session with or without Chad. I also shared with her an idea I had about how to engage Chad. I shared with her an important truth about adolescents, which is that no adolescent likes their parents or any other adults planning their futures for them, such as shipping them off to boarding schools or a residential treatment centers. I asked Kimberly what she thought about my sending him a text from the session regarding how unfair I thought it was that plans were being made for possibly sending him to a boarding school and that I felt his voice should be represented here and be heard as part of the decision-making process. She thought it would be worth trying, since she and Paul were seriously thinking about boarding school. At the same time, I shared with her that I would empathize with Chad in the text message about how uncomfortable going for counseling has been for him in the past, a real drag, and that I wanted to spare him from further misery if he should decide not to come next session. Finally, I would let him know that I would just go along with whatever his parents decided would be best for him if he chose not to come. Kimberly and I also thought we should send this message to him via e-mail a few times over the week as well.

The First Official Conjoint Family Session

Not only did Paul show up to our second session, but we had a special guest appearance by Chad. Chad came into the session like an attorney ready to defend his position against being shipped off to a boarding school. He was polite and respectful toward his parents and me. Since Chad wielded all of the power and was in charge of the family mood, I felt it behooved me to meet with him first alone to try to build an alliance with him. I began our conversation by complimenting him on his courageousness for taking a stand and wanting to take charge of his future, as well as taking a big responsible step by showing up for our session and not blowing me off! Chad propped his head back and smiled. Rather than delving right into the boarding school topic or discussing other difficulties, I wanted to come to know him better by his key strengths. Chad shared with me that among his friends he is known as the "King of COD and *World of Warcraft*." He went on to add that they call him this because he is "the master of making the most enemy kills in a single game" of *Call of Duty*. His house record was "75 kills" in one COD game. His house record of kills with *World of Warcraft* was 50. With the *World of Warcraft* online game, Chad also boasted about how he throws his opponents off with his multiple avatars (online characters), playing at a more advanced level then his friends and other players, being a member of a clan, and how he and his fellow clan members pull off several well-planned raids a week, mixing up the times they attack. I asked him what his secret was about how he was so successful in this game with "taking out" enemy players and he shared with me that he combines "good intuition, lightening quick reflexes, and I have a sixth sense." Chad was beaming with joy while boasting about his high level of skill as a gamer.

At this point in the session, I shifted gears and asked him about his other talents and he shared with me that he was really into graphic art design, website design, computer technology, and animation. I asked him the next time to bring in some of his best graphic art and animation work to share with me. Chad also shared with me that he has earned "good bucks" making websites for both friends, other kids at school, and adults.

Finally, Chad did acknowledge that he used to be a good baseball player up until age 12 and when the "pitching got too fast to hit the ball," he decided to end his baseball career. Chad shared with me that it was at this point, when he hung up his baseball career, his father had "checked out of my life." Since the drawbridge door had just opened for me, I decided to shift gears and seize the opportunity to explore this issue with Chad. With a sad look on his face, he shared with me that he and his father used to have "a very tight relationship," did a lot of activities together, but that abruptly changed after he gave up baseball career, which was, "My dad's number one passion in life." From that point on, the two men had drifted apart from one another and only come together to argue about "poor school grades, not doing my homework, falling asleep in class, swearing at my mom, refusing to cooperate, and being on the computer too long playing *World of Warcraft* or spending too much time playing COD and other X-Box games." I shared with Chad my crazy thought that had just popped into my mind, which was that all of these complaints and behaviors are examples of his protesting about how he did not like the way things were in the family and that he wished the family situation could return back to how things were with him and his dad in the past and where there was more peace and fewer arguments in the family. Chad agreed and openly admitted that "to avoid conflicts and putdowns" from his dad he escaped into his on- and offline gaming worlds, where he felt "respected, connected with other people like me, and indestructible." I asked Chad if I could help him try to re-establish a new and more positive relationship with his father. Chad acknowledged that he would really appreciate that but he thought it would be difficult because his father is "stubborn and holds grudges." I shared with him that it will be hard work but if we all work together as a team we have a good shot at pulling it off. I also pointed out that he was so used to thriving in chaos, managing the unexpected and high stress situations with his COD and *World of Warcraft* wealth of experience and training, which will help him to cope with the challenge of trying to reconcile with his father. Chad agreed that these games had toughened him up to better cope with high levels of unpredictability and stress.

Just prior to meeting the parents, I wanted to find out a little bit about the depths of Chad's on- and offline video-gaming habit and other habits he may engage in. He reported daily playing four or five hours right after school, sometimes a few hours late at night into the early morning hours during the week, and stretches of six or seven hours on the weekend days mostly with friends. The longest period of abstinence reported was two days because their PC crashed. When offline and involved in other activities, Chad has a tendency to daydream about his success in these games and gets irritated when there are obstacles put up to playing, like "family dinner, doctor's appointments, and homework assignments having to be done." I asked him if he could see himself cutting back on his gaming if it meant having a better relationship with his dad, more peace in the house, and doing a little better in school. I also asked him to think of any privileges he would like me to fight for with his parents. Chad agreed to think about these two things in the waiting room while I met with his parents.

Last, I explored with Chad if he was into other online activities or partied with weed (marijuana), drank, or got into any other drugs, or self-harmed in any other way. Chad openly admitted that he had smoked weed and drank a few times with his friends just to "cop a buzz, but not to get totally ripped." Chad found that this impaired both his on- and offline gaming abilities and always likes to be "on top of my game when I play." He also tried online gambling a few times but lost every time and decided to permanently discontinue this activity. Chad never got into "the cutting thing"; however, he told me he knew some girls at school that did this. I complimented him for being so open and honest with me.

When I met alone with the parents, I shared with them how much I had enjoyed getting to know Chad, and how he had opened up about some of his issues and concerns. I shared with Paul Chad had voiced a desire to bring back the former closer relationship he used to have with him and that he misses it very much. Kimberly smiled and shared that she would love to see that again. Even Paul responded begrudgingly that he would want that too but he needed to see "a better attitude and more respect from Chad." Using baseball metaphors and lingo, I asked Paul what would be one step over the next week that he could take to hit a homerun with Chad, something that he will really notice and appreciate. Paul shared that he could "check in with him about his day, talk to him with a nicer tone of voice, and take an interest in Chad's graphic art design and animation work." I also asked Paul to take a ride back in my imaginary time machine to one of his best college baseball games where his team leadership abilities really stood out. After accessing the game using all of his senses, including color and motion, Paul described how while his team had their last time at batting he got their clean-up hitter [fourth batter] and co-star player Tony, who had been in a hitting slump fired up to drive in the winning run so their team could win the game. I asked him how he got Tony fired up and Paul said to him, "You are the main man, make it happen, we've got this game in the bag!" Apparently, Tony "clobbered a line shot hit into a centerfield seam," which easily drove in the winning run from second base. When asked how he had individually performed in the game, Paul shared that he had "three hits that drove in three runs." I asked him what his secret was for having such a fine performance and Paul said, "Being totally focused, patient, and waiting for the perfect meaty gift pitch." Paul lit up as he reminisced about this big game that gave his team the league championship. I shared with Paul that he could have made a fine coach and that I believed he could use his uplifting words to inspire Chad to turn his situation around so that his family could be a winning team too. Kimberly chimed in that she would love for them to become a winning family team. Paul agreed.

Prior to ending the family session, we went over the blueprint for change plan as a group and consent forms were signed so I could collaborate with the school social worker Barbara and some of Chad's concerned teachers. In beginning the goal-setting process with them, I asked them to play around with the idea that if they left our meeting today completely satisfied, and while driving off, their situation had changed beyond their wildest dreams, how will things be different? Kimberly shared that Paul and Chad would argue less and have a closer relationship, which out of all of her best hopes was her number one wish. Chad reported that he and his father would be getting along much better and his parents would stop nagging and complaining so much. Both parents reported that Chad would be reducing his time playing on- and offline video-games, be staying on top of his school work, and earning himself better grades. When asked to rate each parties' behavior after they noticed all of these changes beginning to happen when they returned home after our first family session today, what would their ratings be on a scale from 1 to 10, with 1 being totally optimistic that things will continue to improve and 10 you feel that the situation is better enough. The parents rated the situation at a 6. After sharing with the parents that they were 60% of the way toward that 10, I asked them, "What are you going to do over the next week to get up to that lucky 7?" Both Paul and Kimberly shared that they would work on greatly reducing their nagging, lecturing, and arguing with Chad. Chad rated his situation at a 5 because he recognized how hard it will be to cut back on his on- and offline video-gaming and get caught up with his school work. His goal for achieving a 6 over the next week was to try to cut back on his on- and offline video-gaming and try and spend more time on his school work. Chad also shared that the privilege he would like to earn as a result of getting up to that 6 would be getting one of his "ear pierced." Paul chimed in and said that he and his mom will let him know "after seeing some great effort with no attitude" on his part over the week if he "earns it."

Since Chad had not been on ADD medication for a year there was no need at this point to bring in a psychiatrist. It also was unclear the role of the excessive on- and offline video-gaming behavior was playing in producing ADD-like behavior, since these symptoms occurred as Chad got more heavily involved in this activity. The parents also questioned whether Chad really had ADD as well. The family agreed to continue family therapy and established the following well-formulated treatment goals:

- Father and son session time devoted to resolving their conflicts and strengthening their relationship.
- Chad will cut back on his on- and offline video-gaming time (one hour less of gaming hours on week days, no late night playing, and two hours less on weekend days) as an experiment.

- The parents will reduce and work towards eliminating their nagging and yelling behaviors in response to Chad's willingness to reduce his on- and offline video-gaming time.
- Chad will take steps to stay on top of his homework assignments and pick up his grades in school.
- A collaborative meeting with Chad's social worker and teachers would be initiated by Kimberly to begin addressing his academic decline, any learning issues, or conflicts with his teachers.

I complimented all family members on their openness and willingness to work together like a championship baseball team. I also underscored the many responsible steps Chad was already taking to help himself out and to help turn the family situation around. Paul was complimented on his willingness to come and how he has so much to offer Chad in the way of his leadership abilities, inspirational words of wisdom, and how to persevere when faced with challenging situations. Kimberly was also complimented for her managerial abilities in that she had successfully rounded up all of the family team members to come to our meeting and work hard together. Since we had had such a productive session and I wanted to be careful not to prescribe family members too complicated therapeutic experiments to do, I offered the following choices:

- Kimberly would be in charge of a family mood makeover with spearheading a parental effort to keep the family atmosphere more positive and peaceful, minus nagging, lectures, putdowns, and arguing.
- Building on Paul's idea of approaching Chad differently and taking an interest in his life and natural talents, he was asked to pull some other surprises over the next week in relationship to his son that will shock him in a positive way.
- Chad was asked to conduct a secret mission of trying to discover what positive effects his cutting back on his on- and offline video-gaming had on his relationships with his parents and with getting his school work done over the next week.

I cautioned the family about how in family members' best efforts to change their situations there will be bumps in the road that they may need to carefully negotiate and it will require solid teamwork. I also encouraged them to be on their toes for inevitable setbacks and slipping back into their old problematic ways of interacting and old habits, like increasing video-gaming and distancing from the family as a form of escape. Finally, we wrapped up the session with the family offering feedback to me about their perceptions of our first official family meeting. Both parents reported that they were more hopeful and would hold off pursuing boarding schools at this point. Chad had a sigh of relief on his face when he heard this. Chad shared, "It was sweet!" He further added that he felt that I was different than the other "shrinks" he had been "forced to see" in the past. We scheduled our next appointment and Kimberly planned to call Barbara to set up a meeting with Chad's teachers.

The First School Collaborative Meeting

Present in our first school collaborative meeting were Barbara, Kimberly, Chad (sporting a newly pierced ear), and Mrs. Dillard and Mr. Finch, his English and History teachers respectively. Chad has both of these classes back to back first thing in the morning every day. Both teachers complained about: Chad's "lack of participation" in their classes, his "D and F grades on quizzes and tests," his "missing assignments," and "falling asleep" in their classes sometimes. When asked about his strengths and what he does well at in their classes, both teachers shared that they thought he was an "excellent writer." The teachers both admitted that it was Chad's writing ability that was sparing him from failing their classes. They inquired with both Kimberly and Chad why they thought the grades had taken a major "nose dive" lately. Kimberly pointed out that they are now working on reducing Chad's involvement with his on- and offline video-gaming time so that school work gets done more consistently and he gets enough sleep. Chad openly admitted that some nights he is up late playing online video-games, which was making it difficult for him to get up in the mornings and staying awake in their classes. Barbara and the teachers strongly encouraged Kimberly to crack down on the video-gaming situation and for Chad to work with his parents on this as well. They also pointed out that his junior level grades are very important when it comes to trying to get into the kind of technical skill colleges he might like. Barbara shared with the group how talented Chad was with graphic art design and animation.

Both Mrs. Dillard and Mr. Finch were willing to drop most of Chad's bigger past assignments that were overdue if he would make a commitment to stay on top of his current homework, prepare better for quizzes and tests, and participate more in their classes. Chad agreed to put more time and energy into performing better in their classes. We discovered from Barbara that Chad was getting mostly A and high B grades in his other classes. Prior to ending our meeting, I offered the teachers the experiment of daily keeping track of the responsible steps Chad will be taking in their classes so that we can discuss what further progress he had made in our next meeting. We scheduled our next collaborative meeting for one month later.

The Second Conjoint Family Session

The family came in smiling and very pleased with their team effort. Paul proudly proclaimed, "The way our family team played over the week we could have beaten any team in the World Series!" I was eager to learn from family members what was giving them the winning edge. Paul reported that Chad's behavior was excellent in that he regularly was doing his homework without reminders, there was "no attitude" or explosive behavior, he spoke to him and Kimberly in a respectful way, there were no arguments, and he earned his pierced ear! I explored with Chad if he was aware of how he pulled off these big steps. Chad pointed out that he wants to have better relationships with his parents and more peace in the family. He also complimented his father for talking to him and taking an interest in him again. Kimberly praised both Paul and Chad for trying to get along better and avoiding arguments. She further added that not only had Chad kept with the contract regarding time limitations playing on- and offline video-games but he would come to her for support when he would feel anxious and craving to play for longer periods of time and later in the night. Chad discovered, as hard a sacrifice as it was, that cutting out the late night online-gaming was helping him to sleep better, easily catch the school bus in the mornings, and not fall asleep in class. The parents rated Chad and their situation overall at an 8! Chad was so proud of himself that he rated himself two steps higher on the scale at a 7.

I asked the two men if they felt comfortable meeting alone with me to work on further strengthening their relationship. Both Paul and Chad thought this was a good idea. I asked Chad the following tough question, "What is missing in your relationship with your father that if it were present, would make a big difference for you?" Chad started to tear up and courageously shared with his father how he missed the closeness they used to have in their relationship and doing things together. Paul moved right next to Chad and put his arm around him to comfort him. Chad looked at his father and told him how he felt that since he had given up baseball that Paul had rejected him. Paul shared with Chad that he had been disappointed about it but it did not mean that he would stop loving him. He felt that Chad had drifted away from him and his mother by spending most of his free time playing video-games and family time was not important to him anymore. Paul also shared with Chad how proud of him he was with his major behavioral overhaul over the past week and how impressed he was with his graphic art design and animation work. Chad smiled and thanked his dad for noticing that he was really trying. I encouraged the two men to talk face-to-face about how they want to re-invent their relationship with one another, including both what they want to add new or reinstate from the past. Chad shared with his father that he would like them to find some fun activities to do together like wall-climbing and camping. Paul shared that he would enjoy doing those activities with Chad as well. He also asked Chad if he could teach him how to make better graphics for his Apple keynote presentation slides for work. After hearing this, a light bulb had lit up in my mind and I thought, why not put Chad in charge of mentoring his dad over the next week to help him to begin to develop some skills in graphic art design? Both men pulled out their iPhone calendars and typed in daily training session times they agreed to over the next week where Chad would serve as his father's mentor and teacher. Paul devoted an hour for each training session. I shared my house rules about Paul having to be a respectful student and good listener, and not challenging Chad's teaching abilities. I also recommended that Paul draw from his recipe for baseball performance success of really "focusing and being patient" while trying to master these new skills. They both laughed and looked forward to implementing the experiment.

After a mini-intersession break, we reconvened as a whole group. I complimented all family members on their excellent progress and shared with them the old adage, "If it works, don't fix it." I encouraged them to increase doing what was working, such as: having positive family interactions, Chad's continuing to cut back on his video-game time and staying on top of his school work, and Paul and Chad continuing to work on strengthening their relationship. As a vote of confidence to the family, I asked them when they would like to come back, in two or three weeks, and they chose to schedule our next appointment in two weeks. I predicted that sometimes things happen when we least expect them and that there may be a minor setback on their vacation from counseling but to remember that we could not have a slip if we had not already made great headway. Three therapeutic experiments were offered:

- Kimberly is to pull out her imaginary magnifying glass and daily notice what further progress each family member is making. She can either write her observations down or make mental notes of them to discuss in our next session.
- Chad will serve as Paul's mentor/teacher over the next week teaching him graphic art design skills
- Chad was to keep track daily of what he does that works to help him to successfully reduce further his on- and offline video-gaming

The Third Conjoint Family Session

Two weeks later, the family came in with a glowing progress report. Paul kicked off our conversation by pointing out that "Chad is a great teacher!" Apparently, Paul was able to master some basic graphic art design skills, thanks to Chad's teaching abilities and "tremendous patience" with him. I asked Chad what he thought about his father as a student. Chad shared that although his father "struggled at times" and even made "silly mistakes," overall he felt that he did "a good job." Both men shared that the experience was fun and Paul felt that he had learned a lot in a short amount of time. I asked if they had planned to continue the training sessions and Paul voiced a strong desire to continue them. In fact, Paul offered to pay Chad for helping him improve the graphics in his Apple keynote presentation slides. Chad welcomed this opportunity.

Kimberly reported that there has been a major family climate change. The home atmosphere is much more positive, upbeat, and peaceful. When asked about what is working, she shared that the two men are growing much closer and doing things together outside of the home on the weekends, such as: wall-climbing at their health club, running errands, and they even went to the movies together once. Chad reported that he had reduced his on- and offline video-gaming time to one hour after school, the late night gaming had stopped, and on the weekends, he was down to one or two hours of playing with friends. I asked him what his secret was of how he was able to pull that off. Chad shared that he has enjoyed spending more time with his father on the weekends, especially doing the wall-climbing with him. He also had to start doing some weekend service work for the colleges he was applying to who were looking for this important life experience in their applicants' backgrounds. Chad was working in a neighborhood soup kitchen for the homeless eight hours on the weekends. Chad had shared with me that this service work job was hard to come by and he had found it through the help of an adult friend of his parents'. He felt that his high school career-planning department "really sucked" and the counselor Ms. Jackson who ran it did not do such a great job of helping students find service work opportunities in their community. The parents chimed in how responsible Chad had become with doing the service work, doing his homework, and improving his school grades significantly. They rated Chad at a 9 for all of the great strides he was making in all areas of his life. Chad gave himself a 9 as well.

In revisiting the service work situation with Chad, I shared with him an idea I had that would tap his graphic art design and website construction skills. I explored with Chad if we were able to work out with Ms. Jackson his having the opportunity to assist her with constructing a special website which would list service work opportunities and assist students with placements, could he see himself getting involved with such a project? Chad thought this was a "sweet opportunity!" I had Chad and the parents sign off on a consent form so I could speak with Ms. Jackson about the idea. I encouraged Chad to create a proposal and some prototypes of what such a website would look like, its text, and other unique features and services offered for students. The parents thought this would be a great opportunity for Chad to make a difference at his school and also look great for the colleges he was applying to.

To help cover the back door with the family, I asked them, "What would you have to do to go backwards at this point?" All family members confidently stated that they could not fathom this happening due to their tremendous progress. However, they were able to reflect on how things used to be with family arguments, Chad's feeling rejected by his father, Paul's yelling a lot, and Chad's excessive use of video-gaming to escape from his parents.

After our intersession break, I complimented all family members on their tremendous progress. I encouraged them to keep doing what was working and for Chad to approach Ms. Jackson when he is prepared to discuss this project with her. When asked when they wanted to come back for a check-up, they decided to schedule an appointment a month down the road.

The Second School Collaborative Meeting

Present at our second school collaborative meeting were Paul, Kimberly, Chad, Barbara, Mrs. Dillard, Mr. Finch, and Ms. Jackson. Across the board all school staff highly praised Chad's 360-degree turnaround academically and behaviorally. He was now consistently completing and turning in his homework, scoring high on quizzes and tests, and getting A grades on all of his papers. He was no longer falling asleep in class, clashing with his peers, or mouthing off to his teachers. However, the most exciting news was Ms. Jackson's accepting Chad's proposed service work website! Apparently, he had put together a very attractive website design with beautiful graphics. Ms. Jackson pointed out that she could use a lot of help with identifying and placing students in service work sites in the community and welcomed Chad's assistance with this. In fact, she was going to talk to Chad's dean about seeing if he could get extra school credit hours for his time devoted to this important project. All the adults around the table shared with Chad how impressed they were with his great progress and stepping up to help students learn about and land service work opportunities in the community. We all agreed that it was not necessary to schedule another collaborative meeting.

The Fourth and Final Family Session

A month later, the family came in reporting further great progress. Chad was now actively involved with Ms. Jackson in launching his new website and locating potential service work sites in the community. It was also worked out with the dean that he will earn credit hours for all of his time with helping Ms. Jackson and fellow students. In fact, the dean had called Kimberly to tell her what a "fine son" she had for coming up with this project and "stepping up as a student leader." Chad smiled and shared how excited he was about this new project. The other great news was that Chad was growing out of playing on- and offline video-games during the week and on the weekends. He was now only playing two or three hours a week and, instead, either working on his service work project and other school work, or hanging out with his new wall-climbing friends that he met at their health club. I asked Chad if it felt strange for him to be spending much more time in the offline world doing other activities and he shared with all of us that he has come to like it better than living in the video-gaming world. Both Paul and Kimberly shared how proud they were of Chad. Kimberly also shared that she was so delighted how close Paul and Chad were now. Chad agreed.

To help further consolidate the family gains, I asked them the following future-oriented question: "Let's say we decide to have a reunion party one year from today, when we get together again what further changes that you made will you be most eager to share with me?" The parents shared that "Chad will be attending one of his choice colleges." Chad shared that he had "stopped on- and offline video-gaming" since he had "outgrown this activity." I fell out of my chair out of amazement in response to his future report of kicking his video-gaming habit for good. Everyone laughed. Chad also said that he will have "made some new friends at school, including having a girlfriend!"

After a short intersession break, I complimented all family members on their tremendous progress and how much I enjoyed learning about their future of success. We mutually agreed to terminate. I shared with the family that I have an open door policy and if they should ever need a tune-up to feel free to call me. I also pointed out that I like to check in with families down the road to find out what further progress they have made and not to be surprised when I call them.

Treatment Follow-Up

I spoke with Chad and his mother at 6 and 12 months on the telephone. At 6 months, Chad was getting ready to head off for his first choice college. Kimberly had nothing but positive things to say about Chad's individual and the family's progress. Chad shared with me that his school service work project was a hit success and proved to be a valuable resource for students seeking out service work opportunities. Chad also reported that he had "completely stopped playing on- and offline video-games." I congratulated him on this really great accomplishment. He further added that he had "much more important things to do with my time." I asked him what his consultation fee was if I needed him to come in and help me with another young person hooked on offline and online video-gaming. Chad said, "No charge for you, dude!"

When I spoke with Chad and his mother at the one-year mark, I was met with another glorious progress report. Chad was eager to share with me the best news of all which was his having a girlfriend. Chad really loved his college and he was performing quite well academically. Kimberly shared with me how proud she was of her son. I wished them well.

Reflections on the "King of the Castle" or just the "King of COD and World of Warcraft" Case

Mark: I think this case nicely illustrates our whole point of working mainly with strengths and resources, of helping to expand the healthy parts of our clients as a way to grow out of their problems. In my view, the two basic therapeutic processes here were the reparation of the father–teen bond and the utilization of Chad's graphic design abilities in a positive way, up to a point where the self-destructive video-gaming habit had no space in the family's life; it had, in a way, become irrelevant.

Matthew: Yes, in looking back, the four key levers for change with this case were as follows: (1) using a paradoxical letter to engage Chad, which fit nicely with his initial high psychological reactance level to participating in family therapy; (2) since Chad had tremendous power in his family, seeing him alone first to build an alliance tactically paid off in that it reduced his defensiveness; (3) seizing the therapeutic opportunity to capitalize on Chad's disclosing how painful his father's emotional withdrawal from him had been by working to strengthen the father-Chad bond; and (4) utilizing Chad's computer savvy skills to empower him to design and run an on- and offline service work website for other students.

Mark: The other interesting aspect to me about this case is that you did this resource-oriented work without minimizing or ignoring the problems. Both the excessive video-gaming and poor school performance were discussed openly and frankly both during the family sessions and the school meetings, and their progress was monitored throughout therapy. But they did not become the "one-and-only" important topic, but were framed implicitly as simple obstacles in the way to Chad's personal goals: to get closer to his father again and to move on to the college he wants to go to. For me, this is the essential element of a collaborative approach towards working with addictions: it is not about taking a moral stance against the self-destructive habit, but about discovering with our clients what their goals are, figuring out with them how to reach them, and helping them to reduce their self-destructive habits if they are in their way.

Matthew: I am with you 100% about clients taking the lead in defining the goals for treatment. Once they bear witness to all of the benefits of reducing some of the consequences of engaging in their self-destructive habits, they will eventually arrive at the conclusion that it is time to move on from their beloved habits and continue to improve the quality of their lives any positive way they can.

Mark: Another aspect of the treatment process I would like to highlight is how you created the *solution-determined system*. You had to put a lot of effort into getting the family into therapy and this only happened after a number of phone calls, of invitation letters, and an individual session with Chad's mother. Close cooperation with the school system, including collaborative meetings with all the involved school staff, struck me as the other important element.

Matthew: I like to think of the solution-determined system as a healing tribe of concerned others in our client's social ecology. Each member, including the referring person, family members and/or intimate partners, extended family members, close friends, the client's adult inspirational others, and the involved helping professionals from larger systems possess valuable strengths, talents, and resources that can help us to co-create a therapeutic context ripe for change. By regularly having family–school collaborative meetings with school professionals, particularly if our teen clients are experiencing difficulties in that context, can help build solid bridges from school to home and ensure clear communications.

Mark: As to the decision to start the first conjoint family meeting with Chad, and not with the parents or the whole family, I would say it goes against most family therapists' clinical lore, which would prescribe to start the session seeing the parents first. Would you have made the same therapeutic decision if you had not seen Chad's mother alone in the previous meeting or if you only spoke to her or her husband on the telephone?

Matthew: Yes, I would have pursued the same clinical course of action whether I had seen or spoken to either parent on the telephone. Over my professional career as a family therapist, I have found it to be much more productive when I have seen powerful adolescents in charge of the family mood first before seeing the parents alone. This has several advantages: (1) it provides you with a wonderful opportunity to build a meaningful connection with the young person and gain therapeutic leverage, (2) we can learn firsthand what is in it for him or her to participate in family therapy, (3) he or she will not feel like the therapist is conspiring or plotting with the parents behind his/her back, and (4) he or she can become an agent of change and be given therapeutic experiments to try out with their family.

Mark: The other point I would like to touch on is related to the police involvement after the big fight with Chad. I have often seen parents who are very reluctant to take such measures, even in the face of extreme behavior by their teenage kids. What I often do in those cases is to work with the parents to enable them to take this firm position, for instance becoming willing to call the police if necessary, or to discuss boarding school as a practical option and not as a mere threat. Seen from the stages of change model (Prochaska et al., 2006), this means helping parents to move from a contemplative to the determination and action stage vis-à-vis their kid. The one message I usually emphasize in these situations is that parents need to keep "an iron fist in a velvet glove," that is, to be firm and set limits in a very calm manner, which makes it easier, in turn, to promote the caring aspect of the parent–teen relationship. Any thoughts about that?

Matthew: Yes, with tyrannical and powerful adolescents, parents typically are intimidated by them and may make threats but don't follow through; they may acquiesce, or dig in more and adopt a "my way or the highway" approach, or grow down in age and be like big kids. All of these approaches are examples of how parents fuel oppositional defiant behavior with their kids. In contrast, Omer (2004) has shown that when parents start being less emotionally reactive by using nonviolent Gandhian tactics, this parental stance can curtail most challenging adolescent behaviors. I think one reason why this parenting strategy works so well is that it is hard for kids to be intimidating and win the power struggle when they don't have sparring partners. When parents can calmly, firmly, and consistently set limits as a unified team, it is quite difficult for kids to win the battle of power and control. Furthermore, when kids know that they can count on their parents to be emotionally and physically available to them and they demonstrate their love and appreciation for them, they are less likely to be explosive and rebel against them. This was the case for Chad. He was protesting against his father's rejecting him and longing to rekindle the kind of close relationship they used to have together in the past.

Mark: In most cases we are able to successfully reduce the problematic habits by promoting positive alternatives and improving meaningful relationships. Sometimes, however, other things improve but the problems stay basically the same. Thinking of Chad, it could have been possible that while hanging out more with his dad or working on the service work website project he would still spend too many hours at night videogaming. What would you have done in that case?

Matthew: Here is where I would make strategic use of confusion à la TV detective *Columbo*. I would put on my ruffled trench coat and scratch my head with a confused look on my face and ask Chad, "Help me out Chad, I am really confused here. With tears, you told me that you longed to have a closer relationship with your dad, you made it quite clear that you were not going to allow your parents to send you away, and that you wanted to get into the top college you were shooting for, and yet you have made some choices with your actions that can make all of these goals and wishes not happen, can you please help me understand this? Maybe I am missing something here." It is very hard, even for the most resistant client, not to want to help out the confused and bungling therapist! Other helpful questions that are helpful to ask are: "Is there something that we have not talked about that you think I need to know about?" or "Prior to coming here for the first time, was there something that you told yourself that you were not going to bring up in our meetings together?" The *Columbo* tactics and the above questions can help us uncover the *not yet said* (Anderson, 1997) or secrets that may be blocking a more complete symptom/problem-free client situation from occurring.

Mark: One last question. I am impressed by how much you were able to accomplish in one conjoint family session. How much time do you schedule for the first family meeting?

Matthew: It is pretty standard for me to see a family for the first time for about an hour. However, I may go over a little bit (15–20 minutes) if some important client material is being discussed. I think it has a lot to do with pacing, session focus, and efficiency. When you have a packed client schedule, you need to make a lot happen in a short amount of time. A mother I had once consulted with in a live family demonstration interview had said to a researcher interviewing her about the experience regarding my therapeutic in-session activity had said: "He knows where he will go and won't go within his framework and he is in charge… but you are free to be who you are within his framework."

9

WORKING WITH RELUCTANT AND COMPLICATED MULTI-HABIT-DEPENDENT CLIENTS AND COUPLE AND FAMILY SYSTEMS

> For every complex problem there is a simple solution that is wrong.
> *George Bernard Shaw*

Introduction

What do we do when the habit or multi-habit-dependent partner or family members refuse to participate in sessions? How do we work with dual-habit-dependent partner couples and families presenting with multi-habit-dependent family members? Is it possible to change the multi-habit-dependent partner or family member indirectly through his or her concerned partner or parents, or with the help of key members from their social network? In this chapter, we will provide in-depth answers to these questions and offer highly practical therapeutic strategies and tactics to either facilitate the engagement of the reluctant identified client in attending sessions or change him or her indirectly without participating in couple or family therapy.

We begin the chapter discussing how we have expanded our therapeutic approach when working with complicated and complex couple and family systems by integrating ideas from complexity theory and the fields of conflict resolution and negotiation and organizational consulting. This will be followed by a discussion of several effective engagement strategies to employ with reluctant clients. Next, we cover how to intervene effectively with referring professionals, concerned couple partners, parents, other family members, and concerned members from the reluctant clients' social networks when they are unwilling to participate in couple and family sessions.

Expanding the Possibilities: Matching Complexity with Complexity to Navigate Through Intractable Problem Mazes

In the spirit of the wise fourteenth century English philosopher William of Ockham, who once said, "It is vain to do with more what can be done with fewer" (Stokes, 2002, p. 55), when beginning with new couples and families we try to keep things tentative and simple with our initial impressions and therapeutic strategies and gradually build in more complexity if what we are thinking and doing is not producing the kind of changes the clients desire (Beyebach, 2009; Beyebach & Rodríguez Morejón, 1999; Selekman, 2005, 2006, 2009, 2010). However, with couples and families presenting with key reluctant partners or family members absent from sessions, partners and family members with multi-habit dependencies, and with seemingly intractable and chronic difficulties, keeping things simple by using approaches that are too formulaic or rely heavily on simple solution strategies often falls way short with these complicated clinical situations. Some of the reasons why these challenging couples and families do not respond well to straightforward therapeutic approaches are as follows: they present with layers of complexity;

they behave as random and nonlinear systems; couple partners and family members have high psychological reactance levels when presented with the threat of change; they may be so demoralized by their intractable and chronic difficulties and multiple treatment failures that they cannot identify any past helpful coping and problem-solving strategies or entertain future problem-free realities; the partners or family members may be so disconnected from one another that a change in one person fails to effect a change in the other; and their conflicts and problem-maintaining interactions may be so entrenched that they are impervious to straightforward therapeutic change strategies. Therefore, with these challenging couples and families we have expanded our collaborative strengths-based brief family therapy model to incorporate ideas from: the *positive deviance* model developed by Richard Pascale and Jerry and Monique Sternin (Pascale, Sternin, & Sternin, 2010); the *obliquity problem-solving* approach from economist and researcher John Kay (2011); the innovative *attractor landscape of conflict model* developed by Peter Coleman and his colleagues at the International Center for Cooperation and Conflict Resolution at Columbia University and in Munich, Germany (Coleman, 2011); *complexity theory* (Holman, 2010; Johnson, 2007); and practical ideas from organizational consultants and researchers on near-miss crisis situations, managing uncertainty and intractable and complex problem situations, and wisdom gained from our failures and successes (Edmondson, 2011; Gino & Pisano, 2011; Mauboussin, 2009, 2011; McGrath, 2011; Pascale, Sternin, & Sternin, 2010; Sargut & McGrath, 2011; Schlesinger, Kiefer, & Brown, 2012; Tinsley, Dillon, & Madsen, 2011).

The positive deviance approach of Pascale and his colleagues has been successfully used to resolve highly complex and seemingly intractable local and international level problem situations in a counter-intuitive way. They believe that the solutions already exist in the community and the key to problem resolution is to identify who the individual *positive deviants* or outliers are that have already met with success at constructively managing the problem or similar difficulties in the past. Next, they try to figure out with the individual positive deviants and other stakeholders involved what is the thinking and action steps behind what drives these exception patterns (solution-building and maintaining patterns), and what they need to do to begin implementing what works (Pascale et al., 2010). This is why we find it so beneficial to actively collaborate with the key resource people from our clients' social networks because it could be an adult inspirational other, a close friend, a relative, or a concerned helping professional from a larger system who has already come up with a highly creative idea or solution for the presenting problem that may be worthwhile discussing and/or implementing.

Kay (2011) and Coleman (2011) contend that with complex problem situations it is critical to first identify and respect the complexities and then simplify the action steps. Through experimentation, discovery, and embracing uncertainty, knowledge is gained by stumbling upon what works, listening for the clients' "not yet said," seizing anomalies, epiphanies, serendipitous events to build on, and other opportunities in sessions, and determining, based on the clients' feedback, what to stop doing that is unproductive and, instead, moving the session in a different direction. As therapists, we need to adopt a pluralistic and flexible therapeutic stance by borrowing ideas from other models.

To know whether you can trust a particular therapeutic hunch or intuitive judgment, cognitive psychology researcher and Nobel Prize winner Daniel Kahneman (2011a, b) would contend that the therapist must answer two important questions:

- "Are my judgments based on experiencing some regularity to certain couple or family patterns of interactions or other dynamics observed over time to enable predictions of new therapeutic actions that are more likely to be successful at removing these barriers to change?"
- "Have I gained enough experience working with and securing good feedback from this couple or family to know the mistakes I may be making and what I need to do differently?"

These questions can help prevent what he refers to as "illusions of validity and skill" or therapeutic overconfidence.

Coleman (2011), who works with highly complex and intractable local, national, and international conflict situations, recommends that we strive to limit negativity and to create a climate of hope and possibilities with the clients, while simultaneously identifying and disrupting the destructive beliefs, attitudes, patterns of interaction, and traps that may undermine the change process and keep the situation stuck. He further recommends that we intervene on multiple levels of the client system and that our interventions are well thought out and sustainable. Finally, it is important to remember that complex systems can spontaneously move from order to disorder and back again even after implementing well-timed and seemingly sound change strategies (Johnson, 2007; Mauboussin, 2011; Sargut & McGrath, 2011).

The Role of the Therapist when Working with Complex and Multi-Habit-Dependent Couples and Families

When working with complex and multi-habit-dependent couples and families, therapists need to be fully present and provide ample space for clients to share their treatment expectations, preferences, theories of change, and details about their past unsuccessful attempted solutions. Such details must include what former therapists and treatment program staff did that was upsetting in order to avoid inadvertently replicating them. Furthermore, we have to carefully listen and observe for any deviations from the norm reported by the clients; try to uncover in collaboration with the clients what they think the root causes of any of these deviations from the norm were; carefully read the clients' feedback in response to our therapeutic interventions; be flexible and adaptive, and learn from our mistakes and failures. Finally we need to be on the alert for client concerns and near-miss crisis situations each session and address them immediately, being prepared in any given session to change tactics or strategies when necessary. Every obstacle or negative outcome we experience in the therapeutic process with our clients can be viewed as a *gift* and opportunity for evidence and learning in informing our need to shift gears and try something new, target our interventions at different system's levels, or bring in other resources from their social networks to aid in the change effort.

We need to be careful not to be too overconfident with our therapeutic approaches and interventions when clients start to make progress because they could be near-miss crisis situations masquerading as successes, in that the clients' positive responses to particular interventions could be possibly more due to luck or flukes rather than to our well-timed interventions or clinical brilliance. Kahneman (2011b) cautions us to be careful not to create for ourselves a false reality that makes too much sense. This is why it is important to critically analyze with our clients what specifically led to their improvement and successes (Dorner, 1997; Kay, 2011; Kahneman, 2011a; Kahneman, Lovallo, & Sibony, 2011; Sargut & McGrath, 2011; Selekman, 2009; Tinsley et al., 2011). Furthermore, we need to take the time to critically analyze our mistakes and failures and ask ourselves:

- "If I had another shot at conducting that session all over again, what would I have done differently?"
- "What have I learned from this mistake or failure that I will put to use the next time I see this couple or work with a family like this again in the future?"

At the same time, when working with these challenging couples and families, we need to give ourselves permission to take risks and trust our intuition or instincts about what is worthwhile exploring and trying out.

Effective Strategies for Engaging Reluctant Multi-Habit-Dependent Clients and their Partners and/or Family Members

As we have indicated throughout this book, it is hard to engage the habit-dependent individual, let alone multi-habit-dependent clients and their partners and/or family members. In some cases, the partners and some of the other family members are plagued by habit dependencies and other difficulties which can make these cases quite complex and a challenge to work with for even the most seasoned of therapists. For the habit-dependent clients, their partners, and family members, their therapists pose a threat by trying to change or take away their beloved habits that have benefited them in multiple ways, and that they will protect at all costs. Often, these clients have had negative past inpatient and outpatient treatment experiences where they felt mismanaged and misunderstood, and had had little say in the goal-setting and treatment planning process, which further exacerbated and perpetuated their difficulties. For the partners and family members who have become accustomed to and organized around the client's serious habit difficulties and consequences, any change induced by a therapist or a treatment team can be a threat as well to the couple or family system's equilibrium (see the case example of Gino later in the chapter). In situations where it is brought to our attention by couple partners or parents that the multi-habit-dependent client is reluctant to attend the initial couple or family session there are three different strategies that can be employed that can pave the way for engagement. They are: *tracking and disrupting problem-maintaining interactions that undermine engagement, establishing direct communications with the multi-habit-dependent client,* and the *use of letters.*

Tracking and Disrupting Problem-Maintaining Interactions that Undermine Engagement

Before attempting to directly intervene with the reluctant multi-habit-dependent client, we like to give the concerned couple partner or parent seeking help the benefit of the doubt that through some adjustments we can empower him or her to engage the client for couples or family therapy. Once we have gathered on the telephone from the partner or parent clear pictures of all of his or her attempted solutions for trying to get the client to come to the session, such as pleading, bribing, and making threats, we will be able to identify together several points to disrupt these unproductive patterns that are inadvertently maintaining the client's protest not to attend treatment with him or her. The most concerned partner or parent can be offered the following five strategies to experiment with to get the reluctant client to join in couple or family therapy sessions:

- Identify and experiment with past successful strategies that have fostered cooperation and trust with the client in the past, and try using one or more of them to counter the client's negativity or reluctance to attend couple or family sessions.
- Have the partner or parent experiment with changing his or her words, tone of voice, nonverbal posture and instead experiment with a softer or more loving way of gaining the client's cooperation and willingness to attend sessions with him or her.
- If past successful change strategies do not work, and changing the way he or she interacts with the client fails to make a difference as well, explore with the partner or parent what surprising and novel things he or she could try that may provoke a change in the client.
- If this strategy fails to work, the therapist can recommend tactics to experiment with to help disrupt unproductive interactions with the client, such as declaring him- or herself as the problem to try to elicit the client's empathy, concern, and desire to help him or her out in a couple or family session.
- A final strategy to try is to have the partner or parent ask the client to invite his or her closest friends to accompany him to the couple or family session.

WORKING WITH RELUCTANT AND COMPLICATED CLIENTS

Establishing Direct Communications with the Multi-Habit-Dependent Client in their Homes or Locations of Choice

Typically, one or a combination of the above strategies succeeds at engaging the reluctant multi-habit-dependent client. However, if this fails to work, we will attempt to establish direct communications with the client. For some clients, offering to do a home visit or meet them in some other neutral or safe location may be less threatening than going to a therapist's office. Once the client agrees to meet with the therapist in his or her home or in some other location of their choice, he or she should begin with rapport-building and getting to know the client by his or her strengths, talents, passions, and hobbies. Showing that you are willing to go the extra mile to engage them with your outreach efforts conveys to the client that you really care and are unlike former therapists who gave up on his or her concerns about treatment. This positive and non-threatening meeting can help set the engagement process in motion.

Another closely related strategy is to see if the client would feel comfortable meeting with you and one or two alumni who used to have the same kind of difficulties and who successfully conquered their habits. The alumni can truly empathize with the costs and struggles the client may be grappling with. They also can share their wisdom and expertise about how they conquered their habits and have successfully stayed quit. Furthermore, if the client is unemployed or doing poorly at school, the alumni may be able to assist them with securing employment and with improving their school work. Finally, if the client and alumni make a meaningful connection they can participate in couple and family sessions and serve as an effective relapse prevention support team between sessions (Selekman, 2005, 2006, 2009).

Use of Letters

We use letters in couples and family therapy in a variety of ways. For the purpose of this chapter, we will limit our discussion to how letters can serve as a powerful intervention strategy for engaging and re-engaging reluctant clients, partners, and key absent family members who wield a great deal of power and control in their families and are reluctant to participate in family therapy. The letters can be sent to the reluctant client via e-mail, text message, or in hardcopy form. Depending on the client's preferred way of communicating with others.

Sometimes, a simple and straightforward letter of invitation that emphasizes the positives is enough to make a difference and get the reluctant identified client, couple partner, or family member into therapy. We use these simple letters if our assessment is that the main reason for the identified client's reluctance to attend counseling is that he or she is demoralized by unsuccessful previous therapy and/or by the constant criticism and belittling by his or her parents.

In other cases it is preferable to combine highlighting the positive with a clear message about how much is at stake with therapy, spelling out the possible negative consequences of not attending the session. This strategy only works if the engaged parent or couple partner is not already using threats unsuccessfully, in which case a letter like this would only be *more of the same* (Fisch, Weakland, & Segal., 1982). The case example of Kyle illustrates how the use of a letter via texting helped engage a reluctant husband who was abusing marijuana and alcohol, gambling on- and offline, and spent hours on the Internet bidding on *e-Bay* items and visiting porn sites. Kyle, Rhonda's husband, had been in marital therapy twice before with her and did not like it. The childless couple had been married for 15 years and had shared many positive life experiences together. Despite Rhonda's best efforts to change the way she interacted with Kyle (she had tried all five of the engagement strategies described earlier in the chapter) to engage him to join her in seeing me, he dug in and told her to go by herself. From the session, Kyle was sent the following text message in letter format:

Dear Kyle,

Today, in reflecting on her positive memories about you and the past, Rhonda had shared with me a couple of very exciting and adventurous trips the two of you had gone on together. Wow! The scuba trip in the Great Barrier Reef off the coast of Australia sounded really awesome! Rhonda also shared with me how you reminded her of *Lawrence of Arabia* when she had rode on the camel with you in the Moroccan desert! While telling me about these wonderful and romantic times together, I could tell that Rhonda really loves you and will fight to save her marriage to you. I must say you have a really wonderful wife who is quite devoted to you. I have worked with similar couples like you and Rhonda and the wives ended up getting burned out, giving up on their marriages, and either ended them or had affairs. In your case, I hope neither one of these situations occurs for your sake because you have a wife that really loves and cares about you a lot but you can never tell with these situations.

I am sending you this text letter in an attempt to wave the red flags with you saying that together we should really try to prevent the dire from happening here. Please excuse me for being little bit selfish here but I would really like to hear from you about your experience of the Australian scuba diving adventure and camel riding experiences and any other past positive memories you have about your relationship with Rhonda. Since I have seen Rhonda twice, I am happy to balance things out and see you twice or if you would prefer, I could see you with Rhonda, whatever feels most comfortable for you.

If you wish to come in for those individual sessions, please call me at your earliest convenience and I will try and get you in this week. My telephone number is _____. I have scheduled with Rhonda a session for the three of us for next Wednesday night. Please let me know if that evening works for you as well or if you would like to schedule an individual session time that works better with your schedule.

I am really looking forward to meeting you!

Best Wishes,
Matthew D. Selekman, MSW

The next day I received a call from Kyle stating that he decided that he would feel more comfortable seeing me the first time with Rhonda. He also shared with me that it made him feel "real happy" after reading the text letter to know that Rhonda still loved him. I underscored that and told him that I was delighted that we could work together with her to protect all of the wonderful things and experiences that they shared in their relationship. Kyle came to our next appointment highly motivated to saving his marriage and willing to examine the role his habits had played in serving as distance regulators in the emotional and sexual intimacy areas of their relationship. Kyle had "felt guilty" about this. In exploring what he had not liked about his past marital therapy experiences, both "the therapists were females" and he had felt "they had taken Rhonda's side" and "blamed" him for their relationship difficulties. Kyle shared with me that he was happy I was a male therapist and appeared to be neutral and not take anyone's side.

Sometimes the assessment of the family situation and the stage of readiness for change that the identified client is currently in will dictate whether or not a more direct and straightforward communication with him or her via a letter will not make a difference. In those situations, we sometimes use paradoxical letters that give non-attendance a positive connotation and prescribe it (Andolfi, 1980; Rohrbaugh, Tennen, Press, & White, 1981; Selvini-Palazzoli, Cecchin, Prata, & Boscolo, 1978; Stanton & Todd, 1982). In using these provocative letters it is important to always attribute noble intentions to the client's refusal to participate in therapy, and also to carefully evaluate the likely impact the letter may have on the family, foreseeing possible negative reactions and ways to handle them.

Andres and his wife came to see me (MB), worried about their 18-year-old son Paco, who had dropped out of school three years ago and was not working, was abusing marijuana, alcohol, and other substances, and was verbally abusive with his parents and his 14-year-old brother Mateo. As the parents explained, Paco had always been jealous of Mateo, who was described as a "nice, well-behaved kid" and who excelled on his school soccer team. However, academically, Mateo was a very poor student. Paco had been seen by a psychiatrist two years ago and had been put on medication, which he refused to take; since then, he had refused to see any other therapist and spent days locked up in his bedroom, or out on the streets doing drugs with friends. He had refused to come to see me for therapy and would not speak to me on the telephone. After the initial session with his parents and his brother Mateo, I decided to try and engage him with the following letter:

Dear Paco,

I am Mark Beyebach, the therapist your parents saw last week. After a long conversation with them, and your brother Mateo, I am writing you to let you know how impressed I am with how well you are doing the hard job you have taken on. It is clear to me that you are sacrificing your own life and your own future for the sake of your brother. By playing the "black sheep" of the family you are making your brother shine and look like the family angel. I think for the time being it is necessary for you to continue to make this sacrifice, so that your parents keep distracted and do not focus on Mateo's serious academic problems. It is also important for the time being that you do not join our meetings, so that you can keep on being the family scapegoat. If you wish, I can keep you updated via mail of what is discussed in our meetings here.

Yours sincerely,
Mark Beyebach, PhD

According to the parents' report, Paco was very upset when he had received my letter, and in fact did not sleep at home the next two nights. Later it was discovered he had been out partying with friends. When he eventually returned home, he declared that he wanted to go to the next family session, to "show the stupid therapist that he was wrong!" Following my instructions, the parents had said to him that maybe it was not a good idea that he attended the session, which increased Paco's resolve to do so. I decided to see him alone and after some tense minutes, we found some common ground to begin therapy together.

Intervening Indirectly through the Referring Professional, Couple Partner, Family Members, and Key Social Network Members when the Identified Client is Absent

All is not lost if, in spite of our persistent outreach efforts, we are unable to engage the reluctant client for couple or family therapy sessions. Most importantly, just having the most concerned or motivated member or members of the client system present in sessions can be enough leverage to engage for treatment and indirectly change the reluctant client (Boscolo & Bertrando, 1993; Fisch & Schlanger, 1999; Hedges, 2005; Selekman, 2009; Smith & Meyers, 2004; Szapocznik, Hervis, & Schwartz, 2003; Szapocznik & Kurtines, 1989; Szapocznik & Williams, 2000; Weakland, 1983).

Creating a Climate Ripe for Building Cooperative Partnerships and Transformative Conversations with Referring Professionals

Often, the idea that the client has a "problem" comes from somebody outside their home, such as an employer, a school psychologist or some other school personnel, a physician or pediatrician, a probation officer, a child protective worker, or a friend of the concerned couple partner or parent. Once alarmed by the client's behavior and/or if in a power position to enforce response and action, these professionals will encourage the concerned partner or parents to pursue couple or family therapy to try and ameliorate the identified "problem(s)." The more extreme and long-standing the identified problems or behaviors are described to be, the more likely multiple helping professionals representing diverse larger systems will be called in as well to coalesce around the identified client and his or her partner and/or family to make sure steps are being taken to resolve their difficulties. Anderson (1997) and Anderson and Goolishian (1988, 1991) refer to the family–multiple helper system as a *problem-determined system*. However, we prefer to think of the family–multiple helper system as a *solution-determined system*, in that the referring person, other involved helping professionals, or concerned members of the client's social network are potential allies that possess the necessary competencies and creativity to co-construct high quality solutions with the clients (Selekman, 2009, 2010).

Since the identified client may not think he or she has a problem, is reluctant to surrender their beloved habits, and is in the *precontemplation* stage of readiness for change, he or she will resist efforts to change him or her. The mistake here is that the referring person and other involved helping professionals are gearing their treatment recommendations and interventions for a client who is in the *action stage* of readiness for change, which is destined to fail for a client who is in the *precontemplative stage*. This can lead not only to the client being even more reluctant to participate in any form of counseling but to further exacerbating his or her habit difficulties, demoralization for all parties involved, and to the intensification of the conflicts in their couple and family relationships. Therefore, it is critical that the therapist actively collaborates with the referring person and the involved helping professionals as early in treatment as possible to learn about their main concerns, expectations, theories of change, and best hopes for treatment outcome. This will provide an opportunity to gain access to a kaleidoscopic view of the identified problem situation, introduce some alternative constructions or viewpoints, and to build cooperative partnerships with the referring person and other professionals. In addition, having the concerned partner, parents, and other concerned members from the reluctant client's social network present at this meeting affords them with the opportunity to share their concerns, preferences, and unique needs that they would like help with from the referring person and other involved helping professionals from larger systems. We have witnessed in these family–multiple helper collaborative meetings family members, key members from the reluctant client's social network, and involved helping professionals spontaneously agreeing to partner up in the various social contexts the client is having difficulties in, such as at the workplace, at the school, or even in the community. The bonus for the therapist is having concerned others working for you outside the office and between couple and family therapy sessions helping the reluctant client make better choices and reduce problematic behaviors without having him or her attending therapy. For the sake of brevity, we will limit our discussion to two common scenarios that occur in the referring person–therapeutic system interactions and how to work productively with each of these situations.

The Referring Person and the Couple Partner or Parents are the Customers

With clinical situations in which the referring person and the couple partner or parents are customers for change and are in the *action stage* of readiness for change, while the client is reluctant to attend couple or family therapy, we need to intervene with both the concerned referring person and the committed members of the client system simultaneously. With the referring person, we need to first build a positive relationship and assess his or her problem views, theories of change, best hopes and goals for the identified client, and expectations for therapy with the client and their couple partner or family. From a non-expert position and in a tentative manner, the therapist can introduce alternative explanations for the identified client's behavior and disguised information about similar clients he or she worked with in the past who presented with the same kind of behaviors and yet did not have a diagnosable DSM-IV mental health disorder or an addiction. Reframing of negative behaviors or symptoms can be used sparingly as well. However, the therapist has to carefully read the feedback from the referring person to see if these alternative explanations are acceptable or come close to fitting his or her beliefs or views. If this begins to create some doubt that there is a problem warranting immediate clinical attention, the doubt can be increased by expanding on the construction of the client's behavior that seems to resonate the most with the referring person, which may lead to a shift from pushing for treatment and to just monitoring the behavior of concern. It may be mutually decided that the referring person will contact the couple partner or the parents and explain that they may have jumped the gun with their concerns with pushing for counseling and instead will monitor the situation.

If it appears that the couple partner or parents would still like to have a session to discuss matters, we will meet with them and, using the same strategy as with the referring person, conduct the session in a similar way. In addition, we will explore with the couple partner or the parents what is going well in their relationships with the identified client and in other areas of his or her life, as well as sharing what specifically they may be doing that is contributing to their son or daughter's positive and responsible behaviors. This will further help neutralize the idea that there is a "problem," requiring professional attention. All it may take is a single session with a couple partner or the parents to close the door on the need for counseling. However, if the couple partner or parents are still concerned about any aspect of the identified client's self-destructive habits or with any other difficulties, we will conduct a detailed assessment of all of their attempted solutions, and offer them useful therapeutic tools and strategies for disrupting enabling patterns of interaction and coach them to reward responsible and other non-problem habit behaviors (O'Farrell &Fals-Stewart, 2006; Smith & Meyers, 2004).

The Referring Person is the Customer and the Couple Partner or Parents and the Client are not even Window-Shoppers for Counseling

In clinical situations where we are faced with a room full of *precontemplators*, other habit-dependent partners or family members, who often present as *no problem-problem couples and families* (Eastwood, Sweeney, & Piercy, 1987; Prochaska, Norcross, & DiClemente, 2006; Selekman, 2005), we need not panic or think this is our worst nightmare! Instead, we need to look at the leverage we have been given by the referring professionals' power to mandate them to go for counseling. This is particularly true for court-ordered, child protective, work-related mandatory management, and alternative to school suspension case situations. One big advantage for therapists working with clients who are being forced to go for counseling is that it sets up a beautiful split where the therapist can become the ally and the referring professional by default becomes the heavy person putting them through this terrible ordeal. Once we secure permission from the clients to meet with or communicate with the referring professional, we can begin to build a collaborative partnership with him or her and find out the reasons for making the referral, the consequences for the identified client, couple partner, or parents not participating in counseling, and what specifically needs to change that would indicate that the clients would no longer have to go for counseling.

After securing this valuable information, it can be communicated to the couple partner or parents and to the identified client. This may be just enough to gain compliance to attend counseling. In our initial couple and family sessions, we strive to build strong therapeutic alliances with the partners or each family member and convey loudly and clearly that we empathize with their dilemma about being forced to see us and that we will work really hard to get the referring professional off their backs. It is helpful to share with them what steps the referring professional needs to see them take to satisfy his or her treatment expectations so that they would no longer have to go for counseling. Through the use of future-oriented questions and projecting the clients two or three months down the road, we like to have all participants describe in great detail any other steps they see themselves taking in the future that will really surprise the referring professional! We can explore with and have them imagine what kind of differences and positive effects these future changes will have on them individually and in their relationships. Using curiosity, we can find out if any of their reported changes are already happening. If so, we can have them experiment with and increase their positive solution-building patterns of thinking, feeling, and behaving as a way of getting the referring professional off their backs. We also like to make it clear to our clients that we will be their advocates and fight for and negotiate any special needs or requests they may have directly with the referring professional and with other helping professionals from larger systems that may be involved. Finally, we strongly recommend to the clients that we invite the referring professional and any other involved helping professionals to our sessions to bear witness to and hear about the positive changes they are making. This will lead to the referring professional and other involved helpers being less alarmed about the client's and other family members' behavior and can reduce clients' lengths of stay in treatment.

With some cases, in spite of our best efforts to successfully engage the couple partner or the parents, the identified client may still refuse to attend our sessions. When faced with this clinical dilemma, we have had some success simultaneously working with the couple partner or parents and intervening directly with the referring professional, who may be feeling stuck with the identified client and may welcome our support and fresh ideas. We will first track with the referring professional his or her typical ways of interacting (tone of voice and what specifically is said) with the identified client. We will map this circular interaction out on a pad of paper or flip chart so that the referring professional can visually see how he or she is stuck doing *more-of-the-same* with what he or she says to or does with the identified client. This can be newsworthy for the referring professional and can offer us many locus points for pattern intervention. We can ask the referring professional the miracle question, find out about any pieces of the miracle that have already happened that can be amplified or increased, and have him or her speculate what miracle-like behaviors the identified client would like to see from him or her. Then as an experiment, the referring professional should pretend to engage in the miracle-like behaviors over the next week and notice how the client responds. We can offer them other therapeutic experiments to try as well. Sometimes, simply by changing either the referring professional's problem-maintaining beliefs about or negative interactions with the identified client may be enough to alter problematic behavior or dissolve the idea that there is a "problem" requiring immediate therapeutic intervention. Once the referring person is less alarmed and no longer sees the necessity and urgency for the identified client and other family members to be in counseling, any initial treatment process can stop at that point, as the problem has dissipated (Anderson, 1997; Anderson & Goolishian, 1988).

If in spite of all of our efforts of offering the referring professional alternative ways of viewing and interacting with the identified client and he or she is still pressing us to engage the client for treatment but it proves to be futile, we need to work with the couple partner or the parents alone or with key resource people from identified client's social network to try to gain therapeutic leverage and indirectly change him or her through their efforts. Strengthening the couple partner's or parents' coping abilities, encouraging them to pursue their personal goals and enjoyable and meaningful activities, no matter what the identified client says or does, and empowering them to only interact with the identified client in constructive and positive ways can not only facilitate his or her engagement into treatment but possibly lead to him or her making quite dramatic changes (Meyers, 2012; Selekman, 2009; Smith & Meyers, 2004).

Working Alone with the Most Concerned Couple Partners, Parents, or other Family Subsystems

When we only have the couple partner, parents, and or other concerned family members presenting themselves for treatment, rather than viewing this as a major treatment dilemma, instead we can look at how this situation provides some important advantages for the therapist and all concerned parties involved. Often, the people who come to the initial session without the reluctant client fall somewhere between being in the *contemplative* and *action stages* of readiness for change. Therefore, they recognize that there is a problem that they would like resolved and may eventually be ready to partner up with their therapists to experiment with novel change strategies. Those participants in the action stage will be armed with treatment goals and be very clear what specifically they want to see changed with the identified client first. Having at least one member from the reluctant client's system present in our couple or family sessions may be all that it takes to change him or her through indirect means. During this individual session time with couple partners or parents, therapists can use role-playing as an effective experiential way to teach positive communication skills and strategies for disrupting problem-maintaining interactions with the habit-dependent person. Thus, couple partners and parents are empowered to be the agents of change (Meyers, 2012; Smith & Meyers, 2004). The following three playful therapeutic experiments can also be successfully employed with concerned couple partners, the parents, and with the participating reluctant client's siblings.

Being Mysterious and Arbitrary

In clinical situations where the reluctant client wields all of the power and control in the couple or family system, the *being mysterious and arbitrary* therapeutic experiment can dramatically alter this couple or family dynamic. For the habit or multi-habit-dependent partner or adolescent, they discover that their habit(s) can serve the functions of disempowering intimate others, hold them hostage, and it allows them to control and dominate them so as to get their way when necessary. Therefore, their decision to boycott couple and family sessions is to protect their power positions and habits at all costs.

The couple partner or parents are to discontinue tip-toeing around the identified client, set goals for themselves, and suddenly become mysterious with making plans, with their comings and goings in and out of the home, and when they eventually do return back home and are asked where they went, the arbitrary response to the identified client is, "Oh, I just felt like going out." They are not to furnish any other information if interrogated. Not only can this intervention successfully get reluctant clients into treatment but they may become desperate enough after losing their power and control grip with their partner or parents to solicit advice and support from the therapists about how to manage this dilemma. Even if this positive outcome does not occur, the couple partner and the parents will no longer feel like hostages and feel empowered.

Doing Something Novel and Surprising

The *doing something novel and surprising* therapeutic experiment is very similar to and more expansive than the *being mysterious and arbitrary* experiment (de Shazer, 1988, 1991; Selekman, 2005, 2009, 2010). With this therapeutic experiment, the couple partner or the parents can be as creative and off-the-wall as they want to be with their novel and surprising responses to the identified client's provocative and difficult behaviors. We have had couple partners and parents putting on disguises, dancing and singing, saying and doing strange things, and putting on Academy Award performances. Similar to the results with the *being mysterious and arbitrary* experiment, the reluctant client may enter couple or family treatment with concerns that their partner or parents were "going crazy" and seeking the therapist's help with his or her concern. On a cautionary note, we do not use either the *being mysterious and arbitrary* or the *doing something novel and surprising* therapeutic experiment with potentially violent partners or those with a history of this behavior. We also will not use these experiments with parents who have a history of being excessively punitive.

Putting the Siblings in Charge of the Habit or Multi-Habit-Dependent Parent's Happiness for a Day

As mentioned earlier about how family members may become indoctrinated and succumb to emotional and behavioral difficulties themselves from feeling out of control and invalidated, one powerful way the siblings can inject positive emotion into their relationships with the habit or multi-habit-dependent parent is to *be in charge of their parent's happiness for a day*. The other bonuses with this therapeutic experiment is it can help improve sibling conflict and rivalry difficulties, the younger and older children can take a break from parental limit-testing and their own unproductive habits, and it reduces stress and enabling behaviors that only serve to maintain the parent's habit difficulties. The therapist meets alone with the siblings and has each of them come up with specific things that they can do separately and together that they know that the habit or multi-habit-dependent parent will really appreciate and notice. Some of the ideas siblings have come up with are: preparing together for the parent a special dinner of some favorite dishes, putting together a nice card or letter listing all of the qualities and aspects of the parent that they appreciate, and engaging the parent in a fun activity that they used to enjoy doing in the past together. This therapeutic experiment can pave the way for the habit-dependent parent to be willing to accompany their "wonderful" children to a family session. It does not always work and we prepare them for this possibility, but sometimes we have been able to schedule a spontaneous family session in the home in the evening of the day that the experiment had been successfully implemented and the initially reluctant parent was willing to participate.

Working with Dual-Habit-Dependent Couples and Multi-Habit Dependent-Family Member Families

One of the toughest clinical dilemmas is working with dual-partner habit-dependent couples and multi-habit-dependent family member families. Since both partners and habit-dependent family members reinforce each other's habit behaviors and other difficulties, a change in one partner, family member, or family relationship may not change others, may further exacerbate the others' habit behaviors and difficulties, and/or lead to a couple or family crisis occurring (Birchler, Fals-Stewart, & O'Farrell, 2005, 2008; O'Farrell & Fals-Stewart, 2006; Selekman, 2005, 2009). Therefore, to help simplify matters, it may make sense to work with smaller subsystems of the family separately and establish separate treatment goals and work projects for a while until the overall couple or family situation becomes less chaotic and more stable. Once that occurs, we can bring couple partners and family members back together to consolidate gains, establish joint treatment goals, and discuss relapse prevention teamwork. However, it is important to remember that even after separating the partners and family members, some preliminary work may be necessary to gradually advance them through the stages of readiness for change until they are ready to take action and commit to the change process.

If change is not occurring after splitting up the couple or working with individuals or subsystems in the family, we will use more indirect therapeutic interventions like the *negative consequences of change* (Fisch & Schlanger, 1999; Fisch et al., 1982; Watzlawick, Weakland, & Fisch, 1974) and *the therapeutic debate* (Sheinberg, 1985). We will caution the couple partners and family members about changing too quickly since their habits have become so central in their lives and we want to protect them from the discomfort of shaking things up with a sudden and dramatic change to the couple or family equilibrium.

The Negative Consequences of Change

Closely related to restraint from immediate change is exploring the negative consequences of change for each partner or the family members (Fisch et al., 1982). Here, the therapist can wonder aloud what the specific costs or disadvantages would be for each partner or family member if alcohol, drugs, cutting, eating-distressed habits, excessive Internet use, video-gaming, or gambling suddenly stopped. Some examples of potential consequences of change the therapist can be curious about are as follows: would the couple partners be forced to face their unresolved conflicts; without the aid of Ecstasy would a couple partner become less confident about his or her ability to perform sexually in the relationship; or would a more emotionally vulnerable family member become so depressed that he or she would entertain taking his or her life?

The Therapeutic Debate

A final way we like to intervene with these highly entrenched and complicated couple and family situations is to use the *therapeutic debate* consultation team format (Papp, 1983; Selekman, 2006, 2009; Sheinberg, 1985). With the assistance of two colleagues observing the therapist and the couple or family working together, around 40 minutes into the hour the team members can enter the therapy room and have a debate regarding the dilemmas of change. The team members can represent the position of each partner or with a family, one team member can represent the parents' position and the other team member can represent the adolescent's position. Each team member has the therapeutic maneuverability and freedom to put himself or herself out on a limb with sharing the various reasons stability or no change is important for one or both couple partners or certain family members, such as protecting one's power position, the secondary gains of having serious difficulties, or how and why change could be catastrophic for the couple relationship, particularly if the glue that kept the couple together was the great pleasure they derived from regularly "getting stoned" together. The therapist is free to be neutral, actively participate in the debate, or support the couple or family members' pro-change positions. Often, the couple partners and family members end up not only joining the debate to challenge team members' views but may divulge secrets or share other important material that they had never talked about before with one another that have served as constraints or blocks for individual, couple, or family change happening. This consultation team format is very effective with stuck couple and family case situations and can have a liberating effect on the therapeutic system.

Organizing a Social Ecology: The Power of Utilizing Key Resource People from the Reluctant Client's Social Network to be the Agents of Change

Another valuable resource we can tap when the Herculean efforts of the therapist, couple partner, the parents, and other family members to try to engage the reluctant client do not work is enlisting the services of the key concerned members from his or her social network. This can include important adult inspirational others, close friends, known *weak link* acquaintances, and extended family members the reluctant client is closest to. Coleman (2011) refers to the concerned others from the client's social network as *integrative catalysts*, in that they have strong and positive relationships with the client, are not entangled in the couple and family problem-maintaining dynamics and conflicts, and pose no threat to him or her.

Koch and Lockwood (2010) have found in their research and business consulting work that there are many advantages to strengthening one's relationships with members of the *weak link network*, in that it is an untapped resource that can open the door for all kinds of positive possibilities for people. Weak link resource people are acquaintances from one's school, workplace, local community, or friendly individuals we had met at a party, at the health club or recreational center, or through other friends in the past and we had good feelings about but never took the time to develop stronger relationships with them. They also can be people that we had heard about who attend one's school, work at the same place, share similar hobbies and interests as us, and have good reputations as important, insightful, and interesting people to get to know. The weak link resource people also can be recruited by couple partners or parents to help provide additional support for the identified client to help prevent relapses and to help build new meaningful relationships. Once the reluctant client is successfully engaged, we can explore with him or her who their key weak link people are and encourage more involvement with them, which can help expand their social support system, serve as positive peer influences, and move them away from negative peers or friends who may be part of the habit problem maintenance system.

One effective way we like to employ the services of concerned members of the reluctant client's social network is to have them conduct *secret mission projects* as a non-threatening and indirect way to engage him or her for treatment. While conducting collaborative meetings with the couple partner, family members, concerned members from the client's social network, and involved helping professionals, we explore which social network members have the strongest connection and most leverage with the identified client. We want to find out how to capture his or her attention best in terms of what they like to talk about or do together with these key social network resource people. Once we have this important information, the identified key resource people can plan secret mission projects, which are activities that the reluctant client typically enjoys doing with them and can create a relaxed climate that can gain his or her trust and increase his or her willingness to go to a counseling session with them. The case example below illustrates how secret mission projects conducted separately by two key members from the client's social network paved the way to his involvement in family therapy.

Casey, 18, had dropped out of high school his junior year and had refused to get work. According to the parents, Casey spends his evenings and daytimes smoking marijuana, drinking, playing online war games, and engaging in on- and offline gambling with his friends. Casey had had several outpatient counseling experiences with his parents in the past but would only attend a session or two and then refuse to go again. The parents felt completely dethroned by Casey and were at a loss for what to do. I had seen the parents twice and thought it was time to expand the treatment system. I asked them to think of what key leverage people from Casey's or the family's social networks we could recruit to help us turn their son's situation around. Rodger, Casey's father, shared that his younger brother Bill used to go fishing with Casey every weekend when Casey was in his mid-teens and it was a positive experience for both of them. Bill used to serve as part of an elite US Navy force and would share stories with Casey about his adventures around the world. They had not seen each other for a year because of Bill's frequent work trips. At times in the past, Rodger thought Bill was closer to his son than he was. Rodger contacted Bill from the session and arranged a meeting with him to discuss the possibility of not only participating in our sessions but also to bring back the tradition of taking Casey fishing again. He also shared with him about the secret mission project idea of using his powerful leverage with Casey to get him to participate in our family sessions and begin to take steps to turn his life around. Bill agreed to help out in any way he could. He contacted Casey to see if he would like to join him fly fishing in Montana over a weekend. Casey was very excited to hear from Bill and agreed to go with him on this spectacular fishing trip in Montana. The weekend was a hit success in that Casey shared with Bill some potential future career interest areas and he liked the idea of having his uncle participate in family sessions with his parents. As a result of Bill's regular participation in our family sessions, he inspired Casey to get his GED, attend a local junior college, helped him to find a good job with a close friend of his, and helped facilitate the strengthening of Rodger's relationship with Casey. Bill used his authority and leverage with Casey to get him to commit to abandoning his self-destructive habits and showing his parents more respect in order to be able to keep his job with his friend.

Case Examples

"I Became My Worst Nightmare!" Taking Back Control "With a Little Help from my Friends"

Raquel, 17, was referred to me (MS) by her school social worker Ms. Robson for cutting, suspected drug use, academic performance decline, peer conflict difficulties, and depression. The peer conflicts were related to rumors circulating around the school that Raquel is a "Ho!" (whore) because she was very sexually active, was sexting a lot and making provocative and sexually charged home videos with some friends that ended up on the Internet. When asked about and sharing her concerns with Raquel, Ms. Robson was met with responses like: "Oh, we were just having some fun," "I don't want to talk about it," or "It is none of your business!" However, there had been times in her counseling sessions that she disclosed feeling "used and hurt" by boys. Ms. Robson's theory was that Raquel's sexually acting out behaviors was related to "the lack of having an emotionally loving father figure and the mother's distancing from her as well due to her alcohol use."

Ms. Robson also shared with me that Raquel's parents were divorced and the biological father Peter was a recovering alcoholic and substance abuser. He had been in inpatient chemical dependency treatment for cocaine and alcohol abuse once when Raquel was 12. According to Ms. Robson, the father was inconsistent with visitations and child support. He also has had legal difficulties related to inside trading deals for his company. At times, Raquel wondered if her father was using drugs again. She suspected that Raquel was not very close to her father. Raquel had disclosed once to Ms. Robson that she also worried about her mother's drinking. Apparently, when Raquel confronts her mother about drinking too much wine, and drinking and driving, she would get defensive with her and downplay her drinking. Sylvia, Raquel's mother, had a new husband, Stuart, and Raquel reported that she talks very little to him and they rarely do things together one-on-one or as a family because he works all of the time or goes on dates with her mother. Ms. Robson also reported that Raquel had been in family therapy twice before and after her parents had divorced for depression and cutting when she was 13. Finally, we agreed to regularly communicate with one another about Raquel's school functioning and regarding her progress in family therapy.

The First Family Session

Sylvia and Raquel came to the first session on time. I began the session by getting to know the family members by learning about their strengths. Sylvia loved reading fiction books, going to the movies, and gourmet cooking with Stuart. Raquel used to perform and sing, liked "to chill" with friends, and communicate with her friends on *Facebook*. I explored with the family what specifically they wanted to change. Sylvia expressed her concerns about Raquel's cutting, use of marijuana, and her grades slipping in school. We first began with the cutting issue and how Sylvia managed it. Raquel chimed in, "Well, yelling at me about it doesn't help!" I explored with Raquel what specifically she would like her mother to say or do that could help the most. She went on to say, "Yelling and going ballistic on me just makes it worse. Oh, just forget about it... you never really listen anyways. I feel I can't talk to you." I shared with Raquel that she could be a helpful guide to her mother about what she could do differently that would really help. She said, "First, you could really try to listen to me about what's making me upset or why I cut myself." Sylvia felt that she tries to get Raquel to open up to her but, she "never does." I took a risk and explored with Raquel what she thought some of the roadblocks were that prevented her and her mother from communicating better. Raquel shared, "Try her drinking." Sylvia chimed in that Raquel thought she had a drinking problem. Sylvia went on to say that she may have "a few glasses of wine in the evening," but that was the extent of her drinking. Raquel then responded with, "What about all of those nights with your friends when you go out and come home ripped!" Sylvia was visibly getting upset and said, "You really don't know what you're talking about and besides, honey, we are here for you."

At this point in the session, I decided to shift gears and take our conversation in a more positive direction by asking the miracle question. Sylvia began by sharing that her ideal miracle scenario would be the following: "Raquel stopped cutting, she would be doing her homework without reminders, and she would open up more to me about what's going on in her life." When asked about how those changes would make a difference for her, Sylvia shared that she would "worry about and argue less with her and be less stressed out." I turned to Raquel and asked her, "How does a more chilled out mom sound to you?" Raquel shared chuckling, "That would be cool." I finally got Raquel to laugh and lighten up. I asked her what effect would a more "chilled out mom" have on her. Raquel shared with us that she would be "less stressed out" as well. She went on to say, "I won't have to worry about when my mom goes out drinking and driving." Sylvia abruptly chimed in and turned to me and said, "She really is over-exaggerating about my drinking ... I don't drink every day or am out driving drunk!"

I changed direction at this point and asked both of them if any pieces of the miracle had already started to happen a little bit. Raquel pointed out that she had gotten a "B" grade on a math test, which was a big improvement for her. To help emphasize this sparkling moment for her, I asked, "Are you aware of how you pulled that off?" Raquel responded with, "I studied for once and had asked for help from my teacher so I could really get how to do the problems." She also acknowledged that asking for help from a teacher was really different for her. Sylvia complimented Raquel and asked her why she had not told her about it. Raquel shared that she had forgotten to. I asked Raquel if there were any other miracle-like surprises with her schoolwork. She reported that she had completed some back assignments for her English class as well. When asked about how she had pulled that off, Raquel had responded with "I don't want to fail my English class and have to go to summer school." I complimented Raquel and shared with her that I was very impressed with how responsible she was being in taking big steps to turn around her school situation. She could not identify any other pretreatment miracle-like occurrences with her mother or in their relationship. Sylvia also could not think of any miracles that were starting to happen in her relationship with Raquel.

At this point in the session, I met alone with Sylvia. I revisited all of her attempted solutions for managing Raquel's challenging behaviors. Sylvia said she had tried everything from yelling, lecturing, taking privileges away, and grounding but "nothing worked." She also pointed out to me how angry she is with Raquel's biological father Peter for "not regularly paying child support, canceling visitations at the last moment," and not backing her up with disciplining her when she gets out of hand. Apparently, when Raquel does spend time with Peter he "always brings his new girlfriend and it's all about spending money on her and playtime, it is not about having a concerned fatherly conversation about cutting, use of marijuana, and poor grades." I asked if Sylvia would feel okay if I met with Peter and involved him in some sessions with Raquel. She thought this would be a great idea. Sylvia felt that they could use a lot of work on their relationship because he has "let her down a lot since the divorce." When asked about what had led to her divorce from Peter, Sylvia shared that they "argued all of the time in front of Raquel, he used to drink and do cocaine, blow a lot of money, and it became highly toxic for everyone." I asked her about Raquel's relationship with her new husband Stuart and she said that he was nice to her but they had not really connected that well. She wished that they both had a closer relationship and despite her Herculean efforts to try to be the bridge between them, "neither one budges to meet the other half way." When asked if this was a goal that she wished us to pursue, Sylvia responded with, "Absolutely!" Apparently, when he was asked to attend our family session, Stuart felt that Sylvia needed to first work on gaining more leverage and strengthening her relationship with Raquel before entering family therapy. Raquel did not want Stuart to participate in family therapy with her at this time.

From a one-down position and using curiosity, I revisited with Sylvia why she thought Raquel was so concerned about her drinking. She said that it happens when you are around it all of the time. I explored with Sylvia what she meant by this. Sylvia went on to add that her "father, uncles, and grandfather drank a lot and were alcoholics." Apparently, her father, one of the uncles, and the grandfather had died from "alcoholism-related liver problems." On Peter's side of the family, his father was an alcoholic and he had an older brother Paul who died from a heroin overdose. I shared with Sylvia that maybe out of love and concern for her, Raquel does not want alcoholism to claim her life as well, since it had gotten the best of her maternal grandfather, other relatives, and her father Peter. She pointed out that occasionally she "might drink a little too much wine" but tries "to not over do it because of my family background." Sylvia shared that to her knowledge Raquel stays away from alcohol. I also explored with Sylvia if she thinks that Raquel might think that she has the green light to use marijuana since she has claimed Sylvia drinks too much and seems to be powerless to change this situation. Sylvia was intrigued by my question and had never thought about the situation in that way. I put myself out on a limb and took a big risk with Sylvia and asked her if I could get Raquel to commit to stopping her use of marijuana and cutting herself, would she be willing to greatly reduce her use of wine? Sylvia agreed to try but made it clear to me that Stuart and her really loved wine and gourmet cooking and her social life with close friends was regularly going out for dinners and/or drinks. I shifted gears and restrained her from immediate change and asked her to think about whether or not she should taper down on her alcohol consumption even if the stress and worry this produces for Raquel may contribute to her cutting and marijuana use. Sylvia abruptly changed her position and made it quite clear that she was "willing to do anything to help" her daughter.

I encouraged her to experiment with injecting more positive emotion into her relationship with Raquel by initiating conversations with her about daily high points at school, with her friendships, and find things that she might like to do with her, such as grabbing a cup of coffee, going shopping, or pampering themselves together with getting their nails done and/or pedicures. Sylvia shared with me that she was not doing enough fun mother–daughter activities with Raquel. She thought this could work because she had a tendency to "nag and focus too much on problems with Raquel rather than talk about good stuff." When asked what her initial treatment goal was, Sylvia wanted to work on both reducing her "nagging" behavior and finding some "meaningful activities" she could do with Raquel. To get a rating on Sylvia's nagging behavior over time, I asked her the following question: "If Raquel were sitting in that empty chair over there and I asked her, 'On a scale from 10 to 1, with 10 not nagging at all, and 1 nagging all of the time, where would you have rated your mom's nagging behavior a month ago?', what do you think Raquel would have said?" Sylvia said, "A minus 3!" We laughed together and I responded with, "You mean you would get a subterranean rating?!" Sylvia laughed. To get a current baseline, she felt that Raquel would presently have rated her "at a 2." I explored with Sylvia how she thinks she was able to advance upward to a 2. Sylvia shared that she has been trying to reduce her nagging behavior because she was discovering that it often led to an argument with Raquel which in turn led to her not doing her homework. I complimented Sylvia on her ability to come to that realization and to try to steer clear from fueling arguments and power struggles with Raquel. I offered Sylvia an experiment of paying close attention daily to the various things she will do to avoid caving into nagging. Her other goal for herself over the next week was to come up with at least one fun and/or meaningful activity that she will do with Raquel. Sylvia believed that if she could pull these two objectives off that that would take her up to a 3 on the scale.

I met alone with Raquel to see how I could be helpful to her. Although Raquel had been talking to Ms. Robson at school about her mother's drinking, she wished that I could "fix this problem." She went on to say that her "mom lies a lot and was not honest" with me about her drinking problem and that she "worries a lot about her being killed in a car accident." I mapped out on a flip chart in my office how, when multiple family members (showing her father Peter, Sylvia, and Raquel as part of the family map) are plagued by habit difficulties (Peter's past and possible current drinking and drug use, Sylvia's drinking, and Raquel's marijuana use, cutting, and sexually risky behaviors, which I was made aware of by Ms. Robson), they end up mutually reinforcing each other's habits by perpetuating vicious worry, guilt, and blame interactions with one another that serve as the habits' life support systems. Raquel felt this made a lot of sense and shared with me that when she worries or feels guilty after getting into an argument with her mother or her father she had a tendency to "want to cut or get stoned."

To help redirect the focus back on Raquel, I asked her if there was anything that we did not talk about in the company of her mother that she thought we needed to talk about, such as her use of alcohol or other drugs, and anything else she was up to or was stressing her out. Raquel took a risk with me and shared how she went to "RAVE parties" with her close friends and had "done Ecstasy, cocaine, and *Special-K* [Ketamine] a few times and sometimes got drunk." She also reported having "made out with some older guys" that she had "met at the RAVE parties." We discussed the importance of practicing safe sex and she claimed that she "always used protection." The other two things her mother was not aware about was her sexting (sending provocative and scantily clothed pictures of herself) on her *iPhone* to some popular boys at her school and putting out on the Internet some "wild videos" of her and a friend dressed provocatively dancing in an erotic way.

I learned later that she was crawling out of her bedroom window around midnight the night of weekend RAVE parties and her mother and Stuart had no idea what she was doing. She also would arrange in her pillows in a human form under the covers to make it look like she was cuddled up. Apparently, she would sleep like this normally so from a distance her mother or Stuart would not think she was missing.

Beginning with Raquel's drug use, I wanted to find out if smoking weed and doing the other drugs she mentioned was a regular recreational activity or whether it happened infrequently. Raquel contended that she did not buy or deal weed and only smoked on the weekends with friends (sharing bowls of weed or a blunt) when it was available. She had been smoking weed since the age of 13. Raquel reported really liking Ecstasy because it made her feel "more sexy and free at the RAVE parties." She felt that cocaine made her feel "real jumpy" and she "didn't like it." Her two experiences with *Special-K* were "really freaky" and she stopped using it. Raquel made it quite clear to me that she was not hooked on any of these drugs and has gone at least a week or two without using any drugs without any craving to use. I explored with her what she did instead of drug use during those periods of abstinence. Raquel shared that keeping busy, steering clear from "certain people and places, and no drama" with her "friends" helped. I asked her if she had observed any costs to using weed or Ecstasy and Raquel felt there were times with the weed that she would forget to call people or to do school assignments. With the Ecstasy she once had a real scare where this guy at a RAVE party was feeling her off on the dance floor and she was worried that he might try to rape her while she was intoxicated because "he was so creepy." After hearing this, I shared with her a story of a former client her age who had something similar happen to her at a RAVE party and the guy who was feeling her off inappropriately did end up raping her when she had left the party. Raquel appeared troubled by this true story. We discussed all of the risks with going to RAVE parties, such as the combination of dancing, drinking, and drugging on the blood pressure and the heart and how some men slip terrible drugs like GHB and *roofies* (Rohypnol) in young women's drinks and end up taking advantage of them and being powerless to stopping them.

Next, we discussed the meaning of her sexting and exposing herself on the Internet with provocative and erotic videos. Raquel loved all of the attention she was getting from the boys around the school and all of the e-mails she was receiving from males around the world. I explored with her why getting "all of the attention" this way was so significant to her and how it was benefiting her. Raquel pointed out that she attracted some "really cute guys" by doing this and it made her "feel special." I was curious about what feeling special and how her sexually provocative behavior fit into Raquel's life story. Raquel shared with me that prior to the sexting, videos, and going to RAVE parties she felt both "insignificant to and rejected" by the boys at her school. She also had not had a boyfriend for a long time. Closely related to her feelings of being insignificant and rejected, Raquel disclosed that she could not count on her father to show up for visitations and show his love for her. While talking about her shaky relationship with her father, I asked if she would like to do some sessions with him alone to try to strengthen their relationship. Raquel felt that it would be a waste of time because her father will always put his girlfriend and work before her. Apparently, when her father failed to show up for visitations or invalidated her in other ways, this would lead to a cutting episode, which for Raquel served at times as a form of self-punishment or she would use it to ward off painful feelings.

In an attempt to establish a well-formulated initial treatment goal with Raquel, I asked her what specifically would she like to change first other than her mother's drinking behavior. Raquel made it very clear to me that this was still most important to address, however she did ask for help with how to not let the girls at school, whom she said were like the "Plastics" from the movie *Mean Girls*, get to her emotionally. Apparently, when they would harass or spread nasty rumors about her both around the school and online calling her a "Ho" or "a slut" or post other awful things about her, it would set the stage for a "cutting" episode, "getting stoned," or "sexually fooling around" with boys and young men. Closely related to this, she wanted to learn how to be less reactive to and not cave into surrendering to the habits when both her mother and biological father would invalidate her. Raquel shared her ambivalence with me about giving up these habits because she said they were like her "good friends." When asked what she meant by "good friends," Raquel pointed out how she could always count on these habits "to blot out bad thoughts and feelings" and make her "feel better." Conversely, she also recognized how her habits were costing her in a negative way, such as her contracting the HPV virus from her sexual promiscuous behavior, the weed was making her forgetful with remembering to do school assignments, and she had some bad looking scars on her arms and legs from the cutting that she was not happy about. In fact, one boy that she really liked rejected her after seeing her scars and thinking she was "crazy." I found out later from Raquel that her mother was not aware that she had contracted the HPV virus because this diagnosis had been made by a physician at a free youth clinic that provides confidential assessment, education, and treatment for adolescents and their partners who have contracted sexually transmitted diseases. Raquel was frightened to discover that some adolescent females and women can develop pre-cervical cancerous conditions from HPV.

To get a rating on how committed Raquel was to conquering each of these habits, I constructed three different scales. Raquel was asked on a scale from 10 to 1, with 10 being totally committed to conquering habit A = cutting, B = getting stoned, C = sexually fooling around and 1 a little bit committed to conquering each of these habits, where would she had rated herself prior to and after the miracle happened. Raquel, prior to the miracle happening on Scale A, had rated herself at a 4, on Scale B at a 2, and on Scale C at a 2. After the miracle happened, Raquel rated herself on Scale A at a 7, on Scale B at a 5, and on Scale C at an 8. I first explored with Raquel was she aware of how specifically she got herself to steps higher up on Scale A to the lucky 7. Raquel responded with being really "troubled by my scars as being a turn off" and "feeling ashamed by" what she had done to herself. She further added that the cutting and sexually acting out behaviors were the highest up on her lists to change. With Scale B, Raquel was concerned about her loss of short-term memory problem, not only being able "to remember to do school assignments" but "forgetting about important things" her friends had said to her as well. It was these concerns that were making Raquel feel the need to take a closer look at whether or not weed was a friend or foe to her. Finally, on Scale C contracting the HPV virus and being called "a Ho" by her peers was starting to get to her as well. Additionally, she had shared with me that she had stopped going to RAVE parties, sexting, and making the provocative videos with her friends because these activities were really costing her in all areas of her life.

I complimented Raquel on her incredible ability to recognize how what used to work for her with her trusty habits was starting to backfire for her and that on her own she was slowly but surely taking back control of her life from them. I also pointed how habits are like Academy Award performers in that initially they appear to be friends but in reality end up being foes that can wreak a lot of havoc in a person's life. Finally, I had shared with Raquel that habits do not surrender easily and that it will take hard work, being on your toes, and having slips even after short and long stretches of having good self-control to conquer them for good. Before setting our goals for the next week, Raquel asked me about some tools she could try out to help her not to cave into her habits when they were trying to take control of her. I taught her *urge-surfing* and because she loved popcorn the *Taking a Trip to Popcorn Land* mindfulness food meditation. Raquel set the following goals for herself over the next week:

- In her efforts to get up to an 8 on Scale A, she was going to remind herself through self-talk about feeling "ashamed about" her scars and wanting to stop disfiguring herself. Raquel also planned to use urge-surfing and the Taking a Trip to Popcorn Land meditation.
- In trying to advance herself to a 6 on Scale B, she was going to play in her mind the self-talk tape, "Stop! You don't like not being able to remember things!" Raquel also planned to use urge surfing and Taking a Trip to Popcorn Land meditation to help her not caving in to "getting stoned." Finally, she planned to try and stay away from certain people and places where "weed was present."
- In her efforts to advance herself to a 9 on Scale C, she was going to remind herself how seeking love through fooling around and one-night stands with guys cost her big time with her contracting the HPV virus and gaining the reputation of being a "Ho" at school, which she did not like. She also planned to tell her friends that she was making videos and sexting with that she decided to stop doing these activities.

Since we were well over our time, I did not take an intersession break but just had Sylvia come back in and join us so we could wrap up. I complimented both Raquel and her mother in conveying to me their love and concern for one another and willingness to take big steps toward improving their relationship. I reiterated that the changes they are trying to make will require hard work, perseverance, patience with one another, and teamwork. I shared with them that I was looking forward to hearing what further progress they made the next time we got together. Before we parted, I asked Sylvia and Raquel what the session was like for them. Sylvia shared that she found the session to be very helpful and was proud of Raquel for agreeing to go with her for family counseling. Raquel reported that she really liked the meeting and felt that this session was different from her work with other family counselors. When asked to elaborate on the differences, she said that her former therapists "sided with" her parents versus her. They also "spent more time" with her parents and were "not interested in" her "opinions." We scheduled our next appointment.

Phone Conversation with Ms. Robson

I updated Ms. Robson on the results of my first family session. On Ms. Robson's end, she shared with me that Raquel had told her that she liked me and was hoping I could help her mother regarding her drinking. She also reported that Raquel had gotten into a big argument with another female student who was harassing her about being a "Ho." Ms. Robson was aware that this type of name-calling really got to Raquel. Raquel had shared with her that she was committed to trying to change her reputation at school for being flirtatious and provocative with the boys. I shared with Ms. Robson that I was feeling quite optimistic about being able to help Raquel conquer her self-destructive habits.

The Second Family Session

Not only did the family show up late for the session but Stuart had come with Sylvia and Raquel. Apparently, Sylvia got a DUI (Driving Under the Influence) violation, lost her driver's license for 9 months, and was ordered by the judge to do 72 hours of DUI counseling. Therefore, Stuart had to drive them to our session. When asked to join us in the family session, Stuart declined and wished to stay in the lobby finishing up some work. Sylvia and Raquel did not look very happy. The atmosphere in my office felt heavy, like dark grey clouds hovering over our heads. I commented on the climate in the room and Raquel voiced that she was very upset with her mother. Sylvia's temper flared and she countered with, "What about the bag of marijuana I found in your bedroom closet?! You don't think I am upset about that?" Raquel responded with, "That had been in there for a long time and besides it's not mine... I was holding it for a friend." Sylvia came back with, "Don't you realize, it is illegal, and Stuart and I could get into trouble with the police for just having it in the house!" Raquel responded with, "Talk about illegal, what about you getting busted for drinking and driving!" Since this interaction was spiraling out of control, I asked Raquel to step out so I could meet with her mother alone.

Sylvia shared with me that she had had only three glasses of wine and really felt like she should not have been given a DUI by the police officer. She was planning to get Stuart's lawyer involved to challenge the charge. Sylvia also was upset about having to see a psychologist for 72 hours who would just be educating her about alcoholism being a disease, which she felt she already knew from her family of origin and extended family experience. Apparently, she had already had "one boring session" with the psychologist. At this point, I was really curious to hear Stuart's views on this situation. Sylvia invited Stuart to join us. It turned out that Stuart also supported Sylvia's position about wrongly being arrested and charged. He was going to see if he could get his lawyer to challenge the DUI charge and get her out of the DUI counseling as well. While listening to Stuart, I was saying to myself that "This is enabling at its best!" Finally, we get some legal leverage to aid Sylvia in addressing what may be a drinking problem, particularly with her being genetically predisposed to becoming alcohol dependent and Stuart is colluding with and protecting Sylvia from taking responsibility for this difficulty. They also both felt that "Raquel was really the problem" and that I should see her individually. They were clearly a united front couple. Although it would have been nice to partner up with the DUI counselor and regularly collaborate, I felt that because Sylvia was so defensive about her drinking and upset about getting the DUI that she would have balked at my idea to have her sign a consent form, so I did not pursue this.

Next, Sylvia shared with me that not only did she find a bag of marijuana in Raquel's bedroom closet but the day after she had gotten the DUI, she and her daughter got into a big argument and Raquel ran away from home for two days. Sylvia was panic-stricken and had called the police who eventually found Raquel with some of her friends at a party that had been raided where drugs and alcohol were found. After she was brought to their home by the police, another argument erupted which resulted in Raquel's inflicting a big and deep cut into her left forearm. Stuart rushed her to the local emergency room and she had to have stitches because the bleeding would not stop. I provided empathy and support and pointed out how volatile the situation was right now for her, Stuart, and Raquel. I agreed with Sylvia and Stuart that I should see Raquel and her separately for a little while until some of the tension and conflict subsides.

Before inviting Raquel in, I explored with Sylvia if she was able to make headway with her goal of reducing her nagging behavior. Sylvia pointed out to me that she had really tried hard to avoid nagging over the week and felt that she had achieved her goal of reaching a 3 on the scale. In fact, Sylvia said that they were getting along really well and they even went shopping and had dinner together. I took the time to elicit from Sylvia all of the details about the positive interactions and experiences she was having with Raquel earlier in the week. Temporarily, Sylvia remained positive and complimentary of Raquel's efforts to behave better. Sylvia reported that Raquel had shared with her that she had gotten an 'A' on a Math test, which was one of her weakest subjects. She was really pleased by this. In addition to not nagging, Sylvia tried real hard to be positive and more playful with Raquel. However, this more upbeat conversation came to an abrupt halt and Sylvia moved into sharing with me how everything unraveled with their relationship Thursday night when she returned home from the police station and they had their big argument. After Raquel had run away that night, Sylvia had gone through her bedroom and had found the bag of marijuana in her closet. This had made both her and Stuart quite upset.

With the limited remaining session time, I met alone with Raquel. Raquel had been crying in the waiting room while I was meeting with her mother and Stuart. I explored with her what was behind her tears. She started to cry again while telling me how hard she had been "trying to turn things around" earlier in the week and how she had "totally lost it" after finding out about her mother's DUI situation and the "big argument" they had Thursday night. She went on to add, "I felt so angry with my mom, how she does not care how I feel about her drinking… she could have been killed driving or killed someone on the streets. I said to myself, 'Fuck it and fuck her!'" To help normalize for Raquel her relapsing situation, I shared with her how habits strike when we reach this state of anger and frustration, and feel like surrendering.. Raquel agreed. She decided to get highly "ripped on weed by bonging" at a close friend's house the first night she had run away. According to Raquel, her friend Carmen's mother greatly disliked Sylvia because of past negative interactions they had had and did not call her to let her know that she was safe and at their house. On the second night at her friend's party, not only did she smoke a lot of weed but she did shots of vodka and made out with a guy from her high school. The cutting habit got the best of her shortly after being brought home by the police and following a lecture and big argument with her mother and Stuart. Apparently, Raquel had never cut herself so deeply before. We discussed how she was triple teamed by the habits that had infiltrated her mind and brainwashed her to relinquish her self-control to them. Raquel agreed and said, "I became my worst nightmare!" I pointed out to Raquel that habits are devilish and like to make their prey feel and act like their worst nightmare. They also like to make their victims feel guilty and ashamed, which can lead to more cutting, drugging, and sexually risky behavior. I shared with her that when under the habits' spell you become part of a vicious, self-perpetuating cycle.

Before moving on to coming up collaboratively with a new and tighter plan of action for staying on track, I revisited with Raquel the high points and sparkling moments of her earlier in the week positive roll she was on at standing up to the habits. According to Raquel, on Scale A, she contended that she shot up to a 9 by not entertaining once any thoughts or urges to cut herself. When asked about how she made this happen, she played in her mind her self-talk tape of "I am tired of feeling ashamed by my scars and turning off people." She also kept very busy during her free time and regularly practicing the use of urge-surfing and the Taking a Trip to Popcorn Land mindfulness meditation. On Scale B, Raquel felt she had made it up to a 7 because twice she said, "No!" to friends who wanted to "party with weed" after school. On Scale C, Raquel had felt that she had made it up to a 9 after turning down a close friend who had asked her to sneak out with her Tuesday night to go to a RAVE party. She also reminded herself that she was very upset and worried about having contracted the HPV virus and tired of being called a "Ho" at school and how she really wants to achieve a dramatic reputation change at school. I made a big deal about and amplified and consolidated all of Raquel's great work earlier in the week, which had not been erased by her slips on Thursday and Friday nights. I also underscored that not only did Raquel successfully take charge of the habits earlier in the week but that the slips that did occur go with the territory of change and they are a sign she is making good headway. Raquel smiled and looked relieved. Although the slips had made Raquel feel that she had gotten knocked down by the habits a few notches downward on each of the scales, she did not feel she fell below a 5 on any of them. I thought this was a great indication that she had not lost all of her hope and self-confidence about being able to conquer the habits.

One adjustment we made as far as relapse prevention work goes was for Raquel to start using the *My Positive Trigger Log* so she could keep track of what she and concerned others did that triggered positive emotion for her and warded off habit strikes. Raquel also was asked to identify high-risk, worst-case scenario situations where the habits were most likely to strike and three constructive steps she could take to stay on track and prevent temporary derailments from occurring with each of the scenarios. She did a nice job with this exercise. Raquel was going to continue to use urge-surfing and the Taking a Trip to Popcorn Land meditation to help her to stay on track as well. In an effort to provide additional support for her, I offered the idea of bringing in two former youth alumni to the next session who used to have similar difficulties as her to share their wisdom and expertise about how they conquered their habits and have stayed quit for over two years. Raquel thought this was an "awesome idea" since most of her friends did drugs and some of them cut themselves as well. I shared with her that I need to get written consent from her mother and my alumni's parents to do this. Since most of her friends used drugs and/or self-harmed, I also wanted to find out if there were any weak link potential resource people from her social network that could be involved for added support. Her only friends at school who she had not socialized with and who did not use drugs or self-harm were Stella and Carol. I encouraged Raquel to work on strengthening her relationships with Stella and Carol and ask them if she would like to hang out or do something fun together. Raquel thought this was a good idea in that she had to build some new friendships if there was any hope for her to conquer her habits.

Finally, I let Raquel know that we were going to structure our sessions so that I saw her separately from her parents. Raquel thought this could be a good idea as well. I shared with Raquel a great quote from the Rock singer Janis Joplin, "Don't compromise yourself, you're all that you got." Raquel liked the quote and had once heard Janis Joplin in the past and thought that she had a "cool voice." I pointed out to Raquel that neither she nor I could change the mother's drinking situation and that it was most important that she take care of herself, and that was all she had control of.

After reconvening Sylvia and Stuart, I reiterated for everyone that although it was a rough week that slips go with the territory of change and they all were able to see through the muck that some positive things did occur earlier in the week. I underscored those important steps that both Sylvia and Raquel had made. We mutually agreed that I would see Raquel and the parents separately for a while. Sylvia and Raquel signed off on my significant other consent form so I could bring in the two former youth alumni who were now upstanding citizens in their lives and habit-free. Both Sylvia and Stuart thought this could be a helpful idea. Raquel was excited to meet the alumni. I wished Sylvia good luck with the lawyer and her court situation. I also asked her to pull out her imaginary magnifying glass over the next week and carefully look daily for any encouraging steps she observed Raquel taking with her, Stuart, or individually. Everyone left in better spirits and more hopeful about their situation.

Surprise Telephone Call from Raquel's Father, Peter

A few days after our tough family session, I received a call from Peter to see if we could do a family session with just him and Raquel. Before agreeing to do this, I asked if I could check it out with Sylvia and Raquel. He had been contacted twice by Sylvia after Raquel had both run away and when she was taken to the emergency room for stitches after cutting deep into her arm. Peter shared with me that he was glad that I was addressing Raquel's cutting and marijuana use and Sylvia's drinking. He further added that he believed that Sylvia had a drinking problem and how when they were married they drank and did a lot of drugs together. Peter was very pleased to learn that I was a certified addiction counselor and was going to help Raquel not become an "addict" and an "alcoholic" like him. He disclosed to me that he had been "in drug rehab" and attends both Narcotics Anonymous (NA) and Alcoholics Anonymous (AA) meetings.

After hanging up with Peter, I called Sylvia and Raquel to see if it would be okay to do a family session with Peter. Both Sylvia and Raquel were okay with it. I called Peter back to set up an appointment for two weeks down the road.

Brief Telephone Conversation with Ms. Robson

I wanted to alert Ms. Robson about Raquel and her mother's rough week. Ms. Robson was well aware of the situation because she had spoken to Sylvia two times because Raquel had not showed up at school on Thursday and Friday. She was also concerned about "Raquel's severe decline." Apparently, earlier in the week, Raquel had been in "great spirits" and "did not have any squabbles with any peers." I pointed out that our last session finished on a positive note and that I had scheduled a family session with Peter and Raquel. Ms. Robson was glad to hear that. She shared with me that she will continue to provide individual and group sessions with Raquel for added support.

The Third Family Session

Present at the third family session was Sylvia, Stuart, Raquel, Paula, and Rod. The family was introduced to Paula and Rod who were the two alumni I had invited to the session to provide added support for Raquel. Both Paula and Rod briefly shared their stories of courage and how they conquered their habits. Paula shared with the family that she used to cut herself daily, a few times a day, for three years. Along with that, she had gotten pregnant after having sex with an older guy at a RAVE party and her parents made her get an abortion. She also used to smoke a lot of marijuana over a four year period. When asked by Sylvia how she had conquered these serious habits, Paula pointed out that one of her best friends was raped and killed after attending a RAVE party and another friend who had been cutting herself accidentally severed a vein while intoxicated on alcohol and marijuana and bled to death before the paramedics had arrived to her home. At this point, Paula drummed up the courage to say, "Enough is enough!" After that day, she completely made a lifestyle overhaul by abandoning her drug-using and cutting friends, began making new friends, got involved with yoga and mindfulness meditation, and started taking school much more seriously. Paula had been accepted into her first choice college in the fall. All family members voiced how impressed they were by Paula's amazing turnaround.

Rod jokingly said to the family that Paula's story was tough to beat. Rod shared that he had been cutting and heavily abusing alcohol and marijuana since age 14 when he was trying to "come out" to his parents about being gay. His parents were staunch Catholics and kicked him out of the house. For close to a year, Rod lived out on the streets. Finally, his parents let him come back home. Upon returning home, he and his father got into a big argument about changing his sexual orientation and he died from a sudden heart attack. Feeling guilty for his father's death, Rod tried to take his life by slicing his wrists. After this family crisis, he and his mother grew closer together and Rod had to go back into the closet about being gay in order not to lose his mother's love again. Rod was forced to live a double life, which consisted of being underground on the weekends with his other gay and lesbian friends and during the week "acting straight." Although he was now 18 and completely stopped cutting, drinking, and smoking weed, he reported still feeling the need to "act straight" around his mother because he did not want to run the risk of losing her love again. Thanks to Paula turning him on to yoga and mindfulness meditation he has found more inner peace and was much happier about his life. Rod shared with us that he was going to be attending a major university in the fall. Similar to the reaction the family had towards Paula, they were in awe and emotionally captured by Rod's story of courage. In fact, Sylvia had shed some tears and empathized with Rod's dilemma with his mother. She also commented, "Now I understand why Raquel worries so much about me." Raquel chimed in, "I don't want to lose you too." I encouraged them to hug one another.

At this point in the session, I asked to meet alone with Raquel, Paula, and Rod. In addition to yoga and mindfulness meditation, I invited Paula and Rod to share what else they were doing to stay quit. Paula started taking art classes to further improve her painting skills and going for long bicycle rides with her new non-drug-using friends. Rod was regularly attending a Young Person's NA group and a confidential support group for gay and lesbian youth at a local social service agency. He also got back into playing guitar again. They both felt that the recipe for staying quit was filling up one's free time with as many healthy and constructive activities as possible. When asked about having any slips, since they had made a commitment to change, both Paula and Rod reported having had a few slips. However, they were able to quickly get back on track because they knew who to call that would support them and to meditate immediately to help center themselves and quiet their minds. Raquel identified her non-drug-abusing and non-self-harming friends Stella and Carol that she could call for support in a crisis. Both Paula and Rod offered themselves to serve as supportive sponsors for Raquel if she ever was feeling vulnerable or in a high-risk situation. Prior to wrapping up our time together, both Paula and Rod offered to take Raquel to the mindfulness meditation center and yoga studio that they used. I thought this was a great idea and planned to bring this terrific opportunity idea to Sylvia and Stuart. Raquel thought this was an "awesome idea!" She also let me know that she had had a great week rating herself at an 8–9 on all the habit scales and was getting along much better with her mother.

Before meeting with Sylvia and Stuart, I asked Raquel if there was anything else she was concerned about or wanted to ask Paula and Rod about. Raquel took a risk with them and brought up her worries about her mother's drinking problem and being so reactive to it. Paula shared that her father was a recovering alcoholic and how she and her mother used to plead with him about getting help for his drinking and it never worked. In fact, for Paula it only made her feel more out of control and want to go smoke weed and cut herself. Finally, she and her mother had learned through attending an Al-Anon meeting the principle of "detaching with love." Once she and her mother "stepped back and stopped enabling" they started coping better and eventually her father got help for his drinking. Raquel found the "detaching with love" idea helpful and planned to experiment with it over the next week.

I met alone with Sylvia and Stuart. They both thanked me for bringing in Paula and Rod and felt that they could be a big help to Raquel. Sylvia was in a much better mood. When asked what further progress Raquel had made, she said that they had had two very positive conversations over coffee and she observed several times Raquel working hard on her homework. Raquel also took another big and courageous step with her mother. She gave her all of her drug paraphernalia, an old bag of marijuana that had been stashed away in her bedroom and together they flushed it down the toilet. Raquel gave her mother some razor blades she had hidden in her bedroom which she had been using for cutting herself. She also took a risk with her and shared with her that she used to go to RAVE parties, be very sexually active, and had contracted the HPV virus because she was not practicing safe sex. Although Sylvia was troubled by this information, she offered to take her to the pediatrician's office to further evaluate the HPV virus situation. Raquel told her mother about the free youth clinic she had been going to that had a physician and a nurse practitioner who were regularly monitoring the situation. Sylvia was glad to hear that Raquel was being responsible with this situation and requested that she keep her posted on the status of her condition. Raquel agreed to do this.

I asked Sylvia what specifically she was doing differently with Raquel that promoted all of these big responsible steps. All week Sylvia had refrained from nagging and being critical of Raquel. On the nagging scale, she felt that she had shot up to an 8. Another bright spot over the week was Stuart and Raquel going out for pizza one night. According to Stuart, they had a nice meal together and he felt since this evening they had been talking more. I amplified and consolidated all of the parents' reported gains.

On a negative note, Sylvia shared with me that Peter had gotten into legal hot water with some inside trading deal and will more than likely have to do jail time. Sylvia had not told Raquel about this situation. However, Peter had told Sylvia that he would have to cancel our scheduled family session. As soon as Peter knows more about his situation, he had planned to meet with Raquel and tell her about it. Sylvia also suspected that Peter was using cocaine again because he was having financial difficulties and behind on his child support payments. She also shared with me that although she could not legally get out of the DUI situation that the counseling sessions were not that bad and she had been reflecting more lately on how alcoholism had wreaked havoc in her family of origin, extended family, marriage to Peter, and relationship with Raquel.

I took a brief intersession break and then reconvened the family. Just as I was about to talk, Sylvia thanked Paula and Rod for coming and not only hoped that they would join us in future sessions but also help Raquel stay on track between sessions. Raquel chimed in and shared that they had invited her to join them at both the yoga studio and at their mindfulness meditation center. Both Sylvia and Stuart thought this was a great idea and gave Raquel the okay to go with them. I underscored all of the positive changes that had occurred after the previous tough week and shared how this was an example of their resilience and ability to bounce back quickly as a family team.

Peter Calls to Cancel our Family Session

Two days later, I received a call from Peter that he had been charged for illegal inside trading with a company and extortion and was looking at 5–10 years of jail time, according to his attorney. On top of this, he shared that Sylvia was going after him legally for getting behind on his child support payments as well. Peter was planning to call Raquel and let her know about his situation. He also shared with me that he had gotten off the wagon with his cocaine use and had had a prolonged relapsing situation occur. Although Peter had gotten back on track after this difficult relapsing episode, he felt like his "whole world was caving in." I asked him if he was at risk for trying to take his life and he assured me that he was depressed but was not planning to try to take his life. I also explored with Peter if he had contacted his NA and AA sponsors. According to Peter, his NA sponsor was on his way over to his apartment as we spoke. I wished him good luck with everything and shared with him that I was totally committed to helping Raquel turn her life around. He thanked me for being there for Raquel.

The Fourth Family Session

Present at the fourth family session were Stuart, Sylvia, Raquel, Paula, and Rod. After I asked what further progress they had made, Sylvia had a glowing report for Raquel. She had noticed that Raquel consistently did her homework without any reminders, they did not have one argument, and she went out with Stuart twice and they both had a good time. Stuart chimed in that he really enjoyed having dinner with Raquel and getting to know her better as a person. Raquel felt the same way and mentioned that she had not given Stuart "a fair shake in the past." Raquel reported that she really loved going to do yoga and meditation with Paula and Rod. Rod also took her to an NA meeting, which Raquel felt was enlightening and helpful. Raquel also shared that she really enjoyed going a recent Friday night outing to dinner and a movie with Paula and Rod. In fact, both Paula and Rod shared with Sylvia that they thought Sylvia had a wonderful daughter and was fun to hang out with. Sylvia agreed. Raquel was sporting a big smile on her face and looking at her mother said, "See, I'm not so bad." Both Sylvia and Stuart responded with, "We know that." Raquel shared with the group that she was hovering around a 10 on all of her habit scales. In addition to all of the positive observations and behaviors reported, Raquel was staying away from certain people and places, regularly practicing urge-surfing and meditation, and was now taking a hip-hop dance class to stay on track. She also got together three times with Stella and they had a lot of fun together. I learned that Stella had turned Raquel on to "ceramic making," which has become a new hobby for her to engage in after school or on the weekends.

The only dip in the road and shaky situation for Raquel was learning from her father about his having to go to jail for a long time. However, she not only had a meaningful and supportive conversation with her mother about the situation but called both Paula and Rod for added support, which really helped stave off a potential relapse. Everyone acknowledged how proud they were of Raquel and how well she had handled the bad news. Raquel also thanked Stuart again for being very understanding and supportive with helping her constructively manage this emotionally upsetting situation. Sylvia shared that "Stuart had really stepped up quite a bit with Raquel in a fatherly way when it was needed most."

Sylvia also shared that she was making a commitment to try and abstain from alcohol use while in DUI counseling and because she knew her drinking was upsetting to Raquel. Raquel shared with her mother that she greatly appreciated her willingness to do this. In fact, Stuart was helping out with this situation by keeping alcohol out of the home and not drinking himself.

I briefly met alone with Raquel, Paula, and Rod. Both Paula and Rod congratulated her for having an excellent week. I shared with Raquel that she was really flexing her muscles over the past week showing the habits that she was a real tough force to reckon with and may have driven them out of town! Everyone laughed and Rod chimed in with, "I wouldn't want to mess with you, if I were a habit!" We discussed how successfully she was taking all of the time and energy she used to use to fuel the habits and enable them to dominate her life to taking charge of her life by channeling this time and energy into engaging in healthy and constructive activities and into building a solid support system for herself. She reported that "detaching with love" had been helping her to not allow worries about her mother starting to drink again get the best of her. Raquel reported feeling much more self-confident and excited about the future. Like Paula and Rod, she wanted to go to college and study journalism.

I had a sudden flash of an idea that I wanted to present to Raquel that I thought could bring her and her mother closer together and help the latter stay on track with protecting her sobriety. I asked if Raquel could see herself setting side some daily time for one week to teach her mother how to do urge-surfing and mindfulness meditation. Raquel thought this was great idea. I invited Sylvia in to join us and Raquel took charge of presenting the idea of mentoring her mother in a daily ritual for one week. Sylvia thought it would be great to learn other ways for maintaining her sobriety. They decided to have the training sessions after school before dinner. I laid down the ground rules regarding Sylvia's need to protect the training session time and being a respectful student while Raquel taught her the mechanics of doing urge-surfing and mindfulness meditation.

Next, I reconvened Stuart, Sylvia, Raquel, Paula, and Rod after a brief intersession break. I used this time to amplify and consolidate all of their gains. As a vote of confidence to the family, I offered them the option of coming back in either three or four weeks. The family elected to come back in three weeks. I encouraged them to keep doing more of what works and for Sylvia and Raquel to try and break their scales with further great achievements individually and in their relationships.

The Fifth Family Session

Present in our fifth family session were Stuart, Sylvia, Raquel, and Stella. Paula and Rod had commitments and could not attend. Raquel not only introduced me to Stella but had brought in two beautiful ceramic bowls she had made with her. The parents shared that they really liked Stella and was glad that Raquel was friends with her. Other positive family changes that occurred was both Sylvia and Stuart spending more quality time with Raquel, having nice conversations, shopping, and going on long bicycle rides. Sylvia shared that Raquel was an excellent teacher and she had found both the urge-surfing and mindfulness meditations to be very helpful for protecting her sobriety and staying on track. Raquel smiled and thanked her mom for the compliment. Raquel was spending a lot of time hanging out with Stella and Carol. She also was attending weekly her hip-hop class and Paula and Rod's yoga class and their meditation center.

Sylvia announced with the help of her DUI counselor she had gone for six weeks without one sip of alcohol. Stuart vouched for Sylvia because he had been keeping close tabs on her. Sylvia had steered clear from certain restaurants and friends where a lot of drinking would occur. She also purchased a family membership at a health club that offered yoga classes and gave the classes a try. Sylvia reported liking yoga a lot. Her hope was that Raquel would go to the classes with her. Raquel shared that she planned to start going to the health club and take classes with her the next week. Since she was getting quite good with the basic yogic poses, I encouraged Raquel to serve as a mentor again for her mother and daily work with her to master the basic yogic poses. Both Raquel and Sylvia liked this idea.

After a brief intersession break, I amplified and consolidated all of the family members' gains. I thanked Stella for coming and being a good friend to Raquel. Since they appeared to do so well while on vacation from counseling, I asked the family when they would like to come back in five or six weeks. The family chose six weeks. I encouraged them to keep doing more of what works and keep track of any new steps they will take to further improve their family life.

Brief Telephone Conversation with Ms. Robson

I contacted Ms. Robson to update her on Raquel and her family's tremendous progress. Ms. Robson was quick to tell me that Raquel had made a 360-degree turnaround emotionally, behaviorally, and academically. Because of Raquel's changes she no longer is experiencing peer harassment and she was doing superior work in all of her classes. We both discussed how important the mother's changes with the drinking and more positive interactions had been for Raquel. I added that her bonding with Stuart and all of the support she was getting from positive peers also played a part in Raquel's transformation. I shared with Ms. Robson that unless there were any concerns reported to me by Raquel or the family I will probably terminate with them after our next visit. Ms. Robson had no problem with that and planned to offer continued support for Raquel at school if she needed it.

The Sixth and Final Family Session

For our sixth and final session only Sylvia, Stuart, and Raquel attended. When asked what further progress they had made, Sylvia pointed out that it was a great vacation break from counseling. Raquel was pulling in excellent grades in all of her classes, she was staying quit from drug use, there were no cutting episodes, and no arguments. Raquel and Stuart were growing much closer and he was teaching her how to play tennis. She continued to make good use of her solid support team of Paula, Rod, Stella, and Carol. On three occasions, they all went out for dinner and hung out together. One night, Sylvia hosted a BBQ party as a way to thank Paula, Rod, Stella, and Carol for being such a big support for Raquel and contributing to her success.

During the break period, Sylvia, Stuart, and Raquel went on a family road trip to visit colleges on the east coast that she was interested in. They also built into the road trip a fun vacation at Cape Cod. Sylvia did not have one slip with alcohol use and was going strong. Raquel chimed in that she was very proud of her mother. Stuart pointed out how they had learned to cook and eat gourmet dinners without any alcohol use.

When asked what they would have to do that would make their situation go backwards for them at this time, not one family member could fathom this happening because they felt so confident about their continued progress. I encouraged Raquel to continue to make maximum use of her solid support team of Paula, Rod, Stella, and Carol. After complimenting all the family members on their great work, we mutually agreed to terminate.

Telephone Follow-Up

I contacted Sylvia and Raquel at 6 and 12 months. At 6 months, I had learned that Raquel had gotten into one of the colleges she wanted to go to. Raquel had not had one cutting or drug use episode. She also had been dating a boy from another high school who was a star football player. Sylvia was working on getting her driver's license back and was finishing up her DUI counseling, which she felt had helped her to remain abstinent from alcohol. Sylvia reported that her relationship with Raquel was much stronger. Stuart and Raquel's relationship bond was much stronger as well.

At 12 months, I could only reach Sylvia. Raquel was away at college and doing very well there. According to Sylvia, there were no reports of cutting or drug use. Raquel's boyfriend attended the same college. Sylvia really liked Raquel's boyfriend and felt that they were very compatible as a couple, especially because he was "a jock" and totally opposed to drug use. Sylvia was delighted to share with me that she had continued to remain abstinent from alcohol use and became a real "yoga junky."

Reflections on "I Became My Worst Nightmare!" Taking Back Control "With a Little Help From my Friends" Case

Mark: The therapy with Raquel and her family is an excellent example of a complex case, where we have three people presenting with serious habit difficulties, all in a different stage of readiness to change. I would like to highlight your productive use of *therapeutic curiosity*. With Raquel you gently explored why getting all of the attention with her sexual behaviors was so significant to her and how it was benefiting her. With Sylvia, you started by wondering aloud with both her and Raquel what the barriers were in their relationship. Your non-judgmental stance allowed you to engage both women in these therapeutic conversations and to carefully test the limits of their readiness for change. I wonder if you could have used more of this strategy in the first session, inviting Raquel to expand more on how her mother's alcohol use was a problem for her, or in a more positive way inquiring during the miracle conversation what other ways Sylvia's reducing her alcohol usage could help and benefit Raquel. Also, when Sylvia and Stuart presented in the second session denying any alcohol problem, you may have asked something along the lines of why alcohol use may have been connected to such negative things as her relatives' deaths from alcohol-related liver illnesses, her DUI arrest, or her daughter's marijuana use.

Matthew: I think the reason why I avoided being too pushy with having Sylvia consider reducing her alcohol use too soon was that I was fearful I would chase her out the door! I was also up against a united front couple here that was quite adamant about Raquel being the problem and there was a lot of psychological reactance from Sylvia when her drinking was discussed. My experience in the past of working with other families where one or both parents had substance abuse difficulties is that after striving to build alliances with them, the first step is to tap their competencies and past successes as parents to help resolve their kids' presenting problems. If this straightforward approach does not work and the parents' substance abuse impairment is getting in the way of implementing change strategies with their kids, then I will go indirect and make strategic use of confusion in the spirit of TV detective *Columbo*. I might introduce a line of questioning like, "This might sound like an off-the-wall idea, but I wonder if your daughter thinks that she has the green light to party with weed when she observes the two of you downing a few cocktails daily in the evenings. Who knows, she may not be thinking like that but I wonder what you guys think?" This may open the door for parents to look at their substance abuse and entertain the idea that it may be a barrier for their kids' changing. However, we have to be mindful of the fact that if you cross the bridge too prematurely and begin even gently and respectfully addressing the parents' substance abuse issues, you run the risk of them getting defensive, dropping out or completely pulling the plug on family therapy.

Mark: In my view, another important issue is how you worked with the interactions of the self-destructive habits of mother and daughter. In the first session you asked Sylvia if she would be willing to reduce her use of wine to help Raquel reduce her marijuana use; later, you used positive steps that were taken by Raquel to reinforce and promote Sylvia's

	changes and vice versa. At the same time, you tried to avoid that a slip by one of them did induce a setback in the other. I like to describe this as "cheating with circularity"; we want the improvements of one person to have a positive effect on the other; but we want the setback by one to not negatively influence the other.
Matthew:	Yes, I took a risk attempting to negotiate a *something for something* contract with a parent who clearly was in the precontemplation stage of readiness for change. This is more likely to foster cooperation with a parent in the preparation stage, since he or she is knocking on the door to taking action. I have even had some parents in the past who were in the contemplation stage willing to enter into this contract with their sons or daughters. On the up side of things with Sylvia, my therapeutic move did provide important assessment information regarding her high psychological reactance level and being in the precontemplation stage with her drinking.
Mark:	In the third and fourth sessions, you explained to Raquel that neither she nor you could change the mother's drinking situation and that it was most important that she take care of herself, as that was all she had control of. This paved the way for Raquel's later embracing the "detaching with love" principle and is a wonderful example of how we can make use of circularity to induce changes in one person by helping the other one to change her part in the interaction. Working with the parents and couple partners of persons with self-destructive habits, I often find that the only real change in their ineffective attempted solutions is to shift gears completely and give a clear message that they have given up on their offspring, and relinquish any attempts to force her or him to change. However, I also find that this is not easy to do for most concerned others and furthermore, that is usually not enough to *pretend* to do it, but they really have to change themselves emotionally in order to be able to detach from the habit-dependent person. How do you help clients do that in these situations?
Matthew:	Many of these couple partners, parents, and concerned relatives truly believe if they persist harder with their enabling attempted solutions that eventually they will succeed at stabilizing the identified clients' self-destructive habits. We need to approach them with loving kindness and compassion and empathize with their dilemmas. In keeping things simple, we can attempt to get partners and parents to try out an Al-Anon meeting and learn the principle of detaching with love. We also could try having them list the advantages and disadvantages of relentlessly persisting with their enabling behaviors. If this does not help create any new possibilities, we can use the pattern interruption strategy of exaggerating the problem-maintaining interaction pattern by having the couple partner or parents increase its frequency and duration. Another possibility is to externalize the self-destructive habit and how it brainwashes the partner or parents to keep engaging in unproductive interactions in order to keep the problem life support system intact. The

next step would be to organize the couple partner and parents to join forces with the identified client against it so together they can thwart it and dismantle its life support system.

Mark: Your invitation to Raquel to mentor her mother on mindfulness meditation techniques obviously brought them closer together and empowered both of them in their efforts to stay quit from their self-destructive habits. I use the "mentoring your parent" experiment a lot in my clinical work, but when I talk with my structural family therapy-oriented colleagues they object to this intervention because they think it gives the adolescent too much power. What would your response be to professionals like this that voice this concern?

Matthew: For structural therapists, I would argue that this is one way to challenge and disrupt the disengagement family pattern that may be fueling the adolescent's self-destructive behaviors. Minuchin (1986) contends that family therapists need to engage in three important operations: challenge the symptom-bearer, challenge the family structure, and challenge the family belief system. This family connection-building ritual accomplishes all three. The adolescent has an opportunity to shine and show the parents how competent he or she is and can be non-problematic; it builds in more closeness and infuses positive emotions into the parent–teen relationship; and last, the parents' outmoded belief system is altered by having this positive experience with their son or daughter.

Mark: One other intervention that you employed that made a big difference with this case was the use of two of your former clients. I sometimes invite clients with whom I am working who are in the advanced stages of the change process to join me as guest consultants to help inspire stuck clients who were grappling with similar difficulties. However, I am more reluctant to invite alumni. I feel that coming back into a therapeutic setting again, even to help someone else out, could be a way to bring "problems" back into their lives again. On the other hand, it is clear that there are clients who really take pride in helping others. So, how do you determine what alumni to invite?

Matthew: I try to match up alumni who have experienced and conquered similar self-destructive habits of the client. These are young people that have confidently stayed quit from and continue to do so for at least a year and are functioning well in all areas in their lives. I would not even consider alumni who have had some serious prolonged relapsing situations post-treatment. I also think about alumni's communication styles and key strengths as well when matching them up with clients. Using alumni in couple or family therapy is a great therapeutic option when all of the identified client's friends have serious self-destructive habit problems as well. It is a therapeutic option that many clients are eager to try out and, in some cases, has led to life-long friendships growing out of their experiences working together. In Raquel's case, Paula and Rod succeeded at establishing a meaningful and strong connection with her and were instrumental in paving the way for her treatment success.

When a Family Tsunami Strikes: A Budding Crisis that had Masqueraded as Family Progress

Gino, 19, was referred to me (MS) by Dr. Spinelli who had been working with his father Giuseppe for the past two years for depression, alcohol abuse, and his gambling and sex addictions. Giuseppe was born in Sicily and immigrated to the United States with his family when he was 10. Dr. Spinelli shared with me that he felt like he was the male counterpart of Dr. Jennifer Melfi on the popular TV show *The Sopranos* and that Giuseppe was like Tony Soprano, in that he was rugged, intimidating-looking, and fit the mobster mold. According to Dr. Spinelli, Giuseppe and his older brother took over ownership of his father's restaurants and boutique hotels. His marriage to Lola had been on the rocks for close to 20 years because of her alcoholism problems, the lack of sexual intimacy in their relationship, his cyber-sex and involvement with prostitutes, and his gambling problem. The couple had numerous unsuccessful marital therapy experiences and had been in family therapy together to address both Gino's and his older brother Paolo's substance abuse difficulties. Paolo had been kicked out of the house when he was 18 and has little contact with the family. The oldest sibling Maria was a successful businesswoman, married, and lived out of state with her family. She had emotionally cut herself off from her parents since graduating from college. Maria limited her visits to her parents and Gino to holiday times.

Gino, since early adolescence, had been abusing alcohol, marijuana, and cocaine, and gambling. In spite of Gino's habit difficulties, he was able to graduate high school with B+/A− grade point average and had aspirations about going to college. He recently was psychiatrically hospitalized for a suicide attempt after a long stretch from not having access to cocaine and having a gambling debt of $10,000 hanging over his head. Dr. Spinelli was Gino's attending psychiatrist at the hospital. When asked about the family dynamics and the role they played in enabling Gino to continue to abuse drugs and to gamble, Dr. Spinelli described one reoccurring pattern that reinforces these difficulties. He described an "acceptance–rejection pattern of interaction between Giuseppe and Gino" in which the former expresses his strong desire for Gino to take over the family restaurant and hotel businesses in the future and then, when he gets into trouble or is irresponsible with drugs and gambling, Giuseppe calls him "a loser, gives him the silent treatment for days," and talks about having his nephew take over the family businesses instead. For Gino, hearing and experiencing this with his father "shatters him" and fuels his self-destructive habits. To further complicate matters, Gino cannot count on his mother to be emotionally available to support him due to her problems with depression and alcoholism. However, he did cherish the times when she was sober and they could talk. I also learned that Giuseppe sometimes "gives Gino money to buy drugs or pay off gambling debts." This pattern also served as part of the habit maintenance problem life support system as well.

Dr. Spinelli thought it would be a great idea for me to meet Gino in the hospital prior to our first family therapy session. Gino and I were able to establish good rapport. I also invited Dr. Spinelli to join our first family therapy session, and he agreed to attend.

The First Family Session

The same day Gino was discharged from the hospital we held our first family therapy session. Gino was much less agitated than the day I had first met him on the hospital unit with Dr. Spinelli. Giuseppe and Lola began arguing intensely as soon as they walked into my office. He was upset with Lola because she had been drinking before our session. I could smell the alcohol on Lola's breath. Lola was upset with her husband for spending the night out "with hookers." Gino tried to get his parents to stop yelling at one another and turned to me and said, "You see what I have to put up with!" After Gino had shared this, Giuseppe shared with Gino, "Yeah, you don't think all of your problems and counseling doesn't stress us out! When are you going to grow up!" Gino asked me if he could leave the room. Lola chimed in, "Don't leave honey… your father is more upset with me than you." Gino, in looking at his father said, "Maybe if you cared more about mom rather than going to Vegas all of the time and messing around with all of those women she would be happier." Giuseppe got out of his chair to hit Gino and Dr. Spinelli and I immediately jumped out of our chairs to prevent him from striking Gino in the face. Seeing how toxic and volatile it is working with this family group together, we decided to meet with them separately.

Out of respect for Giuseppe's being the head of the household, we began meeting alone with him first. Giuseppe apologized for losing his cool. We stressed the importance of establishing a no-violence contract in the household. Although Giuseppe had struck Gino in the past after he got into legal trouble with drug possession as a minor and having to help him pay off gambling debts, he contended that he had not laid a finger on Gino for years. We explored with Giuseppe what he has done instead of using physical means to discipline Gino. Giuseppe reported that sometimes he would go for long drives or walks when upset or hang out with his friends at the bar of one of their restaurants. We wanted to make sure that Giuseppe would commit to not hurting Gino or Lola no matter what they said or did. He agreed to work on his "hot temper" with both of us.

I explored with Giuseppe what his vision and best hopes were for Gino. Giuseppe shared with us that his older son Paolo was slated to take over the family businesses before Gino but because "his life took a terrible nosedive with drug use and gambling" and he was "caught stealing a grand [$1000]" from one of his restaurants, he had to kick him out of the house. According to Giuseppe, "now history was repeating itself" and he felt that Gino was "going down the same path as Paolo" and he too cannot be counted on to take over the family businesses. Giuseppe disclosed that this was "a big worry" of his and fueled his depression. He went on to share that he started working in his father's restaurants as a teenager and "learned the ropes through hard work and many personal sacrifices," such as giving up his "number one passion of boxing competitively." Giuseppe went on to add that his "biggest mistake was treating" his sons "like princes," by giving them whatever they wanted and "letting them slide from having to work on a regular basis at the restaurants" like he had to. I asked Giuseppe, "How did he know that Gino is not different from Paulo in wanting to pursue a more successful future for himself?" Giuseppe chimed in with, "But the path that he is on right now is in the opposite direction." Dr. Spinelli pointed out that with a lot of encouragement, structure, and a change of lifestyle he believed Gino was capable of being a successful adult. In sharing the psychological evaluation IQ test scores with us, Dr. Spinelli pointed out that Gino tested to be in the "superior range intellectually" and had "a long track record academically of being a B+/A student grade-wise." Giuseppe agreed that Gino was "very intelligent" and could have "a bright future." He shared with us that Gino probably "inherited his uncle's genes who had taught physics at a major university in the old country." We also learned that Gino served as the captain of his high school debate team and led them to several big victories in statewide and out-of-state competitions.

Using the future, I had Giuseppe close his eyes and imagine seeing in his mind Gino at 25 years of age coming over for Sunday dinner at their home now living on his own, and competently running the family company, and I asked him the following questions:

1. "What will you be talking about together?"
2. "What valuable words of wisdom will you be offering Gino about running the company?"
3. "How will you be supporting Gino in his leadership role and keep the company going strong?"
4. "What strengths and talents will you come to know about Gino as a successful manager?"
5. "What will it mean to you and how will it make a difference in your relationship with Gino to be proud of him?"

While listening to these questions, Giuseppe started to smile and his affect dramatically changed in a positive way. In responding to these questions, he became more hopeful about the future possibilities for Gino. I asked if it would be okay to bring Gino back in to hear Giuseppe's responses to my questions. Giuseppe agreed to try it out. Much to our surprise, Giuseppe began by apologizing to Gino for losing his temper with him. This appeared to surprise Gino as well in that his father would rarely apologize to him when angry with him. I explained to Gino the future scenario and shared the questions again. I asked Gino to give his father his undivided attention while listening to his responses to the questions. Giuseppe shared that he would be finding out how things were going for him in his management role and asking him if he had any questions about running the business. He also would ask him if he had a new woman in his life and how the relationship was going. In response to the second question, Giuseppe would share with Gino what had worked for him as a manager that brought the best out in his employees' performances and marketing strategies that paid off. I was curious to know what Giuseppe's secret recipe for success was in bringing out the best in his employees. He said that he would be "very supportive, complimentary, and try and accentuate their unique strengths." I made a mental note about how we could use this in Giuseppe's relationship with Gino.

With question number three, Giuseppe would let Gino know that he will always try to make himself available to him in a consultative support role if Gino was experiencing any management difficulties. In response to question number four, the strengths and talents Giuseppe will come to know with Gino was "his ability to inspire and motivate others to be all that they could possibly become." Gino was smiling when he heard this.

Finally, in response to the last question, Giuseppe shared that he used to be proud of Gino "leading his debate team to victory" and "pulling in those great grades." With "Gino's future success running our family business, I will be very proud of him and if my father were around, it would have brought him great joy to see his grandson shine and uphold the Calabrese family name in the restaurant business." Again, Gino was smiling and appeared to like the sound of this. I explored with Gino what his thoughts and reactions were to the positive things his father was saying about him and his bright future. Gino shared that he was blown away by what his father had said and that it made him feel happy to learn that his father believed in him. We discussed if Gino's future vision for himself paralleled his father's. Apparently, when Gino was much younger he worked some weekends in the restaurant and at times could see himself running the show in the future. He also was quite impressed with his father's great business sense and had looked up to him for all that he accomplished and for upholding the Calabrese family name with restaurants and hotels. According to Giuseppe, this was the first time he had heard this from his son.

We discussed the father's concerns with the path Gino had been on for some time with abusing substances and gambling and not being able to achieve his future vision for him. Gino shared that all of his dad's "putdowns," getting his "head chewed off," and being told he was "a loser" had greatly contributed to his negative view of himself and the use of substances to "get rid of bad thoughts and feelings" and "the rush feelings" he got from gambling, particularly when he would win.

As a helpful way to move this conversation from potentially digressing into a blame–counter-blame destructive interaction, I co-constructed the problem into "the terrible nosedive pattern of drug abuse and gambling," which had been wreaking havoc in the Calabrese family for some time. I shared with the family that this pattern had gotten the best of Paolo, Gino, and at times Giuseppe and Lola. Giuseppe mentioned that he had two nephews who were also being pushed around by the same pattern. To help raise the emotional bar in the room and get the two men fired up to putting a stop to this pattern's reign over them by allowing it to undermine the Calabrese legacy of the men keeping the family company name as one of the best in the business, I raised the dilemma with the two men of what they could do together to help *take out* or *knock off* (using mob terminology) the pattern for good. Gino shared that he could commit to working with his father at least five days a week learning the ropes of running both restaurants and hotels. I shared with Gino that keeping busy like that would help keep him out of trouble and that I thought it was a great idea. Giuseppe also thought it was a great idea. In addition, he also thought that maybe for the first few months while Gino was trying "to stay clean and sober and not gamble" he could "manage his money for him" so that he would "not be tempted to blow it on drugs or gambling." Out of concern for his mother, Gino encouraged his dad to treat his mother in a more respectful and loving way and that it may have a positive effect on her drinking problem. Giuseppe said he would think about this suggestion. I interjected that Lola was part of the family team and keeping her strong and confident was a necessity. I encouraged the men to strive to be a team, to keep the lines of communication open, and remind themselves that it is "the terrible nosedive pattern of drug abuse and gambling" that is the villain here, not one of them or Lola. I pointed out that these patterns are very powerful, do not die easily, and they tend to strike the most when there is a lot of negativity, pessimism, and blaming in families. I encouraged them both to keep track over the next week of the various things they will do as individuals and a team to stand up to the pattern and not let it get the best of them. Surprisingly, the two men left the room with their arms around one another and their heads up.

With the remaining session time, we met briefly with Lola. Lola inquired with us about "what kind of magic had we worked" with the two men. She told us "they were smiling" and seemed to be "getting along better." We briefed Lola on what was discussed with the two men and how "the terrible nosedive pattern of drug abuse and gambling" was the real culprit in their family story. Lola agreed and talked about how the pattern had gotten the best of her marriage, her abuse of alcohol and pills, Paolo, Gino, her older brother Luigi, and two of Giuseppe's nephews. She further added that this pattern probably was contributing to why Maria limited her contact with them as well. We explored with Lola what she thought she could do as a team member and in joining forces with Giuseppe and Gino to help conquer the oppressive pattern. Lola shared with us that she felt out of control with her drinking and occasionally would take tranquilizers to help her to sleep better some nights. Since Dr. Spinelli was also an addictions specialist, he shared the dangers of combining alcohol and tranquilizers with Lola. He also offered her the opportunity to have her detoxed so that she could be in better shape to handle the family crusade against the pattern that was destroying her family. Lola said that she would think about the detox idea and would try to stay out of the house more by socializing with friends and try get back into playing golf at their country club. She felt that engaging in these activities would help her to reduce her use of alcohol and not feel so depressed about her life. At this point we ran out of time and we had to wrap up with the whole family.

We complimented the family on their ability to bounce back after a rough start and do some great work as a family team in their efforts to take back control of their lives from "the nosedive pattern of drug abuse and gambling" and upholding the Calabrese family name. I underscored the importance of solid teamwork, backing one another up, and recognizing that hard work and keeping busy can be the recipe for success. However, I did caution them on taking the change process nice and slow and to not be discouraged if slips occur, which often go along with embarking as a family into new territory. I went on to say that change can be threatening and uncomfortable when family members have relied for a long time on their habits to cope and to make them feel better. Finally, I reiterated the family therapeutic experiment of them keeping track of the various steps they will take individually and as a family group to stand up to the drug abuse and gambling. I asked them to keep track of their useful self-talk and self-generated problem solving and coping strategies that seemed to work at blocking "the nosedive pattern" attacks and preventing habit slips.

The Second Family Session

Present at the second family session were Giuseppe, Lola, and Gino. Dr. Spinelli could not attend our family session because of a client emergency. The good news was that Lola came to our session clean and sober. Gino had ended up working six days at two of his father's restaurants. He also steered clear from his drug-using and gambling friends by staying home Friday and Saturday nights. Giuseppe was very complimentary of Gino's efforts to turn his life around. He even had kind words for Lola in her efforts to greatly reduce her alcohol consumption, get out of the house more, and playing golf with her friends. I asked them what else they had done to achieve victories over "the nosedive pattern of drug use and gambling." Apparently, Gino took a big step one day when he had intense craving to score some cocaine but instead sought his father out for support. Another positive step he took on another day when craving to use alcohol and drugs was to go back to the restaurant to work after he had already had completed his shift there. I shared with him that this should be his mantra, "keeping busy, keeps me out of trouble." I pointed out how that mantra had helped out one of my former alcoholic clients. I amplified and consolidated all of the family's gains. Next, I asked if I could meet alone with Gino.

I began by complimenting Gino on all of his great strides toward turning his life around. He shared with me that it was a really rough week, particularly dealing with craving to use and "turning down" running with his "crew" of partying friends. Gino did a nice job of identifying all of his triggers for using and wanting to gamble. I taught him both the sound and the Taking a Trip to Popcorn Land meditations and how to do urge-surfing as effective ways to quiet his mind and help him to constructively manage craving and prevent slips from happening. I also gave him the *positive trigger log* to fill out and use over the next week as well. For added support, I encouraged him to contact Cocaine Anonymous (CA) to see if there was a meeting he could attend in his community. Since most of his friends used drugs and gambled, I asked him if he had any weak link acquaintances from high school, at the restaurants, or through other friends who did not use or gamble. Gino identified a former debate team member named Eric who he had liked but they never hung out socially. Apparently, he had heard that Eric was a pre-law major at a local university. I encouraged Gino to contact him and expand his social network. Gino thought this was a good idea.

We revisited the family company situation and if this line of work was a true career path he wanted for himself. Gino was ambivalent about it in that he wanted to keep the family tradition of the son's taking over the business through the generations but he also had thought about going to college and eventually going to law school. I shared with him that a lot of schools offer evening and weekend part-time programs for working students. Gino said it would be difficult to juggle both but that it was a possibility. I asked him if he thought his father would support this. Gino felt that his father would support the idea of applying to local colleges but not to out-of-state schools. I encouraged him to explore with Eric what his college experience has been like.

Before bringing in Gino's mother, I asked him if he had any other worries or concerns that had not been talked about. Gino was worried that his parents were "going to divorce." According to Gino, for years they have been "arguing" and his father is always "cheating on" his mother. He also felt sorry for her and was worried about her "excessive drinking." I empathized with Gino's dilemma of being continuously exposed to his parents' arguing and his mother's excessive drinking. However, I cautioned him about the dangers of getting entangled in his parents' marital conflicts and trying to save his mother and how all of this stress could compromise his own sobriety. I encouraged him to use his new coping tools when stressed out or pushed around by the worrying thoughts. Finally, I shared with him that I would try to do all I could to help his parents with their marital issues and his mother's drinking problem.

I spent the last part of the session with Lola. I began by exploring with her what she had been doing to reduce her use of alcohol. Lola "spent a lot of time out of the home socializing with friends, started working out at the health club, and played golf one time." She also quit taking tranquilizers. Lola shared with me that she had thought about the detox idea but wanted to hold off for now to see if she can "maintain just cutting back." On the bright side of things with her marital relationship, Giuseppe and Lola "went out for dinner one night and had a romantic evening." I explored with her how they got this to happen and she said that by refraining from drinking and "being dressed to kill was a turn on for Giuseppe." The couple went a whole week without one big argument.

I asked Giuseppe to join us to explore with him what was working in his relationship with Lola. Giuseppe shared that Lola was "a real knockout" the night they went out and it was "a real romantic evening." He also complimented Lola on her efforts to greatly reduce her alcohol consumption and get out of the house more. I asked the couple if they wanted to contract to work on changing one particular difficulty in their relationship. They mutually agreed to work on changing their arguing problem. I asked them the following goal-setting question, "Let's say you leave my office today and once you have walked through my door heading out to your car something feels strange, your arguing problem has been completely zapped away. What will you notice that is happening instead when the two of you are communicating with one another that specifically will be helping you get along much better?" Giuseppe shared that Lola is no longer nagging or blaming him about something. He also shared that when that happens he will have "more loving feelings for Lola and want to spend more time with her." Lola shared that she will be his "number one woman, there would be no more hookers" or Giuseppe's "spending late evening hours visiting porn sites on the Internet." Instead, Lola shared that they would be "more sexually intimate with one another." She would "no longer feel lonely in the nights." I asked them to rate the arguing situation on a scale from 1 to 10, with 10 being a very little arguing and 1 all of the time one month prior to seeing me. They both rated the arguing situation at a 1. I then asked what would they have rated the arguing situation after last week and Lola said they were at a 5 and Giuseppe said a 6. When asked what specifically they were doing that led to the 50% and 60% improvement on their respective scales, they both shared that there was no blaming, more affection giving, no nagging or complaining, and the atmosphere was more upbeat. In setting a goal for the next week, I asked the partners to identify what steps each of them were going to take over the next week to get one step higher on their scales to 6 and 7 respectively. Giuseppe said that he would continue to be "more loving" toward Lola and "take her out dancing," which they had not done in a long time together. Lola said that she would continue to refrain from nagging and complaining and limit her alcohol use as much as possible. I briefly met with each partner alone and had each of them come up with two positive secret surprises they could pull over the next week that they think the partner would notice and really appreciate. They were not allowed to tell the partner what the surprises were and they will compare notes in the next session.

After a brief intersession break, I complimented the family on doing an excellent job of out-smarting and frustrating the "the nosedive pattern of drug abuse and gambling." I gave all family members a big "high-five" for their excellent teamwork. I encouraged Gino to remember his mantra, "Keeping busy, keeps me out of trouble," to practice using the meditations and urge-surfing, and to fill in the positive trigger log. He should aslo put to use what he learns that works. Also, I encouraged Gino to contact Eric to get together for added support and to further strengthen their relationship.

We discussed a variety of worst-case scenarios that could potentially occur over the week and the concrete steps family members will take to diffuse each of these situations. Finally, I cautioned the family that changes were happening so quickly that they may be due for some bumps in the road or a setback and to be on their toes ready as a team to constructively manage these potential challenging situations.

Emergency Telephone Call from Dr. Spinelli

Three days prior to my next session with the Calabrese family, I received an emergency call from Dr. Spinelli. I had been trying to get a hold of him since my last family session to update him on the family's progress. According to Dr. Spinelli, Giuseppe had been arrested for physically assaulting his wife, Lola had moved in with one of her older sisters, and Gino experienced a prolonged relapse in which he had free-based (smoked) a large quantity of cocaine combined with downing a lot of hard liquor. Apparently, he had witnessed the battery situation and tried to break it up and got slugged in the face by Giuseppe who was quite intoxicated at the time on alcohol. Gino called the police out of fear his father would kill his mother. After the police took his father away, Lola, also heavily intoxicated on alcohol, packed her suitcases and most valuable possessions and had Gino take her over to her sister's house. After dropping his mother off, Gino went to score his cocaine and he came home and free-based it all away. When Giuseppe had gotten released from jail with the help of his attorney, he found Gino passed out on the couch with his pipe and a half-filled bottle of Jack Daniels whiskey and called 911. Dr. Spinelli put Gino on a chemical dependency unit of a hospital that he attended at after he was medically stable. He pointed out that Gino was lucky to be alive because he could have had a stroke. What was really perplexing to Dr. Spinelli and me was the fact that up until the crisis occurred the family members were all getting along really well with one another.

I was completely blown away with how extreme and dramatic this family situation had unraveled. It was like a tsunami had struck the family! The situation was a real-life example of complexity theory in action, moving suddenly from order to disorder and back to stability. This was also an example of how what seemingly appears to be treatment progress can be masquerading as a severe crisis that was right on the cusp of happening. In reflecting on this family tsunami crisis, I wondered if my desire for conjoint family sessions and pushing for too much intimacy too early in the treatment process was too threatening to family members, in that there was such a long history between them of being emotionally hurt by one another and distrusting of each other's hidden intentions and agendas, which may have contributed to the negative backlash and crisis occurring. Finally, by my efforts to reduce or eliminate the very habits that had served the family members well in terms of providing emotional insulation and distance in their relationships also posed a threat to the equilibrium of the family system.

Dr. Spinelli and I discussed the situation and where to go clinically from here. He requested that I see Gino individually at the hospital and continue to work with him after he is discharged. As far as Giuseppe goes, Dr. Spinelli planned to see him individually "to address his anger management and his multiple addiction problems." Lola had shared with Dr. Spinelli that she was planning to divorce Giuseppe because of his violent behavior and repeated cheating on her. Prior to the battering incident, Lola found out through a friend that she had seen Giuseppe with what was described as a hooker going into a hotel together. Apparently, Lola confronted Giuseppe about this when he was intoxicated and he slapped her hard in the face and then she hit him back, which led to his punching her in the face. Gino tried to wrestle his dad away from his mother and got slugged in the process. This is when he had called the police. There was a restraining order placed on Giuseppe to stay away from Lola.

Gino had told Dr. Spinelli that he needed to move out of the house, stop working for his father, and go to college. I totally agreed with this game plan. Since Gino was very close with his maternal uncle Sal, it was mutually decided that he could live at his house until he is completely self-sufficient and capable of living on his own. Sal owned a successful paint shop and planned to put Gino to work there.

Dr. Spinelli and I both agreed after this major tsunami-like family crisis that having family members together in conjoint family therapy would be too toxic and it would be better to see them individually. Out of respect and concern for Lola, I shared with Dr. Spinelli that I would follow-up with her to see if she needed any support during these rough family times. He agreed that my checking in with Lola would be a kind and caring thing to do.

Individual Session with Gino

Gino was in a good place when I met with him on the chemical dependency hospital unit. He had spoken to his mother and learned about the pending divorce. Gino thought this was a good idea because he felt that his parents were incompatible. Although his father had called him a few times, Gino had refused to talk to him. Gino pointed out how he had lost his respect for his father and wanted to emancipate himself completely from him. He now truly understood why Maria cut herself off from the family. Apparently, they had had a few lengthy telephone conversations and some face-to-face visits on the unit thanks to Dr. Spinelli's having written an order in his chart for her to be able to visit. Gino and Maria had always had a close relationship. Gino was the only family member she stayed in contact with.

Gino had shared the great news with me about being accepted at two local universities. He had planned to be a pre-law major and pursue his real career dream. Prior to the family tsunami crisis situation, Gino had scored high on school tests and had applied to four universities. He got the news from his mother who had had her sister pick up the mail from their home. Gino was considering going to the same university that his former debate team member Eric was attending. They had gotten together a few times before Gino had been hospitalized.

We discussed Gino's new living arrangements and future job with Sal. Gino really liked Sal and liked these plans. Once he decided on what university to attend, he was considering moving into a student dorm to be a part of the campus life and to expand his social horizons.

In discussing relapse prevention planning, Gino pointed out that he found the use of the mantra, "Keeping busy, keeps me out of trouble," the sound meditation, urge-surfing, and referring to his positive trigger log to be most useful at keeping him on track. We also collaboratively put together a solid weekly structured plan for success, which included filling up his leisure time with healthy and constructive activities. I had heard about a local CA meeting place that I wanted Gino to look into. I also encouraged him to get a sponsor there as well. Gino planned to follow-up on this after his discharge. Before ending our meeting, Gino gave me his aunt's telephone number so I could check-in with his mother.

Telephone Conversation with Lola

Lola was doing really well. After the family tsunami crisis and drying out from alcohol, she had gone to a woman substance-abuse counselor to work on her drinking problem that she had been referred to by a close friend who was in recovery. She also had contacted Dr. Spinelli who was performing an outpatient detox with her and placed her on disulfiram (antabuse). The other good news was that Lola was regularly attending AA meetings and had a sponsor. Finally, she shared with me that she was interviewing for a management position at a women's clothing store. I commended Lola for taking these courageous steps to turn her life around. She thanked me for continuing to help out Gino. Lola was delighted about Gino's going to college and wanting to eventually become a lawyer. She also was holding off from encouraging Gino to re-connect with his father until he decided on his own to want to do this.

Brief Telephone Conversation with Dr. Spinelli

Dr. Spinelli had called me to let me know that he was discharging Gino from the hospital and that Sal was picking him up. He also shared with me that Lola was receiving an outpatient detox regimen from him and doing quite well in her own treatment with a substance-abuse counselor. Giuseppe was deeply depressed about how he had played a major role in triggering the family tsunami crisis situation and was working hard on his difficulties with anger management, drinking, and gambling. Dr. Spinelli placed him on Prozac.

I also had learned that Gino had picked the same university that his friend Eric was attending and declared his pre-law major right away. I shared with Dr. Spinelli that I would continue with follow-up sessions with Gino until he felt satisfied and ready to stop counseling. We discussed his tight relapse prevention plan as well.

The Second and Later Counseling Sessions with Gino

In our individual counseling session, Gino had shared the great news about the university he had selected. His friend Eric was thrilled about this as well. They had planned the next school year to try to be roommates. He secured a dorm room on campus for the first year. Gino had started working at Sal's paint shop, was attending the local CA meetings, got a sponsor, and was regularly using his relapse prevention tools. In terms of funding his college education, Gino was planning to use his earnings from the job to cover books and living expenses and some trust fund money that his maternal grandfather had set aside for his college education.

In future sessions with Gino, I amplified and consolidated his gains and bore witness with awe to his tremendous growth becoming a responsible and fulfilled adult. I got to meet Eric and uncle Sal on two occasions and it was quite clear that they both cared a lot about Gino and had served as a great support system for him. We started having longer time intervals between sessions after our third visit. I ended up seeing Gino on and off nine more times throughout the year. Gino's sticking to his highly structured plan for success, working, going to college, and high level of commitment to his recovery prevented any future slips from happening. Throughout the treatment process, I let Dr. Spinelli know about Gino's progress and he reciprocated by letting me know how things were going with Giuseppe. We both hoped that down the road Giuseppe could reconcile his relationship with Gino.

Telephone Follow-Up

I spoke to Gino at 6 and 12 months after we had terminated. At 6 months, Gino reported having excellent grades in school and was really enjoying his college experience. He had made many new non-drug-using friends and joined the college debate team. He was still going strong with staying on the recovery track and working for Sal. No drug or gambling slips were reported. He was very proud of his mother who not only was now clean and sober but had carried through with divorcing his father. Gino was still not talking to his father.

At 12 months, I received a similar report from Gino. However, a major change that had occurred was that he had joined his father in a session with Dr. Spinelli where his dad had apologized to him and sought his forgiveness. Gino accepted his father's apologies but would not take his money for college. Gino had felt good about this decision. He was still working for Sal, earning high marks in college, and beginning to investigate law schools for the future. There were no reports of drug use or gambling.

Reflections on the When a Family Tsunami Strikes: A Budding Crisis that had Masqueraded as Family Progress *Case*

Mark: This case clearly shows the intricacies of working with a complicated multi-habit-dependent family system. The initial picture was certainly gloomy but, in spite of it, you were able to begin therapy with your usual unconditional therapeutic optimism, to maneuver to get a number of changes going, and then to maintain your therapeutic presence in the face of an unexpected crisis. Gino eventually managed to get out of the powerful grip of substance abuse and gambling and dramatically change his life, and the parental divorce was a positive outcome as well due to the high level of toxicity of the relationship. This case reminds us that as therapists we only have limited input in the lives of the families we work with, and it is our clients who are the "unsung heroes of therapy" (Duncan & Miller, 2000). I think that one way of looking at what happened with the Calabrese family is that they were only able to move forward once they had truly hit bottom as a family.

Matthew: I agree with you that once the whole family group hit bottom it helped liberate each family member to find their individual life paths and change in their own unique ways. Some of the major challenges of working with complex adaptive systems like the Calabrese family are the *unattended consequences* and our *attentional blindness* cognitive limitation (Mauboussin, 2011; Sargut & McGrath, 2011). Unlike most families we work with where triggering a change in one member can lead to changes in other members, the opposite is true with complex adaptive systems: even a small change can have surprising and catastrophic system-wide negative effects. We saw this in action when I attempted to build in more intimacy and quality time in Giuseppe's relationship with Lola, which resulted in violence and Gino having a serious cocaine relapse. Cognitive research indicates that it is quite difficult if not impossible to observe and comprehend a highly diverse array of relationships from any vantage point, particularly with complex environments (Sargut & McGrath, 2011). The bottom line is that because of our cognitive limitations we can only focus on one thing at a time and can easily lose sight of some individual or relationship in the family that is beginning to unravel or decline in functioning as a result of something new being introduced to the system.

Mark: In the first session, you decided to see Giuseppe first and then move on to strengthen the father–son connection. After your creative and emotional use of the goal-building future projection with Giuseppe, you took the risk of getting Gino in, have him listen to his father's dreams about him, and create common goals from there. My analysis is that this way of operating not only pulled Giuseppe and Gino momentarily closer, but later enabled Gino, who by then felt more competent by having received the support and recognition of his father, to distance from him and start his own differentiated personal journey. On the down side, it seems to me that this way of co-constructing the preferred future privileged Giuseppe's future vision over that of Gino's.

Matthew: In looking back, I think I was accommodating to Giuseppe's role as the head of the family and wielding the power. My experience working with other traditional Italian families is the importance of honoring the father. And on some level I was intimidated by this large and powerful-looking man whom I did not want to upset or challenge in any way. My thinking was to first take people where they were at, build alliances with each of these men, and then work on some positive connection-building in their relationship. Once this preliminary work was accomplished, I would have strived to bring out Gino's voice more and empower him to find his own unique career path and place in the world.

Mark: Externalizing the "terrible nosedive pattern of drug abuse and gambling" allowed you to create a common theme without blaming Gino or anyone else for the drug use and the gambling. I am convinced that this type of externalization is one of the most powerful ways to handle past histories and multi-generational family issues and legacies without losing the focus on future action, strengths, and on solutions. Did you consider constructing a broader pattern that would have included Giuseppe's problems with gambling and women, and Lola's alcohol abuse problem? For example, could you have named "the terrible nosedive pattern into self-destruction," or do you think the family would not have been ready to hear that at that point?

Matthew: In looking back, I think it might it have been premature to imply in any way that Giuseppe and Lola were also being oppressed by this pattern because neither one of them were taking any ownership of their self-destructive habits. Furthermore, I was thinking that my first priority was to help the parents help Gino resolve his difficulties and be careful not to put them on the defensive. If down the road, however, the parents had taken some ownership for their self-destructive habit problems and we had been doing conjoint family therapy together, then I might have extended the new externalized problem pattern frame to include them.

Mark: At a given moment during the first session, Gino shared that he could commit to working with his father at least five days a week. A common way to handle responses like this in a pure solution-focused way would be ask, "How would that be helpful?" Instead, you shared with Gino that keeping busy like that would help keep him out of trouble and that you thought it was a great idea. During the next session, when he had confirmed that things had improved by keeping busy, you shared with him your former client's mantra of how "Keeping busy, keeps me out of trouble" and how you have used these valuable words of wisdom with other clients. The interesting point to me is that when we work this way, we are departing from the radical "not knowing" position of a solution-focused therapist, as we are using our expert knowledge in the territory of self-destructive behaviors to strategically highlight certain exceptions and improvements; at the same time we stay client-focused because we are using this expert knowledge not to lecture or impose our own views, but to work along our clients' views.

Matthew: I frequently make use of former clients' creative ideas and valuable words of wisdom with both new and older clients. My decision to share the "Keeping busy, keeps me out of trouble" mantra with Gino is about giving ourselves permission as therapists to take positive risks with clients to test out the use of certain ideas or therapeutic experiments that we think might work. Klein (2009) has found in his research studying the decision-making of professionals who have to make quick decisions on their feet (firefighters, servicemen and women, emergency room staff), rely heavily on their intuitions and he believes possess a vast reservoir of action scripts in their minds about *what works* with particular crisis and/or problem situations that they regularly tap as roadmaps to solutions.

Mark: To me, the improvements that Giuseppe and Lola reported during the second session were not flukes and I would also rather not see them as "masquerading an impending crisis." In my view, to think of improvements this way paves the way to a distrustful position as therapists, which can undermine our usual stance of taking clients' strengths seriously. Instead, I prefer to ponder if a given improvement does or does not make enough of a difference with a given family. If you asked me to speculate about the possible reasons for the serious backlash after the second session, I would suggest a different explanation. To me, and with the enormous advantage of hindsight, what might have helped in the second session was a specific relapse prevention plan with the marital couple. My hunch is that some "worst-case" scenario discussion with the couple, including how to prevent possible violence and creating an escape plan for Lola, could have made a difference. This might have stood some chances of at least making the relapse situation less dangerous both for Lola and Gino.

Matthew: Yes, I agree with you that earlier in the therapy when Dr. Spinelli and I had discussed a no-violence contract with Giuseppe we failed to explore what three steps Lola and Gino could take if they felt in danger and observed that the father was losing control. I am usually pretty good about covering this base. I think this is another example of the attentional blindness mentioned earlier and the challenges of working with complex and complicated family systems. There is so much to attend to and stay on top of. Furthermore, what seems to work well with complex adaptive systems and the change process is *decoupling* (Sargut & McGrath, 2011), which consists of separating the parts of a system to decrease systemic consequences, such as unexpected events or crises. As early as the first session, I began to use decoupling by seeing individual family members, which made it safe for each member to voice their concerns and best hopes. In looking back, maybe I should not have attempted to work with the parents on intimacy issues as a couple but, instead, have worked with each partner separately maintaining a systemic focus. Interestingly enough, we (Dr. Spinelli and Lola's alcohol counselor) ended up working this way with the family after our family tsunami crisis and it had greatly contributed to their positive treatment outcome.

Mark: One last area I would like to reflect on is the limitations of therapeutic influence and on both the constraints to and opportunities for change.

I feel that one limitation that both therapists and researchers have is that our time frame is necessarily more constricted than that of the families we serve. This means that pretty often what seems to be a therapeutic success at termination and even at follow-up may later turn out to be a failure. For example, a couple's therapy contributes to saving their marriage but eventually translates into the maintenance of an unsatisfactory relationship. It can also work the other way around with a therapeutic failure leading a couple to divorcing and down the road remarrying. To me, this is quite clear with the Calabrese family where the real reconciliation of Gino with his father took place eventually after a massive family and personal crisis.

10
COUPLE AND FAMILY RELAPSE PREVENTION TOOLS AND STRATEGIES

> If you try to shortcut the game, then the game will shortcut you. If you put forth the effort, good things will be bestowed upon you.
>
> *Michael Jordan*

Introduction

Clients with self-destructive habits often present in therapy with long histories of extreme ups and downs in their lives, with many attempts at trying to overcome their problems, and with repeated setbacks in their attempts to conquer them. As we have seen in Chapter 1, the maintenance of self-destructive habits is due both to how they are engraved in the brain and to their inclusion in broader behavioral, cognitive, emotional, and relational patterns that also tend to self-perpetuate. Seen from a complementary perspective, the struggle of trying to restrain from engaging in self-destructive habits is related to the difficulty of learning new alternative behaviors. As Polivy and Herman (2002) have found in their research, 90% of individuals attempting to change a self-destructive habit fail to do so in their first attempt.

Relapses have been defined in many different ways, not only between different types of self-destructive habits, but also within each of them. One framework for understanding and defining relapses comes from the distinction of lapse and relapse developed in substance abuse research (Marlatt & Gordon, 1985) and applied to problem gambling (Ledgerwood & Petry, 2006) as well. A *lapse* (or slip) involves engaging in the self-destructive behavior in a way that constitutes a transgression against personal goals or program rules (for instance, scratching one lottery ticket if abstinence from gambling is the program rule; drinking more than two glasses of wine set as a goal). A *relapse* would be an extended period of resurgence of the self-destructive habit, accompanied by perceived loss of control and a reduction in self-efficacy (for instance, indulging again in several days of gambling; or getting drunk). The process by which a lapse occurs (or not) and then transforms (or not) into a relapse was initially described as a relatively straightforward interplay of high-risk situations, coping skills, and cognitive variables like abstinence self-efficacy and positive outcome experiences (Brownell, Marlatt, Lichtenstein, & Wilson, 1986). In essence, a high-risk situation (for instance, walking into a bar where acquaintances are drinking and snorting cocaine) could be handled with effective coping skills by the person (walk out again; refuse to drink or do a line of cocaine), which would lead to increased self-efficacy and a decreased probability of relapse. If, on the contrary, the person used ineffective coping responses (takes a drink in that bar to calm the craving; fails to refuse friends offering him a line of cocaine to snort), his perception of self-efficacy would decrease and would entertain the possible positive outcomes of engaging in the behavior; once he engaged in it, the abstinence violation effect ("Now that I have done it … I can do more of it") would promote its use further; this, together with the positive short-term effects of the behavior/substance would increase the probability of a full-blown relapse. However, the conflicting findings of research and essentially the inability to predict relapses on the basis of this model have led to a reconceptualization of the process (Marlatt & Witkiewitz, 2005; Witkiewitz & Marlatt, 2004), which is now understood as a multidimensional, complex system in which a number of distal and proximal variables intersect recursively in such a way that "seemingly insignificant changes in levels of risk (for example, slight decreases in mood ratings) kindle a relapse episode, often initiated by a minor cue" (Witkiewitz & Marlatt, 2004, p. 229).

In our view, the realization of cognitive behavioral theorists and researchers that the relapse process might be better understood on the basis of principles of self-organization and dynamical systems theories like complexity and chaos theories, are congruent with our systemic perspective, that emphasizes the equipotentiality and equifinality of human behaviors (Holman, 2010; Johnson, 2007; von Bertalanffy, 1968). The clinical implication is that, as therapists, we should not try to predict relapse a priori, but examine with each and every client–couple/family unit which factors may contribute to and protect them from relapse, and how they change over time and mutually reinforce each other, with an openness to learn from each lapse in order to meet the unique needs of the individual client better.

In any case, from a clinical perspective relapses have negative effects not only because by falling prey to their self-destructive habits clients are again exposed to their psychological and physical impact, even risking their lives by overdosing in the case of drug abuse or by going too far in the case of cutting, but also because of the demoralization that a relapse is likely to bring about. When clients relapse they feel defeated and "back-to-square-one"; they feel incompetent, and lose their recaptured sense of personal agency and control; and they may confirm that as they suspected, the self-destructive habit is "stronger than me." Relapse also can have a direct bearing on the therapeutic relationship, a major predictor of successful therapy (Orford, 2008; Wampold, 2001); if the risk of lapses has not been adequately acknowledged and discussed in therapy, the unwarned client will feel that therapy has failed and that the therapist cannot be trusted, and is likely to feel hopeless and drop out of therapy. In other instances, the relapsing client may wish to stay in therapy, but feels so ashamed and embarrassed about the setback that he or she will cancel a scheduled appointment.

For all of these reasons, relapse prevention should be very high on the agendas of any therapeutic program dealing with self-destructive habits. This also is the case with our collaborative strengths-based brief family therapy approach that takes the possibility of slips and relapses into account from the very beginning of therapy and upholds relapse prevention as an important therapeutic theme throughout the course of treatment. However, if a relapse still occurs, in spite of all of the efforts to prevent it, it is very important to view it as an excellent opportunity to gain wisdom from it. Prochaska and DiClemente (1982, 1985, 1992) have repeatedly demonstrated in their research that relapses are one more phase in the process of change, and therefore one step more in the direction of overcoming the problem. As we often share with our clients, "It is not a shame to have a relapse; it is a shame to have a relapse and not learn from it." We also point out how slips are like wise sages and they offer us valuable wisdom about what we can learn from our mistakes, what specific situations or contexts we need to make better choices in, and where specifically we need to tighten up with the structure. We often reframe for clients that slips are an opportunity for comeback practice, springboards toward further changes, and temporary derailments, and point out to them that they could not be making good headway if they did not have a slip. By doing so, slips will not be perceived by clients as disastrous occurrences and signs that they are back to square one. Sometimes we specifically mention that the sneaky and clever habit will try to use the slip as an attempt to demoralize the identified client and try to brainwash him or her to drop out of therapy. With these situations, we suggest that having at least one more session to learn from it is in fact a better choice. Some examples of the kind of questions we ask clients who have just had a slip, are as follows:

- "What did you learn from that slip on Tuesday that you will put to use the next time you are faced with a similar stressful situation?"
- "What was the most memorable aspect of that slip experience that will make you think twice in the future about caving into getting 'stoned' again?"
- "After this experience, what specifically do you think you/your partner/parents need to put into place that can help minimize the likelihood of future slips?"
- "Let's say you have another slip in a few weeks, what steps will you take to quickly get back on track?"
- "What is the best way your partner/parents should respond to you following a slip?"

Goal-Maintenance and Relapse Prevention is a Couple and Family Affair

Most traditional disease model and Twelve-Step-oriented therapists working with clients deemed addicted to substances, gambling, sex, and so forth often view relapse prevention training as centered mainly on direct work with the individual identified client. Some of these programs and therapists for that matter today still operate from the philosophy of: "Three Strikes, You're Out!" regarding slips and relapses with their clients. However, the *catch-22* for these clients who feel compelled to use substances or engage in their other choice self-destructive habits is that they are being punished for exhibiting the very symptoms of the disorder they have been labeled with. According to Bowen, Chawla, and Marlatt (2011) and Marlatt and Witkiewitz (2005), this aversive approach to treatment may work in the short run but in the long term, clients have been found to return back to problem use patterns.

In these traditional treatment programs, couple and family members may be seen separately in a group setting and are typically educated about their survival role behaviors, signs, and symptoms of the identified clients' *disease*, what can contribute to their having relapses, and the importance of pursuing their own recovery programs with the help of participation in self-groups. However, what is often left overlooked and unchanged by more traditional therapists is how couple partners, family members, and certain members from the identified clients' social networks problem-saturated beliefs, entrenched problem-maintaining patterns of interaction, and attempted solutions are contributing to further perpetuating the identified clients' habit difficulties. This is unfortunate, given that there is an overwhelming body of high-quality research and clinical practice wisdom that shows to what extent these interaction patterns are directly linked to relapses occurring with a wide range of self-destructive behaviors (Ciarrocchi, 2001; Grant, Donahue, & Odlaug, 2011; Kwon, 2011; Ladouceur & Lachance, 2007; Liddle, 2010; Maltz & Maltz, 2010; O'Farrell & Fals-Stewart, 2006; Robin & Le Grange, 2010; Selekman, 2009; Szapocznik, Hervis, & Schwartz, 2003).

Often, the therapists and treatment program staff become the privileged experts offering their choice therapeutic tools and strategies and treatment modalities that they think would be *best* for the habit-dependent person, couple partner, and family members. Also, they may privilege their treatment goals high above what the clients wish to work on changing first. However, by doing so, they disempower the clients and assumes that they lack the necessary skills, strengths, and resourcefulness to generate their own unique coping and problem-solving strategies. It is no surprise to us why clients with habit difficulties tend to have high relapse rates when they receive this type of treatment experience.

Therefore, we believe strongly that relapse prevention is a couple and family affair. In addition, we have found it beneficial to bring into our counseling sessions key concerned members from our habit-dependent clients' social networks as well to help provide them with a strong support system and to offer them a diversity of creative ideas, which can optimize for the generation of multiple high-quality solutions. The habit-dependent person can have the lead voice in sharing with his or her partner, concerned family and social network members what their triggers are for engaging in their habits, how they can support them in the best way possible to stay on track, and how best to respond when they have a slip. Couple partners, family members, concerned friends, adult inspirational others, and other key members from their social networks also will have plenty of floor time to offer their creative ideas, expertise, and wisdom.

We still believe it is critical to devote individual session time to the habit-dependent person to address any individual concerns or struggles he or she may be having, to learn about his or her triggers (both positive and negative), and teach him or her distress management tools and strategies to use when they are alone and in high-risk situations. It is also helpful to use this time to further consolidate his or her gains as well.

Major Relapse Prevention Strategies

Consolidating Questions: Underscoring and Accentuating Storylines of Courage and Success

Relapse prevention begins even before we start discussing relapses, with the use of *consolidating questions*. Consolidating questions are designed to help amplify and consolidate clients' gains in changing their habits and/or their improvements in other presenting problem areas of their lives. They help underscore and accentuate the key courageous steps the identified clients, their partners, and family members have taken as they continue to conquer their difficulties and sustain their new solution patterns of thinking, feeling, and doing that help them to stay on track. The consolidating process begins with amplifying and solidifying any new solution patterns of thinking, feeling, and doing that occur prior to our first couple and family sessions and throughout the course of treatment, being curious about the specifics of *what* has improved. Once we know the details of these improvements, we need to understand *how* the client has been able to generate them. During this "positive blaming" process we ask clients what specific thoughts or actions they have undertaken to bring about their accomplishments, and how other significant others have been helpful (Berg & Reuss, 1997; de Shazer et al., 2007). We also can place clients in the expert advisor role to us and invite them to share what words of wisdom they think we should offer other clients struggling with similar difficulties. This helps consolidate their *news of a difference*. A third way we can consolidate our clients' gains is to have them envision future realities of further success, including positive gains and surprises they would be sharing with us, other past treatment providers, involved helping professionals, and with key members from their social networks. Some examples of consolidating questions are as follows:

- "So, what's better, even a little bit since we spoke on the telephone last week?"
- "Are you aware of how you pulled that off?!"
- "How has that made a difference in your relationship with your partner/daughter?"
- "What other important and pleasant discoveries did you make about your daughter and your relationship with her?"
- "Are you aware of how you took that courageous step to refrain from cutting for three days?"
- "What is your secret so I can share your expertise with other self-harming teens?"
- "Let's say we get together in one week's time and you come in here to share with me that you took some further courageous steps as a couple, what will you tell me you did?"
- "What would you have to do to go backward at this point?"
- "How are you viewing yourself differently now as opposed to when we first started working together?"
- "If I was to work with other parents struggling with similar difficulties that you used to have with your son, what advice and words of wisdom would you want me to share with them?"

- "Let's say we had a reunion party in my office one year from today. What important changes will you share with me that you all had made that will really surprise me and make me fall out of my chair with amazement?"
- "If you were contracted to serve as expert consultants to your former therapists and treatment program staff, what advice and valuable words of wisdom would you offer them in their work with similar families like yours?"

Being Mindful Practitioners

Our ability to stay mindfully present with our clients can play a major role in their ability to stay on track and successfully stave off near-miss or budding crisis situations, which can lead to slips or prolonged relapsing situations occurring. By being mindfully present, we mean being astute observers and generous listeners to everything that occurs within us and between us moment-by-moment with our clients. This includes observing our thoughts, feelings, when we become too attached to limited and narrow views of our clients' problem situations, our reactions to our clients' verbal and nonverbal responses and interactions, and their reactions to us. We need to be curious about contradictions in their verbal and nonverbal communications and be keenly aware of and address client alerts of dissatisfaction with any aspects of the treatment process. We have learned this the hard way; while reviewing cases where clients relapsed and dropped out of therapy, we have found that in most cases clients were giving us clear but unnoticed or unacknowledged clues that they were not satisfied with their therapeutic progress or fearful that they may have a setback. In addition to taking clients' fears about setbacks or lack of progress seriously, we like to make room for them to share any concerns they may have in other areas of their lives (a recent death in the family, an ill parent, a job loss) or regarding their presenting problems, and together with them come up with a solid action plan for addressing their concern areas. At the same time in a given session, we want to listen carefully for clients' storylines of courage, recent epiphanies, anomalies, and serendipitous events and observe for any other opportunities to seize and utilize in co-authoring new solution-determined stories with them. Finally, we need to use ourselves like cameras with wide angle zoom lens, zooming in on micro-events and interactions face-to-face with our clients and zooming out not only to watch ourselves in relationship to the clients but to gain access to the *big picture* of the key patterns that are connected to maintaining the habit difficulties both within the family and across all of their significant relationships. As part of the zooming out process, we also are on the lookout for solution-promoting exception patterns we can seize across the key relationships and contexts the clients interface with that we can utilize to help them stay on track and resolve their other presenting difficulties. Therapists can ask clients the following questions to help address concerns and the *not-yet-said* to prevent future crises or slips:

- "Is there anything we have not talked about up to this point, that unless we address it soon, could lead to a crisis or major setback occurring?"
- "Is there anything else going on outside our target goal areas that any of you are concerned about that could come back to haunt us or derail your progress unless we resolve it now?"
- [Giving a couple a three week vacation from counseling as a vote of confidence] "Let's say two weeks into your vacation from counseling the two of you get into a big argument, what would you have wished we had addressed or resolved before you went on vacation that might have prevented this slip?"
- "Once this issue is resolved, how will that make a difference with your situation?"

An important issue to stress here is that relapses are likely to occur with all kinds of habits, not only self-destructive ones. Therefore, we should not only have in our minds the possibility of relapses with the identified clients, but also discuss and prevent concerned others slipping back into their unproductive and ineffectual solution patterns of interaction as well. For example, a wife is successfully staying away from lottery clubs, but her husband is at risk of getting back into his old habit of over-controlling her; a daughter is successfully coping with her urge to self-harm, but her parents are beginning to fall back into their nagging and belittling behaviors again. In other words, it is also difficult to change for couple partners and family members, and they may need the same kind of help and patient guidance to maintain their changes similar to the work we do with the self-destructive habit clients. We find it useful to determine at what stages of readiness for change couple partners, family members, and involved extended family members presently are in, help them to advance to the next stages, and do relapse prevention work with them as well so that do not fall back into former unproductive problem-maintaining behaviors they used to engage in.

Externalizing Solutions to Thwart Sneaky Habit Strikes

Externalizing solutions questions are specifically designed to further consolidate and sustain favorite, effective, and client-generated coping and problem-solving tools and strategies so as to help make clients impervious to sneaky and surprise habit strikes, particularly when stressful life events, disappointments, or transition periods occur and our clients are most vulnerable to slips. When experiencing a high level of emotional distress or stress, even the most solid of clients can have a minor slip or prolonged relapse and become vulnerable to their old habits. Therefore, it is most beneficial to explore with clients in great detail about what they need to do to further refine and solidify their most useful coping and problem-solving strategies so that if their former habits re-assert their power and try to neutralize or block their positive effects they know how best to respond. It also is helpful to let clients know that habits do not die easily and can strike when they are least expecting it. Finally, clients should be encouraged to use their choice coping and problem-solving strategies more and in all contexts where they may be faced with toxic people and potentially uncomfortable or stressful situations. Some examples of externalizing solutions questions are as follows:

- "In what ways can you call upon and use 'Telling myself to stay chilled' to help you to stay on track and not cave into 'partying' (smoking weed and drinking) when you see your nemesis Amanda at your friend's graduation party?"
- "In addition to 'Telling myself to stay chilled,' what other favorite tools or strategies of yours could you come armed with to the graduation party that could serve as good backups if the old partying habit attempts to neutralize it and seduce you into using?"
- "I understand that you and your partner have been arguing a lot lately outside of 'scheduled complaint session' times, which can set the stage for a possible slip. In what ways can we get back to making or improving upon 'scheduled complaint sessions' effective at decreasing your arguments again?"
- "What inspiring subjects or topics for 'making drawings' and 'writing poetry' can put you in a deep enough creative zone that you are less likely to fall prey to 'cutting's' hypnotic trance induction to carve yourself up when you are stressed out?"
- "In what ways can we further tweak the 'sound meditation' to make it even more effective to help combat all of the work stress you are under right now?"

Couple and Family Constructive Response Planning for Potential Worse-Case Scenarios

An effective way to cover the back door with our clients once they start making progress in second and future sessions is to do *couple and family constructive response planning for worse-case scenarios*. When the identified clients have made it known to their couple partners and family members what specific type of activities, toxic people, and situations could trigger slips or prolonged relapses for them, constructive steps can be identified that each person can take to effectively stabilize the situation and get them back on track. It is most important that the identified clients, couple partners, and family members identify as many possible worst-case scenarios that they can possibly think of that could occur so as to be well prepared for constructively managing each of these possible situations. With crisis-prone couples and families, we will explore what they envision the next crisis could be, where it might occur, who might be involved with it, what steps will the partners and family members take to constructively stabilize the situation, what they will do if this first response strategy does not work (Figure 10.1). This strategy can effectively disrupt a longstanding couple or family pattern. We would like to emphasize that our first choice is always to access the plans that the couple or family can generate on their own with our gentle prompting; we refrain from giving advice, and prefer to stay in the "devil's advocate" position, spelling out difficulties and giving clients room to sort them out. We only suggest our own relapse prevention strategies if our clients are at a given moment unable to create their own plan, if they are fearful that their plan might not be enough or that they may not be able to carry it out as planned, or if we feel that our clients' ideas need to be further enhanced.

Using Peers, Key Social Network Members, and Client Alumni Expert Consultants to Serve as a Natural Relapse Prevention Support System

Research convincingly shows that high-quality social support is highly predictive of long-term abstinence rates across several addictive behaviors (Copello, Orford, Hodgson, & Tober, 2009; Moos, 2007; Witkiewitz & Marlatt, 2004), and in our clinical experience it plays a central role for dealing with any self-destructive habit. To help further empower our clients to stay on track and optimize for their future success, we have them invite their most concerned and committed friends and other key members from their social networks to join us as part of the relapse prevention support team. Having these concerned others working for us, both within and between

Worse-case scenario	Individual steps I will take	The steps we will take *(partner, family members, key resource people from social network)*

Figure 10.1 My/our constructive response plans for worse-case scenarios.

couple or family scheduled sessions in contexts we have limited or no access to, can serve as a powerful support structure to help our clients make good choices, stay on track, and make further progress. These key resource people bring compassion, creativity, and wisdom, which can be tapped and utilized in co-constructing solutions with the couple and family. Over the years, we have witnessed incredible teamwork where close friends have teamed up with the identified clients' adult inspirational others at school or in the community, where clergy and relatives have helped clients land jobs, and where close friends made a commitment to kick their habits to help optimize for the identified clients to conquer their habits. I (MS) once had a client who was struggling to stay quit from drug use, and three of the client's closest friends set up a 24-hour crisis phone call system arrangement to help her not cave into using when feeling vulnerable and at risk. This client had indicated that, thanks to her friends' kindness and tremendous support, she was able to achieve and maintain abstinence from drug use.

When our clients do not have a strong and positive social network of concerned others, we will encourage them to try to identify *weak link* people they can establish contact with and work on building more solid relationships with them (Koch & Lockwood, 2010). These weak link individuals may be friendly acquaintances of the client or have been recommended to them by friends and others as bright, caring, and resourceful people. Once the clients begin to establish better rapport with and more trusting relationships with them, we can explore the possibility of having them also serve as members of the relapse prevention team.

Another valuable resource group of individuals that can be recruited and actively involved as part of the relapse prevention support system are former client alumni consultants who used to struggle with similar difficulties. This is particularly useful in situations where all of the clients' peers are heavily involved with self-destructive habits. Since they successfully conquered their habit difficulties, are now functioning at much higher levels, and often have become upstanding citizens, the client alumni consultants have wisdom regarding not only what it takes for resolving habit difficulties but how best to stay quit from them. They can assist clients with organizational skill development, improving school and work performance, and with finding jobs, and can broaden their horizons by exposing them to positive and healthy leisure activities, hobbies, and service work.

Individual Distress Management Tools and Strategies

Since our habit-dependent clients will not always be in the company of their concerned partners, family, and social network members, or may be distancing themselves due to intense conflicts or big letdowns, it is critical that we arm the clients with a wide range of effective distress management tools and strategies that they could put into place when feeling vulnerable to caving into their old habits or when slips do occur. Once we have accessed our clients' ideas on what the risk situations and possible relapse triggers are, and have helped them spell out and organize their own ideas on how to deal with them, we like to provide some additional resources and share the distress management tools we have found most useful. As part of the distress management skill mastery process, it is most beneficial to practice with clients in our offices step-by-step how to perform each distress management tool or strategy that we expose them to. We find it helpful to give our clients instruction sheets for the major distress management tools and strategies we offer them that they can take home and refer to in case they forget a step or get stuck with the implementation process. This also helps increase treatment adherence. We encourage our clients to practice using the distress management tools and strategies daily, even when they are not feeling vulnerable to slips or are not experiencing emotional distress or stress elevation. It is critical that they become so proficient at using their distress management tools and strategies that they will become integrated into their daily routines and can be used as easily as switching a light on and off. In fact, in the cognitive-behavioral literature *willpower* is often described as a type of muscle, which may be strengthened with practice but can also become fatigued and lead to poor decision-making (Baumeister, Heatherton, & Tice, 1994; Baumeister & Tierney, 2011; Ciarrocchi, 2001). Finally, after offering each new distress management tool and strategy it is important to evaluate with clients how the implementation process went, any difficulties they may have experienced while experimenting with them (intruding thoughts, confusion, difficulty staying focused), and see if they would like to modify the specific distress management tools or strategies they were struggling with to make them more manageable. Some clients, usually in the very advanced stages of their change process, might even prefer not to use any of them, because they feel that doing them reminds them of the problematic habit they not only want to overcome but also want to "forget." Ultimately, clients should choose which distress management tools and strategies they like and have gotten the best results from.

The Structured Plan for Success

In earlier chapters we have underscored the importance of helping our clients establish healthy lifestyles that will give them the inner psychological and physical strength to prevent relapses and to transform their lives. We have found in our clinical practices that when our clients generate a solid and highly structured success plan they not only reduce the likelihood of slips occurring but also tend to have better treatment outcomes. The clients' *structured plans for success* can include the following daily objectives: daily protected quality time with partners or family members; maintaining a healthy diet; getting 8 or more daily hours of sleep; engaging in some form of a daily aerobic exercise (walking, jogging, bicycling, and swimming) for a minimum of 20 minutes or longer; devoting 10–15 minutes daily of mindfulness meditation and/or related practices and 15–20 minutes practicing other choice distress management tools and strategies; leisure time to engage in healthy and meaningful hobbies or activities solo and/or with positive peers (face-to-face offline interactions); pursue unexplored interest areas of curiosity and intrigue; involvement in some form of service work and/or striving to perform at least one random act of kindness per day; striving to make a commitment to steer clear from toxic peers, places, and activities (Figure 10.2). Baumeister and Tierney (2011) have found that one's willpower to stay on track, self-regulating capacities, and choice-making abilities can become compromised when we do not get enough sleep. Therefore, we strongly encourage our clients to try and get an adequate amount of sleep each night, such as 8 or more hours.

As part of their structured plan for success, clients may want to add attending self-help groups like Alcoholics Anonymous (AA), Narcotics Anonymous (NA), or Gamblers Anonymous (GA), and so forth if they think this form of added support would be helpful to build into their daily regime. Once the client in session identifies all of the specific details for their daily objectives, he or she can fill in a *My Structured Plan for Success Worksheet* and take it home to use as the roadmap for success. Prior to ending the couple or family session, it is also critical that clients present their structured plans for success to their partners or parents so that they can gain their support with their efforts to stay on track and transform their lifestyles.

Some clients may be initially reluctant to introduce so many changes to their usual lifestyle, their position being that they want to "get rid" of the problematic habit, but without "messing with the rest" of their lives. We do not see this as resistance, but as a logical reaction given that proposed changes to anyone's lifestyle can be perceived as a threat, and that therefore ambivalence towards any change is understandable. We handle this ambivalence in different ways. On the one hand, it might be necessary to clarify with the client the link between these behavioral and lifestyle changes and the overcoming of the self-destructive habit and the prevention of relapses. On the other hand, we will proceed slowly and take into account in what stage of readiness for change they are currently in not only in relationship to resolving the self-destructive habit but regarding their broader lifestyle changes. A more indirect strategy is not to spell out the structured plan for success as such, but to be extremely attentive to any changes the client performs

	Monday	Tuesday	Wednesday	Thursday	Friday	Saturday	Sunday
6 AM							
7 AM							
8 AM							
9 AM							
10 AM							
11 AM							
12 PM							
1 PM							
2 PM							
3 PM							
4 PM							
5 PM							
6 PM							
7 PM							
8 PM							
9 PM							
10 PM							
11 PM							

Figure 10.2 "My structured plan for success" worksheet.

spontaneously in that direction, even the very small steps, and to consolidate and celebrate these gains with them. This is often the case with healthy habits like going for a walk or working out; clients start to do a little bit of it at their own initiative, and we take the risk of reinforcing and promoting these positive steps further.

Two other important areas that dovetail into clients' structured plans for success are spiritual involvement or engagement and pursuing and/or upholding their core personal values. Spiritual involvement can take many forms, such as: achieving inner peace through regularly meditating and/or using creative visualization, regularly praying, attending a place of worship once a week, pursuing and having peak experiences. Research indicates that spiritual wellness can strengthen psychological functioning, increase hope, optimism, and gratitude levels, and can serve as a resiliency protective factor (Carmody, Reed, Kristeller, & Merriam, 2008; Kristeller, 2010, 2003; McCullough, Emmons, & Tsang, 2002). Mindfulness meditation can serve as a healthy form of spiritual engagement for non-religious clients.

It is important for our clients to share what their core personal values are and how their self-destructive habit(s) and other difficulties have impacted on them in all areas of their lives. Miller, Forcehimes, and Zweben (2011) contend that "Exploring a person's core values can clarify what are often regarded as spiritual or meaning-in-life motivations for change" (p. 348). As part of the goal-setting process, clients may want to establish new values they wish to pursue or revisit their most cherished values in the past and get back on track upholding them, such as: being a more attentive parent devoting more time to his or her daughter, or being more respectful and appreciative toward one's partner (Haidt, 2006; Peterson, 2006; Wilson, Sandoz, Flynn, & Slater, 2010). The clients can then determine the *when* and the *how* (specific behavioral steps), during a given week they will devote time to putting their core values and spiritual involvement into action. In future sessions, consolidating questions will be useful to create *news of a difference* by inviting clients to compare their old problem-maintaining views of self and patterns of behavior with their new transformed selves and solution-maintaining patterns of behavior.

Quieting the Mind: Finding Inner Peace and Happiness with Mindfulness Meditation and other Related Practices

As we have shown throughout this book, clients with self-destructive habits very often complain about their feelings of hopelessness and despair, being out of control, oppressed by negative self-deprecating thoughts, rumination, and unable to find any peace of mind. When our self-destructive-habit clients are stressed out, the brain's alarm system housed in the amygdala is activated by whatever the stressor is that they experience as a threat. Next, their *emotion mind*, which is associated with the fight-or-flight response, takes over and their higher levels of brain functioning, which have to do with complex and rational thinking, become compromised, leading to impaired judgment and more than likely engaging in self-destructive habits. It is our contention that there is no better antidote to counter this emotional hijacking process than mindfulness meditation and related practices.

The mindfulness meditations and related exercises we present in this section can help our clients to quiet their minds, center them, and empower them to see more clearly and make better and healthy decisions when experiencing emotional distress or some other stressor. They also can employ loving-kindness, compassion, and remind themselves of how our minds are like "the sky," and negative emotions and thoughts are fluid, impermanent, will eventually pass, and are only one part of the "now" experience (Wegela, 2009). Finally, we let them know that one of the major benefits of meditating is that it strengthens the part of their brains that increases positive emotions and regulates negative emotions (Fredrickson, 2009; Hanson & Mendius, 2009).

In this section of the chapter, we discuss thirteen mindfulness meditations and related practices that can teach our clients how to find inner peace and happiness: *Six Breaths on Purpose, Urge Surfing, Taking a Trip to Popcorn Land, The Sound Meditation, 5, 4, 3, 2, 1, Cloud and Wave-Watching, Body-Scanning, The Two Gardens Mindfulness Practice for Couples, My Sacred Sanctuary Visualization, Visualizing Movies of Joy and Success, Visualizing the Resilient You in Action, Self-Directed Neuroplasticity*, and *Imagine Yourself as_____ to Stay on Track*. We let our clients know that to achieve mastery of the mindfulness meditations and related practices of their choosing will require a lot of patience, commitment, and practice time. If necessary, we make clear again that this commitment will pay off in their quest for a better, habit-free life. We also need to let them know that it is not uncommon while in the midst of meditating or doing these exercises to experience intruding thoughts, feelings, or uncomfortable bodily sensations. Rather than panic or abandoning the meditations or exercises, we encourage them instead to use this as a wonderful opportunity to practice decentering or self-observing their thoughts, feelings, and bodily sensations and come to know what they really are, temporary, fluid, and like the clouds in the sky, which are in perpetual motion and will eventually clear, revealing their beautiful blue sky selves that are always present. Furthermore, new neuroscience research has indicated that when you put words to your feelings, when you label them, two things occur: activity is stimulated in the prefrontal cortex and lowered in the amygdala alarm circuit. The simple act of labeling to yourself what you are feeling as you are feeling it helps to dampen this overreaction or panic response when experiencing unpleasant feelings while meditating.

However, if clients' distress tolerance is low and they are experiencing a great deal of emotional or physical discomfort while attempting to meditate, we will encourage them to stop and later in the day try one of the visualization strategies or something fun and positive, like cloud-watching, discussed below. This has been the case for some of our past traumatized clients who tend to have very low distress tolerance levels for negative emotion and it is too threatening to close their eyes, sit with, and self-observe their negative thoughts and feelings. These clients may do better with a combination of visualization strategies, cloud- or wave-watching, and learning disputation skills discussed later.

By offering our clients a wide range of different mindfulness mediations and related exercises to choose from, it is our hope that they will find at least a few of them that they will develop confidence in using and will build into their daily schedules practice time. Finally, with each of the mindfulness meditations and exercises we walk the clients step-by-step through how to perform them and give them a written description of how to implement each one of them at home.

Six Breaths on Purpose

This meditation is easy to do and can be quite helpful to clients who have a tendency to worry and/or ruminate too much. When they are being pushed around by their worries or rumination they are to sit down somewhere quiet, get comfortable in a chair, close their eyes, and pay close attention to the rise and fall of each breath. They are to take six long, deep, and deliberate breaths (Wilson & DuFrene, 2012). We have added our own variation to this mindfulness exercise. With the inhalation breathes they can pretend that they are inhaling in whatever is stressing them out (negative thoughts, feelings, and external stressors). With the exhalation breathes, they are to pretend that they are exhaling or externalizing/letting go of their negative thoughts and related feelings and external stressors. Often, clients report feeling very relaxed and like they have quieted their minds after the final breath.

Urge Surfing

Urge surfing was developed by Alan Marlatt and his colleagues at the University of Washington as a powerful mindfulness coping strategy to help substance abusers reduce the likelihood of having slips by strengthening their self-regulatory capacities (Bowen et al., 2011; Marlatt, Bowen, Chawla, & Witkiewitz, 2008). Clients are first instructed to get comfortable in a chair or on a couch in a quiet room. They are told that while doing this mindfulness exercise if they feel like they are having difficulty sitting with their powerful emotions and are fearful of having a slip, they are to stop immediately. With their eyes closed, they are to capture an image in their mind of a person, object, place, or situation that would trigger them to get stoned, drunk, cut, want to gamble, engage in cyber-sex, etc. While using all of their senses, including color and motion, they are to pay close attention to and respond quietly to themselves to the following questions:

- "What emotions are arising?"
- "What thoughts are entering my mind connected to the urge to use?"
- "What does the urge want?"
- "What does it want to change?"
- "If it could speak, what might it say?"
- "Is there a story it has to tell?"
- "Are there images or memories coming up?"
- "What physical sensations am I experiencing?"

- "Where in my body do I feel these sensations the most?"
- "What feels most intolerable about this experience?"
- "Can I stay with it with loving-kindness for myself?"
- "Can I stick with this experience in a kind of curious way?"

Clients are told while doing urge surfing that they are making a choice not to act on any urges or cravings that arise but just staying with them and observing, as best as they can. When a certain intense urge or craving arises, they are to picture in their mind seeing it as a big powerful ocean wave, and imagine seeing themselves riding the wave with their breathe (take an 'in' breathe and an 'out' breathe) as a surfboard to stay right with it. They are to picture themselves successfully keeping their balance on their surfboards as the waves rise and staying on top of them until they lower. They are encouraged to keep maintaining their balance so as not to be wiped out by the urges or cravings. Finally, they are to continue to stay present with the waves, keep their balance on their surfboards, observe urges and cravings but not react to them. The beauty of this mindfulness exercise is that it helps increase clients' self-confidence and distress tolerance levels and they gain a safe, meta-position to their negative thoughts, feelings, bodily distress, urges and cravings as curious observers without having to cave into their self-destructive habits. For some clients who recently achieved abstinence from their habits or are feeling more vulnerable, it may be helpful initially for them to use a kitchen timer and limit their urge surfing practice time to 5 minutes and gradually increase the time as they develop more self-confidence with urge surfing. It is important to let clients know that research indicates that even the most powerful urges or intense emotions often subside at 15–20 minutes (Schwartz & Begley, 2003).

Taking a Trip to Popcorn Land

One easy-to-master food meditation is *Taking a Trip to Popcorn Land*. Clients are first instructed to get comfortable in a chair or on a couch in a quiet room and place one piece of popcorn in their left palms of their hands. Each step is to be done slowly for 2–3 minutes. Next, they are to carefully study the piece of popcorn, looking at its shape, its various indentations, its coloring, and any shadowing around it. The next step is to reach over with the right hand, pick it up, and roll it around the fingertips. While doing so, the clients are to close their eyes immerse themselves in its texture and whatever sensations they experience. Following this step, they are to place the piece of popcorn in their mouths and roll it around their teeth and tongues without biting down on it. They will salivate. After this step, they are to slowly and finely chew the piece of popcorn without swallowing it. They are to pay close attention to its taste (buttery, salty). Finally, they are to swallow the chewed-up piece of popcorn, paying close attention to whatever sensations they experience as it slides down their esophagus. So for 12 minutes they have been totally immersed in the popcorn eating experience and transported to Popcorn Land (Selekman, 2005, 2009, 2010).

Sound Meditation

Clients are first instructed to get comfortable in a chair or on a couch in a quiet room and close their eyes. They are to carefully tune in to each sound they hear around them and simply label them, such as: "I just heard a dog barking outside." The clients are not to try to figure out why they are hearing particular sounds but simply label each one. They are to do this for 12 minutes. A lot of clients become so centered on sound that they fall asleep in our offices or at home where they practice this meditation. However, some clients may respond better to listening to soothing and relaxing music that produces a lot of imagery in their minds. We both like to expose our clients to music that can provide this kind of meditative effect (Selekman, 2005, 2009, 2010).

5, 4, 3, 2, 1

We start as usual, suggesting our clients get comfortable in their chairs. Next, we invite them to pay attention to five different objects in the room one by one. Each of them is to be carefully observed for about 4–5 seconds, carefully noticing their color, size, shape, texture, and so forth. The clients are then asked to pay attention to five sounds; again they are to carefully notice what sounds they hear and anything unique about each one. Next, the clients are to focus on five bodily sensations, carefully noticing each of them, one by one. After this first round, attention will be paid to four objects, four sounds, four bodily sensations; and then three objects, three sounds, three bodily sensations, and so on. The objects, sounds, and bodily sensations can be different in each round, or the same. This exercise is based on the hypnotic work of Milton H. Erickson and is quite useful for helping clients combat rumination and defocus from their negative thoughts and feelings. However, before using it with a more difficult or relapse-prone clients, it is important for them to practice at least for two weeks to see how it works for him or her. Once the clients are trained in this exercise, they may prefer to do only three rounds of the exercise (Dolan, 1991; Isebaert, 2005).

Cloud and Wave-Watching

Two other types of mindfulness experiences we can offer our clients out in nature are: *cloud* and *wave watching*. When being oppressed by negative thoughts and feelings, clients are to get out of their heads, go outside, and carefully study the clouds. Not only are they to pay close attention to their gradual movement but carefully observe the clouds' various shapes. They are to look for identifiable cloud shapes that resemble familiar animals, objects, and human faces and head shapes. We like to have our clients write down their observations of the different recognizable cloud shapes they had observed each time they engage in this fun activity. For the clients, they feel like detectives with their familiar cloud-shape hunting and it becomes a pleasurable mindfulness outlet for them.

Wave watching serves a dual purpose for clients. First, waves serve as a great metaphor for the impermanence of problems and stressful life events. The waves may be powerful when they come crashing into the rocks or reef along the shoreline but once this happens they always reduce in intensity and fall back. Second, sitting by the sea or lakeshore is a relaxing and multi-sensory experience. As the waves come in, often we experience a breeze on our skin. The colors of waves can be beautiful shades of blue and green. The sound of the water both coming ashore and returning back produces a very soothing and relaxing effect on us (Selekman, 2009).

Body Scanning

Body scanning is a highly useful distress management strategy for empowering clients to sooth themselves when they are experiencing feelings of loss of control, unpleasant bodily sensations, and somatic complaints. With this mindfulness exercise, clients may feel more comfortable lying on the office floor or on a couch. They are to first identify somewhere in their bodies where they are experiencing some physical discomfort, tightness, or pain. Next, they are to locate somewhere on their arms, legs, chests, necks where they feel completely relaxed. They are then to go back inside their bodies and find somewhere where they feel relaxed and then revisit the bodily area where they had felt some discomfort or pain. The next step is to go back outside and locate somewhere else on their arms, legs, chests, or necks where they feel totally relaxed. By this time, when they go back inside their bodies and revisit the original bodily area where they felt discomfort or pain it has either greatly subsisted or it has disappeared. Clients often report finding this mindfulness exercise very relaxing, provides inner peace for them, and they have gained a sense of self-confidence by doing it (Bowen et al., 2011; Selekman, 2009).

COUPLE AND FAMILY RELAPSE PREVENTION TOOLS

The Two Gardens Mindfulness Practice for Couples

The Nobel Prize-nominated Buddhist monk Thich Nhat Hanh has come up with a beautiful metaphor for how couples should think about and take care of their relationship on a daily basis, which he calls *two gardens* (Hanh, 2011). He shares with couples that they have two gardens to regularly tend to: one's personal garden and the garden of his or her loved one. The first skill each partner has to cultivate is the art of gardening. He believes in each one of us there are flowers and there is garbage. The garbage consists of anger, fear, and jealousy and if you water it, it will strengthen the negative seeds. However, when we water the flowers of compassion, understanding, and love, we strengthen the positive seeds. When we do not know how to practice selective and mindful watering in our own garden we will lack the wisdom and skill to help water the flowers in our partner's garden. By cultivating our own garden well, we also help to cultivate our partner's garden.

When couples become entrenched in arguing and conflict, the only way to make peace with one another is for the partners to go home to their gardens and cultivate the flowers of peace, compassion, understanding, and joy. Once that is accomplished, each partner can approach the other with compassion and patience. Every attempt by the partners to change is to be acknowledged by showing their love and appreciation for one another. Each partner needs the other's daily attention and watering of his or her positive seeds. Unless this happens on a regular basis, the relationship will wither. Hanh puts it best when he said, "In true love, there is no distinction between the one who loves and the one who is loved. Your suffering is my suffering. Lover and beloved are one" (p. 33).

My Sacred Sanctuary Visualization

The *sacred sanctuary visualization* is another way we can help our clients' center themselves and find inner peace. They are to get comfortable in a chair or on a couch in a quiet room with their eyes closed. Next, they are to imagine in their mind's eye using all of their senses, including color and motion, an image of a beautiful and peaceful place they have escaped to where they are completely safe and liberated from any negative thoughts, feelings, and toxic others. It is helpful for clients to use all of their senses to describe in great detail what their sacred sanctuary looks like, if there is any greenery, flowers, birds, what sounds they hear, and so forth. They have nowhere else to be except living in the miraculous moment in their special sacred sanctuary. They are free to stay in their sacred sanctuary as long as they need to.

Visualizing Movies of Joy and Success

This distress management tool has been highly rated by self-harming adolescents presenting with concurrent self-destructive habit difficulties (Selekman, 2005, 2009; Selekman & Schulem, 2007). Once the clients get comfortable in chairs or on a couch, they are to close their eyes and picture a blank movie screen in their minds. Using all of their senses, including color and motion, they are to project on to the screen a movie of some joyful life experience (a memorable family vacation or outing with close friends; seeing a beautiful art work, building, something out in nature that moved them, going to a memorable concert) or something that they had accomplished that they were very proud of themselves (a stellar athletic, musical, or theatrical performance; a special act of kindness). The client is free to decide which type of movie they wish to practice accessing. What is most important is that the movie they selected is easy to access, triggers a strong dose of positive emotion, and puts them in great spirits after viewing it in their minds. It is critical that they practice using this distress management tool one or two times per day, even during times they are not experiencing emotional distress or stressful life events.

Visualizing the Resilient You in Action

The client is to first get comfortable in a chair, close his/her eyes, and capture a blank movie screen in his/her mind. Next, he/she is to project on to the movie screen using all of his/her senses, including color and motion, a movie showing him/her overcoming or bouncing back quickly from an adverse life event from his/her past. After watching the movie of his/her resilience in action for 10–12 minutes, he/she is to respond to the following questions:

- "What inner resources and key strengths did I call upon to bounce back quickly from this challenging and/or painful life event?"
- "What did I learn about myself and what wisdom did I gain from how I handled the situation?"
- "In what ways can I call upon my inner resources and key strengths to empower me to resolve my current difficulty?"

Whenever our clients are feeling at a loss for how to overcome current life challenges, they can do this visualization exercise to get a quick boost of self-confidence and inner strength to fire them up to address the challenges head on. This visualization is a constant reminder to our clients that they have the strengths and resources to tackle any of life's hurdles that come their way.

Self-Directed Neuroplasticity

Our brains are truly remarkable in that they can rapidly adapt to changes in the environment due to their plasticity and go to great lengths to protect our survival. According to DiSalvo (2011), our brains are "happy" when they are receiving a steady diet of certainty, stability, pattern recognition, and pleasure versus emotional distress or pain. However, because of our brain's make-up and *reward distinction blindness*, it sets us up to regularly pursue pleasurable experiences, some of which can be potentially harmful to and lead us to eventually becoming dependent on self-harming, substance abuse, eating-distressed behavior, gambling, and excessive use of the Internet and cyber-porn for pleasure and/or quick relief from emotional distress or mood regulation. We like to educate our clients about how our primitive brains essentially brainwash us with their powerful deceiving messages into believing that our self-destructive habits are good for us and to keep engaging in them despite serious physical, psychological, social, school, or occupational consequences.

Schwartz and Gladding (2011) encourage their clients to use the power of focused attention to direct their choices and actions, which can rewire their brain circuitry and re-establish their engagement in healthy virtuous habits or activities and the use of many of the coping tools and strategies described in this chapter. They have developed a four-step model for empowering their clients to conquer a wide range of self-destructive habits, including mental health problems like obsessive-compulsive disorder. The four steps are: *label, reframe, refocus,* and *revalue*. With the first step, clients are to identify what their main deceptive brain messages are and the accompanying uncomfortable psychological, physical sensations, or urges they may be experiencing. The second step entails having clients reframe the deceptive brain messages, uncomfortable thoughts, feelings, urges as false brain messages (It's not ME, It's just my BRAIN). The third step consists of having clients focus their attention on accessing or identifying any positive thoughts or feelings they may have in their heads, or getting involved in some positive activity even when the deceptive brain messages, negative emotions, or urges are still pushing them around. Finally, the clients are to step back, see clearly, and reflect on how the negative emotions, thoughts, physical discomfort, and urges are being caused by deceptive brain messages that are not true and are to be dismissed by them.

Imagine Yourself as _____ to Stay on Track

This playful goal-maintenance and fun relapse prevention strategy taps clients' inventiveness, triggers positive emotion, and can help strengthen their confidence levels to stay quit from their self-destructive habits. Research indicates that by making *upward comparisons* or connecting oneself to successful others can energize a person to take action (Martin, Haskard-Zoinierek, & DiMatteo, 2010). Therapists begin this exercise by asking clients to think of their favorite athletes, actors, historic figures, and famous and popular literary characters and comic book super-heroes. Next, we want them to close their eyes and imagine shaking the hands of their admired others, which connects them as one. We want to know as clearly as possible now that they have merged with their admired others and what specifically they had received from them that they will use to stay on track, such as valuable words of wisdom and encouragement and the power of focusing intently on achieving one's objective or goal. This could be having more inner courage, self-confidence, being more focused, having more patience, being more flexible, taking positive risks, and so forth. For example, one of my (MS's) clients, a big Michael Jordan fan, decided to merge with him to help elevate his self-confidence and feel more comfortable with taking positive risks like expanding his horizons to pursue new interests during his leisure time. Like Jordan, the client also felt that he needed to be a better team player with his spouse when it came to making important decisions. By making these adjustments, the client was better able to reduce the likelihood of slips occurring and improved his marital relationship as well.

Other Solution-Enhancement and Goal-Maintenance Tools and Strategies

There are other solution-enhancement and goal-maintenance tools and strategies discussed below: *my positive trigger log, disputation skills, interviewing both sides of the client's ambivalence*, the *chilling out room, the rainy day letter, the treasure chest*, and the use of *self-help groups* for added support. In combination with the therapeutic tools and strategies discussed earlier, they can further empower our clients to conquer and stay quit from their self-destructive habits.

My Positive Trigger Log

The *positive trigger log* is a highly effective relapse prevention and distress management tool. In the addiction field, substance abuse counselors rarely inquire with their clients what their positive triggers are. They and their substance-abusing clients focus most of their attention on negative triggers and high-risk situations. Although it is important for us, the clients' couple partners, parents, and involved members from their social networks to learn this important information, what is just as important is knowing what specifically the clients and concerned others do that triggers positive emotion. It is the positive emotion that is curative, in that it strengthens their immune systems, increases their optimism, hope, and happiness levels, and regular doses of it serve as resiliency protective factor for them (Fredrickson, 2009; Peterson, 2006; ; Selekman, 2009; Selekman & Schulem, 2007; Seligman, 2011).

Clients are given a blank *positive trigger log* (see Figure 10.3) to fill out over a week. They must pay close attention daily to what self-generated coping and problem-solving strategies they come up with and use, and what other members of the solution-determined system do that both helps to prevent them from caving in to their self-destructive habits and triggers positive emotion for them. The last column of the log has them identify which of the coping and problem-solving strategies seemed to help the most. In the next couple and family session, we review the positive trigger log and the clients can circle which of the coping and problem-solving strategies they and others need to increase deploying. We can also determine if there are any particular stressful contexts, where using specific coping and problem-solving could be beneficial. We make copies

Date	What I did	My parents/siblings	Friends	Other involved helpers	Positive thoughts and feelings triggered

Figure 10.3 My positive trigger log.

of our clients' positive trigger logs for our files and give them the originals to carry them around folded up in wallets, backpacks, or briefcases to pull out and remind themselves of their many options when faced with high-risk situations. We also give them extra blank positive trigger logs to take home and fill out when they and concerned others come up with additional coping and problem-solving strategies they wish to write down (Selekman, 2006, 2009).

Disputation Skills

Pioneering positive psychology researcher Martin Seligman contends that one of the best types of skill in life we should all try to master to help us be more resilient and optimistic thinkers, and to lead to more fulfilling lives, are *disputation skills* (Seligman, 2002, 2011; Seligman, Reivich, Jaycox, & Gillham, 1995). By achieving mastery with these important thinking skills and having open and flexible minds, we are less likely to fall prey to rumination, excessive pessimism, catastrophic thinking (when one thing goes wrong anticipating that everything else will go wrong in one's life), depression, and anxiety difficulties. There are three major disputation skills that we like to teach our clients: *playing super-sleuth detectives searching for clues and hard evidence, using the mind as a kaleidoscope to search for alternative explanations,* and *the implications and usefulness of clinging to narrow and rigid views.*

PLAYING SUPER-SLEUTH DETECTIVES SEARCHING FOR CLUES AND HARD EVIDENCE

It greatly helps when teaching this valuable disputation skill to have clients who are fans of detective stories and mysteries. They are much more eager and interested in testing out their abilities as super-sleuth detectives and find that this is a stimulating and fun activity to engage in. Whenever we have clients who come into our offices like trial attorneys eager to prove to us that when things go wrong in their lives it must be due to some character flaws, their personalities, or they are solely to blame for life disappointments or failings. In a playful way, we challenge them to go out like super-sleuth detectives, conduct a thorough investigation interviewing significant others and close friends, and gather as many clues and hard evidence to back up their final explanations for why things are going wrong for them. More often than not, many of our clients come back to the their next meetings with us either empty-handed or with little evidence to support their rigid explanations for their difficulties, and they begin to see how their cases would be dismissed in a court of law due to the lack of evidence to support their positions. Typically, after this experience of playing detectives and seeing how difficult it is to find evidence, they become more open to exploring alternative explanations for their difficulties. For more pessimistic skeptical clients, we will send them out again as detectives to search for those elusive clues and the hard evidence they think is out there. Often, when these clients come back empty-handed again, their rigid explanations begin to unravel and there is more openness to exploring alternative explanations.

USING THE MIND AS A KALEIDOSCOPE TO SEARCH FOR ALTERNATIVE EXPLANATIONS

Most clients are familiar with kaleidoscopes and have fond memories of looking through them and seeing beautiful colored designs and patterns. They observed that there was not just one image but multiple images as they turned and faced it at different objects. Like looking through a kaleidoscope, when we experience life disappointments, losses, interpersonal conflicts, and so forth there are multiple explanations for why all of these things occur, not just one. However, clients are more vulnerable to catastrophic thinking and pessimism, and negativity and have a tendency to adopt a tunnel-vision way of viewing these life experiences and may cling to one narrow explanation for their occurrences. After having clients share their pleasurable past experiences with kaleidoscopes, we have them try out the experiment over the next week of pretending to use their minds as a kaleidoscopes and, with curious minds, focus them in the directions of the very life disappointments or difficulties they are presently struggling with. They are to try to come up with three or more images of explanations for why these life disappointments or difficulties are occurring or just occurred, looking for the roles others are playing or played in these situations. Often, clients find that the metaphor of using one's mind as a kaleidoscope helps them to locate multiple explanations for why their life disappointments or difficulties are occurring or had occurred and feel liberated by their kaleidoscopic experiences.

THE IMPLICATIONS AND USEFULNESS OF CLINGING TO NARROW AND RIGID VIEWS

One major thinking trap that clients plagued by habit difficulties fall prey to is *rumination*. Typically, like a broken record, ruminators replay in their heads all of the details regarding something bad that happened to them and how they blame themselves for it. Rumination can make them vulnerable prey for depression and anxiety difficulties, as well as set the stage for slips and prolonged relapsing situations to occur. Therefore, as a way to help combat this dangerous thinking trap, we actively have clients challenge their narrow and rigid explanations both in session, at home, and in any other contexts they are plagued by these thoughts. Some useful questions to both ask clients and have them ask themselves between sessions are as follows:

- "How can you be absolutely certain that you were totally responsible for _____?"
- "Does dwelling on _____ make you feel more 'chilled' or more bummed out?"
- "You know how they say it takes two to tango. So, how do you know that you are solely responsible for your recent conflict situation with Tony?"
- "Do I honestly think I can have complete control over what Barbara writes on Marnie's *Facebook* wall, or is this a silly delusion?"
- "Is dwelling on my catastrophic fear about Tony breaking up with me making me feel better, or is it really making me feel more out of control?"

Questions like these help clients begin to see how their rigid, negative, and catastrophic thinking gets them into trouble emotionally with themselves and with others in their lives, how they fuel the self-destructive habit and pave the way for relapses. Similar to the other disputation skills discussed, both implications and usefulness help clients develop much more open and flexible minds and be more optimistic with their thinking.

Interviewing Both Sides of the Client's Ambivalence

In the spirit of narrative therapy (Epston, 2000), we will pursue having clients externalize or objectify both sides of their ambivalence regarding the advantages and disadvantages of giving up their choice self-destructive habits. If the client would find it helpful, he or she can come up with a name for each side of his or her ambivalence. Using an empty chair, the client is to pretend to be a reporter covering a story on both sides of the ambivalence. By doing so, he or she can make important discoveries about him- or herself, such as certain thoughts, feelings, memories, and stressors that are barriers for change. Through infiltrating the minds of both sides of their ambivalence, the client can come to see the advantages of changing and the hidden agenda and logic behind why the disadvantage side is trying to maintain the status quo rather than changing.

We also have had couple partners and parents participate in interviewing both sides of the client's ambivalence as another effective way for altering their unproductive and outmoded beliefs and problem-maintaining patterns of behavior. Sometimes we will have couple partners and parents sit in the chair of and put themselves in the shoes of the client's disadvantage side of his or her ambivalence to elicit their compassion and truly gain a deeper understanding of the strong grip the self-destructive habit has had on him or her. An added bonus is that the partner and parents may learn about the various functions the client's self-destructive habits have served for them. Any shift in the client's, partners,' or parents' viewing of the problem situation, can lead to dramatic changes in their interactions.

The Chilling Out Room

The *chilling out room* was specifically designed for adolescents and adults plagued by habit and anger management difficulties (Selekman, 2006, 2009). It is a multi-sensory and pattern intervention strategy that can be implemented in clients' homes. The adolescent or adult is to select a room in a quiet area of their house that will serve as their official *chilling out room*. This is their safe and sacred sanctuary that they are to stay in as long as they need in order to emotionally decompress and center themselves. No couple partners or family members are to disturb them while they are in the chilling out room. In fact, I have the client design an artistic-looking **Do Not Disturb** for their special room. The room must have a window so that colorful and fragrant flowers can be placed near it. The flowers access clients' visual and olfactory sensory modes. There will be an art corner in the room where the client can paint or draw freely or make something out of clay. This activity will access their visual and tactile sensory modes. The nice thing about fresh clay is that it is pleasurable to run your fingers through it and it demands your immediate focus and attention. There will be book, periodical, and music libraries in the room. We encourage clients to decide what books, magazines, personal journals and logs, photo albums, and music they should have that triggers positive emotion. Once we have solid therapeutic alliances with our clients, we will recommend certain books and magazines in line with their life passions or interest areas, and relaxing and contemplative music we would like them to listen to, possibly with the sound meditation. While doing the sound meditation, they can pay close attention to certain sounds and images the music produces in their minds and its physiological effect on their bodies. Some of our clients who like yoga have chosen to use their quiet time in the chilling out room to do yogic breathing and exercises.

Once implemented with couples and families, we have found that couple partners, parents, and siblings have equally benefited from using the chilling out room, particularly when they have had stressful work and school days and need to emotionally and physically decompress before interacting with the habit-dependent partner or adolescent. This is a great way to help prevent negative interactions and enabling behaviors.

The Rainy Day Letter

One therapeutic experiment that we regularly use as part of our relapse prevention strategy is to invite our clients to write a *rainy day letter* to them that they can read during times of distress and/or when they feel at risk of relapsing (Dolan, 1991). In this letter, the client provides support and comfort, shares some supportive words of wisdom, and reminds him- or herself of what constructive actions can be taken to feel better, such as talk to a friend, telephone a relative, go out for a walk, or play certain music. The letter is to be written when the client is in good spirits, feels optimistic and in control of his or her life, and is to be read on "rainy days." It is to be kept in a special place at home where it can be easily accessed when needed.

The Treasure Chest

The *treasure chest* (Dolan, 2000; Isebaert, 2005) or "survival kit" is another strategy to be used in moments of distress and feeling at risk for a relapse, and as a way to get out of a negative situation and empower clients to utilize their personal resources. We ask our clients to fill a chest or box with beautiful and special objects like trinkets, meaningful letters, and pictures that re-connect the client with positive emotional moments, and helpful significant others: the picture of a best friend, a souvenir from an exciting and special vacation, the ring inherited from a loved and highly cherished grandmother, a CD of a favorite group, and any other object that is symbolic of hope and happiness. The "rainy day letter" may be one of the objects in the treasure chest. If the client wishes to do so, she or he can bring the treasure chest into a session to show us its contents and share with us the meaningful stories connected to the objects, which will trigger positive emotion for them. For some clients who spend many hours on the computer or using their digital devices, a "virtual treasure chest," an archive, blog, or personal web page with their pictures, special music or words of advice and support makes more sense.

Another variation we use is the *self-esteem medication* (Herrero de Vega & Beyebach, 2004). We ask our clients to prepare a "medication box" imitating real medications, and fill it with small self-esteem-boosting "tablets" (words of wisdom, specific advice, small souvenirs, etc.), together with instructions on dosages, effects, and incompatibilities with other medications, and so forth. The medication box is easy to carry around when needed.

Self-Help and Support Groups

Our position of encouraging clients, their partners, and family members to attend self-help groups is that it is completely up to them to decide whether or not they can benefit from them. In clinical situations where the clients lack strong support systems, we will recommend to them that they get involved in a self-help group and even considering getting a sponsor. With our clients' written consent, we like to collaborate with their sponsors throughout the course of therapy to help unify our relapse prevention teamwork efforts and help optimize for our clients to stay on the recovery track. If a client, his or her partner, or family members have been told by relatives or friends that certain self-groups can help conquer self-destructive habits, help them to better cope with high levels of stress, and contribute to their own personal growth, we will support their pursuit to get involved in these particular self-help groups by providing them with important contact information for groups in their area. The same is true for other types of support groups they are interested in getting involved with. What is most critical here is our sensitivity and respect for clients' theories of change and what specifically they think will work best for them (Duncan, 2010; Hubble, Duncan, Miller, & Wampold, 2010; Selekman, 2009).

Helpful Strategies for Managing Challenging Couple and Family Situations where Relapses Continue to Occur

Relapses sometimes occur, in spite of our best efforts to co-develop with our clients highly structured and solid relapse prevention plans. Additionally, the couple partners and family members may have continued to persist with their overprotective, super-responsible, overcontrolling, or other enabling behaviors out of fear and anxiety that something dire will happen to the habit-dependent client. For the habit-dependent client, the couple partner's and/or family members' enabling behaviors can trigger negative emotions in him or her, fuel irresponsible behavior, poor choice-making, and eventual relapses in his or her effort to take back control. A vicious and cyclical relapse-promoting pattern of interaction gets set in motion where the unspoken words of the concerned couple partner or family members are: "We will save you from yourself because you are irresponsible and out-of-control." The habit-dependent client's private dialogue is, "I will not let you control me, I will show you!" Ultimately, all parties become deadlocked in an endless power struggle over control, which becomes a game without an end.

With these couple and family dilemmas, there are three strategic therapeutic strategies that we like to employ that can break these rigid patterns of interaction. The first pattern intervention and paradoxical strategy encourages the couple partner or parents to increase their pattern of super-responsible and/or overprotective behaviors, which is called the *compression technique* (Stanton, 1984). The second pattern intervention strategy that redefines the rules of the game and the relationship interactions, is called *declaring impotence* (Andolfi, Angelo, Menghi, & Nicolo-Corigliano, 1983). Finally, we like to recommend to parents of powerful and/or multi-habit-dependent adolescents as a last resort intervention strategy to employ *Gandhian nonviolent passive resistance tactics*, such as staging a *sit-in* in their bedrooms (Omer, 2004). We discuss below each one of these strategies.

The Compression Technique

This strategy is particularly effective with couple partners and parents who are super-responsible and overprotective with the habit-dependent partner or adolescent, and do not respond well to straightforward therapeutic efforts to reduce or eliminate their counter-productive ways of interacting with him or her. Even after giving them plenty of space to share their concerns and recommend what their therapists should try to do differently with them and the identified client, they continue to persist in their unproductive attempted solutions. The *compression technique* encourages them to greatly increase their super-responsible and overprotective interactions with the habit-dependent partner or adolescent out of love and concern for him or her. In fact, they are to wait on him or her hand and foot. The therapist can wonder aloud with the partner or parents what bases they have failed to cover with their partner or adolescent, in terms of being super-responsible for or overprotective with him or her and encourage them to be as comprehensive as possible in their efforts to save their loved one (Stanton, 1984). What eventually happens over time is that the habit-dependent partner or adolescent puts his or her foot down, becomes tired of being smothered, and starts to take responsibility for his or her behavior, including achieving abstinence from his or her choice habits. At this point, he or she is ripe for change and ready to co-develop a tighter and more effective relapse prevention plan.

Declaring Impotence

With some of the couples and families we have worked with, they not only continued to persist in their counter-productive enabling behaviors but they were also feeling completely burned out, demoralized, and experiencing hopelessness and despair. Similar to the highly effective Al-Anon principle of *detaching with love*, we encourage couple partners and parents to accept the fact that they cannot change their habit-dependent partners or young adult/adolescent offspring and to focus their attention, time, and energy on taking care of themselves. They are to approach the habit-dependent partner or young adult/adolescent *declaring impotence* in their inability to change him or her and that they are abdicating this responsibility (Andolfi et al., 1983). As part of this declaration of impotence, the couple partner and parents can let go of everything else they were doing to make the habit-dependent partner or kid's life as comfortable as possible, such as: cooking special meals, washing and drying clothes, being an alarm clock in the mornings to wake him or her up for school or work, being a chauffer, and so forth. When approached by the habit-dependent partner or young adult/adolescent about why they have discontinued their former super-responsible behaviors, partners or parents are to arbitrarily share lines like: "I am emotionally exhausted," "The battle is over, I have surrendered," or "It is my/our turn, I/we need to take care of me/us." They are to avoid at all costs having conversations about or justifying with the habit-dependent person their reasons for pursuing new ways of taking care of themselves and living.

Gandhian Nonviolent Passive Resistance Parental Tactics

When working with multi-habit dependent and tyrannical adolescents who clearly are in charge of the family mood and where the parents are at their wits' end with their efforts to change them, *Gandhian nonviolent passive resistance tactics* can be quite effective (Omer, 2004). Gandhi and later Martin Luther King successfully demonstrated the power in and the widespread changes that can occur when nonviolent passive resistance tactics are employed. One Gandhian tactic that we particularly like to use is the *sit-in*. The parents are to pick times to stage their sit-ins where they are willing and have in some cases a few hours to sit inside their kids' bedrooms in front of their doors as long as it takes for the kids to come up with some realistic and doable solution strategies for changing their habit and other challenging behaviors. They are to let their adolescents know that they are tired with the way the family situation has been and how it is time for a major family overhaul and climate change. In addition, they let their kids know that they are making a commitment to stopping all of their negative and unproductive ways of interacting with them, and they are prepared to sit as long as it takes for their kids to come up with solutions for their problematic behaviors. While sitting, the parents need to agree to refrain from yelling, making threats, lecturing, pleading, and abandoning whatever else they had tried in the past that was unproductive. They are not to react to or flinch when their kids scream out profanities at them or engage in other disrespectful and provocative behaviors with them.

Eventually, the adolescents become tired and discover that they cannot win against passive parents who refuse to be their sparring partners. Once they come up with some novel and realistic ideas for resolving their habit and other challenging behaviors that seem worthwhile trying out, the parents can support their efforts to implement their new change strategies. During the times that their children are putting forth a concerted effort to change and be more responsible and respectful towards them, the parents are to praise their efforts and reward them with high-quality time, engaging in a fun and pleasurable activity their children would like to do with them.

Conclusion

In this chapter, we have presented a plethora of relapse prevention tools and strategies to empower our clients to further consolidate their gains, stay on track, and constructively manage inevitable slips that occur while on the pathway to recovery. It is our contention that relapse prevention training is a couple and family affair, needs to begin in initial sessions, and is a critical dimension to any treatment approach for all five of the self-destructive habits discussed in this book. Clearly, the more well stocked our clients' relapse prevention arsenal is and the more structure they have in their lives, the less likely it is that slips will occur, and we can optimize for their future success at treatment outcome.

11

SELF-DESTRUCTIVE HABITS

Future Directions with Treatment, Training, and Research

> This is not the end. It is not even the beginning of the end. But it is, perhaps, the end of the beginning.
>
> *Winston Churchill*

Introduction

After more than three decades of our working with self-destructive habit clients, their couple partners, and families in both inpatient and outpatient settings, we have experienced with them the many challenges of conquering seemingly intractable and chronic habit difficulties, the bumpy roads and slips while they are striving to remain on the recovery track, as well as experiencing our share of treatment failures with them. In this chapter, we will underscore seven practice guidelines for optimizing the likelihood for successful couple and family treatment with self-destructive habit clients. Next, we will share with readers some of the valuable lessons we have learned and wisdom gained from our treatment failures. The remainder of the chapter will cover our future recommendations for treatment, training, and research.

Doing What Works: Seven Practice Guidelines for Optimizing for Treatment Success

Thanks to the ongoing feedback from our clients throughout the treatment process and at treatment outcome and follow-up, clinical evidence-based practice wisdom, and our professional colleagues' research included in this book, the following seven practice guidelines have grown out about what contributes to treatment success.

Keeping the Focus on and Utilizing Client Strengths and Resources Co-Creates With Them a Therapeutic Context Ripe for Change

Since many self-destructive habit clients experience difficulties with negative emotion, mood regulation and high psychological reactance levels employing therapeutic tools and strategies from solution-focused brief therapy (Berg & Miller, 1992; Berg & Reuss, 1997; de Shazer 1991, 1988; de Shazer et al., 2007), positive psychology (Fredrickson, 2009; Lopez & Snyder, 2009; Peterson, 2006; Peterson & Seligman, 2004; Seligman 2011; Snyder & Lopez, 2007), and motivational-enhancement therapy (Miller & Rollnick, 2002; Rollnick, Mason, & Butler 1999; Rosengren, 2009) can effectively neutralize negative emotions by increasing positive emotion, hope, and optimism levels, reduce psychological reactivity to change, foster cooperative partnerships, and co-create a therapeutic climate ripe for change with them. All of these strengths-based approaches operate from the core assumptions that all clients have the strengths and resources to change and they are truly the experts on their own lives and the kind treatment experiences they wish to have. Therefore, it behooves therapists to view their clients' expertise as a valuable resource to be tapped and utilized to empower them to conquer their self-destructive habit difficulties. This is supported by psychotherapy outcome research that suggests that around 40% of treatment variance is accounted for by what the client brings to the therapeutic encounter (Bohart & Tallman, 2010; Duncan, 2010; Hubble, Duncan, & Miller, 1999; Lambert, 2010; Wampold, 2001). Our collaborative strengths-based brief family therapy model incorporates the best elements of these and other family and individual therapy approaches, client-informed research, and involves actively collaborating with and tapping the expertise of key resource people from clients' social networks to co-construct solutions.

Self-Generated Changing Challenges the Notion that Clients with Self-Destructive Habits have Progressive Diseases and are Incapable of Changing without Treatment

The ever-expanding self-change and single-session brief intervention research literature on self-destructive habit individuals is challenging the traditional illness metaphor and Twelve-Step program philosophy where the professionals are the keepers of the higher truth that *change is not possible without treatment and total abstinence goals* (Klingemann & Klingemann, 2009; Shaffer & Jones, 1989; Sobell, 2010). If anything, as professionals and researchers we should invest the time and energy in learning from these resilient, creative, and resourceful individuals about what their recipes for success have been and teach our clients plagued by self-destructive habits their creative tools and strategies and/or establish treatment program frameworks based on their expertise.

Tailor-Fitting the Therapeutic Relationship and Optimizing for Client Choice-Making Can Greatly Enhance Alliance-Building and Foster Cooperative Partnerships

Research indicates that when substance abusers, clients with other self-destructive habits, and clients in general are given the decision-making power regarding choosing what treatment modalities they wish to pursue, determining the goals for treatment, and when we honor their preferences (unique habit quitting styles, expectations, and visions of change, they will be highly invested in the treatment process and motivated to succeed (Duncan, 2010; Hubble, Duncan, Miller, & Wampold, 2010; Norcross, 2010; Selekman, 2009; Selekman & Schulem, 2007; Wampold, 2001; Whitlock, 2008)). Our blueprint for change plan places clients in the drivers' seats in terms of goal-setting and treatment decision-making, which helps to foster cooperative partnerships with them in their very first couple or family therapy sessions. Clients also are invited to give us end of session feedback each session on the quality of our relationships with them, any adjustments they would like us to make, and their experience of the change process or lack thereof. All of the above therapeutic operations help prevent premature client drop out from occurring and can optimize for positive treatment outcomes.

Self-Destructive Habit Difficulties Call for an Integrative and Flexible Bio-Psychosocial Systemic Approach

As can be seen from many of the challenging case examples presented in this book, one-size-does-not-fit-all with self-destructive habit clients, couple partners, and families. We need to be flexible and integrative and match what we do clinically with the unique needs and characteristics of our clients and with the ever-changing nature of the therapeutic alliance (Friedlander, Escudero, & Heatherington, 2006; Pinsof, 1995), which includes tailor-fitting our relationships with them and using a wide range of therapeutic tools and strategies from different family and individual therapy approaches. By viewing our clients through multiple lenses, it offers us multiple pathways for intervention and helps us to determine with them at what systems levels to target specific change strategies. Even if one is a highly skilled couple or family therapist, it is important with self-destructive habit clients not to lose sight of the powerful role brain systems and neurotransmitters play in fueling and maintaining their clients' habits. We must cover this systems level in couple and family therapy along with altering cognitive distortions that also play a major role in maintaining their difficulties.

We Need to Honor the Multiple Functions and Meanings of our Clients' Self-Destructive Habits

For self-destructive habit clients, their choice habits have unique meanings in their life stories and serve multiple functions for them. Many of these clients describe their habits as gifts or valuable resources for helping them cope with emotional distress, regulate their moods, or just to feel something. Interpersonally, their choice habits may be used to gain more power in an intimate relationship, to control or hurt others, or may be a metaphor for a relationship conflict or harboring a family secret. In many cases, the self-destructive habits often become hidden practices occurring behind the scenes and will be protected by the clients at all costs. This is why it is so important at the very beginning of couple or family therapy to come to know how clients' choice habits have benefited them, how they fit into their life stories, and what would be the disadvantages of their giving them up.

It is Critical to be Sensitive to Trauma and Co-Morbidity Issues with our Self-Destructive Habit Clients, as well as to the Risk of Suicide and Violence

When it is made clear to us by the clients at the beginning of couple and/or family therapy that trauma and co-morbidity has played a significant role in the development and/or maintenance of the self-destructive habits, we need to be mindful of the fact that the choice habits in some cases have served as major or sole coping strategies for them in warding off flashbacks, paralyzing anxiety, or serving as the glue to hold them together emotionally. If we jump the gun and prematurely push for the reduction of their engaging in their choice habits, some clients can become suicidal or may experience other crises. Therefore, we need to carefully gauge with the clients their tolerance and readiness for change levels with addressing and changing their self-destructive habits, establish very small goals, and when the clients are in the preparation and action stages of readiness for change, we can offer replacement coping strategies and perhaps negotiate a tapering down quitting style with their choice habits. In clinical situations where mindfulness meditation and alternative healing methods are not doing the trick and the clients are still experiencing unpleasant psychological and physical distress, we will either use eye movement desensitization and reprogramming (E.M.D.R.) to re-process the traumatic memories (Shapiro, 1989; Shapiro & Forrest, 2004; Shapiro, Kaslow, & Maxfield, 2007) or bring in a psychiatrist to evaluate if the use of medication can benefit the client.

Relapse Prevention Training is a Couple and Family Affair and Must Begin in the First Session and be Continued Throughout the Treatment Process

Relapse prevention is one of the most important therapeutic operations that can optimize for self-destructive habit clients' treatment success. We begin relapse prevention training at the very beginning of couple and family therapy and it continues throughout the entire treatment process. As part of the relapse prevention planning and strategizing process, we actively involve the couple partner, family members, and key and concerned members from their social networks. The more solid and clear the relapse prevention plan is, the more likely the self-destructive habit client will be able to stave off slips and stay on the recovery track. Worst-case scenario planning is an important aspect of the relapse prevention process. It also is critical to normalize for the client, couple partner, and the family how slips are inevitable and part of the change process. We believe slips can offer both our clients and us valuable wisdom about where we need to tighten up with the structure and what specifically to do differently when faced with similar stressful situations.

Lessons Learned from Treatment Failures

In the same way that slips and relapses are valuable teachers for our clients and their families and couple partners, our therapeutic failures over the years have also taught us a number of important lessons. We see the following as the main sources of therapeutic dropout or stagnation.

Failure to Help the Self-Destructive Habit-Dependent Client to Advance to the Next Stage of Readiness for Change

As we have demonstrated throughout this book, the central task of therapy with self-destructive habit clients is not simply to find out what they have to do, but to get them to actually do it (Ciarrocchi, 2001). To this end we use all the joining, consciousness-raising, and motivation-enhancing interventions that we have described in this book. However, in some cases none of these strategies seems to have any effect on the position of our self-destructive-habit clients, who remain in a contemplative or even a precontemplative stage of readiness for change in spite of our best therapeutic efforts. The inability to work therapeutically with clients who are perfectly happy with their self-destructive habit, unaware of their negative consequences, or simply unwilling to take them seriously is linked to broader cultural and social issues which, as we will discuss below, often legitimize and promote the abuse of substances, Internet or other self-destructive activities (Blaszczynski, 2009, 2011; Orford, 2011).

Failure to Engage a Relevant Member of the Client System or to Help the Parents or Couple Partner of the Client to Move in their Stages of Readiness for Change

One way of handling self-destructive habit clients whom we have failed to help to move in their stages of readiness for change is to rely on the support, influence, and even pressure (monitoring and control) of their families or couple partners. For this reason, not being able to engage the relevant members of the client system into therapy is one of the main sources of therapeutic failure. This is especially the case when the self-destructive habit client is an oppositional adolescent; in these situations not including both parents from the first session on, dramatically increases the likelihood of therapeutic stagnation. This is why we have adopted a more proactive approach (Prochaska, Norcross, & DiClemente, 2006), reaching out to the relevant family members (especially to the fathers) and proceeding strategically in order to ensure their commitment to therapy (Santisteban et al., 1996; Szapocznik, Hervis, & Schwartz, 2003; Szapocznik & Kurtines, 1989). In those cases where the father or the mother cannot be engaged in spite of our best effort, or they are simply not available, it is critical to find more effective ways to intervene with those who do come to the sessions.

Failure to Deal with the Complications Related to Multi-Habit-Dependent Self-Destructive Couples and Families

Motivating and supporting key family members or the couple partners are central therapeutic tasks, and one major source of failure has been when parents or couple partners stayed paralyzed by the intimidating nature of their children's or partners' problems and failed to take adequate action (Fisch & Schlanger, 1999). The best way we have found for handling these situations is to "go slow," not just with the self-destructive habit-dependent clients, but with their family members and couple partners also, making sure that we are not asking them to take difficult steps before they are ready to do so. Here, the motivational therapeutic tools and strategies that we have presented for self-destructive habit clients are also useful to enhance the commitment and readiness to change of their concerned others.

Failure to Maintain our Therapeutic Leverage in Complex Networks of Involved Helping Professionals from Larger Systems

Another source of lack of success is when the complexity of the professional helper system exceeds our capacity to make a meaningful difference, especially when we have a peripheral position within the helping system, or get caught in the conflict between family and professionals, or between different groups of professional helpers themselves. We have found that the best way to handle these difficult situations is to keep our collaborative, low-profile stance, but to be very active in reaching out to all parties involved, while at the same time making sure that we give credit for any positive change to all involved parties.

"Self-Destructive Habit Overrides," Powerful Relapses that Unsettle the Therapeutic System and Pave the Way for Family Destruction and Chronic Difficulties

Finally, we have to acknowledge that even with cases that are apparently proceeding smoothly and producing significant clinical changes at all levels, sometimes the self-destructive habit strikes back in unexpected and often very destructive ways—the kind of "self-destructive habit override" illustrated with situations like the Gino case presented in Chapter 9, but also those cases where relapses lead to unnecessary hospitalizations, disempowering clients and families alike. Having learned this the hard way, we now devote an even more substantial part of our therapeutic efforts to relapse prevention with our clients and their couple partners, families, and their concerned resource people from their social networks.

Future Directions for Training and Research

There is a great need for the development of effective treatment methods, prevention initiatives, and treatment outcome research in the relatively new areas of self-harm, gambling, and Internet and cyber-sex abuse (Westphal, 2007). But even in the substance abuse and eating disorder fields, which have a long history of research and treatment, there is still ample space and need for truly effective treatments that serve our clients better (Dennis, Scott, Funk, & Foss, 2005; Dutra et al., 2008; Gutiérrez, 2011; Orford, 2008; Thompson-Brenner, Glass, & Westen, 2003; Von Holle et al., 2008).

Training

Given that we both spend a substantial proportion of our professional time training and supervising therapists, we have given a lot of thought to how we can improve this important part of our work. Indeed, a collaborative strengths-based brief family therapy approach poses some specific challenges for training and dissemination. It should not be seen as a closed model that can be trained from scratch as a whole "package," but more as a process of learning where new therapeutic tools and strategies are progressively incorporated into a framework of respectful and collaborative practice. We strongly believe this for a number of reasons. For one, collaborative strengths-based brief family therapy is an integrative approach, making use of a considerable number of different therapeutic tools and strategies, so that proper use would require a great deal of training to master these different ingredients. A second reason is that therapists' creativity and their willingness to take positive risks is a central feature of our approach, and one that goes beyond the mastery of any number of discrete procedures. Finally, we firmly believe that any therapeutic approach should not only maximize the positive impact of client and relationship factors, but should also bring forth the individual strengths and resources of each individual therapist (Wampold, 2006). Again, this speaks out against the shortcomings of standardization and the abuse of manuals (Duncan & Miller, 2006; Wampold, 2001).

This said, how could training in collaborative strengths-based brief family therapy be further developed? In our view, effective training and supervision requires that we help our trainees and supervisees to develop their own competencies in several areas that are in line with the seven therapy practice principles outlined earlier. More specifically, our experience as trainers and supervisors is that successful training in collaborative strengths-based brief family therapy should improve the following:

- Therapists' skill to focus on and make use of clients' resources and self-generated changing and healing capacities.
- Therapists' presence in session, and their skill to monitor and tailor-fit the therapeutic alliance based on client feedback, especially in conjoint sessions where it is critical to develop a sense of safety and shared purpose. This includes the willingness and skill to strategically engage the relevant members of the client system.
- Therapists' use of self, positive risk-taking, and sensible and adequate personal involvement, together with a willingness to step outside of their usual "comfort zone" in order to better respond to the specific challenges of a particular client situation.
- Therapists' willingness to work in highly volatile chaotic situations in order to contain and channel crisis and relapses.
- Last but not least, familiarity with the range of available therapeutic tools, experiments, rituals, and strategies from which to choose from within our model. Although we see it as secondary to the alliance-building and cooperation-enhancing aspect of our approach, this "skills building" and "tool box" component is always an important part of our trainings.

For us, the central challenge that lies ahead is to produce lasting changes, not only in individual therapists, but in the entire professional culture of agencies and organizations that work with self-destructive habit clients, in order to help them become more collaborative, resource-oriented, context-sensitive and outcome-informed.

Research

We believe that qualitative research studies with self-changers and/or individuals who required just one session and/or minimal treatment to kick their self-destructive habits can offer therapists valuable insights about what works and the development of effective therapeutic change strategies. In fact, intensive qualitative studies with self-changers can aid professionals in co-developing innovative treatment methods and short-term treatment programs based on the expertise and creative strategies of these resourceful and resilient individuals. We are in agreement with Orford (2008), who argues in favor of more research on unaided change versus therapy change, and with Tucker (2008) who contends: " By studying natural resolutions, the cultural and other contextual elements that motivate and sustain positive change begin to emerge with clarity, which is not possible in studies of problem drinkers who seek help" (p. 217).

Although there have been numerous treatment outcome studies with couples and families in the addictions and eating disorder fields, there have been only a few poorly designed and controlled couple and family treatment outcome studies that have been conducted with adolescents and adults presenting with self-harming, problem gambling, and Internet and cyber-sex dependency problems. Those research studies that have been conducted with these last three self-destructive habit difficulties tended to utilize approaches that are based on popular individual therapy models like cognitive-behavioral therapy (Beck, Rush, & Emery., 1979) or dialectical behavioral therapy and/or were more family psycho-educational (Miller, Rathus, & Linehan, 2007). With eating disorders, there are many individual therapy and family therapy treatment studies, but very few outcome studies with couples.

Even the pioneers and researchers behind the empirically supported multidimensional family therapy (Liddle, 2002, 2010) brief strategic family therapy (Szapocznik et al., 2003), functional family therapy (Alexander, Pugh, & Parsons, 1998), and multisystemic therapy (Henggeler, Schoenwald, Borduin, Rowland, & Cunningham, 1998, 2009) models have not conducted treatment outcome studies with youth presenting mainly with self-harming, eating-distressed, problem gambling, and Internet and cyber-sex abuse problems. Most of their adolescent clientele and families in their studies were presenting with a wide range of other externalizing behavioral problems or substance-abuse difficulties.

We are planning to launch a multi-site, well-controlled collaborative strengths-based brief family treatment outcome study with adolescents presenting with one or more of the five self-destructive habits presented in this book. We do not intend to prove the effectiveness of one more competing therapy model to be promoted in the psychotherapy market. Instead, using both quantitative and qualitative process-outcome research methods, our hope is that with the help of the subjects in our study we will be able to pinpoint what aspects of the treatment methodology and process promote self-healing and self-changing processes, to learn about different quitting styles, and to identify specific family relationship changes that effectively stabilize the self-destructive behaviors. We will specifically focus on how certain therapeutic experiments and strategies work in the context of the unfolding therapeutic alliance and on how therapist input, conceptualized in terms of therapeutic presence and interpersonal skill (Anderson, Ogles, Patterson, Lambert, & Vermeersch, 2009; Geller & Greenberg, 2012; Wampold, 2001, 2006) contributes to and promotes the progression of clients and their families along the stages of readiness for change.

Conclusion

In this book we have presented our conceptualization of the territory of self-destructive habits and have shown how our integrative and flexible collaborative strengths-based brief family therapy approach offers therapists a highly pragmatic treatment method for couples and families plagued by self-destructive habit difficulties. We have strongly emphasized the importance of the psychotherapy common factors such as: the establishment, strengthening, and ongoing monitoring of the quality of our therapeutic alliances with our clients, their couple partners, and families; the creation of a therapeutic climate ripe for change; the openness to the constant feedback from our clients' session-by-session; and the ongoing monitoring of therapeutic progress as the key ingredients for producing successful treatment outcomes. In addition, we have provided a long and varied "menu" of therapeutic tools, experiments, and rituals to be used in the context of our therapeutic relationships of choice that we co-create with our clients. Although we have highlighted the promises and the positive impact of these therapeutic positions, strategies and methods, we have also acknowledged and described the bumps in the road that we often find in our work with these most challenging clients. We hope that the ideas brought forth in this book will inspire other therapists to continue improving their practices, and that they will spark the inventiveness and creativity of our readers to the benefit of their self-destructive habit clients, their couple partners, and families.

REFERENCES

Abbott, M. W., & Volberg, R. A. (1996). The New Zealand National Survey of Problem and Pathological Gambling. *Journal of Gambling Studies, 12* (2), 143–160.

Aboujaoude, E. (2011). *Virtually you: The dangerous powers of the e-personality*. New York: Norton.

Aboujaoude, E., Koran, L. M., Gamel, N., Large, M. D., & Serpe, R. T. (2006). Potential markers for problematic Internet use: A telephone survey of 2,513 adults. *CNS Spectrum: The Journal of Psychiatric Medicine, 11* (10), 750–755.

Achab, S., & Khazaal, Y. (2011). Psychopharmacological treatment in pathological gambling: A critical review. *Current Pharmacology, 17,* 1389–1395.

Adler, P. A., & Adler, P. (2011). *The tender cut: Inside the hidden world of self-injury*. New York: New York University.

Agras, W. S., Crow, S., Mitchell, J. E., Halmik, K. A., & Bryson, S. (2009). A 4-year prospective study of Eating Disorder NOS compared with full eating disorder syndromes. *International Journal of Eating Disorders, 42,* 565–570.

Agras, W. S., Walsh, T., Fairburn, C. G., Wilson, G. T., & Kraemer, H. C. (2000). A multicenter comparison of cognitive-behavioral therapy and interpersonal psychotherapy for bulimia nervosa. *Archives of General Psychiatry, 57,* 459–466.

Alexander, J. F., Pugh, C., & Parsons, B. (1998). *Blueprints for violence prevention: Vol. 3. Functional family therapy*. Boulder, CO: Center for the Study and Prevention of Violence.

Allgood, S. M., Parham, K. B., Salts, C. J., & Smith, T. A. (1995). The association between pretreatment change and unplanned termination in family therapy. *American Journal of Family Therapy, 23* (3), 195–202.

Amato, L., Davoli, M., Ferri, M., & Ali, R. (2006). Methadone at tapered doses for the management of opioid withdrawal (Cochrane Review). In: *The Cochrane Library*, Issue 1. Chichester, UK: John Wiley & Sons.

Amen, D. G., & Smith, D. E. (2010). *Unchain your brain: 10 steps to breaking the addictions that steal your life*. Los Angeles, CA: MindWorks Press.

APA. (1994). *Diagnostic and statistical manual of mental disorders* (4th ed., text rev.). Washington, DC: American Psychiatric Association.

Andersen, T. (1991). *The reflecting team: Dialogues about the dialogues about the dialogues*. New York: Norton.

Anderson, C. A., Sakamoto, A., Gentile, D. A., Nobuko, I., Shibuya, A., Yukawa, S., & Kobayashi, K. (2008). Longitudinal effects of violent video games on aggression in Japan and the United States. *Pediatrics, 122* (5), 1067–1072.

Anderson, G., & Brown, R. I. (1984). Real and laboratory gambling, sensation- seeking and arousal. *British Journal of Psychology, 75* (3), 401–410.

Anderson, H. (1997). *Conversation, language, and possibilities: A post-modern approach to therapy*. New York: Basic.

Anderson, H., & Gehart, D. (2007). *Collaborative therapy: Relationships and conversations that make a difference*. New York: Routledge.

Anderson, H., & Goolishian, H. (1988). Human systems as linguistic systems: Evolving ideas about the implications for theory and practice. *Family Process, 27,* 371–393.

Anderson, H., & Goolishian, H. (1991). Thinking about multi-agency work with substance abusers and their families: A language systems approach. *Journal of Strategic and Systemic Therapies, 10* (1), 20–36.

Anderson, T., Ogles, B. M., Patterson, C., Lambert, M. J., & Vermeersch, D. A. (2009). Therapist effects:

REFERENCES

Facilitative interpersonal skills as a predictor for therapist success. *Journal of Clinical Psychology, 65* (7), 755–768.

Andolfi, M. (1980). *Family therapy: An interactional approach*. New York: Plenum.

Andolfi, M., Angelo, C., Menghi, P., & Nicolo-Corigliano, M. (1983). *Behind the family mask: Therapeutic change in rigid family systems*. New York: Brunner/Mazel.

Andover, M. S., Pepper, C. M., & Gibb, B. E. (2007). Self-mutilation and coping strategies in a college sample. *Suicide and Life-Threatening Behavior, 37*, 238–243.

Anker, M. G., Duncan, B. L., & Sparks, J. A. (2009). Using client feedback to improve couple therapy outcomes: A randomized clinical trial in a naturalistic setting. *Journal of Consulting and Clinical Psychology, 77*, 693–704.

Anokhin, A. P., Golosheykin, S., Sirevaag, E., Kristjansson, S., Rohrbaugh, J. W., & Heath, A. C. (2006). Rapid discrimination of visual scene content in the human brain. *Brain Research, 1093*, 167–177.

Anthony, J. C., & Petronis, K. R. (1995). Early-onset drug use and risk of later drug problems. *Drug & Alcohol Dependency, 40*, 9–15.

Arcelus, J., Mitchell, A. J., Wales, J., & Nielsen, S. (2011). Mortality rates in patients with anorexia nervosa and other eating disorders: A meta-analysis of 36 studies. *Archives of General Psychiatry, 68*, 724–731.

Ariely, D. (2008). *Predictably irrational: The hidden forces that shape our decisions*. New York: Harper Collins.

Ariyabuddhiphongs, V. (2012). Adolescent gambling: A narrative review of behavior. *Journal of Mental Health and Addiction*, DOI: 10.1007/511469 0129401–6, Springer/Link.

Azrin, N. H., Sisson, R., Meyers, R., & Godley, M. (1982). Alcoholism treatment by disulfram and community reinforcement therapy. *Journal of Behavioral Therapy and Experimental Psychiatry, 13*, 105–112.

Baker, A., Boggs, T. G., & Lewin, T. J. (2001). Randomized controlled trial of brief cognitive-behavioral interventions among regular users of amphetamines. *Addiction, 96*, 1279–1287.

Baker, A., Lee, N. K., & Clare, M. (2005). Brief cognitive-behavioral interventions for regular amphetamine abusers: A step in the right direction. *Addiction, 100*, 367–378.

Baker, T. B., Piper, M. E., McCarthy, D. E., Majeskie, M. R., & Fiore, M. C. (2004). Addiction motivation reformulated: An affective processing model of negative reinforcement. *Psychological Bulletin, 111*, 33–51.

Barber, J., Luborsky, L., Crits-Christoph, P., Thase, M., Weiss, R., & Frank, A. (1999). Therapeutic alliance as a predictor of outcome in treatment of cocaine dependence. *Psychotherapy Research, 9*, 54–73.

Bartlett, R. C., & Collins, S. D. (2011). *Aristotle's nicomachean ethics*. Chicago, IL: The University of Chicago Press.

Baumeister, R. F. (1996). The crystallization of discontent in the process of major life change. In T. F. Heatherton & J. L. Weinberger (Eds.), *Can personality change?* (pp. 281–297). Washington, DC: American Psychological Association.

Baumeister, R. F., Heatherton, T. F., & Tice, D. M. (1994). *Losing control: How and why people fail at self-regulation*. San Diego, CA: Academic Press.

Baumeister, R. F., & Tierney, J. (2011). *Willpower: Rediscovering the greatest human strength*. New York: Penguin Press.

Beard, K. W. (2008). Internet addiction in children and adolescents. In C. B. Yarnall (Ed.), *Computer research science trends* (pp. 59–70). Hauppauge, NY: Nova Science.

Beard, K. W. (2011). Working with adolescents addicted to the Internet. In K. S. Young & C. Nabuco de Abreu (Eds.), *Internet addiction: A handbook and guide to the evaluation and treatment* (pp. 173–191). Hoboken, NJ: John Wiley.

Beck, A. (1995). Cognitive therapy with personality disorders. In P. Salkovskis (Ed.), *Frontiers in cognitive therapy* (pp. 165–181). New York: Guilford.

Beck, A., Rush, A., & Emery, G. (1979). *Cognitive therapy of depression*. New York: Guilford.

Becoña, E. (1999). *Bases teóricas que sustentan los programas de drogas*. [Theoretical basis for drug abuse prevention.] Madrid, Spain: Plan Nacional de Drogas.

Becoña, E., & Cortés, M. (Eds.). (2008). *Guia clinica de intervención psicologica en addicciones*. [Clinical guide for psychological intervention in addictions.] Madrid, Spain: Socidrogalcohol.

Bercaw, B., & Bercaw, G. (2010). Finding healthy sexuality in recovering relationships. *Family Therapy Magazine, 9* (1), 32–37.

Berg, I. K., & DeJong, P. (1998). *Interviewing for solutions*. Pacific Grove, CA: Brooks/Cole.

Berg, I. K., & Miller, S. D. (1992). *Working with the problem drinker: A solution-focused approach*. New York: Norton.

REFERENCES

Berg, I. K., & Reuss, N. H. (1997). *Solutions step by step: A substance abuse treatment manual.* New York: Norton.

Bergh, C., Brodin, U., Lindberg, G., & Sodersten, P. (2002). Randomized controlled trial of a treatment for anorexia and bulimia. *Proceedings of the National Academic of Sciences, USA, 99,* 9486–9491.

Bergh, C., Eklund, S., Ericksson, M., Lindberg, G., & Sodersten, P. (1996). A new treatment of anorexia nervosa. *Lancet, 348,* 611–612.

Bergh, C., Osgood, M., Alters, D., Maletz, L., Leon, M., & Sodersten, P. (2006). How effective is family therapy for the treatment of anorexia nervosa? *European Eating Disorders Review, 14,* 371–376.

Bertrand, K., Dufour, M., Wright, J., & Lasnier, B. (2008). Adapted couple therapy (ACT) for gamblers: A promising avenue. *Journal of Gambling Studies, 24,* 393–409.

Beutler, L. E., Moleiro, C. M., & Talebi, H. (2002). Resistance. In J. C. Norcross (Ed.), *Psychotherapy relationships that work: Therapists contributions and responsiveness to patients* (pp. 129–143). New York: Oxford University Press.

Beyebach, M. (2000). La tecnica de la externalizacion en el trabajo con trastornos de la alimentación. [Externalization in the treatment of eating disorders.] In N. Gracia-Martin, B. Perez-Rodriguez, & M. Rial-Cascudo (Eds.), *Los trastornos de la alimentacion desde una perspectiva multidisciplinar* (pp. 199–237). Bilbao, Spain: Aldakuntza.

Beyebach, M. (2006). *24 ideas para una psicoterapia breve.* [24 ideas for brief psychotherapy.] Barcelona, Spain: Herder.

Beyebach, M. (2009). Integrative solution-focused brief therapy: A provisional roadmap. *Journal of Systemic Therapies, 28,* 18–35.

Beyebach, M., & Carranza, V. E. (1997). Therapeutic interaction and drop-out: Measuring relational communication in solution-focused therapy. *Journal of Family Therapy, 19* (2), 173–213.

Beyebach, M., & Herrero, M. (2010). *200 tareas en terapia breve.* [200 homework tasks in brief therapy.] Barcelona, Spain: Herder.

Beyebach, M., Piqueras, R., & Rodríguez, A. (1991). Terapia Centrada en las Soluciones: un studio de caso. [Solution focused therapy: A case study.] *Cuadernos de Terapia Familiar, 18,* 61–92.

Beyebach, M., & Rodríguez Morejón, A. (1999). Some thoughts on integration in solution-focused therapy. *Journal of Systemic Therapies, 18* (1), 24–42.

Bien, T. (2010). *The Buddha's way of happiness: Healing sorrow, transforming negative emotion and finding well-being in the present moment.* Oakland, CA: New Harbinger.

Birchler, G. R., Fals-Stewart, W., & O'Farrell, T. J. (2005). Couple therapy for alcoholism and drug abuse. In J. L. Lebow (Ed.), *Handbook of clinical family therapy* (pp. 251–2810). Hoboken, NJ: John Wiley & Sons.

Birchler, G. A., Fals-Stewart, W., & O'Farrell, T. J. (2008). Couple therapy for alcoholism and drug abuse. In A. S. Gurman (Ed.), *Clinical handbook of couple therapy* (4th ed., pp. 523–545). New York: Guilford.

Birmingham, C. L., Gutiérrez, E., Jonat, L., & Beumont, P. (2004). Randomized controlled trial of warming in anorexia nervosa. *International Journal of Eating Disorders, 35,* 234–238.

Birmingham, C. L., Su, J., Hlynsky, J. A., Goldner, E. M., & Gao, M. (2005). The mortality rate from anorexia nervosa. *International Journal of Eating Disorders, 38,* 143–146.

Black, C. (1982). *It will never happen to me.* Denver, CO: MAC Publishing.

Black, D., Belsare, G., & Schosser, S. (1999). Clinical features, psychiatric co-morbidity, and health-related quality of life in persons reporting compulsive computer use behavior. *Journal of Clinical Psychiatry, 60,* 839–843.

Blakeslee, S., & Blakeslee, M. (2007). *The body has a mind of its own: How body maps in your brain help you do almost everything better.* New York: Random House.

Blanco, C., Petkova, E., & Ibanez, A. (2002). A pilot placebo controlled study of fluvoxamine for pathological gambling. *Annals of Clinical Psychiatry, 14,* 9–15.

Blaszczynski, A. (1988). Clinical studies in pathological gambling. Ph. D. Thesis, Sydney, New South Wales, Australia: University of New South Wales.

Blaszczynski, A. (2009). Problem gambling: We should measure harm rather than "causes." *Addiction, 104,* 1070–1074.

Blaszczynski, A. (2011). Harm minimization can be achieved by a symbiosis between government, industry, and individuals. *Addiction, 106,* 10–12.

Blaszczynski, A., & McConaghy, N. (1988). SCL-90 assessed psychopathology in pathological gamblers. *Psychological Reports, 62,* 547–552.

REFERENCES

Blaszczynski, A., & Nower, L. (2002). A pathways model of pathological gambling. *Addiction, 97*, 487–499.

Blaszczynski, A., Steel, Z., & McConaghy, N. (1997). Impulsivity in pathological gambling: The antisocial impulsivist. *Addictions, 92*, 75–87.

Blaszczynski, A., Winter, S. W., & McConaghy, N. (1986). Plasma endorphin levels in pathological gamblers. *Journal of Gambling Behavior, 2*, 3–14.

Block, J. J. (2008). Issues for DSM V: Internet addiction. *American Journal of Psychiatry, 165*, 306–307.

Blomqvist, J. (2010). Self-change from alcohol and drug abuse: Often-cited classics. In H. Klingemann & L. C. Sobell (Eds.), *Promoting self-change from addictive behaviors: Practical implications for policy, prevention, and treatment* (pp. 31–57). New York: Springer.

Blum, R. W., Beuhring, T., Shew, M. L., Bearinger, L. H., Sieving, R. E., & Resnick, M. D. (2000). The effects of race/ethnicity, income, and family structure on adolescent risk factors. *American Journal of Public Health, 90*, 1879–1884.

Bohart, A. C., & Tallman, K. (2010). Clients the neglected common factor in psychotherapy. In B. L. Duncan, S. D. Miller, B. E. Wampold, & M. A. Hubble (Eds.), *The heart and soul of change: Delivering what works in therapy* (2nd ed., pp. 83–113). Washington, DC: American Psychological Association.

Bordin, E. S. (1979). The generalizability of the psychoanalytic concept for the working alliance. *Psychotherapy, 16*, 252–260.

Boscolo, l., & Bertrando, P. (1993). *The times of time: A new perspective in systemic therapy and consultation*. New York: Norton.

Boscolo, L., Cecchin, G., Hoffman, L., & Penn, P. (1987). *Milan systemic therapy: Conversations in theory and practice*. New York: Basic.

Bottlender, M., Kohler, J., & Soyka, M. (2006). The effectiveness of psychosocial treatment approaches for alcohol dependence: A review. *Fortschritteder der Neurologie-Psychiatrie, 74*, 19–31.

Bowen, S., Chawla, N., & Marlatt, G. A. (2011). *Mindfulness-based relapse prevention for addictive behaviors*. New York: Guilford.

Braverman, J., LaBrie, R. A., & Shaffer, H. J. (2011). A taxometric analysis of actual Internet sports gambling behavior. *Psychological Assessment, 23*, 234–244.

Brewer, J., & Potenza, M.N. (2008). The neurobiology of and genetics of impulse control disorders: Relationships to drug addictions. *Biochemical Pharmacology, 75*, 63–75.

Bronfenbrenner, U. (1979). *The ecology of human development: Experiments by nature and design*. Cambridge, MA: Harvard University Press.

Brown, M. Z., Comtois, K. A., & Linehan, M.M. (2002). Reasons for suicide attempts and non-suicidal self-injury in women with borderline personality disorder. *Journal of Abnormal Psychology, 111*, 198–202.

Brown, S., & Lewis, V. (1999). *The alcoholic family in recovery: A developmental model*. New York: Guilford.

Brown, T. G., Seraganian, P., Tremblay, J., & Annis, H. (2002). Process and outcome changes with relapse prevention versus 12-Step aftercare programs for substance abusers. *Addiction, 97*, 677–689.

Brownell, K. D., Marlatt, A., Lichtenstein, E., & Wilson, G. T. (1986). Understanding and preventing relapse. *American Psychologist, 41*, 765–782.

Bruch, H. (1978). *The golden cage: The enigma of anorexia nervosa*. Cambridge, MA: Harvard University Press.

Budney, A. J., & Higgins, S. T. (1998). *A community reinforcement approach: Treating cocaine addiction*. Rockville, MD: NIDA.

Budney, A. J., Moore, B. A., Rocha, H. L., & Higgins, S. T. (2006). Clinical trial of abstinence-based vouchers and cognitive-behavioral therapy for cannabis dependence. *Journal of Consulting and Clinical Psychology, 74*, 307–316.

Budney, A. J., Roffman, R., Stephens, R. S., & Walker, D. (2007). Marijuana dependence and its treatment. *Addiction Science and Clinical Practice, 4*, 4–6.

Budney, A. J., Vandrey, R. G., Hughes, J. R., Moore, B. A., & Bahrenburg, B. (2007). Oral delta-9-tetrahydrocannabinol suppresses cannabis withdrawal symptoms. *Drug and Alcohol Dependence, 86*, 22–29.

Burke, M., & Kraut, R. (2011). Social capital on *Facebook*: Differentiating uses and users. Retrieved from http://www.thoughtcrumbs.com/publications/burke_chi2011_socialcapitaloffacebook.pdf.

Burman, S. (1997). The challenge of sobriety: Natural recovery without treatment and self-help groups. *Journal of Substance Abuse, 9*, 41–61.

Cacioppo, J. T., & Patrick, W. (2008). *Loneliness: Human nature and the need for social connection*. New York: Norton.

REFERENCES

Califano, J. A. (2007). *High society: How substance abuse ravages America and what to do about it.* New York: Public Affairs Press.

Cantwell, P., & Holmes, S. (1994). Social construction: A paradigm shift for systemic therapy and training. *Australian and New Zealand Journal of Family Therapy, 15* (1), 17–26.

Caplan, S. (2007, April). Relations among loneliness, social anxiety, and problematic Internet use. *Cyberpsychology and Behavior, 10,* 234–244.

Carballo, J. L., Fernandez-Hermida, J. R., Secades-Villa, R., Sobell, L. C., Dum, M., & Garcia-Rodriguez, O. (2010). Natural recovery from alcohol and drug problems: A methodological review of the literature from 1999–2005. In H. Klingemann & L. C. Sobell (Eds.), *Promoting self-change in addictive behaviors: Practical implications for policy, prevention, and treatment* (pp. 87–101). New York: Springer.

Carey, K. B., Purnine, D. M., Maisto, S. A., & Carey, M. P. (1999). Assessing readiness to change substance abuse: A critical review of instruments. *Clinical Psychology Science and Practice, 6* (3), 245–266.

Carmody, J., Reed, G., Kristeller, J., & Merriam, P. (2008). Mindfulness, spirituality, and health-related symptoms. *Journal of Psychosomatic Research, 64,* 939–1003.

Carnes, S., & Carnes, P. J. (2010). Understanding cyber-sex in 2010. *Family Therapy Magazine, 9* (1), 10–18.

Carnes, P. J., & Delmonico, D. L. (2007). *In the shadows of the net: Breaking free from compulsive online sexual behavior.* Center City, MN: Hazeldon.

Carr, N. (2010). *The shallows: What the Internet is doing to our brains.* New York: Norton.

Carragher, N., & McWilliams, L. A. (2011). A latent class analysis of DSM-IV criteria for pathological gambling: Results from the National Epidemiological Survey on alcohol and related conditions. *Psychiatry Research, 187* (1 & 2), 185–192.

Carrasco, J. L., Saiz-Ruiz, J., Moreno, I., Hollander, E., & Lopez-Ibor, J. J. (1994). Low platelet MAO activity in pathological gambling. *Acta Psychiatrica Scandinavica, 90,* 427–431.

Carroll, K. M. (1996). Relapse prevention as a psychosocial treatment: A review of controlled clinical trials. *Experimental and Clinical Psychopharmacology, 4,* 46–54.

Carroll, K. M., Easton, C. J., Nich, C., Hunkele, K. A., Keavins, T. M., & Sinha, R. (2006). The use of contingency management and motivational skills-building therapy to treat young adults with marijuana dependence. *Journal of Consulting and Clinical Psychology, 74,* 955–966.

Cerrato, M., Carrera, O., Vazquez, R., Echevarria, E., & Gutiérrez, E. (2012). Heat makes a difference in activity-based anorexia: A translational approach to treatment development in anorexia nervosa. *International Journal of Eating Disorders, 45,* 26–35.

Chaey, C. (2011). Social gaming summit. *Fast Company, 160,* 36.

Chambless, D. L., & Crits-Christoph, P. (2006). What should be validated? In J. C. Norcross, L. E. Beutler, & R. F. Levant (Eds.), *Evidenced-based practices in mental health: Debate and dialogue on the fundamental questions* (pp. 131–160). Washington, DC: American Psychological Association.

Chellappan, S., & Kotikalapudi, R. (2012). How depressives surf the web. *The New York Times, Sunday Review, CLXI* (55), June 17, 805.

Chodron, P. (2010). *Taking the leap: Freeing ourselves from old habits and fears.* Boston, MA: Shambhala.

Christensen, A., & Jacobson, N. S. (2000). *Reconcilable differences.* Ney York: Guilford.

Ciarrocchi, J. W. (2001). *Counseling problem gamblers: A self-regulation manual for individual and family therapy.* San Diego, CA: Academic Press.

Ciarrocchi, J. W. & Richardson, R. (1989). Profile of compulsive gamblers in treatment. *Journal of Gambling Behavior, 5,* 53–65.

Clapper, J. R., Mangieri, R. A., & Piomelli, D. (2009). The endocannabinoid system as a target for the treatment of cannabis dependence. *Neuropharmacology, 56,* 235–243.

Clark, L., Lawrence, A. J., Astley-Jones, F., & Gray, N. (2009). Gambling near-misses enhance motivation to gamble and recruit win-related brain circuitry. *Neuron, 61,* 481–490.

Cloninger, C. R., Sigvardsson, S., Svrakic, D. M. & Przybeck, T. R. (1995). Personality antecedents of alcoholism in a national area probability sample. *European Archives of Psychiatry and Clinical Neuroscience, 245,* 239–244.

Cohen, E., Feinn, R., Arias, A., & Kranzler, H.R., (2007). Alcohol treatment utilization: Findings from the National Epidemiologic Survey on Alcohol and Related Conditions. *Drug and Alcohol Dependence, 86,* 214–221.

REFERENCES

Colahan, M., & Robinson, P. H. (2002). Multi-family groups in the treatment of young adults with eating disorders. *Journal of Family Therapy, 24* (1), 17–30.

Coleman, P. T. (2011). *The five percent: Finding solutions to seemingly impossible conflicts.* New York: Public Affairs.

Commings, D. E., Rosenthal, R. J., Lesieur, H. R., Rugle, L. J., Muhleman, D., Chin, C., Dietz, G., & Gade, R. (1996). A study of the dopamine D2 receptor gene in pathological gambling. *Phamacogenetics, 6,* 223–234.

Connell, G., Mitten, T., & Bumberry, W. (1999). *Reshaping family relationships: The symbolic therapy of Carl Whitaker.* New York: Brunner/Mazel.

Copeland, J., Swift, W., Roffman, R., & Stephens, R. (2001). A randomized controlled trial of brief cognitive-behavioral interventions for cannabis use disorder. *Journal of Substance Abuse Treatment, 21,* 55–64.

Copello, A., Orford, J., Hodgson, R., & Tober, G. (2009). *Social behavior and network therapy for alcohol problems.* London, UK: Routledge.

Corney, W. J., & Cummings, W. T. (1985). Gambling behavior and informational processing biases. *Journal of Gambling Behavior, 1,* 111–118.

Creed, T. A., & Kendall, P. C. (2005). Therapeutic alliance-building behavior within a cognitive-behavioral treatment for anxiety in youth. *Journal of Consulting and Clinical Psychology, 73,* 498–505.

Crisp, A. H. (1997). Anorexia nervosa as flight from growth: Assessment and treatment based on the model. In D. M. Garner & P. E. Garfinkel (Eds.), *Handbook of treatment for eating disorders* (2nd ed.), (pp. 248–277). New York: Guilford.

Crow, S. J., Mitchell, J. E., Roerig, J. D., & Steffen, K. (2009). What potential role is there for medication treatment in anorexia nervosa? *International Journal of Eating Disorders, 42,* 1–8.

Cunningham, J. (2005). Little use of treatment among problem gamblers. *Psychiatric Services, 56,* 1024–1025.

Cunningham-Williams, R. M., Cottler, L. B., Compton, W. M., Spitznagel, E. L., & Ben-Abdallah, A. (2000). Problem gambling and co-morbid psychiatric and substance abuse disorders among drug users recruited from drug treatment and community settings. *Journal of Gambling Studies, 16,* 347–376.

Darbyshire, P. I., Oster, C., & Carrig, H. (2001). The experience of pervasive loss: Children and young people living in a family where gambling is a problem. *Journal of Gambling Studies, 17,* 23–45.

Dare, C., & Eisler, I. (2000). A multi-family group day treatment program for adolescent eating disorders. *European Eating Disorders Review, 8,* 4–18.

D'Amore, K., & Lloyd-Richardson, E. (2008). *Non-suicidal self-injury among college students: Integrating qualitative and quantitative findings.* Paper presented at the International Society for the Study of Self-Injury, Harvard University, Cambridge, MA, June.

D'Angelli, A. R., Grossman, A. H., & Salter, N. P. (2005). Predicting the suicide attempts of lesbian, gay, and bisexual youth. *Suicide Life-Threatening Behavior, 35* (6), 646–660.

Davis, R. A. (2001). A cognitive-behavioral model of pathological Internet use. *Computers in Human Behavior, 17,* 187–195.

Dawson, D. A., Goldstein, R. B., & Grant, B.F. (2007). Rates and correlates of relapse among individuals in remission from DSM-IV alcohol dependence: A 3-year follow-up. *Alcoholism, Clinical and Experimental Research, 31,* 2036–2045.

Dawson, D. A., Grant, B. F., Stinson, F. S., Chou, P. S., Huang, B., & Roan, W. J. (2005). Recovery from DSM-IV alcohol dependence: United States 2001–2002. *Addiction, 100,* 281–292.

DeCaria, C. M., Hollander, E. H., Grossman, R., Wong, C. M., Mosowich, S. A., & Chersasky, S. (1996). Diagnosis, neurobiology, and treatment of pathological gambling. *Journal of Clinical Psychiatry, 57,* 80–84.

Dedmon, J. (2003). *Is the Internet bad for your marriage?* Study by the American Academy of Matrimonial Lawyers, Chicago, IL [News Release]. Retrieved January 15, 2011, from http://www.expertclick.com/NewsReleaseWire/default.cfm?Action=ReleaseDetail &ID=3051.

DeFrain, J., & Stinnett, N. (1992). Building on inherent strengths in families: A positive approach for psychologists and counselors. *Topics in Family Psychology and Counseling, 1* (1), 15–26.

Dell'Osso, B., Hadley, S., Allen, A., Baker, B., Chaplin, W. E., & Hollander, E. (2008). Ecitalopram in the treatment of impulse-compulsive Internet usage disorder: An open label trial followed by a double-blind discontinuation phase. *Journal of Clinical Psychiatry, 69* (3), 452–456.

Delmonico, D. L., & Griffin, E. J. (2011). Cyber-sex addiction and compulsivity. In K. S. Young &

REFERENCES

C. Nabuco de Abreu (Eds.), *Internet addiction: A handbook and guide to evaluation and treatment* (pp. 113–135). Hoboken, NJ: John Wiley.

Denizet-Lewis, B. (2009). *America anonymous: Eight addicts in search of a life*. New York: Simon & Schuster.

Dennis, M. L., Godley, S. H., Diamond, G., Tims, F. M., Babor, T., Donaldson, J., ... Funk, R. (2004). The cannabis youth treatment (CYT) study: Main findings from randomized trials. *Journal of Substance Abuse Treatment, 27*, 197–213.

Dennis, M. L., Scott, C. K., Funk, R., & Foss, M. A. (2005). The duration and correlates of addiction and treatment careers. *Journal of Substance Abuse Treatment, 28*, 51–52.

de Shazer, S. (1985). *Keys to solutions in brief therapy*. New York: Norton.

de Shazer, S. (1988). *Clues: Investigating solutions in brief therapy*. New York: Norton.

de Shazer, S. (1991). *Putting difference to work*. New York: Norton.

de Shazer, S. (1994). *Words were originally magic*. New York: Norton.

de Shazer, S., Dolan, Y., Korman, H., Trepper, T., McCollum, E., & Berg, I.K. (2007). *More than miracles: The state of the art of solution-focused brief therapy*. Binghamton, NY: Haworth.

de Shazer, S., & Isebaert, L. (2003). The Bruges model: A solution-focused approach to problem drinking and substance abuse. *Journal of Family Psychotherapy, 14*, 43–52.

De Vega, J. A. (1996). Terapia familiar and toxicomanias. [Family therapy and addictions.] In J. Navarro & M. Beyebach (Eds.), *Avances en terapia familiar sistemica* (pp. 273–298). Barcelona, Spain: Paidos.

Diamond, G. S., Liddle, H. A., Wintersteen, M. B., Dennis, M. L., Godley, S. H., & Tims, F. (2006). Early therapeutic alliance as predictor of treatment outcome for adolescent cannabis users in outpatient treatment. *American Journal on Addictions, 15*, 26–33.

Dimeff, L. A., Baer, J. S., Kivlahan, D. R., & Marlatt, G. A. (1999). *Brief screening and intervention for college students: A harm reduction approach*. New York: Guilford.

DiSalvo, D. (2011). *What makes your brain happy and why you should do the opposite*. Amherst, NY: Prometheus Books.

Ditmar, H. (2005). Compulsive buying—A growing concern: An examination of gender, age, and endorsement of materialistic values as predictors. *British Journal of Psychology, 96*(4), 467–491.

Ditmar, H., Long, K., & Bond, R. (2007). When a better self is only a button click away: Associations between materialistic values, emotional and identity-related buying motives, and compulsive buying tendency online. *Journal of Social and Clinical Psychology, 26*(3), 334–361.

Dodge, E., Hodes, M., Eisler, I., & Dare, C. (1995). Family therapy for bulimia nervosa in adolescents: An exploratory study. *Journal of Family Therapy, 17*, 59–78.

Doidge, N. (2007). *The brain that changes itself: Stories of personal triumph from the frontiers of brain science*. New York: Viking.

Dolan, Y. (1991). *Resolving sexual abuse*. New York: Norton.

Dolan, Y. (2000). *Beyond survival: Living well is the best revenge*. London, UK: Brief Therapy Press.

Dorner, D. (1997). *The logic of failure: Recognizing and avoiding error in complex situations*. New York: Basic Books.

Duckworth, A. L., Steen, T. A., & Seligman, M. E. P. (2005). Positive psychology in clinical practice. *Annual Review of Clinical Psychology, 1*, 629–651.

Duncan, B. L. (2010). *On becoming a better therapist*. Washington, DC: American Psychological Association.

Duncan, B. L., Hubble, M. A., & Miller, S. D. (1997). *Escape from babel: Toward a unifying language of psychotherapy*. New York: Norton.

Duncan, B. L., & Miller, S. D. (2000). *The heroic client: Doing client-directed, outcome-informed therapy*. San Francisco, CA: Jossey-Bass.

Duncan, B. L., & Miller, S. D. (2006). Treatment manuals do not improve outcomes. In J. C. Norcross, L. E. Beutler, & R. F. Levant (Eds.), *Evidenced-based practices in mental health* (pp. 140–149). Washington, DC: American Psychological Association.

Duncan, B. L., Miller, S. D., & Sparks, J. (2000). Exposing the mythmakers. *Family Therapy Networker, March/April*, 24–53.

Duncan, B. L., Miller, S. D., Wampold, B. E., & Hubble, M. A. (Eds.). (2010). *The heart and soul of change: Delivering what works in therapy* (2nd ed.). Washington, DC: American Psychological Association.

Dunican, K. C., & Del Dotto, D. (2007). The role of olanzapine in the treatment of anorexia nervosa. *The Annals of Pharmacotherapy, 41*, 111–115.

Durrant, M., & Coles, D. (1991). The Michael White approach. In T. C. Todd & M. D. Selekman (Eds.),

REFERENCES

Family therapy approaches with adolescent substance abusers (pp. 135–175). Needham Heights, MA: Allyn & Bacon.

Dutra, L., Stathopoulou, G., Basden, S. L., Leyro, T. M., Powers, M. B., & Otto, W. (2008). A meta-analytic review of psychosocial interventions for substance use disorders. *American Journal of Psychiatry, 165*, 179–187.

Dweck, C. S. (2006). *Mindset: The new psychology of success*. New York: Ballantine.

Dyer, J., Gregerson, H., & Christensen, C. M. (2011). *The innovator's DNA: Mastering the five skills of disruptive innovators*. Boston, MA: Harvard Business Review Press.

Earle, R. H., & Bell, M. E. (2010). The tsunami: Adolescents, technology, and pornography. *Family Therapy Magazine, 9* (1), 18–22.

Eastwood, M., Sweeney, D., & Piercy, F. P. (1987). The "no problem-problem": A family therapy approach for first-time adolescent substance abusers. *Family Relations, 36*, 125–128.

Ebaugh, H. R. F. (1988). *Becoming an ex: The process of role exit*. Chicago, IL: University of Chicago.

Echeburúa, E., Baez, C., & Fernández-Montalvo, J. (1996). Comparative effectiveness of three therapeutic modalities in the psychological treatment of pathological gambling: long-term outcome. *Behavioural and Cognitive Psychotherapy, 24*, 51–72.

Echeburúa, E., & Fernández-Montalvo, J. (2005). Psychological treatment of slot-machine pathological gambling: New perspectives. *Journal of Gambling Studies, 21*, 21–26.

Echeburúa, E., González-Ortega, I., De Corral, P., & Polo-López, R. (2011). Clinical gender differences among adult pathological gamblers seeking treatment. *Journal of Gambling Studies, 27*, 215–227.

Eddy, K. T., Dorer, D. J., Franko, D. L., Tahilani, B. S., Thompson-Brenner, H. & Herzog, D. (2008). Diagnostic crossover in anorexia nervosa and bulimia nervosa: Implications for DSM-V. *American Journal of Psychiatry, 165*, 245–250.

Edmondson, A. C. (2011). Strategies for learning from failure. *Harvard Business Review, 89* (4), 48–58.

Edwards, G., Orford, J., Egert, S., Guthrie, S., Hawker, A., & Taylor, C. (1977). Alcoholism: A controlled trial of "treatment" and "advice." *Journal of Studies on Alcohol, 36*, 1004–1031.

Eisler, I. (2005). The empirical and theoretical base of family therapy and multiple-family day therapy for adolescent anorexia nervosa. *Journal of Family Therapy, 27*, 104–131.

Eisler, I., Dare, C., Hodes, M., Russell, G. F., Dodge, E., & Le Grange, D. (2000). Family therapy for adolescent anorexia nervosa: The results of a controlled comparison of two family interventions. *Journal of Child Psychology and Psychiatry, 41*, 727–736.

Eisler, I., Dare, C., Russell, G. F., Szmukler, G., Le Grange, D., & Dodge, E. (1997). Family and individual therapy in anorexia nervosa: A 5-year follow-up. *Archives of General Psychiatry, 54*, 1025–1030.

Ellingstad, T. P., Sobell, L. C., Sobell, M. B., Eickleberry, C., & Golden, C. J. (2006). Self-change: A pathway to cannabis resolution. *Addictive Behaviors, 31* (3), 519–530.

EMCDDA (2005). The state of the drug problems in Europe: Annual 2005 report. *European Monitoring Centre for Drugs and Drug Addiction*.

Emmons, R. A. (2007). *Thanks! How the new science of gratitude can make you happier*. New York: Houghton-Mifflin.

Emmons, R. A., & McCullough, M. E. (2004). *The psychology of gratitude*. New York: Oxford University.

Epling, W. F. & Pierce, W. D. (1991). *Solving the anorexia puzzle: A scientific approach*. Toronto, Canada: Hogrefe & Huber.

Epling, W. F., Pierce, W. D., & Stefan, L. A. (1983). A theory of activity-based anorexia. *International Journal of Eating Disorders, 3*, 27–46.

Epstein, E. E., & McCrady, B. S. (2002). Couple therapy in the treatment of alcohol problems. In A. S. Gurman & N. Jacobson (Eds.), *Clinical handbook of marital therapy* (3rd ed., pp. 597–628). New York: Guilford.

Epston, D. (1998). *Catching up with David Epston: Collection of narrative papers, 1991–1996*. Adelaide, South Australia: Dulwich Centre.

Epston, D. (2000). *Crafting questions in narrative therapy practice*. Workshop presented at the Evanston Family Therapy Institute, Evanston, IL, May.

Erlich, E., Erlich, L. H., & Pepper, G. B. (Eds.). (1994). *Karl Jaspers: Basic philosophical writings*. Atlantic Highlands, NJ: Humanities Press.

Escudero, V. (2011). *Adolescentes y familias en conflicto: Terapia familiar centrado en la alianza terapeutica. Manual de tratamiento*. [Adolescents and families in conflict: Alliance-centered family therapy.] Coruna, Spain: Fundacion Meninos.

Fairburn, C. G. (1985). Cognitive-behavioral treatment in bulimia. In D. M. Garner & P. E. Garfinkel (Eds.), *Handbook of psychotherapy for anorexia and bulimia*. New York: Guilford.

Fairburn, C. G. (2008). Eating disorders: The transdiagnostic view and cognitive-behavioral therapy. In C. G. Fairburn (Ed.), *Cognitive-behavioral therapy and eating disorders*. New York: Guilford.

Fairburn, C. G., & Bohn, K. (2005). Eating disorders NOS (EDNOS): An example of the troublesome "not otherwise specific" (NOS) category in DSM-IV. *Behavior Research and Therapy, 43*, 691–701.

Fairburn, C. G., Cooper, Z., Shafran, R., Bohn, K., & Hawker, D.M. (2008). Clinical perfectionism, core low self-esteem, and interpersonal problems. In C. G. Fairburn (Ed.), *Cognitive-behavior therapy and eating disorders* (pp. 197–220). New York: Guilford.

Fairburn, C. G., & Harrison, P. J. (2003). Eating disorders. *Lancet, 361* (9355), 407–416.

Fairburn, C. G., Jones, R., Peveler, R. C., Carr, S. J. Solomon, R. A., & O'Connor, M. E., ... Hope, R. A., (1991). Three psychological treatments for bulimia nervosa: A comparative trial. *Archives of General Psychiatry, 48*, 463–469.

Fairburn, C. G., Kirk, J., O'Connor, M., & Cooper, P. J. (1986). A comparison of two psychological treatments for bulimia nervosa. *Behavior Research and Therapy, 24*, 629–643.

Fallon, P., & Wonderlich, S. A. (1997). Sexual abuse and other forms of trauma. In D. M. Garner & P. E. Garfinkel (Eds.), *Handbook of treatment for eating disorders* (2nd ed., pp. 394–414). New York: Guilford.

Fals-Stewart, W., Birchler, G. R., & O'Farrell, T. J. (1996). Behavioral couples therapy for male substance-abusing patients: Effects on relationship adjustment and drug-abusing behavior. *Journal of Consulting and Clinical Psychology, 64*, 959–972.

Fals-Stewart, W., O'Farrell, T. J., & Hooley, J. M. (1999). Relapse among married or cohabiting substance-abusing patients: The role of perceived criticism. *Behavior Therapy, 32*, 787–801.

Family Safe Media (2010). Pornography statistics. Retrieved from http://www.familysafemedia.com/pornography_statistics.html, January 13, 2011.

Favazza, A. R. (1998). *Bodies under siege: Self-mutilation and body modification in culture and psychiatry*. Baltimore, MD: Johns Hopkins University.

Favazza, A. R., & Selekman, M. D. (2003). *Self-injury in adolescents*. Annual Spring Conference of the Child and Adolescent Centre, Department of Psychiatry, University of Western Canada, London, Ontario, Canada, April.

Faye, P. (1995). The addictive characteristics of the behavior of self-mutilation. *Journal of Psychosocial Nursing and Mental Health Service, 33* (6), 36–39.

Ferentz, L. (2011). It's not about the food. *Psychotherapy Networker, 35* (1), 40–55.

Ferri, M., Amato, L., & Davoli, M. (2006). Alcoholics Anonymous and 12-Step programs for alcohol dependence. *The Cochrane Library*, Issue 3, Art. No.: CD005032. DOI: 10.1002/14651858. CD005032.pub2.

Fiorillo, C. D., Tobler, P. N., & Schultz, W. (2003). Discrete coding of reward probability and uncertainty by dopamine neurons. *Science, 299*, 1898–1902.

Fisch, R., & Schlanger, K. (1999). *Brief therapy with intimidating cases: changing the unchangeable*. San Francisco, CA: Jossey-Bass.

Fisch, R., Weakland, J. H., & Segal, L. (1982). *The tactics of change: Doing therapy briefly*. San Francisco, CA: Jossey-Bass.

Fisch, R., Weakland, J. H., Watzlawick, P., Segal, L., Hoebel, F. C., & Deardorff, C. M. (1975). *Learning brief therapy: An introduction manual*. Palo Alto, CA: Mental Research Institute.

Fishman, H. C. (1993). *Intensive structural therapy: Treating families in their social context*. New York: Basic Books.

Fletcher, A. C., Steinberg, L., & Williams-Wheeler, M. (2004). Parental influences on adolescent problem behavior: Revisiting Stattin and Kerr. *Child Development, 75*, 781–796.

Forster, E. M. (1909/1997). *The machine stops*. London, UK: Andre Deutsch Limited. (Originally published in *The Oxford and Cambridge Review*, November 1909.)

Fowler, J. S., Volkow, N. D., Kassed, C. A., & Chang, L. (2007). Imaging the addicted human brain. *Science Practice Perspectives, 3* (2), 4–16.

Frank, J. D. (1973). *Persuasion and healing: A comparative study of psychotherapy* (2nd ed.). Baltimore, MD: John Hopkins University Press.

Frascella, J., Potenza, M. N., Brown, L. L., & Childress, A. R. (2010). Shared brain vulnerabilities open the way for nonsubstance addictions: Carving addiction at a new joint? *Annals of the Academy of Sciences, 1187*, 294–315.

Frederickson, B. L. (2009). *Positivity: Groundbreaking research reveals how to embrace the hidden strengths of positive emotions, overcome negativity, and thrive*. New York: Crown.

Freeman, J., Epston, D., & Lobovits, D. (1997). *Playful approaches to serious problems: Narrative therapy with children*. New York: Norton.

Friedlander, M. L., Escudero, V., & Heatherington, L. (2006). *Therapeutic alliances in couple and family therapy: An empirically-informed guide to practice*. Washington, DC: American Psychological Association.

Friedlander, M. L., Escudero, V., Heatherington, L., & Diamond, G. M. (2011). Alliance in couple and family therapy. *Psychotherapy, 48*, 25–33.

Friedman, S. (Ed.). (1995). *The reflecting team in action: Collaborative practice in family therapy*. New York: Guilford.

Fulkerson, J. A., Story, M., Mellin, A., Leffert, N., Neumark-Sztainer, D., & French, S. A. (2006). Family dinner meal frequency and adolescent development: Relationships with developmental assets and high risk behaviors. *Journal of Adolescent Health, 39*, 337–345.

Funk, J. B. (2005). Children's exposure to violent video games and desensitization to violence. *Child and Adolescent Psychiatric Clinics in North America, 14* (3), 387–404.

Furman, B., & Ahola, T. (1992). *Solution talk: Hosting therapeutic conversations*. New York: Norton.

Gable, S. L., Reis, H. T., Impett, E. A., & Asher, E. R. (2004). Capitalizing on daily positive events. *Journal of Personality and Social Psychology, 87*, 228–245.

García, A. (2006). *El Proceso de cambio en terapia centrada en las soluciones: La perspectiva de los clients*. [The process of change in solution-focused therapy: Clients' perspective.] Unpublished Master's dissertation.

Gardner, H. (1993). *Multiple intelligence: The theory in practice*. New York: Basic Books.

Garfield, S.L. (1996). Some problems associated with "validated" forms of psychotherapy. *Clinical Psychology: Science and Practice, 3*, 218–229.

Garfield, S. L. (1998). Some comments on empirically supported treatments. *Journal of Consulting and Clinical Psychology, 66*, 121–125.

Garfinkel, P. E., & Garner, D. M. (1982). *Anorexia nervosa: A multidimensional approach*. New York: Brunner/Mazel.

Garner, D. M. (1993). Pathogenesis of anorexia nervosa. *Lancet, 341*, 1631–1635.

Garner, D. M., Vitousek, K. M., & Pike, K. M. (1997). Cognitive-behavioral therapy for anorexia nervosa. In D. M. Garner & P. E. Garfinkel (Eds.), *Handbook of treatment for eating disorders* (2nd ed., pp. 94–144). New York: Guilford.

Garrido, M. F., Jaén, P. R., & Domínguez, A. (2011). *Ludopatia y relaciones families: Clinica y Tratamiento*. [Gambling and family relationships: Clinical signs and treatment.] Barcelona, Spain: Paidos.

Geller, S. M., & Greenberg, L. S. (2012). *Therapeutic presence: A mindful approach to effective therapy*. Washington, DC: American Psychological Association.

Gentile, D. A., Choo, H., Liau, A., Sim, T., Li, D., Fung, D., & Khoo, A. (2011). Pathological video game use among youth: A two-year longitudinal study. *Pediatrics, 127*, 319–329.

George, E., Iveson, C., & Ratner, H. (1999). *Problem to solution: Brief therapy wit individuals and families*. London, UK: Brief Therapy Press.

Gibson, L. (2010). The nature of loneliness. *University of Chicago Magazine, 103* (2), 38–41.

Gino, F., & Pisano, G. P. (2011). Why leaders don't learn from success. *Harvard Business Review, 89* (4), 68–76.

Gomes, K., & Pascual-Leone, A. (2009). Primed for change: Facilitating factors in problem gambling treatment. *Journal of Gambling Studies, 25*, 1–17.

Gooding, P., & Tarrier, N. (2009). A systematic review and meta-analysis of cognitive-behavioral interventions to reduce problem gambling: Hedging our bets? *Behavior Research and Therapy, 47*, 592–607.

Gossop, M., Marsden, J., Stewart, D., & Kid, T. (2003). The National Treatment Outcome Study (NTORS): 4–5 year follow-up Results. *Addiction, 98*, 291–303.

Gossop, M., Marsden, J., Stewart, D., & Treacy, S. (2002). Change and stability of change after treatment of drug misuse: Two-year outcomes from the National Treatment Outcome Research Study in the United Kingdom. *Addictive Behaviors, 27*, 155–166.

Gottman, J. M. & Gottman, J. S. (2008). Gottman method couple therapy. In A. S. Gurman (Ed.), *Clinical handbook of couple therapy* (pp. 138–167). New York: Guilford.

REFERENCES

Gottman, J. M., Schwartz Gottman, J., & DeClaire, J. (2006). *10 lessons to transform your marriage*. New York: Crown.

Goudriaan, A. E., Oosterlaan, J., deBeurs, E., & Van Den Brink, W. (2004). Pathological gambling: A comprehensive review of bio-behavioral findings. *Neuroscience and Behavioral Review, 28*, 123–141.

Grall-Bonnec, M., Wainstein, L., Augy, J., Bouiu, G., Feuillet, F., Vénisse, J. L., Sébille-Rivain, V. (2011). Attention deficit hyperactivity disorder among pathological and at-risk gamblers seeking treatment: a hidden disorder. *European Addiction Research, 17*, 231–240.

Grant, J. E., Brewer, J. A., & Potenza, M. N. (2006). The neurobiology of substance and behavioral addictions: CNS spectrums. *The International Journal of Neuropsychiatric Medicine, 11* (12), 924–930.

Grant, J. E., Donahue, C. B., & Odlaug, B. L. (2011). *Overcoming impulse control problems: A cognitive-behavioral therapy program*. New York: Oxford University Press.

Gratz, K. L., & Chapman, A. L. (2007). The role of emotional responding and childhood maltreatment in the development and maintenance of deliberate self-harm among male undergraduates. *Psychology of Men and Masculinity*, (1), 1–14.

Gratz, K. L., & Chapman, A. L. (2009). *Freedom from self-harm: Overcoming self-injury with skills from DBT and other treatments*. Oakland, CA: New Harbinger.

Greenfield, D. (1999). Psychological characteristics of compulsive Internet use. *Cyber-Psychology and Behavior, 2*, 403–412.

Greenfield, D. (2011). The addicted properties of Internet usage. In K. S. Young & C. Nabuco de Abreu (Eds.), *Internet addiction: A handbook and guide to evaluation and treatment* (pp. 135–155). Hoboken, NJ: John Wiley.

Gregson, D., & Efran, J. S. (2002). *The Tao of sobriety: Helping you to recover from alcohol and drug addiction*. New York: Thomas Dunne Books.

Grilo, C. M. (2002). Binge-eating disorder. In C. G. Fairburn & K. D. Brownwell (Eds.), *Eating disorders and obesity: A comprehensive handbook* (2nd ed., pp. 178–182). New York: Guilford.

Grun, L., & McKeigue, P. (2000). Prevalance of excessive gambling before and after introduction of a national lottery in the United Kingdom: Another example of the single distribution theory. *Addiction, 95*, 959–966.

Gutiérrez, E. (2009). Terapia con lo imprescindible. [Minimal therapy.] Workshop held at the Universidad Pontificia de Salamanca, Salamanca, Spain.

Gutiérrez, E. (2011). Anorexia nervosa: La rata o el divan? [Anorexia nervosa: The rat or the couch?] *Accion Psicologica, 8*, 57–71.

Gutiérrez, E., Cerrato, M., Carrera, O., Portillo, M. P., Cerrato, M., Vasquez, R., & Echevarria, E. (2008). Heat reversal of activity-based anorexia: Implications for the treatment of anorexia nervosa. *International Journal of Eating Disorders, 41*, 594–601.

Gutiérrez, E., Vazquez, R., & Boakes, R. A. (2002). Activity-based anorexia: Ambient temperature has been a neglected factor. *Psychonomic Bulletin & Review, 9*, 239–249.

Haidt, J. (2006). *The happiness hypothesis: Finding modern truth in ancient wisdom*. New York: Basic Books.

Haines, J., & Williams, C. L. (2003). Coping and problem-solving of self-mutilators. *Journal of Clinical Psychology, 59*, 1097–1106.

Haley, J. (1963). *Strategies of psychotherapy*. New York: Grune & Stratton.

Haley, J. (1973). *Uncommon therapy: The psychiatric techniques of Milton H. Erickson*. New York: Grune & Stratton.

Haley, J. (1976). *Problem-solving therapy: New strategies for effective family therapy*. San Francisco, CA: Jossey-Bass.

Haley, J. (1983). *Ordeal therapy*. San Francisco, CA: Jossey-Bass.

Halmi, K. A., Agras, W. S., Mitchell, J., Wilson, G. T., Crow, S., & Bryson, S. W. (2002). Relapse predictors of patients with bulimia nervosa who achieved abstinence through cognitive-behavioral therapy. *Archives of General Psychiatry, 5* (12), 1105–1109.

Halvorson, H. G. (2010). *Succeed: How we can reach our goals*. New York: Hudson Street Press.

Han, D. H., Lee, Y. S., Yang, K. C., Kim, E. Y., Lyoo, I. K., & Renshaw, P. F. (2007). Dopamine genes and reward dependence in adolescents with excessive Internet video game play. *Journal of Addiction Medicine, 1* (3), 133–138.

Hanh, T. N. (1998). *The heart of Buddha's teaching: Transforming suffering into peace, joy, and liberation*. New York: Broadway.

REFERENCES

Hanh, T. N. (2001). *Anger: Wisdom for cooling the flames.* New York: Riverhead.

Hanh, T. N. (2011). After the honeymoon. *Buddhadharma: The Practitioner's Quarterly,* Fall, 26–33.

Hanson, R., & Mendius, R. (2009). *Buddha's brain: The practical neuroscience of happiness, love, and wisdom.* Oakland, CA: New Harbinger.

Hartman, A., Herzog, T., & Driunkman, A. (1992). Psychotherapy of bulimia nervosa: What is effective? A meta-analysis. *Journal of Psychosomatic Research, 36,* 159–167.

Hawton, K., & Rodham, K. (2006). *By their own young hand: Deliberate self-harm and suicidal ideas in adolescents.* London, UK: Jessica Kingsley.

Hawton, K., Townsend, E., Avensman, E., Gunnel, D., Hazell, P., & House, A. (2006). Psychosocial and pharmacological treatments for deliberate self-harm. *Cochrane Library, 3,* 1–61.

Hayes, S. C., Strosahl, K. D., & Wilson, K. G. (1999). *Acceptance and commitment therapy: An experiential approach to behavior change.* New York: Guilford.

Heath, N. L., Schaub, K., Holly, S., & Nixon, M. K. (2009). Self-injury today: Review of population and clinical studies in adolescents. In M. K. Nixon & N. L. Heath (Eds.), *Self-injury in youth: The essential guide to assessment and intervention* (pp. 9–29). New York: Routledge.

Heath, N. L., Toste, J. R., Nedecheva, T., & Charlebois, A. (2008). An examination of non-suicidal self-injury among college students. *Journal of Mental Health Counseling, 30,* 137–156.

Hedges, F. (2005). *An introduction to systemic therapy with individuals: A social constructionist approach.* Basingstoke, UK: Palgrave Macmillan.

Hendrick, S., Isebaert, L., & Dolan, Y. (2012). Solution-focused brief therapy in alcohol treatment. In C. Franklin, T. S. Trepper, W. J. Gingerich, & E. E. McCollum (Eds.), *Solution-focused brief therapy: A handbook of evidence-based practice* (pp. 264–278). New York: Oxford University Press.

Henggeler, S. W., Schoenwald, S. K., Borduin, C., Rowland, M. D., & Cunningham, P. B. (1998). *Multisystemic treatment of antisocial behavior in children and adolescents.* New York: Guilford.

Henggeler, S. W., Schoenwald, S. K., Borduin, C. M., Rowland, M. D., & Cunningham, P. B. (2006). Juvenile drug court: Enhancing outcomes by integrating evidence-based treatments. *Journal of Consulting and Clinical Psychology, 74,* 42–54.

Henggeler, S. W., Schoenwald, S. K., Borduin, C. M, Rowland, M. D., & Cunningham, P.B. (2009). *Multisystemic therapy for antisocial behavior in children and adolescents* (2nd ed.). New York: Guilford.

Herrero de Vega, M., & Beyebach, M. (2004). Losungsorientierte selbstwertgefuhl-gruppen. *Zeitschrift fur Systemische Therapie and Beratung, 22,* 239–246.

Herzog, D. B., Greenwood, D. N., Dorer, D. J., Flores, A. T., Ekeblad, E. R., & Richards, A. (2000). Mortality in eating disorders: A descriptive study. *International Journal of Eating Disorders, 28,* 20–26.

Herzog, D. B., Keller, M. B., Lavori, P. W., & Sacks, N. R. (1991). The course and outcome of bulimia nervosa. *Journal of Clinical Psychiatry, 52,* 4–8.

Higgins, S. T., Budney, A. J., Bickel, W. K., Foerg, F. E., Donham, R., & Badger, D. J. (1994). Incentives improve outcome in outpatient behavioral treatment of cocaine abusers. *Archives of General Psychiatry, 51,* 568–576.

Higgins, S. T., Budney, A. J., Bickel, W. K., Hughes, J. R., Foerg, F. E., & Badger, D. J. (1993). Achieving cocaine abstinence with a behavioral approach. *American Journal of Psychiatry, 150,* 763–769.

Higgins, S. T., & Silverman, K. (Eds.). (1999). *Motivating behavior change among illicit drug-abusers: Research on contingency management interventions.* San Diego, CA: Academic Press.

Hilt, L., & Nolen-Hoeksema, S. (2008). *Functions of non-suicidal self-injury in young adolescent girls.* Paper presented at the International Society for the Study of Self-Injury Conference, Harvard University, Cambridge, MA, June.

Hjerth, M. (2005). New developments in solution-focused thinking. Workshop held at the Masters degree programme in Family Therapy and Systemic Interventions, Universidad Pontificia de Salamanca, Salamanca, Spain.

Hodgins, D. C., & el-Guebaly, N. (2000). Natural and treatment-assisted recovery from gambling problems: A comparison of resolved and active gamblers. *Addiction, 95* (5), 777–789.

Hodgins, D. C., & el-Guebaly, N. (2004). Retrospective and prospective reports of precipitants to relapse in pathological gambling. *Journal of Consulting and Clinical Psychology, 72,* 72–80.

Hodgins, D. C., Peden, N., & Cassidy, E. (2005). The association between comorbidity and outcome in pathological gambling: A respective follow-up of recent quitters. *Journal of Gambling Studies, 21* (3), 255–271.

REFERENCES

Hoffman, L. (2002). *Family therapy: An intimate journey*. New York: Norton.

Holden, N. L. (1990). Is anorexia nervosa an obsessive compulsive disorder? *British Journal of Psychiatry, 157,* 1–5.

Hollander, M. (2008). *Helping teens who cut: Understanding and ending self-injury*. New York: Guilford.

Hollerman, J. R., & Schultz, W. (1998). Dopamine neurons report and error in temporal prediction of reward during learning. *Nature and Neuroscience,* 1, 304–309.

Hollis, J. F., Gullion, C. M., Stevens, V. J., Brantley, P. J., Appel, L. J., Ard, J. D. … Svetkey, L. P. (2008). Weight loss during the intensive intervention phase of the weight-loss maintenance trial. *Journal of Preventative Medicine, 35* (2), 118–126.

Holman, P. (2010). *Engaging emergence: Turning upheaval into opportunity*. San Francisco, CA: Berrett-Koehler.

Holy Bible, The (1994). 21st century King James version: Containing the old testament and the new testament. Gary, SD: 21st Century King James Bible Publishers.

Hsu, L. K. (1997). Can dieting cause an eating disorder? *Psychological Medicine, 27,* 509–513.

Hubble, M. A., Duncan, B. L., & Miller, S. D. (Eds.). (1999). *The heart and soul of change: What works in therapy*. Washington, DC: American Psychological Association.

Hubble, M. A., Duncan, B. L., Miller, S. D., & Wampold, B. E. (2010). Introduction. In B. L. Duncan, S. D. Miller, B. E. Wampold, & M. A. Hubble (Eds.), *The heart and soul of change: Delivering what works in therapy* (pp. 23–47). Washington, DC: American Psychological Association.

Huebner, H. F. (1993). *Endorphins, eating disorders, and other addictive behaviors*. New York: Norton.

Huestis, M. A., Gorelick, D. A., Heishman, S. J., Preston, K. L., Nelson, R. A., Moolchan, E. T., & Frank, R. A. (2001). Blockade of effects of smoked marijuana by the CBI-selective cannabinoid receptor antagonist SR141716. *Archives of General Psychiatry, 58,* 322–328.

Hunt, G. M., & Azrin, N. H. (1973). A community reinforcement approach to alcoholism. *Behavior Research and Therapy, 11,* 91–104.

Iacoboni, M. (2008). *Mirroring people: The new science of how we connect with others*. New York: Farrar, Straus, & Giroux.

Isebaert, L. (2005). *Kurzzeittherapie ein praktisches Handbuch: Die gesundheitsorientierte kognitive Therapie*. Stutgart, Germany: Thieme.

Italie, L. (2012). YouTubers beg: Am I pretty? *The Daily Post,* May 17, 8.

Jacob, F. (2001). *Solution-focused recovery from eating-distress*. London, UK: Brief Therapy Press.

Jacobs, D. F. (1988). Evidence for a common dissociative-like reaction among addicts. *Journal of Gambling Studies, 4* (1), 2737.

Jacobson, C. M. & Gould, M. (2007). The epidemiology and phenomenology of non-suicidal self-injurious behavior among adolescents: A critical review of the literature. *Archives of Suicide Research, 11,* 129–147.

Jacobson, N. S., & Christensen, A. (1996). *Integrative couple therapy*. New York: Norton.

Jacques, C., Ladouceur, R., & Ferland, R. (2000). Impact of availability on gambling: A longitudinal study. *Canadian Journal of Psychiatry, 45,* 810–815.

Johnson, N. (2007). *Simply complexity: A clear guide to complexity theory*. Oxford, UK: One World.

Johnston, L. D., O'Malley, P. M., Bachman, J. G., & Schulenberg, J. E. (2012). *Monitoring the Future national results on adolescent drug use: Overview of key findings, 2011*. Ann Arbor: Institute for Social Research, The University of Michigan.

Joiner, T. (2005). *Why people die by suicide*. Cambridge, MA: Harvard University Press.

Joiner, T., Petit, J. W., Walker, R. L., Voelz, Z. R., Cruz, J., & Rudd, M. D. (2002). Perceived burdensomeness and suicidality: Two studies on the suicide notes of those attempting and completing suicide. *Journal of Social and Clinical Psychology, 21,* 531–545.

Joseph, S. (2011). *What doesn't kill us: The new psychology of post-traumatic growth*. New York: Basic Books.

Kabat-Zinn, J. (1994). *Wherever you go, there you are: Mindfulness meditation in everyday life*. New York: Hyperion.

Kadden, R. M., Litt, M. D., Cooney, N. L., Kabela, E., & Getter, H. (2001). Prospective matching of alcoholic clients to cognitive-behavioral therapy or interactional group therapy. *Journal of Studies on Alcohol, 62,* 359–369.

Kafka, M. P., & Hemen, J. (2003). Hyper-sexual desire in males with paraphilia-related disorders? *Sexual Abuse: A Journal of Research and Treatment, 15,* 307–321.

Kahn, J. (2011). The visionary: A digital pioneer questions what technology has wrought. *The New Yorker, 137* (20), 46–53.

REFERENCES

Kahneman, D. (2011a). *Thinking fast and slow*. New York: Farrar, Straus and Giroux.

Kahneman, D. (2011b). The surety of fools. *The New York Times Magazine, CLXI* (55,567), October 23, 30–33, 62.

Kahneman, D., Lovallo, D., & Sibony, O. (2011). Before you make that big decision ... *Harvard Business Review, 89* (6), 51–60.

Kalischuk, R. G., Nowatzki, N., Cardwell, K., Klein, K., & Solowoniuk, J. (2006). Problem gambling and its impact on families: A literature review. *International Gambling Studies, 6*, 31–60.

Källmén, H., Andersson, P., & Andren, A. (2008). Are irrational beliefs and depressive mood more common among problem gamblers than no-gamblers? A survey of Swedish problem gamblers and controls. *Journal of Gambling Studies, 24*, 441–450.

Kandel, D. B. (1996). *Stages and pathways of drug involvement: Examining the gateway hypothesis*. Cambridge, UK: Cambridge University Press.

Karlsen, F. (2011). Entrapment and near miss: A comparative analysis of psych-structural elements in gambling games and massively multi-player online role-playing games. *International Journal of Mental Health and Addiction, 2*, 193–207.

Kauer, J. A., & Malenka, R. C. (2007). Synaptic plasticity and addiction. *Nature Reviews and Neuroscience, 8*, 844–858.

Kay, J. (2011). *Obliquity: Why our goals are best achieved indirectly*. New York: Penguin Press.

Keel, P. K., Mitchell, J. E., Miller, K. B., Davis, T. L., & Crow, S. J. (1999). Long-term outcomes of bulimia nervosa. *Archives of General Psychiatry, 56* (1), 63–69.

Kemperman, I., Russ, M. J., & Shearin, E. (1997). Self-injurious behavior and mood regulation in borderline patients. *Journal of Personality Disorders, 11*, 146–157.

Kessler, R. C. (2004). The epidemiology of dual diagnosis. *Biological Psychiatry, 56*, 63–69.

Kessler, R. C., Costello, E. J., Merikangas, K. R., & Ustun, T.B . (2001). Psychiatric epidemiology: Recent advances and future directions. In R. W. Mandersscheid & M. J. Henderson (Eds.), *Mental Health, United States 2000* (pp. 45–78). Washington, DC: U.S. Government Printing Office.

Kessler, R. C., Crum, R. M., Warner, L. A., Nelson, C. B., Schulenberg, J., & Anthony, J. C. (1997). Lifetime co-occurrence of DSM-III-R alcohol abuse and dependence with other psychiatric disorders in the National Co-Morbidity Survey. *Archives of General Psychiatry, 54*, 313–321.

Keys, A., Brozek, J., Heshel, A., Mickelsen, O., & Taylor, H. L. (1950). *The biology of human starvation*. Minneapolis, MN: University of Minnesota.

Kiesler, D. J. (1966). Some myths of psychotherapy research and the search for a paradigm. *Psychological Bulletin, 65*, 110–136.

King, R. A., Schwab-Stone, M., Fisher, M. J., Greenwald, S., Kramer, R. A., Goodman, S. H., Lahey, B. B., & Gould, M. S. (2001). Psychosocial risk behavior correlates of youth suicide attempts and suicidal ideation. *Journal of the American Academy of Child and Adolescent Psychiatry, 40* (7), 837–846.

Kirby, K. C., Marlowe, D. B., Festinger, D. S., Garvey, K. A., & La Monaca, V. (1999). Community reinforcement training for family and significant others of drug abusers: A unilateral intervention to increase treatment entry of drug abusers. *Drug and Alcohol Dependence, 56*, 85–96.

Klein, G. (2009). *Streetlights and shadows: Searching for the keys to adaptive decision-making*. Cambridge, MA: The MIT Press.

Klerman, G. L. (1986). The National Institute of Mental Health Epidemiological Catchment Area (NIMH-ECA) program. *Social Psychiatry and Psychiatric Epidemiology, 21*, 159–166.

Klingborg, T. (2009). *The overflowing brain: Information overload and the limits of working memory*. Oxford, UK: Oxford University.

Klingemann, H. (1991). The motivation for change from problem alcohol and heroin use. *British Journal of Addiction, 86*, 727–744.

Klingemann, H., & Klingemann, J. (2009). How much treatment does a person need?: Self-change and the treatment system. In P. M. Miller (Ed.), *Evidence-based addiction treatment* (pp. 267–287). Burlington, MA: Academic Press.

Klingemann, H., & Sobell, L. C. (Eds.) (2010). *Promoting self-change from addictive behaviors: Practical implications for policy, prevention, and treatment*. New York: Springer.

Klonsky, E. D. (2011). About self-injury. Retrieved from http://www.isssweb.org/aboutnssi.php.

Klonsky, E. D. (2007a). The functions of deliberate self-injury: A review of the empirical evidence. *Clinical Psychology Review, 27*, 226–239.

Klonsky, E. D. (2007b). Non-suicidal self-injury: An introduction. *Journal of Clinical Psychology, 63*, 1039–1043.

Klonsky, E. D., & Muehlenkamp, J. J. (2007). Self-injury: A research review for the practitioner. *Journal of Clinical Psychology, 63*, 1045–1056.

Ko, C. H., Liu, G. C., Hsiao, S., Yen, J. Y., Yang M. J., Lin, W. C. ... Chen, C. S. (2009). Brain activities associated with gaming urge of online gaming addiction. *Journal of Psychiatric Research, 43*, 739–747.

Ko, C. H., Yen, J. Y., Chen, C. C., Chen, S. H., Wu, K., & Yen, C. F. (2006). Tridimensional personality of adolescents with Internet addiction and substance use experience. *Canadian Journal of Psychiatry, 51* (14), 887–894.

Ko, C. H., Yen, J. Y., Chen, C. S., Chen, C. C., & Yen, C. F. (2008). Psychiatric co-morbidity of Internet addiction in college students: An interview study. *CNS Spectrums: The Journal of Psychiatric Medicine, 13* (2), 147–153.

Koch, R., & Lockwood, G. (2010). *Super Connect: The power of networks and the strength of weak links*. London, UK: Little, Brown.

Kolhatkar, S. (2011). Cheating incorporated. *Bloomberg Businessweek, February 14–20*, 60–66.

Kozak, A. (2009). *Wild chickens and petty tyrants: 108 metaphors for mindfulness*. Boston, MA: Wisdom.

Kral, R., & Kowalski, K. (1989). After the miracle: The second stage in solution-focused therapy. *Journal of Strategic and Systemic Therapies, 8*, 73–76.

Krampe, H., Stawicki, S., Wagner, T., Bartels, C., Aust, C., & Rugher, E. (2006). Follow-up of 180 alcoholic patients for up to 7 years after outpatient treatment: Impact of alcohol deterrents on outcome. *Alcoholism: Clinical and Experimental Research, 30*, 86–95.

Kranzler, H. R., & Van Kirk, J. (2001). Efficacy of naltrexone and acamprosate for alcoholism treatment: A meta-analysis. *Alcoholism: Clinical and Experimental Research, 25*, 1335–1341.

Kraut, R., Patterson, M., Lundmark, V., Kiesler, S., Mukopadhyay, T., & Scherlis, W. (1997). Internet paradox: A social technology that reduces social involvement and psychological well-being? *American Psychologist, 53*, 1017–1031.

Krishnan, M., & Orford, J. (2002). Gambling and the family: From the stress-coping-support perspective. *Journal of Gambling Studies, 14*, 83–90.

Kristeller, J. L. (2003). Mindfulness, wisdom, and eating: Applying a multi-domain model of mediation effects. *Journal of Constructivism in the Human Sciences, 8*, 107–118.

Kristeller, J. L. (2010). Spiritual engagement as a mechanism of change in mindfulness and acceptance-based therapies. In R. A. Baer (Ed.), *Assessing mindfulness and acceptance processes in clients: Illuminating the theory and practice of change* (pp. 155–184). Oakland, CA: Context.

Krystal, H. (1982). Alexithymia and psychoanalytic treatment. *International Journal of Psychoanalytic Psychotherapy, 9*, 353–388.

Kwon, J. H. (2005). The Internet game addiction of adolescents: Temporal changes and related psychological variables. *Korean Journal of Clinical Psychology, 24*, 267–280.

Kwon, J. H. (2011). Toward the prevention of adolescent Internet addiction. In K. S. Young & C. Nabuco de Abreu (Eds.), *Internet addiction: A handbook and guide to evaluation and treatment* (pp. 223–245). Hoboken, NJ: John Wiley.

Kwon, J. H., Chung, C. S., & Lee, J. (2009). The effects of escape from self and interpersonal relationships on the pathological use of Internet games. *Community Mental Health Journal, 47* (1), 113–121.

Labrador, F. J., Echeburúa, E., & Becoña, E. (2000). *Guia para la eleccion de tratamientos psicologicos efectivos: Hacia una nueva psicología clinica*. Madrid, Spain: Dykinson.

LaBrie, R., & Shaffer, H. J. (2011). Identifying behavioral markers of disordered Internet sports gambling. *Addiction Research & Theory, 19*, 56–65.

Ladouceur, R.. & Lachance, S. (2007). *Overcoming your pathological gambling workbook*. New York: Oxford University.

Ladouceur, R., Sylvain, C., & Boutin, C. (2001). Cognitive treatment of pathological gambling. *Journal of Nervous and Mental Disease, 189*, 774–780.

Ladouceur, R., & Walker, M. (1996). A cognitive perspective on gambling. In P. M. Salkovskis (Ed.), *Trends in cognitive and behavioral therapies* (pp. 89–120). New York: Wiley.

REFERENCES

Laessle, R.G ., Kittl, S., & Fichter, M. (1987). Major affective disorders in anorexia nervosa and bulimia: A descriptive diagnostic study. *Psychiatry, 151*, 785–789.

Lam, L. T., & Peng, Z. W. (2010). Effect of pathological use of the Internet on adolescent mental health: A prospective study. *Archives of Pediatrics and Adolescent Medicine, 164* (10), 901–906.

Lambert, M. J. (2010). *Prevention of treatment failure: The use of measuring, monitoring, and feedback in clinical practice.* Washington, DC: American Psychological Association.

Langer, E. (1975). "The illusion of control." *Journal of Personality and Social Psychology, 32*, 311–328.

Lanier, J. (2011). *You are not a gadget: A manifesto.* New York: Alfred Knopf.

Lasegue, C. (1873). On hysterical anorexia. *Medical Times and Gazette, 2*, 265–266.

Lebow, J. L. (2005). Family therapy at the beginning of the twenty-first century. In J. L. Lebow (Ed.), *Handbook of clinical family of clinical family therapy* (pp. 1–14). Hoboken, NJ: John Wiley & Sons.

Ledgerwood, D. M., & Petry, N. M. (2006). What do we know about relapse in pathological gambling? *Clinical Psychology Review, 26*, 216–228.

Lee, C. (2011). This man is addicted to sex. *Newsweek*, December 5, 50–55.

Leff, J., & Vaughn, C. (1985). *Expressed emotion in families: Its significance for mental illness.* New York: Guilford.

Le Grange, D., & Lock, J. (2007). *Treatment manual for bulimia nervosa: A family-based approach.* New York: Guilford.

Le Grange, D., & Lock, J. (2010). Family-based treatment for adolescents with bulimia nervosa. In C. M. Grilo & J. E. Mitchell (Eds.), *The treatment of eating disorders* (pp. 372–388). New York: Guilford.

Le Grange, D., & Schmidt, U. (2005). The treatment of adolescents with bulimia nervosa. *Journal of Mental Health, 14*, 587–597.

Lesieur, H. R. & Blume, S. B. (1991). When lady luck loses: Women and compulsive gambling. In N. Van Der Bergh (Ed.), *Feminist perspectives on addiction* (pp. 181–197). New York: Springer.

Leung, L. (2007). Stressful life events, motives for Internet use, and social support among digital kids. *CyberPsychology and Behavior, 10* (2), 204–214.

Levine, M. (2006). *The price of privilege: How parental pressure and material advantage are creating a generation of disconnected and unhappy kids.* New York: HarperCollins.

Lewis, S. P., & Santor, D. A. (2010). Self-harm reasons, goal achievement, and prediction of future self-harm. *Journal of Nervous and Mental Disease, 198*, 362–369.

Lewis, V., Allen-Byrd, L., & Rouhbakhsh, P. (2004). Understanding successful family recovery in treating alcoholism. *Journal of Systemic Therapies, 23*, 39–51.

Liddle, H. A. (2002). *Multidimensional family therapy for adolescent cannabis users.* (Cannabis Youth Treatment Series, Vol. 5.) Rockville, MD: Center for Substance Abuse Treatment.

Liddle, H. A. (2010). Treating adolescent substance abuse using multidimensional family therapy. In J. R. Weisz & A. E. Kazdin (Eds.), *Evidenced-based psychotherapies for children and adolescents* (pp. 416–435). New York: Guilford.

Liddle, H. A., Rodriquez, R. A., Dakof, G. A., Kanzki, E., & Marvel, F. A. (2005). Multidimensional family therapy: A science-based treatment for adolescent drug abuse. In J. Lebow (Ed.), *Handbook of clinical family therapy* (pp. 128–163). New York: John Wiley & Sons.

Lindberg, A., Fernie, B. A., & Spada, M. (2011). Metacognitions in problem gambling. *Journal of Gambling Studies, 27*, 73–81.

Linden, D. J. (2011). *The compass of pleasure: How our brains make fatty foods, orgasm, exercise, marijuana, generosity, vodka, learning, and gambling feel so good.* New York: Viking.

Linden, R. D., Pope, H. G., & Jonas, J. M. (1986). Pathological gambling and major affective disorder: Preliminary findings. *Journal of Clinical Psychiatry, 47* (4), 201–203.

Linehan, M. M. (1993). *Cognitive-behavioral treatment in borderline personality disorder.* New York: Guilford.

Lingford-Hughes, A., & Nutt, D. (2003). Neurobiology of addiction and implications for treatment. *The British Journal of Psychiatry, 182*, 97–100.

Lipchik, E. (2002). *Beyond technique in solution-focused therapy: Working with emotions and the therapeutic relationship.* New York: Guilford.

Lloyd-Richardson, E. E., Perrine, N., Dierker, L., & Kelley, M. L. (2007). Characteristics and functions of non-suicidal self-injury in a community sample of adolescents. *Psychological Medicine, 37*, 1183–1192.

REFERENCES

Lobo, D. S., & Kennedy, J. L. (2009). Genetic aspects of pathological gambling: A complex disorder with shared genetic vulnerabilities. *Addiction, 104*, 1454–1465.

Lobsinger, C., & Beckett, L. (1996). *Odds to break even: A practical approach to gambling awareness*. Sydney, New South Wales, Australia: Relationships Australia, Inc.

Lock, J., & Le Grange, D. (2005). *Help your teenager beat an eating disorder*. New York: Guilford.

Lock, J., Le Grange, D., Agras, W. S., & Dare, C. (2001). *Treatment manual for anorexia nervosa: A family-based approach*. New York: Guilford.

Lofthouse, N., Muehlenkamp, J. J., & Adler, R. (2008). Non-suicidal self-injury and co-occurrence. In M. K. Nixon & N. L. Heath (Eds.), *Self-injury in youth: The essential guide to assessment and intervention* (pp. 59–78). New York: Routledge.

Lopez, S. J., & Snyder, C. R. (Eds.). (2009). *Oxford handbook of positive psychology* (2nd ed.). New York: Oxford University Press.

Lorains, F. K., Gulishaw, S., & Thomas, S. A. (2011). Prevalence of comorbid disorders in problem and pathological gambling: Systematic review and meta-analysis of population surveys. *Addiction, 106* (3), 490–498.

Lorenz, V. C., & Shuttlesworth, D. E. (1983). The impact of pathological gambling on the spouse of the gambler. *Journal of Community Psychology, 11*, 67–76.

Lorenz, V. C., & Yaffee, R. A. (1986). Pathological gambling: Psychosomatic, emotional and marital difficulties as reported by the gambler. *Journal of Gambling Behavior, 2*, 40–49.

Lorenz, V. C., & Yaffee, R. A. (1989). Pathological gamblers and their spouses: Problems in interaction. *Journal of Gambling Behavior,5*, 113–126.

Lottery Vendor Data (2008). www.gtech.com/site_resources/pdfs/USLotteriesWhitePaperFinal.pdf.

Lowenstein, T. (2005). *Buddhist inspirations: Essential philosophy, truth, and enlightenment*. London, UK: Duncan Baird.

Lubman, D. L., Yücel, M., & Hall, W. D. (2007). Substance use and the adolescent brain: A toxic combination? *Journal of Psychopharmacology, 21* (8), 792–794.

Lund, I. (2011). Irrational beliefs revisited: Exploring the role of gambling preferences in the development of misconceptions in gamblers. *Addiction Research & Theory, 19*, 40–46.

Lundahl, B. W., Kunz, C., Brownwell, C., Tollefson, D., Burke, B. L. (2010). A meta-analysis of motivational interviewing: Twenty-five years of empirical studies. *Research on Social Work Practice, 20*, 137–160.

Lynskey, M. T., Heath, A. C., Bucholz, K. K., Slutske, W. S., Madden, P. A. F., Nelson, E. C., … Martin, N. G. (2003). Escalation of drug use in early-onset cannabis users versus co-twin controls. *Journal of the American Medical Association, 289*, 427–433.

Lyubomirsky, S. (2007). *The how of happiness: A scientific approach to getting the life you want*. New York: Penguin Press.

MacKillop, J., Amlung, M. T., Few, L. R., Ray, L. A., Sweet, L., & Munafo, M. R. (2011). Delayed reward discounting and addictive behavior: A meta-analysis. *Psychopharmacology, 216*, 305–321.

Madanes, C. (1981). *Strategic family therapy*. San Francisco, CA: Jossey-Bass.

Madanes, C. (1984). *Behind the one-way mirror: Advances in the practice of strategic therapy*. San Francisco, CA: Jossey-Bass.

Maisel, E., Epston, D., & Borden, A. (2004). *Biting the hand that starves you: Inspiring resistance to anorexia/bulimia*. New York: Norton.

Malchiodi, C. A. (Ed.). (2003). *Handbook of art therapy*. New York: Guilford.

Malchiodi, C. A. (Ed.). (2008). *Creative interventions with traumatized children*. New York: Guilford.

Maltz, J. (2011). Recipe for life. *Psychotherapy Networker, 35* (1), 18–27.

Maltz, W. (2009). Out of the shadows: What's the prevalence of porn doing to our psyches? *Psychotherapy Networker, 33* (6), 26–36.

Maltz, W., & Maltz, L. (2010). *The porn trap: The essential guide to overcoming problem problems caused by pornography*. New York: Harper.

Marceaux, J. C., & Melville, C. L. (2011). Twelve-step facilitated versus mapping-enhanced cognitive-behavioral therapy for pathological gambling: A controlled study. *Journal of Gambling Studies, 27*, 171–190.

Marche, S. (2012,). Is *Facebook* making us lonely? *The Atlantic, 309* (4), 60–70.

Marijuana Project Research Group (2004). Brief treatments for cannabis dependence: Findings from a randomized multi-site trial. *Journal of Consulting and Clinical Psychology, 72*, 455–466.

REFERENCES

Markel, H. (2011). *An anatomy of addiction: Sigmund Freud, William Halsted, and the miracle drug cocaine*. New York: Pantheon Books.

Marlatt, G. A. (1978). Craving for alcohol, loss of control and relapse: A cognitive-behavioral analysis. In P. A. Nathan, G. A. Marlatt, & T. Loberg (Eds.), *Alcoholism: New directions in behavioural research and treatment* (pp. 271–274). New York: Plenum.

Marlatt, G. A. (Ed.). (1998). *Harm-reduction: Pragmatic strategies for managing high-risk behaviors*. New York: Guilford.

Marlatt, G. A., Bowen, S., Chawla, N., & Witkiewitz, K. (2008). Mindfulness-based relapse prevention for substance abusers: Therapist training and therapeutic relationships. In S. F. Hick & T. Bien (Eds.), *Mindfulness and the therapeutic relationship* (pp. 107–122). New York: Guilford.

Marlatt, G. A., & Gordon, J. R. (1985). *Relapse prevention: Maintenance strategies in the treatment of addictive behaviors*. New York: Guilford.

Marlatt, G. A., & Witkiewitz, K. (2005). Relapse prevention for alcohol and drug problems. In G. A. Marlatt & D. M. Donovan (Eds.), *Relapse prevention: Maintenance strategies in the treatment of addictive behaviors* (pp. 1–45). New York: Guilford.

Martin, L. R., Haskard-Zoinierek, K. B., & DiMatteo, M. R. (2010). *Health behavior change and treatment adherence: Evidenced-based guidelines for improving healthcare*. New York: Oxford University Press.

Martinez, F., LeFloch, V., Gaffie, B., & Villejoubert, G. (2011). Reports of wins and risk-taking: An investigation of the mediating effect of the illusion of control. *Journal of Gambling Studies, 27*, 271–285.

Martino, S., Carroll, K. M., Nich, C., & Rounsaville, B. J. (2006). A randomized controlled pilot study of motivational interviewing for patients with psychotic and drug use disorders. *Addiction, 101*, 1479–1492.

Mauboussin, M. J. (2009). *Think twice: Harnessing the power of counter-intuition*. Boston, MA: Harvard Business.

Mauboussin, M. J. (2011). Embracing complexity. *Harvard Business Review, 89* (9), 89–92.

Maude-Griffin, P. M., Hohenstein, J. M., Humfleet, G. L., Reilly, P. M., Tusel, D. J., & Hall, S. M. (1998). Superior efficacy of cognitive-behavioral therapy for urban crack cocaine abusers: Main and matching effects. *Journal of Clinical and Consulting Psychology, 66*, 832–837.

McCauley, K. T. (2009). Addiction is a disease, not a choice. In C. Fisanick (Ed.), *Addiction: Opposing viewpoints* (pp. 33–39). Detroit, MI: Greenhaven Press.

McCollum, E., Stith, S. M., & Thomsen, C. J. (2012). Solution focused brief therapy in the conjoint couples treatment of intimate partner violence. In C. Franklin, T. S. Trepper, W. J. Gingerich, & E. E. McCollum (Eds.), *Solution-focused brief therapy: A handbook of evidence-based practice* (pp. 130–143). New York: Oxford University Press.

McCrady, B .S. (2004). To have but one true friend: Implications for practice and research on alcohol use disorders and social networks. *Psychology of Addictive Behaviors, 18*, 113–121.

McCrady, B. S. & Epstein, E. E. (1995). Marital therapy in the treatment of alcoholism. In A. S. Gurman & N. Jacobson (Eds.), *Clinical handbook of marital therapy* (2nd ed., pp. 369–393). New York: Guilford.

McCrady, M. S., Epstein, E. E., Cook, S., Jensen, N., & Hildebrandt, T. (2009). A randomized trial of individual and couple behavioral alcohol treatment for women. *Journal of Consulting and Clinical Psychology, 77*, 243–256.

McCrady, B. S., Epstein, E. E., & Kahler, C. W. (2004). Alcoholics Anonymous and relapse prevention as maintenance strategies after conjoint behavioral alcohol treatment for men: 18-months outcomes. *Journal of Consulting and Clinical Psychology, 72*, 870–878

McCrady, B. S., Hayaki, J., Epstein, E. E., & Hirsch, L. S. (2002). Testing hypothesized predictors of change in conjoint behavioral alcoholism treatment for men. *Alcoholism: Clinical and Experimental Research, 26*, 463–470.

McCrady, B. S., Noel, N. E., Abrams, D. B., Stout, R. L., Nelson, H. F., & Hay, W. M. (1986). Comparative effectiveness of three types of spouse involvement in outpatient behavioral alcoholism treatment. *Journal of Studies on Alcohol,47*, 459–467.

McCrady, B. S., Stout, R., Noel, N. E., Abrams, D. B., & Nelson, H. F. (1991). Effectiveness of three types of spouse-involved behavioral alcoholism treatment. *British Journal of Addictions, 86*, 1415–1424.

McCullough, M. E., Emmons, R. A., & Tsang, J. (2002). The grateful disposition: A conceptual and empirical topography. *Journal of Personality and Psychology, 82*, 112–127.

McDermott, D. & Snyder, C. R. (1999). *Making hope happen: A workbook for turning possibilities into reality*. Oakland, CA: New Harbinger.

REFERENCES

McGee, D., Del Vento, A., & Bavelas, J. B. (2005). An interactional model of questions as therapeutic interventions. *Journal of Marital and Family Therapy*, 31, 371–384.

McGowan, K. (2010). The new quitter. *Psychology Today*, 43 (4), 78–84.

McGrath, R. G. (2011). Failing by design. *Harvard Business Review*, 89 (4), 76–86.

McKeel, J. (2011). What works in solution-focused brief therapy. In C. Franklin, T. S. Trepper, W. J. Gingerich, & E. E. McCollum (Eds.), *Solution-focused brief therapy: A handbook of evidence-based practice* (pp. 130–143). New York: Oxford University Press.

McLellan, A. T., Lewis, D. C., O'Brien, C. P., & Kleber, H. D. (2000). Drug dependence, a chronic medical illness: Implications for treatment, insurance, and outcomes evaluation. *Journal of the American Medical Association*, 284 (13), 1689–1695.

McQueen, J., Howe, T. E., Allan, L., Mains, D., & Hardy, V. (2011). Brief interventions for heavy alcohol users admitted to general hospital wards. *Cochrane Database of Systematic Reviews* 2011, Issue 8. Art. No.: CD005191.

Melville, K. M., Casey, L. M., & Kavanagh, D. J. (2007). Psychological treatment drop-out among pathological gamblers. *Clinical Psychology Review*, 27, 944–958.

Melville, C. L., Davis, C. S., Matzenbacher, D. L., & Clayborne, J. (2004). Node-link mapping-enhanced group treatment for pathological gambling. *Addictive Behaviors*, 29, 73–87.

Messerly, J. G. (2009). Online game playing can be addictive. In C. Fisanik (Ed.), *Addiction: Opposing viewpoints* (pp. 40–48). Farmington Hills, MI: Greenhaven Press.

Meyers, R. J. (2012). *CRAFT: The community reinforcement and family training model*. Workshop presented at the Haymarket Center's Summer Institute on Addictions, Elmhurst, IL, June.

Meyers, R. J., Miller, W. R., Smith, J. E., & Tonigan, J. (2002). A randomized trial of two methods for engaging treatment-refusing drug users through concerned significant others *Journal of Consulting and Clinical Psychology*, 70 (5), 1182–1185.

Michel, B., & Nock, M. (2008). *The pain paradox: Understanding analgesia in NSSI*. Paper presented at the International Society for the Study of Self-Injury Conference, Harvard University, Cambridge, MA, June.

Milby, J. B., Schumacher, J. E., Raczynski, J. M., Caldwell, E., Engle, M., & Michael, M. (1996). Sufficient conditions for effective treatment of substance-abusing homeless persons. *Drug and Alcohol Dependence*, 431, 39–47.

Millar, H. R. (1998). New eating disorder service. *Psychiatric Bulletin*, 22, 751–754.

Miller, A. L., Rathus, J. H., & Linehan, M. M. (2007). *Dialectical behavior therapy with suicidal adolescents*. New York: Guilford.

Miller, D. (2005). *Women who hurt themselves: A book of hope and understanding*. New York: Basic Books.

Miller, M. C. (2007). Is 'Internet addiction' a distinct mental disorder? *Harvard Mental Health Letter*, 24 (4), 8.

Miller, W. R., Forcehimes, A. A., & Zweben, A. (2011). *Treating addictions: A guide for professionals*. New York: Guilford.

Miller, W. R., Meyers, R. J., & Tonigan, J. (1999). Engaging the unmotivated in treatment for alcohol problems: A comparison of three strategies for intervention through family members. *Journal of Consulting and Clinical Psychology*, 67 (5), 688–697.

Miller, W. R., & Rollnick, S. (2002). *Motivational interviewing: Preparing people for change* (2nd ed.). New York: Guilford.

Miller, W. R., Walters, S. T., & Bennett, M. E. (2001). How effective is alcoholism treatment? *Journal of Studies on Alcohol*, 62, 211–220.

Minuchin, S. (1974). *Families and family therapy*. Cambridge, MA: Harvard University Press.

Minuchin, S. (1986). Four-day live supervision training in structural family therapy. Clinical intensive training at the Gestalt Integrated Family Therapy Institute, Chicago, IL, April.

Minuchin, S., & Fishman, H. C. (1981). *Family therapy techniques*. Cambridge, MA: Harvard University Press.

Minuchin, P., Colapinto, J., & Minuchin, S. (1998). *Working with families of the poor*. New York: Guilford.

Minuchin, S., Rosman, B. L., & Baker, L. (1978). *Psychosomatic families: Anorexia nervosa in context*. Cambridge, MA: Harvard University Press.

Mitchell, J. E., Specker, S. M., & de Zwaan, M. (1991). Co-morbidity and medical complications of bulimia nervosa. *Journal of Clinical Psychiatry*, 52 (10), 13–20.

REFERENCES

Mokdad, A. H., Marks, J. S., Stroup, D. F., & Gerberding, J. L. (2004). Actual causes of death in the United States. *Journal of the American Medical Association, 291* (10):1238–1245.

Monti, P. M., Miranda, R., Nixon, K., Sher, K. J., Swartzwelder, H. S., Tapert, S. F. … Crews, F. T. (2005). Adolescence: Booze, brains, and behavior. *Alcohol Clinical Experimental Research, 29,* 207–220.

Moore, T. H. M., Zammit, S., Lingfor-Hughes, T. R. E., Jones, P. B., Burke, M., & Lewis, G. (2007). Cannabis use and risk of psychotic or affective mental health outcomes: A systematic review. *Lancet, 370,* 319–328.

Moos, R. H. (2007). Theory-based processes that promote remission of substance abuse disorders. *Clinical Psychology Review, 27,* 537–551.

Moos, R. H., Schaefer, J., Andrassy, J., & Moos, B. (2001). Outpatient mental healthcare, self-help groups, and patients' one-year treatment outcomes. *Journal of Clinical Psychology, 57* (3), 273–287.

Morton, R. (1689). *Phtisiologia seu exercitations de Phthisi.* London, UK: Smith.

Moyer, A., Finney, J. W., Swearingen, C. E., & Vergun, P. (2002). Brief interventions for alcohol problems: A meta-analytical review of controlled investigations in treatment-seeking and non-treatment-seeking populations. *Addiction, 97,* 279–292.

Muehlenkamp, J., & Gutiérrez, P. M. (2004). An investigation of differences between self-injurious and suicide attempts in a sample of adolescents. *Suicide and Life-Threatening Behavior, 34,* 12–24.

Muehlenkamp, J. J., Yates, B., & Alberts, A. (2004). *Gender and racial differences in self-injury.* Paper presented at the Annual American Association of Suicidology Conference, Miami, FL, April.

Müller, C. A. & Banas, R. (2011). Disulfiram: An anti-craving substance? *American Journal of Psychiatry, 168* (1), 98.

Mutschler, J., Buhler, M., Grosshans, M., Diehl, A., Mann, K., & Kiefer, F. (2010). Disulfiram: An option for the treatment of pathological gambling? *Alcohol and Alcoholism, 45,* 214–216.

Nardone, G., Milanese, R., & Verbitz, T. (2005). *Prison of food: Research and treatment of eating disorders.* London, UK: Karnac.

Nardone, G., Verbitz, T., & Milanese, R. (1999). *The prisons of food: Strategic solution-oriented research and treatment of eating disorders.* London, UK: Karnac.

Nardone, G., & Watzlawick, P. (1990). *L'Arte del cambiamento.* [The art of change.] Florence, Italy: Ponte alle Grazie.

Nasser, M. (2004). Dying to live: Eating disorders and self-harm behavior in a cultural context. In J. L. Levitt, R. A. Sansone, & L. Cohn. (Eds.), *Self-harm behavior and eating disorders: Dynamics, assessment, and treatment* (pp. 15–31). New York: Brunner-Routledge.

National Campaign to Prevent Teen and Unplanned Pregnancy (2008). Sex and tech. Retrieved from http://www.thenationalcampaign.org/sextech/PDF/SexTech-Summary.pdf, January 4, 2011.

National Institute on Drug Abuse (1999). *Principles of drug addiction treatment: A research-based guide* (2nd ed.). NIH Publication 09-418..

Neret, G. (1994). *Salvador Dali 1904–1989.* Berlin, Germany: Benedict Taschen.

Newham Asian Women's Project (2004). *Silent scream: Young Asian women and self-harm.* London, UK: Hoxton-Printhouse.

Nock, M. K., Joiner, T., Gordon, K. H., Lloyd-Richardson, E., & Prinstein, M. J. (2006). Non-suicidal self-injury among adolescents: Diagnostic correlates and relation to suicide attempts. *Psychiatry Research, 144* (1), 65–72.

Nock, M. K., & Prinstein, M. J. (2005). Contextual features and behavioral functions of self-mutilation among adolescents. *Journal of Abnormal Psychology, 114* (1), 140–146.

Norcross, J. C. (2010). The therapeutic relationship. In B. L. Duncan, S. D. Miller, B. E. Wampold, & M. A. Hubble (Eds.), *The heart and soul of change: Delivering what works in therapy* (2nd ed., pp. 113–143). Washington, DC: American Psychological Association.

Norcross, J. C., Beutler, L. E., & Levant, R. F. (Eds.). (2006). *Evidenced-based practices in mental health: Debate and dialogue on the fundamental questions.* Washington, DC: American Psychological Association.

Norrholm, S. D., Bibb, J. A., Nestler, E. J., Ouimet, C. C., Taylor, J. R., & Greengard, P. (2003). Cocaine-induced proliferation of dendritic spines in nucleus accumbens is dependent on the activity of cyclin-dependent kinase-5. *Neuroscience, 116,* 19–22.

Nylund, D., & Corsiglia, V. (1994). Becoming solution-focused forced in brief therapy: Remembering something important we already know. *Journal of Systemic Therapies, 13* (1), 5–13.

REFERENCES

Odlaug. B. L., Marsh, P. J., Kim, S. W., & Grant, J. E. (2011). Strategic versus non-strategic gambling: Characteristics of pathological gamblers based on gambling preferences. *Annals of Clinical Psychiatry, 23,* 105–112.

O'Farrell, T. J., & Fals-Stewart, W. (2002). Behavioral couples and family therapy for substance abusers. *Current Psychiatry Reports, 4,* 371–376.

O'Farrell, T. J., & Fals-Stewart, W. (2003). Alcohol abuse. *Journal of Marital and Family Therapy, 29,* 121–146.

O'Farrell, T. J., & Fals-Stewart, W. (2006). *Behavioral couples therapy for alcoholism and drug abuse.* New York: Guilford.

O'Farrell, T. J., Hooley, J., Fals-Stewart, W., & Cutter, H. S. (1998). Expressed emotion and relapse in alcoholic patients. *Journal of Consulting and Clinical Psychology, 66,* 744–752.

O'Hanlon, W. H. (1987). *Taproots: Underlying principles of Milton H. Erickson's therapy and hypnosis.* New York: Norton.

O'Hanlon, W. H., & Weiner-Davis, M. (1989). *In search of solutions: A new direction in psychotherapy.* New York: Norton.

Olmstead, T. A., Sindelar, J. L., Easton, C. J., & Carroll, K. M. (2007). The cost-effectiveness of four treatments for marijuana dependence. *Addiction, 102,* 1443–1453.

Omer, H. (2004). *Nonviolent resistance: A new approach to violent and self-destructive children.* Cambridge, UK: Cambridge University Press.

Onnis, L. (1988). *Famiglia e malattia psicomattica: L'orientamento sistemico.* [Family and psychosomatic illness: The systemic approach.] Roma, Italy: NIS.

Orford, J. (2008). Asking the right questions in the right way: The need for a shift in research on psychological treatments for addiction. *Addiction, 103* (6), 875–885.

Orford, J. (2011). *An unsafe bet? The dangerous rise of gambling and the debate we should be having.* London, UK: Wiley-Blackwell.

Orford, J., & Edwards, G. (1977). *Alcoholism: A comparison of treatment and advice with a study of the influence of marriage.* New York: Oxford University Press.

Orimoto, L., & Vitousek, K. (1992). Anorexia nervosa and bulimia nervosa. In P. W. Wilson (Ed.), *Principles and practices of relapse prevention* (pp. 85–127). New York: Guilford.

Osuch, E. A., & Payne, G. W. (2008). Neurobiological perspectives on self-injury. In M. K. Nixon & N. L. Heath (Eds.), *Self-injury in youth: An essential guide to assessment and intervention* (pp. 79–110). New York: Routledge.

Ougrin, D., Ng, A., & Low, J. (2008). Therapeutic assessment based on cognitive-analytic therapy for young people presenting with self-harm: A pilot study. *Psychiatry Bulletin, 32,* 423–426.

Ougrin, D., Zundel, T., & Ng, A. V. (2010). *Self-harm in young people: A therapeutic assessment manual.* London, UK: Hodder Arnold.

Pallesen, S., Mitsem, M., Kvale, G., Johnsen, B., & Mode, H. (2005). Outcome of psychological treatments of pathological gambling: A review and meta-analysis. *Addiction, 100,* 1412–1422.

Papp, P. (1983). *The process of change.* New York: Guilford.

Park, S. K., Kim, J. Y., & Cho, C. B. (2008). Prevalence of Internet addiction and correlations with family factors among South Korean adolescents. *Adolescence, 43* (172), 895–909.

Pascale, R., Sternin, J., & Sternin, M. (2010). *The power of positive deviance: How unlikely innovators solve the world's toughest problems.* Boston, MA: Harvard Business.

Paus, T. (2005). Mapping brain maturation and cognitive development during adolescence. *Trends in Cognitive Science, 9,* 60–68.

Pennebaker, J. W. (2004). *Writing to heal: A guided journal for recovering from trauma and emotional upheaval.* Oakland, CA: New Harbinger.

Pérez Opi, E., & Landarroitajáuregui, J. R. (1995). Teoría de pareja: Introducción a una terapia sexológica sistémica. *Revista de Sexología, 70–71,* 5–207.

Peterson, C. (2006). *A primer in positive psychology.* New York: Oxford University Press.

Peterson, P. L., Hawkins, J. D., & Catalano, R. F. (1992). Evaluating comprehensive drug risk reduction interventions: Design challenges and recommendations. *Evaluation Review, 16,* 579–602.

Peterson, C., & Seligman, M. E. P. (2004). *Character strengths and virtues: A handbook and classification.* New York: Oxford University Press/American Psychological Association.

REFERENCES

Petry, N. (2003). Patterns and correlates of Gamblers' Anonymous attendance in pathological gamblers seeking professional treatment. *Addictive Behaviors, 28*, 1049–1062.

Petry, N. M. (2005). Stage of change in treatment-seeking pathological gamblers. *Journal of Consulting and Clinical Psychology, 73*, 312–322.

Petry, N. M. (2009). Disordered gambling and its treatment. *Cognitive and Behavioral Practice*, 457–467.

Petry, N. M., Peirce, J. M., & Stitzer, M. L. (2005). Effect of prize-based incentives on outcomes in stimulant abusers in outpatient psychosocial treatment programs: A National Drug Abuse Treatment Clinical Trials network Study. *Archives of General Psychiatry, 62*, 1148–1156.

Petry, N. M., Stintson, F. S., & Grant, B. F. (2005). Co-morbidity of DSM-IV pathological gambling and psychiatric disorders: Results from the National Epidemiologic Survey on Alcohol and Related Conditions. *Journal of Clinical Psychiatry, 66*, 564–574.

Petry, N. M., Weinstock, J., Ledgerwoo, D. M., & Morasco, B. (2008). A randomized trial of brief interventions for problem and pathological gambling. *Journal of Consulting and Clinical Psychology, 76*, 318–328.

Pietrusza, C., Rothenberg, P., & Whitlock, J. (2011). *Reaching out: The role of formal and informal disclosure in non-suicidal self-injury cessation.* Poster presented at the International Society for the Study of Self-Injury Sixth Annual Conference, New York, NY, June.

Pike, K. M., Walsh, B. T., Vitousek, K., Wilson, G. T., & Bauer, J. (2003). Cognitive behavioral therapy in the post-hospitalization treatment of anorexia nervosa. *American Journal of Psychiatry, 160* (11), 2046–2049.

Pinsof, W. M. (1995). *Integrative problem-centered therapy*. New York: Basic Books.

Plante, L. G. (2007). *Bleeding to ease the pain: Cutting, self-injury, and the adolescent search for self.* Westport, CT: Praeger.

Polivy, J. (2001). The false hope syndrome: Unrealistic expectations of self-change. *International Journal of Obesity and Related Metabolic Disorders, 25*, 80.

Polivy, J. (2010). The natural course and outcome of eating disorders and obesity. In H. Klingemann & L. C. Sobell (Eds.), *Promoting self-change in addictive behaviors: Practical implications for policy, prevention, and treatment* (pp. 119–126). New York: Springer.

Polivy, J., & Herman, C. (2002). Causes of eating disorders. *Annual Review of Psychology, 53*, 187–213.

Polk, E., & Liss, M. (2007). Psychological characteristics of self-injurious behavior. *Personality and Individual Differences, 43*, 567–577.

Pope, H. G., Gruber, A. J., Hudson, J. L., Cohane, G., Huestis, M. A., & Yurgelun-Todd, D. (2003). Early onset cannabis use and cognitive deficits: What is the nature of the association? *Drug and Alcohol Dependence, 69*, 303–310.

Potenza, M. N. (2006). The neurobiology of pathological gambling and drug addiction: An overview and new findings. In T. W. Robbins, B. J. Everitt, & D. J. Nutt (Eds.), *The neurobiology of addiction: New vistas.* Oxford, UK: Oxford University.

Potenza, M. (2008). The neurobiology of pathological gambling and drug addiction: An overview and new findings. *Philosophical Transactions of the Royal Society, 363*, 3181–3189.

Price, R. K., Risk, N. K., & Spitznagel, E. L. (2001). Remission from drug abuse over a 25-year period: Patterns of remission and treatment use. *American Journal of Public Health, 7*, 1107–1113.

Prochaska, J. O., & DiClemente, C. C. (1982). Transtheoretical therapy: Toward a more integrative model of change. *Psychotherapy: Theory, Research, and Practice, 19*, 276–288.

Prochaska, J. O., & DiClemente, C. C. (1985). Common processes of self-change in smoking, weight control, and psychological distress. In S. Shiffman & T. A. Wills (Eds.), *Doping and substance abuse* (pp. 345–363). San Diego, CA: Academic Press.

Prochaska, J. O. & DiClemente, C. C. (1992). *Stages of change in the modification of of problem behaviors*. Newbury Park, CA: Sage.

Prochaska, J. O., DiClemente, C. C., & Norcross, J. C. (1992). In search of how people change: Applications to addictive behaviors. *American Psychologist, 47*, 1102–1114.

Prochaska, J. O, Norcross, J. C., & DiClemente, C. C. (2006). *Changing for good: A revolutionary six-stage program for overcoming bad habits and moving your life positively forward.* New York: Harper-Collins.

Project MATCH Research Group (1997). Matching patients with alcohol disorders to treatments: Clinical implications from Project MATCH. *Journal of Mental Health, 7*, 589–602.

Quick, E. K. (1996). *Doing what works in brief therapy: A strategic solution-focused approach.* Burlington, MA: Academic Press.

REFERENCES

Quinn, J. (2009). Americans' gambling $100 billion in casinos like rats in a cage. Retrieved from http://www.marketoracle.co.uk/UserInfo-James Quinn.html, October 22, 2011.

Raimo, E. B. & Schukit, M. A. (1998). Alcohol dependence and mood disorders. *Addictive Behaviors, 23* (6), 933–946.

Raub, T.D. (2012). Returning from relapse. *Renew Magazine, July/August*, 56–59.

Rawson, R. A., Marinelli-Casey, P., & Anglin, M. D. (2004). A multisite comparison of psychosocial approaches for the treatment of methamphetamine dependence. *Addiction, 99*, 708–717.

Rawson, R. A., McCann, M. J., & Flammino, F. (2006). A comparison of contingency management and cognitive-behavioral approaches for stimulant-dependent individuals. *Addiction, 101*, 267–274.

Raymond, N. C., Coleman, E., & Miner, M. H. (2003). Psychiatric co-morbidity compulsive/impulsive traits in compulsive sexual behavior. *Comprehensive Psychiatry, 44*, 370–380.

Razzano, L. A., & Pashka, N. (2012). *Evidenced-based treatment for co-occurring mental health and substance use disorders*. Workshop presented at Haymarket Center's Summer Institute on Addictions, Elmhurst, IL, June.

Rinpoche, L. Z. (1993). *Transforming problems into happiness*. Boston, MA: Wisdom Publications.

Robbins, M. S., Turner, C. W., Alexander, J. F., & Perez, G. A. (2003). Alliance and drop-out in family therapy for adolescents with behavior problems: Individual and systemic effects. *Journal of Family Psychology, 17*, 534–544.

Roberts, J. (2004). Compulsive spending younger generations. *Futurist, 32* (2), 2.

Robin, A. L., & Le Grange, D. (2010). Family therapy for adolescents with anorexia nervosa. In J. R. Weisz & A. E. Kazdin (Eds.), *Evidenced-based psychotherapies for children and adolescents* (2nd ed., pp. 345–359). New York: Guilford.

Robins, L. N. (1993). Vietnam veterans' rapid recovery from heroin addiction: A fluke or normal expectation? *Addiction, 88*, 1041–1054.

Robins, L. N., Helzer, J. E., Hesselbrock, M., & Wish, E. (1980). Vietnam veterans three years after Vietnam: How our study changed our view of heroin. In L. Brill & C. Winick (Eds.), *Yearbook of substance use and abuse* (pp. 213–230). New York: Human Science Press.

Rohrbaugh, M., Tennen, H., Press, S., & White, L. (1981). Compliance, defiance, and therapeutic paradox: Guidelines for strategic use of paradoxical interventions. *American Journal of Orthopsychiatry, 51*, 454–467.

Roland, J. (1985). Questionstorming: Outline of the method. Pynthanics. Retrieved from, http://pynthan.org/documents/questorming.html, September 13, 2011.

Rolland, J. (1994). *Families, illness, and disability*. New York: Basic Books.

Rollnick, S., Mason, P., & Butler, C. (1999). *Health behavior change: A guide for practitioners*. Edinburgh, Scotland: Churchill Livingstone.

Ropelato, J. (2009). Internet pornography statistics. Retrieved from http://internet-filter-reviewtoptenreviews.com/internet pornography statistics.html, January 24, 2011.

Rosen, L. D., Cheever, N. A., & Carrier, L. M. (2012). *iDisorder: Understanding our obsession with technology and overcoming its hold on us*. New York: Palgrave Macmillan.

Rosen, S. (1982). *My voice will go with you: The teaching tales of Milton H. Erickson*. New York: Norton.

Rosengren, D. B. (2009). *Building motivational interviewing skills: A practitioner workbook*. New York: Guilford.

Roth, A., & Fonagy, P. (2005). *What works for whom? A critical review of of psychotherapy research*, (2nd ed.). New York: Guilford.

Rumpf, H. J., Bischof, G., & John, U. (2010). Remission without formal help: New directions in studies using survey data. In H. Klingemann & L. C. Sobell (Eds.), *Promoting self-change in addictive behaviors: Practical implications for policy, prevention, and treatment* (pp. 73–86). New York: Springer.

Rush, B., Veldhuizen, S., & Adlaf, E. (2007). Mapping the prevalence of problem gambling and its association with treatment. *Journal of Gambling Issues, 20*, 193–213.

Russell, G. (1979). Bulimia nervosa: An ominous variant of anorexia nervosa. *Psychological Medicine, 9*, 429–448.

Russell, G. F., Szmukler, G. I., Dare, C., & Eisler, I. (1987). An evaluation of family therapy in anorexia nervosa and bulimia nervosa. *Archives of General Psychiatry, 44*, 1047–1057.

Ryan, T., & Xenos, S. (2011). Who uses *Facebook*? An investigation of the big five: Shyness, narcissism, loneliness, and *Facebook* usage. *Computers and Human Behavior, 27* (5), 1658–1664.

Ryle, A., & Kerr, I. (2002). *Introduction to cognitive-analytic therapy: Principles and practice*. New York: John Wiley.

REFERENCES

Saal, D., Dong, Y., Bonci, A., & Malenka, R .C. (2003). Drugs of abuse and stress trigger a common synaptic adaptation in dopamine neurons. *Neuron, 37*, 577–582.

Safer, D. L., Telch, C. F., & Agras, W. S. (2001). Dialectical behavior therapy for bulimia nervosa. *American Journal of Psychiatry, 158* (4), 632–634.

Salecl, R. (2010). *The tyranny of choice*. London, UK: Profile Books.

Sansone, R. A., Levitt, J. L., & Sansone, L. A. (2004). Psychotropic medications, self-harm behavior, and eating disorders. In J. L. Levitt, R. A. Sansone, & L. Cohn (Eds.), *Self-harm behavior and eating disorders: Dynamics, assessment, and treatment* (pp. 245–259). New York: Brunner-Routledge.

Santisteban, D. A., Coatsworth, J. D., Perez-Vidal, A., Kurtines, W. M., Schwartz, S., & Laperriere, A. (2003). Efficacy of brief strategic family therapy in modifying Hispanic-adolescent behavior problems and substance use. *Journal of Family Psychology, 17*, 123–133.

Santisteban, D. A., Muir, J., Mena, M. P., & Mitrani, V. B. (2003). Integrative borderline adolescent family therapy: Meeting the challenges of treating adolescents with borderline personality disorder. *Psychotherapy: Theory, Research, Practice, and Training, 40* (4), 251–264.

Santisteban, D. A., Szapocznik, J., Perez-Vidal, A., Kurtines, W., Murray, E. J., & La Pierriere, A. (1996). Efficacy of interventions for engaging youth and familias into treatment and some variables that may contribute to differential effectiveness. *Journal of Family Psychology, 10*, 35–44.

Sargut, G., & McGrath, R. G. (2011). Learning to live with complexity: How to make sense of the unpredictable and the undefinable in today's hyper-connected business world. *Harvard Business Review, 89* (9), 68–76.

Satir, V. (1983). *Conjoint family therapy*. Palo Alto, CA: Science & Behavior.

Satir, V. (1988). *The new people-making*. Palo Alto, CA: Science & Behavior.

Schlesinger, L. A., Kiefer, C. F., & Brown, P. B. (2012). *Just start: Take action, embrace uncertainty, and create the future*. Boston, MA: Harvard Business.

Schroeder, S. R., Oster-Granite, M. L., & Thompson, T. (2002). Self-injurious behavior: Gene, brain, and behavior relationships. *Research in Developmental Disabilities, 23* (5), 367–368.

Schultz, W. (2003). Discrete coding of reward probability and uncertainty by dopamine neurons. *Science, 299*, 1898–1902.

Schwartz, B. (2004). *The paradox of choice: Why more is less*. New York: Harper Collins.

Schwartz, J. M., & Begley, S. (2003). *The mind and the brain: Neuroplasticity and the power of mental force*. New York: Regan Books.

Schwartz, J. M., & Gladding, R. (2011). *You are not your brain: The 4-step solution for changing bad habits, ending unhealthy thinking, and taking control of your life*. New York: Avery.

Scott, V. M., Mottarella, K. E., & Lavooy, M. J. (2006). Does virtual intimacy exist? A brief exploration into reported levels of intimacy in online relationships. *Cyber-Psychology and Behavior, 9* (6), 759–761.

Selekman, M. D. (2005). *Pathways to change: Brief therapy with difficult adolescents* (2nd ed.). New York: Guilford.

Selekman, M. D. (2006). *Working with self-harming adolescents: A collaborative strengths-based therapy approach*. New York: Norton.

Selekman, M. D. (2009). *The adolescent and young adult self-harming treatment manual: A collaborative strengths-based brief therapy approach*. New York: Norton.

Selekman, M. D. (2010). *Collaborative brief therapy with children*. New York: Guilford.

Selekman, M. D., & Schulem, H. (2007). The self-harming adolescents and their families expert consultants project: A qualitative study. Unpublished manuscript.

Selekman, M., Wilson, J., & Beyebach, M. (2005). *Therapeutic moments that count: Practicing outside your comfort zone*. Workshop held at the Annual Psychotherapy Networker Conference, Washington, DC, March.

Seligman, M. E. P. (2002). *Authentic happiness*. New York: The Free Press.

Seligman, M. E. P. (2011). *Flourish: A visionary new understanding of happiness and well-being*. New York: The Free Press.

Seligman, M. E. P., Reivich, K., Jaycox, L., & Gillham, J. (1995). *The optimistic child: A revolutionary program that safeguards children against depression and builds lifelong resilience*. New York: Houghton-Mifflin.

Selvini-Palazzoli, M., Boscolo, L., Cecchin, G., & Prata, G. (1978). *Paradox and counter-paradox: A new model in the therapy of the family in schizophrenic transaction*. New York: Jason Aronson.

REFERENCES

Selvini-Palazzoli, M., Boscolo, L., Cecchin, G., & Prata, G. (1980). Hypothesizing—circularity—neutrality: Three guidelines for the for the conductor of the session. *Family Process, 19* (1), 3–13.

Selvini-Palazzoli, M., Cirillo, S., Selvini, M., & Sorrentino, A. M. (1998). *Ragazze anoressiche e bulimiche*. Milan, Italy: Raffaello Cortina.

Shaffer, H. J. (2010). Considering the unimaginable: Challenges to accepting self-change or natural recovery from addiction. In H. Klingemann & L.C. Sobell (Eds.), *Promoting self-change from addictive behaviors: Practical implications for policy, prevention, and treatment* (pp. ix–xiii). New York: Springer.

Shaffer, H. J., Hall, M. N., & Vanderbilt, J. (1999). Estimating the prevalence of disordered gambling behavior in the United States and Canada; A research synthesis. *American Journal Public Health, 89*, 1369–1376.

Shaffer, H. J., & Jones, S. B. (1989). *Quitting cocaine: The struggle against impulse*. Lexington, MA: Lexington Books.

Shaffer, H. J., LaBrie, R. A., & LaPlante, D. A. (2004). Laying the foundation for regional exposure to social phenomena: Considering the case of legalized gambling as a public health toxin. *Psychology of Addictive Behaviors, 18*, 40–48.

Shaffer, H. J., Martin, R., Kleschinsky, J., & Neporent, L. (2012). *Change your gambling, change your life: Strategies for managing your gambling and improving your finances, relationships, and health*. San Francisco, CA: Jossey-Bass.

Shapiro, F. (1989). Eye movement desensitization: A new treatment for post-traumatic stress disorder. *Journal of Behavioral Therapy and Experimental Psychiatry, 20*, 211–217.

Shapiro, F., & Forrest, M. S. (2004). *EMDR: The breakthrough therapy for overcoming anxiety, stress, and trauma*. New York: Basic Books.

Shapiro, F., Kaslow, F., & Maxfield, L. (2007). *Handbook of EMDR and family processes*. New York: John Wiley.

Sharples, T. (2008). Teens' latest self-injury fad: Self-embedding. *Time* Magazine Archive. Retrieved from http://www.time.com/time/printout/0.8816,1865995,00.html, December 17, 2008.

Sharry, J., Madden, B., & Darmody, M. (2004). *Becoming a solution-focused detective*. Binghamton, NY: Haworth.

Shelef, K., Diamond, G. M., Diamond, G. S., & Liddle, H. A. (2005). Adolescent and parent alliance and treatment outcome in multidimensional family therapy. *Journal of Consulting and Clinical Psychology, 73*, 689–698.

Shermer, M. (2011). *The believing brain: How we construct beliefs and reinforce them as truths*. New York: Times Books.

Sheinberg, M. (1985). The debate: A strategic technique. *Family Process, 24* (2), 259–271.

Siegel, D. J. (2007). *The mindful brain: Reflection and attunement in the cultivation of well-being*. New York: Norton.

Siegel, D. J. (2010a). *The mindful therapist: A clinician's guide to mindsight and neural integration*. New York: Norton.

Siegel, D. J. (2010b). *Mindsight: The new science of personal transformation*. New York: Bantam Books.

Siegel, R. D. (2010). *The mindfulness solution: Everyday practices for for everyday problems*. New York: Guilford.

Silverman, K., Svikis, D., Wong, C. J., Hampton, J., Stitzer, M. L., & Bigelow, E. A. (2002). Reinforcement-based therapeutic workplace for the treatment of drug abuse: Three-year abstinence outcomes. *Experimental and Clinical Psychopharmacology, 10*, 228–240.

Sinha, R., Easton, C., Renee-Aubin, L., & Carroll, K. M. (2003). Engaging young probation-referred marijuana-abusing individuals in treatment: A pilot trial. *American Journal of Addiction, 12*, 314–324.

Skinner, K. B. (2005). *Treating pornography addiction: The essential tools for recovery*. Provo, UT: Growth Climate, Inc.

Slutske, W. S. (2006). Natural recovery and treatment-seeking in pathological gambling: Results of two US national surveys. *American Journal of Psychiatry, 163*, 297–302.

Slutske, W. S., Eisen S., True, W. R., Lyons, M. J., Goldberg, J., & Tsuang, M. (2000). Common genetic vulnerability for pathological gambling and alcohol dependence in men. *Archives of General Psychiatry, 57*, 666–673.

Smart, R. G. (2010). Natural recovery or recovery without treatment from alcohol and drug problems as seen from survey data. In H. Klingemann & L. C. Sobell (Eds.), *Promoting self-change from addictive behaviors: Practical implications for policy, prevention, and treatment* (pp. 59–71). New York: Springer.

REFERENCES

Smedslund, G., Berg, R. C., Hammerstrom, K. T., Steiro, A., Leiknes, K. A., Dahl, H. M., & Karlsen, K. (2011). Motivational interviewing for substance abuse. *Cochrane Database of Systematic Reviews* 2011, Issue 5, Art.No.: CD008063.

Smith, J. E., & Meyers, R. J. (2004). *Motivating substance abusers to enter treatment: Working with family members*. New York: Guilford.

Smith, R. F. (2003). Animal models of preadolescent substance abuse. *Neurotoxicol Teratology*, 25, 291–301.

Smock, S. A., Trepper, T. S., Wetchler, J. L., McCollum, E. E., Ray, R., & Pierce, K. (2008). Solution-focused group therapy for level 1 substance abusers. *Journal of Marital and Family Therapy*, 34, 93–106.

Snyder, C. R., & Lopez, S. J. (2007). *Positive psychology: The scientific and practical explorations of human strengths*. Thousand Oaks, CA: Sage.

Sobell, L. C. (2010). The phenomenon of self-change: Overview and key issues. In H. Klingemann & L. C. Sobell (Eds.), *Promoting self-change from addictive behaviors: Practical implications for policy, prevention, and treatment* (pp. 1–30). New York: Springer.

Sobell, L. C., Cunningham, J. A., & Sobell, M. B. (1996). Recovery from alcohol problems with and without treatment: Prevalence in two population surveys. *American Journal of Public Health*, 86 (7), 966–972.

Sobell, L. C., Ellingstad, T. P., Sobell, M. B. (2000). Natural recovery from alcohol and drug problems: Methodological review of the research with suggestions for future directions. *Addiction*, 95 (5), 749–764.

Sobell, L. C., & Sobell, M. B. (2011). *Group therapy for substance use disorders*. New York: Guilford.

Sobell, L. C., Sobell, M. B., & Agrawal, S. (2002). Self-change and dual recoveries among individuals with alcohol and tobacco problems: Current knowledge and future directions. *Clinical and Experimental Research*, 26, 1936–1938.

Sprenkle, D. H., Davis, S. D., & Lebow, J. (2009). *Common factors in couple and family therapy: The overlooked foundation for effective practice*. New York: Guilford.

Srisurapanont, M., & Jarusuraisin, N. (2002). Opioid antagonists for alcohol dependence. *Cochrane Library*, Issue 2. Chichester, UK: John Wiley.

Stall, R., & Biernacki, P. (1986). Spontaneous remission from the problematic use of substances: An inductive model derived from a comparative analysis of the alcohol, opiate, tobacco, and food/obesity literature. *The International Journal of the Addictions*, 21 (1), 1–23.

Stanton, M. D. (1984). Fusion, compression, diversion, and the workings of paradox: A therapeutic systemic change. *Family Process*, 23 (2), 135–167.

Stanton, M. D., & Todd, T. C. (1982). *The family therapy of drug abuse and addiction*. New York: Guilford.

Steel, Z., & Blaszczynski, A. (1996). The factorial structure of pathological gambling. *Journal of Gambling Studies*, 12, 3–20.

Steinberg, L., Fletcher, A., & Darling, N. (1994). Parental monitoring and peer influence on adolescent substance abuse. *Pediatrics*, 93, 1060–1064.

Steinberg, M. A. (1993). Couples treatment issues for recovering male compulsive gamblers and similar dyads. *Journal of Gambling Studies*, 9, 153–167.

Steinglass, P., Bennett, L. A., & Wolin, S. J. (1993). *The alcoholic family*. New York: Basic Books.

Steinhausen, H. C. (2009). Outcome of eating disorders. *Children and Adolescent Psychiatric Clinics of North America*, 18, 255–242.

Stephens, R. S., Roffman, R. A., & Curtin, L. (2000). Comparison of extended versus brief treatments for marijuana use. *Journal of Consulting and Clinical Psychology*, 68, 898–908.

Stinnett, N., & O'Donnell, M. (1996). *Good kids: How you and your kids can successfully navigate the teen years*. New York: Doubleday.

Stokes, P. (2002). *Philosophy: 100 essential thinkers*. New York: Enchanted Lion Book.

Stucki, S., & Rihs-Middel, M. (2007). Prevalence of adult problem and pathological gambling between 2000 and 2005: An update. *Journal of Gambling Studies*, 23, 245–257.

Substance Abuse and Mental Health Services Administration (2012). *Results from the 2011 National Survey on Drug Use and Health: Summary of national findings*, NSDUH Series H-44, HHS Publication No. (SMA) 12-4713. Rockville, MD: Substance Abuse and Mental Health Services Administration.

Suler, J. (2004). The online disinhibition effect. *Cyber-Psychology and Behavior*, 7, 321–326.

Suurvali, H., Hogins, D., Toneatto, T., & Cunningham, J. (2008). Treatment-seeking among Ontario problem gamblers: Results of a population survey. *Psychiatric Service*, 59, 1343–1346.

REFERENCES

Sylvain, C., Ladouceur, R., & Boisvert, J.M. (1997). Cognitive and behavioral treatment of pathological gambling: A controlled study. *Journal of Consulting and Clinical Psychology, 65,* 727–732.

Szapocznik, J., Hervis, O., & Schwartz, S. (2003). *Brief strategic family therapy for adolescent drug abuse.* Therapy manuals for drug addiction, manual 5. Bethesda, MD: U.S. Department of Health and Human Services, National Institutes of Health, and National Institute on Drug Abuse.

Szapocznik, J., & Kurtines, W. M. (1989). *Breakthroughs in family therapy with drug-abusing and problem youth.* New York: Springer.

Szapocznik, J., Kurtines, W. M., Foote, F., Pérez-Vidal, A., & Hervis, O. E. (1983). Conjoint versus one person family therapy: Some evidence for effectiveness of conducting family therapy through one person. *Journal of Consulting and Clinical Psychology, 51,* 889–899.

Szapocznik, J., Kurtines, W. M., Foote, F., Pérez-Vidal, A., & Hervis, O. E. (1986). Conjoint versus one person family therapy: Further evidence for the effectiveness of conducting family therapy through one person. *Journal of Consulting and Clinical Psychology, 54,* 395–397.

Szapocznik, J., & Williams, R. A. (2000). Brief strategic family therapy: Twenty-five years of interplay among theory, research, and practice in adolescent behavior problems and drug abuse. *Clinical Child and Family Psychology Review, 3,* 117–134.

Taffel, R. (2009). *Childhood unbound: Saving our kids best selves—confident parenting in a world of change.* New York: The Free Press.

Tamminga, C. A., & Nestler, E. J. (2006). ¡Pathological gambling: Focusing on the addiction, not the activity. *American Journal of Psychiatry, 163,* 180–181.

Tatarsky, A. (2007). *Harm-reduction psychotherapy: A treatment for drug and alcohol problems.* Lanham, MD: Rowman & Littlefield.

Taylor, C. (2010). *Enough! A Buddhist approach to finding release from addictive patterns.* Ithaca, NY: Snow Lion Publications.

Teesson, M., Degenhardt, L., Lynskey, M., & Hall, W. (2005). The relationships between substance use and mental problems: Evidence from longitudinal studies. In T. Stockwell, P. J. Grunewald, J. Toumbourou, & W. Loxley (Eds.), *Preventing harmful substance use: The evidence-base for policy and practice* (pp. 43–51). New York: John Wiley.

Thompson-Brenner, H., Glass, S., & Westen, D. (2003). A multidimensional meta-analysis of psychotherapy for bulimia nervosa. *Clinical Psychology: Science and Practice, 10,* 269–287.

Tidwell, L., & Walther, J. B. (2002). Computer-mediated communication effects on disclosure, impressions, and interpersonal evaluations: Getting to know one another a bit at a time. *Human Communication Research, 28,* 317–348.

Tinker, J. E. & Tucker, J. A. (1997a). Environmental events surrounding natural recovery from obesity. *Addictive Behaviors, 22,* 571–575.

Tinker, J. E., & Tucker, J. A. (1997b). Motivations for weight loss and behavior change strategies associated with natural recovery from obesity. *Psychology of Addictive Behaviors, 11,* 98–106.

Tinsley, C. H., Dillon, R. L., & Madsen, P. M. (2011). How to avoid catastrophe. *Harvard Business Review, 89* (4), 90–100.

Tomm, K. (1987a). Interventive interviewing: Part I. Strategizing as a fourth guideline for the therapist. *Family Process, 26* (1), 3–13.

Tomm, K. (1987b). Interventive interviewing: Part II. Reflexive questioning as a means to enable self-healing. *Family Process, 26* (1), 167–183.

Tomm, K. (1988). Interventive interviewing: Part III. Intending to ask lineal, circular, strategic, and reflexive questions. *Family Process, 27,* 1–15.

Toneatto, T. (1999). Cognitive psychopathology of problem gambling. *Substance Use and Misuse, 34,* 1593–1604.

Toneatto, T. (2008). A cognitive behavioral analysis of Gamblers' Anonymous. *Journal of Gambling Issues, 21,* 68–79.

Toneatto, T., & Brennan, J. (2002). Pathological gambling in treatment-seeking substance abusers. *Addictive Behavior, 27,* 465–469.

Toneatto, T., & Dragonetti, R. (2008). Effectiveness of community-based treatment for problem-gambling: A quasi-experimental evaluation of cognitive-behavioral versus Twelve Step therapy. *The American Journal of Addictions, 17,* 298–303.

REFERENCES

Toneatto, T., & Ladouceur, R. (2003). Treatment of pathological gambling: A critical review of the literature. *Psychology of Addictive Behaviors, 17*, 284–292.

Toneatto, T., & Nett, J. C. (2010). Natural recovery from problem gambling. In H. Klingemann & L. C. Sobell (Eds.), *Promoting self-change in addictive behaviors: Practical implications for policy, prevention, and treatment* (pp. 113–118). New York: Springer.

Towfigh, E., & Glöckner, A. (2011). GAME OVER: Empirical support for soccer bets regulations. *Psychology, Public Policy, and Law, 17* (3), 475–506.

Tracy, S. W., Kelly, J. F., & Moos, R. (2005). The influence of partner status, relationship quality, and relationship stability on outcomes following intensive substance use disorder treatment. *Journal of Studies on Alcohol, 66*, 497–505.

Trungpa, C. (1984). *Shambhala: The sacred path of the warrior*. Boston, MA: Shambhala.

Tuchfeld, B. S. (1981). Spontaneous remissions in alcoholics: Empirical observations and theoretical implications. *Journal of Studies on Alcohol, 42*, 626–641.

Tucker, J. A. (2008). Different pathways to knowledge about different pathways to recovery: A comment on the people awakening study. *Addiction, 103*, 216–217.

Turkle, S. (2011). *Alone together: Why we expect more from technology and less from each other*. New York: Basic.

Turner, N. E. (2000). Randomness, does it matter? *Journal of Gambling Issues*, (2), Retrieved from: http://www.camh.net

UK Alcohol Treatment Trial (2005). Cost-effectiveness of treatment for alcohol problems: Findings of the randomized UK alcohol treatment trial (UKATT). *British Medical Journal, 331*, 527–528.

Vaillant, G. E. (1983). *The natural history of alcoholism*. Cambridge, MA: Harvard University Press.

Vaillant, G. E. (2003). A 60-year follow-up of alcoholic men. *Addiction, 98*, 1043–1051.

Vaillant, G. E., & Milofsky, E. S. (1984). Natural history of male alcoholism: Paths to recovery. In D. W. Goodwin, K. T. Dusen, & S. A. Mednick (Eds.), *Longitudinal research on alcoholism* (pp. 53–71). New York: Kluwer-Nijhoff Publishing.

Van der Ham, T., Stien, D. C., & van Engeland, H. (1994). A four-year prospective follow-up study of 49 eating disordered adolescents: Differences in course of illness. *Acta Psychiatrica Scandinavica, 90*, 229–235.

Van der Kolk, B. A. (2009). *Trauma, attachment, and the body*. One-day workshop presented in Evanston, IL, November.

Van der Kolk, B. A., McFarlane, A. C., & Weisaeth, L. (2007). *Traumatic stress: The effects of overwhelming experience on mind, body, and society*. New York: Guilford.

Van der Kolk, B. A., Roth, S., Pelcovitz, D., Sunday, S., & Spinazzola, J. (2005). Disorders of extreme stress: The empirical foundation of complex trauma adaptation. *Journal of Traumatic Stress, 18*, 389–399.

Vanderlinden, J., Norre, J., & Vandereycken, W. (1992). *A practical guide in the treatment of bulimia nervosa*. New York: Brunner/Mazel.

Vanderlinden, J., & Vandereycken, W. (1997). *Trauma, dissociation, and impulse dyscontrol in eating disorders*. New York: Taylor & Francis.

Vanderlinden, J., Vandereycken, W., & Claes, L. (2007). Trauma, dissociation, and impulse dyscontrol: Lessons from the eating disorders field. In E. Vermetten, M. J. Dorahy, & D. Spiegel (Eds.), *Traumatic dissociation: Neurobiology and treatment* (pp. 317–331). Arlington, VA: American Psychiatric Association.

Van Elburg, A. A., Hillebrand, J. G., Huyser, C., Snoek, M., Kas, M. J. H., Hoek, H. H., & Adam, R. A. H. (in press). Mandometer treatment not superior to treatment as usual for anorexia nervosa. *International Journal of Eating Disorders*. DOI: 10.1002/eat.20918.

Vaughn, C., & Leff, J. (1976). The influence of family and social factors on the course of psychiatric illness: A comparison of schizophrenic and depressed neurotic patients. *British Journal of Psychiatry, 29*, 125–137.

Volberg, R. A. (1994). The prevalence and demographics of pathological gamblers: Implications for public health. *American Journal of Public Health, 84*, 237–241.

Volberg, R. A. (2004). Fifteen years of problem gambling prevalence research. What do we know? Where do we go? *The Electronic Journal of Gambling Issues: eGambling, 10*, doi: 10.4309/jgi.2004.10.12

Von Holle, A., Pinheiro, A. P., Thornton, L. M., Klump, K. L., Berrettini, W. H., & Brandt, H. (2008). Temporal patterns of recovery across eating disorder subtypes. *Australian and New Zealand Journal of Psychiatry, 42*, 108–117.

Waldorf, D. (1983). Natural recovery from opiate addiction: Some social-psychological processes of untreated recovery. *Journal of Drug Issues, 13* (2), 237–280.

REFERENCES

Walker, D. D., Roffman, R. A., Stephens, R. S., Berguis, J., & Kim, W. (2006). Motivational-enhancement therapy for adolescent marijuana users: A preliminary randomized controlled trial. *Journal of Consulting and Clinical Psychology, 74*, 628–632.

Walsh, B. W. (2006). *Treating self-injury: A practical guide.* New York: Guilford.

Walther, J. B. (2007). Selective self-presentation communication: Hyper-personal dimensions of technology. *Computers and Human Behavior, 23*, 2538–2557.

Wampold, B. E. (2001). *The great psychotherapy debate: Models, methods, and findings.* London, UK: Lawrence Erlbaum.

Wampold, B. E. (2006b). What should be validated? The psychotherapist. In J. C. Norcross, L. E. Beutler, & R. F. Levant (Eds.), *Evidence-based practices in mental health: Debate and dialogue on the fundamental questions* (pp. 200–208). Washington, DC: American Psychological Association.

Wampold, B. E., Mondin, G. W., Moody, M., Stich, F., Benson, K., & Ahn, H. (1997). A meta-analysis of outcome studies comparing bona fide psychotherapies: Empirically, "All must have prizes." *Psychological Bulletin, 12*, 203–215.

Watkins, P. C., Scheer, J., Ovnicek, M., & Kolts, R. (2006). The debt of gratitude and indebtedness. *Cognition and Emotion, 20* (2), 217–241.

Watzlawick, P. (1993). *Brief strategic therapy.* Workshop held at the Universidad Pontificia de Salamanca, Salamanca, Spain.

Watzlawick, P., Beavin, J. H., & Jackson, D. D. (1967). *Pragmatics of human communication.* New York: Norton.

Watzlawick, P., Weakland, J. H., & Fisch, R. (1974). *Change: Principles of problem formation and problem resolution.* New York: Norton.

Weakland, J. H. (1983). Family therapy with individuals. *Journal of Strategic and Systemic Therapies, 2*, 25–33.

Wedig, M. M., & Nock, M.K. (2007). Parental expressed emotion and adolescent self-injury. *Journal of the American Academy of Child and Adolescent Psychiatry, 46* (9), 1171–1178.

Weiner-Davis, M., de Shazer, & Gingerich, W. (1987). Building on pretreatment change to construct the therapeutic solution: An exploratory study. *Journal of Marital and Family Therapy, 13* (4), 359–363.

Weisz, J. R., Weiss, B., Han, S.S., Granger, D.A., & Morton, T. (1995). Effects of psychotherapy with children and adolescents revisited: A meta-analysis of treatment outcome studies. *Psychological Bulletin, 117*, 450–468.

Welch, G., Hall, A., & Renner, R. (1990). Patient subgrouping in anorexia nervosa using psychologically-based classification. *International Journal of Eating Disorders, 9*, 311–322.

Welte, J. W., Barnes, G. M., Tidwell, M. O., & Hoffman, J. H. (2009). The association between problem gambling and conduct disorders in a national survey of adolescents and young adults in the United States. *Journal of Adolescent Health, 45*, 396–401.

Welte, J. W., Barnes, G. M., Tidwell, M. O., & Hoffman, J. H. (2011). Gambling and problem gambling across the life-span. *Journal of Gambling Studies, 27*, 49–61.

Welte, J. W., Barnes, G. M., Wieczorek, W. F., Tidwell, M. O., & Parker, J. (2001). Alcohol and gambling pathology among US adults: Prevalence, demographic patterns, and co-morbidity. *Journal of Studies on Alcohol, 62*, 706–712.

Westphal, J. R. (2007). Are the effects of gambling treatment overestimated? *International Journal of Mental Health and Addiction, 5* (1), 65–79.

Whitaker, C. (1989). *Midnight musings of a family therapist.* New York: Norton.

White, M. (2007). *Maps of narrative practice.* New York: Norton.

White, M. (2011). *Narrative practice: Continuing the conversation.* New York: Norton.

White, M., & Epston, D. (1990). *Narrative means to therapeutic ends.* New York: Norton.

Whitfield, S. (1992). *Magritte.* Brussels, Belgium: Ludion.

Whitlock, J. (2008). Non-suicidal self-injury and recovery: What students say about why they started, how they stopped, and what they learned along the way. Workshop presented at the Creating Healthy Community Conference, University of Michigan, Ann Arbor, MI, March.

Whitlock, J., Eckenrode, J., & Silverman, D. (2006). Self-injurious behaviors in a college population. *Pediatrics, 117*, 1939–1948.

Whitlock, J., & Knox, K. (2007). The relationship between suicide and self-injury in a young adult population. *Archives in Pediatrics and Adolescent Medicine, 161* (7), 634–640.

REFERENCES

Whitlock, J., Muehlenkamp, J., & Eckenrode, J. (2008). Variation in non-suicidal self-injury: Identification and latent classes in a college population in emerging adults. *Journal of Clinical Child and Adolescent Psychology, 37* (4), 725–735.

Whitlock, J., & Selekman, M. D. (2012). Non-suicidal self-injury across the lifespan. In M. Nock (Ed.), *Oxford handbook of suicide and self-injury*. New York: Oxford University Press, in press.

Williams, A. L. & Merten, M. J. (2008). A review of online social networking profiles by adolescents: Implications for future research and intervention. *Adolescence, 43* (170), 253–274.

Wilson, G. T., Fairburn, C. G., & Agras, W. S. (1997). Cognitive-behavioral therapy for bulimia nervosa. In D. M. Garner & P. E. Garfinkel (Eds.), *Handbook of treatment for eating disorders* (2nd ed., pp. 67–93). New York: Guilford.

Wilson, K., & DuFrene, T. (2012). *The wisdom to know the difference: An acceptance and commitment therapy workbook for overcoming substance abuse*. Oakland, CA: New Harbinger.

Wilson, K., Sandoz, E. K., Flynn, M. K., & Slater, R. N. (2010). Understanding, assessing, and treating values processes in mindfulness and acceptance-based therapies. In R. A. Baer (Ed.), *Assessing mindfulness and acceptance processes in clients: Illuminating the theory and practice of change* (pp. 77–106). Oakland, CA: Context.

Wilson, W., Mathew, R., Turkington, T., Hawk, T., Coleman, R. E., & Provenzale, J. (2000). Brain morphological changes and early marijuana use: A magnetic resonance and position emission tomography study. *Journal of Addictive Disorders, 19*, 1–22.

Winick, C. (1962). Maturing out of narcotic addiction. *Bulletin on Narcotics, 14*, 1–7.

Winters, J., Fals-Stewart, W., O'Farrell, T. J., Birchler, G. R., & Kelly, M. L. (2002). Behavioral couples therapy for female substance-abusing patients: Effects on substance use and relationship adjustment. *Journal of Consulting and Clinical Psychology, 70*, 344–355.

Witkiewitz, K., & Marlatt, G. A. (2004). Relapse prevention for alcohol and drug problems: That was Zen, this is Tao. *American Psychologist, 59* (4), 224–235.

Witkiewitz, K., & Marlatt, G. A. (Eds.). (2007). *Therapist's guide to evidence-based relapse prevention*. London, UK: Academic Press.

Wohl, M. J. A., & Sztainert, T. (2011). Where did all of the pathological gamblers go? Gambling symptomatology and stage of change predict attrition in longitudinal research. *Journal of Gambling Studies, 27*, 155–169.

Woodside, D. B., Garfinkel, P. E., Lin, E., Goering, P., Kaplan, A. S., & Goldbloom, D. S. (2001). Comparisons of men with full or partial eating disorders, men without eating disorders, and women with eating disorders in the community. *American Journal of Psychiatry, 158* (4), 570–574.

Wosnitzer, R. & Bridges, A. (2007, May). *Aggression and sexual behavior in best-selling pornography: A content analysis update*. Paper presented at the Annual Meeting of the International Communications Association.

Yates, T. M. (2004). The developmental psychopathology of self-injurious behavior: Compensatory regulation in post-traumatic adaptation. *Clinical Psychology Review, 24*, 35–74.

Yen, J. Y., Yen, C. F., Chen, C. C., Chen, S. H., & Ko, C. H. (2007). Family factors of Internet addiction and substance use experience in Taiwanese adolescents. *Cyber-Psychology and Behavior, 10* (3), 323–329.

Yoo, H. J. (2004). Attention-deficit hyperactivity symptoms and Internet addiction. *Psychiatry and Clinical Neurosciences, 58*, 487–494.

Young, K. S. (1998). *Caught in the Net: How to recognize the signs of Internet addiction and a winning strategy for recovery*. Hoboken, NJ: John Wiley.

Young, K. S. (2007). Cognitive-behavior therapy with Internet addicts: Treatment outcomes and implications. *Cyber-Psychology and Behavior, 10* (5), 671–679.

Young, K. S. (2011). Clinical assessment of Internet-addicted clients. In K. S. Young & C. Nabuco de Abreu (Eds.), *Internet addiction: A handbook and guide to evaluation and treatment* (pp. 19–35). Hoboken, NJ: John Wiley.

Young, K. S., & Rogers, R. (1997). The relationship between depression and Internet addiction. *Cyber-Psychology and Behavior, 1*(1), 25–28.

Zanker, C. (2009). Anorexia nervosa and the body image myth. *Eating Disorders Review, 17*, 327–330.

INDEX

Aboujaoude, E. 204
absent clients 241
abstinence 9, 12, 15, 26, 310; celebrating habit-free days 75; gambling 182, 183–4; self-change 5, 22; self-efficacy 6; social support 291; substance abuse 145, 149, 150; urge surfing 297
Acceptance and Commitment Therapy 29
"accomplices" 142
acquiescence 15
adapted couples therapy (ACT) 179
addiction: brain processes 18; co-morbidity 7; disease model 22; gambling 176, 177; Internet and cyber-sex dependency 4, 204, 212; positive trigger log 301; self-harm 86, 87; sexual 209; substance abuse 145; "switching addiction model" 7
Adler, P. 84
Adler, P. A. 84
adolescents: art therapy 68–72; chilling out room 304–5; compulsive shopping 208; conversational questions 44–5; coping sequence questions 43; cyber-bullying 218–19; dance performances 78; failure to engage parents 312; imaginary time machine 65–8; Internet and cyber-sex dependency 4, 207, 209, 211, 215, 217–18, 219–34; multi-habit dependencies 249–84; online gaming 207–8; parental role 111; parents mentored by 61, 227, 228, 269; positive sticky notes 63; relapse prevention 306–8; secret surprise 63; seeing separately 51–2; self-change 26; self-harm 82, 86, 87, 89–90, 93–4; service work 65; stress 3; substance abuse 146, 150, 157–8; subsystem work with parents 50–1; *Values-in-Action Inventory of Strengths for Youth* 73, 74; *see also* children; young adults
"afterglow effect" 34
agency thinking 80
Ahola, Tapani 201
Alberts, A. 83
alcohol abuse: abstinence violation 15; access to alcohol 11; brain processes 19; case examples 20–1, 161, 167–8; celebrating habit-free days 75; co-morbidity 6, 151; cognitive processes 12; cyber-sex dependency 214; eating disorders 118; gambling 180, 190, 195; impact on the brain 144–6; medication 148; multi-habit dependencies 270–1, 273–7, 279, 282; multiple substance use 151; online disclosure 207; parental 51, 69, 94, 96–105, 108, 158, 249, 251–2, 256–8, 260, 262, 264–8; pathways model 12, 13; prevalence 144; relapse 285; relational factors 13; self-change 22, 23–4; self-harm 84; social pressures 9; treatment 26, 148, 149–50, 154, 155
alcohol behavior couples therapy 149
Al-Anon 49, 262–3, 268, 307
Alcoholics Anonymous (AA) 75, 104, 107, 148, 260, 279, 293
alexithymia 87
alumni 239, 259, 260–2, 263, 264, 269, 292
ambivalence 304
amenorrhea 113
Anderson, H. 242
anger management difficulties 58, 278
anorexia 10, 13, 112–13, 115; assessment questions 119–20; biological processes 114, 115; case example 125–43; co-morbidity 6; cognitive processes 12; diagnosis 118; family dynamics 120; functions of 10; pathways to 115–16; preoccupation 8; prevalence 112; recovery rates 116; relational factors 13; treatment 116–17, 121–5; *see also* eating disorders
"anthropological task" 124
anti-depressants 88
anti-social personality disorder 10
anxiety 3, 11, 13; eating disorders 123; gambling 176; Internet and cyber-sex dependency 4, 212, 213; self-harm 86; substance abuse 151
anxiety disorders: co-morbidity 6, 7; cyber-sex dependency 213; eating disorders 118; self-harm 88, 89; substance abuse 146
appreciation days 74, 164, 165, 169
Arcelus, J. 114
Aristotle 1, 5–6
arousal 11, 13, 86, 176

346

INDEX

art therapy 31, 68–72
"ascetic anorectics" 124
Asher, E. R. 74, 216
assessment: eating disorders 118–20; gambling 179–81; Internet and cyber-sex dependency 211–14; self-harm 91–3; substance abuse 151–2
Astley-Jones, F. 177
attention deficit disorder (ADD) 3, 7, 13, 210, 213, 219, 224
attention deficit hyperactivity disorder (ADHD) 7, 180, 210, 213
attentional blindness 281, 283
attractor landscape of conflict model 236
attributional style 175
attunement 34
authors, favorite 79
autistic spectrum disorders 213
availability bias 175

Baker, T. B. 16
Baumeister, R. F. 23, 293
Beard, K. W. 211
Becoña, E. 146
behavioral couples therapy 149
"being mysterious and arbitrary" experiment 245, 246
Bercaw, B. 211, 215
Bercaw, G. 211, 215
Berg, Insoo Kim 5, 153, 154, 201–2
Berra, Yogi 174
Bertrand, K. 179
best hopes questions 41–2
binge-drinking 85, 90; see also alcohol abuse
binge-eating 3, 4, 112, 113–14, 118; co-morbidity 6; dopamine receptors 7; gambling 177; pathways to 14, 116; treatment 121, 123; see also bulimia; eating disorders
biological processes 7, 15, 30; eating disorders 114–15, 117; gambling 177–8; Internet and cyber-sex dependency 210–11; substance abuse 145–6; see also brain
Blanco, C. 176
Blaszczynski, A. 7, 11, 12–14, 176, 177
body image distortion 113, 116
body scanning 185, 298
Bond, R. 208
"booster" sessions 118
borderline personality disorder 6, 10, 86, 88, 89
Bowen, S. 287
brain 16–20, 295, 311; gambling 177–8; habitual behavior 6; Internet and cyber-sex dependency 210–11; malfunction of the reward system 12; mindfulness meditation 295–6; self-directed neuroplasticity 300; substance abuse impact on the 144–6; see also neurotransmitters
Bridges, A. 209
brief strategic family therapy 89, 149, 315
brief therapy 29, 117, 122, 148, 155; see also collaborative strengths-based brief family therapy; solution-focused brief therapy
Brown, L. L. 207–8
Brown, M. Z. 85
Bruch, Hilde 113
Buddhism 4–5, 28–9
Budney, A. J. 148
bulimia 10, 113, 115; assessment questions 119–20; "booster" sessions 118; co-morbidity 6; cognitive-behavioral therapy 211; deception 9; diagnosis 118; functions of 121; maintenance factors 16; pathways to 14, 116; prevalence 112; recovery rates 116; relational factors 13; self-harm 85–6, 91; treatment 117, 121–5; see also eating disorders
burning 83, 90, 91

Cacioppo, J. T. 207
caffeine 3, 145
cannabis 13, 144, 145, 146, 147–8, 149; see also marijuana
Carnes, Patrick 209, 210
Carnes, S. 210
Carrier, L. M. 205
Carrig, H. 181
case examples: eating disorders 125–43; gambling 187–203; Internet dependency 219–34; multi-habit dependencies 239–40, 248, 249–84; self-harm 94–111; substance abuse 159–73
Catalano, R. F. 146
celebrating habit-free days 75, 138, 139
Chaey, C. 208
change 2, 5, 168; circularity 268; negative consequences of change intervention 246–7; research 314; resistance to 15; self-harm 110; visions of 39, 40; see also readiness for change; self-change
Chawla, N. 287
Cheever, N. A. 205
Chellappan, S. 4
Chen, C. C. 215
Chen, S. H. 215
children: art therapy 69; conversational questions 44; goal-setting 140; Internet use 4, 213; multi-habit dependent parents 246; of problem gamblers 182, 188, 194; subsystem work with parents 50–1; see also adolescents; family; siblings
Childress, A. R. 207–8
chilling out room 75, 80, 304–5
choreography 77
Christensen, A. 178
chronicity 16, 17, 22
Chung, C. S. 215
Churchill, Winston 309
Ciarrocchi, J. W. 28, 176, 178–9, 183
cigarettes 3, 18
circle of caring others 58
"circularity bias" 14
Clark, L. 177

347

INDEX

classical conditioning 11
client-attempted solutions questions 39–40
client-directed, outcome-informed therapy 31
client expertise questions 36–9
client importance questions 41
Cloninger, C. R. 13
cloud-watching 185, 296, 298
co-morbidity 1, 6–7, 311; alcohol abuse 151; eating disorders 118–19; gambling 176, 179–80; Internet and cyber-sex dependency 213–14; personality disorders 10; self-harm 88; substance abuse 151
cocaine 13, 145, 149, 155, 263; addictive potential 18; case example 159–73; multi-habit dependencies 270, 275, 277; prevalence 144; relapse 285; self-change 21
cognitive-behavioral therapy (CBT) 31; coping skills 156; decision-making using dice 141–2; eating disorders 116–17, 122, 123; gambling 178, 179; Internet and cyber-sex dependency 211; relapse 286; research studies 315; self-harm 89; substance abuse 149
cognitive dissonance 12
cognitive limitations 281
cognitive processes 12, 17, 30, 311; eating disorders 122; gambling 178, 184
coin tossing experiment 130, 132, 133, 140, 141–2
Coleman, Peter 236, 237, 247
collaborative language systems therapy 31
collaborative strengths-based brief family therapy 2, 16, 27–9, 31–59, 310; client feedback 54–5; clients' choice habits to inform clinical decision-making 55–8; co-creating a therapeutic climate ripe for change 33–5; intersession break 54; interviewing for possibilities 35–49; relapse prevention 286; research 315; risk management 58–9; self-harm 89; session format 32; solution-determined system membership 52–4; subsystem work 49–52; training 313–14
"collage of the heart" 157
Columbo tactics 108, 161, 233, 267
Commings, D. E. 177
community reinforcement approaches (CRA) 31, 148–9
compassion 36, 268, 292, 295, 299, 304
complexity 235–6, 237
complexity theory 236, 277–8, 286
compliment box 62–3
compression technique 306–7
compulsive shopping 208, 211
Comtois, K. A. 85
conditioning 11, 12, 17
confidence: eating disorders 124, 135; mindfulness exercises 297, 298, 300; questions 40
conjoint therapeutic project 154–5
consent form 52, 53
consolidating questions 288–9
constructive habits 55–8
constructive response planning 290–1

contingency management (CM) 149
controlled behavior 9, 12, 182
coping mechanisms 11, 13
coping questions 203
coping responses 285
coping sequence questions 43
coping skills training 148, 156, 171–2
coping strategies 26, 30, 36, 290, 301, 311
core personal values 294–5
cortisol 115
counter-regulation 15
couple partners: art therapy 68–72; celebrating habit-free days 75; conversational questions 44; cyber-sex 211; drama experiments 77–8; dual-habit dependent couples 246–7; eating disorders 124, 125–43; experiments and rituals 61–5; externalization of the problem 48; failure to engage 312; gambling 178–9, 181–2, 184, 185–203; imaginary time machine 66–8; Internet and cyber-sex dependency 26, 215; interviewing the client's ambivalence 304; multi-habit dependencies 235–6, 238–40, 242–4, 246–7, 312–13; pessimism 43; relapse prevention 287–8, 290–1, 306–7, 311; relational approach 29; scaling questions 41; self-generated pretreatment change 33–4, 36; self-harm 93; session format 32; solution-determined system membership 52–4; substance abuse 147, 149–50, 151, 152–3, 158–73; subsystem work 49–50, 245–6; "Two Garden" mindfulness practice 169, 299; violence prevention plans 58–9
courage 36, 37–8, 56, 78, 194
cravings 10, 18, 19, 75; cyber-sex dependency 214; gambling 175, 191–2, 195; self-harm 86; substance abuse 145, 165, 275
crazy and absurd ideas 63–4
creativity 61, 143, 292, 315
cultural issues 110
cutting 13, 82–3, 84, 88, 90, 91; case example 94–111; multi-habit dependencies 249, 251–2, 254–5, 257–62; *see also* self-harm
cyber-bullying 57, 206, 218–19
cyber-sex dependency 4, 13, 204, 205, 206, 208–9; brain processes 19, 210–11; co-morbidity 7, 213–14; disease model 22; DSM-IV classification 6; family and couple dynamics 215; maintenance factors 15; multi-habit dependencies 270, 276; research 211, 313, 315; self-change 21, 25–6; treatment strategies 215–19; virtuous habits 57

D'Amore, K. 87
dance performances 78
Darbyshire, P. I. 181
Davis, S. D. 29
De Shazer, Steve 141, 201–2
deception 9, 181, 189
decisional balancing processes 23, 26
decoupling 283

delay strategies 156
delayed reward discounting 175
delicious dish experiment 64
Dell'Osso, B. 212
Delmonico, David 209
depression 4, 6, 7, 11, 13; eating disorders 118; gambling 179–80, 201; gratitude letter and visit 76–7; Internet and cyber-sex dependency 212, 213; multi-habit dependencies 249, 270; self-harm 86, 88, 89; substance abuse 146, 151
"detaching with love" strategy 49, 262, 264, 268, 307
detectives, playing 303
Diagnostic and Statistical Manual-IV (DSM-IV) 5, 6, 88; eating disorders 113, 114, 118; gambling 174–5; Internet and cyber-sex dependency 211–12; substance abuse 145
dialectical behavior therapy (DBT) 89, 117, 118, 315
diaries 23, 56, 78, 98, 99
DiClemente, C. C. 50, 202, 286
dieting 9, 11, 12; biological processes 114; functions of 121; pathways model 12, 115–16; relational factors 13
digital technology 2, 4, 72, 204–5, 216; *see also* Internet dependency
DiSalvo, D. 300
disarmament 184, 186, 194, 195
disease model 5, 15, 22, 287
disputation skills 296, 302–4
dissociation 13, 176, 180, 206, 208
distress management 89–90, 292–306
Ditmar, H. 208
Doidge, N. 6
"doing something novel and surprising" experiment 245–6
Dolan, Yvonne 203
dopamine 7, 11, 12, 16–18; gambling 177; impulse control disorders 13; online gaming 207–8; pornography 210; self-destructive habit maintenance loop 19; substance abuse 145; uncertainty 177
drama 77–8
drawing out oppressive thoughts 70
dreams 71
drink *see* alcohol abuse
drug sensitization 145, 146
dual-habit dependent couples 246–7
Dufour, M. 179
Duncan, B. L. 54, 143

e-mails 216
eating disorders 112–43; assessment 118–20; biology of 114–15; case example 125–43; co-morbidity 118–19; cognitive dissonance 12; counter-regulation 15; dieting 9, 11; differences between 10; disease model 22; DSM-IV classification 6; family and couple dynamics 120–1, 125; functions of 119–20, 121, 123, 125; multiple paths to 115–16; pathways model 13, 14; prevalence 112; relapse 16; research 116–18, 313, 314–15; self-change 21, 25; self-harm 88, 91–2, 94; social pressures 12; starvation syndrome 12; treatment strategies 121–5; virtuous habits 57; *see also* anorexia; bulimia; obesity
Ebaugh, H. R. F. 23
economic upheaval 3
Ecstasy 253
editorial reflection 54, 59, 98, 102
Edwards, G. 26
ego-syntonic nature of self-destructive habits 9
emotional disengagement 181
emotions 16, 17, 69, 295; *see also* negative emotions; positive emotions
empathy 36, 74–5
empirically supported treatments (ESTs) 27
endorphins 7, 19, 86, 88, 115, 210
epiphanies 36, 38, 75, 76, 236, 289
episodic self-harmers 90
Erickson, Milton H. 298
existential loss 181
experiential therapy 31
experimenters (self-harm) 90
experiments and rituals 30, 59, 60–81; art therapy 68–72; drama 77–8; eating disorders 124; editorial reflection 54; family/couple connection-building 61–5, 269; gambling 185, 193–4; imaginary time machine 65–8; Internet and cyber-sex dependency 216, 218, 228; positive psychology 72–7; pretreatment 33; referring professionals 244; self-harm 98–9, 103, 108; substance abuse 154, 157, 158–9, 166–7; subsystem work 49, 50, 245–6; written word 78–80
exposure 178, 179, 185
expressive writing therapy 31
externalization of the problem 47–8, 268; eating disorders 117, 122; farewell letter 79; gambling 179, 183, 195, 202; multi-habit dependencies 282; oppressive thoughts 70; substance abuse 146, 155
externalization solutions questions 290
eye movement desensitization and reprogramming (E.M.D.R.) 311

Facebook 4, 206, 207, 209
family: art therapy 68–72; conversational questions 44; digital technology-free days 216; drama and dance experiments 77, 78; eating disorders 116, 120–1, 124–5, 141; experiments and rituals 61–5; externalization of the problem 48; failure to engage 312; gambling 181–2; importance of 10; Internet and cyber-sex dependency 215; intersession break 54; maintenance factors 16; multi-habit dependencies 235–6, 238–41, 246–7, 312–13; protective factors 14; recovery cycle 17;

INDEX

family (*cont.*):
  relapse prevention 287–8, 290–1, 306–8, 311; relational approach 29; self-generated pretreatment change 33–4, 36; self-harm 89, 93–4; session format 32; solution-determined system membership 52–4; substance abuse 147, 152–3, 157–8; subsystem work 49–52, 245–6; violence prevention plans 58–9; *see also* couple partners; parents
family-multiple helper system 242
family service work 65
family therapy: connection-building ritual 269; eating disorders 117, 118, 120, 121, 125; self-harm 89; substance abuse 149, 150; subsystem work 141; *see also* collaborative strengths-based brief family therapy
famous guest consultants experiment 62
farewell letter 79, 132, 193, 194
fast-food consumption 3
Favazza, A. R. 84, 88
fear about the future 3
feedback from clients 28, 32, 44, 54, 314, 315; case examples 164; multi-habit dependencies 237; substance abuse 150; tailor-fitting the therapeutic relationship of choice 34
film 77–8
Fiore, M. C. 16
5, 4, 3, 2, 1 exercise 298
follow-up 107, 139–40, 151, 170, 200, 230, 266
followers (self-harm) 90
Forcehimes, A. A. 294–5
forgiveness 186, 199, 211, 280
Forster, E. M. 204
Frascella, J. 207–8
Freud, Sigmund 21
functions of self-destructive habits 10, 20–1, 55, 311; eating disorders 119–20, 121, 123, 125; self-harm 83–4; substance abuse 152, 155
Furman, Ben 201
future-oriented questions 46–7, 154, 170, 173, 183, 230, 244
future selves 66–7

Gable, S. L. 74, 216
Gamblers Anonymous (GA) 135, 178, 183, 293
gambling 174–203; access to facilities 11; assessment 179–81; biology of 177–8; brain processes 19; case examples 126–8, 130–1, 135, 142, 161–2, 165–8, 187–203; co-morbidity 6, 7, 176, 179–80; cognitive-behavioral therapy 211; cognitive dissonance 12; controlled 9, 12, 182; deception 9; differences between gamblers 10; disease model 22; dopamine receptors 7; DSM-IV classification 6; eating disorders 118, 119; family and couple dynamics 181–2; functions of 10; "gambler's fallacy" 19–20, 175, 176, 184; maintenance factors 16; multi-habit dependencies 248, 270–1, 273–7, 281, 282; multiple faces of 174–5; multiple paths to 176–7; parental 51; pathways model 12, 13, 14; prevalence 174; relapse 16, 285; research 178–9, 313, 315; self-change 21, 25; social pressures 9, 12; substance abuse 151; treatment strategies 182–7; virtuous habits 58
Gandhian nonviolent passive resistance 233, 306, 307–8
gender: eating disorders 113; gambling 176; oppression of women 100, 111; self-harm 82
genetic factors 177
Gibson, L. 207
Gladding, R. 300
glass of wishes 63
goals 26, 32; asking children 140; couple/family choreography 77; eating disorders 141; experiments and rituals 60; future-oriented questions 46; goal-setting questions 41–3; Internet dependency 224, 231; multi-habit dependencies 246, 255; substance abuse 163; subsystem work 50, 52
Goolishian, H. 242
Gottman, J. M. 74
Gottman, J. S. 74
Grant, B. F. 180
gratitude collages 72
gratitude letter and visit 76–7
gratitude log 74–5
Gray, N. 177
guilt: eating disorders 123; gambling 181, 183; multi-habit dependencies 252; parents 51; substance abuse 105

habit diaries 56, 78, 98, 99
habit-free days 75
habits 5–6
Hall, M. N. 174
Halsted, William 21
HALT exercise 123
Hanh, Thich Nhat 169, 299
happiness 72, 74, 246, 301
harm-reduction 5–6, 31, 92, 211
Hawkins, J. D. 146
healthy eating 27, 117, 121–2, 293
heavy self-harmers 91, 92
Hemen, J. 213
Herman, C. 285
heroin 144
Hollis, J. F. 25
hope 32, 66–7, 237, 301, 309
Hubble, M. A. 54
humor journal 80

Ibanez, A. 176
iDisorder 205
illusions of control 175, 176, 177, 184
imaginary feelings X-ray machine 69
imaginary time machine 65–8, 157
imagination questions 46–7
"imagine yourself as..." exercise 301
Impett, E. A. 74, 216
impotence, declaring 306, 307

350

INDEX

impulse control disorders 13, 58; cognitive-behavioral therapy 211; DSM-IV classification 6; gambling 174–5; Internet and cyber-sex dependency 213; self-harm 87, 88
impulsivity 11, 13; gambling 176, 177, 180; substance abuse 147
Inception (movie) 46
inertia failure 15
infidelity websites 206
integrated borderline adolescent family therapy 89
integrative approach 310–11, 313–14
integrative behavioral couple therapy 178
integrative catalysts 247
Internet dependency 3, 4, 204–34, 312; assessment 211–14; brain processes 210–11; case examples 219–34; co-morbidity 213–14; compulsive shopping 208; dark side of the Internet 204–7; disease model 22; DSM-IV classification 6; family and couple dynamics 215; gaming 207–8, 219–34; multi-habit dependencies 248; research 211, 313, 315; self-change 21, 25–6; treatment strategies 215–19; virtuous habits 57; *see also* cyber-sex dependency
Internet gambling 174, 205
interpersonal therapy (IPT) 117, 118
interviewing for possibilities *see* questions
inventions 61–2
invisible couple/family inventions 61–2
Isebaert, Luc 5

Jacob, Frederike 123
Jacobs, D. F. 176
Jacobson, N. S. 178
Jaspers, Karl 34
Joiner, T. 84–5, 86
Joplin, Janis 259
Jordan, Michael 285, 301
Joseph, Stephen 87–8

Kafka, M. P. 213
Kahneman, Daniel 236–7
kaleidoscope, using the mind as a 303
Karolinska Institute 117
Kay, Alan 60
Kay, John 236
Kemperman, I. 86
Kennedy, J. L. 177
Kettering, Charles 39
key resource people 247–8, 259, 287–8, 291–2
Keys, Ancel 114–15
King, Martin Luther 307
Klein, G. 283
Klingborg, T. 210
Klingemann, H. 22
Klingemann, J. 22
Knox, K. 85
Ko, C. H. 207–8, 213, 215
Koch, R. 247
Kolts, R. 75

Kotikalapudi, R. 4
Kwon, J. H. 207, 208, 215

lack of control 8, 147; *see also* loss of control
Lambert, M. J. 54
Lanier, Jaron 207
lapses *see* slips
Lasnier, B. 179
Lavooy, M. J. 206
Lawrence, A. J. 177
Lebow, J. L. 29
Ledgerwoo, D. M. 179
Lee, J. 215
legal issues 151, 180, 204
leisure time 293
letter of advice 80
letters to clients 239–41
life passions 38, 56, 170–1, 212, 305
lifestyle changes 24, 27, 293–4
Linden, David 16, 18, 20, 177
"linearity bias" 15
Linehan, M. M. 85
Lipchik, Eve 202
living sculpture 197
Lloyd-Richardson, E. E. 87
Lobo, D. S. 177
Lockwood, G. 247
loneliness 4, 127, 207
Long, K. 208
loss of a loved one 67–8
loss of control 8, 28; body scanning 298; eating disorders 114; gambling 175; Internet and cyber-sex dependency 212; relapse 285; self-harm 85, 91
Lynskey, M. T. 146

maintenance factors 15–16, 116, 182
maintenance loop 18–19
Majeskie, M. R. 16
Maltz, L. 211
Maltz, W. 211
marijuana 12, 144, 155, 156, 223; case examples 161, 162; multi-habit dependencies 248, 253, 256, 257–62, 267; self-harm 94–8, 101; *see also* cannabis
marital conflict 16, 24, 99; eating disorders 120, 125; gambling 181; Internet and cyber-sex dependency 206; multi-habit dependencies 276; substance abuse 158, 159, 160–1, 163, 171
Markel, Howard 21
Marlatt, G. A. 156, 286, 287, 296
maximizers 208
McCarthy, D. E. 16
McCollum, E. 202
McConaghy, N. 176
McQueen, Steve 209
medication 3–4, 19, 311; anti-depressants 88; eating disorders 116; gambling 177n2; self-esteem medication box 305–6; substance abuse 148, 150, 155

INDEX

meditation: sound 275, 279, 297, 305; substance abuse 24; "Taking a Trip to Popcorn Land" 166, 167, 193, 255, 258–9, 275, 297; *see also* mindfulness meditation
mental health problems 8, 13; gambling 174; substance abuse 146, 151
mentoring of parents by adolescents 61, 227, 228, 269
Merten, M. J. 207
metacognitions 175
metaphors 143, 146, 170–1, 202–3
methadone 148
methamphetamines 144, 145, 149
Michel, B. 86
Miller, A. L. 89
Miller, D. 85
Miller, M. C. 205
Miller, S. D. 54, 143
Miller, W. R. 22, 294–5
mindfulness meditation 24, 26, 28–9, 31, 295–300; eating disorders 123; gambling 185; mindful practitioners 289–90; multi-habit dependencies 261, 263–5, 269; self-harm 89; structured plan for success 293; "Two Garden" practice 169, 299
"Minnesota experiment" 114–15
Minuchin, S. 269
miracle questions 41, 42, 128–9, 140, 141, 157, 244, 250
miracle story mural 70
mood disorders 6, 7, 213
Moore, T. H. M. 146
Moos, R. H. 146
motivational-enhancement therapy 31, 89, 211, 309
motivational interviewing (MI) 148, 149, 179
Mottarella, K. E. 206
movies of joy and success 102, 103, 104, 108, 166–7, 299
Muehlenkamp, J. J. 83
multi-family psychoeducational groups 89
multi-habit dependencies 41, 214, 235–84; case examples 239–40, 248, 249–84; key resource people 247–8; referring professionals 242–4; relapse prevention training 171–2; role of the therapist 237; subsystem work 245–6; treatment failures 312–13; treatment strategies 238–41
multidimensional family therapy 89, 149, 211, 315
multisystemic therapy 149, 315
murals 69–70
music 70, 77–8, 297, 305
"musical themes" 170–1

nagging 142; eating disorders 121, 127, 131; Internet dependency 224, 225; multi-habit dependencies 252, 257, 262, 276–7
Narcotics Anonymous (NA) 260, 263, 293
Nardone, Giorgio 124
narrative therapy 31, 79, 304; creativity 143; eating disorders 117; gambling 202; metaphors and rituals 203
narrow and rigid views 303–4
negative consequences of change intervention 246–7
negative emotions 28, 30, 32, 306, 309; deceptive brain messages 300; mindfulness meditation 295, 296; self-harm 84
negative metacognitions 175
neuronal model 11
neuronal pathways 6
neuroscience 31, 295
neurotransmitters 11, 17–18, 19, 31, 145, 177n2, 311; *see also* dopamine
news of a difference 44, 75, 288, 295
newspaper headline experiment 79–80
nightmare question 43–4, 154–5, 183
nihilistic fear about the future 3
Nock, M. K. 85, 86
Norcross, J. C. 50, 202
Nower, L. 7, 11, 12–14, 177
numbing of feelings 83, 85, 86, 95

obesity 4, 25, 78, 113; *see also* eating disorders
obliquity problem-solving approach 236
obsessive-compulsive disorder: co-morbidity 6, 7, 10; cognitive-behavioral therapy 211; cyber-sex dependency 213; eating disorders 118; self-directed neuroplasticity 300; self-harm 88, 89
Omer, H. 233
online disinhibition effect 205–6
operant conditioning 11
optimism 32, 72, 74, 301, 309
Orford, J. 1–2, 26, 314
Oster, C. 181
our happiest moments documentary 77–8
Outcome Rating Scale (ORS) 54
Ovnicek, M. 75
oxytocin 19, 210

Palo Alto Mental Research Institute (MRI) 28, 31, 123
parents: art therapy 69; celebrating habit-free days 75; conversational questions 44–5; eating disorders 118, 120, 125; failure to engage 312; gambling 185; imaginary time machine 65–8; Internet and cyber-sex dependency 4, 26, 211, 213, 215, 217–18, 219–33; interviewing the client's ambivalence 304; mentored by adolescent children 61, 227, 228, 269; multi-habit dependencies 238–41, 249–84, 312–13; pessimism 43; positive sticky notes 63; relapse prevention 306–8; scaling questions 41; secret surprise 63; self-harm 89–90, 93, 94–111; siblings 52; substance abuse 19, 147, 150, 152–3, 157–8; subsystem work 50–1, 245–6; *see also* family
Parker, Charlie 144
Pascale, Richard 236
passions 38, 56, 170–1, 212, 305

INDEX

the past, bringing back the best from 65–6
past successes 37
pathological gambling, definition of 174–5
pathway thinking 80
pathways model 11–15, 115–16, 147, 177
pattern disruption intervention strategies 8, 122, 155–6, 185, 211, 219, 268
peers: eating disorders 116; peer pressure 12; protective factors 14; relational approach 29; solution-determined system membership 52; substance abuse 147, 155, 156–7; *see also* social networks
Pennebaker, J. W. 78
perceived risk 147
percentage questions 48–9
perfectionism 123
personality disorders 10
pessimism 43–4, 47, 111, 303
Peterson, Christopher 73, 80
Peterson, P. L. 146
Petkova, E. 176
Petry, N. M. 178, 179, 180
Pinsol, Bill 142
Piper, M. E. 16
planning out y perfect day experiment 73
playfulness 46, 64, 69
pleasure-seeking 7, 83, 84
Polivy, J. 25, 285
pornography *see* cyber-sex dependency
"positive blaming" 33, 288
positive deviance model 236
positive emotions 30, 32, 72, 246, 309; case examples 128, 164, 173; compliment box 63; e-mails 216; gratitude letter and visit 76–7; gratitude log 74; humor journal 80; mindfulness meditation 295, 299, 301; parent-adolescent bond 51; positive trigger log 301; success stories 80; treasure chest 305–6
positive psychology 28–9, 31, 72–7, 309
positive sticky notes 63
positive trigger log 102–3, 104, 166, 259, 275, 277, 279, 301–2
post-traumatic stress disorder (PTSD) 6, 13, 75, 87, 88, 119
Potenza, M. N. 207–8
practice guidelines 309–12
preoccupation 8, 175
presuppositional questions 41, 42
pretreatment: client expertise questions 36–7; co-creating a therapeutic climate ripe for change 33–5
primary caretakers 51
problem-clarification questions 39
problem gambling, definition of 174, 175
"problem talk" 203
problem-tracking questions 39, 41
Prochaska, J. O. 22, 50, 202, 286
protective factors 14, 17, 27, 146–7, 301
Przybeck, T. R. 13
psychoeducation 89, 143, 315; eating disorders 121–2; gambling 184, 202; sex therapy 217
psychosis 146
public pledges 24, 26
purgative anorectics 113, 118
purging 3, 113, 114, 121, 123

question-storming 64–5
questions 35–49; client expertise 36–9; *Columbo* tactics 108, 161, 233, 267; conversational 44–5; coping 203; coping sequence 43; eating disorders 119–20; externalization of the problem 47–8; future-oriented 46–7, 154, 170, 173, 183, 230, 244; gambling 180–2; goal-setting 41–3; Internet and cyber-sex dependency 214; multi-habit dependencies 272; percentage 48–9; pessimistic sequence 43–4; problem clarification and visions of change 39–41; relapse prevention 288–9, 290; self-harm 92–3; slips 286–7; substance abuse 151–3; "three questions for a happy life" 157; *see also* scaling questions
quick-fix solutions 3–4

rainy day letter 305
rapport 33
reactance levels 35, 60, 236, 309
readiness for change 22, 28, 29, 202, 311; action stage 51–2, 54, 101, 110, 114, 155, 218, 232, 245; contemplative stage 60, 113, 154, 180, 245, 268, 312; experiments and rituals 60; externalization of the problem questions 47; future research 315; gambling 179; Internet and cyber-sex dependency 218; maintenance stage 52, 218; multi-habit dependencies 267; precontemplative stage 50–1, 60, 157, 242, 268, 312; preparation stage 51–2, 54, 101, 110, 113–14, 155, 162, 218, 268; questions 39, 40; relapse prevention 290; substance abuse 156; tailor-fitting the therapeutic relationship of choice 35; termination stage 218; *see also* change
recovery 5, 16, 17; eating disorders 116, 117; gambling 182; substance abuse 147–8, 149–50
referring professionals 109, 242–4, 313
regular self-harmers 91
reinforcement 15, 16, 86
Reis, H. T. 74, 216
relapse 1, 8, 9, 285–308, 311–12; alcohol abuse 150; eating disorders 116, 117, 118, 139–40; future-oriented questions 46–7; gambling 178, 179, 182, 183, 184, 185, 191, 196, 203; individual distress management tools and strategies 292–306; maintenance factors 15, 16; major prevention strategies 288–92; multi-habit dependencies 171–2, 277, 283; prevention plans 26; "self-destructive habit overrides" 313; self-harm 86–7; substance abuse 145, 146, 147, 149, 151, 166, 171–2; *see also* slips
relational factors 11, 13, 24, 29

relaxation 123, 193
reluctance to enter treatment 238–41, 242–4
reparation 185, 186
research 22, 313, 314–15; eating disorders 116–18; gambling 178–9; Internet and cyber-sex dependency 211; self-harm 88–90; substance abuse 147–51
resilience 38, 56; positive psychology experiments 72; positive trigger log 301; substance abuse 147; trauma survivors 87, 88
resources 32, 37, 309–10, 314
restrictive anorectics 10, 113, 118, 121
Reuss, N. H. 5, 153, 154
reversal questions 44–5
reward distinction blindness 300
risk and risk taking 11, 14, 146–7, 177, 186
risk management 58–9
rituals *see* experiments and rituals
Roffman, R. 148
Rollnick, S. 22
Rosen, S. 205
rumination 8, 72, 84, 200; disputation skills 302, 303–4; eating disorders 124, 128; mindfulness meditation 296, 298
Russ, M. J. 86

sacred sanctuary visualization 299
safety 28, 109
scaling questions 41, 42–3; eating disorders 129, 131, 133, 134–5, 138; gambling 186, 190, 199; Internet dependency 224; multi-habit dependencies 254–5, 258, 276–7; self-harm 97; substance abuse 162–3, 165, 171
Scheer, J. 75
schemas 12
schizophrenia 142
school environment 147
school meetings 103–4, 109–10, 225, 226, 229, 231–2
Schulem, H. 24
Schultz, W. 145, 177
Schwartz, J. M. 300
Scott, V. M. 206
secret mission projects 49, 248
secret surprise 63, 98, 99–100, 194, 277
Selekman, M. D. 24, 83–4, 90
self-battery 83, 84, 90
self-change 2, 5, 21–3, 310; alcohol abuse 23–4; eating disorders 25; gambling 25; implications for clinical practice 26–7; Internet and cyber-sex dependency 25–6; research 314; self-harm 24–5; substance abuse 23–4
self-directed neuroplasticity 300
self-efficacy 6, 30, 285
self-esteem 13, 23; eating disorders 116, 117, 118, 124; gambling 176; Internet and cyber-sex dependency 213; mentoring ritual 61; self-esteem medication box 305–6; service work 65; substance abuse 147
self-fulfilling prophecies 15, 171, 173, 182

self-harm 4, 11, 82–111; assessment 91–3; brain processes 19; case example 94–111; co-morbidity 6, 88; cognitive processes 12; couple and family dynamics 93–4; differences between self-harmers 10; DSM-IV classification 6; eating disorders 119; functions of 10, 83–4; maintenance factors 15, 16; methods of 82–3; multi-habit dependencies 249, 251–2, 254–5, 257–62; online disclosure 207; pathways model 13, 14; practice classification system 90–1; relapse 16; research 88–90, 313, 315; self-change 21, 24–5; substance abuse and 85–7; suicide distinction 84–5; trauma 87–8; virtuous habits 57
self-help groups 75, 293, 306; *see also* Alcoholics Anonymous; Gamblers Anonymous; Narcotics Anonymous
self-regulation 2, 15, 28, 58, 87, 213, 293
Seligman, Martin 302
serendipitous events and practices 36, 38–9, 56, 236, 289
serotonin 19, 88, 210
service work 65, 218, 228, 229–30, 231, 293
severe self-harmers 91, 92
sex: addiction to 7, 270; eating disorder case example 130, 138, 139, 142; offline desires and fantasies 216–17; *see also* cyber-sex dependency; sexually risky behaviors
sexting 209, 249, 253, 255
sexual abuse: cyber-sex dependency 213; eating disorders 116, 124; self-harm 87, 91, 92
sexual orientation 85, 261
sexuality, female 124
sexually risky behaviors: eating disorders 119; gambling 177; Internet 206; multi-habit dependencies 249, 253–5, 258, 262; self-harm 85, 88, 91
Shaffer, H. J. 174
Shame (movie) 209
Shaw, George Bernard 235
Shearin, E. 86
shopping 208
siblings 52, 62, 241; eating disorders 125; multi-habit dependencies 246, 248; substance abuse 158; *see also* children
significant other consent form 52, 53
Sigvardsson, S. 13
sit-ins 307–8
six breaths on purpose 296
Skinner, K. B. 213
sleep 27, 75, 86, 293
slips (lapses) 56, 151, 203, 285, 286–7, 312; habit diaries 78; multi-habit dependencies 255, 258, 259, 261, 274; self-harm 86, 98, 105; substance abuse 164; *see also* relapse
Slutske, Wendy 175
smoking 9
social networking sites 4, 205, 207, 209
social networks 58, 236; gambling 185; key resource people 247–8, 259, 287–8, 291–2;

INDEX

relapse prevention 291–2, 311; reluctant clients 242; substance abuse 150, 156; *see also* peers
social pressures 9, 12
social skills training 148
social support 2, 16, 17; negative 30; relapse prevention 291–2; self-help groups 306; substance abuse 147; weak link network 247–8
solution-determined system 52–4, 109, 231–2, 242, 301
solution-focused brief therapy 28, 31, 140–1, 148, 201–2, 203, 309
soul collages 71–2
sound meditation 275, 279, 297, 305
spiritual involvement 27, 294, 295
Sprenkle, D. H. 29
Stages of Readiness for Change model *see* readiness for change
Steinberg, M. A. 179
Stephens, R. S. 148
Sternin, Jerry 236
Sternin, Monique 236
sticky notes 63
Stintson, F. S. 180
story murals 69–70
strengths 32, 36, 56, 314; eating disorders 124; Internet and cyber-sex dependency 212, 231; key strengths and resources questions 37; multi-habit dependencies 272–3; "musical themes" 170–1; positive psychology experiments 72; practice guidelines 309–10; top signature 74; *Values-in-Action Inventory* 73, 74
stress 3, 116
stressors 2, 16, 295
structural therapy 269
structured plan for success 166, 167, 279, 280, 293–5
substance abuse 3, 4, 144–73, 312; access to drugs 11; assessment 151–2; biology of 145–6; brain processes 18, 19; case examples 20–1, 159–73; celebrating habit-free days 75; co-morbidity 6, 151; cognitive processes 12; controlled 9; cyber-sex dependency 214; dopamine receptors 7; DSM-IV classification 6; eating disorders 118; family and couple dynamics 152–3; functions of 152, 155; gambling 176, 177, 180; maintenance factors 15, 16; monitoring by parents 19; multi-habit dependencies 248, 249, 252–3, 256–62, 267, 270–1, 273–7, 281; multiple paths to 146–7; online disclosure 207; parental 69, 158, 249, 250, 263, 267; pathways model 12, 13; positive trigger log 301; preoccupation 8; prevalence 144; preventive function of family time 4; relapse 16, 285; research 147–51, 313, 314–15; self-change 21–2, 23–4; self-harm 84, 85–7, 88, 90–2, 94–8, 101, 110; social pressures 12; subsystem work 51; treatment strategies 153–9; virtuous habits 57

subsystem work 49–52, 109, 245–6; eating disorders 118, 141; substance abuse 151
success stories 80
suicide 58, 67, 84–5, 88, 92; case examples 101, 261; classification of self-harmers 91; eating disorders 112; multi-habit dependencies 270; online disclosure 207
Suler, J. 205
super-sleuth detectives, playing 303
superhero cartoon strip 72
surrealist art solutions 70–1
Svrakic, D. M. 13
"switching addiction model" 7
System of the Observation of Therapeutic Alliances (SOFTA) 28
systemic couples therapy (SCT) 179
systemic therapy 14, 29

tailor-fitting the therapeutic relationship of choice 34–5
"Taking a Trip to Popcorn Land" meditation 166, 167, 193, 255, 258–9, 275, 297
"teachable moments" 154, 184, 192, 202
temperature 115, 122
temptation, building a fence around 183
termination of therapy 107, 230, 266
therapeutic alliance 2, 27, 28, 243–4, 310, 315; client feedback 44, 54–5; eating disorders 121; self-harm 89; substance abuse 154; subsystem work 109; training 314
therapeutic climate 33–5, 242, 309, 315
therapeutic curiosity 267
therapeutic debate 246, 247
therapeutic presence 34
therapeutic relationship of choice 34–5
"three questions for a happy life" 157
thrill-seeking 14, 83–4, 185
Tierney, J. 23, 293
time machine 65–8, 157
Toneatto, T. 178, 183
top signature strengths 74
training 313–14
trauma 11, 311; eating disorders 116, 119; self-harm 87–8, 92
treasure chest 305–6
treatment 1–2, 7, 19–20, 26–7; client choice-making 310; eating disorders 112, 116–18, 120, 121–5; expectations and preferences 40, 237, 310; failures 312–13; gambling 178–9, 182–7; integrative approach 310–11; Internet and cyber-sex dependency 211, 215–19; multi-habit dependencies 238–41; pathways model 14; relapse prevention 287; self-harm 89; substance abuse 147–51, 153–9; *see also* family therapy
triggers 49, 56, 172; gambling 180, 183; habit diaries 78; multi-habit dependencies 275; relapse prevention 291; self-harm 86, 98, 102, 103; substance abuse 164, 165, 167; *see also* positive trigger log

355

INDEX

trust and mistrust 10; eating disorders 127–8, 129, 134, 135–6, 142–3; gambling 181, 182, 186, 188–9, 191, 195; Internet and cyber-sex dependency 215; substance abuse 154, 163, 171
Tucker, J. A. 314
Turkle, S. 4, 204–5
Turner, N. E. 25, 202
Twain, Mark 31
Twelve-Step programs 5, 22, 148, 178, 287, 310
"two chair machine" 192, 195, 198, 202
"Two Garden" mindfulness practice 169, 299
two-step tango strategy 50, 154, 183

uncertainty 177, 236
urge surfing 156, 255, 258–9, 263–5, 275, 277, 279, 296–7
urges 185

values 294–5
Values-in-Action Inventory of Strengths (VIA) 73, 74
Vanderbilt, J. 174
video-games 4, 11, 18, 20–1; multi-habit dependencies 248; online 205, 207–8, 219–34; superhero cartoon strip 72; virtuous habits 57; *see also* Internet dependency
violence: case examples 271, 277, 278; Internet and cyber-sex dependency 212; substance abuse 158; video-games 208; violence prevention 58–9
virtuous habits 55–8; gambling 185; Internet and cyber-sex dependency 215–16; substance abuse 157
visions of change 39, 40
visualization 26, 80, 296; movies of joy and success 102, 103, 104, 108, 166–7, 299; resilient you in action 300; sacred sanctuary 299

Walker, D. 148
Walsh, B. W. 88
Wampold, B. E. 54
Watkins, P. C. 75
wave-watching 185, 296, 298
weak link network 247–8, 259, 275, 292
Weinstock, J. 179
Whitlock, J. 83–4, 85, 87
William of Ockham 235
Williams, A. L. 207
willpower 292–3
Winter, S. W. 176
withdrawal symptoms 10, 15; gambling 175; Internet and cyber-sex dependency 212, 214; self-harm 86; substance abuse 145, 150, 155
Witkiewitz, K. 286, 287
worst-case scenario planning 56, 58–9, 312; gambling 198; multi-habit dependencies 259, 277, 283; relapse prevention 290–1; substance abuse 165–6, 172
Wosnitzer, R. 209
Wright, J. 179
writing experiments 78–80

Yates, B. 83, 87
Yen, C. F. 215
Yen, J. Y. 215
yoga 24, 57, 100, 261, 263, 266, 305
Yoo, H. J. 210
you at your best story 80
young adults: art therapy 68–72; gambling 174; imaginary time machine 65–8; parents mentored by 61; stress 3; substance abuse 144, 146, 149, 150; *see also* adolescents
Young, K. S. 211, 212

Zweben, A. 294–5